ZAGAT
2013
Philadelphia Restaurants

LOCAL EDITOR
Michael Klein with Drew Lazor

STAFF EDITOR
Yoji Yamaguchi

Published and distributed by
Zagat Survey, LLC
76 Ninth Avenue
New York, NY 10011
T: 212.977.6000
E: philadelphia@zagat.com
plus.google.com/local

ACKNOWLEDGMENTS

We're grateful to our local editors, Michael Klein, restaurant columnist for the *Philadelphia Inquirer* and multimedia producer for philly.com/food. He's edited this Survey since 1993. Also, Drew Lazor, a longtime Philadelphian who writes about food, drink, movies and music. We also sincerely thank the thousands of people who participated in this survey – this guide is really "theirs."

We also thank Eva Bacon, Anne Bauso, Melissa Brice, Suzanne and Norman Cohn, Katharine Critchlow, Jack and Mia Dorazio, Pete Dorazio, Ali and Gregg Dorazio, Maureen Fitzgerald, Lisa and Tom Haflett, Karen Hudes, Loretta and Tom Jordan, Leah Kauffman, Jodi and Alan Klein, Diane Klein, Jennifer, Rachel, Lindsay, Jackie and Harry Klein, Craig LaBan, Michele Laudig, Mike Lima, Karen and Dan McFaul, Rick Nichols, Carol and Ben Preston, Mike Romeo, Sybil Rothstein, Cheldin Barlatt Rumer, Rebecca Salois, Richard Vague, Wendy Warren, Romy Weinberg and Justin Wineburgh, as well as the following members of our staff: Anna Hyclak (editor), Brian Albert, Sean Beachell, Maryanne Bertollo, Reni Chin, Larry Cohn, Nicole Diaz, Kelly Dobkin, Jeff Freier, Alison Gainor, Matthew Hamm, Justin Hartung, Marc Henson, Ryutaro Ishikane, Natalie Lebert, Mike Liao, Vivian Ma, Caitlin Miehl, James Mulcahy, Polina Paley, Albry Smither, Amanda Spurlock, Chris Walsh, Jacqueline Wasilczyk, Thomas Wysocki, Hannah Yang, Sharon Yates, Anna Zappia and Kyle Zolner.

ABOUT ZAGAT

In 1979, we asked friends to rate and review restaurants purely for fun. The term "user-generated content" had yet to be coined. That hobby grew into Zagat Survey; 33 years later, we have loyal surveyors around the globe and our content now includes nightlife, shopping, tourist attractions, golf and more. Along the way, we evolved from being a print publisher to a digital content provider. We also produce marketing tools for a wide range of corporate clients, and you can find us on Google+ and just about any other social media network.

Our reviews have always been based on public opinion surveys. The ratings reflect the average scores given by the survey participants who voted on each establishment. The text is based on quotes from, or paraphrasings of, the surveyors' comments. Phone numbers, addresses and other factual data were correct to the best of our knowledge when published in this guide.

JOIN IN: To improve our guides, we solicit your comments - positive or negative; it's vital that we hear your opinions. Just contact us at **nina-tim@zagat.com.** We also invite you to share your opinions at plus.google.com/local.

©2012 Zagat Survey, LLC
ISBN-13: 978-1-60478-513-5
ISBN-10: 1-60478-513-6
Printed in the
United States of America

Contents

OTHER USEFUL LISTS

Special Features:

Ratings & Symbols

	Name	Symbols	Cuisine	Zagat Ratings			
				FOOD	DECOR	SERVICE	COST

Area, Address & Contact

Tim & Nina's ◑ *Deli*   ▽ 24 | 10 | 13 | $17

University City | 3333 Chestnut St. (S. 34th St.) | 215-555-1234 | www.zagat.com

Review, surveyor comments in quotes

"It's always sunny" at this neon-lit University City deli where law school and Wharton students "get down to business" on "awesome" sandwiches and hoagies, including the "felony" cheesesteak/cheesecake combo "wid onions"; Zagat *père*'s "spot-on Rocky Balboa impersonations" compensate for "minimal" service and decor.

Ratings

Food, Decor & **Service** are rated on a 30-point scale.

26 – 30   extraordinary to perfection

21 – 25   very good to excellent

16 – 20   good to very good

11 – 15   fair to good

0 – 10   poor to fair

▽   low response | less reliable

Cost

The price of dinner with a drink and tip; lunch is usually 25% to 30% less. For unrated **newcomers,** the price range is as follows:

I $25 and below   E $41 to $65

M $26 to $40   VE $66 or above

Symbols

◑   serves after 11 PM

Ⓢ Ⓜ   closed on Sunday or Monday

⊘   no credit cards accepted

Maps

Index maps show the restaurants with the highest Food ratings in those areas.

About This Survey

- 1,441 restaurants covered
- 13,179 surveyors
- 61 notable openings
- Meals out per week per surveyor: 2.5 (vs. 3.1 nationally)
- Top Rated: **Fountain** (Food, Decor, Service), **Buddakan** (Popularity)
- No. 1 Newcomer: **Vedge**

SURVEY STATS: Thirty percent say they're spending more per meal, 61% say the same and only 9% say less . . . Philadelphians report leaving an average tip of 19.6%, among the highest in our major U.S. markets . . . Fifty-four percent make reservations online or via e-mail; 39% still phone . . . According to 59%, texting, tweeting, e-mailing or talking on a cell phone while at the table is rude and inappropriate . . . Service remains the biggest dining-out drawback (cited by 66%), followed by noise (16%) and prices (6%) . . . Favorite cuisines: Italian (30%), American (15%), French (12%) and Japanese (9%) . . . On a 30-point scale, Philadelphia gets a 23 for culinary creativity, 19 for hospitality, 24 for choice/diversity and 18 for table availability.

HOT NEIGHBORHOODS: East Passyunk (**Birra, Stateside**); Fairmount (**Alla Spina, Hickory Lane, La Calaca Feliz, Lemon Hill, Paris Wine Bar**); Fishtown (**Pickled Heron, Loco Pez**); Main Line (**Paramour, Pescatore**).

EXPANSIONS: Notable names who added to their empires include Stephen Starr (**Il Pittore, Route 6**); Marc Vetri (**Alla Spina**); Marcie Turney and Valerie Safran (**Jamonera**); Munish Narula (**Tashan**); Luca Sena (**Spiga**).

NEW BLOOD: Le Bec Fin's new French Laundry–sourced crew (Walter Abrams and Nicolas Fanucci) took over for retired founder Georges Perrier; *Top Chef* winner Kevin **Sbraga**'s eponymous American dresses up the Avenue of the Arts; Rich Landau and Kate Jacoby's vegan specialist **Vedge** adds style to Washington Square West.

QUICK BITES: Fried chicken, donuts and coffee are dished up at South Philly's **Federal Donuts**; Neapolitan pizza options expanded with **In Riva** in East Falls and South Street's **Nomad Pizza**; Philly's first **Shake Shack** is serving its burgers and shakes in Rittenhouse.

Philadelphia, PA
October 8, 2012

Michael Klein

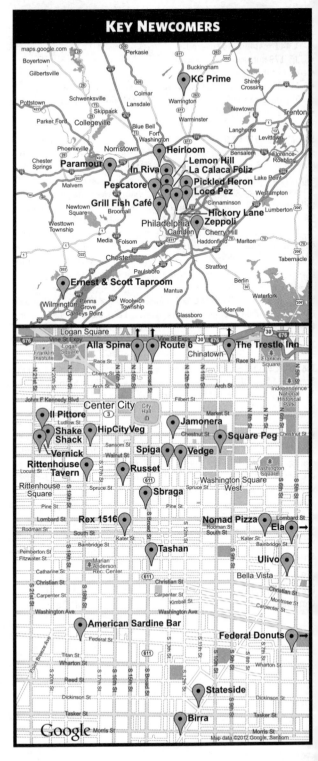

KEY NEWCOMERS

maps.google.com

KC Prime

Heirloom
Lemon Hill
La Calaca Féliz
Paramour
In Riva
Pickled Heron
Loco Pez
Pescatore
Grill Fish Café
Hickory Lane
Zeppoli

Philadelphia

Ernest & Scott Taproom

Logan Square

Alla Spina — Route 6 — The Trestle Inn

Il Pittore — Jamonera

Shake Shack — HipCityVeg — Square Peg

Vernick — Spiga — Vedge

Rittenhouse Tavern — Russet

Sbraga

Rex 1516 — Nomad Pizza — Ela

Tashan — Ulivo

American Sardine Bar

Federal Donuts

Stateside

Birra

Google   Map data ©2012 Google, Sanborn

Key Newcomers

Our editors' picks among this year's arrivals. See full list at p. 38.

Alla Spina | *Italian* | Marc Vetri's industrial-chic Fairmount gastropub

American Sardine Bar | *American* | Point Breeze gastropub

Birra | *Italian* | Trendy pizzeria on the East Passyunk strip

Ela | *New American* | Molecular gastronomy in Queen Village

Ernest & Scott Taproom | *New American* | Wilmington gastropub

Federal Donuts | *Amer./Dessert* | Chicken and donuts in South Philly

Grill Fish Café | *Vietnamese* | West Philly sibling of Vietnam

Heirloom | *New American* | Farm-to-table cuisine in Chestnut Hill

Hickory Lane | *New American* | American bistro in Fairmount

HipCityVeg | *Vegan* | Vegan fast food in Rittenhouse Square

Il Pittore | *Italian* | Upscale Rittenhouse Italian

In Riva | *Italian* | Industrial-chic spot near Schuylkill River in East Falls

Jamonera | *Spanish* | Midpriced tapas at this Wash West wine bar

KC Prime | *Steak* | Upscale steakhouse in Warrington

La Calaca Feliz | *Mexican* | Midpriced Fairmount sibling of Cantina Feliz

Lemon Hill | *New American* | Fairmount corner tap serving locavore fare

Loco Pez | *Mexican* | Hipster Mex in a retro rec-room setting in Fishtown

Nomad Pizza | *Pizza* | Pies from a big-bellied oven near South Street

Paramour | *New American* | Upscale New American in the Wayne Hotel

Pescatore | *Italian* | Seafood-centric Italian BYO in Bala Cynwyd

Pickled Heron | *French* | Farm-to-table Gallic BYO in Fishtown

Rex 1516 | *Southern* | Jet Wine Bar's Rittenhouse sibling

Rittenhouse Tavern | *American* | Upscale brasserie in Rittenhouse

Route 6 | *Seafood* | Stephen Starr's fish house in Fairmount

Russet | *New American* | Farm-to-table BYO in Rittenhouse

Sbraga | *American* | Top Chef winner's spot near Kimmel Center

Spiga | *Italian* | Modern small plates in Wash West

Square Peg | *American* | Edgy Wash West diner from Cuba Libre crew

Stateside | *American* | Lively small-plates joint in East Passyunk

Tashan | *Indian* | Upscale Avenue of the Arts Indian

The Trestle Inn | *Amer.* | Hipster bar in a former strip club in Callowhill

Ulivo | *Italian* | Queen Village newcomer

Vedge | *Vegan* | Vegan newcomer in Washington Square West

Vernick Food & Drink | *American* | High-end Rittenhouse spot

Zeppoli | *Italian* | Vetri alum Joey Baldino's Collingswood BYO

Most Popular

This list is plotted on the map at the back of this book.

1. Buddakan | *Asian*
2. Amada | *Spanish*
3. Iron Hill Brewery | *American*
4. Zahav | *Israeli*
5. Vetri | *Italian*
6. Barbuzzo | *Mediterranean*
7. El Vez | *Mexican*
8. Parc | *French*
9. Morimoto | *Japanese*
10. Fountain | *Continental/French*
11. Alma de Cuba | *Nuevo Latino*
12. Osteria | *Italian*
13. Pat's Steaks | *Cheesesteaks*
14. Bibou | *French*
15. J.B. Dawson's/Austin's | *Amer.*
16. Geno's Steaks | *Cheesesteaks*
17. Talula's Garden | *American*
18. 10 Arts | *American*
19. One Shot Coffee | *American*
20. Nifty Fifty's | *Diner*

21. White Dog Cafe | *Eclectic*
22. Blackfish | *American/Seafood*
23. Distrito | *Mexican*
24. Devon Seafood | *Seafood*
25. Butcher & Singer | *Steak*
26. Wm. Penn Inn | *Amer./Cont.*
27. Yangming | *Chinese*
28. Jim's Steaks | *Cheesesteaks*
29. Lacroix | *Eclectic*
30. Ooka Japanese | *Japanese*
31. Dilworthtown Inn | *American*
32. Tinto | *Spanish*
33. Sabrina's Café | *Eclectic*
34. Chifa | *Chinese/Peruvian*
35. The Prime Rib | *Steak*
36. Reading Term. Mkt. | *Eclectic*
37. Fork | *American*
38. Cuba Libre | *Cuban*
39. Estia | *Greek*
40. Big Fish Grill | *Seafood*

MOST POPULAR CHAINS

1. Chickie's & Pete's | *Pub Food*
2. Cheesecake Factory | *Amer.*
3. Bonefish Grill | *Seafood*
4. Five Guys | *Burgers*
5. The Capital Grille | *Steak*

6. Bahama Breeze | *Caribbean*
7. Maggiano's | *Italian*
8. P.F. Chang's | *Chinese*
9. The Melting Pot | *Fondue*
10. Fogo de Chão | *Brazilian*

Many of the above restaurants are among the Philadelphia metropolitan area's most expensive, but if popularity were calibrated to price, a number of other restaurants would surely join their ranks. To illustrate this, we have added two lists comprising 80 Best Buys on page 16.

Top Food

29 Fountain | *Continental/French*
Vetri | *Italian*
Birchrunville Store | *Fr./Italian*
Bibou | *French*

28 Sycamore | *American*
Fond | *American*
Paloma | *French/Mexican*
Bluefin | *Japanese*
Vedge | *Vegetarian*
Sketch | *Burgers*
Talula's Table | *European*
Morimoto | *Japanese*
Amada | *Spanish*
Sovana Bistro | *Med.*
Little Fish | *Seafood*
Domani Star | *Italian*
Ela | *American*
Capogiro | *American/Dessert*
Majolica* | *American*

27 Zahav | *Israeli*

Di Nic's | *Sandwiches*
Osteria | *Italian*
Daddy Mims | *Creole*
Tre Scalini | *Italian*
John's Roast Pork | *Sandwiches*
The Prime Rib | *Steak*
Popi's Italian Rest. | *Italian*
Matyson | *American*
Honey | *American*
Buddakan | *Asian*
Restaurant Alba | *American*
August | *Italian*
Sola | *American*
Washington House | *Amer.*
Le Virtù | *Italian*
Oishi | *Asian*
Lacroix | *Eclectic*
Funky Lil' Kitchen | *American*
Chickie's Italian Deli | *Italian*
Sbraga | *American*

BY CUISINE

AMERICAN (NEW)

28 Sycamore
Fond
Ela
Majolica
27 Matyson

AMERICAN (TRAD.)

27 Washington House
26 Kimberton Inn
25 William Penn Inn
General Warren Inne
24 City Tavern

ASIAN

27 Buddakan
Oishi
Umai Umai
25 Nectar
Sampan

BARBECUE

25 El Camino Real
Sweet Lucy's
63 Bistro
24 Bomb Bomb BBQ
22 Percy Street Barbecue

CHEESESTEAKS

26 Tony Luke's
Chink's Steaks
25 Dalessandro's
Chubby's Steaks
Steve's Prince/Steaks

CHINESE

26 Chun Hing
25 Han Dynasty
Sang Kee Duck House
CinCin
Abacus

CONTINENTAL

29 Fountain
26 Duling-Kurtz House
25 William Penn Inn
23 Farmicia

ECLECTIC

27 Lacroix
Augusto's
26 Reading Terminal Mkt.
25 Bistro 7
24 AllWays Café

Excludes places with low votes; * indicates a tie with restaurant above

FRENCH

- 29 Birchrunville Store
- 26 Cochon
- Savona
- 23 Beau Monde
- 21 Amuse

FRENCH (BISTRO)

- 29 Bibou
- 28 Sovana Bistro
- 26 Bistrot La Minette
- 25 Spring Mill
- 23 Bistro St. Tropez

GREEK

- 27 Kanella
- 25 Dmitri's
- Estia
- Olive Tree Med. Grill
- 24 Zorba's Taverna

INDIAN

- 26 Shere-E-Punjab
- Amans
- 25 Tashan
- 24 Saffron
- 23 Ekta

ITALIAN

- 29 Vetri
- Birchrunville Store
- 28 Domani Star
- 27 Osteria
- Tre Scalini

JAPANESE

- 28 Bluefin
- Morimoto
- 27 Doma
- 26 Ooka Japanese
- Zama

MEDITERRANEAN

- 28 Sovana Bistro
- 27 Barbuzzo
- 25 Paradiso
- Arpeggio
- 19 Bella

MEXICAN

- 28 Paloma
- 26 Tequilas
- Lolita

- 25 El Camino Real
- Distrito

MIDDLE EASTERN

- 27 Zahav
- 26 Bitar's
- 25 Alyan's
- 24 Kabul
- 23 Maoz Vegetarian

PIZZA

- 27 Santucci Square Pizza
- 26 Rustica
- Ariano
- Tacconelli's
- Famous Mack's

SEAFOOD

- 28 Little Fish
- 26 Blackfish
- 25 Clam Tavern
- Fish
- Gallo's Seafood

SOUL/SOUTHERN

- 26 Relish
- Carversville Inn
- 25 Honey's Sit 'n Eat
- Marsha Brown Creole
- 24 Ms. Tootsie's

SOUTH AMERICAN

- 27 Fogo de Chão
- 26 Tierra Colombiana
- Chifa
- Chima
- 25 Na Brasa

STEAKHOUSES

- 27 The Prime Rib
- Fogo de Chão
- 26 Morton's Steak
- The Capital Grille
- Seven Stars Inn

THAI

- 27 Nan
- 26 Chabaa Thai
- 25 Thai Orchid
- Thai L'Elephant
- Tamarind

VEGAN/VEGETARIAN

28 Vedge
27 Blue Sage
24 AllWays Café
   Blackbird Pizzeria
23 Maoz Vegetarian

VIETNAMESE

26 Vietnam Rest.
25 Vietnam Café
24 Nam Phuong
   Pho 75
   Le Viet

BY SPECIAL FEATURE

BREAKFAST

29 Fountain
27 Lacroix
26 Tierra Colombiana
   Reading Terminal Mkt.
25 Cafe Lift

NEWCOMERS (RATED)

28 Vedge
   Ela
27 Sbraga
26 Il Pittore
25 Federal Donuts

BRUNCH

29 Fountain
27 Lacroix
26 Kimberton Inn
   Fork
25 William Penn Inn Rest.

PEOPLE-WATCHING

28 Sycamore
   Fond
   Vedge
   Morimoto
   Amada

BYO

29 Birchrunville Store
   Bibou
28 Sycamore
   Fond
   Talula's Table

POWER LUNCH

29 Fountain
26 The Capital Grille
25 Del Frisco's
24 Parc
22 Table 31

CHILD-FRIENDLY

28 Capogiro Gelato
27 Tre Scalini
26 Tierra Colombiana
   Duling-Kurtz House
   Seven Stars Inn

PRIVATE ROOMS

27 The Prime Rib
   Lacroix
   Dilworthtown Inn
26 Tierra Colombiana
   Morton's Steak

CLASSIC PHILLY

26 Reading Terminal Mkt.
24 Oyster House
   City Tavern
23 Ralph's
20 Melrose Diner

QUICK BITES

28 Sketch
   Ela
27 John's Roast Pork
   Paesano's Philly Style
26 Royal Tavern

HOTEL DINING

29 Fountain (Four Seasons)
27 The Prime Rib (Radisson)
   Lacroix (Rittenhouse)
26 Duling-Kurtz House
   Delmonico's (Hilton)

QUIET CONVERSATION

29 Fountain
   Birchrunville Store
   Bibou
28 Sycamore
   Fond

MEET FOR A DRINK

28 Vedge
   Ela
27 Osteria
   The Prime Rib
   Sbraga

SMALL PLATES

27 Honey
   Modo Mio
25 19 Bella
   Distrito
   Teca

TRANSPORTING EXPERIENCES

29 Vetri
   Birchrunville Store
28 Paloma Mexican
   Morimoto
27 Le Virtù

TRENDY

29 Vetri
28 Vedge

   Morimoto
   Amada
   Little Fish

WINNING WINE LISTS

29 Fountain
   Vetri
28 Vedge
   Amada
   Ela

BY LOCATION

AVENUE OF THE ARTS

27 Sbraga
   Fogo de Chão
26 Morton's Steak
   The Capital Grille
25 Estia

BELLA VISTA

29 Bibou
28 Paloma
   Little Fish
   Santucci Square Pizza
26 Royal Tavern

BUCKS COUNTY

28 Domani Star
27 Honey
   Washington House
   Oishi
   Blue Sage

CHESTER COUNTY

29 Birchrunville Store
28 Talula's Table
   Sovana Bistro
   Majolica
27 Daddy Mims Creole BYOB

CHESTNUT HILL

26 Night Kitchen Bakery
25 CinCin
24 Osaka
   Mica
23 Cafette

CHINATOWN

27 Di Nic's
26 Nan Zhou
   Reading Terminal Mkt.
   Vietnam Rest.
25 Sang Kee Duck House

DELAWARE COUNTY

28 Sycamore
26 Capriotti's Sandwich Shop
   Charlie's Hamburgers
   Nick's Old Original Roast Beef
   Tony Luke's

FAIRMOUNT

27 Umai Umai
25 Figs
   Sabrina's Café
   Trio
24 Zorba's Taverna

LANCASTER/ BERKS COUNTIES

27 Green Hills Inn
26 Lily's on Main
   Gibraltar
   Belvedere Inn
   Gracie's

LOGAN SQUARE

29 Fountain
27 Doma
26 Chima
25 Swann Lounge
24 Phillips Seafood

MAIN LINE

27 Restaurant Alba
   Sola
   Frankie's Fellini Café
26 Savona
   Antonella's Italian Kitchen

MANAYUNK

26 Chabaa Thai Bistro
25 Han Dynasty
   Agiato
24 Couch Tomato Café
   Hikaru

MONTGOMERY COUNTY

28 Bluefin
27 Funky Lil' Kitchen
26 Blackfish
   Rist. San Marco
   Ooka Japanese

NORTHEAST PHILLY

27 Santucci Square Pizza
26 Chink's Steaks
   Tony's Place
25 Grey Lodge Pub
   Steve's Prince/Steaks

NORTHERN LIBERTIES

27 Modo Mio
   Paesano's Philly Style
26 Rustica
25 Koo Zee Doo
   El Camino Real

OLD CITY

28 Amada
27 Franklin Fountain
   Buddakan
26 La Famiglia
   Radicchio Cafe

QUEEN VILLAGE/ SOUTH STREET

28 Ela
26 Cochon
   Bistrot La Minette
   Core De Roma
25 La Fourno

RITTENHOUSE

28 Capogiro Gelato
27 The Prime Rib

Matyson
Lacroix
Tinto

SOUTH PHILLY

27 John's Roast Pork
   Popi's Italian
   August
   Chickie's Italian Deli
   Paesano's Philly Style

UNIVERSITY CITY

28 Capogiro Gelato
27 Nan
26 Marigold Kitchen
25 Han Dynasty
   Distrito

WASHINGTON SQUARE WEST

29 Vetri
28 Vedge
   Morimoto
   Capogiro Gelato
27 Barbuzzo

NEW JERSEY

28 Zeppoli
27 Sagami
   Sapori
   Arugula
   Filomena Lakeview

DELAWARE

28 Green Room
27 Mikimotos
   Culinaria
   Soffritto Italian Grill
26 Capriotti's Sandwich Shop

Top Decor

<u>28</u>
Fountain
Nineteen
Vedge
R2L

<u>27</u>
Buddakan
Talula's Garden
Bella Tori
Del Frisco's
Lacroix
Morimoto
Dilworthtown Inn
Water Works
Paramour
The Prime Rib

<u>26</u>
Butcher & Singer
Union Trust
Nectar
Marsha Brown Creole
Black Bass
Harvest Seasonal Grill

The Dandelion
Kimberton Inn
Cuba Libre
Alma de Cuba
Firebirds Wood Fired Grill
Savona
Firecreek
Estia
Duling-Kurtz House
Parc
Washington House
City Tavern

<u>25</u>
General Warren Inne
Birchrunville Store
Tashan
William Penn Inn
Pod
Joseph Ambler Inn
Vetri
The Capital Grille

OUTDOORS

Catherine's/General Store
Frankford Hall
General Warren Inne
Inn at Phillips Mill
Le Virtù
Moshulu

Nineteen
Olce Pizza Grille
Parc
Rouge
Talula's Garden
Water Works

PRIVATE ROOMS

Alla Spina
Buddakan
Butcher & Singer
Del Frisco's
Lacroix
Le Bec Fin

Nineteen
Paramour
The Prime Rib
Tashan
Union Trust
Zahav

ROMANCE

Alma de Cuba
Bibou
Birchrunville Store Cafe
Buddakan
Butcher & Singer
Del Frisco's

Fountain
Lacroix
Nineteen
Talula's Garden
Tashan
Vetri

SIDEWALK SCENES

a.kitchen
Alma de Cuba
Amada
Audrey Claire
Bar Ferdinand
Bridget Foy's

Cantina Dos Segundos
Cantina Los Caballitos
Continental
Devon Seafood
Parc
Rouge

Top Service

28 Fountain
Birchrunville Store
Vetri
Lacroix
Vedge
Talula's Table

27 Bibou
The Prime Rib
Dilworthtown Inn
Fond
Washington House

26 Fogo de Chão
Duling-Kurtz House
Sovana Bistro
Morimoto
Davio's
The Capital Grille
Farm & Fisherman
Barclay Prime
Honey

Osteria
General Warren Inne
Zahav
Victor Café

25 Relish
Paloma
Chima
Swann Lounge
Talula's Garden
William Penn Inn
Morton's Steak
Grey Lodge Pub
Chun Hing
Buddakan
August
Fleming's Prime Steak
Seven Stars Inn
Ristorante Pesto
Cucina Forte
Il Pittore

Best Buys

1. Franklin Fountain
2. La Colombe
3. Capogiro Gelato
4. Green Line
5. Charlie's Hamburgers
6. Anthony's Italian Coffee
7. Rybread
8. B2
9. Rustica
10. Ishkabibble's
11. California Tortilla
12. Bravo
13. Maoz Vegetarian
14. Nan Zhou
15. Di Nic's
16. Chickie's Italian Deli
17. Luigi's Pizza Fresca
18. Jake's Wayback Burgers
19. Night Kitchen Bakery
20. Blackbird Pizzeria
21. Capriotti's Sandwich Shop
22. Federal Donuts
23. John's Roast Pork
24. BRGR Joint
25. Chink's Steaks
26. Sketch
27. Five Guys
28. Qdoba
29. PrimoHoagies
30. Paesano's Philly Style
31. Steve's Prince/Steaks
32. Lee's Hoagie House
33. Bonté Wafflerie
34. Isaac's
35. Bitar's
36. Tony's Place
37. Famous Mack's
38. Gino's Burgers & Chicken
39. Delancey Street Bagels
40. Abner's Cheesesteaks

OTHER GOOD VALUES

A Full Plate
Alyan's
Anne's Kitchen Table
Antonella's Italian Kitchen
Baja Fresh Mexican Grill
Bobby's Burger Palace
Café L'Aube
Cafe Lift
Campo's Deli
Capriccio Cafe & Espresso Bar
Cosmi's Deli
Dalessandro's
Elevation Burger
Freddy & Tony's
Geno's Steaks
Green Eggs Café
Grindcore House
Gryphon Coffee Co.
Honest Tom's Taco Shop
Hot Diggity

Jim's Steaks
Jose's Tacos
Jules Thin Crust
Larry's Steaks
M Kee
Mugshots Coffeehouse & Cafe
Pat's King of Steaks
Peace A Pizza
Pho Cali
Pho Ha
Pho 75
Pho Xe Lua
Pure Fare
Reading Terminal Mkt.
Santucci Square Pizza
Singapore Kosher Vegetarian
Slack's Hoagie Shack
Steve's Prince of Steaks
Su Xing House
Tony Luke's

OTHER USEFUL LISTS*

LOCATION MAPS

---

*These lists include low vote places that do not qualify for top lists. All restaurants are in the Philadelphia area unless otherwise noted (LB=Lancaster/Berks Counties; NJ=New Jersey Suburbs; DE=Wilmington/Nearby Delware).

Special Features

Listings cover the best in each category and include names, locations and Food ratings. Multi-location restaurants' features may vary by branch.

BREAKFAST

Fountain	**Logan Sq**	29
Green Room	**Wilmington/DE**	28
Lacroix	**Rittenhouse**	27
Tierra Colombiana	**N Philly**	26
Reading Term. Mkt.	**Chinatown**	26
Barrington Coffee	**Barrington/NJ**	26
Bird-in-Hand	**Bird-in-Hand/LB**	25
Cafe Lift	Callowhill	25
Honey's Sit	**N Liberties**	25
Sabrina's Café	**Bella Vista**	25
Morning Glory	**Bella Vista**	25
Metro. Diner	**N Wales**	24
Famous 4th St. Deli	**multi.**	24
Parc	Rittenhouse	24
Hawthornes	**Bella Vista**	24
La Colombe	**Rittenhouse**	24
Hank's Place	**Chadds Ford**	23
Pop Shop	**Collingswood/NJ**	23
a.kitchen	**Rittenhouse**	23
Capriccio	**Rittenhouse**	23
Nineteen	**Ave of the Arts**	23
Blueplate	**Mullica Hill/NJ**	23
Ben & Irv's	**Huntingdon Vly**	23
Nifty Fifty's	**multi.**	23
Ants Pants Cafe	**SW Center City**	22
Full Moon	**Lambertville/NJ**	22
Keating's	**Del Riverfront**	22
Mastoris	**Bordentown/NJ**	22
Winnie's Le Bus	**Manayunk**	21
Ponzio's	**Cherry Hill/NJ**	21
Marathon Grill	**multi.**	21
Ardmore Station	**Ardmore**	20
Trolley Car	**Mt Airy**	20
Mayfair Diner	**NE Philly**	20
Darling's	**multi.**	20
Melrose Diner	**S Philly**	20
Mal's American Diner	**Skippack**	20
Hymie's	**Merion Station**	19

Down Home	**Chinatown**	19
Little Pete's	**Rittenhouse**	19
Ruby's Diner	**multi.**	19
Murray's Deli	**Bala Cynwyd**	19
Mrs. Marty's Deli	**Media**	18

BRUNCH

Fountain	**Logan Sq**	29
Green Room	**Wilmington/DE**	28
Lacroix	**Rittenhouse**	27
Olce Pizza Grille	**Lansdale**	26
Kimberton Inn	**Kimberton**	26
Aunt Berta's	**Oaklyn/NJ**	26
Fork	**Old City**	26
William Penn Inn	**Gwynedd**	25
Cafe Lift	**Callowhill**	25
The Tortilla Press	**Collingswood/NJ**	25
Figs	**Fairmount**	25
Morning Glory	**Bella Vista**	25
Krazy Kat's	**Montchanin/DE**	25
Swann Lounge	**Logan Sq**	25
Spring Mill	**Conshohocken**	25
Robin's Nest	**Mt Holly/NJ**	25
Las Cazuelas	**N Liberties**	24
Parc	**Rittenhouse**	24
Bella Tori	**Langhorne**	24
Continental	**Old City**	24
Cantina Caballitos/Segundos	**multi.**	24
Monk's Cafe	**Rittenhouse**	24
Hawthornes	**Bella Vista**	24
Yardley Inn	**Yardley**	24
Mixto	**Wash Sq W**	24
Bay Pony Inn	**Lederach**	24
Cuba Libre	**Old City**	24
N. 3rd	**N Liberties**	23
Beau Monde	**Qn Village**	23
Monsu	**Bella Vista**	23
Moshulu	**Del Riverfront**	23
Cock 'N Bull	**Lahaska**	23
Standard Tap	**N Liberties**	23
White Dog	**Univ City**	23

SPECIAL FEATURES

Popi's Italian	**S Philly**	27	Nectar	**Berwyn**	25
Fuji Japanese	**Haddonfield/NJ**	27	CinCin	**Chestnut Hill**	25
Washington Hse.	**Sellersville**	27	Deep Blue	**Wilmington/DE**	25
Le Virtù	**E Passyunk**	27	Smith/Wollensky	**Rittenhouse**	25
NEW Sbraga	**Ave of the Arts**	27	Del Frisco's	**Ave of the Arts**	25
Dilworth. Inn	**West Chester**	27	Sampan	**Wash Sq W**	25
Talula's Garden	**Wash Sq W**	27	Olive Tree	**Downingtown**	25
Terra Nova	**Sewell/NJ**	27	**NEW** Ulivo	**Qn Village**	25
NEW Pescatore	**Bala Cynwyd**	27	Palm Rest.	**Ave of the Arts**	25
Il Fiore	**Collingswood/NJ**	27	**NEW** Tashan	**Ave of the Arts**	25
Fogo de Chão	**Ave of the Arts**	27	Pizza By Elizabeths	**Greenville/DE**	25
La Famiglia	**Old City**	26	Oyster Hse.	**Rittenhouse**	24
Blackfish	**Conshohocken**	26	Union Trust	**Wash Sq W**	24
Morton's	**multi.**	26	Moonstruck	**NE Philly**	24
Capital Grille	**Ave of the Arts**	26	Phillips Sea.	**Logan Sq**	24
Moro	**Wilmington/DE**	26	Bonefish Grill	**multi.**	24
Ooka	**multi.**	26	Pod	**Univ City**	24
Savona	**Gulph Mills**	26	Mica	**Chestnut Hill**	24
Giumarello	**Westmont/NJ**	26	Francisco's	**Wash Crossing**	24
Piccolina Tosc.	**Wilmington/DE**	26	Pietro's Prime	**West Chester**	24
Delmonico's	**Wynnefield**	26	Bella Tori	**Langhorne**	24
Ariano	**Media**	26	Rist. Panorama	**Old City**	24
Saloon	**Bella Vista**	26	Georges'	**Wayne**	24
Dom. Hudson	**Wilmington/DE**	26	Firecreek	**Downingtown**	24
Chifa	**Wash Sq W**	26	Le Castagne	**Rittenhouse**	24
Barclay Prime	**Rittenhouse**	26	Pizzeria Stella	**Society Hill**	24
Kimberton Inn	**Kimberton**	26	Black Bass	**Lumberville**	24
Charcoal BYOB	**Yardley**	26	Cantina Feliz	**Ft Washington**	24
Butcher/Singer	**Rittenhouse**	26	Susanna Foo's	**Radnor**	24
Sullivan's Steak	**multi.**	26	Gemelli on Main	**Manayunk**	24
Chima	**Logan Sq**	26	Big Fish Grill	**multi.**	24
Belvedere Inn	**Lancaster/LB**	26	Le Viet	**Bella Vista**	24
Fleming's Prime	**Marlton/NJ**	26	Marg. Kuo	**Wayne**	24
Stella Sera	**Chestnut Hill**	26	Parc Bistro	**Skippack**	24
Fleming's Prime	**Radnor**	26	J.B. Dawson's/Austin's	**multi.**	24
NEW Fish	**Wash Sq W**	25	Marg. Kuo Mandarin	**Malvern**	24
Harvest	**Glen Mills**	25	Toscana 52	**Feasterville**	24
Estia Restaurant	**Ave of the Arts**	25	P.F. Chang's	**multi.**	24
Paradiso	**E Passyunk**	25	10 Arts	**Ave of the Arts**	24
Firebirds	**multi.**	25	Charlie Brown's	**Woodbury/NJ**	23
General Warren Inne	**Malvern**	25	McCormick/Schmick	**multi.**	23
Ruth's Chris	**multi.**	25	Log Cabin	**Leola/LB**	23

Steak 38 | **Cherry Hill/NJ**	23
Blue Pear | **West Chester**	23
a.kitchen | **Rittenhouse**	23
Varalli | **Ave of the Arts**	23
NEW Route 6 | **Fairmount**	23
Radice | **Blue Bell**	23
Aperto | **Narberth**	23
Benihana | **Pennsauken/NJ**	23
White Dog | **Wayne**	23
Farmer's Daughter | **Blue Bell**	23
JG Domestic | **Univ City**	23
Girasole | **Ave of the Arts**	23
Azie | **multi.**	23
Nineteen | **Ave of the Arts**	23
Blue Bell Inn | **Blue Bell**	23
Dettera | **Ambler**	23
Dandelion | **Rittenhouse**	23
R2L | **Rittenhouse**	23
Blue2O | **Cherry Hill/NJ**	22
Square 1682 | **Rittenhouse**	22
Palace of Asia | **multi.**	22
Treno | **Westmont/NJ**	22
Columbus Inn | **Wilmington/DE**	22
Thai Kuu | **Chestnut Hill**	22
Brandywine Prime | **Chadds Ford**	22
NEW KC Prime | **Warrington**	22
NEW La Calaca Feliz | **Fairmount**	22
NEW Walnut St. Supper Club | **Wash Sq W**	22
NEW Ella's Amer. Bistro | **Wayne**	22
Blackbird | **Collingswood/NJ**	22
NEW Paramour | **Wayne**	22
Erawan Thai | **multi.**	22
Legal Sea Foods | **King of Prussia**	22
Perch Pub | **Ave of the Arts**	22
Table 31 | **Logan Sq**	22
Pizzicato | **multi.**	22
Matador | **Wayne**	21
Fare | **Fairmount**	21
Water Works | **Fairmount**	21
NEW McKenzie Brew | **multi.**	21
NEW 401 Diner | **Conshohocken**	21
Amuse | **Ave of the Arts**	21
Ted's Montana | **Warrington**	21
Ponzio's | **Cherry Hill/NJ**	21

Verdad Rest. | **Bryn Mawr**	21
Marathon Grill | **multi.**	21
Broad Axe Tav. | **Ambler**	21
Pub/Penn Valley | **Narberth**	20
Chops Restaurant | **Bala Cynwyd**	20
Hokka Hokka | **Chestnut Hill**	20
Opa | **Wash Sq W**	20
NEW Hickory Lane | **Fairmount**	20
Aneu | **Berwyn**	19
Spamps | **Conshohocken**	19
Xilantro | **Wayne**	18
Tavern 17 | **Rittenhouse**	18
Newtown Grill | **Newtown Sq**	18
Serafina | **Rittenhouse**	16
NEW In Riva | **E Falls**	-
NEW Kris | **S Philly**	-
Le Bec Fin | **Rittenhouse**	-
NEW Rex 1516 | **Rittenhouse**	-
NEW Rittenhouse Tavern | **Rittenhouse**	-
NEW Russet | **Rittenhouse**	-
NEW Vernick Food/Drink | **Rittenhouse**	-

BYO

Birchrunville Store | **Birchrunville**	29
Bibou | **Bella Vista**	29
Fond | **E Passyunk**	28
Paloma | **Bella Vista**	28
Bluefin | **E Norriton**	28
Tomo Sushi | **Glassboro/NJ**	28
Talula's Table | **Kennett Sq**	28
Masamoto | **Glen Mills**	28
Luna Rossa | **Turnersville/NJ**	28
Little Fish BYOB | **Bella Vista**	28
Domani Star | **Doylestown**	28
Zeppoli | **Collingswood/NJ**	28
Capogiro Gelato Artisans | **E Passyunk**	28
Majolica | **Phoenixville**	28
Sagami | **Collingswood/NJ**	27
Sapori | **Collingswood/NJ**	27
Orchard | **Kennett Sq**	27
Daddy Mims | **Phoenixville**	27
Su Xing House | **Rittenhouse**	27
Tre Scalini | **E Passyunk**	27
Spice Thai | **Doylestown**	27

Sprig & Vine | **New Hope**	27	Nan Zhou | **Chinatown**	26
Arugula | **Sewell/NJ**	27	La Locanda | **Voorhees/NJ**	26
Kitchen Consigliere | **Collingswood/NJ**	27	Cucina Forte | **Bella Vista**	26
Matyson | **Rittenhouse**	27	Mélange | **Haddonfield/NJ**	26
Fuji Japanese | **Haddonfield/NJ**	27	Manon | **Lambertville/NJ**	26
Hinge | **Port Richmond**	27	Olce Pizza Grille | **Lansdale**	26
August | **S Philly**	27	Mercato | **Wash Sq W**	26
Sola | **Bryn Mawr**	27	Antonella's | **Bryn Mawr**	26
Oishi | **Newtown**	27	Ariano | **Media**	26
Funky Lil' Kitchen | **Pottstown**	27	L'Angolo | **S Philly**	26
Pasta Pomodoro | **Sewell/NJ**	27	Brother's Pizza | **Cinnaminson/NJ**	26
Tokyo Mandarin | **multi.**	27	Ristorante Castello | **Blue Bell**	26
TreVi | **Glenside**	27	Coriander | **Voorhees/NJ**	26
Santucci Square Pizza | **multi.**	27	Bonjung | **Collegeville**	26
Blue Sage | **Southampton**	27	Blue Claw Crab | **Burlington/NJ**	26
Bona Cucina | **Upper Darby**	27	Shere-E-Punjab | **Drexel Hill**	26
Fieni's Ristorante | **Voorhees/NJ**	27	Tre Famiglia | **Haddonfield/NJ**	26
Jasmine Oriental | **Medford/NJ**	27	Kabuki | **King of Prussia**	26
Umai Umai | **Fairmount**	27	Tacconelli's | **multi.**	26
Frankie's Fellini | **Berwyn**	27	Charcoal BYOB | **Yardley**	26
Modo Mio | **N Liberties**	27	Amani's BYOB | **Downingtown**	26
Paesano's Philly Style | **N Liberties**	27	La Viola Ovest | **Rittenhouse**	26
		Femmina Italian Grill | **Medford/NJ**	26
NEW Pescatore | **Bala Cynwyd**	27		
Singapore Kosher | **Chinatown**	27	High Street Caffe | **West Chester**	26
Pumpkin | **SW Center City**	27		
Augusto's | **Warminster**	27	Nunzio | **Collingswood/NJ**	26
Il Fiore | **Collingswood/NJ**	00	Aunt Berta's | **Oaklyn/NJ**	26
Farm/Fisherman | **Wash Sq W**	27	Lolita | **Wash Sq W**	26
Oriental Pearl | **Haddonfield/NJ**	27	Bistro/Marino | **Collingswood/NJ**	26
IndeBlue | **Collingswood/NJ**	27	Tokyo Hibachi | **Deptford/NJ**	26
Doma | **Logan Sq**	27	Bobby Chez | **multi.**	25
De Lorenzo's | **Fairless Hills**	26	Koo Zee Doo | **N Liberties**	25
NEW Heirloom | **Chestnut Hill**	26	Nick's Pizzeria/Steak | **multi.**	25
Blackfish | **Conshohocken**	26	Tratt. Giuseppe | **Newtown Sq**	25
Catherine's | **Unionville**	26	Han Dynasty | **multi.**	25
Marigold Kitchen | **Univ City**	26	Dream Cuisine | **Cherry Hill/NJ**	25
Fat Tomato Grill | **Berlin/NJ**	26	Trattoria Totaro | **Conshohocken**	25
Radicchio Cafe | **Old City**	26	Inn/Phillips Mill | **New Hope**	25
Rustica | **N Liberties**	26	Cross Culture | **multi.**	25
Ooka | **Willow Grove**	26	Akira | **multi.**	25
Sakura Spring | **Cherry Hill/NJ**	26	Black Lab Bistro | **Phoenixville**	25
Chabaa Thai | **Manayunk**	26	Megu | **multi.**	25
Cochon | **Qn Village**	26	Dmitri's | **multi.**	25
Izumi | **E Passyunk**	26	Geechee Girl | **Germantown**	25
Hamilton's | **Lambertville/NJ**	26	Kinnaree | **Horsham**	25
		Thai Orchid | **Blue Bell**	25

Fellini Cafe | **Media**	25
Cafe Lift | **Callowhill**	25
Kaya's | **Havertown**	25
Sorrento's | **Lafayette Hill**	25
Honey's Sit | **N Liberties**	25
Scannicchio's | **S Philly**	25
Arpeggio | **Spring Hse**	25
19 Bella | **Cedars**	25
The Tortilla Press | **Collingswood/NJ**	25
Figs | **Fairmount**	25
Alyan's | **South St.**	25
Sabrina's Café | **multi.**	25
Carlucci's Grill | **Yardley**	25
Abacus | **Lansdale**	25
Green Eggs | **multi.**	25
Station House | **Haddon Hts/NJ**	25
Angelo's | **Mt Laurel/NJ**	25
Little Café | **Voorhees/NJ**	25
Kingdom/Vegetarians | **Chinatown**	25
Bunha Faun | **Malvern**	25
FuziOn | **Worcester**	25
Ota-Ya | **multi.**	25
Bruno's Rest./Pizza | **Haddonfield/NJ**	25
Elements Cafe | **Haddon Hts/NJ**	25
Thai L'Elephant | **Phoenixville**	25
Avalon | **West Chester**	25
Tamarind | **South St.**	25
Sammy Chon's K-Town | **multi.**	25
Trio | **Fairmount**	25
Olive Tree | **Downingtown**	25
NEW Ulivo | **Qn Village**	25
Zakes Cafe | **Ft Washington**	25
Ishkabibble's | **South St.**	25
Bistro 7 | **Old City**	25
Sweet Lucy's | **NE Philly**	25
Thai Orchid | **Berwyn**	25
Ray's Cafe | **Chinatown**	25
The Kibitz Room | **Cherry Hill/NJ**	25
63 Bistro | **N Wales**	25
New Harmony | **Chinatown**	25
Kisso Sushi | **Old City**	25
Dim Sum Garden | **Chinatown**	25
Duck Sauce | **Newtown**	25
Circles | **multi.**	25

La Locanda/Ghiottone | **Old City**	25
Porcini | **Rittenhouse**	25
Siri's | **Cherry Hill/NJ**	24
Ritz Seafood | **Voorhees/NJ**	24
Christine's Rest. | **Yardley**	24
El Sitio Grill & Cafe | **Collingswood/NJ**	24
Taq. La Veracruz. | **Bella Vista**	24
Hot Diggity! | **South St.**	24
Melograno | **Rittenhouse**	24
Gino's Pizza | **Norristown**	24
Kabobeesh | **Univ City**	24
Fellini Cafe | **Newtown Sq**	24
Norma's | **Cherry Hill/NJ**	24
Bocelli | **Gwynedd**	24
Las Cazuelas | **N Liberties**	24
Zorba's Taverna | **Fairmount**	24
Club Diner | **Bellmawr/NJ**	24
Alfred's Tomato | **Blackwood/NJ**	24
Sazon | **N Liberties**	24
Audrey Claire | **Rittenhouse**	24
British Chip Shop | **Haddonfield/NJ**	24
Casta Diva | **Rittenhouse**	24
Francisco's | **Wash Crossing**	24
From the Boot | **multi.**	24
Ariana's Ristorante | **N Wales**	24
Sal/Joe's Spaghetti | **Maple Shade/NJ**	24
Avalon Pasta | **Downingtown**	24
Famous 4th St. Deli | **multi.**	24
Chlöe | **Old City**	24
Barone's/Villa Barone | **multi.**	24
Kabul Afghan | **Old City**	24
Angelino's | **Fairmount**	24
Café Estelle | **N Liberties**	24
Saffron | **multi.**	24
Anthony's Creative | **Haddon Hts/NJ**	24
Kunkel's | **Haddon Hts/NJ**	24
Banana Leaf | **Chinatown**	24
Mikado | **Cherry Hill/NJ**	24
Cap'n Cat Clam Bar | **Voorhees/NJ**	24
Sannie | **NE Philly**	24
Casona | **Collingswood/NJ**	24

Joe's Peking | **Marlton/NJ**	24
Vito's Pizza | **multi.**	24
Lee How Fook | **Chinatown**	24
La Viola | **Rittenhouse**	24
Little Tuna | **Haddonfield/NJ**	24
Pho Eden | **Cherry Hill/NJ**	24
Il Cantuccio | **N Liberties**	24
Café L'Aube | **Fairmount**	24
Lee's Hoagie | **multi.**	24
Chiangmai | **Conshohocken**	24
Trax Rest. | **Ambler**	24
Day by Day | **Rittenhouse**	24
Hunan Rest. | **Ardmore**	24
Marg. Kuo Mandarin | **Malvern**	24
Gnocchi | **South St.**	24
Fountain Side | **Horsham**	23
Siam Thai | **Lambertville/NJ**	23
Salento | **Rittenhouse**	23
Hank's Place | **Chadds Ford**	23
Alfredo | **Berwyn**	23
SLiCE | **multi.**	23
One Shot Coffee | **N Liberties**	23
Animo Juice | **Haddonfield/NJ**	23
Monsu | **Bella Vista**	23
Il Giardino | **Spring Hse**	23
Bacco | **Doylestown**	23
Fayette St. | **Conshohocken**	23
Back Porch Cafe | **Skippack**	23
Sang Kee Noodle | **Cherry Hill/NJ**	23
That's Amore | **Collingswood/NJ**	23
Westmont Family Rest. | **Westmont/NJ**	23
Silverspoon | **Wayne**	23
Bellini Grill | **Rittenhouse**	23
Jong Ka Jib | **E Oak Lane**	23
Toscana | **Mullica Hill/NJ**	23
Frank's Time Out | **Berlin/NJ**	23
Aperto | **Narberth**	23
Cafette | **Chestnut Hill**	23
Ariana | **multi.**	23
Piccolo Tratt. | **multi.**	23
Almaz Café | **Rittenhouse**	23
Cake | **Chestnut Hill**	23
Isaac's | **multi.**	23
Branzino | **Rittenhouse**	23
Athena | **Glenside**	23
Mi Lah Veg. | **Rittenhouse**	23
Cafe Du Laos | **S Philly**	23
Ekta Indian Cuisine | **multi.**	23
Blueplate | **Mullica Hill/NJ**	23
943 | **Bella Vista**	23
Cafe Preeya | **Huntingdon Vly**	23
A Full Plate | **N Liberties**	23
La Pergola | **Jenkintown**	23
Kuzina/Sofia | **Cherry Hill/NJ**	23
Shiao Lan Kung | **Chinatown**	23
Vitarelli's | **Cherry Hill/NJ**	23
Luigi's Pizza Fresca | **Marlton/NJ**	23
Pat's Pizza | **multi.**	23
White Elephant | **Huntingdon Vly**	23
Caffe Galleria | **Lambertville/NJ**	23
Rick's | **Lambertville/NJ**	23
Minar Pal. | **Wash Sq W**	23
La Na Thai | **Media**	23
Zacharias | **Worcester**	23
Tiffin | **multi.**	22
Arugula | **Huntingdon Vly**	22
Joe Pesce | **Collingswood/NJ**	22
Jules Thin Crust | **multi.**	22
Jasmine Asian | **Glenside**	22
Tampopo | **multi.**	22
Full Moon | **Lambertville/NJ**	22
Effie's | **Wash Sq W**	22
Johnny's Pizza | **Cherry Hill/NJ**	22
Thai Basil | **Collingswood/NJ**	22
El Azteca | **Mt Laurel/NJ**	22
Cucina Carini | **Mt Laurel/NJ**	22
Mirna's Café | **multi.**	22
NEW Pure Fare | **Rittenhouse**	22
Med. Grill | **multi.**	22
Thai Kuu | **Chestnut Hill**	22
Cafe Fontana | **Maple Shade/NJ**	22
Chez Elena Wu | **Voorhees/NJ**	22
Da Vinci Ristorante | **E Passyunk**	22
Jamaican Jerk | **Ave of the Arts**	22
A La Maison | **Ardmore**	22
Cool Dog Cafe | **Cherry Hill/NJ**	22
Blackbird | **Collingswood/NJ**	22
Erawan Thai | **multi.**	22
Charles Plaza | **Chinatown**	22

CELEBRITY CHEFS

Masaharu Morimoto	Delmonico's | **Wynnefield** 26
Morimoto | **Wash Sq W** 28	Kimberton Inn | **Kimberton** 26
Erin O'Shea	Vietnam Rest. | **Chinatown** 26
Percy St. BBQ | **South St.** 22	Gracie's | **Pine Forge** 26
Nunzio Patruno	Bobby Chez | **multi.** 25
Nunzio | **Collingswood/NJ** 26	Bird-in-Hand | **Bird-in-Hand/LB** 25
Guillermo Pernot	Geechee Girl | **Germantown** 25
Cuba Libre | **Old City** 24	William Penn Inn | **Gwynedd** 25
Eric Ripert & Nathan Volz	Villa di Roma | **Bella Vista** 25
10 Arts | **Ave of the Arts** 24	La Esperanza | **Lindenwold/NJ** 25
Douglas Rodriguez	Honey's Sit | **N Liberties** 25
Alma de Cuba | **Rittenhouse** 25	Scannicchio's | **S Philly** 25
Kevin Sbraga	Spasso Italian Grill | **Old City** 25

Masaharu Morimoto
  Morimoto | **Wash Sq W** 28

Erin O'Shea
  Percy St. BBQ | **South St.** 22

Nunzio Patruno
  Nunzio | **Collingswood/NJ** 26

Guillermo Pernot
  Cuba Libre | **Old City** 24

Eric Ripert & Nathan Volz
  10 Arts | **Ave of the Arts** 24

Douglas Rodriguez
  Alma de Cuba | **Rittenhouse** 25

Kevin Sbraga
  NEW Sbraga | **Ave of the Arts** 27

Joe Scarpone
  NEW Ulivo | **Qn Village** 25

Michael Schulson
  Sampan | **Wash Sq W** 25

Bryan Sikora
  a.kitchen | **Rittenhouse** 23

Christopher Siropaides
  Georges' | **Wayne** 24

Greg Smith
  Table 31 | **Logan Sq** 22

Michael Solomonov
  Zahav | **Society Hill** 27
  NEW Federal Donuts | **S Philly** 25

Brad Spence
  Amis | **Wash Sq W** 26

Daniel Stern
  R2L | **Rittenhouse** 23

Francis Trzeciak
  Birchrunville Store | **Birchrunville** 29

Marc Vetri & Jeff Michaud
  Vetri | **Wash Sq W** 29
  Osteria | **N Philly** 27
  NEW Alla Spina | **Fairmount** 25

CHILD-FRIENDLY

Capogiro Gelato Artisans | **multi.** 28

Sagami | **Collingswood/NJ** 27

Tre Scalini | **E Passyunk** 27

Tierra Colombiana | **N Philly** 26

Gibraltar | **Lancaster/LB** 26

Ooka | **multi.** 26

Bitar's | **Bella Vista** 26

Delmonico's | **Wynnefield** 26

Kimberton Inn | **Kimberton** 26

Vietnam Rest. | **Chinatown** 26

Gracie's | **Pine Forge** 26

Bobby Chez | **multi.** 25

Bird-in-Hand | **Bird-in-Hand/LB** 25

Geechee Girl | **Germantown** 25

William Penn Inn | **Gwynedd** 25

Villa di Roma | **Bella Vista** 25

La Esperanza | **Lindenwold/NJ** 25

Honey's Sit | **N Liberties** 25

Scannicchio's | **S Philly** 25

Spasso Italian Grill | **Old City** 25

Arpeggio | **Spring Hse** 25

The Tortilla Press | **Collingswood/NJ** 25

Harry's Savoy | **Wilmington/DE** 25

Sabrina's Café | **Bella Vista** 25

Haydn Zug's | **E Petersburg/LB** 25

Yangming | **Bryn Mawr** 25

Teca | **West Chester** 25

Ota-Ya | **Lambertville/NJ** 25

Tamarindos | **Broad Axe** 25

Shiroi Hana | **Rittenhouse** 25

Sweet Lucy's | **NE Philly** 25

The Kibitz Room | **Cherry Hill/NJ** 25

Stoudts Black Angus | **Adamstown/LB** 25

Devon Seafood | **Rittenhouse** 24

Siri's | **Cherry Hill/NJ** 24

Mamma Maria | **E Passyunk** 24

Bomb Bomb BBQ | **S Philly** 24

Moonstruck | **NE Philly** 24

Kabobeesh | **Univ City** 24

Fellini Cafe | **Newtown Sq** 24

Rangoon | **Chinatown** 24

Norma's | **Cherry Hill/NJ** 24

Maggiano's | **multi.** 24

Las Cazuelas | **N Liberties** 24

Corner Bistro | **Wilmington/DE** 24

Feby's Fish. | **Wilmington/DE** 24

Pub | **Pennsauken/NJ** 24

Famous 4th St. Deli | **Qn Village** 24

SPECIAL FEATURES

Adobe Cafe	**Roxborough**	21
Snockey's Oyster	**S Philly**	21
Mad Mex	**multi.**	21
HAVANA	**New Hope**	21
DiNardo's	**Old City**	21
Jack's Firehse.	**Fairmount**	21
Ponzio's	**Cherry Hill/NJ**	21
Otto's Brauhaus	**Horsham**	21
Rock Bottom	**King of Prussia**	21
The Plough & the Stars	**Old City**	21
Baja Fresh	**multi.**	21
Winberie's	**Wayne**	21
Bridget Foy's	**South St.**	21
Marathon Grill	**multi.**	21
Broad Axe Tav.	**Ambler**	21
Inn of the Hawke	**Lambertville/NJ**	20
Qdoba	**multi.**	20
Ardmore Station	**Ardmore**	20
Trolley Car	**Mt Airy**	20
Dave/Buster's	**Del Riverfront**	20
Kildare's	**West Chester**	20
Mayfair Diner	**NE Philly**	20
Darling's	**multi.**	20
Melrose Diner	**S Philly**	20
Hymie's	**Merion Station**	19
Christopher's	**Wayne**	19
Hard Rock	**Chinatown**	19
Persian Grill	**Lafayette Hill**	19
Down Home	**Chinatown**	19
Little Pete's	**multi.**	19
Mexican Post	**Wilmington/DE**	19
Ruby's Diner	**multi.**	19
Primavera Pizza	**Ardmore**	19
Johnny Mañana's	**E Falls**	19
McGillin's	**Wash Sq W**	18
Gullifty's	**Rosemont**	17
Plate	**Ardmore**	16
Elephant/Castle	**Rittenhouse**	15

ENTERTAINMENT

Green Room	**Wilmington/DE**	28
Prime Rib	**Rittenhouse**	27
Filomena Lake.	**Deptford/NJ**	27
Filomena Italiana	**Clementon/NJ**	27

Singapore Kosher	**Chinatown**	27
Tierra Colombiana	**N Philly**	26
Rist. San Marco	**Ambler**	26
Reading Term. Mkt.	**Chinatown**	26
Kimberton Inn	**Kimberton**	26
Creed's	**King of Prussia**	26
Sullivan's Steak	**multi.**	26
High Street Caffe	**West Chester**	26
William Penn Inn	**Gwynedd**	25
Deep Blue	**Wilmington/DE**	25
Harry's Savoy	**Wilmington/DE**	25
Joseph Ambler Inn	**N Wales**	25
Rose Tree Inn	**Media**	25
Swann Lounge	**Logan Sq**	25
Mamma Maria	**E Passyunk**	24
Norma's	**Cherry Hill/NJ**	24
Tex Mex Connect.	**N Wales**	24
Marrakesh	**South St.**	24
Bistro Romano	**Society Hill**	24
City Tavern	**Old City**	24
Bay Pony Inn	**Lederach**	24
Mendenhall Inn	**Mendenhall**	24
Cuba Libre	**Old City**	24
Silk City	**N Liberties**	24
Beau Monde	**Qn Village**	23
D'Angelo's	**Rittenhouse**	23
High Note Cafe	**S Philly**	23
Cock 'N Bull	**Lahaska**	23
White Dog	**Univ City**	23
La Collina	**Bala Cynwyd**	23
Tai Lake	**Chinatown**	23
Blue Bell Inn	**Blue Bell**	23
Eulogy Belgian	**Old City**	23
Chickie's/Pete's	**multi.**	23
Manayunk Brew.	**Manayunk**	22
Victor Cafe	**S Philly**	22
Rembrandt's	**Fairmount**	22
Jamaican Jerk	**Ave of the Arts**	22
Half Moon	**Kennett Sq**	22
Four Dogs	**West Chester**	22
Bahama Breeze	**multi.**	22
HAVANA	**New Hope**	21
Bourbon Blue	**Manayunk**	21

FIREPLACES

Wash. Cross. Inn | **Wash Crossing**	22
Gables | **Chadds Ford**	22
St. Stephens Green | **Fairmount**	22
NEW Paramour | **Wayne**	22
Wash. St. Ale | **Wilmington/DE**	22
Mastoris | **Bordentown/NJ**	22
Sly Fox | **Royersford**	22
Scoogi's | **Flourtown**	21
NEW McKenzie Brew | **Berwyn**	21
HAVANA | **New Hope**	21
Rode's Fireside | **Swedesboro/NJ**	21
Mandarin Buffet | **Cherry Hill/NJ**	21
Bridgid's | **Fairmount**	21
The Plough & the Stars | **Old City**	21
P.J. Whelihan's | **Medford Lkes/NJ**	21
High St. Grill | **Mt Holly/NJ**	21
Landing | **New Hope**	21
Inn of the Hawke | **Lambertville/NJ**	20
Dublin Square | **Cherry Hill/NJ**	20
Hokka Hokka | **Chestnut Hill**	20
Kildare's | **multi.**	20
Black Sheep Pub | **Rittenhouse**	20
Freight House | **Doylestown**	20
Molly Maguire's | **Phoenixville**	19
Ladder 15 | **Rittenhouse**	19
Spamps | **Conshohocken**	19
Fadó Irish | **Rittenhouse**	18
McGillin's | **Wash Sq W**	18
Newtown Grill | **Newtown Sq**	18
Elephant/Castle | **Rittenhouse**	15
NEW Nomad Pizza | **South St.**	—

GREEN/LOCAL/ORGANIC

NEW Vedge | **Wash Sq W**	28
Zeppoli | **Collingswood/NJ**	28
Honey | **Doylestown**	27
NEW Sbraga | **Ave of the Arts**	27
Talula's Garden | **Wash Sq W**	27
Farm/Fisherman | **Wash Sq W**	27
NEW Heirloom | **Chestnut Hill**	26

Agiato | **Manayunk**	25
Mica | **Chestnut Hill**	24
NEW Lemon Hill | **Fairmount**	23
Farmer's Daughter | **Blue Bell**	23
NEW Paramour | **Wayne**	22
Fare | **Fairmount**	21
NEW HipCityVeg | **Rittenhouse**	—
NEW In Riva | **E Falls**	—
NEW Pickled Heron | **Fishtown**	—
NEW Russet | **Rittenhouse**	—
NEW Spiga | **Wash Sq W**	—
NEW Vernick Food/Drink | **Rittenhouse**	—

HISTORIC PLACES

Birchrunville Store | **Birchrunville**	29
Green Room | **Wilmington/DE**	28
John's Roast Pork | **S Philly**	27
Washington Hse. | **Sellersville**	27
Dilworthtown Inn | **West Chester**	27
La Famiglia Rist. | **Old City**	26
Ristorante San Marco | **Ambler**	26
Catherine's | **Unionville**	26
Marigold Kitchen | **University City**	26
Duling-Kurtz Hse. | **Exton**	26
Seven Stars Inn | **Phoenixville**	26
Tequilas | **Rittenhouse**	26
Cucina Forte | **Bella Vista**	26
Limoncello Ristorante | **West Chester**	26
Reading Term. Mkt. | **Chinatown**	26
Kimberton Inn | **Kimberton**	26
Tacconelli's | **Port Richmond**	26
Carversville Inn | **Carversville**	26
Belvedere Inn | **Lancaster/LB**	26
Slate Bleu | **Doylestown**	26
Dalessandro's | **Roxborough**	25
Clam Tavern | **Clifton Heights**	25
Inn/Phillips Mill | **New Hope**	25
William Penn Inn | **Gwynedd**	25
Marsha Brown | **New Hope**	25
General Warren Inne | **Malvern**	25
Dante & Luigi's | **Bella Vista**	25
Joseph Ambler Inn | **N Wales**	25
Yangming | **Bryn Mawr**	25
Haydn Zug's | **E Petersburg/LB**	25

SPECIAL FEATURES

Pressroom | **Lancaster/LB** ⎤

NEW Russet | **Rittenhouse** ⎤

HOTEL DINING

Best Western Inn
Palace of Asia | **Ft Wash** 21⎤

Black Bass Hotel
Black Bass | **Lumberville** 24⎤

Brick Hotel
Brick Hotel Rest. | **Newtown** 22⎤

Chestnut Hill Hotel
Chestnut Grill | **Chestnut Hill** 22⎤

Clarion Inn at Mendenhall
Mendenhall Inn | **Mendenhall** 24⎤

Crowne Plaza Center City
Elephant/Castle | **Rittenhouse** 15⎤

DoubleTree Mount Laurel
GG's Restaurant | 25⎤
Mt Laurel/NJ

Duling-Kurtz House & Country Inn
Duling-Kurtz Hse. | **Exton** 26⎤

Four Seasons Hotel
Fountain | **Logan Sq** 29⎤
Swann Lounge | **Logan Sq** 25⎤

General Warren Inne
General Warren Inne | **Malvern** 25⎤

Hilton Philadelphia City Ave.
Delmonico's | **Wynnefield** 26⎤

Holiday Inn Lansdale
1750 Bistro | **Lansdale** 25⎤

Hotel du Pont
Green Room | **Wilmington/DE** 28⎤

Hyatt at the Bellevue
Palm Rest. | **Ave of the Arts** 25⎤
Nineteen | **Ave of the Arts** 23⎤

Hyatt Regency at Penn's Landing
Keating's | **Del Riverfront** 22⎤

Inn at Montchanin Village
Krazy Kat's | **Montchanin/DE** 25⎤

Inn at Penn
Penne | **Univ City** 18⎤

Inn at Phillips Mill
Inn/Phillips Mill | **New Hope** 25⎤

Joseph Ambler Inn
Joseph Ambler Inn | **N Wales** 25⎤

Lambertville House Hotel
Caffe Galleria | 23⎤
Lambertville/NJ

Le Méridien Philadelphia
Amuse | **Ave of the Arts** 21⎤

Loews Philadelphia Hotel
SoleFood | **Wash Sq W** 25⎤

Morris House Hotel
M Restaurant | **Wash Sq W** 23⎤

The Palomar
Square 1682 | **Rittenhouse** 22⎤

Penn's View Hotel
Rist. Panorama | **Old City** 24⎤

Radisson Plaza-Warwick Hotel
Prime Rib | **Rittenhouse** 27⎤
Tavern 17 | **Rittenhouse** 18⎤

Rittenhouse Hotel
Lacroix | **Rittenhouse** 27⎤
Smith/Wollensky | **Rittenhouse** 25⎤

Ritz-Carlton Hotel
10 Arts | **Ave of the Arts** 24⎤

Sheraton City Center Hotel
Phillips Sea. | **Logan Sq** 24⎤

Sheraton University City
Sang Kee Noodle | **Univ City** 23⎤

Wayne Hotel
NEW Paramour | **Wayne** 22⎤

William Penn Inn
William Penn Inn | **Gwynedd** 25⎤

LATE DINING

(Call for closing hours)

NEW Loco Pez | **Fishtown** 29⎤

NEW Ela | **Qn Village** 28⎤

Capogiro Gelato Artisans | 28⎤
multi.

Franklin Fountain | **Old City** 27⎤

Buddakan | **Old City** 27⎤

Barbuzzo | **Wash Sq W** 27⎤

Cap'n Cats Clam Bar | 27⎤
Deptford/NJ

Royal Tavern | **Bella Vista** 26⎤

Nick's Old Original | **multi.** 26⎤

Village Whiskey | **Rittenhouse** 26⎤
Tony Luke's | multi. 26⎤

Francesco's Cucina | **Berlin/NJ** 26⎤

Bailey's Bar & Grille | **Levittown** 26⎤

Grey Lodge | **NE Philly** 25⎤

Dalessandro's | **Roxborough** 25⎤

Memphis Tap | **Port Richmond** 25⎤

El Camino Real | **N Liberties** 25⎤

Alla Spina | **Fairmount** 25⎤

NEW Tapestry | **Qn Village** 25⎤

Larry's Steaks | **Wynnefield** 25⎤

Stone Rose | **Conshohocken** 25⎤

Chubby's Steaks | **Roxborough** 25⎤

South Philly Tap | **S Philly** 25⎤

SPECIAL FEATURES

Phily Diner | **Runnemede/NJ** 22

St. Stephens Green | **Fairmount** 22

Victory Brewing | **Downingtown** 22

Charcoal Pit | **Wilmington/DE** 22

Duffer's Mill | **Marcus Hook** 22

Baby Blues | **Univ City** 22

Brauhaus Schmitz | **South St.** 22

Perch Pub | **Ave of the Arts** 22

Wash. St. Ale | **Wilmington/DE** 22

Phil's Tav. | **Blue Bell** 22

45th St. Pub | **multi.** 22

Bahama Breeze | **King of Prussia** 22

Mastoris | **Bordentown/NJ** 22

Isaac Newton's | **Newtown** 22

Alstarz | **Bordentown/NJ** 22

Metro Diner | **Brooklawn/NJ** 21

NEW The Trestle Inn | **Callowhill** 21

Matador | **Wayne** 21

Grace Tav. | **SW Center City** 21

Exeter Family Rest. | **Reading/LB** 21

Trappe Tavern | **Trappe** 21

Mad Mex | **multi.** 21

McKenzie Brew | **multi.** 21

Imperial Inn | **Chinatown** 21

HAVANA | **New Hope** 21

Hollywood Cafe | **Woodbury Hts/NJ** 21

Dead Presidents Pub | **Wilmington/DE** 21

Slate | **Rittenhouse** 21

Bourbon Blue | **Manayunk** 21

JD McGillicuddy's | **multi.** 21

Benny the Bum's | **NE Philly** 21

Chestnut7 | **Chestnut Hill** 21

Zocalo | **Univ City** 21

Pepperoncini | **Phoenixville** 21

Stoney's British Pub | **Wilmington/DE** 21

Hop Angel | **NE Philly** 21

Byblos | **Rittenhouse** 21

Rock Bottom | **King of Prussia** 21

Ott's | **multi.** 21

Cedar Hollow Inn | **Malvern** 21

Bridget Foy's | **South St.** 21

Medport Diner | **Medford/NJ** 21

P.J. Whelihan's | **multi.** 21

Broad Axe Tav. | **Ambler** 21

NEW Broad St. Diner | **S Philly** 21

Landmark Amer. | **multi.** 20

Frankford Hall | **Fishtown** 20

Pub/Penn Valley | **Narberth** 20

Palace Diner | **Berlin/NJ** 20

Kid Shelleen's | **Wilmington/DE** 20

Nodding Head | **Rittenhouse** 20

Barnaby's Aston | **Media** 20

NEW American Sardine | **S Philly** 20

Local 44 | **Univ City** 20

Brick House | **Willow Grove** 20

Kitchen Bar | **Abington** 20

Dublin Square | **Bordentown/NJ** 20

Clancy's Pub | **Brooklawn/NJ** 20

Dublin Square | **Cherry Hill/NJ** 20

Clancy's Pub | **Sewell/NJ** 20

Fergie's Pub | **Wash Sq W** 20

Farmers' Cabinet | **Wash Sq W** 20

Minella's Diner | **Wayne** 20

Dave/Buster's | **Del Riverfront** 20

Kildare's | **multi.** 20

Copabanana | **multi.** 20

Silver Diner | **Cherry Hill/NJ** 20

Golden Dawn Diner | **Burlington/NJ** 20

Mayfair Diner | **NE Philly** 20

Triumph Brewing | **multi.** 20

MaGerks | **Ft Washington** 20

Darling's | **multi.** 20

Penn Queen Diner | **Pennsauken/NJ** 20

Q BBQ | **Old City** 20

Black Sheep Pub | **Rittenhouse** 20

Melrose Diner | **S Philly** 20

Brittingham's | **Lafayette Hill** 20

Chris' Jazz Cafe | **Ave of the Arts** 19

Christopher's | **Wayne** 19

Little Pete's | **multi.** 19

Oregon Diner | **S Philly** 19

Gigi | **Old City** 19

Connie Mac's | **Pennsauken/NJ** 19

The Coastline | **Cherry Hill/NJ** 19

Molly Maguire's | **Phoenixville** 19

London Grill | **Fairmount**	19
Cooperage | **Wash Sq W**	19
Abner's | **Univ City**	19
Tír na nÓg | **Logan Sq**	19
Ladder 15 | **Rittenhouse**	19
Más Mexicali | **West Chester**	19
KC's Alley | **Ambler**	19
Irish Pub | **multi.**	19
Pub/Passyunk | **E Passyunk**	18
Kite/Key | **Fairmount**	18
Fadó Irish | **Rittenhouse**	18
Joy Tsin Lau | **Chinatown**	18
McGillin's | **Wash Sq W**	18
Country Squire Diner | **Broomall**	18
NEW Barcade | **Fishtown**	18
MilkBoy Coffee | **Wash Sq W**	18
Club House Diner | **Bensalem**	18
Ten Stone | **SW Center City**	18
Tavern 17 | **Rittenhouse**	18
New Wave | **Qn Village**	18
Sage Diner | **Mt Laurel/NJ**	18
Taylors | **Williamstown/NJ**	18
Gullifty's | **Rosemont**	17
Public Hse./Logan | **Logan Sq**	17
Urban Saloon | **Fairmount**	16
Elephant/Castle | **Rittenhouse**	15
NEW Ernest/Scott Taproom | **Wilmington/DE**	-
NEW Industry | **S Philly**	-
NEW Jamonera | **Wash Sq W**	-
Mac's Tavern | **Old City**	-
NEW Morgan's Pier | **Del Riverfront**	-
NEW SoWe Bar Kitchen | **SW Center City**	-

MEET FOR A DRINK

NEW Loco Pez | **Fishtown**	29
NEW Vedge | **Wash Sq W**	28
NEW Ela | **Qn Village**	28
Osteria | **N Philly**	27
Prime Rib | **Rittenhouse**	27
NEW Stateside | **E Passyunk**	27
NEW Sbraga | **Ave of the Arts**	27
Barbuzzo | **Wash Sq W**	27
Terra Nova | **Sewell/NJ**	27
Tinto | **Rittenhouse**	27

Royal Tavern | **Bella Vista**	26
Morton's | **multi.**	26
Capital Grille | **Ave of the Arts**	26
Village Whiskey | **Rittenhouse**	26
Zama | **Rittenhouse**	26
Bistrot/Minette | **Qn Village**	26
Tequilas | **Rittenhouse**	26
Giumarello | **Westmont/NJ**	26
Doghouse Burgers | **Downingtown**	26
Piccolina Tosc. | **Wilmington/DE**	26
Delmonico's | **Wynnefield**	26
Chifa | **Wash Sq W**	26
Bailey's Bar & Grille | **Levittown**	26
Amis | **Wash Sq W**	26
Davio's | **Rittenhouse**	26
Toscano's | **Bordentown/NJ**	26
Butcher/Singer | **Rittenhouse**	26
Fork | **Old City**	26
Grey Lodge | **NE Philly**	25
Memphis Tap | **Port Richmond**	25
El Camino Real | **N Liberties**	25
NEW Fish | **Wash Sq W**	25
Alma de Cuba | **Rittenhouse**	25
Harvest | **Glen Mills**	25
GG's Restaurant | **Mt Laurel/NJ**	25
NEW Alla Spina | **Fairmount**	25
Earth Bread | **Mt Airy**	25
Firebirds | **multi.**	25
Nectar | **Berwyn**	25
Mile High Steak & Seafood | **Glen Mills**	25
Deep Blue | **Wilmington/DE**	25
Del Frisco's | **Ave of the Arts**	25
Joe Santucci's | **NE Philly**	25
Sampan | **Wash Sq W**	25
Garces Trading | **Wash Sq W**	25
Supper | **South St.**	25
Swann Lounge | **Logan Sq**	25
NEW Tashan | **Ave of the Arts**	25
Zavino | **Wash Sq W**	25
Oyster Hse. | **Rittenhouse**	24
Bomb Bomb BBQ | **S Philly**	24
Capers/Lemons | **Wilmington/DE**	24

Union Trust | **Wash Sq W**	24
Moonstruck | **NE Philly**	24
Jimmie Kramer's Peanut | **Reading/LB**	24
Bonefish Grill | **multi.**	24
Pod | **Univ City**	24
Metro. Diner | **N Wales**	24
Coco's | **Wash Sq W**	24
Pietro's Prime | **West Chester**	24
Warmdaddy's | **S Philly**	24
2 Fat Guys | **multi.**	24
Parc | **Rittenhouse**	24
Rist. Panorama | **Old City**	24
Tria Wine Room | **Univ City**	24
Tria | **Wash Sq W**	24
Bobby's Burger | **Univ City**	24
Continental | **Old City**	24
Cantina Caballitos/Segundos | **E Passyunk**	24
Anthony's Pizza | **multi.**	24
Monk's Cafe | **Rittenhouse**	24
Georges' | **Wayne**	24
Kennett Restaurant | **Qn Village**	24
Hawthornes | **Bella Vista**	24
Sidecar | **SW Center City**	24
Pub & Kitchen | **SW Center City**	24
Firecreek | **Downingtown**	24
Pizzeria Stella | **Society Hill**	24
Cantina Feliz | **Ft Washington**	24
Gemelli on Main | **Manayunk**	24
NEW Birra | **E Passyunk**	24
Mixto | **Wash Sq W**	24
Big Fish Grill | **multi.**	24
J.B. Dawson's/Austin's | **multi.**	24
Cuba Libre | **Old City**	24
Las Margaritas | **multi.**	24
Toscana 52 | **Feasterville**	24
P.F. Chang's | **multi.**	24
Three Monkeys Cafe | **NE Philly**	24
Good Dog Bar | **Rittenhouse**	24
10 Arts | **Ave of the Arts**	24
Bar Ferdinand | **N Liberties**	24
Silk City | **N Liberties**	24
Charlie Brown's | **Woodbury/NJ**	23
Arirang | **Langhorne**	23
NEW Lemon Hill | **Fairmount**	23

M Restaurant | **Wash Sq W**	23
Teresa's Next Dr. | **Wayne**	23
Beau Monde | **Qn Village**	23
McCormick/Schmick | **multi.**	23
Steak 38 | **Cherry Hill/NJ**	23
Resurrection Ale | **SW Center City**	23
Blue Pear | **West Chester**	23
a.kitchen | **Rittenhouse**	23
Bell's Tavern | **Lambertville/NJ**	23
Chelsea Tavern | **Wilmington/DE**	23
Varalli | **Ave of the Arts**	23
Zesty's | **Manayunk**	23
Xochitl | **Society Hill**	23
NEW Route 6 | **Fairmount**	23
Standard Tap | **N Liberties**	23
Ollie Gators Pub | **Berlin/NJ**	23
Radice | **Blue Bell**	23
White Dog | **Wayne**	23
Farmer's Daughter | **Blue Bell**	23
Redstone | **Marlton/NJ**	23
Guard House Inn | **Gladwyne**	23
JG Domestic | **Univ City**	23
Jones | **Wash Sq W**	23
Derek's | **Manayunk**	23
Girasole | **Ave of the Arts**	23
Azie | **multi.**	23
Khyber | **Old City**	23
Nineteen | **Ave of the Arts**	23
Belgian Café | **Fairmount**	23
Valanni | **Wash Sq W**	23
Positano Coast | **Society Hill**	23
Dettera | **Ambler**	23
The Twisted Tail | **Society Hill**	23
Continental Mid. | **Rittenhouse**	23
Dandelion | **Rittenhouse**	23
Appalachian Brew. | **Collegeville**	23
R2L | **Rittenhouse**	23
El Rey | **Rittenhouse**	23
Isabella | **Conshohocken**	23
Eulogy Belgian | **Old City**	23
City Tap House | **Univ City**	23
Twenty Manning | **Rittenhouse**	23
Chickie's/Pete's | **multi.**	23
Manayunk Brew. | **Manayunk**	22

Caribou | **Wash Sq W**	22	Amuse | **Ave of the Arts**	21
Square 1682 | **Rittenhouse**	22	Chestnut7 | **Chestnut Hill**	21
Abbaye | **N Liberties**	22	Gypsy Saloon |	21
Treno | **Westmont/NJ**	22	**W Conshohocken**	
Iron Hill | **multi.**	22	Ted's Montana | **Warrington**	21
Devil's Den | **S Philly**	22	Pepperoncini | **multi.**	21
Percy St. BBQ | **South St.**	22	El Fuego | **Rittenhouse**	21
Tango | **Bryn Mawr**	22	Otto's Brauhaus | **Horsham**	21
Max Brenner | **Rittenhouse**	22	Verdad Rest. | **Bryn Mawr**	21
Coyote Cross. | **Conshohocken**	22	Hop Angel | **NE Philly**	21
Brandywine Prime |	22	The Plough & the Stars |	21
Chadds Ford		**Old City**	
La Belle Epoque | **Media**	22	P.J. Whelihan's | **multi.**	21
Maggio's | **Southampton**	22	Campbell's Place | **Chestnut Hill**	21
NEW KC Prime | **Warrington**	22	Broad Axe Tav. | **Ambler**	21
NEW La Calaca Feliz | **Fairmount**	22	Frankford Hall | **Fishtown**	20
NEW Ella's Amer. Bistro | **Wayne**	22	Pub/Penn Valley | **Narberth**	20
St. Stephens Green | **Fairmount**	22	Mission Grill | **Logan Sq**	20
NEW Paramour | **Wayne**	22	Inn of the Hawke |	20
California Pizza |	22	**Lambertville/NJ**	
Plymouth Mtg		Kid Shelleen's |	20
Baby Blues | **Univ City**	22	**Wilmington/DE**	
Brauhaus Schmitz | **South St.**	22	Nodding Head | **Rittenhouse**	20
Catahoula | **Qn Village**	22	**NEW** American Sardine | **S Philly**	20
Perch Pub | **Ave of the Arts**	22	Local 44 | **Univ City**	20
FireStone Roasting |	22	Chops Restaurant |	20
Wilmington/DE		**Bala Cynwyd**	
Phil's Tav. | **Blue Bell**	22	Fergie's Pub | **Wash Sq W**	20
Table 31 | **Logan Sq**	22	Opa | **Wash Sq W**	20
Philadelphia Bar/Rest. |	22	Farmers' Cabinet | **Wash Sq W**	20
Old City		Triumph Brewing | **multi.**	20
Smokin' Betty | **Wash Sq W**	22	MaGerks | **Ft Washington**	20
Pizzicato | **multi.**	22	Q BBQ | **Old City**	20
Alstarz | **Bordentown/NJ**	22	Black Sheep Pub | **Rittenhouse**	20
Revolution Hse. | **Old City**	22	Aneu | **Berwyn**	19
Sly Fox | **Royersford**	22	Gigi | **Old City**	19
Doc Magrogan | **West Chester**	21	Molly Maguire's | **Phoenixville**	19
C19 | **Rittenhouse**	21	Mexican Post | **multi.**	19
Adobe Cafe | **multi.**	21	London Grill | **Fairmount**	19
Matador | **Wayne**	21	Cooperage | **Wash Sq W**	19
Fare | **Fairmount**	21	Sly Fox | **Phoenixville**	19
Water Works | **Fairmount**	21	Tír na nÓg | **Logan Sq**	19
Mad Mex | **multi.**	21	Ladder 15 | **Rittenhouse**	19
NEW McKenzie Brew | **multi.**	21	Más Mexicali | **West Chester**	19
HAVANA | **New Hope**	21	Spamps | **Conshohocken**	19
Slate | **Rittenhouse**	21	Pub/Passyunk | **E Passyunk**	18
Benny the Bum's | **NE Philly**	21	Kite/Key | **Fairmount**	18

Fadó Irish | **Rittenhouse**	18
Xilantro | **Wayne**	18
McGillin's | **Wash Sq W**	18
MilkBoy Coffee | **multi.**	18
Happy Rooster | **Rittenhouse**	18
NEW In Riva | **E Falls**	-⌐

MICROBREWERIES

Earth Bread | **Mt Airy**	25
Stoudts Black Angus | **Adamstown/LB**	25
Coco's | **Wash Sq W**	24
Dock Street Brew. | **Univ City**	24
Appalachian Brew. | **Collegeville**	23
Manayunk Brew. | **Manayunk**	22
Iron Hill | **multi.**	22
Victory Brewing | **Downingtown**	22
NEW McKenzie Brew | **multi.**	21
JD McGillicuddy's | **Ardmore**	21
Rock Bottom | **King of Prussia**	21
Nodding Head | **Rittenhouse**	20
Triumph Brewing | **multi.**	20
Sly Fox | **Phoenixville**	19

NEWCOMERS

Loco Pez | **Fishtown**	29
Vedge | **Wash Sq W**	28
Ela | **Qn Village**	28
Zeppoli | **Collingswood/NJ**	28
Stateside | **E Passyunk**	27
Sbraga | **Ave of the Arts**	27
Pescatore | **Bala Cynwyd**	27
Heirloom | **Chestnut Hill**	26
Il Pittore | **Rittenhouse**	26
Belle Cakery | **E Passyunk**	26
Federal Donuts | **S Philly**	25
Alla Spina | **Fairmount**	25
Tapestry | **Qn Village**	25
Ulivo | **Qn Village**	25
Tashan | **Ave of the Arts**	25
320 Market | **Media**	24
Birra | **E Passyunk**	24
Lemon Hill | **Fairmount**	23
Route 6 | **Fairmount**	23
M Kee | **Chinatown**	23
Honest Tom's Taco | **W Philly**	23
Joe's Crab Shack | **King of Prussia**	23

Bravo! | **Willow Grove**	22
Pure Fare | **Rittenhouse**	22
The Tomato Bistro | **Manayunk**	22
KC Prime | **Warrington**	22
La Calaca Feliz | **Fairmount**	22
Walnut St. Supper Club | **Wash Sq W**	22
Ella's Amer. Bistro | **Wayne**	22
Paramour | **Wayne**	22
The Trestle Inn | **Callowhill**	21
Isabel | **Fairmount**	21
401 Diner | **Conshohocken**	21
Broad St. Diner | **S Philly**	21
American Sardine | **S Philly**	20
Hickory Lane | **Fairmount**	20
Barcade | **Fishtown**	18
Argana Moroccan | **Lansdowne**	-⌐
BlueCat | **Fairmount**	-⌐
Divan Med. Grill | **Qn Village**	-⌐
Ernest/Scott Taproom | **Wilmington/DE**	-⌐
Grill Fish Café | **W Philly**	-⌐
HipCityVeg | **Rittenhouse**	-⌐
Industry | **S Philly**	-⌐
In Riva | **E Falls**	-⌐
Jamonera | **Wash Sq W**	-⌐
Kris | **S Philly**	-⌐
La Petite Dauphine | **Rittenhouse**	-⌐
Little Louie's BBQ | **Collingswood/NJ**	-⌐
Mekong River | **S Philly**	-⌐
Miss Rachel's Pantry | **S Philly**	-⌐
Morgan's Pier | **Del Riverfront**	-⌐
Nomad Pizza | **South St.**	-⌐
Pickled Heron | **Fishtown**	-⌐
Rex 1516 | **Rittenhouse**	-⌐
Rittenhouse Tavern | **Rittenhouse**	-⌐
Russet | **Rittenhouse**	-⌐
Shake Shack | **Rittenhouse**	-⌐
SoWe Bar Kitchen | **SW Center City**	-⌐
Spiga | **Wash Sq W**	-⌐
Square Peg | **Wash Sq W**	-⌐
Vernick Food/Drink | **Rittenhouse**	-⌐

OUTDOOR DINING

Kitchen Consigliere | **Collingswood/NJ**	27
Le Virtù | **E Passyunk**	27
Barbuzzo | **Wash Sq W**	27
Dilworth. Inn | **West Chester**	27
Talula's Garden | **Wash Sq W**	27
Catherine's | **Unionville**	26
Bistrot/Minette | **Qn Village**	26
Izumi | **E Passyunk**	26
Hamilton's | **Lambertville/NJ**	26
Savona | **Gulph Mills**	26
Giumarello | **Westmont/NJ**	26
Olce Pizza Grille | **Lansdale**	26
Chifa | **Wash Sq W**	26
Gracie's | **Pine Forge**	26
Lolita | **Wash Sq W**	26
Fork | **Old City**	26
Koo Zee Doo | **N Liberties**	25
Inn/Phillips Mill | **New Hope**	25
Alma de Cuba | **Rittenhouse**	25
General Warren Inne | **Malvern**	25
Spasso Italian Grill | **Old City**	25
Arpeggio | **Spring Hse**	25
Figs | **Fairmount**	25
Harry's Savoy | **Wilmington/DE**	25
Joseph Ambler Inn | **N Wales**	25
Caffe Aldo | **Cherry Hill/NJ**	25
Teca | **West Chester**	25
Olive Tree | **Downingtown**	25
Morning Glory | **Bella Vista**	25
Spring Mill | **Conshohocken**	25
Robin's Nest | **Mt Holly/NJ**	25
Devon Seafood | **Rittenhouse**	24
Taq. La Veracruz. | **Bella Vista**	24
Maggiano's | **multi.**	24
Audrey Claire | **Rittenhouse**	24
Parc | **Rittenhouse**	24
Tria | **Rittenhouse**	24
Continental | **Old City**	24
Cantina Caballitos/Segundos | **E Passyunk**	24
Anthony's Pizza | **multi.**	24
Pizzeria Stella | **Society Hill**	24
La Viola | **Rittenhouse**	24
City Tavern | **Old City**	24
Bay Pony Inn | **Lederach**	24
Parc Bistro | **Skippack**	24
Cuba Libre | **Old City**	24
Beau Monde | **Qn Village**	23
El Serrano | **Lancaster/LB**	23
Moshulu | **Del Riverfront**	23
Cafette | **Chestnut Hill**	23
Rouge | **Rittenhouse**	23
Derek's | **Manayunk**	23
Branzino | **Rittenhouse**	23
Athena | **Glenside**	23
Nineteen | **Ave of the Arts**	23
Blue Parrot | **Wilmington/DE**	23
Positano Coast | **Society Hill**	23
Pietro's Pizza | **multi.**	23
Continental Mid. | **Rittenhouse**	23
Lilly's/Canal | **Lambertville/NJ**	23
Twenty Manning | **Rittenhouse**	23
333 Belrose | **Radnor**	23
Café Gallery | **Burlington/NJ**	23
Manayunk Brew. | **Manayunk**	22
Caribou | **Wash Sq W**	22
Abbaye | **N Liberties**	22
Chestnut Grill | **Chestnut Hill**	22
Columbus Inn | **Wilmington/DE**	22
Mexican Food | **Marlton/NJ**	22
Tango | **Bryn Mawr**	22
Rembrandt's | **Fairmount**	22
Brasserie 73 | **Skippack**	22
Jamaican Jerk | **Ave of the Arts**	22
Coyote Cross. | **Conshohocken**	22
Four Dogs | **West Chester**	22
Wash. Cross. Inn | **Wash Crossing**	22
Gables | **Chadds Ford**	22
Keating's | **Del Riverfront**	22
Chart House | **Del Riverfront**	22
Wash. St. Ale | **Wilmington/DE**	22
Pizzicato | **Old City**	22
Brick Hotel Rest. | **Newtown**	22
Isaac Newton's | **Newtown**	22
Pattaya | **Univ City**	22
Adobe Cafe | **Roxborough**	21
Bistro La Baia | **SW Center City**	21

Water Works | **Fairmount**	21
HAVANA | **New Hope**	21
Jack's Firehse. | **Fairmount**	21
Bliss | **Ave of the Arts**	21
Zocalo | **Univ City**	21
Otto's Brauhaus | **Horsham**	21
The Plough & the Stars | **Old City**	21
Winberie's | **Wayne**	21
Bridget Foy's | **South St.**	21
Landing | **New Hope**	21
Frankford Hall | **Fishtown**	20
Inn of the Hawke | **Lambertville/NJ**	20
Bella Cena | **Rittenhouse**	20
Freight House | **Doylestown**	20
Tír na nÓg | **Logan Sq**	19
New Wave | **Qn Village**	18
Newtown Grill | **Newtown Sq**	18
Plate | **Ardmore**	16

PEOPLE-WATCHING

NEW Vedge | **Wash Sq W**	28
Morimoto | **Wash Sq W**	28
Amada | **Old City**	28
Little Fish BYOB | **Bella Vista**	28
NEW Ela | **Qn Village**	28
Zeppoli | **Collingswood/NJ**	28
Osteria | **N Philly**	27
Prime Rib | **Rittenhouse**	27
Kitchen Consigliere | **Collingswood/NJ**	27
Matyson | **Rittenhouse**	27
Fuji Japanese | **Haddonfield/NJ**	27
NEW Stateside | **E Passyunk**	27
Buddakan | **Old City**	27
Le Virtù | **E Passyunk**	27
Lacroix | **Rittenhouse**	27
NEW Sbraga | **Ave of the Arts**	27
Barbuzzo | **Wash Sq W**	27
Fieni's Ristorante | **Voorhees/NJ**	27
Talula's Garden | **Wash Sq W**	27
Modo Mio | **N Liberties**	27
Paesano's Philly Style | **multi.**	27
Fogo de Chão | **Ave of the Arts**	27

Tinto | **Rittenhouse**	27
NEW Heirloom | **Chestnut Hill**	26
Capital Grille | **Ave of the Arts**	26
Moro | **Wilmington/DE**	26
Village Whiskey | **Rittenhouse**	26
Zama | **Rittenhouse**	26
Bistrot/Minette | **Qn Village**	26
Izumi | **E Passyunk**	26
Nan Zhou | **Chinatown**	26
Tony Luke's | **S Philly**	26
Tequilas | **Rittenhouse**	26
Limoncello | **West Chester**	26
Harry's Seafood | **Wilmington/DE**	26
Piccolina Tosc. | **Wilmington/DE**	26
Barclay Prime | **Rittenhouse**	26
Amis | **Wash Sq W**	26
Butcher/Singer | **Rittenhouse**	26
Sullivan's Steak | **multi.**	26
Chima | **Logan Sq**	26
Nunzio | **Collingswood/NJ**	26
Fleming's Prime | **multi.**	26
Lolita | **Wash Sq W**	26
Fork | **Old City**	26
Orillas Tapa Bar | **Wilmington/DE**	26
Grey Lodge | **NE Philly**	25
Dalessandro's | **Roxborough**	25
Han Dynasty | **multi.**	25
Memphis Tap | **Port Richmond**	25
El Camino Real | **N Liberties**	25
Megu | **multi.**	25
Dmitri's | **Rittenhouse**	25
Alma de Cuba | **Rittenhouse**	25
Harvest | **Glen Mills**	25
NEW Alla Spina | **Fairmount**	25
Paradiso | **E Passyunk**	25
Earth Bread | **Mt Airy**	25
Nectar | **Berwyn**	25
Harry's Savoy | **Wilmington/DE**	25
Na'Brasa | **Horsham**	25
Smith/Wollensky | **Rittenhouse**	25
Caffe Aldo | **Cherry Hill/NJ**	25
Del Frisco's | **Ave of the Arts**	25

Karma | **Old City**	22
Maggio's | **Southampton**	22
NEW KC Prime | **Warrington**	22
Phily Diner | **Runnemede/NJ**	22
Marco Polo | **Elkins Pk**	22
NEW La Calaca Feliz | **Fairmount**	22
NEW Walnut St. Supper Club | **Wash Sq W**	22
NEW Ella's Amer. Bistro | **Wayne**	22
Blackbird | **Collingswood/NJ**	22
NEW Paramour | **Wayne**	22
Brauhaus Schmitz | **South St.**	22
Catahoula | **Qn Village**	22
Table 31 | **Logan Sq**	22
Smokin' Betty | **Wash Sq W**	22
Chiarella's | **E Passyunk**	22
C19 | **Rittenhouse**	21
Adobe Cafe | **multi.**	21
Metro Diner | **Brooklawn/NJ**	21
Pistachio Grille | **Maple Glen**	21
Jake's/Cooper's | **Manayunk**	21
Hollywood Cafe | **Woodbury Hts/NJ**	21
NEW 401 Diner | **Conshohocken**	21
Slate | **Rittenhouse**	21
Gypsy Saloon | **W Conshohocken**	21
Ted's Montana | **Warrington**	21
Ponzio's | **Cherry Hill/NJ**	21
Pepperoncini | **multi.**	21
El Fuego | **Rittenhouse**	21
Otto's Brauhaus | **Horsham**	21
The Plough & the Stars | **Old City**	21
Campbell's Place | **Chestnut Hill**	21
Hokka Hokka | **Chestnut Hill**	20
Schlesinger's | **Rittenhouse**	20
Le Pain | **Rittenhouse**	20
West Side Gravy | **Collingswood/NJ**	20
Mugshots | **multi.**	19
Chris' Jazz Cafe | **Ave of the Arts**	19
Aneu | **Berwyn**	19
Hard Rock | **Chinatown**	19
Oak Lane Diner | **W Oak Lane**	19

London Grill | **Fairmount**	19
Cooperage | **Wash Sq W**	19
Abner's | **Univ City**	19
Tír na nÓg | **Logan Sq**	19
Ladder 15 | **Rittenhouse**	19
Más Mexicali | **West Chester**	19
World Café | **Wilmington/DE**	19
My Thai | **SW Center City**	19
Kite/Key | **Fairmount**	18
Mrs. Marty's Deli | **Media**	18
Andy's Diner & Pub | **Conshohocken**	18
Xilantro | **Wayne**	18
McGillin's | **Wash Sq W**	18
Beijing | **Univ City**	18
MilkBoy Coffee | **multi.**	18
Tavern 17 | **Rittenhouse**	18
Gullifty's | **Rosemont**	17
Urban Saloon | **Fairmount**	16
Serafina | **Rittenhouse**	16
NEW BlueCat | **Fairmount**	-
NEW Divan Med. Grill | **Qn Village**	-
NEW Grill Fish Café | **W Philly**	-
NEW Industry | **S Philly**	-
NEW In Riva | **E Falls**	-
NEW Kris | **S Philly**	-
Mac's Tavern | **Old City**	-
NEW Mekong River | **S Philly**	-
NEW Morgan's Pier | **Del Riverfront**	-
NEW Rex 1516 | **Rittenhouse**	-
NEW Rittenhouse Tavern | **Rittenhouse**	-
NEW Russet | **Rittenhouse**	-
NEW Shake Shack | **Rittenhouse**	-
NEW Spiga | **Wash Sq W**	-
NEW Square Peg | **Wash Sq W**	-

POWER SCENES

Fountain | **Logan Sq**	29
Green Room | **Wilmington/DE**	28
Morimoto | **Wash Sq W**	28
Amada | **Old City**	28
Zahav | **Society Hill**	27
Osteria | **N Philly**	27
Prime Rib | **Rittenhouse**	27
Buddakan | **Old City**	27

Le Virtù	**E Passyunk**	27
Lacroix	**Rittenhouse**	27
NEW Sbraga	**Ave of the Arts**	27
Talula's Garden	**Wash Sq W**	27
Fogo de Chão	**Ave of the Arts**	27
Farm/Fisherman	**Wash Sq W**	27
Blackfish	**Conshohocken**	26
Morton's	**multi.**	26
Capital Grille	**Ave of the Arts**	26
Piccolina Tosc.	**Wilmington/DE**	26
Saloon	**Bella Vista**	26
Chifa	**Wash Sq W**	26
Barclay Prime	**Rittenhouse**	26
Charcoal BYOB	**Yardley**	26
Butcher/Singer	**Rittenhouse**	26
Sullivan's Steak	**multi.**	26
Fleming's Prime	**multi.**	26
Alma de Cuba	**Rittenhouse**	25
Estia Restaurant	**Ave of the Arts**	25
Paradiso	**E Passyunk**	25
Ruth's Chris	**multi.**	25
Nectar	**Berwyn**	25
Harry's Savoy	**Wilmington/DE**	25
Smith/Wollensky	**Rittenhouse**	25
Caffe Aldo	**Cherry Hill/NJ**	25
Del Frisco's	**Ave of the Arts**	25
Palm Rest.	**Ave of the Arts**	25
NEW Tashan	**Ave of the Arts**	25
Union Trust	**Wash Sq W**	24
Pietro's Prime	**West Chester**	24
Famous 4th St. Deli	**Qn Village**	24
Parc	**Rittenhouse**	24
Georges'	**Wayne**	24
Le Castagne	**Rittenhouse**	24
Toscana 52	**Feasterville**	24
10 Arts	**Ave of the Arts**	24
McCormick/Schmick	**multi.**	23
Blue Pear	**West Chester**	23

NEW Route 6	**Fairmount**	23
White Dog	**Wayne**	23
Redstone	**Marlton/NJ**	23
Guard House Inn	**Gladwyne**	23
JG Domestic	**Univ City**	23
Rouge	**Rittenhouse**	23
Girasole	**Ave of the Arts**	23
Azie	**multi.**	23
Nineteen	**Ave of the Arts**	23
Positano Coast	**Society Hill**	23
Dettera	**Ambler**	23
Continental Mid.	**Rittenhouse**	23
Dandelion	**Rittenhouse**	23
R2L	**Rittenhouse**	23
Square 1682	**Rittenhouse**	22
Brandywine Prime	**Chadds Ford**	22
NEW Paramour	**Wayne**	22
Table 31	**Logan Sq**	22
Doc Magrogan	**West Chester**	21
Matador	**Wayne**	21
Water Works	**Fairmount**	21
Ponzio's	**Cherry Hill/NJ**	21
Chops Restaurant	**Bala Cynwyd**	20
Schlesinger's	**Rittenhouse**	20
Serafina	**Rittenhouse**	16
Le Bec Fin	**Rittenhouse**	-

PRIVATE ROOMS

(Restaurants charge less at off times; call for capacity)

Prime Rib	**Rittenhouse**	27
Lacroix	**Rittenhouse**	27
Green Hills Inn	**Reading/LB**	27
Dilworth. Inn	**West Chester**	27
Tierra Colombiana	**N Philly**	26
Morton's	**multi.**	26
Rist. San Marco	**Ambler**	26
Capital Grille	**Ave of the Arts**	26
Duling-Kurtz Hse.	**Exton**	26
Lily's on Main	**Ephrata/LB**	26
Seven Stars Inn	**Phoenixville**	26
Hamilton's	**Lambertville/NJ**	26

Restaurant	Rating
Savona | **Gulph Mills**	26
Tequilas | **Rittenhouse**	26
Giumarello | **Westmont/NJ**	26
Chophouse | **Gibbsboro/NJ**	26
Saloon | **Bella Vista**	26
Davio's | **Rittenhouse**	26
Creed's | **King of Prussia**	26
Sullivan's Steak | **Wilmington/DE**	26
Vietnam Rest. | **Chinatown**	26
Gracie's | **Pine Forge**	26
Fleming's Prime | **multi.**	26
Fork | **Old City**	26
William Penn Inn | **Gwynedd**	25
Alma de Cuba | **Rittenhouse**	25
Estia Restaurant | **Ave of the Arts**	25
General Warren Inne | **Malvern**	25
Spasso Italian Grill | **Old City**	25
Ruth's Chris | **multi.**	25
Nectar | **Berwyn**	25
CinCin | **Chestnut Hill**	25
Alyan's | **South St.**	25
Harry's Savoy | **Wilmington/DE**	25
Joseph Ambler Inn | **N Wales**	25
Smith/Wollensky | **Rittenhouse**	25
Caffe Aldo | **Cherry Hill/NJ**	25
Pho Xe Lua | **Chinatown**	25
Marg. Kuo Peking | **Media**	25
Shiroi Hana | **Rittenhouse**	25
Avalon | **West Chester**	25
Rose Tree Inn | **Media**	25
Spring Mill | **Conshohocken**	25
Mamma Maria | **E Passyunk**	24
Maggiano's | **multi.**	24
Pod | **Univ City**	24
Meritage | **SW Center City**	24
Feby's Fish. | **Wilmington/DE**	24
Pub | **Pennsauken/NJ**	24
Barone's/Villa Barone | **Moorestown/NJ**	24
Teikoku | **Newtown Sq**	24
Totaro's | **Conshohocken**	24
Back Burner | **Hockessin/DE**	24
Yardley Inn | **Yardley**	24
Bistro Romano | **Society Hill**	24
City Tavern | **Old City**	24
Bay Pony Inn | **Lederach**	24
Cuba Libre | **Old City**	24
10 Arts | **Ave of the Arts**	24
Fountain Side | **Horsham**	23
McCormick/Schmick | **Ave of the Arts**	23
Moshulu | **Del Riverfront**	23
Lamberti's/Tutto Fresco | **Wilmington/DE**	23
Via Napoli | **NE Philly**	23
Ralph's | **Bella Vista**	23
White Dog | **Univ City**	23
Lai Lai Garden | **Blue Bell**	23
Derek's | **Manayunk**	23
La Collina | **Bala Cynwyd**	23
Bistro St. Tropez | **Rittenhouse**	23
Tai Lake | **Chinatown**	23
Shangrila | **Devon**	23
Blue Bell Inn | **Blue Bell**	23
Pietro's Pizza | **South St.**	23
Dettera | **Ambler**	23
August Moon | **Norristown**	23
333 Belrose | **Radnor**	23
Barnsboro Inn | **Sewell/NJ**	23
Square 1682 | **Rittenhouse**	22
Mrs. Robino's | **Wilmington/DE**	22
Iron Hill | **Newark/DE**	22
Chez Elena Wu | **Voorhees/NJ**	22
Tango | **Bryn Mawr**	22
Wash. Cross. Inn | **Wash Crossing**	22
Chart House | **Del Riverfront**	22
Table 31 | **Logan Sq**	22
Brick Hotel Rest. | **Newtown**	22
Adobe Cafe | **Roxborough**	21
Palace of Asia | **Ft Washington**	21
Water Works | **Fairmount**	21
DiNardo's | **Old City**	21
Bourbon Blue | **Manayunk**	21
Jack's Firehse. | **Fairmount**	21

Chops Restaurant | **Bala Cynwyd**	20
Bella Cena | **Rittenhouse**	20
Dave/Buster's | **Del Riverfront**	20
Buca di Beppo | **Exton**	20
Copabanana | **South St.**	20
Fez Moroccan | **Qn Village**	20
Black Sheep Pub | **Rittenhouse**	20
Freight House | **Doylestown**	20
Hard Rock | **Chinatown**	19
World Café | **Univ City**	19
Primavera Pizza | **Ardmore**	19
McGillin's | **Wash Sq W**	18
Ten Stone | **SW Center City**	18
Newtown Grill | **Newtown Sq**	18
Plate | **Ardmore**	16
Le Bec Fin | **Rittenhouse**	-'

PRIX FIXE MENUS

(Call for prices and times)

Fountain | **Logan Sq**	29
Vetri | **Wash Sq W**	29
Birchrunville Store | **Birchrunville**	29
Bibou | **Bella Vista**	29
Fond | **E Passyunk**	28
Paloma | **Bella Vista**	28
NEW Vedge | **Wash Sq W**	28
Talula's Table | **Kennett Sq**	28
Morimoto | **Wash Sq W**	28
Amada | **Old City**	28
Little Fish BYOB | **Bella Vista**	28
Majolica | **Phoenixville**	28
Zahav | **Society Hill**	27
Sapori | **Collingswood/NJ**	27
Orchard | **Kennett Sq**	27
Daddy Mims | **Phoenixville**	27
Prime Rib | **Rittenhouse**	27
Arugula | **Sewell/NJ**	27
Filomena Lake. | **Deptford/NJ**	27
Matyson | **Rittenhouse**	27
Fuji Japanese | **Haddonfield/NJ**	27
Rest. Alba | **Malvern**	27
Washington Hse. | **Sellersville**	27
Oishi | **Newtown**	27
Lacroix | **Rittenhouse**	27

Filomena Italiana | **Clementon/NJ**	27
NEW Sbraga | **Ave of the Arts**	27
Bona Cucina | **Upper Darby**	27
Modo Mio | **N Liberties**	27
Pumpkin | **SW Center City**	27
Tinto | **Rittenhouse**	27
La Famiglia | **Old City**	26
NEW Heirloom | **Chestnut Hill**	26
Blackfish | **Conshohocken**	26
Moro | **Wilmington/DE**	26
Zama | **Rittenhouse**	26
Manon | **Lambertville/NJ**	26
Mercato | **Wash Sq W**	26
Bridget's Steak | **Ambler**	26
Chophouse | **Gibbsboro/NJ**	26
Saloon | **Bella Vista**	26
Dom. Hudson | **Wilmington/DE**	26
Tre Famiglia | **Haddonfield/NJ**	26
Kimberton Inn | **Kimberton**	26
Davio's | **Rittenhouse**	26
High Street Caffe | **West Chester**	26
Nunzio | **Collingswood/NJ**	26
Zento | **Old City**	26
Fleming's Prime | **Radnor**	26
Zinc | **Wash Sq W**	26
Koo Zee Doo | **N Liberties**	25
Dream Cuisine | **Cherry Hill/NJ**	25
William Penn Inn | **Gwynedd**	25
Estia Restaurant | **Ave of the Arts**	25
19 Bella | **Cedars**	25
Nectar | **Berwyn**	25
The Tortilla Press | **Collingswood/NJ**	25
CinCin | **Chestnut Hill**	25
Deep Blue | **Wilmington/DE**	25
Harry's Savoy | **Wilmington/DE**	25
Joseph Ambler Inn | **N Wales**	25
Yangming | **Bryn Mawr**	25
Elements Cafe | **Haddon Hts/NJ**	25
Thai L'Elephant | **Phoenixville**	25

Shiroi Hana | **Rittenhouse**	25
Avalon | **West Chester**	25
Sampan | **Wash Sq W**	25
Zakes Cafe | **Ft Washington**	25
Bistro 7 | **Old City**	25
House/William Merry | **Hockessin/DE**	25
Palm Rest. | **Ave of the Arts**	25
Circles | **S Philly**	25
Spring Mill | **Conshohocken**	25
NEW Tashan | **Ave of the Arts**	25
Ritz Seafood | **Voorhees/NJ**	24
Mamma Maria | **E Passyunk**	24
Moonstruck | **NE Philly**	24
Norma's | **Cherry Hill/NJ**	24
Seasons 52 | **King of Prussia**	24
Sazon | **N Liberties**	24
Mica | **Chestnut Hill**	24
Metro. Diner | **N Wales**	24
Meritage | **SW Center City**	24
Warmdaddy's | **S Philly**	24
Avalon Pasta | **Downingtown**	24
Rist. Panorama | **Old City**	24
Miller's Smorgasbord | **Ronks/LB**	24
Teikoku | **Newtown Sq**	24
Anthony's Creative | **Haddon Hts/NJ**	24
Kunkel's | **Haddon Hts/NJ**	24
Mikado | **multi.**	24
Firecreek | **Downingtown**	24
Yardley Inn | **Yardley**	24
Black Bass | **Lumberville**	24
Fuji Mountain | **Rittenhouse**	24
Little Tuna | **Haddonfield/NJ**	24
Marrakesh | **South St.**	24
Il Cantuccio | **N Liberties**	24
Melting Pot | **multi.**	24
Bay Pony Inn | **Lederach**	24
Mendenhall Inn | **Mendenhall**	24
Cuba Libre | **Old City**	24
P.F. Chang's | **Marlton/NJ**	24
Gnocchi | **South St.**	24
Salento | **Rittenhouse**	23
M Restaurant | **Wash Sq W**	23
Steak 38 | **Cherry Hill/NJ**	23
Moshulu | **Del Riverfront**	23

Fayette St. | **Conshohocken**	23
Varalli | **Ave of the Arts**	23
High Note Cafe | **S Philly**	23
Xochitl | **Society Hill**	23
White Dog | **Wayne**	23
JG Domestic | **Univ City**	23
Derek's | **Manayunk**	23
Girasole | **Ave of the Arts**	23
Bistro St. Tropez | **Rittenhouse**	23
Azie | **Villanova**	23
Nineteen | **Ave of the Arts**	23
Cafe Preeya | **Huntingdon Vly**	23
Blue Bell Inn | **Blue Bell**	23
Kuzina/Sofia | **Cherry Hill/NJ**	23
Positano Coast | **Society Hill**	23
Twenty Manning | **Rittenhouse**	23
Zacharias | **Worcester**	23
Caribou | **Wash Sq W**	22
Square 1682 | **Rittenhouse**	22
Drafting Rm. | **Exton**	22
Mirna's Café | **multi.**	22
Iron Hill | **Maple Shade/NJ**	22
Rist. Primavera | **Wayne**	22
Percy St. BBQ | **multi.**	22
Da Vinci Ristorante | **E Passyunk**	22
A La Maison | **Ardmore**	22
NEW Paramour | **Wayne**	22
Erawan Thai | **Rittenhouse**	22
Roller's/Flying Fish | **Chestnut Hill**	22
Brick Hotel Rest. | **Newtown**	22
Pattaya | **Univ City**	22
C19 | **Rittenhouse**	21
Lambertville Station | **Lambertville/NJ**	21
Lemon Grass Thai | **Univ City**	21
Pistachio Grille | **Maple Glen**	21
Water Works | **Fairmount**	21
La Fontana | **Rittenhouse**	21
Bourbon Blue | **Manayunk**	21
Corner | **Wash Sq W**	21
Marathon Grill | **multi.**	21
Schlesinger's | **Rittenhouse**	20

Fez Moroccan | **Qn Village**	20
The Coastline | **Cherry Hill/NJ**	19
Ladder 15 | **Rittenhouse**	19
My Thai | **SW Center City**	19
Le Bec Fin | **Rittenhouse**	-
NEW Miss Rachel's Pantry | **S Philly**	-

QUICK BITES

NEW Loco Pez | **Fishtown**	29
Sketch | **Fishtown**	28
NEW Ela | **Qn Village**	28
John's Roast Pork | **S Philly**	27
Paesano's Philly Style | **multi.**	27
Royal Tavern | **Bella Vista**	26
Tierra Colombiana | **N Philly**	26
Capriotti's | **multi.**	26
Charlie's Hamburg. | **Folsom**	26
Village Whiskey | **Rittenhouse**	26
Bitar's | **Bella Vista**	26
Tony Luke's | **S Philly**	26
Doghouse Burgers | **Downingtown**	26
Olce Pizza Grille | **Lansdale**	26
Reading Term. Mkt. | **Chinatown**	26
Café Con Choc. | **S Philly**	26
Art of Bread | **Narberth**	26
Night Kitchen Bake | **Chestnut Hill**	26
Stella Sera | **Chestnut Hill**	26
Zento | **Old City**	26
Bobby Chez | **multi.**	25
Grey Lodge | **NE Philly**	25
Memphis Tap | **Port Richmond**	25
NEW Federal Donuts | **S Philly**	25
Earth Bread | **Mt Airy**	25
Larry's Steaks | **Wynnefield**	25
Alyan's | **South St.**	25
Franzone's | **Bridgeport/NJ**	25
Sabrina's Café | **Fairmount**	25
Green Eggs | **S Philly**	25
Steve's Steaks | **NE Philly**	25
The Kibitz Room | **Cherry Hill/NJ**	25

Garces Trading | **Wash Sq W**	25
Zavino | **Wash Sq W**	25
Hot Diggity! | **South St.**	24
NEW 320 Market | **Media**	24
Zorba's Taverna | **Fairmount**	24
British Chip Shop | **Haddonfield/NJ**	24
Jim's Steaks | **multi.**	24
AllWays Café | **Huntingdon Vly**	24
Tria Wine Room | **Univ City**	24
Bobby's Burger | **Univ City**	24
Cantina Caballitos/Segundos | **E Passyunk**	24
Banana Leaf | **Chinatown**	24
Monk's Cafe | **Rittenhouse**	24
Kennett Restaurant | **Qn Village**	24
Hawthornes | **Bella Vista**	24
Couch Tomato Café | **Manayunk**	24
Sidecar | **SW Center City**	24
Pub & Kitchen | **SW Center City**	24
12th St. Cantina | **Chinatown**	24
Five Guys | **multi.**	24
NEW Birra | **E Passyunk**	24
Lee's Hoagie | **multi.**	24
Aqua | **Wash Sq W**	24
Three Monkeys Cafe | **NE Philly**	24
Good Dog Bar | **Rittenhouse**	24
Campo's Deli | **Old City**	24
Dock Street Brew. | **Univ City**	24
Bar Ferdinand | **N Liberties**	24
Silk City | **N Liberties**	24
Pop Shop | **Collingswood/NJ**	23
SLiCE | **multi.**	23
One Shot Coffee | **N Liberties**	23
Forno | **Maple Shade/NJ**	23
South St. Souvlaki | **South St.**	23
Resurrection Ale | **SW Center City**	23
a.kitchen | **Rittenhouse**	23
Sang Kee Noodle | **Univ City**	23
Zesty's | **Manayunk**	23

Maoz Veg. | **multi.**	23
B2 | **E Passyunk**	23
Almaz Café | **Rittenhouse**	23
Cake | **Chestnut Hill**	23
Isaac's | **multi.**	23
Pat's Steaks | **E Passyunk**	23
Ekta Indian Cuisine | **multi.**	23
Blueplate | **Mullica Hill/NJ**	23
A Full Plate | **N Liberties**	23
NEW Honest Tom's Taco | **W Philly**	23
500º | **Rittenhouse**	23
Luigi's Pizza Fresca | **multi.**	23
City Tap House | **Univ City**	23
Nifty Fifty's | **multi.**	23
Chickie's/Pete's | **multi.**	23
Tiffin | **N Liberties**	22
Ants Pants Cafe | **SW Center City**	22
Full Moon | **Lambertville/NJ**	22
Iron Hill | **Lancaster/LB**	22
Dining Car | **NE Philly**	22
Mexican Food | **Marlton/NJ**	22
Brew HaHa! | **multi.**	22
Geno's Steaks | **S Philly**	22
Max Brenner | **Rittenhouse**	22
Maggio's | **Southampton**	22
Bonté Wafflerie | **multi.**	22
St. Stephens Green | **Fairmount**	22
Baby Blues | **Univ City**	22
FireStone Roasting | **Wilmington/DE**	22
Smokin' Betty | **Wash Sq W**	22
Mastoris | **Bordentown/NJ**	22
Revolution Hse. | **Old City**	22
Scoogi's | **Flourtown**	21
NEW 401 Diner | **Conshohocken**	21
Fuel | **multi.**	21
Ponzio's | **Cherry Hill/NJ**	21
El Fuego | **Rittenhouse**	21
Hop Angel | **NE Philly**	21
Giwa | **Rittenhouse**	21
P.J. Whelihan's | **Blue Bell**	21

Gino's Burgers | **King of Prussia**	21
NEW Broad St. Diner | **S Philly**	21
Frankford Hall | **Fishtown**	20
Local 44 | **Univ City**	20
Kitchen Bar | **Abington**	20
Ardmore Station | **Ardmore**	20
Du Jour | **multi.**	20
Trolley Car | **Mt Airy**	20
Schlesinger's | **Rittenhouse**	20
Le Pain | **Rittenhouse**	20
Mayfair Diner | **NE Philly**	20
Triumph Brewing | **Old City**	20
MaGerks | **Ft Washington**	20
Darling's | **multi.**	20
Q BBQ | **Old City**	20
Melrose Diner | **S Philly**	20
Mugshots | **multi.**	19
Hymie's | **Merion Station**	19
Little Pete's | **Rittenhouse**	19
Oregon Diner | **S Philly**	19
Molly Maguire's | **Phoenixville**	19
Mexican Post | **Logan Sq**	19
Hummus | **Univ City**	19
Rosey's BBQ | **Jenkintown**	19
Cooperage | **Wash Sq W**	19
Murray's Deli | **Bala Cynwyd**	19
Más Mexicali | **West Chester**	19
Auspicious | **Ardmore**	19
Pub/Passyunk | **E Passyunk**	18
Mrs. Marty's Deli | **Media**	18
MilkBoy Coffee | **multi.**	18
Tavern 17 | **Rittenhouse**	18
Sage Diner | **Mt Laurel/NJ**	18
Urban Saloon | **Fairmount**	16
Sawatdee | **Rittenhouse**	15
NEW HipCityVeg | **Rittenhouse**	_
NEW Industry | **S Philly**	_
NEW Little Louie's BBQ | **Collingswood/NJ**	_
Mac's Tavern | **Old City**	_
NEW Mekong River | **S Philly**	_
NEW Morgan's Pier | **Del Riverfront**	_
NEW Nomad Pizza | **South St.**	_
NEW Shake Shack | **Rittenhouse**	_

QUIET CONVERSATION

Fountain | **Logan Sq**	29
Birchrunville Store | **Birchrunville**	29
Bibou | **Bella Vista**	29
Sycamore | **Lansdowne**	28
Fond | **E Passyunk**	28
NEW Vedge | **Wash Sq W**	28
Talula's Table | **Kennett Sq**	28
Masamoto | **Glen Mills**	28
NEW Ela | **Qn Village**	28
Zahav | **Society Hill**	27
Honey | **Doylestown**	27
Lacroix | **Rittenhouse**	27
Dilworth. Inn | **West Chester**	27
Talula's Garden | **Wash Sq W**	27
Singapore Kosher | **Chinatown**	27
La Famiglia | **Old City**	26
NEW Heirloom | **Chestnut Hill**	26
Catherine's | **Unionville**	26
Lily's on Main | **Ephrata/LB**	26
La Cena | **Bensalem**	26
Giumarello | **Westmont/NJ**	26
Delmonico's | **Wynnefield**	26
Francesco's Cucina | **Berlin/NJ**	26
Shere-E-Punjab | **multi.**	26
Kimberton Inn | **Kimberton**	26
Charcoal BYOB | **Yardley**	26
Zento | **Old City**	26
Slate Bleu | **Doylestown**	26
La Fourno | **South St.**	25
Inn/Phillips Mill | **New Hope**	25
Cross Culture | **multi.**	25
Geechee Girl | **Germantown**	25
Kinnaree | **Horsham**	25
Amelia's Tea/Holly | **Mullica Hill/NJ**	25
Estia Restaurant | **Ave of the Arts**	25
19 Bella | **Cedars**	25
Thai L'Elephant | **Phoenixville**	25
Trio | **Fairmount**	25
NEW Ulivo | **Qn Village**	25
Bistro 7 | **Old City**	25
Swann Lounge | **Logan Sq**	25

Union Trust | **Wash Sq W**	24
Bocelli | **Gwynedd**	24
Casta Diva | **Rittenhouse**	24
Tavolo | **Huntingdon Vly**	24
Las Bugambilias | **South St.**	24
Bella Tori | **Langhorne**	24
Le Castagne | **Rittenhouse**	24
Yardley Inn | **Yardley**	24
Black Bass | **Lumberville**	24
Parc Bistro | **Skippack**	24
Toscana 52 | **Feasterville**	24
Avenida | **Mt Airy**	23
M Restaurant | **Wash Sq W**	23
Log Cabin | **Leola/LB**	23
Steak 38 | **Cherry Hill/NJ**	23
Blue Pear | **West Chester**	23
Aperto | **Narberth**	23
Cake | **Chestnut Hill**	23
Mi Lah Veg. | **Rittenhouse**	23
Nineteen | **Ave of the Arts**	23
R2L | **Rittenhouse**	23
Farnsworth House | **Bordentown/NJ**	23
La Na Thai | **Media**	23
Braddock's | **Medford/NJ**	22
Palace of Asia | **multi.**	22
Erawan Thai | **multi.**	22
Chiarella's | **E Passyunk**	22
Pistachio Grille | **Maple Glen**	21
Water Works | **Fairmount**	21
Amuse | **Ave of the Arts**	21
Gypsy Saloon | **W Conshohocken**	21
Carriage House | **Voorhees/NJ**	21
Chinnar Indian | **Berwyn**	19
Spamps | **Conshohocken**	19
f**NEW** Divan Med. Grill | **Qn Village**	–
NEW Pickled Heron | **Fishtown**	–
NEW Russet | **Rittenhouse**	–

RAW BARS

Gibraltar | **Lancaster/LB**	26
Village Whiskey | **Rittenhouse**	26
Harry's Seafood | **Wilmington/DE**	26

SPECIAL FEATURES

Creed's	**King of Prussia**	26
NEW Fish	**Wash Sq W**	25
Marsha Brown	**New Hope**	25
Deep Blue	**Wilmington/DE**	25
Caffe Aldo	**Cherry Hill/NJ**	25
SoleFood	**Wash Sq W**	25
Stoudts Black Angus	**Adamstown/LB**	25
Oyster Hse.	**Rittenhouse**	24
Union Trust	**Wash Sq W**	24
Feby's Fish.	**Wilmington/DE**	24
Kunkel's	**Haddon Hts/NJ**	24
Little Tuna	**Haddonfield/NJ**	24
Big Fish Grill	**multi.**	24
Steak 38	**Cherry Hill/NJ**	23
Walter's Steak.	**Wilmington/DE**	23
NEW Route 6	**Fairmount**	23
Nineteen	**Ave of the Arts**	23
Blue2O	**Cherry Hill/NJ**	22
Brandywine Prime	**Chadds Ford**	22
Legal Sea Foods	**King of Prussia**	22
Table 31	**Logan Sq**	22
NEW Doc Magrogan	**multi.**	21
Snockey's Oyster	**S Philly**	21
Riverstone Café	**Exton**	21
Verdad Rest.	**Bryn Mawr**	21
Freight House	**Doylestown**	20
Cooperage	**Wash Sq W**	19

ROMANTIC PLACES

Fountain	**Logan Sq**	29
Vetri	**Wash Sq W**	29
Birchrunville Store	**Birchrunville**	29
Bibou	**Bella Vista**	29
Majolica	**Phoenixville**	28
Zahav	**Society Hill**	27
Osteria	**N Philly**	27
Arugula	**Sewell/NJ**	27
Fuji Japanese	**Haddonfield/NJ**	27
Honey	**Doylestown**	27
August	**S Philly**	27
Washington Hse.	**Sellersville**	27
Le Virtù	**E Passyunk**	27

Lacroix	**Rittenhouse**	27
Dilworth. Inn	**West Chester**	27
Talula's Garden	**Wash Sq W**	27
Umai Umai	**Fairmount**	27
Farm/Fisherman	**Wash Sq W**	27
NEW Heirloom	**Chestnut Hill**	26
Blackfish	**Conshohocken**	26
Catherine's	**Unionville**	26
Marigold Kitchen	**Univ City**	26
Duling-Kurtz Hse.	**Exton**	26
Cochon	**Qn Village**	26
Bistrot/Minette	**Qn Village**	26
Izumi	**E Passyunk**	26
Savona	**Gulph Mills**	26
Giumarello	**Westmont/NJ**	26
Ariano	**Media**	26
Barclay Prime	**Rittenhouse**	26
Charcoal BYOB	**Yardley**	26
Butcher/Singer	**Rittenhouse**	26
Carversville Inn	**Carversville**	26
Stella Sera	**Chestnut Hill**	26
Core De Roma	**South St.**	26
Fork	**Old City**	26
Bistro/Marino	**Collingswood/NJ**	26
Slate Bleu	**Doylestown**	26
Orillas Tapa Bar	**Wilmington/DE**	26
Koo Zee Doo	**N Liberties**	25
Fat Salmon Sushi	**Wash Sq W**	25
Inn/Phillips Mill	**New Hope**	25
Alma de Cuba	**Rittenhouse**	25
Estia Restaurant	**Ave of the Arts**	25
Paradiso	**E Passyunk**	25
General Warren Inne	**Malvern**	25
19 Bella	**Cedars**	25
Nectar	**Berwyn**	25
Figs	**Fairmount**	25
Na'Brasa	**Horsham**	25
Sampan	**Wash Sq W**	25
Trio	**Fairmount**	25
NEW Ulivo	**Qn Village**	25
Bistro 7	**Old City**	25
Agiato	**Manayunk**	25

SPECIAL FEATURES

SENIOR APPEAL

Library IV | **Williamstown/NJ**	26
La Famiglia | **Old City**	26
NEW Heirloom | **Chestnut Hill**	26
Blackfish | **Conshohocken**	26
Morton's | **multi.**	26
Marigold Kitchen | **Univ City**	26
Lily's on Main | **Ephrata/LB**	26
Radicchio Cafe | **Old City**	26
La Locanda | **Voorhees/NJ**	26
Harry's Seafood | **Wilmington/DE**	26
Chophouse | **Gibbsboro/NJ**	26
Francesco's Cucina | **Berlin/NJ**	26
Kimberton Inn | **Kimberton**	26
La Viola Ovest | **Rittenhouse**	26
Femmina Italian Grill | **Medford/NJ**	26
Nunzio | **Collingswood/NJ**	26
Fleming's Prime | **Marlton/NJ**	26
Stella Sera | **Chestnut Hill**	26
Fleming's Prime | **Radnor**	26
Fork | **Old City**	26
Bistro/Marino | **Collingswood/NJ**	26
Koo Zee Doo | **N Liberties**	25
Bird-in-Hand | **Bird-in-Hand/LB**	25
Kinnaree | **Horsham**	25
William Penn Inn | **Gwynedd**	25
Amelia's Tea/Holly | **Mullica Hill/NJ**	25
Honey's Sit | **N Liberties**	25
Estia Restaurant | **Ave of the Arts**	25
General Warren Inne | **Malvern**	25
19 Bella | **Cedars**	25
CinCin | **Chestnut Hill**	25
Harry's Savoy | **Wilmington/DE**	25
Na'Brasa | **Horsham**	25
Carlucci's Grill | **Yardley**	25
Abacus | **Lansdale**	25
Haydn Zug's | **E Petersburg/LB**	25
Pho Xe Lua | **Chinatown**	25
Gallo's Seafood | **NE Philly**	25
Thai L'Elephant | **Phoenixville**	25
Georgine's | **Bristol**	25
The Kibitz Room | **Cherry Hill/NJ**	25
Porcini | **Rittenhouse**	25
Moonstruck | **NE Philly**	24
Nam Phuong | **Bella Vista**	24
Maggiano's | **multi.**	24
Bocelli | **Gwynedd**	24
Phillips Sea. | **Logan Sq**	24
Osaka | **multi.**	24
Bonefish Grill | **multi.**	24
British Chip Shop | **Haddonfield/NJ**	24
Metro. Diner | **N Wales**	24
Casta Diva | **Rittenhouse**	24
Francisco's | **Wash Crossing**	24
Pietro's Prime | **West Chester**	24
Ariana's Ristorante | **N Wales**	24
Avalon Pasta | **Downingtown**	24
Tavolo | **Huntingdon Vly**	24
Pub | **Pennsauken/NJ**	24
Las Bugambilias | **South St.**	24
Bella Tori | **Langhorne**	24
Miller's Smorgasbord | **Ronks/LB**	24
AllWays Café | **Huntingdon Vly**	24
Cheesecake | **Willow Grove**	24
Georges' | **Wayne**	24
Anastasi | **Bella Vista**	24
Yardley Inn | **Yardley**	24
Susanna Foo's | **Radnor**	24
Little Tuna | **Haddonfield/NJ**	24
Good 'n Plenty | **Smoketown/LB**	24
A Taste/Britain | **Wayne**	24
Marg. Kuo | **Wayne**	24
Bay Pony Inn | **Lederach**	24
Parc Bistro | **Skippack**	24
Chiangmai | **Conshohocken**	24
J.B. Dawson's/Austin's | **multi.**	24
Aqua | **Wash Sq W**	24
Mandarin Gdn. | **Willow Grove**	24

Broad Axe Tav. | **Ambler** 21
Gino's Burgers | **King of Prussia** 21
NEW Broad St. Diner | **S Philly** 21
Kitchen Bar | **Abington** 20
Hokka Hokka | **Chestnut Hill** 20
Du Jour | **multi.** 20
Bella Cena | **Rittenhouse** 20
Schlesinger's | **Rittenhouse** 20
Le Pain | **Rittenhouse** 20
Mayfair Diner | **NE Philly** 20
Darling's | **multi.** 20
Mikado | **Ardmore** 20
Melrose Diner | **S Philly** 20
West Side Gravy | **Collingswood/NJ** 20
Hymie's | **Merion Station** 19
Chinnar Indian | **Berwyn** 19
Little Pete's | **Rittenhouse** 19
Oregon Diner | **S Philly** 19
Murray's Deli | **Bala Cynwyd** 19
Spamps | **Conshohocken** 19
Mrs. Marty's Deli | **Media** 18
Country Squire Diner | **Broomall** 18
Newtown Grill | **Newtown Sq** 18
Gullifty's | **Rosemont** 17
Plate | **Ardmore** 16
NEW Argana Moroccan | **Lansdowne** -

SINGLES SCENES

NEW Loco Pez | **Fishtown** 29
Amada | **Old City** 28
NEW Ela | **Qn Village** 28
NEW Stateside | **E Passyunk** 27
Village Whiskey | **Rittenhouse** 26
Tequilas | **Rittenhouse** 26
Chifa | **Wash Sq W** 26
Amis | **Wash Sq W** 26
Sullivan's Steak | **multi.** 26
Orillas Tapa Bar | **Wilmington/DE** 26
Memphis Tap | **Port Richmond** 25
El Camino Real | **N Liberties** 25
Alma de Cuba | **Rittenhouse** 25
NEW Alla Spina | **Fairmount** 25

Earth Bread | **Mt Airy** 25
Deep Blue | **Wilmington/DE** 25
Del Frisco's | **Ave of the Arts** 25
Sampan | **Wash Sq W** 25
Kisso Sushi | **Old City** 25
Zavino | **Wash Sq W** 25
Pod | **Univ City** 24
Tria Wine Room | **Univ City** 24
Tria | **Wash Sq W** 24
Bobby's Burger | **Univ City** 24
Cantina Caballitos/Segundos | **multi.** 24
Kennett Restaurant | **Qn Village** 24
Hawthornes | **Bella Vista** 24
Sidecar | **SW Center City** 24
Pub & Kitchen | **SW Center City** 24
Firecreek | **Downingtown** 24
NEW Birra | **E Passyunk** 24
Mixto | **Wash Sq W** 24
Cuba Libre | **Old City** 24
Good Dog Bar | **Rittenhouse** 24
Dock Street Brew. | **Univ City** 24
Bar Ferdinand | **N Liberties** 24
Silk City | **N Liberties** 24
NEW Lemon Hill | **Fairmount** 23
N. 3rd | **N Liberties** 23
Teresa's Next Dr. | **Wayne** 23
Resurrection Ale | **SW Center City** 23
Raw Sushi | **Wash Sq W** 23
Xochitl | **Society Hill** 23
Standard Tap | **N Liberties** 23
Redstone | **Marlton/NJ** 23
Jones | **Wash Sq W** 23
Derek's | **Manayunk** 23
Azie | **Villanova** 23
Khyber | **Old City** 23
Belgian Café | **Fairmount** 23
Valanni | **Wash Sq W** 23
The Twisted Tail | **Society Hill** 23
Continental Mid. | **Rittenhouse** 23
Appalachian Brew. | **Collegeville** 23

El Rey | **Rittenhouse**	23
Eulogy Belgian | **Old City**	23
City Tap House | **Univ City**	23
Twenty Manning | **Rittenhouse**	23
Chickie's/Pete's | **Bordentown/NJ**	23
Manayunk Brew. | **Manayunk**	22
Devil's Den | **S Philly**	22
Coyote Cross. | **Conshohocken**	22
NEW La Calaca Feliz | **Fairmount**	22
St. Stephens Green | **Fairmount**	22
Brauhaus Schmitz | **South St.**	22
Catahoula | **Qn Village**	22
Smokin' Betty | **Wash Sq W**	22
Revolution Hse. | **Old City**	22
Sly Fox | **Royersford**	22
Matador | **Wayne**	21
Slate | **Rittenhouse**	21
Bourbon Blue | **Manayunk**	21
Chestnut7 | **Chestnut Hill**	21
The Plough & the Stars | **Old City**	21
P.J. Whelihan's | **multi.**	21
Broad Axe Tav. | **Ambler**	21
Frankford Hall | **Fishtown**	20
Mission Grill | **Logan Sq**	20
NEW American Sardine | **S Philly**	20
Fergie's Pub | **Wash Sq W**	20
Opa | **Wash Sq W**	20
Farmers' Cabinet | **Wash Sq W**	20
Triumph Brewing | **Old City**	20
Darling's | **N Liberties**	20
Black Sheep Pub | **Rittenhouse**	20
Mugshots | **multi.**	19
Molly Maguire's | **Phoenixville**	19
Mexican Post | **multi.**	19
Tír na nÓg | **Logan Sq**	19
Ladder 15 | **Rittenhouse**	19
Más Mexicali | **West Chester**	19
World Café | **Wilmington/DE**	19
Pub/Passyunk | **E Passyunk**	18
Kite/Key | **Fairmount**	18
Fadó Irish | **Rittenhouse**	18

MilkBoy Coffee | **multi.**	18
Tavern 17 | **Rittenhouse**	18
Public Hse./Logan | **Logan Sq**	17
Urban Saloon | **Fairmount**	16
NEW In Riva | **E Falls**	–
NEW SoWe Bar Kitchen | **SW Center City**	–
NEW Square Peg | **Wash Sq W**	–

TRANSPORTING EXPERIENCES

Vetri | **Wash Sq W**	29
Birchrunville Store | **Birchrunville**	29
Paloma | **Bella Vista**	28
Morimoto | **Wash Sq W**	28
Le Virtù | **E Passyunk**	27
Lacroix | **Rittenhouse**	27
Farm/Fisherman | **Wash Sq W**	27
La Famiglia | **Old City**	26
Duling-Kurtz Hse. | **Exton**	26
Moro | **Wilmington/DE**	26
Hamilton's | **Lambertville/NJ**	26
Manon | **Lambertville/NJ**	26
Nunzio | **Collingswood/NJ**	26
Koo Zee Doo | **N Liberties**	25
Nectar | **Berwyn**	25
Figs | **Fairmount**	25
El Vez | **Wash Sq W**	25
Krazy Kat's | **Montchanin/DE**	25
Bomb Bomb BBQ | **S Philly**	24
Kabul Afghan | **Old City**	24
Anton's/Swan | **Lambertville/NJ**	24
Le Castagne | **Rittenhouse**	24
Marrakesh | **South St.**	24
10 Arts | **Ave of the Arts**	24
Moshulu | **Del Riverfront**	23
Nineteen | **Ave of the Arts**	23
Positano Coast | **Society Hill**	23
Le Bec Fin | **Rittenhouse**	–

TRENDY

Vetri | **Wash Sq W**	29
NEW Loco Pez | **Fishtown**	29
NEW Vedge | **Wash Sq W**	28
Morimoto | **Wash Sq W**	28

Restaurant	Location	Score
Amada	**Old City**	28
Little Fish BYOB	**Bella Vista**	28
NEW Ela	**Qn Village**	28
Zahav	**Society Hill**	27
Osteria	**N Philly**	27
Matyson	**Rittenhouse**	27
NEW Stateside	**E Passyunk**	27
Buddakan	**Old City**	27
Oishi	**Newtown**	27
NEW Sbraga	**Ave of the Arts**	27
Barbuzzo	**Wash Sq W**	27
Talula's Garden	**Wash Sq W**	27
Terra Nova	**Sewell/NJ**	27
Paesano's Philly Style	**multi.**	27
Tinto	**Rittenhouse**	27
Royal Tavern	**Bella Vista**	26
Capital Grille	**Ave of the Arts**	26
Village Whiskey	**Rittenhouse**	26
Zama	**Rittenhouse**	26
Bistrot/Minette	**Qn Village**	26
Limoncello	**West Chester**	26
Mélange	**Haddonfield/NJ**	26
Piccolina Tosc.	**Wilmington/DE**	26
Chifa	**Wash Sq W**	26
Barclay Prime	**Rittenhouse**	26
Amis	**Wash Sq W**	26
Butcher/Singer	**Rittenhouse**	26
Lolita	**Wash Sq W**	26
Orillas Tapa Bar	**Wilmington/DE**	26
Han Dynasty	**multi.**	25
Memphis Tap	**Port Richmond**	25
El Camino Real	**N Liberties**	25
NEW Fish	**Wash Sq W**	25
NEW Federal Donuts	**S Philly**	25
Alma de Cuba	**Rittenhouse**	25
NEW Alla Spina	**Fairmount**	25
Paradiso	**E Passyunk**	25
Firebirds	**multi.**	25
Vietnam Café	**W Philly**	25
El Vez	**Wash Sq W**	25
Del Frisco's	**Ave of the Arts**	25
Sampan	**Wash Sq W**	25
Morning Glory	**Bella Vista**	25
Garces Trading	**Wash Sq W**	25
Supper	**South St.**	25
NEW Tashan	**Ave of the Arts**	25
Zavino	**Wash Sq W**	25
Hot Diggity!	**South St.**	24
Pod	**Univ City**	24
Pietro's Prime	**West Chester**	24
Parc	**Rittenhouse**	24
Tria Wine Room	**Univ City**	24
Tria	**Wash Sq W**	24
Continental	**Old City**	24
Cantina Caballitos/Segundos	**E Passyunk**	24
Sidecar	**SW Center City**	24
Pub & Kitchen	**SW Center City**	24
Pizzeria Stella	**Society Hill**	24
Cantina Feliz	**Ft Washington**	24
Susanna Foo's	**Radnor**	24
Gemelli on Main	**Manayunk**	24
NEW Birra	**E Passyunk**	24
Mixto	**Wash Sq W**	24
Le Viet	**Bella Vista**	24
Cuba Libre	**Old City**	24
10 Arts	**Ave of the Arts**	24
Bar Ferdinand	**N Liberties**	24
Silk City	**N Liberties**	24
NEW Lemon Hill	**Fairmount**	23
a.kitchen	**Rittenhouse**	23
Xochitl	**Society Hill**	23
NEW Route 6	**Fairmount**	23
White Dog	**Wayne**	23
JG Domestic	**Univ City**	23
Rouge	**Rittenhouse**	23
Azie	**multi.**	23
NEW Honest Tom's Taco	**W Philly**	23
500º	**Rittenhouse**	23
Valanni	**Wash Sq W**	23
Dettera	**Ambler**	23
The Twisted Tail	**Society Hill**	23
Continental Mid.	**Rittenhouse**	23

SPECIAL FEATURES

Landing | **New Hope** 21
Ardmore Station | **Ardmore** 20
Dave/Buster's | **Del Riverfront** 20
Abner's | **Univ City** 19
NEW In Riva | **E Falls** -

VISITORS ON EXPENSE ACCOUNT

Fountain | **Logan Sq** 29
Morimoto | **Wash Sq W** 28
Amada | **Old City** 28
Zahav | **Society Hill** 27
Prime Rib | **Rittenhouse** 27
NEW Sbraga | **Ave of the Arts** 27
Dilworth. Inn | **West Chester** 27
Talula's Garden | **Wash Sq W** 27
Fogo de Chão | **Ave of the Arts** 27
Morton's | **Ave of the Arts** 26
Capital Grille | **Ave of the Arts** 26
Piccolina Tosc. | **Wilmington/DE** 26
Chifa | **Wash Sq W** 26
Barclay Prime | **Rittenhouse** 26
Butcher/Singer | **Rittenhouse** 26
Sullivan's Steak | **multi.** 26
Chima | **Logan Sq** 26
Fleming's Prime | **multi.** 26
Fork | **Old City** 26
Estia Restaurant | **Ave of the Arts** 25
Ruth's Chris | **Ave of the Arts** 25
Smith/Wollensky | **Rittenhouse** 25
Del Frisco's | **Ave of the Arts** 25
NEW Tashan | **Ave of the Arts** 25
Union Trust | **Wash Sq W** 24
Phillips Sea. | **Logan Sq** 24
Pod | **Univ City** 24
Mica | **Chestnut Hill** 24
Bella Tori | **Langhorne** 24
Black Bass | **Lumberville** 24
Gemelli on Main | **Manayunk** 24
10 Arts | **Ave of the Arts** 24
McCormick/Schmick | **multi.** 23

Log Cabin | **Leola/LB** 23
Varalli | **Ave of the Arts** 23
NEW Route 6 | **Fairmount** 23
White Dog | **Wayne** 23
Farmer's Daughter | **Blue Bell** 23
JG Domestic | **Univ City** 23
Azie | **multi.** 23
Nineteen | **Ave of the Arts** 23
R2L | **Rittenhouse** 23
Square 1682 | **Rittenhouse** 22
NEW Paramour | **Wayne** 22
Table 31 | **Logan Sq** 22
Water Works | **Fairmount** 21
Chops Restaurant | **Bala Cynwyd** 20
Le Bec Fin | **Rittenhouse** -

WINNING WINE LISTS

Fountain | **Logan Sq** 29
Vetri | **Wash Sq W** 29
NEW Vedge | **Wash Sq W** 28
Amada | **Old City** 28
NEW Ela | **Qn Village** 28
Osteria | **N Philly** 27
Prime Rib | **Rittenhouse** 27
Le Virtù | **E Passyunk** 27
Lacroix | **Rittenhouse** 27
NEW Sbraga | **Ave of the Arts** 27
Green Hills Inn | **Reading/LB** 27
Barbuzzo | **Wash Sq W** 27
Dilworth. Inn | **West Chester** 27
Fogo de Chão | **Ave of the Arts** 27
Tinto | **Rittenhouse** 27
La Famiglia | **Old City** 26
Morton's | **Ave of the Arts** 26
Capital Grille | **Ave of the Arts** 26
Moro | **Wilmington/DE** 26
Savona | **Gulph Mills** 26
Giumarello | **Westmont/NJ** 26
Piccolina Tosc. | **Wilmington/DE** 26
Saloon | **Bella Vista** 26
Dom. Hudson | **Wilmington/DE** 26
Francesco's Cucina | **Berlin/NJ** 26

SPECIAL FEATURES

Cuisines

Includes names, locations and Food ratings.

AFGHAN

Kabul Afghan	Old City	24
Ariana	multi.	23

AFRICAN

Abyssinia	Univ City	25
Marrakesh	South St.	24
Almaz Café	Rittenhouse	23
Aya's Café	Logan Sq	22
Fez Moroccan	Qn Village	20
NEW Argana Moroccan	Lansdowne	_|

AMERICAN

Sycamore	Lansdowne	28
Fond	E Passyunk	28
NEW Ela	Qn Village	28
Capogiro Gelato Artisans	E Passyunk	28
Majolica	Phoenixville	28
Capogiro Gelato Artisans	multi.	28
Orchard	Kennett Sq	27
Daddy Mims	Phoenixville	27
Matyson	Rittenhouse	27
Honey	Doylestown	27
NEW Stateside	E Passyunk	27
Hinge	Port Richmond	27
Rest. Alba	Malvern	27
Sola	Bryn Mawr	27
Washington Hse.	Sellersville	27
Funky Lil' Kitchen	Pottstown	27
NEW Sbraga	Ave of the Arts	27
Green Hills Inn	Reading/LB	27
Culinaria	Wilmington/DE	27
Dilworth. Inn	West Chester	27
Talula's Garden	Wash Sq W	27
Terra Nova	Sewell/NJ	27
Pumpkin	SW Center City	27
Farm/Fisherman	Wash Sq W	27
Library IV	Williamstown/NJ	26
Relish	W Oak Lane	26
NEW Heirloom	Chestnut Hill	26

Royal Tavern	Bella Vista	26
Catherine's	Unionville	26
Marigold Kitchen	Univ City	26
Fat Tomato Grill	Berlin/NJ	26
Lily's on Main	Ephrata/LB	26
Village Whiskey	Rittenhouse	26
NEW Tony Luke's	multi.	26
Mélange	Haddonfield/NJ	26
Doghouse Burgers	Downingtown	26
Dom. Hudson	Wilmington/DE	26
Blue Claw Crab	Burlington/NJ	26
Chink's Steaks	NE Philly	26
Bailey's Bar & Grille	Levittown	26
Kimberton Inn	Kimberton	26
Charcoal BYOB	Yardley	26
Amani's BYOB	Downingtown	26
High Street Caffe	West Chester	26
Carversville Inn	Carversville	26
Belvedere Inn	Lancaster/LB	26
Aunt Berta's	Oaklyn/NJ	26
Fork	Old City	26
Dalessandro's	Roxborough	25
Bird-in-Hand	Bird-in-Hand/LB	25
Memphis Tap	Port Richmond	25
El Camino Real	N Liberties	25
NEW Federal Donuts	S Philly	25
Black Lab Bistro	Phoenixville	25
Geechee Girl	Germantown	25
William Penn Inn	Gwynedd	25
Harvest	Glen Mills	25
GG's Restaurant	Mt Laurel/NJ	25
Cafe Lift	Callowhill	25
Kaya's	Havertown	25
Honey's Sit	N Liberties	25

Marsha Brown | **New Hope**	25
Earth Bread | **Mt Airy**	25
NEW Tapestry | **Qn Village**	25
Firebirds | **multi.**	25
General Warren Inne | **Malvern**	25
Barry's Steaks | **Wynnefield**	25
Stone Rose | **Conshohocken**	25
Chubby's Steaks | **Roxborough**	25
South Philly Tap | **S Philly**	25
Eclipse Bistro | **Wilmington/DE**	25
Bistro at Cherry Hill | **Cherry Hill/NJ**	25
Harry's Savoy | **Wilmington/DE**	25
Joseph Ambler Inn | **N Wales**	25
Sabrina's Café | **multi.**	25
Green Eggs | **multi.**	25
NEW Green Eggs Café | **Wash Sq W**	25
Haydn Zug's | **E Petersburg/LB**	25
Station House | **Haddon Hts/NJ**	25
Bobby Simone's | **Doylestown**	25
Steve's Steaks | **multi.**	25
Clements Cafe | **Haddon Hts/NJ**	25
Lakes Cafe | **Ft Washington**	25
Shkabibble's | **South St.**	25
Bistro 7 | **Old City**	25
Sweet Lucy's | **NE Philly**	25
Rose Tree Inn | **Media**	25
House/William Merry | **Hockessin/DE**	25
83 Bistro | **N Wales**	25
Garces Trading | **Wash Sq W**	25
Supper | **South St.**	25
Salt & Pepper | **E Passyunk**	25
1750 Bistro | **Lansdale**	25
Swann Lounge | **Logan Sq**	25
Stoudts Black Angus | **Adamstown/LB**	25
Robin's Nest | **Mt Holly/NJ**	25
Pizza By Elizabeths | **Greenville/DE**	25
Christine's Rest. | **Yardley**	24

Bomb Bomb BBQ | **multi.**	24
Claymont Steak | **multi.**	24
NEW 320 Market | **Media**	24
Shady Maple | **E Earl/LB**	24
Jimmie Kramer's Peanut | **Reading/LB**	24
Bonefish Grill | **multi.**	24
Seasons 52 | **multi.**	24
Mica | **Chestnut Hill**	24
Ms. Tootsie's | **multi.**	24
Metro. Diner | **N Wales**	24
Meritage | **SW Center City**	24
Warmdaddy's | **S Philly**	24
Friday Sat. Sun. | **Rittenhouse**	24
Sal/Joe's Spaghetti | **Maple Shade/NJ**	24
2 Fat Guys | **multi.**	24
Chlöe | **Old City**	24
Jim's Steaks | **multi.**	24
Bobby Ray's | **Pennsauken/NJ**	24
Tex Mex Connect. | **N Wales**	24
Miller's Smorgasbord | **Ronks/LB**	24
Gaetano's | **Berlin/NJ**	24
Anton's/Swan | **Lambertville/NJ**	24
Curran's Irish Inn | **Palmyra/NJ**	24
Back Burner | **Hockessin/DE**	24
Cheesecake | **multi.**	24
Knight House | **Doylestown**	24
Kennett Restaurant | **Qn Village**	24
Hawthornes | **Bella Vista**	24
Couch Tomato Café | **Manayunk**	24
Pub & Kitchen | **SW Center City**	24
Firecreek | **Downingtown**	24
Yardley Inn | **Yardley**	24
Black Bass | **Lumberville**	24
Stella Blu | **W Conshohocken**	24
Good 'n Plenty | **Smoketown/LB**	24
Rose Tattoo | **Fairmount**	24
Lee's Hoagie | **multi.**	24
City Tavern | **Old City**	24
Bay Pony Inn | **Lederach**	24

CUISINES

Parc Bistro | **Skippack**	24
J.B. Dawson's/Austin's | **multi.**	24
Mendenhall Inn | **Mendenhall**	24
Trax Rest. | **Ambler**	24
Day by Day | **Rittenhouse**	24
Three Monkeys Cafe | **NE Philly**	24
Good Dog Bar | **Rittenhouse**	24
1906 | **Kennett Sq**	24
Campo's Deli | **Old City**	24
10 Arts | **Ave of the Arts**	24
Ashburner Inn | **NE Philly**	24
Silk City | **N Liberties**	24
211 York | **Jenkintown**	24
Charlie Brown's | **Maple Shade/NJ**	23
Fountain Side | **Horsham**	23
NEW Lemon Hill | **Fairmount**	23
Whistlers Inn | **Cinnaminson/NJ**	23
Race Street Cafe | **Old City**	23
N. 3rd | **N Liberties**	23
Hank's Place | **Chadds Ford**	23
Pop Shop | **Collingswood/NJ**	23
One Shot Coffee | **N Liberties**	23
Log Cabin | **Leola/LB**	23
Resurrection Ale | **SW Center City**	23
Blue Pear | **West Chester**	23
a.kitchen | **Rittenhouse**	23
Moshulu | **Del Riverfront**	23
Fayette St. | **Conshohocken**	23
Back Porch Cafe | **Skippack**	23
Bell's Tavern | **Lambertville/NJ**	23
Chelsea Tavern | **Wilmington/DE**	23
Annie Bailey's | **Lancaster/LB**	23
Tortuga's Mex. | **Collegeville**	23
Westmont Family Rest. | **Westmont/NJ**	23
Randi's | **NE Philly**	23
Silverspoon | **Wayne**	23
Cock 'N Bull | **Lahaska**	23
B2 | **E Passyunk**	23
NEW Route 6 | **Fairmount**	23
Standard Tap | **N Liberties**	23
Lucky's Coffee | **Wilmington/DE**	23
Ollie Gators Pub | **Berlin/NJ**	23
Aperto | **Narberth**	23
White Dog | **multi.**	23
Farmer's Daughter | **Blue Bell**	23
Redstone | **Marlton/NJ**	23
Cafette | **Chestnut Hill**	23
Redstone | **Plymouth Mtg**	23
Guard House Inn | **Gladwyne**	23
Gaetano's/Penny Packer | **Willingboro/NJ**	23
JG Domestic | **Univ City**	23
Jones | **Wash Sq W**	23
Rouge | **Rittenhouse**	23
Whitman Diner | **Turnersville/NJ**	23
Derek's | **Manayunk**	23
Chambers 19 | **Doylestown**	23
Isaac's | **multi.**	23
Khyber | **Old City**	23
Nineteen | **Ave of the Arts**	23
Vintage Bar/Grill | **Abington**	23
Pat's Steaks | **E Passyunk**	23
Blueplate | **Mullica Hill/NJ**	23
Union City Grille | **Wilmington/DE**	23
Blue Parrot | **Wilmington/DE**	23
Blue Bell Inn | **Blue Bell**	23
Dettera | **Ambler**	23
The Twisted Tail | **Society Hill**	23
Black Horse Diner | **Mt Ephraim/NJ**	23
Appalachian Brew. | **Collegeville**	23
R2L | **Rittenhouse**	23
Southwark | **Qn Village**	23
City Tap House | **Univ City**	23
Twenty Manning | **Rittenhouse**	23
333 Belrose | **Radnor**	23
Barnsboro Inn | **Sewell/NJ**	23
Zacharias | **Worcester**	23
Braddock's | **Medford/NJ**	22

Manayunk Brew. | **Manayunk**	22
Square 1682 | **Rittenhouse**	22
Drafting Rm. | **Exton**	22
Iron Hill | **multi.**	22
Dining Car | **NE Philly**	22
Big John's | **Cherry Hill/NJ**	22
Chestnut Grill | **Chestnut Hill**	22
Columbus Inn | **Wilmington/DE**	22
Devil's Den | **S Philly**	22
Iron Abbey | **Horsham**	22
Percy St. BBQ | **multi.**	22
Tango | **Bryn Mawr**	22
Rembrandt's | **Fairmount**	22
Geno's Steaks | **S Philly**	22
Max Brenner | **Rittenhouse**	22
Half Moon | **Kennett Sq**	22
The Taproom & Grill | **Haddonfield/NJ**	22
Four Dogs | **West Chester**	22
Wash. Cross. Inn | **Wash Crossing**	22
Plain/Fancy Farm | **Bird-in-Hand/LB**	22
The Harvest | **Cinnaminson/NJ**	22
NEW Ella's Amer. Bistro | **Wayne**	22
Gables | **Chadds Ford**	22
Cool Dog Cafe | **Cherry Hill/NJ**	22
NEW Paramour | **Wayne**	22
Keating's | **Del Riverfront**	22
Duffer's Mill | **Marcus Hook**	22
Baby Blues | **Univ City**	22
Catahoula | **Qn Village**	22
Perch Pub | **Ave of the Arts**	22
FireStone Roasting | **Wilmington/DE**	22
Phil's Tav. | **Blue Bell**	22
45th St. Pub | **Pennsauken/NJ**	22
Philadelphia Bar/Rest. | **Old City**	22
Smokin' Betty | **Wash Sq W**	22
Mastoris | **Bordentown/NJ**	22
Brick Hotel Rest. | **Newtown**	22
Isaac Newton's | **Newtown**	22
Revolution Hse. | **Old City**	22
Sly Fox | **Royersford**	22
Winnie's Le Bus | **Manayunk**	21
Lambertville Station | **Lambertville/NJ**	21
Adobe Cafe | **multi.**	21
Metro Diner | **Brooklawn/NJ**	21
NEW The Trestle Inn | **Callowhill**	21
NEW Isabel | **Fairmount**	21
Pistachio Grille | **Maple Glen**	21
Fare | **Fairmount**	21
Grace Tav. | **SW Center City**	21
Exeter Family Rest. | **Reading/LB**	21
Jake's/Cooper's | **Manayunk**	21
Wine Thief | **Mt Airy**	21
Trappe Tavern | **Trappe**	21
Mad Mex | **multi.**	21
NEW McKenzie Brew | **multi.**	21
HAVANA | **New Hope**	21
Riverstone Café | **Exton**	21
Hollywood Cafe | **Woodbury Hts/NJ**	21
Dead Presidents Pub | **Wilmington/DE**	21
NEW 401 Diner | **Conshohocken**	21
Slate | **Rittenhouse**	21
Bourbon Blue | **Manayunk**	21
JD McGillicuddy's | **Ardmore**	21
Fuel | **E Passyunk**	21
JD McGillicuddy's | **multi.**	21
Fuel | **Wash Sq W**	21
Rode's Fireside | **Swedesboro/NJ**	21
Benny the Bum's | **NE Philly**	21
Corner | **Wash Sq W**	21
Jack's Firehse. | **Fairmount**	21
Chestnut7 | **Chestnut Hill**	21
Bliss | **Ave of the Arts**	21
Ted's Montana | **Warrington**	21
Elevation Burg. | **Moorestown/NJ**	21
Ponzio's | **Cherry Hill/NJ**	21
Carriage House | **Voorhees/NJ**	21
El Fuego | **multi.**	21
Yellow Submarine | **Maple Shade/NJ**	21
Hop Angel | **NE Philly**	21
Ott's | **multi.**	21
Cedar Hollow Inn | **Malvern**	21

CUISINES

Winberie's | **Wayne**	21
Bridget Foy's | **South St.**	21
P.J. Whelihan's | **multi.**	21
Marathon Grill | **multi.**	21
Broad Axe Tav. | **Ambler**	21
NEW Gino's Burgers | **multi.**	21
High St. Grill | **Mt Holly/NJ**	21
Landing | **New Hope**	21
Landmark Amer. | **multi.**	20
Frankford Hall | **Fishtown**	20
Mission Grill | **Logan Sq**	20
Inn of the Hawke | **Lambertville/NJ**	20
Kid Shelleen's | **Wilmington/DE**	20
Nodding Head | **Rittenhouse**	20
Phoebe's Bar-B-Q | **SW Center City**	20
Barnaby's | **Folsom**	20
Barnaby's Aston | **Media**	20
NEW American Sardine | **S Philly**	20
Local 44 | **Univ City**	20
Qdoba | **Univ City**	20
Colonial Diner | **Woodbury/NJ**	20
More Than Ice Crm. | **Wash Sq W**	20
Brick House | **Willow Grove**	20
Kitchen Bar | **Abington**	20
Trolley Car | **E Falls**	20
Du Jour | **multi.**	20
Trolley Car | **Mt Airy**	20
Schlesinger's | **Rittenhouse**	20
Farmers' Cabinet | **Wash Sq W**	20
Dave/Buster's | **multi.**	20
Copabanana | **multi.**	20
Triumph Brewing | **multi.**	20
MaGerks | **Ft Washington**	20
Darling's | **multi.**	20
Q BBQ | **Old City**	20
NEW Hickory Lane | **Fairmount**	20
Roadhouse Grille | **Skippack**	20
West Side Gravy | **Collingswood/NJ**	20
Freight House | **Doylestown**	20
Mal's American Diner | **Skippack**	20
Brittingham's | **Lafayette Hill**	20
Mugshots | **Fairmount**	19
Chris' Jazz Cafe | **Ave of the Arts**	19
Christopher's | **Wayne**	19
Aneu | **Berwyn**	19
Hard Rock | **Chinatown**	19
Down Home | **Chinatown**	19
The Coastline | **Cherry Hill/NJ**	19
London Grill | **Fairmount**	19
Rosey's BBQ | **multi.**	19
Cooperage | **Wash Sq W**	19
Abner's | **Univ City**	19
Ladder 15 | **Rittenhouse**	19
World Café | **Wilmington/DE**	19
KC's Alley | **Ambler**	19
Irish Pub | **multi.**	19
Great American Pub | **Narberth**	19
Kite/Key | **Fairmount**	18
Harrison Hse. Diner | **Mullica Hill/NJ**	18
NEW Barcade | **Fishtown**	18
MilkBoy Coffee | **Wash Sq W**	18
Happy Rooster | **Rittenhouse**	18
Sorella Rose | **Flourtown**	18
Ten Stone | **SW Center City**	18
Tavern 17 | **Rittenhouse**	18
New Wave | **Qn Village**	18
Taylors | **Williamstown/NJ**	18
Gullifty's | **Rosemont**	17
Public Hse./Logan | **Logan Sq**	17
Plate | **Ardmore**	16
Urban Saloon | **Fairmount**	16
Green Parrot | **Newtown**	16
NEW Ernest/Scott Taproom | **Wilmington/DE**	–
NEW Industry | **S Philly**	–
NEW Little Louie's BBQ | **Collingswood/NJ**	–
Mac's Tavern | **Old City**	–
NEW Miss Rachel's Pantry | **S Philly**	–
NEW Morgan's Pier | **Del Riverfront**	–
NEW Rex 1516 | **Rittenhouse**	–
NEW Rittenhouse Tavern | **Rittenhouse**	–
NEW Russet | **Rittenhouse**	–
NEW SoWe Bar Kitchen | **SW Center City**	–

NEW Square Peg | **Wash Sq W** ⌐

Pressroom Rest. |
   Lancaster/LB ⌐

NEW Vernick Food/Drink | ⌐
   Rittenhouse

ARGENTINEAN

943 | **Bella Vista** 23

ASIAN

Buddakan	**Old City**	27
Umai Umai	**Fairmount**	27
Bunha Faun	**Malvern**	25
Azie	**Media**	23
Jasmine Asian	**Glenside**	22
Asia/Parkway	**Logan Sq**	22
Coconut Bay	**Voorhees/NJ**	21
Old Town Buffet	**multi.**	20

ASIAN FUSION

Shangrila | **Devon** 23

BAKERIES

NEW Belle Cakery	**E Passyunk**	26
Art of Bread	**Narberth**	26
Night Kitchen Bake	**Chestnut Hill**	26
Cake	**Chestnut Hill**	23
Mastoris	**Bordentown/NJ**	22
Ponzio's	**Cherry Hill/NJ**	21
More Than Ice Crm.	**Wash Sq W**	20
Le Pain	**multi.**	20

BARBECUE

El Camino Real	**N Liberties**	25
Sweet Lucy's	**NE Philly**	25
63 Bistro	**N Wales**	25
Bomb Bomb BBQ	**multi.**	24
Whistlers Inn	**Cinnaminson/NJ**	23
Percy St. BBQ	**multi.**	22
Baby Blues	**Univ City**	22
Smokin' Betty	**Wash Sq W**	22
Rode's Fireside	**Swedesboro/NJ**	21
Phoebe's Bar-B-Q	**SW Center City**	20
Q BBQ	**Old City**	20

Rosey's BBQ	**multi.**	19
NEW Little Louie's BBQ	**Collingswood/NJ**	⌐

BASQUE

Tinto | **Rittenhouse** 27

BELGIAN

Monk's Cafe	**Rittenhouse**	24
Teresa's Next Dr.	**Wayne**	23
Belgian Café	**Fairmount**	23
Eulogy Belgian	**Old City**	23
Abbaye	**N Liberties**	22
Iron Abbey	**Horsham**	22
Le Pain	**multi.**	20

BRAZILIAN

Fogo de Chão	**Ave of the Arts**	27
Chima	**Logan Sq**	26
Na'Brasa	**Horsham**	25

BRITISH

British Chip Shop	**Haddonfield/NJ**	24
A Taste/Britain	**Wayne**	24
Dandelion	**Rittenhouse**	23
Stoney's British Pub	**Wilmington/DE**	21

BURGERS

Sketch	**Fishtown**	28
Charlie's Hamburg.	**Folsom**	26
Doghouse Burgers	**Downingtown**	26
Coco's	**Wash Sq W**	24
NEW Bobby's Burger	**multi.**	24
PYT	**N Liberties**	24
Five Guys	**multi.**	24
NEW Jake's Wayback	**multi.**	24
Pop Shop	**Collingswood/NJ**	23
Rouge	**Rittenhouse**	23
500º	**Rittenhouse**	23
Nifty Fifty's	**multi.**	23
Manayunk Brew.	**Manayunk**	22
Rembrandt's	**Fairmount**	22
Charcoal Pit	**multi.**	22
Elevation Burg.	**multi.**	21

CUISINES

BRGR Joint | **Bryn Mawr** 21
NEW Gino's Burgers | **multi.** 21
Ruby's Diner | **multi.** 19
NEW Shake Shack | **Rittenhouse** ┘

BURMESE

Rangoon | **Chinatown** 24

CAJUN

Mélange | 26
  Haddonfield/NJ
High Street Caffe | 26
  West Chester
Rose Tattoo | **Fairmount** 24
Ollie Gators Pub | **Berlin/NJ** 23
Blue Parrot | **Wilmington/DE** 23
Catahoula | **Qn Village** 22
Sly Fox | **Royersford** 22

CALIFORNIAN

NEW Isabel | **Fairmount** 21
El Fuego | **multi.** 21

CARIBBEAN

Tierra Colombiana | **N Philly** 26
Casona | **Collingswood/NJ** 24
Cuba Libre | **Old City** 24
Jamaican Jerk | 22
  Ave of the Arts
Bahama Breeze | 22
  multi.

CHEESESTEAKS

NEW Tony Luke's | 26
  multi.
Chink's Steaks | **NE Philly** 26
Dalessandro's | **Roxborough** 25
Larry's Steaks | **Wynnefield** 25
Chubby's Steaks | **Roxborough** 25
Steve's Steaks | **multi.** 25
Ishkabibble's | **South St.** 25
Claymont Steak | **multi.** 24
Jim's Steaks | **multi.** 24
Gaetano's | **Berlin/NJ** 24
Campo's Deli | **Old City** 24
Whistlers Inn | 23
  Cinnaminson/NJ
Gaetano's/Penny Packer | 23
  Willingboro/NJ
Pat's Steaks | **E Passyunk** 23
Geno's Steaks | **S Philly** 22

Yellow Submarine | 21
  Maple Shade/NJ
Abner's | **Univ City** 19

CHINESE

China House | **Woodbury/NJ** 28
Su Xing House | **Rittenhouse** 27
Tokyo Mandarin | **multi.** 27
Mandarin Oriental | 27
  Mullica Hill/NJ
Singapore Kosher | **Chinatown** 27
Oriental Pearl | 27
  Haddonfield/NJ
Sakura Spring | 26
  Cherry Hill/NJ
South Ocean | **Flourtown** 26
Chun Hing | **Wynnefield** 26
Chifa | **Wash Sq W** 26
China Wok | **Huntingdon Vly** 26
Han Dynasty | **Chinatown** 25
Sang Kee Peking | **multi.** 25
Mandarin Inn | **Sewell/NJ** 25
CinCin | **Chestnut Hill** 25
Abacus | **Lansdale** 25
Yangming | **Bryn Mawr** 25
Kingdom/Vegetarians | 25
  Chinatown
David's Mai Lai Wah | 25
  Chinatown
Marg. Kuo Peking | **Media** 25
Ray's Cafe | **Chinatown** 25
New Harmony | **Chinatown** 25
Marg. Kuo Media | **Media** 25
Dim Sum Garden | **Chinatown** 25
Duck Sauce | **Newtown** 25
Mustard Greens | **Qn Village** 24
Sannie | **NE Philly** 24
Joe's Peking | **Marlton/NJ** 24
Sang Kee Asian | **Wynnewood** 24
Lee How Fook | **Chinatown** 24
Happy Buffet | **Audubon/NJ** 24
Ting Wong | **Chinatown** 24
Marg. Kuo | **Wayne** 24
Mandarin Gdn. | **Willow Grove** 24
Hunan Rest. | **Ardmore** 24
Marg. Kuo Mandarin | **Malvern** 24
P.F. Chang's | **multi.** 24
Sang Kee Noodle | **multi.** 23

Ho Sai Gai	**Chinatown**	23
NEW M Kee	**Chinatown**	23
Tai Lake	**Chinatown**	23
Black Dog Cafe	**Skippack**	23
Shiao Lan Kung	**Chinatown**	23
Ocean Harbor	**Chinatown**	23
Chez Elena Wu	**Voorhees/NJ**	22
Ocean City Rest.	**Chinatown**	22
Charles Plaza	**Chinatown**	22
Wok Chinese	**Rittenhouse**	22
Peking Buffet	**Glassboro/NJ**	21
Imperial Inn	**Chinatown**	21
China Inn	**Norristown**	21
China Royal	**Wilmington/DE**	21
Mandarin Buffet	**Cherry Hill/NJ**	21
Auspicious	**Ardmore**	19
Joy Tsin Lau	**Chinatown**	18
Beijing	**Univ City**	18

COFFEEHOUSES

Barrington Coffee	**Barrington/NJ**	26
La Colombe	**multi.**	24
Café L'Aube	**Fairmount**	24
One Shot Coffee	**N Liberties**	23
Capriccio	**Wash Sq W**	23
B2	**E Passyunk**	23
Anthony's Coffee	**Bella Vista**	23
Almaz Café	**Rittenhouse**	23
Ants Pants Cafe	**SW Center City**	22
Brew HaHa!	**multi.**	22
Bonté Wafflerie	**multi.**	22
Gryphon Coffee	**Wayne**	21
Coffee Works	**Voorhees/NJ**	21
MilkBoy Coffee	**multi.**	18

COLOMBIAN

Tierra Colombiana	**N Philly**	26

CONTINENTAL

Fountain	**Logan Sq**	29
Duling-Kurtz Hse.	**Exton**	26
William Penn Inn	**Gwynedd**	25
Yangming	**Bryn Mawr**	25
FarmiCia	**Old City**	23

Farnsworth House	**Bordentown/NJ**	23
Café Gallery	**Burlington/NJ**	23
Kelly's Seafood	**NE Philly**	21

CREOLE

Daddy Mims	**Phoenixville**	27
High Street Caffe	**West Chester**	26
Marsha Brown	**New Hope**	25
Catahoula	**Qn Village**	22

CUBAN

Tierra Colombiana	**N Philly**	26
Casona	**Collingswood/NJ**	24
Cuba Libre	**Old City**	24

DELIS

The Kibitz Room	**Cherry Hill/NJ**	25
Cosmi's Deli	**S Philly**	25
Famous 4th St. Deli	**multi.**	24
Campo's Deli	**Old City**	24
Ben & Irv's	**Huntingdon Vly**	23
Schlesinger's	**Rittenhouse**	20
Delancey St. Bagels	**Wynnewood**	20
Hymie's	**Merion Station**	19
Murray's Deli	**Bala Cynwyd**	19
Mrs. Marty's Deli	**multi.**	-

DESSERT

Capogiro Gelato Artisans	**multi.**	28
NEW Belle Cakery	**E Passyunk**	26
NEW Federal Donuts	**S Philly**	25
Cheesecake	**multi.**	24
Max Brenner	**Rittenhouse**	22
More Than Ice Crm.	**Wash Sq W**	20
Darling's	**multi.**	20
NEW La Petite Dauphine	**Rittenhouse**	-

DIM SUM

Kingdom/Vegetarians	**Chinatown**	25
New Harmony	**Chinatown**	25
Joe's Peking	**Marlton/NJ**	24
Ocean Harbor	**Chinatown**	23
Imperial Inn	**Chinatown**	21
Joy Tsin Lau	**Chinatown**	18

DINERS

Morning Glory | **Bella Vista**	25
Club Diner | **Bellmawr/NJ**	24
Silk City | **N Liberties**	24
Hank's Place | **Chadds Ford**	23
Nifty Fifty's | **multi.**	23
Phily Diner | **Runnemede/NJ**	22
Mastoris | **Bordentown/NJ**	22
Exeter Family Rest. | **Reading/LB**	21
401 Diner | **Berlin/NJ**	21
New Berlin Diner | **Berlin/NJ**	21
Ponzio's | **Cherry Hill/NJ**	21
Medport Diner | **Medford/NJ**	21
NEW Broad St. Diner | **S Philly**	21
Palace Diner | **Berlin/NJ**	20
Colonial Diner | **Woodbury/NJ**	20
Ardmore Station | **Ardmore**	20
Trolley Car | **multi.**	20
Minella's Diner | **Wayne**	20
Silver Diner | **Cherry Hill/NJ**	20
Golden Dawn Diner | **Burlington/NJ**	20
Mayfair Diner | **NE Philly**	20
Melrose Diner | **S Philly**	20
Little Pete's | **multi.**	19
Oregon Diner | **S Philly**	19
Oak Lane Diner | **W Oak Lane**	19
Ruby's Diner | **multi.**	19
Andy's Diner & Pub | **Conshohocken**	18
Country Squire Diner | **Broomall**	18
Ray's Rest./Malt Shop | **Norristown**	18
Club House Diner | **Bensalem**	18
Sage Diner | **Mt Laurel/NJ**	18

ECLECTIC

Lacroix | **Rittenhouse**	27
Augusto's | **Warminster**	27
Reading Term. Mkt. | **Chinatown**	26
Gracie's | **Pine Forge/LB**	26
Little Café | **Voorhees/NJ**	25
Bistro 7 | **Old City**	25
Corner Bistro | **Wilmington/DE**	24

AllWays Café | **Huntingdon Vly**	24
Tria | **multi.**	24
Continental | **Old City**	24
Totaro's | **Conshohocken**	24
Georges' | **Wayne**	24
Sidecar | **SW Center City**	24
Day by Day | **Rittenhouse**	24
White Dog | **multi.**	23
Cafette | **Chestnut Hill**	23
Cake | **Chestnut Hill**	23
Cafe Preeya | **Huntingdon Vly**	23
A Full Plate | **N Liberties**	23
Continental Mid. | **Rittenhouse**	23
Caffe Galleria | **Lambertville/NJ**	23
Lilly's/Canal | **Lambertville/NJ**	23
Full Moon | **Lambertville/NJ**	22
Roller's/Flying Fish | **Chestnut Hill**	22
Alstarz | **Bordentown/NJ**	22
HAVANA | **New Hope**	21
Gypsy Saloon | **W Conshohocken**	21
Bridgid's | **Fairmount**	21
Campbell's Place | **Chestnut Hill**	21
Pub/Penn Valley | **Narberth**	20
Triumph Brewing | **multi.**	20
Old Town Buffet | **multi.**	20
Gigi | **Old City**	19
World Café | **Univ City**	19
Spamps | **Conshohocken**	19

EGYPTIAN

Aya's Café | **Logan Sq**	22

ETHIOPIAN

Abyssinia | **Univ City**	25
Almaz Café | **Rittenhouse**	23

EURASIAN

Coconut Bay | **Voorhees/NJ**	21

EUROPEAN

Talula's Table | **Kennett Sq**	28
Tria Wine Room | **Univ City**	24
Pub & Kitchen | **SW Center City**	24
Bonté Wafflerie | **multi.**	22

FISH 'N' CHIPS

British Chip Shop | **Haddonfield/NJ** 24

FONDUE

Melting Pot | **multi.** 24

FRENCH

Birchrunville Store | **Birchrunville** 29
Paloma | **Bella Vista** 28
Green Room | **Wilmington/DE** 28
Majolica | **Phoenixville** 28
Green Hills Inn | **Reading/LB** 27
Cochon | **Qn Village** 26
Savona | **Gulph Mills** 26
Manon | **Lambertville/NJ** 26
Art of Bread | **Narberth** 26
Dream Cuisine | **Cherry Hill/NJ** 25
Inn/Phillips Mill | **New Hope** 25
Kinnaree | **Horsham** 25
Agiato | **Manayunk** 25
Robin's Nest | **Mt Holly/NJ** 25
Siri's | **Cherry Hill/NJ** 24
Beau Monde | **Qn Village** 23
Blackbird | **Collingswood/NJ** 22
Paris Wine Bar | **Fairmount** 22
Amuse | **Ave of the Arts** 21
Granite Hill | **Fairmount** 19
🆕 La Petite Dauphine | **Rittenhouse** -|

FRENCH (BISTRO)

Bibou | **Bella Vista** 29
Sovana Bistro | **Kennett Sq** 28
Bistrot/Minette | **Qn Village** 26
Slate Bleu | **Doylestown** 26
Spring Mill | **Conshohocken** 25
Bistro St. Tropez | **Rittenhouse** 23
Caribou | **Wash Sq W** 22
Brasserie 73 | **Skippack** 22
A La Maison | **Ardmore** 22
La Belle Epoque | **Media** 22

GASTROPUB

Barbuzzo | **Wash Sq W** 27
Royal Tavern | **Bella Vista** 26
Memphis Tap | **Port Richmond** 25

Sidecar | **SW Center City** 24
Pub & Kitchen | **SW Center City** 24
Chelsea Tavern | **Wilmington/DE** 23
Standard Tap | **N Liberties** 23
Abbaye | **N Liberties** 22
Devil's Den | **S Philly** 22
St. Stephens Green | **Fairmount** 22
Perch Pub | **Ave of the Arts** 22
Smokin' Betty | **Wash Sq W** 22
Slate | **Rittenhouse** 21
Local 44 | **Univ City** 20
Kildare's | **multi.** 20
Cooperage | **Wash Sq W** 19
Kite/Key | **Fairmount** 18
Urban Saloon | **Fairmount** 16

GERMAN

Brauhaus Schmitz | **South St.** 22
Otto's Brauhaus | **Horsham** 21
Hop Angel | **NE Philly** 21
Frankford Hall | **Fishtown** 20

GREEK

Kanella | **Wash Sq W** 27
Dmitri's | **multi.** 25
Estia Restaurant | **Ave of the Arts** 25
Olive Tree | **Downingtown** 25
Zorba's Taverna | **Fairmount** 24
South St. Souvlaki | **South St.** 23
Westmont Family Rest. | **Westmont/NJ** 23
Athena | **Glenside** 23
Kuzina/Sofia | **Cherry Hill/NJ** 23
Effie's | **Wash Sq W** 22
Lourdas Greek | **Bryn Mawr** 22
Opa | **Wash Sq W** 20

HOAGIES

Lee's Hoagie | **multi.** 24

HOT DOGS

Hot Diggity! | **South St.** 24
Cool Dog Cafe | **Cherry Hill/NJ** 22

CUISINES

ICE CREAM

Capogrio Gelato Artisans	**multi.**	28
Franklin Fountain	**Old City**	27

INDIAN

IndeBlue	**Collingswood/NJ**	27
Coriander	**Voorhees/NJ**	26
Shere-E-Punjab	**multi.**	26
Amans	**Norristown**	26
Cross Culture	**multi.**	25
NEW Tashan	**Ave of the Arts**	25
Saffron	**multi.**	24
Ekta Indian Cuisine	**multi.**	23
Minar Pal.	**Wash Sq W**	23
Sitar India	**Univ City**	23
Tiffin	**multi.**	22
Palace of Asia	**multi.**	22
New Delhi	**Univ City**	22
Karma	**Old City**	22
Palace of Asia	**Ft Washington**	21
Lovash Indian	**South St.**	21
Chinnar Indian	**Berwyn**	19
Khajuraho	**Ardmore**	15

IRISH

Annie Bailey's	**Lancaster/LB**	23
St. Stephens Green	**Fairmount**	22
The Plough & the Stars	**Old City**	21
Dublin Square	**multi.**	20
Fergie's Pub	**Wash Sq W**	20
Kildare's	**multi.**	20
Brittingham's	**Lafayette Hill**	20
Connie Mac's	**Pennsauken/NJ**	19
Molly Maguire's	**multi.**	19
Tír na nÓg	**Logan Sq**	19
Irish Pub	**Rittenhouse**	19
Green Parrot	**Newtown**	16

ISRAELI

Zahav	**Society Hill**	27

ITALIAN

Vetri	**Wash Sq W**	29
Birchrunville Store	**Birchrunville**	29
Luna Rossa	**Turnersville/NJ**	28
Domani Star	**Doylestown**	28
Sapori	**Collingswood/NJ**	27
Tre Scalini	**E Passyunk**	27
Arugula	**Sewell/NJ**	27
Popi's Italian	**S Philly**	27
Kitchen Consigliere	**Collingswood/NJ**	27
Rest. Alba	**Malvern**	27
August	**S Philly**	27
Pasta Pomodoro	**Sewell/NJ**	27
Chickie's Italian Deli	**S Philly**	27
TreVi	**Glenside**	27
Soffritto	**Newark/DE**	27
Fieni's Ristorante	**Voorhees/NJ**	27
Trieste	**Prospect Park**	27
Frankie's Fellini	**Berwyn**	27
Modo Mio	**N Liberties**	27
Paesano's Philly Style	**multi.**	27
NEW Pescatore	**Bala Cynwyd**	27
Il Fiore	**Collingswood/NJ**	27
La Famiglia	**Old City**	26
De Lorenzo's	**Fairless Hills**	26
Rist. San Marco	**Ambler**	26
Fat Tomato Grill	**Berlin/NJ**	26
La Cena	**Bensalem**	26
Moro	**Wilmington/DE**	26
Riverstone	**S Philly**	26
Savona	**Gulph Mills**	26
La Locanda	**Voorhees/NJ**	26
Mélange	**Haddonfield/NJ**	26
La Stanza	**S Philly**	26
Piccolina Tosc.	**Wilmington/DE**	26
Antonella's	**Bryn Mawr**	26
Ariano	**Media**	26
Brother's Pizza	**Cinnaminson/NJ**	26
NEW Il Pittore	**Rittenhouse**	26
Ristorante Castello	**Blue Bell**	26
Saloon	**Bella Vista**	26
Francesco's Cucina	**Berlin/NJ**	26

CUISINES

Ralph's | **Bella Vista**	23
That's Amore | **Collingswood/NJ**	23
Randi's | **NE Philly**	23
Bellini Grill | **Rittenhouse**	23
Frank's Spaghetti | **NE Philly**	23
Café Fiorello's | **West Chester**	23
Toscana | **Mullica Hill/NJ**	23
Radice | **Blue Bell**	23
Nonna's Italian | **West Chester**	23
Anthony's Coffee | **Bella Vista**	23
Piccolo Tratt. | **multi.**	23
Girasole | **Ave of the Arts**	23
Branzino | **Rittenhouse**	23
Bella Tratt. | **Manayunk**	23
943 | **Bella Vista**	23
Teresa's Cafe | **Wayne**	23
Positano Coast | **Society Hill**	23
Pietro's Pizza | **multi.**	23
Brio | **multi.**	23
Luigi's Pizza Fresca | **Burlington/NJ**	23
Vitarelli's | **Cherry Hill/NJ**	23
Luigi's Pizza Fresca | **multi.**	23
Rick's | **Lambertville/NJ**	23
Rist. La Buca | **Wash Sq W**	23
NEW Bravo! | **Willow Grove**	22
Arugula | **Huntingdon Vly**	22
Joe Pesce | **Collingswood/NJ**	22
Cucina Carini | **Mt Laurel/NJ**	22
Treno | **Westmont/NJ**	22
Mrs. Robino's | **Wilmington/DE**	22
Villari's Lake Side | **Sicklerville/NJ**	22
Cafe Fontana | **Maple Shade/NJ**	22
Rist. Primavera | **Wayne**	22
Da Vinci Ristorante | **E Passyunk**	22
Andreotti's Viennese | **Cherry Hill/NJ**	22
Mozzarella Grill | **Sewell/NJ**	22

NEW The Tomato Bistro | **Manayunk**	22
Maggio's | **Southampton**	22
Marco Polo | **Elkins Park**	22
NEW Walnut St. Supper Club | **Wash Sq W**	22
Blackbird | **Collingswood/NJ**	22
Cafe La Fontana | **Hatboro**	22
Table 31 | **Logan Sq**	22
Pizzicato | **multi.**	22
King of Pizza | **Berlin/NJ**	22
Passariello's | **multi.**	22
Al Dente Italiana | **Moorestown/NJ**	22
Chiarella's | **E Passyunk**	22
Basta Pasta | **Skippack**	21
Scoogi's | **Flourtown**	21
Bistro La Baia | **SW Center City**	21
La Fontana | **Rittenhouse**	21
Pasta Pomodoro | **Voorhees/NJ**	21
Caffe Valentino | **S Philly**	21
Roman Delight | **Warminster**	21
Spampinato's | **Conshohocken**	21
Pepperoncini | **multi.**	21
Barnaby's Aston | **Media**	20
Bella Cena | **Rittenhouse**	20
Buca di Beppo | **multi.**	20
Primavera Pizza | **Ardmore**	19
Penne | **Univ City**	18
Serafina | **Rittenhouse**	16
NEW In Riva | **E Falls**	-
NEW Kris | **S Philly**	-
NEW Spiga | **Wash Sq W**	-

JAMAICAN

Jamaican Jerk | **Ave of the Arts**	22

JAPANESE

Bluefin | **E Norriton**	28
Tomo Sushi | **Glassboro/NJ**	28
Morimoto | **Wash Sq W**	28
Umi Japanese | **Somerdale/NJ**	28
Sagami | **Collingswood/NJ**	27
Yokohama | **Maple Shade/NJ**	27
Fuji Japanese | **Haddonfield/NJ**	27
Oishi | **Newtown**	27

Mikimotos | **Wilmington/DE**	27
Tokyo Mandarin | **multi.**	27
Mandarin Oriental | **Mullica Hill/NJ**	27
Doma | **Logan Sq**	27
Ooka | **multi.**	26
Sakura Spring | **Cherry Hill/NJ**	26
Zama | **Rittenhouse**	26
Izumi | **E Passyunk**	26
South Ocean | **Flourtown**	26
Bonjung | **Collegeville**	26
Café Con Choc. | **S Philly**	26
Kabuki | **King of Prussia**	26
Zento | **Old City**	26
Tokyo Hibachi | **Deptford/NJ**	26
Fat Salmon Sushi | **Wash Sq W**	25
Akira | **multi.**	25
Megu | **multi.**	25
A1 | **Fairless Hills**	25
Marg. Kuo Peking | **Media**	25
Ota-Ya | **multi.**	25
Shiroi Hana | **Rittenhouse**	25
Marg. Kuo Media | **Media**	25
Kisso Sushi | **Old City**	25
Blue Pacific | **Lancaster/LB**	24
Osaka | **multi.**	24
Teikoku | **Newtown Sq**	24
Mikado | **multi.**	24
Sannie | **NE Philly**	24
Fuji Mountain | **Rittenhouse**	24
Marg. Kuo | **Wayne**	24
Hikaru | **multi.**	24
Hibachi | **multi.**	24
Marg. Kuo Mandarin | **Malvern**	24
Arirang | **Langhorne**	23
Aki | **Wash Sq W**	23
Raw Sushi | **Wash Sq W**	23
Benihana | **multi.**	23
Lai Lai Garden | **Blue Bell**	23
Azie | **Villanova**	23
August Moon | **Norristown**	23
Jasmine Asian | **Wilmington/DE**	23
Tampopo | **multi.**	22
Chez Elena Wu | **Voorhees/NJ**	22
Makiman Sushi | **multi.**	21

Hokka Hokka | **Chestnut Hill**	20
Mikado | **Ardmore**	20
Fuji Mt. Japanese | **Bryn Mawr**	19
Auspicious | **Ardmore**	19

KOREAN

Doma | **Logan Sq**	27
Sammy Chon's K-Town | **multi.**	25
Jong Ka Jib | **E Oak Lane**	23
August Moon | **Norristown**	23
Tampopo | **multi.**	22
Makiman Sushi | **multi.**	21
Giwa | **Rittenhouse**	21

LAOTIAN

Cafe Du Laos | **S Philly**	23

MALAYSIAN

Rasa Sayang | **Wilmington/DE**	25
Penang | **Chinatown**	25
Banana Leaf | **Chinatown**	24
Aqua | **Wash Sq W**	24

MEDITERRANEAN

Sovana Bistro | **Kennett Sq**	28
Barbuzzo | **Wash Sq W**	27
Gibraltar | **Lancaster/LB**	26
Hamilton's | **Lambertville/NJ**	26
Paradiso | **E Passyunk**	25
Arpeggio | **Spring House**	25
19 Bella | **Cedars**	25
Figs | **Fairmount**	25
Olive Tree | **Downingtown**	25
Audrey Claire | **Rittenhouse**	24
Ariana's Ristorante | **N Wales**	24
Zesty's | **Manayunk**	23
Athena | **Glenside**	23
La Pergola | **Jenkintown**	23
Valanni | **Wash Sq W**	23
Isabella | **Conshohocken**	23
Zacharias | **Worcester**	23
Mirna's Café | **multi.**	22
Med. Grill | **Bryn Mawr**	22
Pistachio Grille | **Maple Glen**	21
Water Works | **Fairmount**	21

CUISINES

Byblos	**Rittenhouse**	21	Matador	**Wayne**	21
Al Dar Bistro	**Bala Cynwyd**	20	Zocalo	**Univ City**	21
Gigi	**Old City**	19	El Fuego	**multi.**	21
Hummus	**multi.**	19	Baja Fresh	**multi.**	21
NEW Divan Med. Grill	**Qn Village**	-	Qdoba	**multi.**	20
NEW Kris	**S Philly**	-	Copabanana	**multi.**	20
			Mexican Post	**multi.**	19

MEXICAN

Más Mexicali	**West Chester**	19
NEW Loco Pez	**Fishtown**	29

Johnny Mañana's | **E Falls** — 19

Xilantro | **Wayne** — 18

Paloma	**Bella Vista**	28
Jose's Tacos	**Callowhill**	26

MIDDLE EASTERN

Tequilas	**Rittenhouse**	26
Café Con Choc.	**S Philly**	26
Lolita	**Wash Sq W**	26
El Camino Real	**N Liberties**	25
La Esperanza	**Lindenwold/NJ**	25
The Tortilla Press	**multi.**	25
Distrito	**Univ City**	25
El Vez	**Wash Sq W**	25
Tamarindos	**Broad Axe**	25
El Tapatio	**Wilmington/DE**	25
Taq. La Veracruz.	**Bella Vista**	24
El Sarape	**multi.**	24
Las Cazuelas	**N Liberties**	24
Taq. La Michoacana	**Norristown**	24
Las Bugambilias	**South St.**	24
Cantina Caballitos/Segundos	**multi.**	24
Cantina Feliz	**Ft Washington**	24
12th St. Cantina	**Chinatown**	24
Las Margaritas	**multi.**	24
Animo Juice	**Haddonfield/NJ**	23
California Tortilla	**multi.**	23
Xochitl	**Society Hill**	23
NEW Honest Tom's Taco	**W Philly**	23
La Tolteca	**multi.**	23
El Rey	**Rittenhouse**	23
El Azteca	**multi.**	22
On the Border	**multi.**	22
Mexican Food	**Marlton/NJ**	22
Coyote Cross.	**Conshohocken**	22
NEW La Calaca Feliz	**Fairmount**	22
El Limon	**Conshohocken**	22
NEW Isabel	**Fairmount**	21

Zahav	**Society Hill**	27
Bitar's	**Bella Vista**	26
Alyan's	**South St.**	25
Norma's	**Cherry Hill/NJ**	24
Kabul Afghan	**Old City**	24
Maoz Veg.	**multi.**	23
Ariana	**multi.**	23
NEW Med. Grill	**Wayne**	22
Al Dar Bistro	**Bala Cynwyd**	20
Persian Grill	**Lafayette Hill**	19
NEW Divan Med. Grill	**Qn Village**	-

MOROCCAN

Marrakesh	**South St.**	24
Fez Moroccan	**Qn Village**	20
NEW Argana Moroccan	**Lansdowne**	-

NEW ENGLAND

NEW Route 6	**Fairmount**	23

NEW MEXICAN

Tortuga's Mex.	**Collegeville**	23
Qdoba	**Univ City**	20

NOODLE SHOPS

Nan Zhou	**Chinatown**	26
Sang Kee Peking	**multi.**	25
Pho 75	**multi.**	24
Sang Kee Noodle	**Univ City**	23

NUEVO LATINO

Alma de Cuba	**Rittenhouse**	25
El Serrano	**Lancaster/LB**	23
Verdad Rest.	**Bryn Mawr**	21

PAKISTANI

Kabobeesh	**Univ City**	24

PAN-ASIAN

Masamoto | **Glen Mills** — 28
Oishi | **Newtown** — 27
Mikimotos | **Wilmington/DE** — 27
Nectar | **Berwyn** — 25
Sampan | **Wash Sq W** — 25
Trio | **Fairmount** — 25
Ritz Seafood | **Voorhees/NJ** — 24
Pod | **Univ City** — 24
Susanna Foo's | **Radnor** — 24
Lai Lai Garden | **Blue Bell** — 23
Shangrila | **Devon** — 23
Jasmine Asian | **Wilmington/DE** — 23

PAN-LATIN

El Sitio Grill & Cafe | **Collingswood/NJ** — 24
Mixto | **Wash Sq W** — 24
Avenida | **Mt Airy** — 23
NEW BlueCat | **Fairmount** — ‑

PENNSYLVANIA DUTCH

Bird-in-Hand | **Bird-in-Hand/LB** — 25
Shady Maple | **E Earl/LB** — 24
Miller's Smorgasbord | **Ronks/LB** — 24
Good 'n Plenty | **Smoketown/LB** — 24
Plain/Fancy Farm | **Bird-in-Hand/LB** — 22

PERSIAN

Persian Grill | **Lafayette Hill** — 19

PERUVIAN

Chifa | **Wash Sq W** — 26
El Serrano | **Lancaster/LB** — 23

PIZZA

Osteria | **N Philly** — 27
Charlie's Pizzeria | **E Norriton** — 27
Santucci Sq. Pizza | **NE Philly** — 27
Rustica | **N Liberties** — 26
Famous/Original King of Pizza | **Cherry Hill/NJ** — 26
Olce Pizza Grille | **Lansdale** — 26

Ariano | **Media** — 26
Tacconelli's | **multi.** — 26
Famous Mack's | **S Philly** — 26
Tony's Place | **NE Philly** — 26
Nick's Pizzeria/Steak | **multi.** — 25
Amato's | **Fairless Hills** — 25
Franzone's | **Bridgeport/NJ** — 25
Angelo's | **multi.** — 25
Joe Santucci's | **NE Philly** — 25
Angelo's Pizza | **Woodbury/NJ** — 25
La Vita's Pizza | **Moorestown/NJ** — 25
Zavino | **Wash Sq W** — 24
Gino's Pizza | **Norristown** — 24
Alfred's Tomato | **Blackwood/NJ** — 24
Bella Pizza Cafe | **Delran/NJ** — 24
Giuseppe's Pizza | **Ambler** — 24
Angelino's | **Fairmount** — 24
Bravo Pizza | **Wayne** — 24
Anthony's Pizza | **multi.** — 24
Couch Tomato Café | **Manayunk** — 24
Blackbird Pizzeria | **Society Hill** — 24
Celebre's | **S Philly** — 24
Pizzeria Stella | **Society Hill** — 24
13th St. Gourmet | **Wash Sq W** — 24
SLiCE | **multi.** — 23
Forno | **Maple Shade/NJ** — 23
Bacco | **Doylestown** — 23
Mama Palma's | **Rittenhouse** — 23
Frank's Time Out | **Berlin/NJ** — 23
Gaetano's/Penny Packer | **Willingboro/NJ** — 23
Pietro's Pizza | **multi.** — 23
Luigi's Pizza Fresca | **multi.** — 23
Pat's Pizza | **multi.** — 23
Marra's | **E Passyunk** — 22
Jules Thin Crust | **multi.** — 22
Johnny's Pizza | **Cherry Hill/NJ** — 22
Cafe Fontana | **Maple Shade/NJ** — 22

CUISINES

Mozzarella Grill	**Sewell/NJ**	22
Maggio's	**Southampton**	22
Healthy Garden	**Voorhees/NJ**	22
California Pizza	**multi.**	22
Pizzicato	**multi.**	22
King of Pizza	**Berlin/NJ**	22
Passariello's	**multi.**	22
Seasons Pizza	**multi.**	21
Peace A Pizza	**Ardmore**	21
Chestnut7	**Chestnut Hill**	21
Peace A Pizza	**multi.**	21
Du Jour	**Haverford**	20
Primavera Pizza	**Ardmore**	19
Gullifty's	**Rosemont**	17
NEW In Riva	**E Falls**	-
NEW Nomad Pizza	**South St.**	-

POLYNESIAN

Moshulu	**Del Riverfront**	23

PORTUGUESE

Koo Zee Doo	**N Liberties**	25

PUB FOOD

Grey Lodge	**NE Philly**	25
Chick's Tavern	**Bridgeport/NJ**	24
Coco's	**Wash Sq W**	24
Monk's Cafe	**Rittenhouse**	24
Good Dog Bar	**Rittenhouse**	24
Dock Street Brew.	**Univ City**	24
N. 3rd	**N Liberties**	23
Teresa's Next Dr.	**Wayne**	23
Skeeter's Pub	**Blackwood/NJ**	23
Chickie's/Pete's	**multi.**	23
Iron Hill	**Maple Shade/NJ**	22
The Taproom & Grill	**Haddonfield/NJ**	22
Victory Brewing	**Downingtown**	22
Wash. St. Ale	**Wilmington/DE**	22
45th St. Pub	**multi.**	22
Alstarz	**Bordentown/NJ**	22

Sly Fox	**Royersford**	22
Trappe Tavern	**Trappe**	21
Dead Presidents Pub	**Wilmington/DE**	21
Rock Bottom	**King of Prussia**	21
The Plough & the Stars	**Old City**	21
Ott's	**multi.**	21
P.J. Whelihan's	**multi.**	21
Landmark Amer.	**multi.**	20
Pub/Penn Valley	**Narberth**	20
Inn of the Hawke	**Lambertville/NJ**	20
Nodding Head	**Rittenhouse**	20
Clancy's Pub	**Brooklawn/NJ**	20
Dublin Square	**Cherry Hill/NJ**	20
Clancy's Pub	**Sewell/NJ**	20
Fergie's Pub	**Wash Sq W**	20
MaGerks	**Ft Washington**	20
Black Sheep Pub	**Rittenhouse**	20
Molly Maguire's	**multi.**	19
Sly Fox	**Phoenixville**	19
KC's Alley	**Ambler**	19
Irish Pub	**multi.**	19
Pub/Passyunk	**E Passyunk**	18
Fadó Irish	**Rittenhouse**	18
McGillin's	**Wash Sq W**	18
Happy Rooster	**Rittenhouse**	18
Gullifty's	**Rosemont**	17
Elephant/Castle	**Rittenhouse**	15

SANDWICHES

Di Nic's	**Chinatown**	27
John's Roast Pork	**S Philly**	27
Capriotti's	**multi.**	26
Nick's Old Original	**multi.**	26
Anne's Kitchen	**Glenside**	26
Tony Luke's	**S Philly**	26
Barrington Coffee	**Barrington/NJ**	26
Night Kitchen Bake	**Chestnut Hill**	26

PrimoHoagies	multi.	25
Hot Diggity!	South St.	24
Bomb Bomb BBQ	Glassboro/NJ	24
Jim's Steaks	multi.	24
Angelino's	Fairmount	24
Lee's Hoagie	multi.	24
Rybread	Fairmount	24
Tree House	Audubon/NJ	23
Capriccio	Wash Sq W	23
Frank's Time Out	Berlin/NJ	23
Isaac's	multi.	23
Pat's Steaks	E Passyunk	23
Ben & Irv's	Huntingdon Vly	23
Slack's Hoagie	multi.	23
NEW Pure Fare	Rittenhouse	22
Geno's Steaks	S Philly	22
Green Line Cafe	multi.	21
Delancey St. Bagels	Wynnewood	20
Mugshots	multi.	19
Country Squire Diner	Broomall	18

SEAFOOD

Little Fish BYOB	Bella Vista	28
Cap'n Cats Clam Bar	Deptford/NJ	27
Library IV	Williamstown/NJ	26
Blackfish	Conshohocken	26
Radicchio Cafe	Old City	26
Gibraltar	Lancaster/LB	26
Hamilton's	Lambertville/NJ	26
Harry's Seafood	Wilmington/DE	26
Bridget's Steak	Ambler	26
Chophouse	Gibbsboro/NJ	26
Creed's	King of Prussia	26
Zinc	Wash Sq W	26
Bobby Chez	multi.	25
Clam Tavern	Clifton Hts	25
NEW Fish	Wash Sq W	25
Dmitri's	multi.	25
Mile High Steak & Seafood	Glen Mills	25
Deep Blue	Wilmington/DE	25
Smith/Wollensky	Rittenhouse	25

Caffe Aldo	Cherry Hill/NJ	25
Gallo's Seafood	NE Philly	25
SoleFood	Wash Sq W	25
Palm Rest.	Ave of the Arts	25
Devon Seafood	Rittenhouse	24
Ritz Seafood	Voorhees/NJ	24
Oyster Hse.	Rittenhouse	24
Phillips Sea.	Logan Sq	24
Bonefish Grill	multi.	24
Feby's Fish.	Wilmington/DE	24
Kunkel's	Haddon Hts/NJ	24
Cap'n Cat Clam Bar	Voorhees/NJ	24
Anastasi	Bella Vista	24
Little Tuna	Haddonfield/NJ	24
Big Fish Grill	multi.	24
McCormick/Schmick	multi.	23
Steak 38	Cherry Hill/NJ	23
Varalli	Ave of the Arts	23
NEW Route 6	Fairmount	23
Branzino	Rittenhouse	23
Athena	Glenside	23
Nineteen	Ave of the Arts	23
Tai Lake	Chinatown	23
NEW Joe's Crab Shack	King of Prussia	23
Kopper Kettle	Langhorne	23
Rist. La Buca	Wash Sq W	23
Chickie's/Pete's	multi.	23
Joe Pesce	Collingswood/NJ	22
Blue2O	Cherry Hill/NJ	22
Lobster Trap	Pennsauken/NJ	22
Marco Polo	Elkins Park	22
Gables	Chadds Ford	22
Legal Sea Foods	King of Prussia	22
Chart House	Del Riverfront	22
Kelly's Seafood	NE Philly	21
NEW Doc Magrogan	multi.	21
Snockey's Oyster	S Philly	21
DiNardo's	Old City	21
Ship Inn	Exton	21
NEW American Sardine	S Philly	20

SMALL PLATES

Honey	Amer.	Doylestown	27
NEW Stateside	Amer.	E Passyunk	27

Modo Mio | Italian | N Liberties 27

Piccolina Tosc. | Italian | 26
Wilmington/DE

Dom. Hudson | Amer. |
Wilmington/DE 26

19 Bella | Med. | Cedars 25

Distrito | Mexican | Univ City 25

Teca | Italian | West Chester 25

Elements Cafe | Amer. | 25
Haddon Hts/NJ

Sampan | Asian | Wash Sq W 25

Friday Sat. Sun. | Amer. | 24
Rittenhouse

Tria | Eclectic | multi. 24

Continental | Eclectic | Old City 24

Stella Blu | Amer. | W
Conshohocken 24

Derek's | Amer. | Manayunk 23

Valanni | Med. | Wash Sq W 23

Continental Mid. | Eclectic | 23
Rittenhouse

C19 | Italian | Rittenhouse 21

Water Works | Med. | Fairmount 21

HAVANA | Amer./Eclectic | 21
New Hope

Riverstone Café | Amer. | Exton 21

SOUL FOOD

Aunt Berta's | Oaklyn/NJ 26

Geechee Girl | Germantown 25

Ms. Tootsie's | multi. 24

Warmdaddy's | S Philly 24

SOUTH AMERICAN

Fogo de Chão | 27
Ave of the Arts

Tierra Colombiana | N Philly 26

Chifa | Wash Sq W 26

Chima | Logan Sq 26

Na'Brasa | Horsham 25

Sazon | N Liberties 24

El Serrano | Lancaster/LB 23

943 | Bella Vista 23

SOUTHERN

Relish | W Oak Lane 26

Carversville Inn | Carversville 26

Aunt Berta's | Oaklyn/NJ 26

Geechee Girl | Germantown 25

Honey's Sit | N Liberties 25

Marsha Brown | New Hope 25

Ms. Tootsie's | multi. 24

Warmdaddy's | S Philly 24

Khyber | Old City 23

The Twisted Tail | 23
Society Hill

Bourbon Blue | Manayunk 21

Jack's Firehse. | Fairmount 21

Chris' Jazz Cafe | Ave of the Arts 19

Down Home | Chinatown 19

Cooperage | Wash Sq W 19

World Café | Wilmington/DE 19

NEW Rex 1516 | Rittenhouse –

SOUTHWESTERN

Adobe Cafe | multi. 21

Mission Grill | Logan Sq 20

SPANISH

Freddy & Tony's | N Philly 29

Amada | Old City 28

Tinto | Rittenhouse 27

Fat Tomato Grill | Berlin/NJ 26

Orillas Tapa Bar | 26
Wilmington/DE

Bar Ferdinand | N Liberties 24

Matador | Wayne 21

Verdad Rest. | Bryn Mawr 21

Gigi | Old City 19

NEW Jamonera | Wash Sq W –

STEAKHOUSES

Prime Rib | Rittenhouse 27

Fogo de Chão | 27
Ave of the Arts

Library IV | Williamstown/NJ 26

Morton's | multi. 26

Capital Grille | 26
multi.

Seven Stars Inn | 26
Phoenixville

Bridget's Steak | Ambler 26

Delmonico's | Wynnefield 26

Chophouse | Gibbsboro/NJ 26

Saloon | Bella Vista 26

Barclay Prime | Rittenhouse 26

Davio's | Rittenhouse 26

Creed's | King of Prussia 26

Butcher/Singer	**Rittenhouse**	26	Amelia's Tea/Holly	**Mullica Hill/NJ**	25
Sullivan's Steak	**multi.**	26	Ray's Cafe	**Chinatown**	25

Butcher/Singer	**Rittenhouse**	26
Sullivan's Steak	**multi.**	26
Chima	**Logan Sq**	26
Fleming's Prime	**multi.**	26
Ruth's Chris	**multi.**	25
Na'Brasa	**Horsham**	25
Smith/Wollensky	**Rittenhouse**	25
Del Frisco's	**Ave of the Arts**	25
Palm Rest.	**Ave of the Arts**	25
Union Trust	**Wash Sq W**	24
Bonefish Grill	**multi.**	24
Pietro's Prime	**West Chester**	24
Pub	**Pennsauken/NJ**	24
Kunkel's	**Haddon Hts/NJ**	24
Hibachi	**multi.**	24
Charlie Brown's	**multi.**	23
Steak 38	**Cherry Hill/NJ**	23
Walter's Steak.	**Wilmington/DE**	23
Union City Grille	**Wilmington/DE**	23
Brandywine Prime	**Chadds Ford**	22
NEW KC Prime	**Warrington**	22
Ted's Montana	**Warrington**	21
Chops Restaurant	**multi.**	20
Spamps	**Conshohocken**	19
Newtown Grill	**Newtown Sq**	18

TAIWANESE

Han Dynasty	**multi.**	25
Ray's Cafe	**Chinatown**	25

TAPAS

Amada	**Old City**	28
Tinto	**Rittenhouse**	27
Orillas Tapa Bar	**Wilmington/DE**	26
Bar Ferdinand	**N Liberties**	24
Matador	**Wayne**	21
Gigi	**Old City**	19

TEAROOMS

Amelia's Tea/Holly	**Mullica Hill/NJ**	25
Ray's Cafe	**Chinatown**	25

TEX-MEX

Tex Mex Connect.	**N Wales**	24
Mad Mex	**multi.**	21

THAI

Spice Thai	**Doylestown**	27
Chabaa Thai	**Manayunk**	26
Kinnaree	**Horsham**	25
Thai Orchid	**Blue Bell**	25
Thai L'Elephant	**Phoenixville**	25
Tamarind	**South St.**	25
Thai Orchid	**Berwyn**	25
NEW Circles	**multi.**	25
Penang	**Chinatown**	25
Siri's	**Cherry Hill/NJ**	24
Teikoku	**Newtown Sq**	24
Chiangmai	**Conshohocken**	24
Aqua	**Wash Sq W**	24
Siam Thai	**Lambertville/NJ**	23
Siam Cuisine	**Doylestown**	23
Cafe Du Laos	**S Philly**	23
Black Dog Cafe	**Skippack**	23
White Elephant	**Huntingdon Vly**	23
La Na Thai	**Media**	23
Thai Basil	**Collingswood/NJ**	22
Thai Kuu	**Chestnut Hill**	22
Erawan Thai	**multi.**	22
Pattaya	**Univ City**	22
Lemon Grass Thai	**Univ City**	21
Mikado	**Ardmore**	20
My Thai	**SW Center City**	19
Sawatdee	**Rittenhouse**	15

TURKISH

NEW Divan Med. Grill	**Qn Village**	–

VEGAN/VEGETARIAN

NEW Vedge	**Wash Sq W**	28
Sprig & Vine	**New Hope**	27
Blue Sage	**Southampton**	27
Singapore Kosher	**Chinatown**	27
Grindcore House	**Qn Village**	26
Kingdom/Vegetarians	**Chinatown**	25
New Harmony	**Chinatown**	25

CUISINES

AllWays Café | Huntingdon Vly — 24

Blackbird Pizzeria | **Society Hill** — 24

Maoz Veg. | **multi.** — 23

B2 | **E Passyunk** — 23

Mi Lah Veg. | **Rittenhouse** — 23

A Full Plate | **N Liberties** — 23

Healthy Garden | **Voorhees/NJ** — 22

Coffee Works | **Voorhees/NJ** — 21

NEW HipCityVeg | **Rittenhouse** — -|

NEW Miss Rachel's Pantry | **S Philly** — -|

VENEZUELAN

Sazon | **N Liberties** — 24

VIETNAMESE

Pho Ha | **Bella Vista** — 26

Vietnam Rest. | **Chinatown** — 26

Vietnam Café | **W Philly** — 25

Pho Xe Lua | **Chinatown** — 25

Nam Phuong | **Bella Vista** — 24

Pho 75 | **multi.** — 24

Pho Eden | **Cherry Hill/NJ** — 24

Le Viet | **Bella Vista** — 24

Vietnam Palace | **Chinatown** — 23

Pho Cali | **Chinatown** — 22

NEW Mekong River | **S Philly** — -|

NEW Grill Fish Café | **W Philly** — -|

Locations

Includes names, locations and Food ratings.

Philadelphia

AVENUE OF THE ARTS

(See map on page 98)

NEW Sbraga | *Amer.* 27

Fogo de Chão | *Brazilian/Steak* 27

Morton's | *Steak* 26

Capital Grille | *Steak* 26

Estia Restaurant | *Greek* 25

Ruth's Chris | *Steak* 25

Del Frisco's | *Steak* 25

Palm Rest. | *Steak* 25

NEW Tashan | *Indian* 25

La Colombe | *Coffee* 24

10 Arts | *Amer.* 24

McCormick/Schmick | *Seafood* 23

Varalli | *Italian* 23

Girasole | *Italian* 23

Nineteen | *Amer./Seafood* 23

Jamaican Jerk | *Jamaican* 22

Perch Pub | *Amer.* 22

Amuse | *French* 21

Bliss | *Amer.* 21

Chris' Jazz Cafe | *Amer.* 19

BELLA VISTA

Bibou | *French* 29

Paloma | *French/Mex.* 28

Little Fish BYOB | *Seafood* 28

Royal Tavern | *Amer.* 26

Bitar's | *Mideast.* 26

Cucina Forte | *Italian* 26

Pho Ha | *Vietnamese* 26

Saloon | *Italian/Steak* 26

Villa di Roma | *Italian* 25

Dante & Luigi | *Italian* 25

Sabrina's Café | *Eclectic* 25

Morning Glory | *Diner* 25

Taq. La Veracruz. | *Mex.* 24

Nam Phuong | *Vietnamese* 24

Anastasi | *Seafood* 24

Hawthornes | *Amer.* 24

Le Viet | *Vietnamese* 24

Monsu | *Italian* 23

Ralph's | *Italian* 23

Anthony's Coffee | *Coffee* 23

943 | *Argentinean/Italian* 23

BREWERYTOWN

Mugshots | *Sandwiches* 19

CALLOWHILL

Jose's Tacos | *Mex.* 26

Cafe Lift | *French/Italian* 25

NEW The Trestle Inn | *Amer.* 21

CHESTNUT HILL

NEW Heirloom | *Amer.* 26

Night Kitchen Bake | *Bakery/Sandwiches* 26

Stella Sera | *Italian* 26

CinCin | *Chinese* 25

Osaka | *Japanese* 24

Mica | *Amer.* 24

Cafette | *Eclectic/New Amer.* 23

Cake | *Bakery/Eclectic* 23

Iron Hill | *Amer.* 22

Chestnut Grill | *Amer.* 22

Thai Kuu | *Asian/Thai* 22

Roller's/Flying Fish | *Eclectic* 22

Chestnut7 | *Amer.* 21

Campbell's Place | *Eclectic* 21

Hokka Hokka | *Japanese* 20

CHINATOWN

(See map on page 98)

Di Nic's | *Sandwiches* 27

Singapore Kosher | *Chinese/Vegetarian* 27

Nan Zhou | *Noodle Shop* 26

Reading Term. Mkt. | *Eclectic* 26

Vietnam Rest. | *Vietnamese* 26

Sang Kee Noodle | *Chinese* 25

Kingdom/Vegetarians | *Chinese/Vegetarian* 25

Pho Xe Lua | *Vietnamese* 25

David's Mai Lai Wah | *Chinese* 25

NEW Sammy Chon's K-Town | *Korean* 25

Ray's Cafe	*Chinese*	25
New Harmony	*Chinese/Vegetarian*	25
Dim Sum Garden	*Chinese*	25
Penang	*Malaysian/Thai*	25
Rangoon	*Burmese*	24
Maggiano's	*Italian*	24
Banana Leaf	*Malaysian*	24
Lee How Fook	*Chinese*	24
12th St. Cantina	*Mex.*	24
Ting Wong	*Chinese*	24
Melting Pot	*Fondue*	24
Ho Sai Gai	*Chinese*	23
Vietnam Palace	*Vietnamese*	23
NEW M Kee	*Chinese*	23
Tai Lake	*Chinese*	23
Shiao Lan Kung	*Chinese*	23
Ocean Harbor	*Chinese*	23
Pho Cali	*Vietnamese*	22
Ocean City Rest.	*Chinese*	22
Erawan Thai	*Thai*	22
Charles Plaza	*Chinese*	22
Imperial Inn	*Chinese*	21
Hard Rock	*Amer.*	19
Down Home	*Southern*	19
Joy Tsin Lau	*Chinese*	18

DELAWARE RIVERFRONT

Hibachi	*Japanese*	24
Moshulu	*Amer.*	23
Keating's	*Amer.*	22
Chart House	*Seafood*	22
Dave/Buster's	*Amer.*	20
NEW Morgan's Pier	*Amer.*	-

EAST FALLS/ MANAYUNK/ ROXBOROUGH

Chabaa Thai	*Thai*	26
Dalessandro's	*Cheesestks.*	25
NEW Han Dynasty	*Chinese*	25
Chubby's Steaks	*Cheesestks.*	25
Agiato	*Italian*	25
Couch Tomato Café	*Amer.*	24
Gemelli on Main	*Italian*	24
Hikaru	*Japanese*	24
Zesty's	*Med.*	23
Derek's	*Amer.*	23

Bella Tratt.	*Italian*	23
Manayunk Brew.	*Pub*	22
NEW The Tomato Bistro	*Italian*	22
Il Tartufo	*Italian*	22
Winnie's Le Bus	*Amer.*	21
Adobe Cafe	*SW*	21
Jake's/Cooper's	*Amer.*	21
Bourbon Blue	*Amer./Southern*	21
JD McGillicuddy's	*Amer.*	21
Trolley Car	*Diner*	20
Kildare's	*Pub*	20
Johnny Mañana's	*Mex.*	19
NEW In Riva	*Italian*	-

EAST OAK LANE

Jong Ka Jib	*Korean*	23

EAST PASSYUNK

Fond	*Amer.*	28
Capogiro Gelato Artisans	*Amer./Dessert*	28
Tre Scalini	*Italian*	27
NEW Stateside	*Amer.*	27
Le Virtù	*Italian*	27
Izumi	*Japanese*	26
NEW Belle Cakery	*Bakery*	26
Paradiso	*Italian*	25
Salt & Pepper	*Amer.*	25
Mamma Maria	*Italian*	24
Cantina Caballitos/Segundos	*Mex.*	24
NEW Birra	*Italian*	24
B2	*Coffee/Vegan*	23
Pat's Steaks	*Cheesestks.*	23
Marra's	*Italian*	22
Geno's Steaks	*Cheesestks.*	22
Da Vinci Ristorante	*Italian*	22
Chiarella's	*Italian*	22
Adobe Cafe	*SW*	21
Fuel	*Health Food*	21
Pub/Passyunk	*Pub*	18

EASTWICK

Chickie's/Pete's	*Seafood*	23

FAIRMOUNT

Umai Umai	*Asian*	27
NEW Alla Spina	*Italian*	25
Figs	*Med.*	25

Restaurant	Score
Sabrina's Café	*Eclectic*	25
Trio	*Asian*	25
Zorba's Taverna	*Greek*	24
Angelino's	*Pizza/Sandwiches*	24
Rose Tattoo	*Amer.*	24
Café L'Aube	*Coffee*	24
Rybread	*Sandwiches*	24
NEW Lemon Hill	*Amer.*	23
LaScala's	*Italian*	24
NEW Route 6	*Seafood*	23
Belgian Café	*Belgian*	23
Luigi's Pizza Fresca	*Italian/Pizza*	23
Rembrandt's	*Amer.*	22
NEW La Calaca Feliz	*Mex.*	22
St. Stephens Green	*Irish*	22
Paris Wine Bar	*French*	22
NEW Isabel	*Californian/Mex.*	21
Fare	*Amer.*	21
Water Works	*Med.*	21
Jack's Firehse.	*Southern*	21
Bridgid's	*Eclectic*	21
NEW Hickory Lane	*Amer.*	20
Mugshots	*Sandwiches*	19
Little Pete's	*Diner*	19
Granite Hill	*Amer.*	19
London Grill	*Amer.*	19
Kite/Key	*Amer.*	18
Urban Saloon	*Pub*	16
NEW BlueCat	*Pan-Latin*	-

FISHTOWN

Restaurant	Score
NEW Loco Pez	*Mex.*	29
Sketch	*Burgers*	28
Ekta Indian Cuisine	*Indian*	23
Frankford Hall	*Amer./German*	20
NEW Barcade	*Amer.*	18
NEW Pickled Heron	*French*	-

GERMANTOWN

Restaurant	Score
Geechee Girl	*Southern*	25

LOGAN SQUARE

(See map on page 98)

Restaurant	Score
Fountain	*Continental/French*	29
Doma	*Japanese/Korean*	27
Chima	*Brazilian/Steak*	26
Swann Lounge	*Amer./French*	25

Restaurant	Score
Phillips Sea.	*Seafood*	24
Percy St. BBQ	*BBQ*	22
Asia/Parkway	*Asian*	22
Table 31	*Italian*	22
Aya's Café	*Egyptian*	22
Mission Grill	*SW*	20
Du Jour	*Amer.*	20
Darling's	*Amer.*	20
Mexican Post	*Mex.*	19
Tír na nÓg	*Pub*	19
Public Hse./Logan	*Amer.*	17

MOUNT AIRY

Restaurant	Score
Earth Bread	*Amer.*	25
Bacio	*Italian*	25
Avenida	*Pan-Latin*	23
Tiffin	*Indian*	22
Wine Thief	*Amer.*	21
Trolley Car	*Diner*	20

NORTHEAST PHILLY

Restaurant	Score
Santucci Sq. Pizza	*Pizza*	27
Chink's Steaks	*Cheesestks.*	26
Tony's Place	*Italian/Pizza*	26
Grey Lodge	*Pub*	25
Steve's Steaks	*Cheesestks.*	25
Gallo's Seafood	*Seafood*	25
Joe Santucci's	*Pizza/Sandwiches*	25
Sweet Lucy's	*BBQ*	25
Macaroni's Restaurant	*Italian*	25
PrimoHoagies	*Sandwiches*	25
Moonstruck	*Italian*	24
Pho 75	*Vietnamese*	24
Cafe Michelangelo	*Italian/Pizza*	24
Jim's Steaks	*Cheesestks.*	24
Sannie	*Chinese/Japanese*	24
Lee's Hoagie	*Sandwiches*	24
Las Margaritas	*Mex.*	24
Three Monkeys Cafe	*Amer.*	24
Ashburner Inn	*Amer.*	24
NEW Jake's Wayback	*Burgers*	24
California Tortilla	*Mex.*	23
Via Napoli	*Italian*	23
Randi's	*Amer./Italian*	23
Frank's Spaghetti	*Italian*	23
Nifty Fifty's	*Diner*	23
Chickie's/Pete's	*Pub*	23

Dining Car	Amer.	22
Kelly's Seafood	Continental/Seafood	21
Benny the Bum's	Seafood	21
Makiman Sushi	Japanese/Korean	21
Hop Angel	Amer./German	21
Dave/Buster's	Amer.	20
Mayfair Diner	Diner	20
NEW Mugshots	Sandwiches	19

NORTHERN LIBERTIES

(See map on page 102)

Modo Mio	Italian	27
Paesano's Philly Style	Italian	27
Rustica	Pizza/Sandwiches	26
Koo Zee Doo	Portuguese	25
El Camino Real	BBQ/Mex.	25
Dmitri's	Greek	25
Honey's Sit	Jewish/Southern	25
Green Eggs	Amer.	25
NEW Circles	Thai	25
Las Cazuelas	Mex.	24
Sazon	Venezuelan	24
Cantina Caballitos/Segundos	Mex.	24
PYT	Burgers	24
Il Cantuccio	Italian	24
Bar Ferdinand	Spanish	24
Silk City	Amer.	24
N. 3rd	Amer.	23
One Shot Coffee	Amer.	23
Standard Tap	Amer.	23
A Full Plate	Eclectic	23
Tiffin	Indian	22
Abbaye	Belgian	22
Darling's	Amer.	20

NORTH PHILLY

Freddy & Tony's	Spanish	29
Osteria	Italian	27
Tierra Colombiana	Colombian/Cuban	26
JD McGillicuddy's	Amer.	21
Qdoba	Mex.	20

OLD CITY

(See map on page 102)

| Amada | Spanish | 28 |
| Franklin Fountain | Ice Cream | 27 |

Buddakan	Asian	27
La Famiglia	Italian	26
Radicchio Cafe	Italian	26
Zento	Japanese	26
Fork	Amer.	26
Han Dynasty	Chinese	25
Spasso Italian Grill	Italian	25
Bistro 7	Eclectic	25
Kisso Sushi	Japanese	25
La Locanda/Ghiottone	Italian	25
Chlöe	Amer.	24
Kabul Afghan	Afghan	24
Rist. Panorama	Italian	24
Continental	Eclectic	24
City Tavern	Amer.	24
Cuba Libre	Cuban	24
Campo's Deli	Cheesestks.	24
Race Street Cafe	Amer.	23
FarmiCia	Continental	23
Ariana	Afghan	23
Khyber	Southern	23
Eulogy Belgian	Belgian	23
Karma	Indian	22
Philadelphia Bar/Rest.	Cheesestks./Seafood	22
Pizzicato	Italian	22
Revolution Hse.	Amer.	22
DiNardo's	Seafood	21
The Plough & the Stars	Pub	21
Triumph Brewing	Amer./Eclectic	20
Q BBQ	BBQ	20
Gigi	Eclectic	19
Mexican Post	Mex.	19
Mac's Tavern	Amer.	-

PORT RICHMOND

Hinge	Amer.	27
Tacconelli's	Pizza	26
Memphis Tap	Amer.	25

QUEEN VILLAGE/ SOUTH ST.

(See map on page 100)

NEW Ela	Amer.	28
Cochon	French	26
Bistrot/Minette	French	26
Grindcore House	Vegetarian	26
Core De Roma	Italian	26

La Fourno	*Italian*	25	La Viola Ovest	*Italian*	26
Dmitri's	*Greek*	25	Butcher/Singer	*Steak*	26
NEW Tapestry	*Amer.*	25	Dmitri's	*Greek*	25
Alyan's	*Mideast.*	25	Alma de Cuba	*Nuevo Latino*	25
Tamarind	*Thai*	25	Smith/Wollensky	*Steak*	25
NEW Ulivo	*Italian*	25	Shiroi Hana	*Japanese*	25
Ishkabibble's	*Cheesestks.*	25	PrimoHoagies	*Sandwiches*	25
Supper	*Amer.*	25	Porcini	*Italian*	25
Hot Diggity!	*Sandwiches*	24	Devon Seafood	*Seafood*	24
Mustard Greens	*Chinese*	24	Oyster Hse.	*Seafood*	24
Ms. Tootsie's	*Soul*	24	Melograno	*Italian*	24
Las Bugambilias	*Mex.*	24	Audrey Claire	*Med.*	24
Famous 4th St. Deli	*Deli*	24	Casta Diva	*Italian*	24
Jim's Steaks	*Cheesestks.*	24	Friday Sat. Sun.	*Amer.*	24
Kennett Restaurant	*Amer.*	24	Famous 4th St. Deli	*Deli*	24
Marrakesh	*Moroccan*	24	Parc	*French*	24
Hikaru	*Japanese*	24	Tria	*Eclectic*	24
Gnocchi	*Italian*	24	Monk's Cafe	*Belgian*	24
Beau Monde	*French*	23	Le Castagne	*Italian*	24
South St. Souvlaki	*Greek*	23	Fuji Mountain	*Japanese*	24
Maoz Veg.	*Mideast./Vegetarian*	23	La Viola	*Italian*	24
Pietro's Pizza	*Pizza*	23	La Colombe	*Coffee*	24
Southwark	*Amer.*	23	Five Guys	*Burgers*	24
Percy St. BBQ	*BBQ*	22	Day by Day	*Amer./Eclectic*	24
Brauhaus Schmitz	*German*	22	Good Dog Bar	*Pub*	24
Catahoula	*Cajun/Creole*	22	Salento	*Italian*	23
Lovash Indian	*Indian*	21	SLiCE	*Pizza*	23
Bridget Foy's	*Amer.*	21	D'Angelo's	*Italian*	23
Copabanana	*Amer./Mex.*	20	a.kitchen	*Amer.*	23
Fez Moroccan	*Moroccan*	20	Mama Palma's	*Italian*	23
New Wave	*Amer.*	18	Bellini Grill	*Italian*	23
NEW Divan Med. Grill	*Turkish*	⌐	Capriccio	*Coffee*	23
NEW Nomad Pizza	*Pizza*	⌐	Rouge	*Amer.*	23
	Almaz Café	*Ethiopian*	23

RITTENHOUSE

(See map on page 98)

	Bistro St. Tropez	*French*	23
Capogiro Gelato Artisans	*Amer./Dessert*	28	Branzino	*Italian/Seafood*	23
	Mi Lah Veg.	*Vegan/Vegetarian*	23
Su Xing House	*Chinese*	27	500º	*Burgers*	23
Prime Rib	*Steak*	27	Pietro's Pizza	*Pizza*	23
Matyson	*Amer.*	27	Continental Mid.	*Eclectic*	23
Lacroix	*Eclectic*	27	Dandelion	*British*	23
Tinto	*Spanish*	27	R2L	*Amer.*	23
Village Whiskey	*Amer.*	26	El Rey	*Mex.*	23
Zama	*Japanese*	26	Twenty Manning	*Amer.*	23
Tequilas	*Mex.*	26	Square 1682	*Amer.*	22
NEW Il Pittore	*Italian*	26	Tampopo	*Japanese/Korean*	22
Barclay Prime	*Steak*	26	**NEW** Pure Fare	*Sandwiches*	22
Davio's	*Italian/Steak*	26	Max Brenner	*Amer./Dessert*	22

Bonté Wafflerie	*Coffee*	22
Erawan Thai	*Thai*	22
Wok Chinese	*Chinese/Seafood*	22
C19	*Italian*	21
La Fontana	*Italian*	21
Slate	*Amer.*	21
El Fuego	*Californian/Mex.*	21
Byblos	*Med.*	21
Giwa	*Korean*	21
Marathon Grill	*Amer.*	21
Nodding Head	*Pub*	20
Qdoba	*Mex.*	20
Schlesinger's	*Deli*	20
Bella Cena	*Italian*	20
Le Pain	*Bakery/Belgian*	20
Black Sheep Pub	*Pub*	20
Little Pete's	*Diner*	19
Ladder 15	*Amer.*	19
Irish Pub	*Pub*	19
Fadó Irish	*Pub*	18
Happy Rooster	*Amer.*	18
Tavern 17	*Amer.*	18
Serafina	*Italian*	16
Sawatdee	*Thai*	15
Elephant/Castle	*Pub*	15
NEW HipCityVeg	*Vegetarian*	-
NEW La Petite Dauphine	*Dessert/French*	-
Le Bec Fin	*French*	-
NEW Rex 1516	*Amer.*	-
NEW Rittenhouse Tavern	*Amer.*	-
NEW Russet	*Amer.*	-
NEW Shake Shack	*Burgers*	-
NEW Vernick Food/Drink	*Amer.*	-

SOCIETY HILL

(See map on page 100)

Zahav	*Israeli*	27
Blackbird Pizzeria	*Pizza/Vegan*	24
Pizzeria Stella	*Pizza*	24
Bistro Romano	*Italian*	24
Xochitl	*Mex.*	23
Positano Coast	*Italian*	23
The Twisted Tail	*Southern*	23

SOUTH PHILLY

John's Roast Pork	*Sandwiches*	27
Popi's Italian	*Italian*	27
August	*Italian*	27
Chickie's Italian Deli	*Italian*	27

Paesano's Philly Style	*Italian*	27
Nick's Old Original	*Sandwiches*	26
Riverstone	*Italian*	26
Tony Luke's	*Cheesestks.*	26
La Stanza	*Italian*	26
L'Angolo	*Italian*	26
Café Con Choc.	*Japanese/Mex.*	26
Famous Mack's	*Pizza*	26
NEW Federal Donuts	*Amer.*	25
Scannicchio's	*Italian*	25
South Philly Tap	*Amer.*	25
Green Eggs	*Amer.*	25
PrimoHoagies	*Sandwiches*	25
Circles	*Thai*	25
Cosmi's Deli	*Deli*	25
Bomb Bomb BBQ	*BBQ/Italian*	24
Pho 75	*Vietnamese*	24
Warmdaddy's	*Soul*	24
Celebre's	*Pizza*	24
SLiCE	*Pizza*	23
High Note Cafe	*Italian*	23
Cafe Du Laos	*Laotian/Thai*	23
Chickie's/Pete's	*Pub*	23
Victor Cafe	*Italian*	22
Devil's Den	*Amer.*	22
Criniti	*Italian*	21
Snockey's Oyster	*Seafood*	21
Caffe Valentino	*Italian*	21
NEW Broad St. Diner	*Diner*	21
NEW American Sardine	*Amer.*	20
Melrose Diner	*Diner*	20
Oregon Diner	*Diner*	19
NEW Industry	*Amer.*	-
NEW Kris	*Med.*	-
NEW Mekong River	*Vietnamese*	-
NEW Miss Rachel's Pantry	*Vegan*	-

SOUTHWEST CENTER CITY

Pumpkin	*Amer.*	27
Meritage	*Amer.*	24
Sidecar	*Eclectic*	24
Pub & Kitchen	*European*	24
Resurrection Ale	*Amer.*	23
Ants Pants Cafe	*Amer.*	22
Grace Tav.	*Amer.*	21
Bistro La Baia	*Italian*	21
Phoebe's Bar-B-Q		20

BBQ/Southern

My Thai | *Thai* — 19

Ten Stone | *Amer.* — 18

NEW SoWe Bar Kitchen | *Amer.* — ⌐

UNIVERSITY CITY

Capogiro Gelato Artisans | *Amer./Dessert* — 28

Marigold Kitchen | *Amer.* — 26

NEW Han Dynasty | *Chinese* — 25

Distrito | *Mex.* — 25

Abyssinia | *Ethiopian* — 25

Kabobeesh | *Pakistani* — 24

Pod | *Asian* — 24

Tria Wine Room | *European* — 24

Bobby's Burger | *Burgers* — 24

Lee's Hoagie | *Sandwiches* — 24

Dock Street Brew. | *Pub* — 24

Sang Kee Noodle | *Chinese* — 23

White Dog | *Eclectic* — 23

IG Domestic | *Amer.* — 23

City Tap House | *Amer.* — 23

Sitar India | *Indian* — 23

Tampopo | *Japanese/Korean* — 22

New Delhi | *Indian* — 22

Baby Blues | *BBQ* — 22

Pattaya | *Thai* — 22

NEW Doc Magrogan | *Seafood* — 21

Lemon Grass Thai | *Thai* — 21

Mad Mex | *Mex.* — 21

Zocalo | *Mex.* — 21

Green Line Cafe | *Sandwiches* — 21

Landmark Amer. | *Amer.* — 20

Local 44 | *Amer.* — 20

Qdoba | *Mex.* — 20

Copabanana | *Amer./Mex.* — 20

Hummus | *Med.* — 19

Abner's | *Cheesestks.* — 19

World Café | *Eclectic* — 19

Beijing | *Chinese* — 18

Penne | *Italian* — 18

WASHINGTON SQUARE WEST

(See map on page 98)

Vetri | *Italian* — 29

NEW Vedge | *Vegetarian* — 28

Morimoto | *Japanese* — 28

Capogiro Gelato Artisans | *Amer./Dessert* — 28

Barbuzzo | *Med.* — 27

Talula's Garden | *Amer.* — 27

Kanella | *Greek* — 27

Farm/Fisherman | *Amer.* — 27

Mercato | *Italian* — 26

Chifa | *Chinese/Peruvian* — 26

Amis | *Italian* — 26

Zinc | *French* — 26

Lolita | *Mex.* — 26

Fat Salmon Sushi | *Japanese* — 25

NEW Fish | *Seafood* — 25

NEW Green Eggs Café | *Amer.* — 25

El Vez | *Mex.* — 25

Sampan | *Asian* — 25

SoleFood | *Seafood* — 25

Garces Trading | *Amer.* — 25

Zavino | *Italian* — 25

Union Trust | *Steak* — 24

Coco's | *Amer.* — 24

Tria | *Eclectic* — 24

Mixto | *Pan-Latin* — 24

Aqua | *Malaysian/Thai* — 24

13th St. Gourmet | *Pizza/Sandwiches* — 24

Aki | *Japanese* — 23

M Restaurant | *Amer.* — 23

LaScala's | *Italian* — 23

Raw Sushi | *Japanese* — 23

Maoz Veg. | *Mideast./Vegetarian* — 23

Capriccio | *Coffee* — 23

Jones | *Amer.* — 23

Valanni | *Med.* — 23

Rist. La Buca | *Italian* — 23

Minar Pal. | *Indian* — 23

Caribou | *French* — 22

Effie's | *Greek* — 22

El Azteca | *Mex.* — 22

Bonté Wafflerie | *Coffee* — 22

NEW Walnut St. Supper Club | *Italian* — 22

Smokin' Betty | *Amer./BBQ* — 22

Fuel | *Health Food* — 21

Makiman Sushi | *Japanese/Korean* — 21

Corner | *Amer.* — 21

El Fuego | *Californian/Mex.* — 21

Qdoba | *Mex.* — 20

Chops Restaurant | *Steak* — 20

More Than Ice Crm. | Amer./Dessert	20
Fergie's Pub | Pub	20
Farmers' Cabinet | Amer.	20
Opa | Greek	20
Le Pain | Bakery/Belgian	20
Cooperage | Amer./Southern	19
Irish Pub | Pub	19
McGillin's | Pub	18
MilkBoy Coffee | Coffee	18
NEW Jamonera | Spanish	-
NEW Spiga | Italian	-
NEW Square Peg | Amer.	-

WEST OAK LANE

Relish | Southern	26
Oak Lane Diner | Diner	19

WEST PHILLY

Vietnam Café | Vietnamese	25
Jim's Steaks | Cheesestks.	24
NEW Honest Tom's Taco | Mex.	23
Green Line Cafe | Sandwiches	21
NEW Grill Fish Café | Vietnamese	-

WYNNEFIELD

Delmonico's | Steak	26
Chun Hing | Chinese	26
Larry's Steaks | Cheesestks.	25
California Pizza | Pizza	22

Philadelphia Suburbs

BUCKS COUNTY

Domani Star | Italian	28
Spice Thai | Thai	27
Sprig & Vine | Vegan	27
Honey | Amer.	27
Washington Hse. | Amer.	27
Oishi | Asian	27
Blue Sage | Vegetarian	27
Augusto's | Eclectic	27
De Lorenzo's | Italian	26
La Cena | Italian	26
Ooka | Japanese	26
Bailey's Bar & Grille | Amer.	26
Charcoal BYOB | Amer./French	26
Carversville Inn | Southern	26
Slate Bleu | French	26
Inn/Phillips Mill | French	25

Cross Culture | Indian	25
Amato's | Pizza	25
Marsha Brown | Creole/Southern	25
Carlucci's Grill | Italian	25
A1 | Japanese	25
Bobby Simone's | Amer.	25
Ota-Ya | Japanese	25
Steve's Steaks | Cheesestks.	25
Villa Barolo | Italian	25
Georgine's | Italian	25
PrimoHoagies | Sandwiches	25
Duck Sauce | Asian/Chinese	25
Christine's Rest. | Amer./Italian	24
El Sarape | Mex.	24
NEW Bonefish Grill | Seafood	24
Francisco's | Italian	24
Bella Tori | Italian	24
Knight House | Amer.	24
Yardley Inn | Amer.	24
Black Bass | Amer.	24
Five Guys | Burgers	24
Lee's Hoagie | Sandwiches	24
J.B. Dawson's/Austin's | Amer.	24
Las Margaritas | Mex.	24
Toscana 52 | Italian	24
P.F. Chang's | Chinese	24
Arirang | Japanese	23
La Stalla | Italian	23
Bacco | Italian/Pizza	23
Siam Cuisine | Thai	23
Cock 'N Bull | Amer.	23
Piccolo Tratt. | Italian	23
Chambers 19 | Amer.	23
Kopper Kettle | Seafood	23
Nifty Fifty's | Diner	23
Chickie's/Pete's | Pub	23
Jules Thin Crust | Pizza	22
On the Border | Mex.	22
Wash. Cross. Inn | Amer.	22
Maggio's | Italian/Pizza	22
NEW KC Prime | Steak	22
Brick Hotel Rest. | Amer.	22
Isaac Newton's | Amer.	22
HAVANA | Amer./Eclectic	21
Roman Delight | Italian	21
Ted's Montana | Amer.	21

NEW Gino's Burgers	*Amer.*	21
Landing	*Amer.*	21
Triumph Brewing	*Amer./Eclectic*	20
Freight House	*Amer.*	20
Club House Diner	*Diner*	18
Green Parrot	*Amer.*	16

CHESTER COUNTY

Birchrunville Store	*French/Italian*	29
Talula's Table	*European*	28
Sovana Bistro	*French/Med.*	28
Majolica	*Amer.*	28
Orchard	*Amer.*	27
Daddy Mims	*Creole*	27
Dilworth. Inn	*Amer.*	27
Capriotti's	*Sandwiches*	26
Catherine's	*Amer.*	26
Duling-Kurtz Hse.	*Continental*	26
Seven Stars Inn	*Steak*	26
Limoncello	*Italian*	26
Kimberton Inn	*Amer.*	26
High Street Caffe	*Cajun/Creole*	26
Han Dynasty	*Chinese*	25
Black Lab Bistro	*Amer.*	25
Teca	*Italian*	25
Thai L'Elephant	*Thai*	25
Avalon	*Italian*	25
Bonefish Grill	*Seafood*	24
Pietro's Prime	*Steak*	24
Mendenhall Inn	*Amer.*	24
1906f	*Amer.*	24
Jake's Wayback	*Burgers*	24
Blue Pear	*Amer.*	23
Café Fiorello's	*Italian*	23
Nonna's Italian	*Italian*	23
Isaac's	*Amer./Sandwiches*	23
Drafting Rm.	*Amer.*	22
Iron Hill	*Amer.*	22
On the Border	*Mex.*	22
Half Moon	*Amer.*	22
Four Dogs	*Amer.*	22
Doc Magrogan	*Seafood*	21
Riverstone Café	*Amer.*	21
Ship Inn	*Seafood/Steak*	21
Pepperoncini	*Italian*	21
Landmark Amer.	*Amer./Pub*	20

Buca di Beppo	*Italian*	20
Kildare's	*Pub*	20
Molly Maguire's	*Pub*	19
Sly Fox	*Pub*	19
Más Mexicali	*Mex.*	19

DELAWARE COUNTY

Sycamore	*Amer.*	28
Masamoto	*Asian*	28
Bona Cucina	*Italian*	27
Trieste	*Italian*	27
Capriotti's	*Sandwiches*	26
Charlie's Hamburg.	*Burgers*	26
Nick's Old Original	*Sandwiches*	26
Tony Luke's	*Cheesestks.*	26
Ariano	*Italian*	26
Shere-E-Punjab	*Indian*	26
Tratt. Giuseppe	*Italian*	25
Clam Tavern	*Seafood*	25
Harvest	*Amer.*	25
Fellini Cafe	*Italian*	25
Kaya's	*Amer.*	25
Firebirds	*Amer.*	25
Mile High Steak & Seafood	*Seafood/Steak*	25
Marg. Kuo Peking	*Chinese/Japanese*	25
Rose Tree Inn	*Amer.*	25
PrimoHoagies	*Sandwiches*	25
Marg. Kuo Media	*Chinese/Japanese*	25
Anthony's Rist.	*Italian*	25
Fellini Cafe	*Italian*	24
NEW 320 Market	*Amer.*	24
Bonefish Grill	*Seafood*	24
Jim's Steaks	*Cheesestks.*	24
Teikoku	*Japanese/Thai*	24
Big Fish Grill	*Seafood*	24
Hibachi	*Japanese*	24
P.F. Chang's	*Chinese*	24
Charlie Brown's	*Steak*	23
Hank's Place	*Diner*	23
Azie	*Asian*	23
Pat's Pizza	*Pizza*	23
Nifty Fifty's	*Diner*	23
Slack's Hoagie	*Sandwiches*	23
La Na Thai	*French/Thai*	23
Iron Hill	*Amer.*	22
Brandywine Prime	*Steak*	22

LOCATIONS

La Belle Epoque	*French*	22
Gables	*Amer.*	22
Duffer's Mill	*Pub*	22
Seasons Pizza	*Pizza*	21
McKenzie Brew	*Amer.*	21
JD McGillicuddy's	*Amer.*	21
Peace A Pizza	*Pizza*	21
Barnaby's	*Amer.*	20
Barnaby's Aston	*Amer./ Italian*	20
Qdoba	*Mex.*	20
Ruby's Diner	*Diner*	19
Mrs. Marty's Deli	*Deli*	18
Country Squire Diner	*Diner*	18
Newtown Grill	*Italian/Steak*	18
NEW Argana Moroccan	*Moroccan*	-

KING OF PRUSSIA

Morton's	*Steak*	26
Capital Grille	*Steak*	26
Kabuki	*Japanese*	26
Creed's	*Seafood/Steak*	26
Sullivan's Steak	*Steak*	26
Ruth's Chris	*Steak*	25
Maggiano's	*Italian*	24
Seasons 52	*Amer.*	24
Cheesecake	*Amer.*	24
Vito's Pizza	*Pizza*	24
Melting Pot	*Fondue*	24
NEW Joe's Crab Shack	*Seafood*	23
California Pizza	*Pizza*	22
Legal Sea Foods	*Seafood*	22
Bahama Breeze	*Caribbean*	22
Peace A Pizza	*Pizza*	21
Rock Bottom	*Pub*	21
Baja Fresh	*Mex.*	21
Gino's Burgers	*Amer.*	21
Ruby's Diner	*Diner*	19

MAIN LINE

Rest. Alba	*Amer.*	27
Sola	*Amer.*	27
Frankie's Fellini	*Italian*	27
NEW Pescatore	*Italian*	27
Savona	*Italian*	26
Doghouse Burgers	*Amer.*	26
Antonella's	*Italian*	26
Amani's BYOB	*Amer.*	26
Art of Bread	*Bakery/French*	26
Amans	*Indian*	26

Fleming's Prime	*Steak*	26
General Warren Inne	*Amer.*	25
Nectar	*Asian*	25
Yangming	*Chinese/Continental*	25
Bunha Faun	*Asian/French*	25
Olive Tree	*Greek*	25
Thai Orchid	*Thai*	25
PrimoHoagies	*Sandwiches*	25
Gino's Pizza	*Pizza*	24
Avalon Pasta	*Italian*	24
Taq. La Michoacana	*Mex.*	24
Saffron	*Indian*	24
Bravo Pizza	*Pizza*	24
Anthony's Pizza	*Pizza*	24
Georges'	*Eclectic*	24
Firecreek	*Amer.*	24
Sang Kee Asian	*Chinese*	24
Tratt. San Nicola	*Italian*	24
Susanna Foo's	*Asian*	24
Five Guys	*Burgers*	24
A Taste/Britain	*Sandwiches*	24
Marg. Kuo	*Chinese/Japanese*	24
Lee's Hoagie	*Sandwiches*	24
Hibachi	*Japanese*	24
Hunan Rest.	*Chinese*	24
Marg. Kuo Mandarin	*Chinese/Japanese*	24
Jake's Wayback	*Burgers*	24
Alfredo	*Italian*	23
Teresa's Next Dr.	*Belgian*	23
Silverspoon	*Amer.*	23
Aperto	*Amer.*	23
White Dog	*Eclectic*	23
Guard House Inn	*Amer.*	23
La Collina	*Italian*	23
Azie	*Asian*	23
Ekta Indian Cuisine	*Indian*	23
Shangrila	*Asian*	23
Teresa's Cafe	*Italian*	23
August Moon	*Japanese/Korean*	23
333 Belrose	*Amer.*	23
Tiffin	*Indian*	22
NEW Jules Thin Crust	*Pizza*	22
Med. Grill	*Med.*	22
Rist. Primavera	*Italian*	22
Tango	*Amer.*	22
A La Maison	*French*	22
NEW Ella's Amer. Bistro	*Amer.*	22

🆕 Paramour | *Amer.*	22
Victory Brewing | *Pub*	22
Lourdas Greek | *Greek*	22
Gryphon Coffee | *Coffee*	21
Matador | *Mex./Spanish*	21
🆕 McKenzie Brew | *Amer.*	21
China Inn | *Chinese*	21
D McGillicuddy's | *Amer.*	21
Peace A Pizza | *Pizza*	21
Elevation Burg. | *Burgers*	21
Verdad Rest. | *Spanish*	21
Cedar Hollow Inn | *Amer.*	21
Vinberie's | *Amer.*	21
RGR Joint | *Burgers*	21
🆕 Landmark Amer. | *Amer./Pub*	20
Pub/Penn Valley | *Eclectic*	20
Qdoba | *Mex.*	20
Chops Restaurant | *Steak*	20
Ardmore Station | *Diner*	20
Du Jour | *Amer.*	20
Minella's Diner | *Diner*	20
Buca di Beppo | *Italian*	20
Delancey St. Bagels | *Bagels/Deli*	20
Mikado | *Japanese/Thai*	20
Al Dar Bistro | *Med.*	20
Hymie's | *Deli*	19
Christopher's | *Amer.*	19
Aneu | *Amer.*	19
Chinnar Indian | *Indian*	19
Fuji Mt. Japanese | *Japanese*	19
Hummus | *Med.*	19
Ruby's Diner | *Diner*	19
Murray's Deli | *Deli*	19
Primavera Pizza | *Pizza*	19
Auspicious | *Chinese*	19
Great American Pub | *Amer.*	19
Cilantro | *Mex.*	18
Ray's Rest./Malt Shop | *Diner*	18
MilkBoy Coffee | *Coffee*	18
Sullifty's | *Amer.*	17
Plate | *Amer.*	16
Khajuraho | *Indian*	15

MONTGOMERY COUNTY

Bluefin | *Japanese*	28
Funky Lil' Kitchen | *Amer.*	27
Charlie's Pizzeria | *Pizza*	27
TreVi | *Italian*	27
Blackfish | *Amer./Seafood*	26

Rist. San Marco | *Italian*	26
Ooka | *Japanese*	26
Anne's Kitchen | *Sandwiches*	26
South Ocean | *Chinese/Japanese*	26
Olce Pizza Grille | *Pizza*	26
Bridget's Steak | *Amer./Steak*	26
Ristorante Castello | *Italian*	26
Bonjung | *Japanese*	26
China Wok | *Chinese*	26
Han Dynasty | *Chinese*	25
Trattoria Totaro | *Italian*	25
Kinnaree | *French/Thai*	25
William Penn Inn | *Amer./Continental*	25
Thai Orchid | *Thai*	25
Sorrento's | *Italian*	25
Arpeggio | *Med.*	25
Stone Rose | *Amer.*	25
19 Bella | *Med.*	25
Joseph Ambler Inn | *Amer.*	25
Na'Brasa | *Brazilian/Steak*	25
Abacus | *Chinese*	25
Tamarindos | *Mex.*	25
Zakes Cafe | *Amer.*	25
PrimoHoagies | *Sandwiches*	25
63 Bistro | *Amer.*	25
1750 Bistro | *Amer.*	25
Spring Mill | *French*	25
El Sarape | *Mex.*	24
Bocelli | *Italian*	24
Osaka | *Japanese*	24
Bonefish Grill | *Seafood*	24
Metro. Diner | *Amer.*	24
From the Boot | *Italian*	24
Ariana's Ristorante | *Med.*	24
Tavolo | *Italian*	24
Giuseppe's Pizza | *Pizza*	24
Tex Mex Connect. | *Tex-Mex*	24
AllWays Café | *Eclectic*	24
Saffron | *Indian*	24
Totaro's | *Eclectic*	24
Anthony's Pizza | *Pizza*	24
Cheesecake | *Amer.*	24
Cantina Feliz | *Mex.*	24
Stella Blu | *Amer.*	24
Lee's Hoagie | *Sandwiches*	24
Bay Pony Inn | *Amer.*	24
Parc Bistro | *Amer.*	24

LOCATIONS

Restaurant	Rating
Chiangmai | *Thai*	24
J.B. Dawson's/Austin's | *Amer.*	24
Trax Rest. | *Amer.*	24
Mandarin Gdn. | *Chinese*	24
Hibachi | *Japanese*	24
P.F. Chang's | *Chinese*	24
Jake's Wayback | *Burgers*	24
211 York | *Amer.*	24
Fountain Side | *Amer./Italian*	23
California Tortilla | *Mex.*	23
Il Giardino | *Italian/Pizza*	23
Bacco | *Italian*	23
Fayette St. | *Amer.*	23
Back Porch Cafe | *Amer.*	23
Tortuga's Mex. | *Mex.*	23
Radice | *Italian*	23
Benihana | *Japanese*	23
Farmer's Daughter | *Amer.*	23
Lai Lai Garden | *Asian*	23
Redstone | *Amer.*	23
Athena | *Greek/Med.*	23
Vintage Bar/Grill | *Amer.*	23
Cafe Preeya | *Eclectic*	23
La Pergola | *Eastern Euro./Mideast.*	23
Blue Bell Inn | *Amer.*	23
Black Dog Cafe | *Asian*	23
Dettera | *Amer.*	23
Appalachian Brew. | *Amer.*	23
White Elephant | *Thai*	23
Ben & Irv's | *Deli*	23
Isabella | *Med.*	23
Slack's Hoagie | *Sandwiches*	23
Zacharias | *Amer.*	23
Tiffin | *Indian*	22
NEW Bravo! | *Italian*	22
Arugula | *Italian*	22
Jules Thin Crust | *Pizza*	22
Jasmine Asian | *Asian*	22
Mirna's Café | *Eclectic/Med.*	22
Iron Hill | *Amer.*	22
Iron Abbey | *Belgian*	22
Brasserie 73 | *French*	22
Coyote Cross. | *Mex.*	22
Marco Polo | *Italian*	22
Cafe La Fontana | *Italian*	22
California Pizza | *Pizza*	22
Phil's Tav. | *Amer.*	22
Sly Fox | *Pub*	22
El Limon | *Mex.*	2
Basta Pasta | *Italian*	2
Pistachio Grille | *Amer./Med.*	2
Palace of Asia | *Indian*	2
Scoogi's | *Italian*	2
Trappe Tavern | *Amer./Pub*	2
NEW Mad Mex | *Mex.*	2
NEW 401 Diner | *Amer.*	2
Gypsy Saloon | *Eclectic*	2
Spampinato's | *Italian*	2
Elevation Burg. | *Burgers*	2
Pepperoncini | *Italian*	2
Otto's Brauhaus | *German*	2
Baja Fresh | *Mex.*	2
P.J. Whelihan's | *Pub*	2
Broad Axe Tav. | *Amer.*	2
Brick House | *Amer.*	20
Kitchen Bar | *Amer.*	20
Dave/Buster's | *Amer.*	20
Old Town Buffet | *Asian/Eclectic*	20
MaGerks | *Pub*	20
Roadhouse Grille | *Amer.*	20
Mal's American Diner | *Amer.*	20
Brittingham's | *Amer./Irish*	20
Persian Grill | *Persian*	19
Molly Maguire's | *Pub*	19
Rosey's BBQ | *BBQ*	19
KC's Alley | *Pub*	19
Spamps | *Eclectic/Steak*	19
Andy's Diner & Pub | *Diner*	18
Sorella Rose | *Amer.*	18

Lancaster/ Berks Counties

ADAMSTOWN

Stoudts Black Angus | *Amer.*	25

BIRD-IN-HAND

Bird-in-Hand | *PA Dutch*	25
Plain/Fancy Farm | *PA Dutch*	22

EAST EARL

Shady Maple | *PA Dutch*	24

EAST PETERSBURG

Haydn Zug's | *Amer.*	25

EPHRATA

Lily's on Main | *Amer.*	26
Isaac's | *Amer./Sandwiches*	23

LOCATIONS

Norma's | *Mideast.* 24
Maggiano's | *Italian* 24
Seasons 52 | *Amer.* 24
NEW Bobby's Burger | *Burgers* 24
Cheesecake | *Amer.* 24
Mikado | *Japanese* 24
Vito's Pizza | *Pizza* 24
Pho Eden | *Vietnamese* 24
McCormick/Schmick | *Seafood* 23
Steak 38 | *Steak* 23
Sang Kee Noodle | *Chinese* 23
Kuzina/Sofia | *Greek* 23
Brio | *Italian* 23
Vitarelli's | *Italian* 23
Pat's Pizza | *Pizza* 23
Blue2O | *Seafood* 22
Palace of Asia | *Indian* 22
Johnny's Pizza | *Pizza* 22
Big John's | *Cheesestks.* 22
Andreotti's Viennese | *Italian* 22
Cool Dog Cafe | *Amer.* 22
California Pizza | *Pizza* 22
Bahama Breeze | *Caribbean* 22
Mandarin Buffet | *Chinese* 21
Ponzio's | *Diner* 21
Baja Fresh | *Mex.* 21
P.J. Whelihan's | *Pub* 21
Dublin Square | *Irish/Pub* 20
Silver Diner | *Diner* 20
The Coastline | *Amer.* 19

CINNAMINSON

Brother's Pizza | *Pizza* 26
NEW Sammy Chon's K-Town | *Korean* 25
Whistlers Inn | *Amer./BBQ* 23
Pat's Pizza | *Pizza* 23
The Harvest | *Amer.* 22

CLAYTON

Nick's Pizzeria/Steak | *Italian/Pizza* 25

CLEMENTON

Filomena Italiana | *Italian* 27
Nifty Fifty's | *Diner* 23

COLLINGSWOOD

Zeppoli | *Italian* 28
Sagami | *Japanese* 27
Sapori | *Italian* 27

Kitchen Consigliere | *Italian* 2
Il Fiore | *Italian* 2
IndeBlue | *Indian* 2
Nunzio | *Italian* 2
Bistro/Marino | *Italian* 2
Bobby Chez | *Seafood* 2
The Tortilla Press | *Mex.* 2
El Sitio Grill & Cafe | *Pan-Latin/Steak* 2
Barone's/Villa Barone | *Italian* 2
Casona | *Cuban* 2
Pop Shop | *Amer.* 2
That's Amore | *Italian* 2
Joe Pesce | *Italian/Seafood* 2
Thai Basil | *Thai* 2
Blackbird | *French/Italian* 2
West Side Gravy | *Amer.* 2
NEW Little Louie's BBQ | *BBQ* –

DELRAN

Bella Pizza Cafe | *Italian/Pizza* 2
Ott's | *Amer./Pub* 2

DEPTFORD

Filomena Lake. | *Italian* 2
Tokyo Mandarin | *Chinese/Japanese* 2
Cap'n Cats Clam Bar | *Seafood* 2
Tokyo Hibachi | *Japanese* 2
Bonefish Grill | *Seafood* 2
Five Guys | *Burgers* 2

EDGEWATER PARK

45th St. Pub | *Pub* 2

GIBBSBORO

Chophouse | *Seafood/Steak* 2

GLASSBORO

Tomo Sushi | *Japanese* 28
Tokyo Mandarin | *Chinese/Japanese* 2
Nick's Pizzeria/Steak | *Italian/Pizza* 2
Bomb Bomb BBQ | *BBQ/Sandwiches* 2
Peking Buffet | *Chinese* 2
Landmark Amer. | *Amer./Pub* 2

HADDONFIELD

Fuji Japanese | *Japanese* 2
Oriental Pearl | *Chinese* 2

Mélange	*Italian/Southern*	26		

Mélange | *Italian/Southern* — 26
Tre Famiglia | *Italian* — 26
Cross Culture | *Indian* — 25
Bruno's Rest./Pizza | *Italian* — 25
British Chip Shop | *British* — 24
Little Tuna | *Seafood* — 24
Animo Juice | *Mex.* — 23
The Taproom & Grill | *Amer./Pub* — 22
P.J. Whelihan's | *Pub* — 21

HADDON HEIGHTS

Station House | *Amer.* — 25
Elements Cafe | *Amer.* — 25
Anthony's Creative | *Italian* — 24
Kunkel's | *Seafood/Steak* — 24

LAMBERTVILLE

Hamilton's | *Med.* — 26
Manon | *French* — 26
NEW Cross Culture | *Indian* — 25
Ota-Ya | *Japanese* — 25
Anton's/Swan | *Amer.* — 24
Siam Thai | *Thai* — 23
Bell's Tavern | *Amer./Italian* — 23
Caffe Galleria | *Eclectic* — 23
Rick's | *Italian* — 23
Lilly's/Canal | *Eclectic* — 23
Full Moon | *Eclectic* — 22
Lambertville Station | *Amer.* — 21
Inn of the Hawke | *Amer.* — 20

LINDENWOLD

La Esperanza | *Mex.* — 25

LOGAN TOWNSHIP

Tokyo Mandarin | *Chinese/Japanese* — 27

MAPLE SHADE

Yokohama | *Japanese* — 27
Tacconelli's | *Pizza* — 26
Sal/Joe's Spaghetti | *Amer./Italian* — 24
Barone's/Villa Barone | *Italian* — 24
Mikado | *Japanese* — 24
Charlie Brown's | *Steak* — 23
Forno | *Pizza* — 23
Iron Hill | *Amer./Pub* — 22

Cafe Fontana | *Italian/Pizza* — 22
Yellow Submarine | *Cheesestks.* — 21
P.J. Whelihan's | *Pub* — 21

MARLTON

Fleming's Prime | *Steak* — 26
Bonefish Grill | *Seafood* — 24
Mikado | *Japanese* — 24
Joe's Peking | *Chinese* — 24
P.F. Chang's | *Chinese* — 24
Redstone | *Amer.* — 23
Pietro's Pizza | *Pizza* — 23
NEW Brio | *Italian* — 23
Luigi's Pizza Fresca | *Italian/Pizza* — 23
Mexican Food | *Mex.* — 22
Pizzicato | *Italian* — 22

MEDFORD

Jasmine Oriental | *Asian/Thai* — 27
Femmina Italian Grill | *Italian* — 26
Illiano Cucina | *Italian* — 24
Braddock's | *Amer.* — 22
Makiman Sushi | *Japanese/Korean* — 21
Ott's | *Amer./Pub* — 21
Medport Diner | *Diner* — 21

MEDFORD LAKES

P.J. Whelihan's | *Pub* — 21

MERCHANTVILLE

The Tortilla Press | *Mex* — 19

MOORESTOWN

Akira | *Japanese* — 25
Megu | *Japanese* — 25
La Vita's Pizza | *Pizza* — 25
Barone's/Villa Barone | *Italian* — 24
Five Guys | *Burgers* — 24
Al Dente Italiana | *Italian* — 22
Passariello's | *Italian/Pizza* — 22
Elevation Burg. | *Burgers* — 21
Old Town Buffet | *Asian/Eclectic* — 20

MOUNT EPHRAIM

Five Guys | *Burgers* — 24
Black Horse Diner | *Diner* — 23

LOCATIONS

MOUNT HOLLY

Robin's Nest | *Amer.* 25
Charlie Brown's | *Steak* 23
High St. Grill | *Amer.* 21

MOUNT LAUREL

Bobby Chez | *Seafood* 25
GG's Restaurant | *Amer.* 25
Angelo's | *Italian/Pizza* 25
El Azteca | *Mex.* 22
Cucina Carini | *Italian* 22
On the Border | *Mex.* 22
Baja Fresh | *Mex.* 21
Sage Diner | *Diner* 18

MULLICA HILL

Mandarin Oriental | *Chinese/Japanese* 27
Amelia's Tea/Holly | *Tearoom* 25
Toscana | *Italian* 23
Blueplate | *Amer.* 23
Pat's Pizza | *Pizza* 23
Harrison Hse. Diner | *Amer.* 18

NATIONAL PARK

Pat's Pizza | *Pizza* 23

OAKLYN

Aunt Berta's | *Soul/Southern* 26

PALMYRA

Curran's Irish Inn | *Amer.* 24

PENNSAUKEN

Pub | *Steak* 24
Bobby Ray's | *Amer.* 24
Benihana | *Japanese* 23
Lobster Trap | *Seafood* 22
45th St. Pub | *Pub* 22
Wild Wings | *Chicken* 21
Penn Queen Diner | *Diner* 20
Connie Mac's | *Irish/Pub* 19

RUNNEMEDE

Antonietta's | *Italian* 23
Pat's Pizza | *Pizza* 23
Phily Diner | *Diner* 22

SEWELL

Arugula | *Italian* 27
Pasta Pomodoro | *Italian* 27
Terra Nova | *Amer.* 27
Bobby Chez | *Seafood* 25
Mandarin Inn | *Chinese* 25

Barnsboro Inn | *Amer.* 23
Mozzarella Grill | *Italian/Pizza* 22
Ott's | *Amer./Pub* 21
P.J. Whelihan's | *Pub* 21
Clancy's Pub | *Pub* 20

SICKLERVILLE

NEW Tony Luke's | *Cheesestks.* 26
Nick's Pizzeria/Steak | 25
    Italian/Pizza
Five Guys | *Burgers* 24
Villari's Lake Side | *Italian* 22

SOMERDALE

Umi Japanese | *Japanese* 28

STRATFORD

Seasons Pizza | *Pizza* 21

SWEDESBORO

Botto's Italian Line | *Italian* 25
Pat's Pizza | *Pizza* 23
Rode's Fireside | *Amer./BBQ* 21

TURNERSVILLE

Luna Rossa | *Italian* 28
Whitman Diner | *Amer.* 23
Nifty Fifty's | *Diner* 23

VOORHEES

Fieni's Ristorante | 27
    Italian/Seafood
La Locanda | *Italian* 26
Coriander | *Indian* 26
Akira | *Japanese/Steak* 25
Little Café | *Eclectic* 25
Ritz Seafood | *Asian/Seafood* 24
Cap'n Cat Clam Bar | *Seafood* 24
Five Guys | *Burgers* 24
Ariana | *Afghan* 23
Chez Elena Wu | *Chinese/Japanese* 22
Healthy Garden | *Pizza* 22
Passariello's | *Italian/Pizza* 22
Pasta Pomodoro | *Italian* 21
Coffee Works | *Coffee* 21
Coconut Bay | *Asian* 21
Carriage House | *Amer./Italian* 21
Baja Fresh | *Mex.* 21

WESTMONT

Giumarello | *Italian* 26
Westmont Family Rest. | *Diner* 23
Treno | *Italian* 22

WILLIAMSTOWN

Library IV | *Steak* — 26
Nick's Pizzeria/Steak | *Italian/Pizza* — 25
Taylors | *Amer.* — 18

WILLINGBORO

Gaetano's/Penny Packer | *Cheesestks./Pizza* — 23

WOODBURY

China House | *Chinese* — 28
Angelo's Pizza | *Pizza* — 25
Charlie Brown's | *Steak* — 23
Colonial Diner | *Diner* — 20

WOODBURY HEIGHTS

Hollywood Cafe | *Amer.* — 21

Delaware

BEAR

Hibachi | *Japanese* — 24

CLAYMONT

Claymont Steak | *Cheesestks.* — 24

EDGEMOOR

Seasons Pizza | *Pizza* — 21

GREENVILLE

Pizza By Elizabeths | *Pizza* — 25
2 Fat Guys | *Amer.* — 24
Brew HaHa! | *Coffee* — 22

HOCKESSIN

House/William Merry | *Amer.* — 25
2 Fat Guys | *Amer.* — 24
Back Burner | *Amer.* — 24

MONTCHANIN

Krazy Kat's | *French* — 25

NEWARK

Soffritto | *Italian* — 27
Capriotti's | *Sandwiches* — 26
Firebirds | *Amer.* — 25
Claymont Steak | *Cheesestks.* — 24
Hibachi | *Japanese* — 24
Iron Hill | *Amer.* — 22
Brew HaHa! | *Coffee* — 22

WILMINGTON

Green Room | *French* — 28
Mikimotos | *Asian/Japanese* — 27

Culinaria | *Amer.* — 27
Moro | *Italian* — 26
Piccolina Tosc. | *Italian* — 26
Harry's Seafood | *Seafood* — 26
Dom. Hudson | *Amer.* — 26
Sullivan's Steak | *Steak* — 26
Orillas Tapa Bar | *Spanish* — 26
Rasa Sayang | *Malaysian* — 25
Eclipse Bistro | *Amer.* — 25
Deep Blue | *Seafood* — 25
Harry's Savoy | *Amer.* — 25
El Tapatio | *Mex.* — 25
Capers/Lemons | *Italian* — 24
Corner Bistro | *Eclectic* — 24
Feby's Fish. | *Seafood* — 24
Anthony's Pizza | *Pizza* — 24
Five Guys | *Burgers* — 24
Big Fish Grill | *Seafood* — 24
Melting Pot | *Fondue* — 24
Hibachi | *Japanese* — 24
Jake's Wayback | *Burgers* — 24
Lamberti's/Tutto Fresco | *Italian* — 23

Chelsea Tavern | *Amer.* — 23
Walter's Steak. | *Steak* — 23
Lucky's Coffee | *Amer.* — 23
Union City Grille | *Steak* — 23
Blue Parrot | *Cajun* — 23
La Tolteca | *Mex.* — 23
Jasmine Asian | *Asian* — 23
Palace of Asia | *Indian* — 22
Mrs. Robino's | *Italian* — 22
Iron Hill | *Amer.* — 22
Columbus Inn | *Amer.* — 22
Brew HaHa! | *Coffee* — 22
Charcoal Pit | *Burgers* — 22
FireStone Roasting | *Amer.* — 22
Wash. St. Ale | *Pub* — 22
Dead Presidents Pub | *Amer.* — 21
China Royal | *Chinese* — 21
Stoney's British Pub | *British* — 21
Kid Shelleen's | *Amer.* — 20
Mexican Post | *Mex.* — 19
World Café | *Amer.* — 19
NEW Ernest/Scott Taproom | *Eclectic* — ‑

LOCATIONS

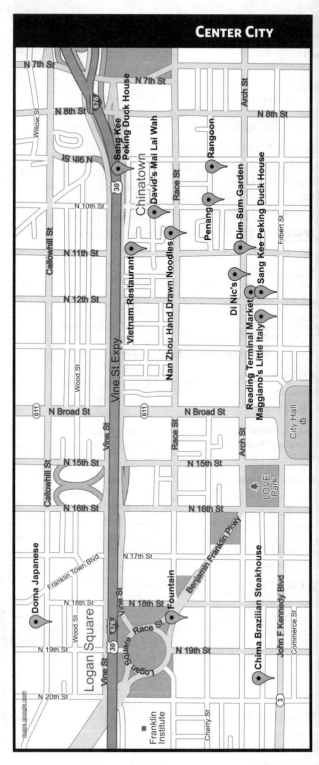

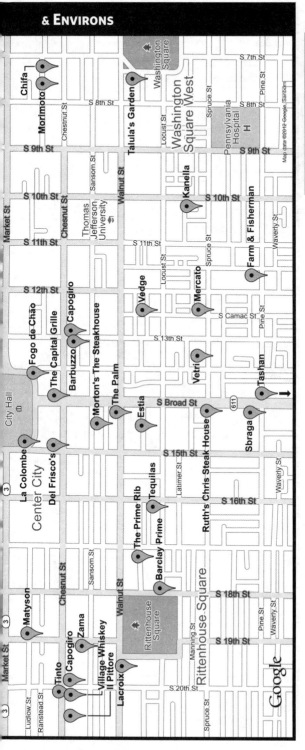

Washington Square West

S 7th St
Pine St
S 8th St
Spruce St
Pennsylvania Hospital
S 9th St

Map data ©2012 Google, Sanborn

Chifa
Morimoto
S 8th St
Chestnut St
S 9th St
Sansom St
S 10th St
Walnut St
S 11th St
Thomas Jefferson University
Talula's Garden
Kanella
Locust St
S 10th St
Spruce St
Waverly St
Farm & Fisherman

S 12th St
Capogiro
Fogo de Chão
The Capital Grille
Barbuzzo
Morton's The Steakhouse
The Palm
Estia
S 13th St
Vedge
Mercato
S Camac St
Pine St
Vetri
Tashan
611
Sbraga

City Hall
Center City
La Colombe
Del Frisco's
S Broad St
S 15th St
Latimer St
Ruth's Chris Steak House
Waverly St

Market St
Chestnut St
Sansom St
Walnut St
The Prime Rib
Tequilas
S 16th St
Barclay Prime

Matyson
Capogiro
Zama
Village Whiskey
Il Pittore
Tinto
Lacroix
Rittenhouse Square
Manning St
S 18th St
Rittenhouse Square
S 19th St
Pine St
Waverly St

Ludlow St
Ransom St
S 20th St
Spruce St
Google

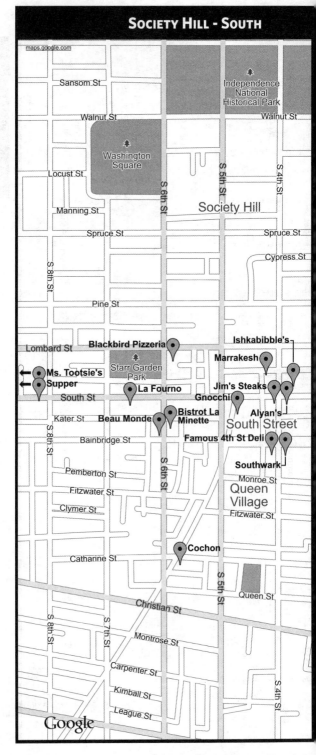

maps.google.com

Sansom St

Walnut St

Walnut St

Independence
National
Historical Park

Washington
Square

Locust St

S 5th St

S 4th St

Society Hill

Manning St

Spruce St

Spruce St

Cypress St

S 6th St

S 8th St

Pine St

Lombard St

Blackbird Pizzeria

Ishkabibble's

Starr Garden
Park

Marrakesh

Ms. Tootsie's
Supper

La Fourno

Jim's Steaks

Gnocchi

Alyan's

South St

Beau Monde

Bistrot La
Minette

South Street

Kater St

Famous 4th St Deli

Bainbridge St

Southwark

S 8th St

Pemberton St

Monroe St

Fitzwater St

Queen
Village

Clymer St

Fitzwater St

Catharine St

Cochon

S 6th St

S 5th St

Queen St

Christian St

S 8th St

S 7th St

Montrose St

Carpenter St

S 4th St

Kimball St

League St

Google

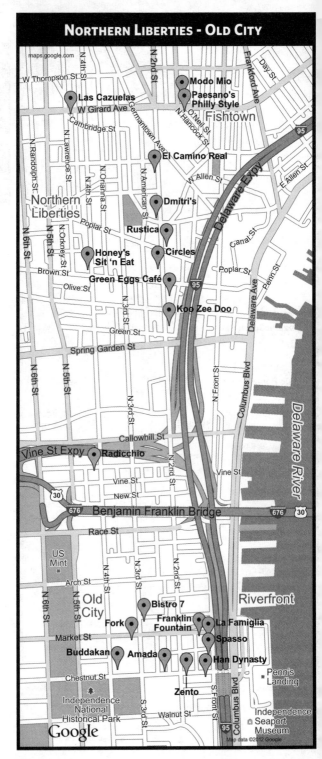

NORTHERN LIBERTIES - OLD CITY

maps.google.com

W Thompson St

W Girard Ave

Las Cazuelas

Cambridge St

Modo Mio

Paesano's Philly Style

Fishtown

N 2nd St

Germantown Ave

N Hancock St

O Neil St

Day St

Frankford Ave

95

Northern Liberties

N Randolph St

N Lawrence St

N Orianna St

N American St

El Camino Real

W Allen St

E Allen St

Delaware Expy

Canal St

Dmitri's

Poplar St

Rustica

Circles

Honey's Sit 'n Eat

Brown St

Olive St

Green Eggs Café

95

Poplar St

Delaware Ave

Penn St

Koo Zee Doo

Green St

Spring Garden St

N 6th St

N 5th St

N 3rd St

N Front St

Columbus Blvd

Delaware River

Callowhill St

Vine St Expy

Radicchio

30

Vine St

New St

N 2nd St

Vine St

676

Benjamin Franklin Bridge

676

30

Race St

US Mint

Arch St

N 4th St

N 3rd St

N 2nd St

Riverfront

Old City

N 6th St

N 5th St

Bistro 7

Fork

Franklin Fountain

La Famiglia

Market St

Spasso

Buddakan

Amada

Han Dynasty

Chestnut St

Zento

S Front St

Penn's Landing

Independence National Historical Park

S 3rd St

Walnut St

Columbus Blvd

95

Independence Seaport Museum

Google

Map data ©2012 Google

Latest openings, menus, photos and more on plus.google.com/local

RESTAURANT
DIRECTORY

Philadelphia

	FOOD	DECOR	SERVICE	COST

Abacus ⓜ Chinese   25 | 22 | 24 | $25

Lansdale | North Penn Mktpl. | 1551 S. Valley Forge Rd.
(Sumneytown Pike) | 215-362-2010

"Foodies in the 'burbs" swear by "creative", "top-notch" Chinese
fare at this BYO "staple" in Lansdale, where manager Joe Chen's
"shtick" makes "everyone from regulars to newbies feel like family", as he steers you to "well-prepared specials"; the prices are
"reasonable", and the "surprisingly elegant" interior, featuring
"huge, beautiful" fish tanks, "belies its strip-mall location."

Abbaye ● Belgian   22 | 18 | 20 | $21

Northern Liberties | 637 N. 3rd St. (Fairmount Ave.) |
215-627-6711 | www.theabbaye.net

Fans of this "no-frills" Belgian "watering hole" on a Northern
Liberties corner laud the "killer" "rotating" beer list", "mouthwatering specials board" and menu that's "good for vegetarians";
"friendly" service from a "rockabilly" staff, "interesting" people-
watching and a vibe that's "welcoming to families" help make it the
neighborhood "Cheers" for many.

Abner's Cheesesteaks ● Cheesesteaks   19 | 13 | 19 | $12

University City | 3813 Chestnut St. (38th Ave.) | 215-662-0100 |
www.abnerscheesesteaks.com

While it "may be bad for your waistline", the "greasy" goodness at this
University City cheesesteak "institution" is "great for your attitude"
(especially "when the hangover calls") and "reasonably priced" to
boot; the "joint" is full of "Penn memorabilia", and many Quaker
alum "love recruiting" on campus "just so they can get lunch here."

Abyssinia Ethiopian   25 | 15 | 18 | $18
Restaurant ● Ethiopian

University City | 229 S. 45th St. (Locust St.) | 215-387-2424 |
www.abyssiniarestaurantpa.com

"Unbelievable" East African tastes are de rigueur at this "quaint",
"soul-warming" University City Ethiopian where you "share a platter" at your own "table" or dine "communally" with a group; critics
caution it's "not the place to go for a quick bite", however, because
service comes at a "leisurely" pace due to "scant" staffers; P.S. you
can mingle with "local hipsters" in the small upstairs bar.

Adobe Cafe Southwestern   21 | 19 | 22 | $24

Roxborough | 4550 Mitchell St. (Leverington Ave.) |
215-483-3947

East Passyunk | 1919 E. Passyunk Ave. (Mifflin St.) | 215-551-2243
www.adobecafephilly.com

"It's Cinco de Mayo every day" at these "friendly", "offbeat"
cantinas in Roxborough and East Passyunk where amigos marvel at
"delish" "spins" on Southwestern chow from kitchens that "really
understand vegetarians"; while some sniff the "trippy" decor is

PHILADELPHIA

| | FOOD | DECOR | SERVICE | COST |

"getting a little worn", that doesn't spoil the "vacation" vibe, which can be turbocharged by pitchers of "awesome" margaritas.

A Full Plate, Café & Catering *Eclectic* ∇ 23 | 20 | 22 | $17

Northern Liberties | 1009 N. Bodine St. (George St.) | 215-627-4068 | www.afullplate.com

Fans predict you'll leave "with a full tummy" from this budget-friendly Southern-tinged Eclectic BYO in Northern Liberties known for "tasty vegetarian and vegan options" and soft drinks served in mason jars; "friendly" service adds to the "enjoyable atmosphere" in the bright, "cute" setting, but some advise "bring an extra bottle of wine with you" because the "homestyle" fare is "worth waiting for – and they do make you wait."

Agiato *Italian* 25 | 23 | 23 | $25

Manayunk | 4359 Main St. (Grape St.) | 215-482-9700 | www.agiatophila.com

"Simple", "delicious" Italian "finger food", including a "worldly selection of cheeses and meats", stars at this "cozy" Manayunk trattoria where you feel like you're "on a European vacation in all the good ways" – i.e. it "doesn't hit your wallet hard" and the "knowledgeable servers don't rush you"; in sum, it's "just the kind of adult venue" Main Street needs; P.S. a post-Survey chef change may not be reflected in the Food score.

Aki *Japanese* 23 | 21 | 20 | $25

Washington Square West | 1210 Walnut St. (12th St.) | 215-985-1838 | www.myakisushi.com

Fans find it "easy to like" this "unpretentious", "affordable" Washington Square West Japanese, citing "crispy", "light" tempura and "friendly" "bartenders" who mix "delicious cocktails", but save highest praise for "awesome" lunch deals and the $24.95 "all-you-can-eat" sushi specials on Wednesdays and Sundays; in sum, it "gets the job done."

a.kitchen *American* 23 | 21 | 21 | $46

Rittenhouse | AKA Rittenhouse Sq. | 135 S. 18th St. (Sansom St.) | 215-825-7030

At this "swanky" American bistro in the AKA Rittenhouse Square, Django alum Bryan Sikora's "forward-thinking fare" yields "a.mazing" "gastronomic rewards", but some caution "plates are generally tapas-sized" so "if you come hungry, you'll leave the same way"; "sexy" digs and a "funky" staff help ramp up the "chic", even if it does get "mind-numbingly loud some nights."

A La Maison ⊠ *French* 22 | 20 | 20 | $43

Ardmore | 53 W. Lancaster Ave. (Ardmore Ave.) | 484-412-8009 | www.alamaisonbistro.com

Opinions vary about this "cozy" French BYO in Ardmore – *amis* say the "first-class" fare in a "lovely", "atmospheric" setting is "just what the Main Line needs"; foes give it a "faux" for Frenchness ("snotty" service notwithstanding) and gripe that it's "loud."

	FOOD	DECOR	SERVICE	COST

Al Dar Bistro *Mediterranean* 20 | 17 | 18 | $31

Bala Cynwyd | 281 Montgomery Ave. (Levering Mill Rd.) |
610-667-1245 | www.aldarbistro.com

"Simply prepared" seafood and "homey" Med mezes are "reliably
tasty" at this long-running, midpriced Main Line "mainstay" run
by a "friendly", "attentive" staff that permits "no surprises" in an
"upbeat (read: "noisy") room teeming with neighborhood "friends"
meeting up; a few purists frown at the "Americanization" of the
cuisine, while road warriors caution that "parking is a bit limited."

Ale House *American* 22 | 18 | 22 | $22

Newton Square | 3570 W. Chester Pike (Newton Street Rd.) |
610-353-1618 | www.alehousenewtondquare.com

After 40-plus years, this "classic" Delco watering hole dishes
out "enjoyable" American "comfort food", including its signature
roast beef sandwich, and "so many beers to choose from" to wash
it down; "nightly specials", "friendly" service and "plenty of TV
screens" in a "comfortable", "casual" setting complete the picture.

Alfredo *Italian* 23 | 20 | 21 | $27

Berwyn | 668 Lancaster Ave. (Waterloo Ave.) | 610-640-2962 |
www.alfredobyo.com

There are "more hits than misses" (such as "solid" pastas and, yes,
the namesake alfredo) at this "charming", moderately priced Main
Line Italian BYO that appeals to a "neighborhood" crowd; it gets
"lively" on weekends, and some warn that "the noise level goes
beyond comfortable decibels."

NEW Alla Spina ● *Italian* ▽ 25 | 25 | 22 | $28

Fairmount | 1410 Mt Vernon St. (Broad St.) | 215-600-0017 |
www.allaspinaphilly.com

Early fans are "blown away" by the "yummy", pork-centric Italian bar
treats and "interesting beers" from "taps galore" at Marc Vetri's
"sexy" North Philly gastropub; the "industrial-looking", graffiti-graced
digs are "over the top", literally, as you can reserve a table atop the
walk-in beer fridge, and while some find it a "little pricey", many
expect it'll be a "favorite for years to come."

The AllWays Café ▣ *Eclectic* 24 | 16 | 22 | $19

Huntingdon Valley | Bethayres Shopping Ctr. | 634 Welsh Rd.
(Huntingdon Pike) | 215-914-2151 | www.allwayscafe.com

Even if "you're not one for health food", this "casual" Huntingdon
Valley Eclectic satisfies with plenty of "wholesome", "appetizing" eats (the butternut squash is "so thick your spoon stands up
by itself") at a "decent price"; "efficient, helpful" counter service
brightens a "bare-bones" space that exudes a "yoga vibe."

Alma de Cuba *Nuevo Latino* 25 | 26 | 24 | $50

Rittenhouse | 1623 Walnut St. (bet. 16th & 17th Sts.) |
215-988-1799 | www.almadecubarestaurant.com

You almost "expect Papa Hemingway" to appear at Stephen Starr and
Douglas Rodriguez's "upscale", "special-occasion" Nuevo

Latino, still "trendy" after a decade-plus in Rittenhouse; brace yourself for "invasive noise levels" generated by "high rollers" who "come for the mojitos" in the "dim" lounge but stay for the "bold flavors" "from land and sea" (e.g. "amazing" ceviche) and "world-class" desserts, all served by a "prompt, attentive" staff in the sleek, contemporary space.

Almaz Cafe *Ethiopian* 23 | 15 | 23 | $17

Rittenhouse | 140 S. 20th St. (Walnut St.) | 215-557-0108
"Tasty", "authentic" Ethiopian plates at "almaz-ing prices" are the draw at Solomon Getnet and Almaz Haile's "pleasant", bi-level Rittenhouse cafe, where they "make you feel right at home" while "educating the masses" about East African cuisine, which is "prepared quickly"; it also serves "delicious" Western breakfast offerings, sandwiches and wraps.

Alyan's Restaurant *Mideastern* 25 | 17 | 21 | $15

South St. | 603 S. 4th St. (South St.) | 215-922-3553
"Yummy" Middle Eastern fare that "never met a piece of garlic it didn't like" is the stuff of "dreams" and "downright cheap" to boot say devotees of this "hole-in-the-wall" just off South Street; while some gripe about "hit-or-miss" service or "outdated" decor, "don't let that stop you" from getting your "falafel fix"; P.S. fans recommend the "pleasant back room."

Amada *Spanish* 28 | 25 | 25 | $53

Old City | 217-219 Chestnut St. (bet. 2nd & 3rd Sts.) | 215-625-2450 | www.amadarestaurant.com
Iron Chef Jose Garces' "rustic yet swanky" Spanish "crown jewel" in Old City "still gets a big olé" for its "fabulous" tapas, "perfectly crafted" sangria and "attentive" service, though it also gets a few jeers for "noise levels" approaching a "soccer match"; fans recommend "bringing a group to justify over-ordering", and since "noshing" makes you "run up a bill", consider the "pig roast" (which must be ordered in advance) or "tasting menus."

Amani's BYOB *American* 26 | 20 | 25 | $41

Downingtown | 105 E. Lancaster Ave. (Wallace Ave.) | 484-237-8179
A "locavore's delight" of "over-the-top delicious" New American fare comes from an open kitchen at Jonathan Amann's midpriced BYO in Downingtown, where wife Jeannine's "helpful" hospitality and a bottle of "your favorite wine" round out a "spectacular meal"; though the "cozy" space can get "noisy", a "fine-dining atmosphere" prevails – "what more could you want?"

Amans Authentic Indian Cuisine *Indian* 26 | 19 | 22 | $22

Norristown | Dekalb Plaza | 2680 Dekalb Pike (Colonial Dr.) | 610-277-5565
"Addictive" naan and a "bargain" buffet that "never disappoints" make this suburban Indian in Norristown "popular" among locals; "welcoming" staffers keep things "friendly without being overbear-

ing" and keep an open line to the kitchen that's "accommodating with the spice level"; P.S. no alcohol served.

Amato's *Pizza*

25 | 22 | 23 | $20

Fairless Hills | Fairway Plaza | 116 Trenton Rd. (Olds Blvd.) | 215-945-6045 | www.amatospizzapa.com

"Phenomenal" thick Sicilian, huge "Brooklyn" pizza and "tasty" "ziti" keep piezani "coming back for more" to this "comfortable" Bucks Italian where the "super-nice" staff makes you feel like you're "visiting the family in their home", the strip-center location behind neon beer signs notwithstanding; another plus: takeout is usually "ready when it should be."

NEW American Sardine Bar ● *American*

20 | 18 | 21 | $24

South Philly | 1801 Federal St. (18th St.) | 215-334-2337 | www.americansardinebar.com

A "paradise" for "hipsters", South Philadelphia Tap Room's "little brother" in South Philly's Point Breeze neighborhood "does not disappoint", dishing out Scott Schroeder's "affordable" American "comfort food" (including a tasty sandwich made from the "under-appreciated" namesake) in a quirky space illumined by "stringed lights"; the grub is "easily washed down with one of the varied rotating beers" doled out by "knowledgeable" bartenders.

Amis Restaurant *Italian*

26 | 22 | 24 | $51

Washington Square West | 412 S. 13th St. (Waverly St.) | 215-732-2647 | www.amisphilly.com

"Order lots of plates and share" the "magical" "peasant cuisine" at Marc Vetri's "hip", "loft-y" "Roman trattoria" around the corner from his "mother ship" in Washington Square West, where "personable" service helps compensate for the "factory"-like din; while it's "more merciful to the wallet" than its elder sibling, some caution you still may "go away hungry or broke, whichever comes first", thanks to small portions that "Jenny Craig" might approve.

Amuse *French*

21 | 24 | 24 | $45

Avenue of the Arts | Le Méridien Philadelphia | 1421 Arch St. (Broad St.) | 215-422-8201 | www.amusephiladelphia.com

This "quiet", "upscale" French in the lobby of Le Méridien near the Convention Center on the Avenue of the Arts elicits lots of "happy faces" with "cocktails" in the bar, "romantic" airs in "cavernous" dining room and "well-executed variations" on Gallic "standards"; while most find the service "pleasant", a few feel there are "not enough servers to provide a seamless experience."

Anastasi Seafood ⊠ *Seafood*

24 | 14 | 22 | $28

Bella Vista | Italian Mkt. | 1101 S. 9th St. (Washington Ave.) | 215-462-0550 | www.anastasiseafood.com

You "cannot get fresher fish anywhere" than this "gem" hidden in the "back of a fish store" in the Italian Market, which finatics swear is the "closest thing Philadelphia has to eating on Cape Cod"; so what if there's "zero ambiance", the fin fare "rocks", the prices are "reasonable" and the "quirky staff keeps the good fun rolling."

Andy's
Diner & Pub 🛇Ⓜ *Diner*

18 | 17 | 21 | $18

Conshohocken | 505 W. Ridge Pike (North Ln.) | 610-940-1444 |
www.andysdinerandpub.com

"Fast and friendly" service rules the day at this 24/7 Conshohocken
diner offering a "huge" menu of "solid" "basics", as well as a salad
bar stocked with "Greek favorites", at "reasonable prices" in
"bright", "standard" digs; cynics find it merely "functional", and
sniff "don't bother Guy Fieri."

Aneu *American*

19 | 23 | 22 | $37

Berwyn | 575 Lancaster Ave. (Old Lancaster Rd.) | 610-251-9600 |
www.aneubistro.com

"Gauzy white drapes", a marble-top bar and exposed brick are
some of the highlights of the "attractive" space at this Main Line
American wine bar, a "nice" venue for "innovative" breakfasts,
"chick lunches" and "quiet" dinners, thanks to "professional"
service and "consistently good" fare; still, it's the happy-hour "bar
menu" and "drink specials" that get the most attention; P.S. there's
a BYO option, but some find the $10 corkage "prohibitive."

Angelino's 🛇 *Italian*

24 | 18 | 22 | $20

Fairmount | 849 N. 25th St. (Parrish St.) | 215-787-9945 |
www.angelinosrap.com

Fairmounters extol the "amazing" pizzas dressed in "fabulous"
sauces and other "tasty" options at this "intimate" BYO Italian
that's run by "nice" folks; throw in tabs that'll "fit a family budget",
a "laid-back", "local vibe" and frequent jazz performances –
"what's not to like?"

Anne's Kitchen Table 🛇 *Sandwiches*

26 | 21 | 23 | $17

Glenside | 11 Wesley Ave. (bet. Bickley & Easton Rds.) |
215-576-1274 | www.anneskitchentable.com

"Just reading the menu" "puts you in good spirits" at this "quaint"
Glenside sandwich "staple" turning out "amazing" renditions of
"your grandma's recipes" offering a "great mix of exciting flavors";
locals "love" the "neighborhood feel" that permeates the "cozy"
space with outdoor seating; P.S. check out the Friday BYO dinners.

Anthony's
Coal Fired Pizza *Pizza*

24 | 20 | 22 | $21

Horsham | 100 Welsh Rd. (Blair Mill Rd.) | 215-657-1113
Wayne | 321 E. Lancaster Ave. (bet. Aberdeen Ave. &
Chamounix Rd.) | 484-580-8022
www.anthonyscoalfiredpizza.com

These links in a regional chain are changing the local "pizza land-
scape" with their "crispy", "top-of-the-line" pies with "charred"
crusts from coal-fired ovens, while their "fantastic", "flavorful"
wings also win praise; some find it a "bit pricey", and others
quibble about "slow" service and the "noise level" in the "industrial" settings, but it "fills up fast" nonetheless, so "get there early."

	FOOD	DECOR	SERVICE	COST

Anthony's Italian
Coffee House *Coffeehouse*

23 | 21 | 22 | $11

Bella Vista | 903 S. 9th St. (Christian St.) | 215-627-2586 |
www.italiancoffeehouse.com

A "classic Italian Market stop", this coffeehouse "hits the spot"
with "dark", "rich" coffees and "perfect" cappuccinos, courtesy
of the "nice" barista, as well as panini, baked goods and gelato;
"quick" service is another plus, but some locals caution "avoid" it
when the "tourists come into town."

Anthony's Ristorante *Italian*

25 | 22 | 23 | $33

Drexel Hill | 4990 State Rd. (Township Line Rd.) | 610-623-6900 |
www.anthonysdrexelhill.net

Though best known for its "banquet accommodations", this Drexel
Hill caterer satisfies even the "tough-to-please" restaurant crowd
with "excellent" "classic" Italian fare at "reasonable prices";
though the scene "can be quiet and romantic or fun and dance-y",
depending on the day, you're always "treated like family" in the
"delightful" environs.

Antonella's Italian Kitchen 🄱 *Italian*

26 | 17 | 24 | $16

Bryn Mawr | 841 Conestoga Rd. (Garrett Ave.) | 610-526-1966 |
www.antonellasitaliankitchen.com

The "fantastic pastas, sandwiches and salads" from this simple,
"family-owned" Main Line BYO Italian eatery-cum-deli are "worth
going out into the cold and rain for" according to fans, and it also
prepares "tasty" platters you can "take home and pretend" you
made yourself; while the setting may be basic, the atmosphere is
"welcoming", and "after just a few visits" the staff "knows your
name and regular order."

Ants Pants Cafe ⊄ *American*

22 | 16 | 20 | $16

Southwest Center City | 2212 South St. (bet. 22nd & 23rd Sts.) |
215-875-8002 | www.antspantscafe.com

G'day, this cash-only cafe down under in Southwest Center City
delivers "delicious" American "brekkie" and lunch with Aussie
twists ("flat whites", "tim tams", "sweet potato fries") that'll "cure
any level of hangover"; many prefer the outdoor seating over the
"small, cramped" room, but wherever you sit, the staff "really
hustles" "without seeming to rush the tables."

A1 Japanese Steak House *Japanese*

25 | 22 | 24 | $34

Fairless Hills | 110 Lincoln Hwy. (Oxford Valley Rd.) |
215-269-1178

A "fabulous" "dinner and a show" is the norm at this "atmosphere"-
heavy, "kid-friendly" Oxford Valley "teppanyaki"-style Japanese
steakhouse where patrons have a "good time having food flung"
at them by "amusing" chefs who "know how to entertain", while
the "courteous", "attentive" staff "keeps the drinks coming"; P.S. it
also serves "affordable, tasty sushi."

	FOOD	DECOR	SERVICE	COST

Aperto ⊠Ⓜ⇱ *American*   23 | 19 | 20 | $44

Narberth | 232 Woodbine Ave. (Montgomery Ave.) |
610-660-0160 | www.apertobyob.com

Watch John Wolferth "prepare" his "top-quality" Euro-inflected
American cuisine ("ethereal oysters") in the open kitchen at his
"cozy" Narbeth BYO tucked away in a "restaurant-challenged"
sliver of the Main Line; although a few feel it "needs to step it up
a bit" on the service front, "above-average" fare at "reasonable
prices" (cash or check only) keep it "always busy."

Appalachian Brewing Co. *American*   23 | 19 | 21 | $25

Collegeville | Collegeville Station | 50 W. 3rd Ave. (Chestnut St.) |
484-973-6064

"Good luck trying to drink in moderation" at this Collegeville
branch of a Harrisburg-based brewpub chain where "delightful"
microbrews "pair perfectly" with selections from an American
"bistro-style menu"; opinions are split on the "cavernous" space
with "classic" exposed rafters ("inviting" to some, "unfinished" to
others), while many find the service "decent, but not exceptional."

Aqua ⊠ *Malaysian/Thai*   24 | 18 | 21 | $26

Washington Square West | 705 Chestnut St. (7th St.) |
215-928-2838 | www.aquamalaysianthai.com

What some say is the "best pad Thai in Philly" and other "tasty",
"semi-exotic" Malaysian-Thai eats make up a menu that "goes on
for pages" at this "cool", "quintessential ma-and-pa" bistro near
Washington Square; though a few claim it's "lost its appeal" after
getting a liquor license, "efficient", "attentive" service and "unexpectedly low" prices continue to make it a "solid" bet and "good
value" overall.

Ardmore Station Cafe *Diner*   20 | 12 | 20 | $17

Ardmore | 6 Station Rd. (Anderson Ave.) | 610-642-2683

For "comfort food" "as good as home, at almost the same cost",
punch your ticket to this "casual" diner across from Ardmore's
SEPTA regional rail station, where "French toast specials" and
other breakfast and lunch choices take you "back to your child-
hood"; while some wish it "had more space", it's "fun to watch
the trains", and the vibe is "kid-friendly to the max", thanks to the
"polite, young" staff.

NEW Argana   - | - | - | I
Moroccan Cuisine *Moroccan*

Lansdowne | 2 N. Lansdowne Ave. (Baltimore Pke.) |
484-461-9595 | www.arganarestaurant.com

Two North African expats are behind this homey Moroccan BYO
in Landsdowne, turning out inexpensive tagines, couscous and kebabs; the space maintains the look and feel of a small-town corner
cafe, but the new residents offer something the former Lansdowne
Diner never did (at least officially): belly dancers.

	FOOD	DECOR	SERVICE	COST

Ariana ● *Afghan* — 23 | 20 | 22 | $27

Old City | 134 Chestnut St. (bet. Front & 2nd Sts.) | 215-922-1535 |
www.restaurantariana.com

These "charming" Afghani BYOs in Old City and Voorhees "consistently deliver" an "explosion of flavors" ("exquisite" sautéed
pumpkin), and best of all, they won't "put a big dent in your
pocket"; a few feel the decor has "room for improvement", but the
"authentic" eats and "friendly" service may tempt you to camp out
on pillows and "break through your 30-minute lunch limit."

Ariana's Ristorante — 24 | 19 | 23 | $29
& Raw Bar *Mediterranean*

North Wales | 981 N. Wales Rd. (Horsham Rd.) | 215-362-7505 |
www.arianaristorante.com

A "neighborhood standard" in North Wales for almost two decades,
this BYO Med offers "high-quality" fare at a "reasonable price point";
"helpful" staffers "with a good sense of humor" "treat you like family"
and help you "look past the decor", which some feel needs "updating."

Ariano *Italian* — 26 | 25 | 24 | $24

Media | 114 S. Olive St. (Baker St.) | 610-892-6944 | www.ariano.net

"Exquisite" gelatos and "unique flat pizzas" (including some "daring" variations) will "blow your taste buds away" at this "rustic"
Italian in Downtown Media, and "friendly" service adds to the
experience; a few complain of "noisy" environs due to "all the tile",
but others rave about the second-floor mural depicting the owner's
"family history" – in sum, it's "not the typical pizza place."

Arirang Hibachi Steak & Sushi *Japanese* — 23 | 24 | 23 | $33

Langhorne | Target Shopping Ctr. | 2329 E. Lincoln Hwy.
(Maple Ave.) | 215-946-2240 | www.partyonthegrill.com

Fans say the "kid-friendly" hibachi shows at this Langhorne link
of a regional Japanese chain are "what you want from your dinner
theater", but it also sports a "quiet tavern setting" where you can
order "well-crafted sushi rolls"; the staff is "friendly", and while
some find it "overpriced", most agree everything's "well executed."

Arpeggio *Mediterranean* — 25 | 19 | 23 | $28

Spring House | Spring House Vill. | 542 Wood Spring Rd.
(Bethlehem Pike) | 215-646-5055 | www.arpeggiobyob.com

"Enticing" Med cuisine, including "flavorful pizzas cooked to
perfection" in a "wood-fired oven", at a "great price point" and "no
reservations" (except for large groups) mean there's "always a line
on weekends" at this "pleasant" BYO in a "lonely shopping center"
in Montco; "friendly, attentive" service, a "comfortable" vibe and
outdoor seating compensate for the somewhat "cramped" space.

Art of Bread Ⓜ *Bakery/French* — 26 | 16 | 19 | $16

Narberth | 920 Montgomery Ave. (Gordon Ave.) | 610-660-8222 |
www.artofbreadbygp.com

"Buttery croissants", "rich quiche", "artful desserts" and other
"amazing" "carbs" are "what zumba is for" quip fans of Georges

Perrier's bakery/French cafe, the "best thing for the Main Line since the train"; so maybe the decor's "average at best" and the service is "uneven" – he still has a "captive audience" in Narberth.

Arugula Ristorante   *Italian*   22 | 22 | 21 | $34

Huntingdon Valley | 1051 County Line Rd. (bet. Princeton Rd. & 2nd St. Pike) | 215-355-5577 | www.ristorantearugula.com

"They do a nice job with whole fish" and "homemade pizzas" at this Italian "hidden gem" in Huntingdon Valley, where the staff "tries really hard" to please in a "beautifully decorated" space; some quip "bring earplugs and learn sign language", for the room can get "noisy" at dinner, and others find it "expensive for a shopping-center restaurant", although BYO helps keep the tabs down.

Ashburner Inn ●   *American*   24 | 22 | 24 | $22

Northeast Philly | 8400 Torresdale Ave. (Ashburner St.) | 215-333-9860 | www.ashburnerinn.com

A "little place with a big heart", this New American is "worth the trip" to the Northeast for "exceptional", "reasonably priced" eats, including an "excellent" chicken-and-blue cheese pizza from the wood-burning oven, and "friendly" service in an attractive "bar-type setting"; on "game days" there's "always a lively crowd" that comes to "watch Philly teams in a Philly environment."

Asia on the Parkway   *Asian*   22 | 19 | 21 | $24

Logan Square | 1700 Benjamin Franklin Pkwy (17th St.) | 215-988-9889 | www.asiaontheparkway.com

"Big portions" of "delish", "reliable" Asian fare are served by a "nice" staff at this "business-lunch" staple near Logan Square; a few detractors find it a "little expensive for what you're getting", but the "large bar" and sidewalk seating are added pluses.

A Taste of Britain ⊠   *Sandwiches*   24 | 21 | 22 | $25

Wayne | Eagle Village Shops | 503 W. Lancaster Ave. (Sugartown Rd.) | 610-971-0390 | www.atasteofbritain.com

"Guys might feel out of place" at this "adorable" Wayne tearoom where Main Line women go with "girlfriends to feel pampered" and remember "their trip to London" over "wonderful" tea sandwiches and scones and a "vast array" of loose teas in a "relaxed" setting; "upbeat", "knowledgeable" service adds to the "enjoyable" experience; P.S. you can buy teas and "British groceries" at the "cute" shop.

Athena Restaurant Ⓜ   *Greek/Mediterranean*   23 | 18 | 22 | $26

Glenside | 264 N. Keswick Ave. (Easton Rd.) | 215-884-1777 | www.athena-restaurant.net

For an "enjoyable", "reasonably priced" "pre-Keswick Theatre" repast, fans tout this "pleasant" Glenside BYO where a "friendly" staff serves up "first-class" Greek and Med fare, including an apps combo that yields "enough to share, but you won't want to"; the outdoor patio is "nice in the summer", and a few will "get it to go" if they "can't eat outside."

	FOOD	DECOR	SERVICE	COST

Audrey Claire ⊄ Mediterranean   24 | 20 | 22 | $36

Rittenhouse | 276 S. 20th St. (Spruce St.) | 215-731-1222 | www.audreyclaire.com

It's "worth the pain" of a "two-hour wait" for the "fantastic", "creative" Med cooking served with "minimal pretension" at Audrey Taichman's BYO "mainstay" in Rittenhouse, where the "open kitchen" "does not disappoint"; "cramped" seating in "spartan" digs sends many to the "excellent" sidewalk tables, where some quip the "buses pass by so closely that SEPTA drivers share your dessert"; P.S. cash only.

August Ⓜ ⊄ Italian   27 | 22 | 25 | $33

South Philly | 1247 S. 13th St. (Wharton St.) | 215-468-5926 | www.augustbyob.com

The "kicked-up, creative" Italian fare at this "adorable", mid-priced South Philly BYO is worthy of "any foodie's list", and the "charming" owners make "everyone who enters feel like a family member"; there's lots of "good karma" in the "homey" setting that "could be your living room" – basically, it's a spot that "clicks" in any month.

August Moon Japanese/Korean   23 | 19 | 22 | $32

Norristown | 300 E. Main St. (Arch St.) | 610-277-4008 | www.augustmoonpa.com

"Families are welcome" at one of Norristown's "best-kept secrets", this Japanese-Korean serving "creative", "moderately priced" fare, and many laud the owners who "go out of their way to be helpful"; the crowd is divided on the "total redo" it underwent in 2011, however, with some praising the "upgrade" and others lamenting the loss of the "BBQ tables."

Augusto's
Restaurant & Catering Ⓜ Eclectic   27 | 21 | 25 | $43

Warminster | 530 Madison Ave. (Nemoral St.) | 215-328-0556 | www.augustocuisine.com

"Downtown quality without the hassle of parking in the city", Augusto Jalon's Eclectic BYO in Warminster is a "diamond in the rough", offering "outstanding", "artistically presented" fare and "knowledgeable" service in a "cozy, warm" setting; "reservations can be difficult to get" and the "price point is high", but most agree it's a "fantastic experience from head to toe."

Auspicious Chinese   19 | 15 | 17 | $24

Ardmore | 11 Cricket Ave. (Lancaster Ave.) | 610-642-1858 | www.newauspicious.com

Surveyors are split on the "new owners" of this "cool" Chinese BYO in Downtown Ardmore: fans give a thumbs-up to "huge portions", "healthy preparations" and "fair prices", while foes find the "plastic" environs, "lackadaisical" service and "mundane" grub decidedly "inauspicious."

	FOOD	DECOR	SERVICE	COST

Avalon Pasta Bistro 🕿Ⓜ *Italian* — 24 | 19 | 23 | $38

Downingtown | 78 W. Lancaster Ave. (Downing Ave.) |
610-873-4200 | www.pastabistro.com

"You'll feel like family" at John Brandt-Lee's BYO set in a "quaint old house" in "sleepy" Downingtown, thanks to his "fabulous" "Italian tapas" that "encourages social interaction" and "helpful" staffers who "try to please"; the chef-owner's "always checking up" on diners, and if you're lucky, he'll even "serve the cheese plate himself"; P.S. cash or check are preferred.

Avalon Restaurant 🕿Ⓜ⇗ *Italian* — 25 | 23 | 24 | $42

West Chester | 312 S. High St. (Dean St.) | 610-436-4100 |
www.avalonrestaurant.net

"Every morsel is delicious" on John Brandt-Lee's "ever-changing" *turista* menu at his "old-world" Italian BYO in West Chester, where you're "made to feel important" by "cheerful" servers, and the "upper deck" "out back" usually makes for a "picture-perfect" evening; some wish it would take credit cards, though, for "who wants to carry cash around these days?"

Avenida Ⓜ *Pan-Latin* — 23 | 21 | 24 | $33

Mount Airy | 7402 Germantown Ave. (Gowen Ave.) |
267-385-6857 | www.avenidarestaurant.com

At this "family-run" Pan-Latin in a "pleasant" old house in Mount Airy, Kim Alvarez's "impeccable" staff wants to "please you" (and ply you with "killer" drinks) while husband Edgar Alvarez's "innovative" "flavors" at "reasonable prices" make it a "good value" ("cha-cha-cha doesn't end with cha-ching"); if the dining room gets "noisy", you can try the "relaxing" outdoor patio in season.

Aya's Café *Egyptian* — 22 | 19 | 22 | $24

Logan Square | 2129 Arch St. (22nd St.) | 215-567-1555 |
www.ayascafe.net

"Affordable", "super-fresh" Egyptian fare served by a "smiling", "attentive" staff in a "comfortable", "chill" setting make this BYO a "great little find" in Logan Square; the "fun" gets going on Saturday nights, when "wonderful musicians" play.

Azie *Asian* — 23 | 24 | 21 | $41

Media | 217 W. State St. (Orange St.) | 610-566-4750 |
www.azie-restaurant.com

Azie on Main *Asian*

Villanova | 789 E. Lancaster Ave. (I-476) | 610-527-5700 |
www.azieonmain.com

"Be prepared to look good and spend a little money" at these "chic, minimalist" Asians in Media and Villanova, where the "sushi is always fresh", the Kobe beef on hot rocks "rocks" and the Sunday buffet is "not to be missed"; "friendly, helpful" service is one more reason many Main Liners use them to "impress those from out of town without taking them into town."

	FOOD	DECOR	SERVICE	COST

Baby Blues BBQ ● *BBQ* | 22 | 20 | 20 | $22 |

University City | 3402 Sansom St. (34th St.) | 215-222-4444 |
www.babybluesphiladelphia.com
'Cuennoisseurs "never get the blues" over the "fall-off-the-bone"
ribs and other "smoky, flavorful" offerings at this "down-home"
branch of a Southern Cal BBQ in University City; it "smells wonderful" in the repurposed brownstone boasting an exhibition kitchen
and dining rooms full of mismatched furniture.

Bacco *Italian* | 23 | 21 | 21 | $27 |

North Wales | 587 Dekalb Pike (Rte. 63) | 215-699-3361
Bacco Bistro *Italian*
Doylestown | Doylestown Shopping Ctr. | 478 N. Main St. (Old
Dublin Pike) | 215-348-9882
"You won't leave hungry" from these "inviting" Italians in the
northern suburbs offering "delicious" "thin-crust pies" and a "great
variety" of "freshly prepared pasta dishes", all at "good price
points"; North Wales boasts an "outdoor patio area" that's packed
at "happy hour", plus a bocce court where you can work off the
carbs, while Doylestown is BYO, which keeps many coming Bacco.

Bacio Italian Restaurante Ⓜ *Italian* | 25 | 19 | 23 | $28 |

Mount Airy | 311 W. Mount Pleasant Ave. (Lincoln Dr.) |
215-248-2740
While it's "easy to overlook" this "unpretentious" Italian BYO in
Mount Airy, fans insist it would be "foolish" to pass by the "consistently good" "standards" and "interesting specials", served by a
"friendly" staff that "accommodates" food restrictions; a few liken
the setting to "eating in someone's basement", but for others, the
"homey" ambiance makes it a "nice place for dates."

Back Porch Cafe ⊅ *American* | 23 | 20 | 22 | $25 |

Skippack | 4000 Skippack Pike (Collegeville Rd.) | 610-584-7870
This "small tourist-town cafe" dishes out "delectable" American
grub at "pretty good prices" in a "comfortable", "homey" setting,
plus a small outdoor patio where you can "enjoy the ambiance of
Skippack Village" in the warmer months; "terrific" service and BYO
are additional pluses.

Bahama Breeze ● *Caribbean* | 22 | 23 | 21 | $28 |

King of Prussia | 320 Goddard Blvd. (Mall Blvd.) | 610-491-9822
You "feel like you're on vacation" (and an "affordable" one at that)
at this "upbeat", "island"-themed chain serving "innovative" Caribbean chow and an "endless" menu of "fruity drinks"; "maybe if you
have enough of them the food gets better" quip critics, who also
kvetch about "long wait times" and "way too much noise", but for
many others it's a "refreshing" option.

Bailey's Bar & Grille ● *American* | 26 | 20 | 24 | $22 |

Levittown | 6922 Bristol-Emilie Rd. (Edgely Rd.) | 215-946-7992
"You feel at home" "gulping domestic beers" and tucking into
"awesome" "crab soup and hot wings" and other American pub

grub at this "laid-back" Levittown "sports bar", where the staff is "always friendly" and the "prices are always right"; "great" live music on the weekends is another plus.

Baja Fresh Mexican Grill *Mexican*   21 | 15 | 19 | $13

Abington | Abington Shopping Ctr. | 1437 Old York Rd. (Susquehanna Rd.) | 215-885-4296
Conshohocken | Plymouth Sq. Shopping Ctr. | 200 W. Ridge Pike (Butler Pike) | 610-828-4524
King of Prussia | 340 W. Dekalb Pike (bet. Henderson Rd. & Pennsylvania Turnpike.) | 610-337-2050
Montgomeryville | 110 Garden Golf Blvd. (Bethlehem Pike) | 215-412-5693
www.bajafresh.com
See review in the New Jersey Suburbs Directory.

Banana Leaf ◑ *Malaysian*   24 | 18 | 21 | $19

Chinatown | 1009 Arch St. (bet. 10th & 11th Sts.) | 215-592-8288
"Give your palate a new adventure without shocking your wallet" at this Malaysian BYO that brings "some much-needed diversity to Chinatown" with an "extensive menu" full of "spicy, flavorful twists"; service is "quick" in the "tropical"-themed setting, which is more suitable for a "casual date" than a "romantic meal."

Bar Ferdinand ◑ *Spanish*   24 | 23 | 22 | $38

Northern Liberties | Liberties Walk | 1030 N. 2nd St. (bet. Girard Ave. & Poplar St.) | 215-923-1313 | www.barferdinand.com
Appealing to "adventurous diners", this "dazzling" tapas specialist in Northern Liberties "isn't your dad's Spanish joint", offering "inspired" small plates with a "wide variety of flavors" and "wonderful" "sangria" in a "sumptuous" space; "gracious" service and monthly live flamenco performances help make it an "awesome date spot", albeit a somewhat "pricey" one.

Barbuzzo ◑ *Mediterranean*   27 | 21 | 24 | $43

Washington Square West | 110 S. 13th St. (Sansom St.) | 215-546-9300 | www.barbuzzo.com
You'd get "fresher" produce only "in the middle of a farmer's field" gush fans of Marcie Turney and Valerie Safran's Med "gem" in Washington Square West, offering "beautiful" fare featuring "locally cultivated ingredients" and "knowledgeable" service; you'll "eat sardines and feel like one too" in the "cramped" space, but for most, it's "well worth it", especially the budino dessert, which is "so good it should be illegal."

🆕 Barcade ◑ *American*   18 | 22 | 19 | $19

Fishtown | 1114 Frankford Ave. (bet. Delaware & Girard Aves.) | 215-634-4400 | www.barcadephiladelphia.com
An "awesome selection of old-school games" and 24 beers on tap will make you "feel like a kid again" at this "hip", warehouse-style "playground" in Fishtown serving "solid" American eats and craft brews to a "cool" crowd; in short, "beer, beef jerky and Battletoads – it doesn't get much better than that."

	FOOD	DECOR	SERVICE	COST

Barclay Prime *Steak*
26 | 25 | 26 | $76

Rittenhouse | The Barclay | 237 S. 18th St. (Locust St.) |
215-732-7560 | www.barclayprime.com

"Big-business types on expense accounts" and other high rollers
head to Stephen Starr's "meat mecca" on Rittenhouse Square,
where "mouthwatering steaks" are served by "professional" servers in a "hip library" setting, and bartenders pour "terrific drinks"
at the "chic bar"; while some decry "overpriced" wines and the
"gimmicky $100 cheesesteak", "any place where you can pick out
your own knife is automatically awesome."

Barnaby's *American*
20 | 21 | 22 | $25

Folsom | 2107 MacDade Blvd. (Kedron Ave.) | 610-522-5400 |
www.barnabysofamerica.com
Media | 5501 Pennell Rd. (bet. Concord & Knowlton Rds.) |
610-558-1929 | www.barnabysaston.com

A crowd that skews "young" heads to these Delaware County
American sports bars for "decent pub fare" at "reasonable" prices
and "great drink specials" poured by "personable" bartenders; although it can get "majorly crowded", the vibe is usually "laid-back"
and the outdoor patio is "awesome after a hard day's
work."

Basta Pasta *Italian*
21 | 18 | 19 | $30

Skippack | 4052 Skippack Pike (bet. Bridge & Collegeville Rds.) |
610-584-0341 | www.bastacabanabar.com

A "wide selection" of "yummy" pasta dishes and some "creative"
pizzas are served in "comfy" environs at this Skippack Italian;
some find it a tad "pricey", but the portions are "plentiful" enough
to provide you with "lunch and dinner the next day"; P.S. many
"love the Cabana Bar in the summer."

Bay Pony Inn ⓜ *American*
24 | 23 | 24 | $42

Lederach | 508 Old Skippack Rd. (Salfordville Rd.) | 215-256-6565 |
www.bayponyinnpa.com

Filial fans "take mom or grandma" to this "upscale" Traditional
American in an "old country inn" in Central Montco for its $21.95
early-bird and other "impeccable" offerings; the owners are "always present" to maintain "professional" service in the "comfortable", "historical" setting, and while a few feel it's "past its prime",
most "have never had a bad experience" here.

Beau Monde ⓜ *French*
23 | 23 | 21 | $30

Queen Village | 624 S. 6th St. (Bainbridge St.) | 215-592-0656 |
www.creperie-beaumonde.com

The crêpes are "phenomenal" at this "romantic" French bistro in
Queen Village, and the "knowledgeable" servers help you build
any combo "your little heart can dream up" without "breaking your
wallet"; the "chic", "bohemian" airs lend it suitable "downtown
charm", and the "sexy" dance club upstairs will help you "burn the
calories from that Nutella crêpe."

	FOOD	DECOR	SERVICE	COST

Beijing Restaurant *Chinese*   18 | 11 | 18 | $16

University City | 3714 Spruce St. (bet. 37th & 38th Sts.) |
215-222-5242 | www.beijingatpenn.com

For "solid" Chinese eats at "reasonable" prices, "Penn students
and hospital employees" ignore the "linoleum" and pack this
University City "staple"; the service is "speedy" (meals are "ready
almost instantly after ordering"), if "never quite friendly."

The Belgian Cafe *Belgian*   23 | 18 | 22 | $25

Fairmount | 601 N. 21st St. (Green St.) | 215-235-3500 |
www.thebelgiancafe.com

"Beer geeks" swoon over this Fairmount "neighborhood haunt" (a
sibling of venerated Monk's Cafe) for its "extensive collection" of
"otherworldly" brews – which could be "intimidating" if it weren't
for "knowledgeable" servers providing "perfect" recommendations; "authentic Belgian mussels", "fantastic burgers" and other
"eclectic takes on hearty bar food" round out the offerings, and
while some find the "dimly lit" interior "lacking", there's "great
outdoor seating."

Bella Cena *Italian*   20 | 18 | 19 | $34

Rittenhouse | 1506 Spruce St. (15th St.) | 215-790-0171 |
www.bellacena-philly.com

Kimmel Center audiences and Rittenhouse locals "feel right
at home" at this "reliable", midpriced trattoria, thanks to a
"well-rounded" menu that "goes beyond pasta and red gravy" and
a staff that gives you "honest" wine pours in "tastefully decorated"
environs; some report "spotty" service, but others appreciate how
the "cost is kept down" thanks to an "affordable" wine list and
corkage-free BYO.

Bella Tori
at the Mansion Ⓜ *Italian*   24 | 27 | 25 | $42

Langhorne | 321 S. Bellevue Ave. (bet. Gilliam & Richardson
Aves.) | 215-702-9600 | www.bellatori.com

"Grab a seat by the fireplace" and you'll be "transported to the
Victorian era" at this "lush", upscale Bucks Italian set in a "wonderful old mansion", where "helpful, unobtrusive" service and
"quality" fare round out an "exceptional dining experience"; BYO
Fridays, a "bountiful" Sunday brunch buffet and $20 early-birds
will "save you money."

Bella Trattoria *Italian*   23 | 21 | 21 | $31

Manayunk | 4258 Main St. (bet. Rector St. & Roxborough Ave.) |
215-482-5556 | www.bellatrattoriapa.com

There's "something for everyone" at this "family- and group-friend-
ly" Manayunk mainstay offering "solid" Italian and "knowledgeable" service in a "friendly environment"; "people-watching" from
the window tables or (weather permitting) sidewalk seating round
out the experience, which you can have "without spending an arm
and a leg."

	FOOD	DECOR	SERVICE	COST

NEW Belle Cakery M _Bakery_   ▽ 26 | 20 | 24 | $17

East Passyunk | 1437 E. Passyunk Ave. (Dickinson St.) |
215-271-2299 | www.bellecakery.com

"Scrumptious" cakes and other "delish" baked goods draw East
Passyunk's post-dinner crowds to this "precious" bakery where
"you feel like you are in a friend's home" while "chatting" up pastry
chef Jessie Prawlucki (of the nearby Fond); it "does not disappoint"
dessert lovers, though some confess "I'm glad I don't live close."

Bellini Grill _Italian_   23 | 20 | 22 | $33

Rittenhouse | 220 S. 16th St. (bet. Locust & Walnut Sts.) |
215-545-1191 | www.bellinigrill.com

"Large-portioned" Italian "standards" at "affordable" prices and
"friendly" service are the draw at this "unpretentious", "welcoming" Rittenhouse BYO whose "cozy" space sports a ceiling "Michel-
angelo himself would be proud of"; still, it's not enough to distract
some from "sardine-like" seating or a "noise level" that rises when
"big groups" show up.

Ben & Irv's _Deli_   23 | 13 | 20 | $19

Huntingdon Valley | Justa Farm Shopping Ctr. | 1962 County Line
Rd. (Davisville Rd.) | 215-355-2000 | www.benandirvs.com

"You're bound to find something you'll like" (or "bump into someone you know") at this old-time" deli in a Huntingdon Valley strip
center where "your bubbe would be so happy" with the "Jewish
soul food" (not to mensch-n the complimentary pickles); so what if
it's "noisy" or the waiters "act like they are doing you a favor"?

Benihana _Japanese_   23 | 21 | 22 | $37

Plymouth Meeting | Plymouth Meeting Mall | 508 W. Germantown
Pike (Plymouth Rd.) | 610-832-5924 | www.benihana.com

While "others have copied" it, fans insist this "family-friendly" teppanyaki trailblazer is still "the best" when it comes to "knife-jug-
gling" and other "utensil acrobatics" by the chefs at the grills; a
few think the show's getting "stale", but for many the "appetizing"
eats and "entertaining" service "never disappoint", making it "perfect for birthdays" or "small get-togethers with friends."

Benny The Bum's ● _Seafood_   21 | 18 | 20 | $30

Northeast Philly | 9991 Bustleton Ave. (bet. Northeast Ave. & Red
Lion Rd.) | 215-673-3000 | www.bennythebums.com

"Enjoy the vibe" at this "quirky", "popular" Northeast Philly seafooder drawing "friendly people" with "reasonably priced" fin fare
and "awesome cocktails"; though some dismiss the eats as "average" and say the "disco"-like digs need an "upgrade", the "huge
bar" with "plenty of TVs" is a popular perch to "watch a game."

Bibou M⊐ _French_   29 | 21 | 27 | $55

Bella Vista | 1009 S. 8th St. (Kimball St.) | 215-965-8290 |
www.biboubyob.com

"You feel obligated to bring your best bottle" to this "intimate"
BYO bistro housed in a former row house in Bella Vista, where

Pierre Calmels creates "soulfully designed" French fare boasting flavors both "subtle and bold", while his wife, Charlotte, will "treat you like mom" did; it's almost "impossible to get a reservation", especially on Sundays, when it offers an "amazing" $45 prix fixe, and remember it's cash only.

Big Fish Grill *Seafood*

24 | 22 | 23 | $32

Glen Mills | Brinton Lakes Shopping Ctr. | 981 Baltimore Pike (bet. Evergreen Dr. & Regency Plaza) | 484-842-1757 | www.bigfishglenmills.com
See review in the Wilmington/Nearby DE Directory.

Birchrunville Store Cafe 🅜Ⓜ⇎ *French/Italian*

29 | 25 | 28 | $57

Birchrunville | 1403 Hollow Rd. (Flowing Springs Rd.) | 610-827-9002 | www.birchrunvillestorecafe.com
"Take a GPS" and head into the "rolling hills of Chester County's horse country", home to Francis Trzeciak's French-Italian "gem" that's "hard to find and harder to forget", thanks to his "inspired" cuisine that was "farm-to-fork before it was cool", served by an "excellent" staff in an "intimate", high-ceilinged setting that lets you "pretend you are in Provence"; BYO makes the "steep" tabs "more palatable" (just don't forget to bring cash).

NEW Birra Ⓜ◑ *Italian*

24 | 19 | 23 | $24

East Passyunk | 1700 E. Passyunk Ave. (17th St.) | 267-324-3127 | www.birraphilly.com
"Mac 'n' cheese pizza" are the "four magic words" at this "family-friendly but still trendy" Italian on East Passyunk's "vibrant" strip, offering "creative spins" on traditional pies, plus brews from an "ever-changing draft selection", served by an "accommodating" staff; sure, "another pizza joint in South Philly sounds boring", but most deem this one an "excellent addition" to the local scene.

Bistro La Baia ⇎ *Italian*

21 | 16 | 20 | $30

Southwest Center City | 1700 Lombard St. (17th St.) | 215-546-0496 | www.bistrolabaia.com
"Consistent", "straightforward" Italian eats and "affordable" prices lead "college students and other value-seekers" to this "cozy" Southwest Center City BYO bistro; "outdoor seating adds to the scorecard" (and allays the "cramped" feeling), and while some report "grumpy" service, others insist the servers are "harmless."

Bistro Romano *Italian*

24 | 25 | 24 | $40

Society Hill | 120 Lombard St. (bet. Front & 2nd Sts.) | 215-925-8880 | www.bistroromano.com
When you want to "wow a date", fans say "nothing can top" the "intimate" "wine cellar" at this "rustic" Italian "hideaway" in Society Hill where "soft lighting", "freakishly attentive service" and "delicious" fare, including an "amazing" tableside Caesar salad, set the stage for a "romantic evening"; it's "cozy", but "not real fancy", and "frequently offered" "promos" help keep tabs in check.

	FOOD	DECOR	SERVICE	COST

Bistro 7 Ⓜ *Eclectic* | 25 | 17 | 22 | $42 |

Old City | 7 N. 3rd St. (Market St.) | 215-931-1560 |
www.bistro7restaurant.com

At his "charming" BYO in Old City, Michael O'Halloran is "at the
top of his game", creating "French-inspired", "farm-to-table" New
American cuisine, including a $50 tasting menu that's worthy of
someone "you're trying to impress"; the "pleasant" staff works the
"tiny" but "classy" quarters with "skill and a smile", even when it's
"congested" with Arden Theater-goers (by the way, "book early").

Bistro St. Tropez *French* | 23 | 20 | 22 | $42 |

Rittenhouse | Marketplace Design Ctr. | 2400 Market St., 4th fl.
(23rd St.) | 215-569-9269 | www.bistrosttropez.com

Fans report Patrice Rames' "civilized" French bistro in Rittenhouse's
Marketplace Design Center is "back to its former glory" since
former sibling Patou closed, and you can "almost taste the sun-
shine" in his "glorious" Provençal "flavors", which are backed by a
"well-thought-out" wine list; "friendly" service and "scenic" views
of the Schuylkill balance quibbles about the "drab" "1990s" setting.

Bistrot La Minette *French* | 26 | 23 | 25 | $52 |

Queen Village | 623 S. 6th St. (Bainbridge St.) | 215-925-8000 |
www.bistrotlaminette.com

Francophiles are "transported" to a "corner in Les Halles" by Peter
Woolsey's Queen Village bistro where some of the "best trained
waiters in the city" serve "soul-warming" French fare and "spot-on"
"drinks" "without the snootiness" in a "charming" setting with a
"cool vibe"; the Sunday evening prix fixe is "a great value", and all
rave about the alfresco "French films" on the "beautiful terrace."

Bitar's Ⓩ *Mideastern* | 26 | 12 | 21 | $14 |

Bella Vista | 947 Federal St. (10th St.) | 215-755-1121

"Amazing", "inexpensive" falafel and hummus served by an "accommodating staff" make this Bella Vista corner Lebanese store a
"healthy" "alternative to the cheesesteak" stands; "don't expect
atmosphere" or rapid speed, as "everything is made to order."

Black Bass Restaurant *American* | 24 | 26 | 23 | $54 |

Lumberville | Black Bass Hotel | 3774 River Rd. (Old Carversville
Rd.) | 215-297-9260 | www.blackbasshotel.com

"Picturesque" Delaware River views and "Colonial ambiance" set
the scene at this 18th-century inn "way out in the country" in Upper Bucks; "innovative" American fare, "attentive" service, a "comfortable" bar with a "great martini list" and a $35 Sunday brunch
with "nonstop champagne refills" complete the picture; P.S. for a
"romantic getaway", you can "stay in one of the upstairs suites."

Black Dog Cafe *Asian* | 23 | 20 | 21 | $28 |

Skippack | 4049 Skippack Pike (bet. Bridge & Store Rds.) |
610-222-9211

This "small but comfortable" Asian BYO tucked into Skippack's
commercial strip delivers "moderate" portions of "tasty" Thai and

Chinese fare in "peaceful" surroundings; clearly, the "attentive" staff provides service with a "personal" touch, and the patio is a "beautiful setting" in season.

Black Lab Bistro ☒ American

25 | 21 | 23 | $36

Phoenixville | 248 Bridge St. (bet. Gay & Main Sts.) | 610-935-5988 | www.blacklabbistro.net

The "tasty offerings" at this "cozy" American BYO in Phoenixville "never disappoint" and will make you "forget the diet"; the staff is "attentive without being obtrusive", and while some clamor about the "din on weekend evenings", most find it "delightful" before "arty movies across the street at the Colonial Theatre."

Black Sheep Pub & Restaurant ◑ Pub Food

20 | 19 | 20 | $23

Rittenhouse | 247 S. 17th St. (Latimer St.) | 215-545-9473 | www.theblacksheeppub.com

"When you want a pint without a lot of fuss", this "old-school" Rittenhouse pub is just the ticket with a "great tap selection" that "keeps the beer geeks happy", "TVs everywhere" and "service with a smile"; "above-average pub fare", including some "unusual combinations", help keep it "always busy."

Blackbird Pizzeria Pizza/Vegan

24 | 15 | 23 | $13

Society Hill | 507 S. 6th St. (bet. Lombard & South Sts.) | 215-625-6660 | www.blackbirdpizzeria.com

"Please your palate and your karma" at this humble walk-up parlor off South Street, where "culinary magicians" conjure up "amazing", "affordable" vegan treats, including "craveable" "artisan" pizzas and a "Philly cheesesteak" you'd never guess "wasn't made with beef"; though some find the "typical pizza joint" digs "run-down" and the service just "ok", it's "highly recommended" by many, including "avid meat and cheese consumers."

Blackfish ☒ American/Seafood

26 | 20 | 25 | $55

Conshohocken | 119 Fayette St. (bet. 1st & 2nd Aves.) | 610-397-0888 | www.blackfishrestaurant.com

If you need a "reason to visit Conshohocken", consider Chip Roman's "date night"–worthy American BYO, where his "exqui-site", "meticulously prepared" cuisine is served by a "professional" staff in a "minimalist" setting; despite gripes about "sardine"-like seating, "noise" and "minuscule" portions, it "lives up to" many fans' "high expectations."

Bliss American

21 | 21 | 21 | $45

Avenue of the Arts | 220 S. Broad St. (bet. Locust & Walnut Sts.) | 215-731-1100 | www.bliss-restaurant.com

Whether at lunch or "pre-theater", you can "watch all of Downtown walk by" at this "centrally located" Avenue of the Arts bistro where "well-prepared" New American cuisine is served by a "prompt, courteous" staff in a "relaxing" "modern" setting; still, a few fault the kitchen for "playing it safe", turning out fare that's "tasty but not outstanding for the price."

	FOOD	DECOR	SERVICE	COST

Blue Bell Inn 🅱 *American*   23 | 21 | 23 | $43

Blue Bell | 601 Skippack Pike (Penllyn-Blue Bell Pike) |
215-646-2010 | www.bluebellinn.com

"Like time traveling back to 1963", this "staid" Montco "institution" may be "old-fashioned", but "that's a good thing" to many,
resulting in a bump in scores since the last Survey for the "reliable"
American fare and "comfortable" digs; the "early-bird special"
rivals "live music" at the "bar" for the favorite activity of "an older
crowd", though "sitting by the fireplace or the outside patio" has
its fans as well.

🆕 BlueCat 🅱Ⓜ *Pan-Latin*   - | - | - | I

Fairmount | 1921 Fairmount Ave. (Uber St.) | 267-519-2911 |
www.bluecatrestaurant.com

This cute corner spot in Fairmount's growing restaurant scene
turns out inventive, inexpensive Pan-Latin cuisine (Chilean
chacareros, arroz con pollo) from its open kitchen; the friendly
husband-and-wife team who run the place named it for their pet
puss, whose likeness hangs from an oversized mural on the wall.

Bluefin 🅱 *Japanese*   28 | 19 | 23 | $43

East Norriton | 2820 Dekalb Pike (Germantown Pike) |
610-277-3917 | www.restaurantbluefin.com

Even after a move into larger, more "engaging new digs" in an East
Norriton strip mall, it's "still hard to get a reservation" at Yong
Kim's Japanese BYO, thanks to what many say is the "freshest,
most creative sushi in the 'burbs", including "insanely delicious"
rolls that "melt like butter"; "smiling", "friendly" service is another
plus, and given the "awesome" fare and "reasonable" prices, many
"can't help but over-order."

Blue Pear Bistro 🅱 *American*   23 | 22 | 23 | $46

West Chester | 275 Brintons Bridge Rd. (Old Wilmington Pike) |
610-399-9812 | www.bluepearbistro.com

"When a meal at the Dilworthtown Inn is too much" for some,
its upmarket sibling across the road outside West Chester "hits
the spot" with "delish", "updated" American "comfort food" and
"friendly" service in a "quaint" historic building with a "nice little
bar"; a few find the portions "tiny" and "overpriced", but most
deem it an "all-around good experience."

Blue Sage   27 | 18 | 24 | $27
Vegetarian Grille 🅱Ⓜ *Vegetarian*

Southampton | 772 2nd St. Pike (Rte. 132) | 215-942-8888 |
www.bluesagegrille.com

You won't find the "founder of the Bacon Appreciation League"
at this Bucks BYO, but many avowed "meatatarians" "worship"
Mike Jackson's "creative" vegetarian cuisine ("not your typical
fake-meat fare") and "celestial" desserts, served by an "accommodating" staff in a "functional but pleasant" room; with prices so "low"
and portions so "filling", they may "need a cart to roll you out.

	FOOD	DECOR	SERVICE	COST

Bobby's
Burger Palace *Burgers*

24 | 20 | 20 | $16

University City | Radian | 3925 Walnut St. (39th St.) |
215-387-0378 | www.bobbysburgerpalace.com

Burgermeisters brave "lines out the door" for Bobby Flay's "big,
juicy, sloppy and delicious" hamburgers, "awesome" milkshakes
and "unbelievable" sweet potato fries, served by a "friendly" staff
at his colorful "fast-food joints"; though some gripe you "pay a
premium" for the Iron Chef's imprimatur, many are happy to "add
crunchify to their vocabulary."

Bobby Simone's
Restaurant *American*

25 | 23 | 23 | $36

Doylestown | 52 E. State St. (Donaldson St.) | 215-340-1414 |
www.ilovebobbys.com

"Out of the way" and "down a charming alley", this "cozy"
American is about "as good as you'll get" in Doylestown aver fans
who tout the "excellent but not highfalutin" fare and "friendly",
"professional" service; it's a "great place to meet", but some find
the tables "too close" together and prefer to sit at the bar "across
the courtyard."

Bocelli *Italian*

24 | 17 | 22 | $35

Gwynedd | 521 Plymouth Rd. (Evans Rd.) | 215-646-9912 |
www.bocellidining.com

"Everything tastes homemade" at this Italian "gem" in the Gwynedd Valley rail station, where "every seat is in view (and smell)
of the kitchen" turning out "top-notch" fare; "close quarters"
notwithstanding, the owners "know how to treat their customers"
and BYO is a "wonderful" plus.

Bomb Bomb
BBQ Grill ☒ *BBQ/Italian*

24 | 18 | 24 | $26

South Philly | 1026 Wolf St. (Warnock St.) | 215-463-1311

"Solid" BBQ and "phenomenal" Italian specialties are "da bomb"
at this "old-school South Philly joint" and its newer Glassboro
sibling, a sandwich-and-'cue specialist; the former is a "neighborhood gem" where waitresses "call you hon'" and the "friendliness
is refreshing", while the latter is a "great place to grab something
fast" near Rowan U.

Bona Cucina Ⓜ� *Italian*

∇ 27 | 16 | 23 | $27

Upper Darby | 66 Sherbrook Blvd. (Marshall Rd.) |
610-623-8811

Hey, your "taste buds don't care about" the "unassuming" digs at
this "quiet" BYO in Upper Darby, but they will be dazzled by the
"fabulous" "classic" Italian flavors coming out of Pat Buonadonna's
kitchen, and fans are fond of the servers "full of personality", although some report they can get "overwhelmed with a full house";
while it's "inexpensive", remember it's cash only.

	FOOD	DECOR	SERVICE	COST

Bonefish Grill *Seafood* `24 | 22 | 23 | $36`

Willow Grove | Regency Sq. | 1015 Easton Rd. (Fitzwatertown Rd.)
215-659-5854
Exton | 460 W. Lincoln Hwy. (Whitford Rd.) | 610-524-1010
Newtown Sq. | 4889 W. Chester Pike (bet. Crum Creek & Rock
Ridge Rds.) | 610-355-1784
NEW Langhorne | 500 Oxford Valley Rd. (Commerce Blvd.) |
215-702-1312
www.bonefishgrill.com
Fans insist "you wouldn't know" this midpriced Outback-sibling
seafooder is a chain given its "reliable" fin fare from a menu offering "plenty of choices", all served by a "professional" staff amid
"attractive" decor; though it's often "crowded and noisy", many
deem it a "pleasant dining experience" "if the city is not an option."

Bonjung Japanese *Japanese* `26 | 21 | 22 | $30`

Collegeville | Collegeville Station | 50 W. Third Ave. (Walnut St.) |
610-489-7022 | www.bonjungsushi.com
Sushiphants "dream about the tuna sundae" and other rolls at
this "pretty" Collegeville Japanese BYO, while Seoulmates dig the
"tasty" "Korean specialty items"; "warm" service and a "pretty"
interior make up for its location in a "large nondescript building",
and while this "guilty pleasure" is "not cheap", it's "highly recommended" by many for a "date-night" destination.

Bonté Wafflerie & Café *Coffeehouse* `22 | 14 | 18 | $12`

Rittenhouse | 130 S. 17th St. (bet. Sansom & Walnut Sts.) |
215-557-8510
Washington Square West | 922 Walnut St. (bet. 9th & 10th Sts.) |
215-238-7407
www.bontewaffles.com
Fans swear "nothing beats" the "rich", "authentic" Belgian waffles
("crisp outside, gooey inside") washed down with "solid cups of
joe" at these affordable Center City cafes, where you can "wrap
yourself in a warm blanket" on a "lazy Sunday" to "chill" and "people-watch" among "students with laptops"; "friendly" servers will
"point you in the right direction" if you want to "be experimental."

Bourbon Blue ● *American/Southern* `21 | 21 | 20 | $30`

Manayunk | 2 Rector St. (Main St.) | 215-508-3360 |
www.bourbonblue.com
"Creative" "New Orleans–style" fare, "cheap bar specials every
night" and a "classy" "Mardi Gras" vibe win praise for this "cool"
Manayunk New American–Southerner; it's set in a building with a
"good view of the canal" and lots of "old-world charm", where the
"personable" owner "makes you feel like a guest in his home" –
which can "get loud" when there's a "party going on downstairs."

Brandywine Prime *Steak* `22 | 22 | 21 | $48`

Chadds Ford | Chadds Ford Inn | 1617 Baltimore Pike (Rte. 100) |
610-388-8088 | www.brandywineprime.com
After a day of "antiquing" or "traipsing through Longwood Gardens", fans recommend Dan Butler's "upscale casual" steakhouse

	FOOD	DECOR	SERVICE	COST

in the old Chadds Ford Inn, where "beautifully done" steaks and "interesting" entrees, "pleasing decor" and "efficient" service make for a "comfortable night out"; while some grouse that it's "overpriced", most report a "positive experience."

Branzino Italian Ristorante *Italian/Seafood* | 23 | 19 | 22 | $42 |

Rittenhouse | 261 S. 17th St. (bet. Locust & Spruce Sts.) | 215-790-0103 | www.branzinophilly.com

The "namesake fish is simple and amazing" and other Italian dishes are made "with love" at this BYO in Rittenhouse, where servers handle crowds with "aplomb" and get you "out in time for the show" (though some feel "rushed"); "white tablecloths" and "sparkling chandeliers" give it an "upscale" feel, and the "lovely garden" is a "summer delight."

Brasserie 73 *French* | 22 | 24 | 23 | $46 |

Skippack | 4024 Skippack Pike (Mensch Rd.) | 610-584-7880 | www.brasserie73.net

"You feel like you're in Paris" at this "cozy" French brasserie in Skippack, savoring "wonderful" Gallic fare in a "beautiful", "quiet" dining room with a "gorgeous" "white marble fireplace"; outdoor seating provides "people-watching" opportunities in the warmer months, and while a few think it's "too expensive for the suburbs", the "generous drinks" may help ease the sting.

Brauhaus Schmitz ● *German* | 22 | 22 | 21 | $31 |

South St. | 718 South St. (7th St.) | 267-909-8814 | www.brauhausschmitz.com

"Achtung, baby!" exclaim hordes about this "rollicking" Deutscher on South Street, where Jeremy Nolen's German fare is the "real deal", while the "enticing" beer and schnapps selection is "something to marvel upon" (when you're not admiring "waitresses in dirndls"); "beautiful" reclaimed woods and exposed brick throughout impart a Bavarian "beer hall" vibe "without the kitsch", and the only *defekt* is the "din."

Bravo Pizza *Pizza* | 24 | 13 | 23 | $12 |

Wayne | 128 N. Wayne Ave. (Lancaster Ave.) | 610-688-6898 | www.gotbravo.com

For "delicious" thin-crust pizza, "even better calzones" and other "quick bites" before or after a movie, Main Liners tout this humble "sidewalk pizza place" that's been on the North Wayne Avenue strip seemingly "forever"; though some say the takeout-oriented digs are "not great for dining", the staff is "helpful even when the place is crazy busy."

NEW Bravo! Cucina Italiana *Italian* | 22 | 24 | 23 | $27 |

Willow Grove | Willow Grove Park Mall | 2500 W. Moreland Rd. (Center Ave.) | 215-657-1131 | www.bravoitalian.com

The "pretty" Roman ruins setting "sure beats the food court" at this family-friendly Italian chain link in Willow Grove Park mall, offering "yummy" eats in "good portions", which are served by a caring staff; critics contend that it's more about "quantity but not quality" and find it "hit-or-miss."

BRGR Joint *Burgers*

21 | 15 | 20 | $12

Bryn Mawr | 1011 W. Lancaster Ave. (Bryn Mawr Ave.) | 484-380-3465 | www.brgrjoint.com

"Come hungry" to this "affordable" Bryn Mawr burger spot that seems to be trying to "bust your gut" with "large", "delicious" hamburgers and "amazing sweet potato fries" washed down with "heaven-sent" milkshakes amid a motif of pirates and tattoos; "friendly" service seals the deal.

Brick Hotel Restaurant *American*

22 | 23 | 21 | $38

Newtown | The Brick Hotel | 1 E. Washington Ave. (State St.) | 215-860-8313 | www.brickhotel.com

The "charming" glassed-in porch is "prime" real estate at this "historic" New American in Newtown Borough that's been "around forever" as a popular venue for "family gatherings", thanks to a "great Sunday brunch"; there's a menu "option for everyone", but critics accuse it of "resting on its laurels", deeming the fare "uneven" and "overpriced", and the service "slow."

Brick House Tavern & Tap ● *American*

20 | 21 | 19 | $26

Willow Grove | 2402 Easton Rd. (Pennsylvania Tpke.) | 215-675-5767 | www.brickhousetavernandtap.com

"Definitely a guy's place", this "sports bar" chain link in Willow Grove rocks as a "man cave" complete with "La-Z-Boys", TVs and "fire pits", offering "tons of beer options" and a menu of "basically nothing but meat"; some dub it a "classier Hooters", and opinions are split over the "friendly" servers – they're an "absolute joy" to admirers, while others grouse that they "care more about their looks than their service."

Bridget Foy's ● *American*

21 | 19 | 22 | $31

South St. | 200 South St. (2nd St.) | 215-922-1813 | www.bridgetfoys.com

The sometimes wacky "South Street scene" plays out in front of the "terrific" covered porch at this "welcoming" New American "neighborhood standby" that's still popular after 35 years for its "eclectic", "well-prepared" chow that's "served with pleasure"; it attracts a "chill" bar crowd ("none of whom are 22 years old, drunk and pierced"), and while a few deem it "midlevel", others consider it a "good adult option."

Bridget's Steakhouse *Steak*

26 | 23 | 23 | $52

Ambler | 8 W. Butler Ave. (Main St.) | 267-465-2000 | www.bridgetssteak.com

Carnivores call this "upscale" steakhouse the "crown jewel" of Ambler for its "top-notch" steaks, "wonderful martinis", "amiable service" and "romantic" setting, all of which add up to a "memorable" experience; critics, though, find it hard to forget the "noisy" bar scene or the prices, which they deem "too high for a suburban joint" (although BYOB Sundays can help).

	FOOD	DECOR	SERVICE	COST

Bridgid's *Eclectic*

| 21 | 16 | 20 | $27 |

Fairmount | 726 N. 24th St. (Meredith St.) | 215-232-3232 |
www.bridgids.com

"Solid", "well-executed" Eclectic "comfort food" is "still a bargain"
at this "cozy" Fairmount corner tap where the front room is a
"locals' bar" and the "homey" dining room in back makes you feel
like you're "visiting your relatives"; "don't expect your typical Bud,
Miller or Coors", but an "impressive" lineup of "amazing craft
beers", which make it "worth stopping by more than once."

Brittingham's ◐ *American/Irish*

| 20 | 18 | 22 | $26 |

Lafayette Hill | 640 Germantown Pike (Joshua St.) |
610-828-7351 | www.brittinghams.com

Irish and the "honorary Irish" alike head to this "friendly" "local
watering hole" in Lafayette Hill for a "pint and a plate of chips"
or other selections from a "well-rounded menu" of American and
Irish pub grub, all at "decent" prices; things get "loud" when bands
play, and it's time to "get comfortable with your neighbors."

Broad Axe Tavern ◐ *American*

| 21 | 21 | 21 | $31 |

Ambler | 901 W. Butler Pike (Skippack Pike) | 215-643-6300 |
www.broadaxetavern.com

A "beautifully restored" "centuries-old roadhouse" is home to this
Montco New American tavern, a "casual" dining option offering
"well-executed", "reasonably priced" pub standards and "amiable"
service in a "cool atmosphere"; some find the fare "unimaginative",
however, and suggest that it's really the "tremendous beer selection" that "makes the trip worth the effort."

NEW Broad Street Diner ⊠Ⓜ◐ *Diner*

| 21 | 17 | 21 | $17 |

South Philly | 1135 S. Broad St. (Ellsworth St.) | 215-825-3636
Fans are cheering the revival of this "upbeat" South Philly 24/7
diner, declaring it a "huge upgrade from the previous version",
where "cheap", "delicious" "standards" are served with a "smile"
by an "efficient" staff; the digs are "clean", and regulars report
"much improved bathroom spaces"; P.S. it's BYO.

B2 ⊟ *Coffeehouse/Vegan*

| 23 | 20 | 20 | $11 |

East Passyunk | 1500 E. Passyunk Ave. (Dickinson St.) | 215-271-5520
South Philly's "tattooed" crowd makes a beeline to this "comfortable" East Passyunk coffeehouse for "awesome" smoothies and
"good ol' fashioned home cooking" served by "lovely" "baristas";
while some quip "you could eat the hipster atmosphere with a
spoon", many agree that if you're "vegan" or suffer "any kind of
allergy", "this is the place for you."

Buca di Beppo *Italian*

| 20 | 20 | 21 | $31 |

Wynnewood | 260 E. Lancaster Ave. (Chatham Rd.) | 610-642-9470
Exton | 300 Main St. (Bartlett Ave.) | 610-524-9939
www.bucadibeppo.com

"Bring a wheelbarrow" for the "leftovers" from the "family-style"
feeds at this "fun" Italian chain dishing out "huge portions" of

"consistent" eats at "reasonable prices"; "endearing" old photos and "kitschy" decor "will keep you talking", and while critics
dismiss it as a "*Jersey Shore*-style parody" serving "factory food", it
remains a popular "fallback" option for "families with kids."

Buddakan ● *Asian*   27 | 27 | 25 | $57

Old City | 325 Chestnut St. (4th St.) | 215-574-9440 |
www.buddakan.com
Still "buzzing" after 15 years, Stephen Starr's "sexy", "swanky"
Old City Asian earns Philadelphia's Most Popular title thanks to
"creative", "exceptionally flavorful" food (oh those "amazing"
edamame ravioli) served by a "professional" staff in a "beautiful",
"Buddhist-chic" setting; sure, the "lively crowd" and "thumping"
"techno-beats" prompt some to "pray to Buddha for peace" and
your wallet will end up "significantly lighter", but most agree the
experience is "well worth it."

Bunha Faun Ⓜ *Asian/French*   ▽ 25 | 14 | 21 | $33

Malvern | 152 Lancaster Ave. (Conestoga Rd.) | 610-651-2836 |
www.bunhafaun.net
There's "always something special" cooking at this "low-key"
French-Asian BYO in Malvern that's earned a "loyal following"
with "reasonably priced" fare that "never wavers in quality" and
"friendly" service; many think the digs "could be spruced up", but
most regard it as an "excellent value" nonetheless.

Butcher & Singer *Steak*   26 | 26 | 25 | $67

Rittenhouse | 1500 Walnut St. (15th St.) | 215-732-4444 |
www.butcherandsinger.com
You expect to see "Don Draper and Roger Sterling at the next table" at this "chic" Stephen Starr steakhouse in Rittenhouse, whose
"supper-club" motif takes you "back to the classic Hollywood era"
while "oozing warmth and charm"; the "mouthwatering" steaks
and "excellent" stuffed hash browns are a "cut above" the norm,
while "outstanding" service and "stellar" bartenders further help
ensure an "impeccable" "upscale dining" experience.

Byblos Restaurant & Bar ● *Mediterranean*   21 | 19 | 20 | $26

Rittenhouse | 114 S. 18th St. (bet. Chestnut & Sansom Sts.) |
215-568-3050 | www.byblosphilly.com
"Tasty" eats and "friendly" service are only part of the story at this
"clubby", "swanky" Rittenhouse Med that also boasts an "awesome" hookah bar and DJs spinning thumping "techno" beats to
a "funky crowd"; critics object to the "unpleasant volume" of the
music and find the fare merely "average", but others recommend it
for a "fun night if you're in the mood."

Café Con   ▽ 26 | 19 | 22 | $17
Chocolate Ⓜ *Japanese/Mexican*

South Philly | 2100 S. Norwood St. (Snyder Ave.) | 267-639-4506 |
www.cafeconchocolate.com
"Amazing" Oaxacan hot chocolate and "wonderful", "made-to-order" Mexican and Japanese eats emerge from the kitchen of

his "informal", affordable cantina in South Philadelphia run by friendly and genuine" folks; the space is "teeny-tiny" and hours an be irregular, so "call ahead to confirm" and good luck "finding place to park."

Cafe Du Laos *Laotian/Thai* ▽ 23 | 18 | 23 | $28

South Philly | 1117 S. 11th St. (bet. Ellsworth St. & Washington Ave.) | 215-467-1546 | www.cafedulaos.com

Flavorful" Laotian and Thai dishes are "executed well" and served by a "fast, attentive" staff at this storefront on the edge of South Philly's Italian Market; the "soothing", "low-lit" space full of "beautiful wood" works equally well as a "romantic timeout" or a place o go "with some friends", and BYO adds to its "good value."

Café Fiorello's *Italian* ▽ 23 | 19 | 21 | $30

West Chester | 730 E. Gay St. (bet. Bolmar St. & Westtown Rd.) | 610-430-8941 | www.fiorellosinwestchester.com

At this "small", homey trattoria in West Chester, "real-deal" Italian are at "reasonable prices" is served by "friendly" staffers who don't speak English that well" but "make you feel like you're sitting at the family dinner table"; "don't worry about trying to decide what to eat", they "will tell you what you want."

Cafe La Fontana *Italian* 22 | 19 | 22 | $36

Hatboro | 58 S. York Rd. (Byberry Rd.) | 215-672-8118 | www.cafelafontanarestaurant.com

Consistently satisfying", this "nice neighborhood find" in Hatboro offers "tasty" Italian fare and "knowledgeable" service in a white-tablecloth" setting that's "classy, but not over the top"; reasonable prices", BYO on Mondays and Tuesdays and a weekday lunch salad bar make it easy on the wallet.

Café L'Aube *Coffeehouse* ▽ 24 | 19 | 23 | $15

Fairmount | 1631 Wallace St. (bet. 16th & 17th Sts.) | 215-235-2720 | www.cafelaube.com

ean Luc Fanny's "true French style" shines through in his "locally roasted coffees", "excellent crêpes" and sandwiches made on fresh baguettes", all served by a "helpful" staff at his Fairmount afe; the "welcoming" setting is an "awesome place to hang out" or sit down and "get work done" over free WiFi.

Cafe Lift Ⓜ ⊄ *French/Italian* 25 | 20 | 21 | $17

Callowhill | 428 N. 13th St. (Hamilton St.) | 215-922-3031 | www.cafelift.com

Fresh ingredients" get a "nice twist" at Mike Pasquarello's "unassuming" American brunch/lunch cafe in the loft district between North Philly and Northern Liberties that's "overrun with crowds" thanks to "awesome" eats such as the "unreal" stuffed French oast; "pleasant" service, a "chill vibe", "cool art on the walls" of he industrial space and a clientele that skews "young" round out he "hip" scene.

	FOOD	DECOR	SERVICE	COST

Cafe Michelangelo ● *Italian/Pizza* ▽ 24 | 20 | 22 | $22

Northeast Philly | 11901 Bustleton Ave. (Byberry Rd.) |
215-698-2233 | www.cafemichelangelo.com

For pastas and brick-oven pizzas even an "Italian grandmom"
will find "close to home", this long-running Italian in Northeast
Philadelphia is a solid bet; "reasonable prices" and "very nice"
service are further pluses, and the outdoor dining (complete
with bocce court) presents a "unique environment" amid the
local strip malls.

Cafe Preeya Ⓜ *Eclectic* ▽ 23 | 18 | 22 | $38

Huntingdon Valley | Village Ctr. | 2651 Huntingdon Pike (Red Lion Rd.) |
215-947-6195 | www.cafepreeya.com

This Thai-influenced Eclectic BYO located in a Huntingdon
Valley strip center may be "small, but it's big on the delivery",
namely, a "diverse menu" of "consistently" good chow that can
"easily rival pricier" "Downtown" spots; "reasonable prices"
help compensate for service that can be "slow" and decor
that's merely "acceptable."

Cafette *Eclectic/New American* 23 | 19 | 23 | $27

Chestnut Hill | 8136 Ardleigh St. (Hartwell Ln.) | 215-242-4220 |
www.cafette.com

"Fresh", "wholesome" New American-Eclectic cuisine and
"friendly" service make this "unpretentious", "charming" BYO
located off the main drag in Chestnut Hill "worth finding"; you
feel like you're at "a friend's house" in the "relaxing", "incredibly cozy" setting, especially on the "delightful" patio with a
"bottle of wine."

Caffe Valentino *Italian* ▽ 21 | 17 | 21 | $35

South Philly | 1245 S. 3rd St. (Wharton St.) | 215-336-3033 |
www.caffevalentino.com

Fans promise that "your taste buds will thank you" for the
"trip to Puglia" by way of this "overlooked" South Philadelphia
Italian BYO that wins praise for its "perfectly cooked whole
grilled branzino" and other "reasonably priced" dishes; "nice
big windows bring in a lot of natural light" to the brightly colored,
two-story space.

Cake Ⓜ *Bakery/Eclectic* 23 | 23 | 21 | $23

Chestnut Hill | 8501 Germantown Ave. (Highland Ave.) |
215-247-6887 | www.cakeofchestnuthill.com

Set in a "former Victorian greenhouse" in Chestnut Hill, this
bakery-cum-Eclectic "takes the cake" with its "wonderful" baked
goods, "pleasant" brunches and "delicious" breakfast and lunch
fare; the "atmosphere is relaxing" in the "charming venue", which
is "decorated beautifully" with flora in the warmer months, and the
service is "friendly", all of which make it a "real find"; P.S. it serves
dinner Thursdays and Fridays.

	FOOD	DECOR	SERVICE	COST

California Pizza Kitchen *Pizza*

22 | 18 | 20 | $23

King of Prussia | King of Prussia Mall | 470 Mall Blvd. (DeKalb Pike) | 610-337-1500
Plymouth Meeting | Plymouth Meeting Mall | 514 W. Germantown Pike (Hickory Rd.) | 610-828-8232
Wynnefield | Target Shopping Plaza | 4040 City Ave. (Old Lancaster Rd.) | 215-473-7010
www.cpk.com

"Pizzas and salads are the perfect combinations" for many fans of this "well-oiled" national Italian chain whose "diverse menu can satisfy any taste" and "fresh" creations "don't present themselves as manufactured"; "come early if you don't want to wait" and be prepared for "lots of noise" in the "family-friendly" settings, and while the service is "friendly", some critics find it a bit too "California."

California Tortilla *Mexican*

23 | 18 | 22 | $12

Northeast Philly | 10000 Roosevelt Blvd. (Red Lion Rd.) | 215-543-5713
Royersford | 1836 E. Ridge Pike (Township Line Rd.) | 610-831-1113
www.californiatortilla.com

Boasting a selection of hot sauces that could "last you a life-time", these links of an affordable Mexican chain are "always jammed" with amigos who "count on it" for "beer-can-size burritos" as well as other *comida* "made to order with fresh ingredients", served by a "peppy staff"; some find the "utilitarian" spaces "too small", and besides, service is "fast" and there's always takeout.

Campbell's Place *Eclectic*

21 | 18 | 19 | $32

Chestnut Hill | 8337 Germantown Ave. (Bethlehem Pike) | 215-242-1818 | www.campbellsplace.com

"Not the place if you want quiet" advise aficionados, this "cozy" Chestnut Hill watering hole is a "true pub" pouring an "impressive selection of draft beers" to go along with a menu of "satisfying" Eclectic pub fare, including "top-notch" burgers; while a few report that the "wait is sometimes long", others appreciate the "welcoming" vibe, courtesy of the "über-friendly owners and staff."

Campo's Deli ⊅ *Cheesesteaks*

24 | 14 | 19 | $13

Old City | 214 Market St. (Strawberry St.) | 215-923-1000 | www.camposdeli.com

For a "taste of Philly" in "touristy" Old City, fans tout this deli that "holds up strong" to "stiff competition" with its "awesome cheesesteaks", "excellent hoagies" or "pepper and eggs like grandma used to make"; some critics, however, find it "over-priced" and grouse about the cash-only policy, "limited seating" and occasional "rudeness."

	FOOD	DECOR	SERVICE	COST

Cantina Dos Segundos ● *Mexican* — 24 | 21 | 21 | $24

Northern Liberties | 931 N. 2nd St. (Laurel St.) | 215-629-0500 |
www.cantinadossegundos.com

Cantina Los Caballitos ● *Mexican*

East Passyunk | 1651 E. Passyunk Ave. (Morris St.) |
215-755-3550 | www.cantinaloscaballitos.com

Mexican fare is "made with love" and served by a staff that "treats
you like friends" at these "quirky" "hot spots" in Northern Liberties
and East Passyunk; "legendary margaritas", "loud, loud" music and
a "chill but lively" vibe make them two of the city's more popular
weekend "hangouts", where you can "observe hipster mating hab-
its", and outdoor seating takes them to the "next level."

Cantina Feliz Ⓜ *Mexican* — 24 | 22 | 23 | $36

Fort Washington | 424 S. Bethlehem Pike (Morris Rd.) |
215-646-1320 | www.cantinafeliz.com

Expect a "mob scene" at this "high-energy" Mex in Fort Washington run by two Jose Garces alums, where "inventive", "tasty" fare
and "yummy" margaritas are served by "friendly", "knowledgeable" folks; it gets "noisy" in the colorful space graced with Day of
the Dead murals, and complaints about "high prices" are balanced
by raves over the white sangria ("if heaven doesn't have it, then I
don't want to go").

The Capital Grille *Steak* — 26 | 25 | 26 | $65

Avenue of the Arts | 1338 Chestnut St. (Broad St.) | 215-545-9588
King of Prussia | 236 Mall Blvd. (Goddard Blvd.) | 610-265-1415
www.thecapitalgrille.com

An "upscale crowd" indulges its "carnivorous cravings" at this
"clubby" national steakhouse chain, a "slice of red meat heaven"
where the "awesome" steaks are "expertly prepared", "superb"
bartenders pour "terrific" drinks and the "service is always stellar";
most agree it's "worth the splurge", so "bring lotsa money" for a
"night to remember."

Capogiro Gelato — 28 | 16 | 21 | $9
Artisans ● *American/Dessert*

University City | Radian Apartments | 3925 Walnut St. (40th St.) |
215-222-0252
Rittenhouse | 117 S. 20th St. (Sansom St.) | 215-636-9250
Washington Square West | 119 S. 13th St. (Sansom St.) |
215-351-0900
East Passyunk | 1625 E. Passyunk Ave. (Morris St.) | 215-462-3790
www.capogirogelato.com

Surveyors swoon over this dessert chain's "decadent", "silky rich"
gelato made with "fresh, local" and "seasonal" ingredients, served
by a "congenial" staff "generous with samples" of the "myriad
flavors"; many tout it as a post-dinner stop to "really impress a
date" (though it also serves a limited menu of New American fare),
and while a few carp about "pricey", "small portions", for most it's
a "treat" well worth the "extra time on the treadmill."

	FOOD	DECOR	SERVICE	COST

Capriccio Cafe & Espresso Bar *Coffeehouse*

▽ 23 | 18 | 21 | $12

Washington Square West | 840 Walnut St. (bet. Arch & Cherry Sts.) | 215-928-3458

Capriccio @ Cafe Cret *Coffeehouse*

Rittenhouse | 110 N. 16th St. (bet. Arch & Cherry Sts.) | 215-735-9797
www.capricciocafe.com

"If you're going to give in to the temptation of carbs", fans tout this Rittenhouse cafe and Wash West outlet for "mouthwatering" baked goods, "tasty" sandwiches and "satisfying" coffee; it's run by "nice" folks, though some shrug and deem it a "good but not great option" when you're looking for a "convenient meal."

Capriotti's Sandwich Shop *Sandwiches*

26 | 14 | 23 | $13

Exton | 117 E. Swedesford Rd. (Pottstown Pike) | 610-363-7095
Glen Mills | 301 Byers Dr. (Baltimore Pike) | 610-361-0300
Kennett Square | 877 E. Baltimore Pike (Village Dr.) | 610-444-4475
Springfield | 141 S. State Rd. (Springfield Rd.) | 484-472-6257
West Chester | 607 E. Market St. (bet. Bolmar & Worthington Sts.) | 610-719-0270
www.capriottis.com

"Awesome", "gigantic" subs such as the turkey Bobbie (i.e. "Thanksgiving on a bun") are the calling card of this national sandwich chain with locations in the western 'burbs and Delaware; there "no ambiance" to speak of (it's a "take-out place", essentially), but service comes "with a smile."

Caribou Cafe *French*

22 | 21 | 21 | $35

Washington Square West | 1126 Walnut St. (bet. 11th & 12th Sts.) | 215-625-9535 | www.cariboucafe.com

"It's all here" for fans of this Washington Square West bistro – "wonderful country French" fare, an "extensive wine list" and surroundings brimming with "art deco fabulousness", including a "beautiful bar"; the staff "accommodates pre-theater crowds" and makes you feel like you "might be in Paris", while in summer, "hipsters turn the sidewalk into the Left Bank east."

Carlucci's Grill *Italian*

25 | 21 | 25 | $26

Yardley | 1633 Big Oak Rd. (Oxford Valley Rd.) | 215-321-9010 | www.carluccisitaliangrill.com

Fans of this Italian BYO "tucked away" in a Bucks shopping center declare it "many notches above" the "red-gravy joints" Downtown, thanks to "outstanding" "homestyle" fare (including "gluten-free" offerings) that's "reasonably priced"; although some say the digs are "nothing fancy", you get "a touch of the old world" from the "entertaining" staff that "treats you like old friends."

Carversville Inn Ⓜ *Southern*

26 | 24 | 25 | $42

Carversville | 6205 Fleecydale Rd. (Aquetong Rd.) | 215-297-0900 | www.carversvilleinn.com

"Creative" Southern stylings (including what many say is the "best rack of lamb in the area") are on offer at this "delightful find" in the "charming" Central Bucks village of Carversville; the "unpretentious" Colonial inn is a "step back in time", complete with "creaky floorboards that make it sound like a ghost's in the kitchen", although most agree there's nothing spooky about the "friendly, helpful" service.

Casta Diva 🗷Ⓜ⇱ *Italian*   24 | 20 | 22 | $43

Rittenhouse | 227 S. 20th St. (Locust St.) | 215-496-9677 | www.castadivabyob.com

"Viva la Diva!" exclaim devotees of this "cozy", cash-only Italian BYO "jewel" in a townhouse just off Rittenhouse Square whose "artfully presented" Italian fare "doesn't casta lot" so "you won't want to skip a single course" and the "professional" staff pays "special attention to your wines"; fans insist "if you don't enjoy this, you are in a really bad mood."

Catahoula *Cajun/Creole*   22 | 16 | 20 | $26

Queen Village | 775 S. Front St. (Fitzwater St.) | 215-271-9300 | www.catahoulaphilly.com

You feel like you're "back in the Big Easy" at this "low-key" Queen Village tap whose "fun" interpretations of Cajun-Creole cuisine and "cool outdoor seating" make it just right for a "date night" or "guys' or gals' night out"; the "friendly", "helpful" staff helps "get the good times rollin'."

Catherine's Restaurant Ⓜ *American*   26 | 22 | 24 | $44

Unionville | General Store | 1701 W. Doe Run Rd. (Rte. 162) | 610-347-2227 | www.catherinesrestaurant.com

For a "romantic" dinner in Chester County's "horse country", even city slickers recommend this "charming" mom-and-pop New American BYO in a former general store near Kennett Square, where a "knowledgeable" staff serves "fabulous" fare from a "clever but not precious" menu; a "relaxed, elegant" setting completes the "special" experience that most agree is "worth the price."

Cedar Hollow Inn   21 | 18 | 21 | $41
Restaurant & Bar ◑ *American*

Malvern | 2455 Yellow Springs Rd. (Rte. 29) | 610-296-9006 | www.cedarhollowinn.com

Housed in a "quaint" 19th-century inn off the main drag in Malvern, this "neighborhood haunt" attracts a "nice bar crowd" with "tasty" New American grub, "friendly" service and theme nights in a "comfortable" setting; while some think the "kitchen needs some inspiration", others regard it as a "fine standby."

Celebre's Pizzeria ◑ *Pizza*   24 | 14 | 22 | $16

South Philly | Packer Park Shopping Ctr. | 1536 Packer Ave. (Broad St.) | 215-467-3255 | www.celebrespizza.com

For a "true South Philly experience", piezani look no further than this "old-school" pizzeria near the stadium complex whose "fantastic" pies are "nothing fancy but made with love"; while most deem the digs merely "average", "fast" service means fans can "grab a bite before a game or concert" knowing they "won't miss a moment" of the action.

Chabaa Thai Bistro Thai   26 | 21 | 24 | $31

Manayunk | 4371 Main St. (Grape St.) | 215-483-1979 | www.chabaathai.com
Thai food "doesn't get more authentic" than Moon Krapugthong's "awesome" creations on offer at her mod-looking BYO in the "heart of Manayunk", served by a "helpful" staff that "cares about its guests"; "word has spread" and now it's "always packed", so you may have to wait "even with reservations", but most agree the fare is "worth it."

Chambers 19 Bistro & Bar American   23 | 19 | 23 | $26

Doylestown | 19 N. Main St. (bet. Court & State Sts.) | 215-348-1940 | www.chambers19.com
After a "day spent shopping" or "visiting museums", many head to this New American on Doylestown's main drag offering "consistently good" fare at "reasonable" prices and "accommodating" service in a "peaceful" environment; its adjacent bar, the Other Side, attracts a "different crowd every night" with "generous drinks" and "live entertainment."

Charcoal BYOB Ⓜ American   26 | 20 | 25 | $35

Yardley | 11 S. Delaware Ave. (River Rd.) | 215-493-6394
Chefs-brothers Mark and Eric Plescha are "masters of sous vide" at their "innovative" New American BYO in Yardley, offering a "constantly changing menu" of "amazing", locavore-friendly fare, served by a "capable, attentive" staff; while some feel the "food is at odds with the surroundings" (a "former lunch spot"), it does offer a "wonderful view" of the Delaware River.

Charles Plaza Chinese   ▽ 22 | 17 | 24 | $22

Chinatown | 234 N. 10th St. (Vine St.) | 215-829-4383
Vegetarian offerings "that dreams are made of" and other "healthy" Mandarin dishes ("no beef, no pork") are "prepared with great pride" and served by a "friendly" staff at "delightful" chef-owner Charles Chen's Chinatown eatery; you "might pay a little more" than usual, but most agree the "consistent quality" and "attractive" setting make it a "fantastic buy."

Charlie Brown's Steakhouse Steak   23 | 21 | 22 | $29

Springfield | 1001 Baltimore Pike (Lincoln Ave.) | 610-604-7410
See review in the New Jersey Suburbs Directory.

Charlie's Hamburgers ⊄ Burgers   26 | 14 | 23 | $10

Folsom | 336 Kedron Ave. (MacDade Blvd.) | 610-461-4228
"You can just taste the homemade love" in the "no-nonsense, bang-for-your-buck" hamburgers and "great" shakes from this "old-school" Delco "institution" dating back to 1935; if some find the digs "questionable", fans insist the setting is "part of the charm", leaving just one lament: "wish they would offer french fries"; P.S. now open every day.

| | FOOD | DECOR | SERVICE | COST |

Charlie's Pizzeria *Pizza*   ▽ 27 | 11 | 22 | $16

East Norriton | Swede Square Shopping Ctr. | 107 W. Germantown Pike (bet. Penn Sq. & Swede Rds.) | 610-275-1403

The "rich-tasting" signature "red-top pizza" with lots of chunky to-mato sauce and a smattering of cheese is a "multiple-napkin treat" at this half-century-old parlor in an East Norriton strip center; the jury's hung on the counter guys ("friendly" vs. "not friendly"), and some suggest the ambiance makes takeout an "excellent" option.

Chart House *Seafood*   22 | 24 | 22 | $52

Delaware Riverfront | Penn's Landing | 555 S. Columbus Blvd. (Spruce St.) | 215-625-8383 | www.chart-house.com

"Yes, it's touristy", but "you can't beat" the Delaware Riverfront location of this "beautiful" seafooder chain link where the water views make for a "gorgeous panorama"; while critics deem it "over-priced" and "average", for many others, "properly strong" drinks, the signature chocolate lava cake and "super" salad bar make it worthy of a "celebration."

The Cheesecake Factory *American*   24 | 22 | 23 | $30

King of Prussia | Pavilion at King of Prussia Mall | 640 W. Dekalb Pike (bet. Allendale & Mall Rds.) | 610-337-2200

Willow Grove | Willow Grove Park Mall | 2500 W. Moreland Rd. (Easton Rd.) | 215-659-0270

www.thecheesecakefactory.com

The signature cheesecake is "just an added bonus" at this "family"-oriented American chain whose "gimongous menu" of "super-sized" dishes is "as fat as a fashion magazine" and inspires fans to wait "an hour or more for a table" in "noisy", "neo-Egyp-tian" meets "Tuscan" digs; a "knowledgeable" staff working "tag team"–style keeps the "assembly line" moving.

Chestnut Grill & Sidewalk Cafe *American*   22 | 21 | 22 | $28

Chestnut Hill | Chestnut Hill Hotel | 8229 Germantown Ave. (Southampton Ave.) | 215-247-7570 | www.chestnuthillgrill.com

"Homemade" Traditional American basics seem to taste even better on the "scenic" front porch "overlooking the action on the Avenue" at this "chestnut" in Chestnut Hill, the "perfect place for brunch" on a "sunny day"; though opinions are split on the interior dining room ("warm and homey" vs. "drab and dark"), "generous portions", "top-quality ingredients" and "spot-on" service make it a "standby" for "village natives."

Chestnut7 ◐ *American*   21 | 22 | 21 | $29

Chestnut Hill | 8201 Germantown Ave. (Hartwell Ln.) | 215-247-7777 | www.chestnut7.com

For "casual, affordable dining", fans tout this Chestnut Hill public house for its "awesome" pizzas and other "tasty" American eats, served by a "super-friendly" staff in an "open", "airy" space; "lots of screens" give it a "sports-bar" feel, and the "lively bar scene" can get "too loud" for some, but the "beautiful" outdoor patio of-fers refuge when the weather's nice.

	FOOD	DECOR	SERVICE	COST

Chiangmai *Thai* — 24 | 18 | 21 | $25

Conshohocken | 108 Fayette St. (1st Ave.) | 610-397-1757 |
www.mychiangmaicuisine.com

Many tout this "charming" Conshy BYO as their "go-to Thai place
in the 'burbs", thanks to "fabulous, authentic" flavors from a
kitchen that's "not afraid to spice it up"; "reasonable" prices and
"knowledgeable" service help make up for "cramped seating" and
"basic" decor, and "speedy takeout is another plus.

Chiarella's Ristorante *Italian* — ▽ 22 | 20 | 22 | $27

East Passyunk | 1600 S. 11th St. (Tasker St.) | 215-334-6404 |
www.chiarellasristorante.com

Most agree Gordon Ramsay's *Restaurant Impossible* visit "improved
things" at this BYO in East Passyunk, though loyalists insist the
"well-cooked" Italian grub "was never the problem"; the setting is
"family-friendly", and in nice weather you can "snag an outdoor seat."

Chickie's & Pete's ◑ *Pub Food* — 23 | 22 | 22 | $26

Northeast Philly | 4010 Robbins Ave. (bet. Charles & Mulberry Sts.) |
215-338-3060
South Philly | 1526 Packer Ave. (15th St.) | 215-218-0500
Bensalem | Parx Casino | 2999 Street Rd. (Tillman Dr.) | 267-525-7333
NEW Warrington | 500 Easton Rd. (bet. Elm & Garden Aves.) |
215-343-5206
Eastwick | 8500 Essington Ave. (Arrivals Rd.) | 215-492-0569
Chickie's & Pete's Cafe *Pub Food*
Northeast Philly | Roosevelt Plaza | 11000 Roosevelt Blvd. (bet. Red Lion &
Woodhaven Rds.) | 215-856-9890
www.chickiesandpetes.com

"Crab fries rule" at this "high-decibel", Philadelphia-centric
sports-bar chain (voted the city's Most Popular Chain), which is
"loaded with TVs" to "yell at" and "decent" fried food to douse
with "beer, beer, beer"; though critics dismiss it as a "Chuck
E. Cheese's for adults", with takes on the service ranging from
"friendly" to "subpar", most consider it a "great place to get together with friends" – as long as they're "Philly fans."

Chickie's Italian Deli ☒ *Italian* — 27 | 14 | 23 | $13

South Philly | 1014 Federal St. (10th St.) | 215-462-8040 |
www.chickiesdeli.net

Hoagarts swear by this "friendly" deli outside the Italian Market in
South Philly, serving "some of the best hoagies" around, including
the "must-have" veggie, made with "Sarcone's bread" and "fresh,
delicious" ingredients that make them "entirely worth the calorie
consumption"; though it's "strictly takeout", "great parking" is a
plus in this part of town.

Chifa *Chinese/Peruvian* — 26 | 25 | 24 | $51

Washington Square West | 707 Chestnut St. (7th St.) |
215-925-5555 | www.chifarestaurant.com

From the complimentary "cheesy" pandebono bread to the
"melt-in-your-mouth pork belly buns", Jose Garces' "energetic"

Peruvian-Chinese hybrid in Wash West "transports you to a neighborhood in Lima" as you "share tastes with your companions"; though some gripe about the "noise level" in the "stunningly different" space complete with cabanas and an opium den–like lounge, the "attentive" staff makes you feel "like you're the only one there"; P.S. dinner only.

Chima Brazilian Steakhouse *Brazilian/Steak*
26 | 24 | 25 | $60

Logan Square | 1901 John F. Kennedy Blvd. (20th St.) | 215-525-3233
You're in "the eye of a delicious meat storm" at this "comfy", contemporary-looking Brazilian steakhouse near Logan Square, where sword-bearing gauchos who are "second to none" deliver "tender, juicy steaks, chops and sausages" to your table until you can't "see straight"; cognoscenti counsel "come hungry" and "don't fill up at the salad bar."

China Inn *Chinese*
▽ 21 | 16 | 22 | $22

Norristown | 2614 W. Ridge Pike (bet. Clearfield Ave. & Trooper Rd.) | 610-539-1600
The "friendly" staff "always remembers you" at this "basic" Chinese spot in Norristown and brings your order "fast"; "reasonable" prices and a "decent" menu offering "a few better choices" than most competitors make it a "favorite" of many.

China Wok *Chinese*
▽ 26 | 21 | 24 | $19

Huntingdon Valley | 773 Huntingdon Pike (San Gabriel Ave.) | 215-379-1322 | www.chinawokathuntingdon.com
Locals in the Huntingdon Valley area swear by this strip-mall Chinese for "good, cheap" renditions of the usual suspects and service that's "on point" and gets you "in and out" as quickly as you need; affordable prices are another reason many dub it their "go-to" place.

Chink's Steaks Ⓩ *Cheesesteaks*
26 | 14 | 22 | $13

Northeast Philly | 6030 Torresdale Ave. (bet. Benner & Higbee Sts.) | 215-535-9405 | www.chinksteaks.com
"Memorable" cheesesteaks "without the silly South Philly drama" are the lure at this "retro" Northeast Philly sandwichery whose "lines prove its great value", the potentially "offensive" name notwithstanding; while a few are cool to the "World War II"–vintage "diner decor", for others it adds to the "great nostalgic feel."

Chinnar Indian Cuisine *Indian*
▽ 19 | 14 | 19 | $20

Berwyn | Swedesford Plaza | 416 W. Swedesford Rd. (Contention Ln.) | 610-251-2526 | www.chinnarindian.com
"Tons of options" for vegetarians, a "speedy" lunch buffet and "friendly" service are the draws at this Indian in a Berwyn strip mall off Route 202; some complain of "hit-or-miss" chow, while others feel the decor "could be more exciting", but for many, it remains a "standby", especially for "takeout."

Chlöe 🅩Ⓜ *American* | 24 | 18 | 23 | $38

Old City | 232 Arch St. (bet. 2nd & 3rd Sts.) | 215-629-2337 | www.chloebyob.com

Chefs-owners Mary Ann Ferrie and Dan Grimes "care about what you eat" and it shows on the "creative", "market-driven" New American menu at their "adorable", "antiques-filled" BYO across from the Betsy Ross House, a refuge "from the hustle and bustle of Old City"; "genuine" service is another plus, and while "no rezzies is a drag" for some, most declare this spot a "winner."

Chops Restaurant *Steak* | 20 | 21 | 21 | $54

Bala Cynwyd | 401 E. City Ave. (bet. Monument Rd. & Presidential Blvd.) | 610-668-3400
Washington Square West | 700 Walnut St. (bet. 7th & 8th Sts.) | 215-922-7770
www.chops.us

"Solid" steaks and "above-average" service in "handsome" settings, plus "great happy-hour prices", win praise for Palm alum Alex Plotkin's upscale meateries in Bala Cynwyd and in a former bank on Washington Square; critics, however, contend that the fare "doesn't match expectations" or the "high prices", and accuse them of "taking their audiences for granted."

Chris' Jazz Cafe 🅩Ⓓ *Southern* | 19 | 18 | 20 | $34

Avenue of the Arts | 1421 Sansom St. (bet. Broad & 15th Sts.) | 215-568-3131 | www.chrisjazzcafe.com

"Amazing" live jazz and "perfectly shaken martinis" in a "speakeasy" atmosphere are one way to win over a "date" at this "chill", midpriced joint off the Avenue of the Arts; the service is "on-point" and the Southern fare is "tasty", and while the space may be "tight", "that's how a good jazz bar is supposed to be."

Christine's Restaurant *American/Italian* | 24 | 23 | 24 | $33

Yardley | 385 Oxford Valley Rd. (Heacock Rd.) | 215-369-2930 | www.christinesofyardley.com

Fans tout this Yardley Italo-American as "one of the better BYOs in the area", offering "wonderful" breakfasts, lunches and dinners at "reasonable" prices in a white-tablecloth setting; it's a popular venue for "groups and special events", but some warn that it gets "too noisy to have a romantic dinner."

Christopher's Ⓓ *American* | 19 | 16 | 20 | $29

Wayne | 108 N. Wayne Ave. (Lancaster Ave.) | 610-687-6558 | www.christophersaneighborhoodplace.com

This "user-friendly" New American eatery-cum–"neighborhood bar" in Downtown Wayne caters to the "family crowd" from "after day care" until "bedtime", when it "becomes a hangout for young adults"; "lots of different choices" on the menu will appeal to "even the pickiest of eaters", while the exposed-brick interior lets "suburban moms feel like they're in Center City", and "moderate" prices seal the deal for most.

	FOOD	DECOR	SERVICE	COST

Chubby's Steaks ● *Cheesesteaks* — 25 | 13 | 21 | $15

Roxborough | 5826 Henry Ave. (Wendover St.) | 215-487-2575
"Leave the tourist landmarks" behind and "mix it up with the locals" over "excellent overstuffed cheesesteaks" at this "diner-type"
Roxborough mainstay; "don't expect elegant decor" or fancy
service – just sandwiches that are "juicy beyond belief", "amazing
cheese fries", beer in frosted mugs and "plenty of napkins."

Chun Hing Restaurant *Chinese* — 26 | 15 | 25 | $21

Wynnefield | Pathmark Shopping Ctr. | 4160 Monument Rd.
(Conshohocken Ave.) | 215-879-6270
Going on 35 years, this "old-time" "Columns-A-and-B" Chinese
off City Avenue in Wynnefield is still worthy of "important family
events" thanks to "heaven-sent dumplings" and other "excellent"
Sichuan offerings, owners who "know their customers by first
name" and a staff so quick it seems like the "food appears before
you order it"; few seem to mind there's "no ambiance" to speak of.

CinCin *Chinese* — 25 | 20 | 23 | $34

Chestnut Hill | 7838 Germantown Ave. (Springfield Ave.) |
215-242-8800 | www.cincinrestaurant.com
"Fabulous", "consistent" Mandarin dishes imbued with a "fine-dining"
"French flair", including "unique specials", are why this "upscale"
Chinese landmark is "packed nightly" with folks from Chestnut
Hill and beyond; manager Henry Lee and staff provide "friendly"
service in the "tasteful" setting, which a few find too "old-school",
while others report that "parking can be a problem."

Circles ⓜ *Thai* — 25 | 12 | 18 | $23

South Philly | 1516 Tasker St. (Hicks St.) | 267-687-1778
Northern Liberties | 812 N. 2nd St. (Poplar St.) | 267-687-1309 ⓜ
Alex Boonphaya and his "Thai magic show" play six days a week at
his "cute" BYO in South Philly's Point Breeze and its new Northern
Liberties outpost; at the original, "fresh, inspiring" and "reasonably
priced" grub is "ferried across the street" from the kitchen by a
"caring" staff (which a few knock as "unpolished"), and with "little
to no decor" to speak of, "delivery service only ups the appeal."

City Tap House ● *American* — 23 | 23 | 22 | $25

University City | Radian Apartments | 3925 Walnut St. (40th St.) |
215-662-0105 | www.citytaphouse.com
An "amazing selection of craft beers", "awesome" brick-oven pizzas, a "huge outdoor terrace" – this New American gastropub in
University City is "not your average watering hole"; in the "jazzy"
dining room, a "friendly" staff attends to a "mix of students and
professionals", and live music "adds to the positive environment."

City Tavern *American* — 24 | 26 | 24 | $41

Old City | 138 S. 2nd St. (Walnut St.) | 215-413-1443 |
www.citytavern.com
"If it was good enough for Franklin and Adams", this rebuilt
18th-century "Colonial" in Old City should appeal to modern-day

"tourists" with "shamelessly authentic" Traditional American "home cooking", a "laid-back" vibe and servers in period costumes; while it's a step "back in time", wags note that "prices have kept up with inflation" – still, the consensus is that "everyone should try it once."

Clam Tavern *Seafood*

25 | 17 | 23 | $32

Clifton Heights | 339 E. Broadway Ave. (Edgemont Ave.) | 610-623-9537
Though it feels like you're "walking into 1966", finatics insist this Delco "classic" "never gets old", thanks to "solid seafood without any pretense", including "amazing" baked clams, and "fast, friendly" service from the staff and the owner, who'll "go above and beyond for his patrons"; most agree "you get what you pay for" at this "neighborhood gem."

Club House Diner ➊ *Diner*

18 | 15 | 19 | $18

Bensalem | 2495 Street Rd. (bet. Knights & Mechanicsville Rds.) | 215-639-4287
Fans of this heavily mirrored, "middle of the road" 24/7 Bensalem diner rave about the "friendly" staff, "awesome" salad bar and "spot-on" grub, while detractors find the fare "hit-or-miss", the service "rushed" and the digs in need of an "upgrade"; but almost all agree you "get a lot of food for your money."

C19 *Italian*

∇ 21 | 18 | 22 | $34

Rittenhouse | 267 S. 19th St. (Rittenhouse Sq.) | 215-545-0441 | www.c19philly.com
A proponent of the "Slow Food and farm-to-table" movements, chef-owner Andrea Luca Rossi prepares "tasty" Venetian small plates featuring "local, fresh" ingredients at his "welcoming" eatery a block from Rittenhouse Square; the toque offers "great" recommendations from the wine list and the staff provides "attentive but not obtrusive" service in the intimate, rustic space.

Cochon ⓜ⇱ *French*

26 | 19 | 22 | $42

Queen Village | 801 E. Passyunk Ave. (Catharine St.) | 215-923-7675 | www.cochonbyob.com
At Gene and Amy Giuffi's porcine-themed French BYO in Queen Village, "all things pig are done wonderfully" and served by a "knowledgeable, down-to-earth" staff in an "intimate" bistro setting (tin ceiling, tile walls); "reservations are necessary" because you are "not the only one who loves it", so bring cash and wear good walking shoes because you may have to "park on the street four blocks away."

Cock 'N Bull Restaurant *American*

23 | 23 | 24 | $35

Lahaska | Peddler's Vill. | 164 Peddler's Vill. (bet. Rtes. 202 & 263) | 215-794-4000 | www.peddlersvillage.com
Seems like this "quaint" Traditional American has been in Peddler's Village "for-eh-ver", dishing out "hearty meals" of "comfort food" ("mouthwatering prime rib"), including Sunday brunch and Thursday dinner buffets, to "regiments of regulars" in an

"antiques"-filled, "old-world" setting; the "caring" staff is "always a help", and while some dismiss the "Colonial" theme as "tourist trapola", others find the historical reenactors "entertaining."

Coco's ● American   ▽ 24 | 15 | 22 | $22

Washington Square West | 112 S. 8th St. (Sansom St.) | 215-923-0123 | www.cocosphilly.com

"Delish burgers" and other "good ol' bar favorites", "cheap beer" (30-plus varieties) and "attentive" service are the selling points of this lively pub in the middle of Jeweler's Row in Wash West, a convenient, budget-friendly stop for ticket-holders at the Walnut Street Theatre; 10 TVs keep sports fans happy, and tolerable decibels mean that "waiters don't have to use sign language."

Continental Mid-town   Eclectic   23 | 24 | 21 | $35

Rittenhouse | 1801 Chestnut St. (18th St.) | 215-567-1800

"Amazing martinis" and "tapas-style" Eclectic dishes are served with "a twist of fun" at Stephen Starr's "too-cool-for-school", "mid-century modern" Rittenhouse Square diner, where an "awesome" rooftop deck snags a "hip" "professional crowd" and swing seats make you "feel like a celebrity" amid a "circus atmosphere"; admirers applaud the "sexy" servers, but some critics find them "aloof."

The Continental   Eclectic   24 | 22 | 22 | $35

Old City | 138 Market St. (2nd St.) | 215-923-6069 | www.continentalmartinibar.com

"Still a classic" after nearly 20 years in business, Stephen Starr's first restaurant maintains its "quintessential Philly stomping ground" status thanks to a "great location" in Old City, "inventive" Eclectic dishes (such as the "often-imitated" cheesesteak eggrolls) and "spot-on" martinis; servers know the midpriced menu "front and back", and even if the "neo-diner" space is "just too darn loud" sometimes, it's "great for people-watching."

Cooperage Wine   19 | 20 | 20 | $26
and Whiskey Bar ● American/Southern

Washington Square West | Curtis Ctr. | 601 Walnut St. (7th St.) | 215-226-2667 | www.cooperagephilly.com

"Not your brother's frat boy bar", this "hidden gem (literally)" in the "oddest location" in a corner of the Curtis Center on Washington Square caters to a "wide clientele" with "upscale" Southern bar fare plus a "great selection" of craft beers and whiskeys; the "rustic" setting is "cool", though a few find it merely "cold", but most warm to the "knowledgeable" service and "exceptional" happy-hour specials.

Copabanana ● American/Mexican   20 | 16 | 18 | $21

South St. | 344 South St. (4th St.) | 215-923-6180
University City | 4000 Spruce St. (40th St.) | 215-382-1330
www.copabanana.com

"Noisy but nice", this "iconic" Mexi-American duo is a "staple of the Philly bar scene", plying a mix of "locals and university" types with "killer" margaritas, "yummy" Spanish fries, "dee-lishous" burgers and "sublime" people-watching; critics, though, feel they have "suffered with time" and "need an overhaul in all categories."

Core De Roma Ⓜ *Italian*   26 | 18 | 25 | $33

South St. | 214 South St. (2nd St.) | 215-592-9777 | www.corederoma.us

"Excellent homemade pastas and sauces made with a light touch" are the hallmark of this "unassuming" Roman-style Italian, a "reasonably priced", "serious option in the playground they call South Street"; "Papa Gigi" Pinti and staff make you "feel at home" in the "cozy" space (which a few find "cheesy"), another reason it's a popular "family favorite"; P.S. it serves alcohol but BYO is allowed.

The Corner *American*   21 | 20 | 20 | $32

Washington Square West | 102 S. 13th St. (Drury St.) | 215-735-7500

An "energetic kitchen" creates "great takes on traditional bar food" at this "happening" Wash West New American, which some fans feel "deserves more love" than it gets; the "unique drinks" on the "great little cocktail menu" are a "pleasant surprise" and help make up for sometimes "inconsistent" fare, while the "modern", rustic setting is upped by a rooftop deck and "amazing music selections."

Cosmi's Deli *Deli*   ▽ 25 | 8 | 20 | $11

South Philly | 1501 S. 8th St. (Dickinson St.) | 215-468-6093 | www.cosmideli.com

This "quintessential" South Philly deli builds what devotees say are the "best cheesesteaks" and "hoagies" in town, made with "local bread" and "plentiful" meats, "for a good price"; the staff has a "nice attytood", and while the decor is pretty much "card tables", "you're not going for the atmosphere."

Couch Tomato Cafe *American*   24 | 17 | 21 | $17

Manayunk | 102 Rector St. (Main St.) | 215-483-2233 | www.thecouchtomato.com

"Fresh", "healthy" American grub and "delish" "gourmet" pizzas, made with "locally grown" ingredients, are served by a "perky" staff at this Manayunk eatery; while the "cute" space may work for an "easy date", some find it "cramped", though the "outside seating is beautiful" in warmer weather; P.S. for fancier dining, there's Tomato Bistro upstairs.

Country Squire Diner ◗ *Diner*   18 | 13 | 20 | $17

Broomall | 2560 W. Chester Pike (bet. Alameda & Sproul Rds.) | 610-353-0550 | www.countrysquirediner.com

"If you're looking for a real diner, look no further" than this "retro" eatery in Broomall, where "solid" grub is served by "old-school waitresses" who "make you feel right at home", and there's lots of "sugary goodness" coming out of what some say is the "best bakery for miles around"; so maybe it's "nothing fantastic" – the prices are "fair" and it "gets the job done."

	FOOD	DECOR	SERVICE	COST

Coyote Crossing *Mexican*

22 | 22 | 20 | $32

Conshohocken | 800 Spring Mill Ave. (8th Ave.) | 610-825-3000 |
www.coyotecrossing.com

Sitting on the "amazing" outdoor patio with an "outstanding"
margarita or mojito at this Conshy Mex is "the way life should be"
according to amigos; the *comida* is "likable", though a few find it
"pricey" and "yuppified", and while the staff is "friendly", some say
the "service could be better."

Creed's Seafood & Steaks 🖾 *Seafood/Steak*

26 | 23 | 25 | $54

King of Prussia | 499 N. Gulph Rd. (Pennsylvania Tpke.) |
610-265-2550 | www.creedskop.com

A "throwback to an earlier time of fine dining", this "upscale
surf 'n' turf" in King of Prussia delivers "remarkable" steaks and
seafood "the way it should be" in a "country-inn ambiance" that
doesn't feel "dowdy"; "professional" servers and "bartenders with
personality" help make it a good venue for a "business meeting."

Criniti *Italian*

21 | 20 | 23 | $29

South Philly | 2611 S. Broad St. (Shunk St.) | 215-465-7750 |
www.crinitirestaurant.com

Benito Criniti "makes you feel welcome" at his son Massimo's
Italian "red-gravy slugger" "close to the stadiums" in South Philly,
where acolytes testify you "can't get better food for the price";
while some say it's "not much for ambiance", others find the converted church with a "big stained-glass window" way "cool."

Cross Culture *Indian*

▽ 25 | 21 | 24 | $29

Doylestown | 64 W. State St. (bet. Hamilton & Main Sts.) |
215-489-9101 | www.crosscultureindiancuisine.net

See review in the New Jersey Suburbs Directory.

Cuba Libre *Cuban*

24 | 26 | 22 | $41

Old City | 10 S. 2nd St. (Market St.) | 215-627-0666 |
www.cubalibrerestaurant.com

They're Havana good time at this "romantic" Cuban in Old City,
where "large fans, indoor trees and Caribbean color schemes" are
so "transporting" "you forget you're in Philly"; amigos talk up the
"interesting" menu, "awesome" Sunday brunch, "massive" rum bar
and "pleasant" service, plus late-night "salsa dancing" that makes
you wish you had rhythm.

Cucina Forte 🅼 *Italian*

26 | 19 | 25 | $36

Bella Vista | 768 S. 8th St. (Catharine St.) | 215-238-0778 |
www.cucinaforte.com

"Light-as-a-feather" gnocci "reigns supreme" on the menu of
Maria Forte's midpriced BYO in a Bella Vista row house, where the
"spitfire" chef prepares Italian "comfort food at its best"; you "feel
like you're visiting family" in the tchotchke-filled room, where the
staff tries to "make your dining experience a memorable one."

| | FOOD | DECOR | SERVICE | COST |

Daddy Mims
Creole BYOB Ⓜ *Creole*

27 | 20 | 23 | $39

Phoenixville | 154 Bridge St. (bet. Church Ave. & Main St.) |
610-935-1800 | www.daddymims.com

At his "sexy" Creole BYO in Phoenixville, chef-owner John Mims
"puts his heart and soul into every meal", including his "fan-
cied-up" tasting menus, "four courses of decadence"; fans praise
the "knowledgeable" staff, though a few say the service feels
"rushed" at times, and the "softly lit" space is "ultracomfortable."

Dalessandro's Steaks
& Hoagies ❶ *Cheesesteaks*

25 | 11 | 20 | $13

Roxborough | 600 Wendover St. (Henry Ave.) | 215-482-5407 |
www.dalessandros.com

Even under new ownership, this "stark" cheesesteakery in
Roxborough hasn't "lost the neighborhood feel" and locals take
their "out-of-town guests" to sit "shoulder-to-shoulder" on
"tiny-tush" counter stools for one of its "meaty" "behemoths";
the "friendly" staff will get you out "quickly", but you may have to
"clear your schedule" for the ensuing "food coma" anyway.

The Dandelion *British*

23 | 26 | 23 | $38

Rittenhouse | 124 S. 18th St. (Sansom St.) | 215-558-2500 |
www.thedandelionpub.com

At Stephen Starr's "beautifully outfitted" U.K. pub in Rittenhouse,
the "corny but irresistible" decor drives home an "Anglophile" concept that's "oversaturated with kitsch" and slightly "pricey"; good
thing service is "attentive", and the food tastes "better than British
food in Britain", with the "are-you-kidding-me fish 'n' chips" and
"rare beers" eliciting an "Edwardian" experience "without the rain."

D'Angelo's Ristorante
Italiano ⌧❶ *Italian*

23 | 20 | 23 | $42

Rittenhouse | 256 S. 20th St. (bet. Locust & Spruce Sts.) |
215-546-3935 | www.dangeloristorante.com

For a "great evening out", fans tout this "upscale yet family-oriented"
Italian off Rittenhouse Square, a "throwback in the best sense",
with "top-notch" fare, "friendly" service and the occasional "bal-
lad" from Sal D'Angelo; while a few quip that "1980 called and
wants its decor back", for most, it's "always a pleasure."

Dante & Luigi's Ⓜ *Italian*

25 | 20 | 23 | $41

Bella Vista | 762 S. 10th St. (Catharine St.) | 215-922-9501 |
www.danteandluigis.com

When it's time to "impress the in-laws", fans tout this
"old-school", "white-tablecloth" Italian operating in the "heart" of
South Philly since 1899, whose "addictive" "red sauce"-style "classics" are "worth every calorie" (the "osso buco promotes world
peace"); "professional" service and "owners who care" make you
feel like "you're eating in someone's house", but keep in mind cash
is preferred (there's a surcharge for credit cards).

	FOOD	DECOR	SERVICE	COST

Darling's Diner ● _American_

20 | **18** | **19** | **$19**

Northern Liberties | Piazza at Schmidt's | 1033 N. 2nd St.
(Germantown Ave.) | 267-239-5775

Darling's Cafe ● _American_

Logan Square | 2100 Spring St. (21st St.) | 215-496-9611
www.darlingsdiner.com

For "inexpensive" "diner standards done right", including "cheese-cake and pie from heaven", "hipsters" and "families" alike head to this 24/7 "neighborhood staple" in Northern Liberties and its Logan Square sibling, both done up in "'50s coffee-shop decor"; despite complaints about service that's "all attitude with nothing to back it up", the tables remain "jam-packed."

Dave & Buster's _American_

20 | **22** | **20** | **$28**

Delaware Riverfront | Pier 19 N. | 325 N. Columbus Blvd.
(Callowhill St.) | 215-413-1951 ●

Northeast Philly | Franklin Mills Mall | 1995 Franklin Mills Circle
(Woodhaven Rd.) | 215-632-0333

Plymouth Meeting | Plymouth Meeting Mall | 500 W. Germantown Pike
(bet. Hickory & Plymouth Rds.) | 610-832-9200
www.daveandbusters.com

Release your inner "big kid" at this "family-friendly" arcade chain where you "kick back and let loose" while tucking into "standard" American "bar food" (although some just "come to play, not eat"); the service is "friendly" and there's "something for everyone" on the menu and in the arcade, offering "great bang for the buck" in terms of "entertainment" value.

David's Mai Lai Wah ● _Chinese_

25 | **13** | **19** | **$20**

Chinatown | 1001 Race St. (10th St.) | 215-627-2610

"It's 2 AM", and chances are your "drunk friends are in Chinatown" at this "faithful" Chinese noodle house, a "late-night staple" that "steps up to the plate" with "memorable" "soups" and "traditional dishes"; seating might be "a tad tight", but you get "good service most of the time", plus "a lot of food for your money."

Da Vinci Ristorante ▣ _Italian_

∇ **22** | **20** | **23** | **$41**

East Passyunk | 1533 S. 11th St. (Tasker St.) | 215-336-3636 |
www.davinciristorante.net

For an "old-style experience", aficionados head to this BYO near the Singing Fountain on the East Passyunk strip that's "as Italian as it gets", with a staff that seems to be "right off the boat" and "freshly made" piatti that are a "terrific value"; a few find the pictures of Leonardo throughout the dining area "kinda cheesy", but for others they're a "nice conversation piece."

Davio's Northern
Italian Steakhouse _Italian/Steak_

26 | **25** | **26** | **$55**

Rittenhouse | Provident Bank Bldg. | 111 S. 17th St. (bet. Chestnut & Sansom Sts.) | 215-563-4810 | www.davios.com

An "eclectic crowd", from "power brokers" to couples seeking "romance", heads to this "white-tablecloth" "splurge" in a restored

	FOOD	DECOR	SERVICE	COST

bank in Rittenhouse for "fabulous" steaks and "creative" Italian dishes beyond the "red-sauce normalcy", backed by an "impressive" wine list; the "gracious" staff makes you "feel like a VIP" in the "elegant" setting with a "vibrant bar scene."

Day by Day Ⓜ *American/Eclectic* 　　24 | 16 | 20 | $20

Rittenhouse | 2101 Sansom St. (21st St.) | 215-564-5540
"Decadent brunch offerings" and "amazing baked goods" mean you have to get to this "long-standing" Rittenhouse American-Eclectic lunch-and-bruncher "right when it opens" or "expect to wait"; though some find "nothing special" about the space and report that service can be "a bit flaky", the majority is "hooked."

Delancey Street Bagels *Bagels/Deli* 　20 | 12 | 16 | $11

Wynnewood | Wynnewood Shopping Ctr. | 50 E. Wynnewood Rd. (Lancaster Ave.) | 610-896-8837 | www.delanceystreetbagels.com
Noshers are in "bagel heaven" at this "reliable", "no-frills" spot where Main Liners "grab" a "shmear or sandwich" to go or "leisurely eat" with their paper to the soundtrack of "neighbors' conversations" and "screaming kids"; while a few kvetch "this is not your New York bagel, except maybe for the prices", most are "glad it's in the neighborhood."

Del Frisco's Double 　　　　25 | 27 | 25 | $69
Eagle Steak House *Steak*

Avenue of the Arts | 1426 Chestnut St. (15th St.) | 215-246-0533 | www.delfriscos.com
There's "a lot of eye candy" at this "old-money" steakhouse in a "grand" former bank off the Avenue of the Arts, including a "cool" repurposed vault, "runway-worthy socialites", "celebrities" and a "wine tower" – but cynics sniff "if you're not part of the scene", "prepare to be scenery"; while the menu is a "carnivorous tour de force", it includes "wonderful options for vegetarians", so "go hungry with a full wallet."

Delmonico's Steakhouse Ⓩ *Steak* 　26 | 22 | 25 | $64

Wynnefield | Hilton Philadelphia City Ave. | 4200 City Ave. (Stout Rd.) | 215-879-4000 | www.hilton.com
Though a "little pricey", the "top-notch" steaks are "worth it" say fans of this upscale meatery in the Hilton in Wynnefield, where the "friendly" staff provides "impeccable" service; a few find the "view of the hotel lobby" a letdown, but the "warm, welcoming" atmosphere inside compensates.

De Lorenzo's Pizza *Italian* 　　26 | 15 | 21 | $21

Fairless Hills | 914 Trenton Rd. (Vermillion Ln.) | 215-295-8313
Amici advise "bring an empty stomach" to this "neighborhood" Italian in Fairless Hills whose "mighty tasty" "thin-crust" Trenton-style tomato pies and "red-sauce" dishes are "made with love", and "too large" portions provide "lunch and dinner the next day"; even though some describe the digs as "straight out of the '70s", the joint is "always full of families" willing to "drive an hour" "up I-95."

	FOOD	DECOR	SERVICE	COST

Derek's *American*   23 | 22 | 22 | $38

Manayunk | 4411 Main St. (bet. Gay & Levering Sts.) |
215-483-9400 | www.dereksrestaurant.com

Derek Davis' New American small and large plates are "creative"
yet "welcoming", and the "vino list is sure to please wine drinkers"
at his Manayunk eatery; an "upbeat" yet "soothing" vibe in an "upscale" setting, a "comfortable" bar, "unpretentious" staff and tabs
that "don't break the bank" result in many "happy people."

Dettera *American*   23 | 24 | 22 | $57

Ambler | 129 E. Butler Ave. (bet. Lindenwold & Ridge Aves.) |
215-643-0111 | www.dettera.com

For "Downtown quality" in "little ol' Ambler", fans tout this "stunning", "upscale" New American where an "amazing two-story bar"
and "outdoor fireplace" set the stage for a "fine wine selection"
and "imaginative" dishes, served by an "awesome" staff; while
many come to "see and be seen", the ambiance is "relaxed", although some tense up at "prices reflecting a Center City attitude."

Devil's Den ◑ *American*   22 | 21 | 21 | $23

South Philly | 1148 S. 11th St. (Ellsworth St.) | 215-339-0855 |
www.devilsdenphilly.com

Chef Paul Trowbridge's "devilishly delicious" New American fare
goes just right with the "awesome" "draft list" and "flight" specials
at this gastropub in South Philly whose "romantic" fireplace is a
"treasure" (as opposed to the "creepy bathrooms with Beelzebubs
painted everywhere"); while the "waiters know their beer", some
find them "slow and rude" and suggest they "could try smiling."

Devon Seafood Grill *Seafood*   24 | 23 | 23 | $47

Rittenhouse | 225 S. 18th St. (bet. Locust & Walnut Sts.) |
215-546-5940

"First-class" seafood and "people-watching" are the big draws at
this "lively", "clubby" fish house where you can "pretend you're
hip" while dining among the "Rittenhouse Square crowd"; some
report the "arched tile ceiling" and "active bar" scene "magnify
voices", so try "booths along the wall" for a "date-night whisper"
(sidewalk seating is also a "plus") and hope the server with the
"homemade biscuits" "makes another stop."

Dilworthtown Inn *American*   27 | 27 | 27 | $61

West Chester | 1390 Old Wilmington Pike (Birmingham Rd.) |
610-399-1390

"History surrounds a fabulous meal" at this New American housed
in an 18th-century inn near West Chester, whose status as a
"special-occasion" destination never wanes thanks to "fabulous"
food and an "incredible" wine list served by "tuxedoed" waiters,
with "large fireplaces" providing a "warm feeling throughout" the
"rustic", "romantic" setting; it's "expensive", but most agree "you
get what you pay for."

	FOOD	DECOR	SERVICE	COST

Dim Sum Garden *Chinese*
25 | 7 | 16 | $14

Chinatown | 59 N. 11th St. (Filbert St.) | 215-627-0218
You say "xio long bao", we say "soup dumplings" – either way, they "steal the show" at this storefront Chinese BYO under a train trestle in Chinatown; fans suggest you "ignore the fluorescent lights and bus-stop atmosphere", for it's "far better than it looks", and "fast" service will permit you to order "sum more" for takeout.

Di Nardo's Famous Crabs *Seafood*
21 | 15 | 20 | $37

Old City | 312 Race St. (bet. 3rd & 4th Sts.) | 215-925-5115 | www.dinardos.com
The "garlic crabs smack you with flavor" at this "friendly", "old school" Old City crabhouse with a "genuine" "family-restaurant-of-yore vibe", and to those who find the digs "super-dated", fans retort "who needs a posh setting while they're wearing a bib and cracking crabs"; other critics find it "overpriced" and "overrated", but for many it remains a "dependable" option for "comfort seafood."

Di Nic's *Sandwiches*
27 | 12 | 21 | $12

Chinatown | Reading Terminal Mkt.1 | 136 Arch St. (bet. 11th & 12th Sts.) | 215-923-6175
"Perfection on a roll" is how fans describe the roast pork sandwich at this newly relocated and expanded stand at Reading Terminal Market, which doles out "tender" Italian sandwiches "so moist that half will drip down your shirt"; even though the service is "efficient", it's "always mobbed", so you'll need "patience while you wait in line", but most agree it's "worth it" to enter "pig heaven."

The Dining Car ●⇄ *American*
22 | 17 | 23 | $18

Northeast Philly | 8826 Frankford Ave. (bet. Academy Rd. & Pennypack St.) | 215-338-5113 | www.thediningcar.com
For the "classic diner experience", this 24-hour Northeast Philly "staple" satisfies "low-budget" loyalists with "huge portions" of "homestyle comfort food" and "lots of goodies" from the in-house bakery; though some say the "traditional" setting is "nothing to write home about", "efficient", "pleasant" service makes up for it.

Distrito *Mexican*
25 | 25 | 23 | $43

University City | 3945 Chestnut St. (40th St.) | 215-222-1657
At his "hip", "upbeat" University City cantina, Jose Garces' "inventive riffs" on "snack-y haute" Mexican cuisine yield "tapas-size" entrees "perfect for sharing" but "so delicious you want to keep them to yourself"; "knowledgeable" servers provide "spot-on recommendations", while "Pepto-Bismol pink walls", *lucha libre* masks", a four-top set up in a VW bug and a karaoke room add to the "circuslike" "party vibe" that's fueled by "festive margaritas."

NEW Divan
Mediterranean Grill *Mediterranean/Turkish*
– | – | – | I

Queen Village | 622 S. 6th St. (Bainbridge St.) | 215-278-2928
The chef from the former Divan Turkish Kitchen has set up a new Med-Turkish BYO across town in a contemporary storefront off

South Street, bringing generous portions and wallet-friendly prices along with him; the casual dining room is simply and stylishly decorated with marble and tile.

Dmitri's ⊅ *Greek* | 25 | 16 | 21 | $33 |

Queen Village | 795 S. 3rd St. (Catharine St.) | 215-625-0556
Rittenhouse | 2227 Pine St. (23rd St.) | 215-985-3680
Northern Liberties | 944 N. 2nd St. (Laurel St.) | 215-592-4550
www.dmitrisrestaurant.com

Afishionados gladly sit "elbow-to-elbow" to savor "awesome seafood" "prepared as simply as possible" at these "informal" Med tavernas, whose prices are "friendly to the wallet" and help most overlook what some describe as "consistently inconsistent" service from a "hipster" staff; the Queen Village original is BYO and cash-only, while Northern Liberties is also BYO but accepts credit cards and Fitler Square takes plastic and has a liquor license (got that?).

Dock Street Brewing Company Restaurant ⊠ *Pub Food* | 24 | 18 | 18 | $24 |

University City | 701 S. 50th St. (Baltimore Ave.) | 215-726-2338 | www.dockstreetbeer.com

At this University City brewpub, "awesome" wood-fired pizzas are paired with "fantastic" house brews, making it a "Penn favorite"; while some dismiss the "hipsterfied" digs in a former firehouse as "roadhouse meets Costco", the "enthusiastic bartenders" will give you a good "excuse to stick around."

Doc Magrogan's Oyster House *Seafood* | 21 | 21 | 21 | $32 |

West Chester | 117 E. Gay St. (bet. Matlack & Walnut Sts.) | 610-429-4046
University City | 3232 Sansom St. (34th St.) | 215-382-3474
www.docmagrogans.com

Fans report this "traditional seafood place" in West Chester "swells like a blowfish" on Monday nights when it offers its "one-buck-a-shuck" special on a "huge selection of oysters"; "courteous" service and a "great drink menu" also make it a "local favorite"; P.S. it recently opened a new location in University City.

Doghouse Burgers *American* | 26 | 17 | 21 | $18 |

Downingtown | 24 E. Lancaster Ave. (bet. Manor & Wallace Aves.) | 610-269-9381 | www.doghouseburgers.com

Fans roll over and beg for the "awesome", "made-to-order" burgers and "great dogs of the no-legged variety" at this casual Downingtown burger joint; the original's rough-hewn wood-and-stone interior is "small", but there's "nice" outdoor seating that makes for a "great hangout" in warmer weather.

Doma Japanese Restaurant *Japanese/Korean* | 27 | 23 | 25 | $34 |

Logan Square | 1822 Callowhill St. (18th St.) | 215-564-1114 | www.domarestaurant.com

Fans of this Japanese-Korean BYO in Logan Square "could eat here every day and not get bored", thanks to an "enormous menu" that ranges from "fresh", "inventive" sushi to "outstanding" bibimbop, served by an "attentive, but laid-back" staff; there's a "casual" vibe in the "sleek" setting that's about as "big as a minute", but that doesn't deter devotees from "coming in for more."

Domani Star *Italian* 28 | 19 | 25 | $35

Doylestown | 57 W. State St. (bet. Hamilton & Main Sts.) | 215-230-9100
While the meatballs may be "to die for", "every dish on the menu is a hit" at this "convivial" Italian BYO in Downtown Doylestown, where the "fresh", "tasty" fare is "served with a smile" and "lives up to the prices" (especially the Sunday–Thursday dinner prix fixe, a "steal" of a deal); some report "cramped", "noisy" environs, but most declare it a "winner."

Down Home Diner *Southern* 19 | 13 | 18 | $19

Chinatown | Reading Terminal Mkt. | 51 N. 12th St. (bet. Arch & Filbert Sts.) | 215-627-1955
"Cops, shoppers, workmen and conventioneers" rub elbows at Jack McDavid's "kitschy" Southern "icon" in Reading Terminal Market whose "fresh", "homestyle" country cooking carries a "reasonable" price tag; the jury's still out on a 2011 renovation with a "barn motif", but it's still "kid-friendly" and a fine stop for breakfast before wandering the aisles.

The Drafting Room *American* 22 | 19 | 23 | $31

Exton | Colonial 100 Shops | 635 N. Pottstown Pike (Ship Rd.) | 610-363-0521 | www.draftingroom.com
"Über-friendly" staffers "know your name (most of the time)" at this "cozy", beer-centric New American in Exton whose "incredible selection" of suds and "interesting specials" bolster a "creative", "varied" menu that works for "everyday" dining; the "bar side" leans toward "fun", and though some say it gets "loud" on the weekends, it's usually "not obnoxious."

Duck Sauce ☒ *Asian/Chinese* 25 | 19 | 23 | $25

Newtown | 127 S. State St. (bet. Mercer & Penn Sts.) | 215-860-8879
The "unique" Chinese and Asian fare at Tony Huang's "busy" Newtown BYO is "not the same ol', same ol'" and "doesn't disappoint"; it's set in an old house that's brimming with "charm", though some think it "could use some more square footage", so regulars advise "get there early or be prepared to wait", even in spite of "prompt", "efficient" service.

Duffer's Mill ● *Pub Food* 22 | 22 | 23 | $22

Marcus Hook | 1600 Naamans Creek Rd. (Delaware Expy.) | 610-859-0011 | www.dufferspa.com
"Friendly" staffers and "fair prices" at this golf-themed Delco sports bar makes it suitable as a "19th hole", a "hangout spot" for "watching a game" or a "fun place to take the family"; though some find the pub fare merely "decent", amenities such as free shuttle buses until last call on Fridays and Saturdays make it a "winner" in the eyes of many.

Du Jour Cafe & Market *American*

20 | 17 | 17 | $27

Haverford | Haverford Sq. | 379 Lancaster Ave. (bet. Station & Woodside Rds.) | 610-896-4556
Logan Square | Commerce Sq. | 2001 Market St. (bet. 20th & 21st Sts.) | 215-735-8010 Ⓢ
www.dujourmarket.com

Surveyors are split over this New American duo in Haverford and Logan Square, with fans praising it as an "easygoing" lunch stop, with "reliable" eats and servers who "try to please"; critics find it "overpriced" and suspect it "can't decide if it's a restaurant or an expensive deli"; the Main Line location offers all-day dining plus Sunday brunch, while its city sibling serves breakfast and lunch weekdays only.

Duling-Kurtz House Restaurant *Continental*

26 | 26 | 26 | $58

Exton | Duling-Kurtz House & Country Inn | 146 S. Whitford Rd. (Commerce Dr.) | 610-524-1830 | www.dulingkurtz.com

The "grand meals" in a "charming old farm setting" at this Continental near Exton are "what historical dining is all about in Philadelphia" declare devotees; "first-rate" dishes come in "superb presentations", and "every wish and need are attended to" by the "old-school" staff, so while it's "expensive", for any "special occasion" it's "always a delight."

Earth Bread+Brewery Ⓜ *American*

25 | 21 | 22 | $22

Mount Airy | 7136 Germantown Ave. (Durham St.) | 215-242-6666 | www.earthbreadbrewery.com

"Earth Bread + Heavenly" could be the nickname of this "socially conscious" brewpub in Mount Airy whose "handcrafted" suds are surpassed only by "amazing flatbreads"; "versatile for families, date nights or singles", it has a "neighborhood feel" with "funky", "recycled" decor that "plays up the earth theme", and while the staff is "friendly", some grouse about "slow" service.

Effie's Ⓜ *Greek*

22 | 17 | 21 | $29

Washington Square West | 1127 Pine St. (Quince St.) | 215-592-8333 | www.effiesrestaurant.com

"If you like culinary adventure", this "traditional" Greek BYO in Washington Square West is the "way to go" for "straightforward" fare that makes you feel like "someone's grandma is in the kitchen"; the "intimate" environs can feel "cramped", but for most it's "worth the inconvenience"; P.S. in warmer weather, "sitting in the courtyard is fun."

Ekta Indian Cuisine *Indian*

23 | 12 | 19 | $24

Fishtown | 250 E. Girard Ave. (Marlborough St.) | 215-426-2277
Bryn Mawr | 1003 W. Lancaster Ave. (Warner Ave.) | 610-581-7070
www.ektaindianrestaurant.com

"Delicious" vindaloo and other Indian choices come in "huge" portions that are "perfect to share" at these "pleasant" BYO twins; some say the storefront digs at the original Fishtown location

	FOOD	DECOR	SERVICE	COST

"aren't much to look at", though the Bryn Mawr sibling is more "cozy", and most all agree the "reasonably priced" food is "well worth" a trip to either.

NEW Ela 🅜● American — 28 | 24 | 25 | $50

Queen Village | 627 S. 3rd St. (Bainbridge St.) | 267-687-8512 | www.elaphilly.com

Jason Cichonski (ex Lacroix) is "wowing everyone" at his upscale-casual Queen Village New American with "inventive", "molecular cuisine" featuring "interesting pairings of textures and flavors" (the "liquid cookie dough dessert is to die for"); while some caution that "small plates lead to expensive dinners", it's nonetheless a "great neighborhood spot" that impresses "without trying to be too cool for school."

El Azteca 🅩 Mexican — 22 | 14 | 21 | $20

Washington Square West | 714 Chestnut St. (bet. 7th & 8th Sts.) | 215-733-0895

Amigos abound for these "nothing-fancy" Mexican twins in Mount Laurel and Wash West that are "better than the big chains" with "authentic", "consistently good" *comida*, "reasonable prices" and an offer to BYOT (bring your own tequila); the staff is "friendly", the vibe is "comfortable, not uppity" and the decor? – well, "it's one of those places you can't judge by looks."

El Camino Real ● BBQ/Mexican — 25 | 23 | 23 | $20

Northern Liberties | 1040 N. 2nd St. (bet. Girard Ave. & Poplar St.) | 215-925-1110 | www.bbqburritobar.com

A "delicious mix" of Mexican and Texas BBQ grub backed by "dangerous" margaritas at this "bustling" Northern Liberties cantina "makes you feel like you're in the Southwest"; the "lively" atmosphere feeds off "hipster energy", "fast, efficient" service and bartenders "generous" with their pours, while low prices also help maintain "strong crowds", but diehards "especially appreciate" the "late hours."

Elephant & Castle ● Pub Food — 15 | 16 | 16 | $26

Rittenhouse | Crowne Plaza Philadelphia Ctr. City | 1800 Market St. (18th St.) | 215-751-9977 | www.elephantcastle.com

As English pubs go, this spacious chain link at the Crowne Plaza on Market Street works as a "gathering place" for the "after-work" crowd, offering a solid "beer selection", "quick" service, "lots of TVs" and "outdoor tables"; detractors dismiss the "frat-style" grub, but others find it "dependable."

Elevation Burger Burgers — 21 | 13 | 19 | $12

Wynnewood | Wynnewood Shopping Ctr. | 50 E. Wynnewood Rd. (Penn Rd.) | 610-645-7704

Collegeville | 201 Plaza Dr. (Evansburg Rd.) | 610-831-1360

NEW Willow Grove | 3945 Welsh Rd. (Blair Mill Rd.) | 215-659-1008 www.elevationburger.com

Those who like their "guilty pleasure" "without a side of heartburn" tout the "healthy" fare at this "fast-paced" organic burger chain, where "grass-fed beef" and veggie options abound, and "olive oil-fried" fries are "made in front of your eyes"; while a few complain about an "overwhelmed" staff and "hospital-cafeteria" decor, the "thick shakes" "made with hand-dipped ice cream" sweeten the experience for most.

El Fuego *Californian/Mexican*   21 | 16 | 19 | $16
Rittenhouse | 2104 Chestnut St. (21st St.) | 215-751-1435
Washington Square West | 723 Walnut St. (8th St.) | 215-592-1901 🗷
"Freshly prepared" Mexi-Cali standards featuring local ingredients can be washed down with "big, fruity margaritas" at these "friendly" twins in Rittenhouse and Wash West; while a few say it's "nothing to write home about", others consider these industrial-looking spots a "notch up from the chains."

NEW Ella's American   ▽ 22 | 25 | 20 | $37
Bistro 🗷 *American*
Wayne | 214 Sugartown Rd. (Lancaster Ave.) | 610-964-3552
Fans are fond of the "fresh", "stylishly comfortable" dining room at this "upscale" New American in a Wayne strip mall, and many think the "quality and diversity" of the fare, which is served by a "gracious" staff in a "festive" setting, make it an "exciting new addition" to the Main Line; P.S. a post-Survey chef change may not be reflected in the Food score.

El Limon *Mexican*   ▽ 22 | 9 | 20 | $15
Conshohocken | 103 Fayette St. (Elm St.) | 610-567-0120
Conshy connoisseurs "love this tiny gem", a "friendly", "no-frills" taqueria on the main drag serving "burritos the size of your head", "delicious tacos and Mexican Coca-Cola"; no one wants to "let the secret out that you don't have to go to Norristown for authentic" *comida,* but with the "free margaritas" at this BYO, all bets are off.

El Rey *Mexican*   23 | 20 | 22 | $29
Rittenhouse | 2013 Chestnut St. (bet. 20th & 21st Sts.) |
215-523-9999 | www.elreyrestaurant.com
At Stephen Starr's "funky" faux dive in Rittenhouse, the "reasonably priced", "classically tasty" Mexican fare is "not too heavy" and goes down even easier at "happy hour" ("$1 tacos? yes, please"); descriptions of the service range from "attentive" to "spaced-out", and while many report "mucho noise" in the main dining area – the "young crowd" doesn't seem to mind.

El Sarape *Mexican*   24 | 21 | 23 | $31
Blue Bell | 1380 Skippack Pike (DeKalb Pike) | 610-239-8667 |
www.elsarapebluebell.com

Los Sarapes *Mexican*
Horsham | Horsham Center Sq. | 1116 Horsham Rd. (Limekiln Pike) | 215-654-5002 | www.lossarapeshorsham.com
Chalfont | 17 Moyer Rd. (Butler Ave.) | 215-822-8858 |
www.lossarapes.com 🅼
With "real-deal" Mexican cooking and a sterling "selection of tequilas", this "upscale" suburban trio is "always busy", and "out-

tanding" service reflects "family ownership"; some carp that it's "cramped" and that you can "expect to drop some dollars", but for most taste – "unexpectedly different, savory and satisfying" – makes up for it."

El Vez ⬤ Mexican   25 | 25 | 23 | $37

Washington Square West | 121 S. 13th St. (Sansom St.) | 215-928-9800 | www.elvezrestaurant.com

It's "always a party" at Stephen Starr's "flavorful, flashy" Wash West Mexican with "quirky decor" ("the bike rotating over the bar harks back to an old Elvis movie") and a "hip" clientele indulging in "knee-weakening" guacamole, plus blood-orange margaritas and other "awesome girl drinks"; it plays "upscale without being pretentious" but the "raucous atmosphere" leads some to wonder "how do the servers not all have laryngitis?"

Erawan Thai Cuisine Thai   22 | 15 | 21 | $23

Chinatown | 925 Arch St. (10th St.) | 215-922-7135 | www.erawanchinatown.com

Rittenhouse | 123 S. 23rd St. (Sansom St.) | 215-567-2542 | www.erawanphilly.com

These independently owned Thais in Rittenhouse and Chinatown deliver "solid goods" "always with a smile" in "unassuming", "no-frills" settings; "combination lunches" and BYO help keep costs "reasonable."

Estia Restaurant Greek   25 | 26 | 24 | $52

Avenue of the Arts | 1405 Locust St. (bet. Broad & 15th Sts.) | 215-735-7700 | www.estiarestaurant.com

"Put on your finest face" before heading to this Greek "splurge" off the Avenue of the Arts "because you will see and be seen here" and be "treated like royalty" amid "old-world" environs that "transport" you to a "taverna in Mykonos"; a "fantastic selection" of "fresh", "exotic" fish, "amazing" lamb and more complete the picture; P.S. the express lunch and three-course pre-theater menus are "winners."

Eulogy Belgian Tavern ⬤ Belgian   23 | 17 | 20 | $26

Old City | 136 Chestnut St. (2nd St.) | 215-413-1918 | www.eulogybar.com

One of the "biggest and baddest beer lists" in town can be found at this midpriced Belgian tavern in Old City, where "well-schooled" bartenders make "wonderful recommendations" among 300 bottled brews and 21 on tap (hint: "they don't want to make you a cocktail"); it's "always so crowded it hurts", and some say table service can be "hit-or-miss", but "amazing mussels" and "crispy fries" compensate.

Fadó Irish Pub ⬤ Irish/Pub Food   18 | 20 | 18 | $25

Rittenhouse | 1500 Locust St. (15th St.) | 215-893-9700 | www.fadoirishpub.com

"Capturing the essence of an Irish pub", this Rittenhouse Square corner tap "takes you across the pond" with boxties, mussels and other "light meal" options to pair with a "solid" beer lineup; its "small rooms" with "lots of nooks and crannies" are "so comfortable you never want to leave" (especially if soccer is on), though on Friday and Saturday DJ nights the "noise level is more suited to twentysomethings."

Famous 4th Street Delicatessen *Deli*   24 | 16 | 20 | $23
Queen Village | 700 S. 4th St. (Bainbridge St.) | 215-922-3274
Rittenhouse | 38 S. 19th St. (Chestnut St.) | 215-568-3271
www.famous4thstreetdelicatessen.com
"Quality and gluttony combine" at this "cramped", "no-fuss" 1920s-style Jewish deli in Queen Village and its similarly subway-tiled Rittenhouse branch, which dish out "redonkulous" "bowls of soup big enough to swim in" and sandwiches "zaftig" enough "to serve an elephant"; the former is a "favorite haunt of city politicos" who keep the "fast", "efficient" staff on its toes – it's "as close as Philly gets to New York."

Famous Mack's Boardwalk Pizza *Pizza*   26 | 15 | 22 | $14
South Philly | 2700 S. Hutchinson St. (Oregon Ave.) | 215-755-7553
"You don't have to travel miles to the boardwalk" for "thin, crispy" "Shore pizza" insist fans of this South Philly offshoot of a popular Wildwood, NJ, pizzeria; the "kind" owner turns out "delicious", "cheap" pies in the tiny space, saving you the "one-hour drive and gas money" – just "take it home" and have a "stay-cation."

Fare *American*   21 | 23 | 22 | $35
Fairmount | 2028 Fairmount Ave. (Corinthian St.) | 267-639-3063
www.farerestaurant.com
"Calming", "eco-friendly design" serves as a backdrop for "local", "healthy spins" on New American fare at this "charming" bistro in Fairmount whose "organic", "gluten free"–friendly philosophy extends to the wine list; "knowledgeable" service is another plus, and while some dissenters find the execution, well, "fair", however "well meaning", others consider it a "great neighborhood addition."

Farm & Fisherman Ⓜ *American*   27 | 21 | 26 | $56
Washington Square West | 1120 Pine St. (Quince St.) |
267-687-1555 | www.thefarmandfisherman.com
"Farm to table without being silly" is how fans describe this "lovely", upmarket New American BYO in Wash West where Joshua Lawler (ex NY State's Blue Hill at Stone Barns) creates "beautiful preparations" of "locally sourced" fare, while wife Colleen oversees the "friendly" staff; the space is "lovely", and while it may be too "intimate" for some, admirers "never want to leave."

The Farmers' Cabinet ☾ *American*   20 | 24 | 22 | $44
Washington Square West | 1113 Walnut St. (12th St.) | 215-923-1113
"Straight out of a ragtime movie", this "dark", "rustic" speakeasy in Wash West helps "knit-cap-wearing hipsters" "channel their inner Daisy or Tom Buchanan", pouring a "crazy collection" of "expertly

crafted" cocktails and Euro beers, which are toted by a "super-engaging" staff in a "Prohibition" setting that's "fantastic without being kitschy"; the "local", "sustainable" New American fare is "fresh" and "interesting", but many just "go for the drinks."

Farmer's Daughter *American*

23 | 23 | 23 | $41

Blue Bell | Normandy Farm | 1401 Morris Rd. (DeKalb Pike) | 215-616-8300 | www.normandygirl.com

The "cute" dining room at Blue Bell's Normandy Farm Hotel is dishing out "tasty", "adventurous" New American flavors for the "business-lunch" crowd and "upscale" Sunday brunchers (who sing the praises of the "great" raw bar); a redo of its drink list "pushed it past the typical golf club bar", and Thursday "live music and specials" keep locals "coming back."

FarmiCia Ⓜ *Continental*

23 | 22 | 22 | $35

Old City | 15 S. 3rd St. (bet. Chestnut & Market Sts.) | 215-627-7885 | www.farmiciarestaurant.com

Loyalists give "a thumbs-up" to this "uncomplicated" Continental in Old City from the Metropolitan Bakery crew for its "farm-to-table" approach that's "not in your face", plus "fabulous drinks" and "drool-worthy desserts"; it can get "crazy busy" (Sunday brunch is an especially "tough reservation"), but the staff is "friendly", if sometimes "flighty", and the "simple" digs are "comfortable."

Fat Salmon Sushi *Japanese*

25 | 23 | 22 | $31

Washington Square West | 719 Walnut St. (7th St.) | 215-928-8881 | www.fatsalmonsushi.com

"Creative", "affordable" sushi that "melts in your mouth" and "phat lunch specials" make Jack Yoo's "sleek" Wash West Japanese a "favorite" of Jefferson "med students and faculty", while "date-nighters" groove on the "sexy" "vibe" and wide range of Japanese beers; while service is usually "fast", "long waits" are to be expected unless you "call ahead or go early."

Fayette Street Grille Ⓜ *American*

23 | 17 | 24 | $36

Conshohocken | 308 Fayette St. (bet. 3rd & 4th Aves.) | 610-567-0366 | www.fayettestreetgrille.com

"Reservations are a must" for chef Douglas Runyen's "creative" three-course prix fixe dinners at his "informal" New American BYO in the "heart" of Conshohocken; it's the "kind of place where everyone knows your name" but given the open kitchen and happy chatter in the compact space, some complain that "one must scream to have a conversation."

NEW Federal Donuts *American*

25 | 13 | 20 | $12

South Philly | 1219 S. 2nd St. (Manton St.) | 267-687-8258 | www.federaldonuts.com

"Leave your willpower" at the door of this "minimalist" South Philly New American that does "three things to perfection" – "finger-lickin' good" Korean-style fried chicken, "unusual" donuts that inspire a "sugar high for days" and drip coffee – but serves only until "the limited supply runs out"; so make a "mad dash" here, but "be prepared to wait in line" anyway; P.S. a Center City location is planned for fall 2012.

Fellini Cafe *Italian*

25 | 22 | 25 | $29

Media | 106 W. State St. (Olive St.) | 610-892-7616 | www.felliniscafe.com

Fans insist you "can't really go wrong" at this "date night"–worthy BYO "fave" on Media's State Street strip, where "huge portions" of "hearty" Italian chow seem even larger in the "close quarters" and "intuitive" waiters create a "romantic" vibe on Mondays when they "break out in arias at a moment's notice"; while some gripe about the "loud" acoustics, others point out that "nobody can hear your misbehaving child."

Fellini Cafe Newtown Square *Italian*

24 | 18 | 21 | $28

Newtown Sq. | St. Albans Shopping Ctr. | 3541 W. Chester Pike (Rte. 252) | 610-353-6131 | www.fellinicafenewtownsquare.com

"Large portions" of "solid" "red-sauce" Italian at a "great price" is the draw at this "small" BYO in Newtown Square that comes "highly recommended for its specials" (which some warn can be "pricey"); a tidy business-appropriate "light lunch" trade "during the week" segues into "hectic" mode at dinnertime, and some warn the staff "tends to move you on" when it gets "crowded."

Fergie's Pub ◐ *Irish/Pub Food*

20 | 19 | 23 | $22

Washington Square West | 1214 Sansom St. (bet. 12th & 13th Sts.) | 215-928-8118 | www.fergies.com

With "no TVs" on the premises, this "old school" Irish pub in Wash West could be "your cup of Guinness" when you want to "escape the beer-guzzling football crowd" and just "hang" peacefully after a "tough day at work"; "down-to-earth" staffers offer "no pretension" as they guide you to solid "drinks" and grub, including some "great vegetarian selections."

Fez Moroccan Restaurant *Moroccan*

20 | 21 | 20 | $30

Queen Village | 620 S. 2nd St. (bet. Bainbridge & South Sts.) | 215-925-5367 | www.fezrestaurant.com

For a "culinary adventure", fans recommend this "intimate" Moroccan "hideaway" in Queen Village, where you "eat with your hands" and sit on cushions "like royalty" over "stunningly inexpensive" seven-course feasts ($25) capped by hookahs and weekend belly dancers; while detractors grouse that it's "not easy on the back" and find the scene a bit "cheesy", others tout it as an "awesome" "ice-breaking" first-date destination.

Figs Ⓜ⊅ *Mediterranean*

25 | 18 | 22 | $29

Fairmount | 2501 Meredith St. (25th St.) | 215-978-8440 | www.figsrestaurant.com

While the "space is small, flavor is not" at Mustapha Rouissiya's "reasonably priced", cash-only Med BYO on a "sun-drenched corner" in Fairmount, a "neighborhood favorite" for its "cosmopolitan" menu, including "marvelous" weekend brunch offerings, and "polite" service in a "European bistro"; cognoscenti counsel "be prepared to wait" even with a reservation.

Firebirds Wood Fired Grill *American*   25 | 26 | 24 | $32

Chadds Ford | Garnet Valley Plaza Ctr. | 91 Wilmington W. Chester Pike (Watkin Ave.) | 484-785-6880 | www.firebirdsrestaurants.com

"Too good for a strip mall" and yet "not as pricey as some other classic" steakhouses, this "happening" chain with branches in Chadds Ford and Newark offers "swoon-worthy", "wood-fired" beef and "spot-on" service in "rustic", "ski lodge-like" settings; whether you "bring a date" or go with a "group of colleagues", most agree it's "well worth a visit."

Firecreek Restaurant + Bar *American*   24 | 26 | 23 | $42

Downingtown | 20 E. Lancaster Ave. (Brandywine Ave.) | 610-269-6000 | www.firecreek-restaurant.com

Though this New American is set in a "refurbished mill" overlooking Brandywine Creek in Downingtown, "you feel like you're in Center City" from the "edgy" "flavor combinations", as well as the concomitant "sticker shock"; a "romantic, rustic" setting and "friendly" service add to its charm, and while it's "not 'wow' for the price" to some, to others it's "swanky enough to make you glad you didn't drive into the city."

NEW Fish *Seafood*   25 | 21 | 23 | $51

Washington Square West | 1234 Locust St. (13th St.) | 215-545-9600 | www.fishphilly.com

Mike Stollenwerk's "gone upscale" with his seafooder's "move" to "modern" digs on a Washington Square West corner, and admirers aver there's "even more to love" at one of the "best raw bars in the city"; amid a new focus on small plates and "cocktails", "inspired" "twists" and "flavor combinations" are still "showing us something new" (while signature skate wing remains) and the staff maintains its "laid-back but attentive" mien.

Five Guys Burgers & Fries *Burgers*   24 | 14 | 20 | $13

Bala Cynwyd | 77 E. City Ave. (bet. Belmont Ave. & Conshohocken State Rd.) | 610-949-9005
Rittenhouse | 1527 Chestnut St. (bet. 15th & 16th Sts.) | 215-972-1375
Warminster | 864 W. Street Rd. (York Rd.) | 215-443-5489
Wayne | 253 E. Swedesford Rd. (Valley Rd.) | 610-964-0214
www.fiveguys.com

See review in the New Jersey Suburbs Directory.

500° ⊠ *Burgers*   23 | 16 | 19 | $15

Rittenhouse | 1504 Sansom St. (bet. 15th & 16th Sts.) | 215-568-5000 | www.500degrees.com

"Mouthwatering" burgers on "beautiful buns" and "addictive" truffle fries make Rouge's sibling one of the "best guilty pleasures in Center City", which comes at a "fraction of the price of the big names in town", and its "well-organized" take-out service is a boon to those who chafe in the "spartan" "storefront" setting; it's open until 3 AM Thursdays–Saturdays, and night owls warn of "crazy long" lines when the "late-night drunk crowd" rolls in.

Fleming's Prime Steakhouse & Wine Bar *Steak*

26 | 25 | 25 | $62

Radnor | Radnor Financial Ctr. | 555 E. Lancaster Ave. (Radnor-Chester Rd.) | 610-688-9463 | www.flemingssteakhouse.com

Fans ponder "what's not to love" about these suburban links of the "clubby", "testosterone-filled" steakhouse chain where "premium" beef is schlepped by "seasoned waiters" who take "customer service to old-time levels" amid "elegant" surroundings; whether it's a full-on, "expense-account" dinner "splurge" or just "awesome happy-hour drinks and noshes", most "go home happy."

Fogo de Chão *Brazilian/Steak*

27 | 25 | 26 | $63

Avenue of the Arts | Widener Bldg. | 1337 Chestnut St. (bet. Broad & Juniper Sts.) | 215-636-9700 | www.fogodechao.com

"You'd better be hungry" before heading to the all-you-can-eat "carnivore's orgy" at this Brazilian steakhouse in a grand former bank off the Avenue of the Arts, where "gauchos" proffer "giant swords" loaded with "delicious" meat "hot off the grill", complemented by a "first-class" salad bar (but "filling up" there is a "rookie mistake"); though not cheap it's "worth it", and if you "still have room for dessert, you didn't do it right."

Fond 🈺 Ⓜ *American*

28 | 20 | 27 | $49

East Passyunk | 1617 E. Passyunk Ave. (Tasker St.) | 215-551-5000 | www.fondphilly.com

"Over-the-top terrific" sums up surveyors' sentiments about this high-end BYO on the East Passyunk strip, where "every bite" of Lee Styer's New American cooking and Jessie Prawlucki's "heavenly desserts" "takes your breath away", while Tory Keomanivong's "enthusiastic" servers are "genuinely caring"; it's an overall "memorable" experience, and a move to a new location (with a bar) later in 2012 may resolve the "space issue."

Fork *American*

26 | 22 | 24 | $48

Old City | 306 Market St. (bet. 3rd & 4th Sts.) | 215-625-9425 | www.forkrestaurant.com

This "intimate" Old City New American "never gets stale" thanks to "sophisticated" fare, "friendly", "knowledgeable" service and "elegant" environs, all of which are sure to please "your most discerning friends", a "romantic date" or "business" guest; while the Food score may not reflect a post-Survey chef change, fans expect it will continue to "live up to high expectations."

Fountain Restaurant *Continental/French*

29 | 28 | 28 | $82

Logan Square | Four Seasons Hotel | 1 Logan Sq. (Benjamin Franklin Pkwy.) | 215-963-1500 | www.fourseasons.com

Philadelphia's No. 1 for Food, Decor and Service, the Four Seasons' "formal but comfortable" French-Continental standout makes you "feel like royalty" with "fabulous" "feasts" of "succulent, creative" fare and "impeccable" service in a "beautiful" setting; "you feel rich just being there", though maybe less so after you leave – but "go ahead and splurge" since most agree it's the "standard by which all other restaurants should be judged."

Fountain Side
Seafood & Grill   *American/Italian*

23 | 19 | 22 | $31

Horsham | 537 Easton Rd. (Meetinghouse Rd.) | 215-957-5122 | www.fountainsidegrill.com

Franco Frederico and crew "take good care of the patrons" at this "roomy" yet "charming" Italo-American BYO located in a Horsham strip mall; "above-average" eats, "reasonable" prices and the little things ("moody lights", "white tablecloths") add up to an "elegant dining experience" suitable for "special occasions."

Four Dogs Tavern   *American*

22 | 21 | 20 | $30

West Chester | 1300 W. Strasburg Rd. (Telegraph Rd.) | 610-692-4367 | www.thefourdogstavern.com

"Above-average" New American "comfort food at comfortable prices" and "friendly" service win praise for this "rustic" "secret getaway" in West Chester, where "you could hang out all day" on the "outdoor patio" with your "pup" and "other well-behaved dogs" in warm weather, or with a two-legged buddy at the bar; though a few find the fare "hit-or-miss", many consider it "worth the trip."

NEW 401 Diner   *Diner*

21 | 18 | 20 | $21

Conshohocken | 401 Fayette St. (4th St.) | 484-351-8029 | www.401conshydiner.com

The crew from nearby Isabella have "vastly improved" this "cozy" Conshohocken BYO diner now serving "upscale", "health-conscious" "comfort food" mainly from "locally sourced ingredients" that gets a "thumbs-up" from fans; the redone digs feature "funky" recycled church pews and hand-tiled tables, and service comes with a side of "diner sass."

Francisco's on the River   ☒ *Italian*

24 | 21 | 22 | $45

Washington Crossing | 1251 River Rd. (Green St.) | 215-321-8789 | www.franciscosontheriver.com

A "lovely view" of the Delaware River is the backdrop to this "charming" Washington Crossing Italian BYO, where chef-owner Francisco Argueta and his "friendly" staff "do it right"; some find it "overpriced" and gripe about the "extremely leisurely pace" of service, but others insist it's "always satisfying."

Frankford Hall   ◐ *American/German*

20 | 25 | 20 | $24

Fishtown | 1210 Frankford Ave. (Girard Ave.) | 215-634-3338 | www.frankfordhall.com

Stephen Starr's "cool" German-style indoor-outdoor biergarten pumps up Fishtown's "hipster population" with "great beers, sausages, burgers" and "giant soft pretzels"; "Ping-Pong and jenga" games, "long wooden tables", "fire pits and heaters" are "clutch" for maintaining primo "people-watching" even in "cold weather."

	FOOD	DECOR	SERVICE	COST

Frankie's Fellini Café *Italian*   27 | 18 | 25 | $26

Berwyn | 678 Lancaster Ave. (Waterloo Ave.) | 610-647-1737 |
www.frankiesfellinicafe.com
"Fabulous", "filling" Italian "home cooking" "packs 'em in" at
Frankie Chiavaroli's "unassuming" BYO trattoria in a strip mall
across from the Berwyn train station; while it's a bit "tight on
space" and "always crowded", the "involved" owner and "accommodating" staff "aim to please" with "personable" service.

The Franklin Fountain ●⊘⊟ *Ice Cream*   27 | 25 | 24 | $10

Old City | 116 Market St. (Letitia St.) | 215-627-1899 |
www.franklinfountain.com
In summer the "line snakes around the corner" at this "old-fashioned" parlor in Old City, where "rich", "exquisitely fresh" scoops
"made from scratch" and "insane" sundaes are served by cos-
tumed servers in tin-ceilinged environs oozing with "nostalgia";
the "wait can be excruciating" but the reward is a "truly artistic
experience" with a cherry on top.

Frank's Spaghetti House Ⓜ *Italian*   23 | 17 | 21 | $20

Northeast Philly | 7602 Castor Ave. (Glendale Ave.) | 215-745-6020
The "aroma of garlic gently caresses you" as you enter this
"no-frills" ,"red-sauce" pasta joint in Northeast Philly, ideally with
an "empty stomach", since the portions of "down-home" Italian
grub are "giant"-size; the owner "keeps the staff on its toes", so
service is "speedy" while the tabs go "easy on your wallet."

Freddy & Tony's Restaurant *Spanish*   ∇ 29 | 19 | 26 | $18

North Philly | 201 W. Allegheny Ave. (2nd St.) | 215-634-3889
"Sinfully" "fantastic" *comida* (including "pork chops that are
better than sex") "takes center stage" at this "low-key", "authentic" Spanish that's occupied a North Philly corner since 1980;
"super-cheap prices" and "attentive" service contribute to the
"family-friendly environment."

The Freight House Ⓢ Ⓜ *American*   20 | 22 | 19 | $43

Doylestown | Doylestown SEPTA Station | 194 W. Ashland St.
(Lafayette St.) | 215-340-1003 | www.thefreighthouse.net
The "fantastic setting" of this New American "inside an old freight
train terminal" at the Doylestown SEPTA station is a popular "place
to be seen" for a "nice dinner out", notably on the patio; critics,
though, rail about "pricey" eats and a "noisy" "pickup" scene of
"wall-to-wall cougars and old men" Thursdays–Sundays.

Friday Saturday Sunday *American*   24 | 20 | 24 | $42

Rittenhouse | 261 S. 21st St. (bet. Locust & Spruce Sts.) |
215-546-4232 | www.frisatsun.com
Four decades young, this "charming", "unfussy" Traditional American "institution" off Rittenhouse Square "welcomes everyone
like a regular" while "managing to retain a fresh approach" with
signature mushroom soup and rack of lamb and "affordable" wine

list; though some grouse that the tables are not much bigger than "your fifth grade desk", "charming" service and a "romantic" vibe help compensate.

From The Boot *Italian* 24 | 18 | 22 | $28

Lafayette Hill | 517 Germantown Pike (Kerper Rd.) | 610-834-8680
Ambler | 110 E. Butler Ave. (York St.) | 215-646-0123 |
Blue Bell | Whitpain Shopping Ctr. | 1502 Dekalb Pike (Yost Rd.) | 610-277-3500
www.fromtheboot.com

A "whiff of garlic when the door opens sets the tone" at this "upbeat" suburban trio where "reasonably priced" Italian "home cooking" "like grandma used to make" and "friendly" service are "worth the line"; fans urge toting "two bottles of wine" to Lafayette Hill and Blue Bell, which are BYO (Ambler has a bar) – "one to drink while waiting and one for dinner."

Fuel *Health Food* 21 | 14 | 20 | $17

East Passyunk | 1917 E. Passyunk Ave. (Juniper St.) | 215-468-3835
Washington Square West | 1225 Walnut St. (13th St.) | 215-922-3835
www.fuelphilly.com

"Healthy", "guilt-free" dishes "under 500 calories" "that actually taste good" are the draw at this New American fast-food duo run by Q102 DJ Rocco, whose "affordable" lineup of "salads, wraps and smoothies" are right for a "quick bite" in East Passyunk and Wash West; one caveat – if you're not into "fist-pump music", which the staff "plays nonstop", consider "delivery or takeout."

Fuji Mountain Japanese Restaurant ● *Japanese* 24 | 20 | 22 | $33

Rittenhouse | 2030 Chestnut St. (bet. 20th & 21st Sts.) | 215-751-0939 | www.fujimt.com

"Impressive sushi boats" and "special rolls" join other "standard", "reasonably priced" Japanese "options" and a "vast sake selection" at this bi-level in Rittenhouse that's "kicking-it-old-school great with no pretensions"; service is "friendly", "not overbearing" while the ambiance is "comfortable", and though some find the surroundings "nondescript", others insist the "karaoke rooms are a must-see."

Fuji Mountain Japanese Restaurant & Bar *Japanese* 19 | 16 | 20 | $33

Bryn Mawr | 14 N. Merion Ave. (Lancaster Ave.) | 610-527-7777 | www.fujimountainrestaurant.com

Fans praise the "attentive", "pleasant" staff at this "adorable" Bryn Mawr Japanese where the atmosphere is "always welcoming"; detractors, however, find the sushi merely "passable" and the atmosphere "bland", insisting "there are better options on the Main Line."

FOOD	DECOR	SERVICE	COST

Funky
Lil' Kitchen 🗷Ⓜ *American*

27 | 21 | 24 | $35

Pottstown | 232 E. King St. (Penn St.) | 610-326-7400 |
www.funkylilkitchen.com

Michael Falcone's "inventive" New American grub "hits the mark"
at his "friendly" "hidden gem" of a BYO in Pottstown; the mood
is "romantic" in the "shoebox-size" digs, and while the menu is
"limited", it "changes frequently" and "everything is consistently
excellent", making "each visit a new experience" that's "worth the
schlep" for "city folks"; P.S. open Wednesday–Saturday.

The Gables at
Chadds Ford Ⓜ *American*

22 | 22 | 22 | $46

Chadds Ford | 423 Baltimore Pike (Brintons Bridge Rd.) |
610-388-7700 | www.thegablesatchaddsford.com

It "feels like you're in a barn" – and "that's right, you are" – at this
Chadds Ford New American on the grounds of a onetime dairy
producer dating back to the late 1800s; with a boisterous bar,
"welcoming" fireplace in winter and "charming", "grottolike patio",
it attracts "the beautiful people of Chester County" with "innovative" fare, though a few haven't warmed up to the recent "change
in ownership" and find it "uneven" for "pricey" tabs.

Gallo's Seafood *Seafood*

25 | 20 | 23 | $29

Northeast Philly | 8101 Roosevelt Blvd. (Holme Circle) |
215-333-0484 | www.gallosseafood.com

"You may have to wait in line with all the seniors" for "early-bird"
specials, but the crab cakes and other "straightforward" seafood
specialties are "fresh" and "melt in your mouth" at this "homey"
yet huge Northeast Philly "mainstay"; there's "something for everyone", including a "burger bar" for "landlubbers", all at "reasonable prices", and "warm", "courteous" service that goes "above
and beyond" gives it a "mom-and-pop feel."

Garces Trading
Company *American*

25 | 20 | 22 | $43

Washington Square West | 1111 Locust St. (11th St.) |
215-574-1099 | www.garcestradingcompany.com

Iron Chef Jose Garces' "pricey" New American "eatery-cum-gourmet
grocery" in Wash West teams "delightful" service with "fantastic"
charcuterie, "delish" pizzas, "duck fat fries" and "nightly specials"
"without pretension"; insiders advise "go with a group so you can
share" – just beware the "deafening" din amplified by subway tiles;
P.S. it's integrated with a state-owned wine and spirits store so you
can save bucks by BYOing your first bottle with no corkage.

Geechee
Girl Rice Café Ⓜ *Southern*

▽ 25 | 19 | 21 | $28

Germantown | 6825 Germantown Ave. (Carpenter Ln.) |
215-843-8113 | www.geecheegirl.com

Valerie Erwin's tribute to Low Country cuisine at her "humble"
but "cute" Germantown BYO might be "Philly's best claim to be

part of the Carolinas", as the reasonably priced, "down-home" cuisine comes with a side of "Southern hospitality"; leisurely service, which sometimes includes visits from the chef, ensures a "relaxed" time, but if you have somewhere else to be, "make your plans accordingly."

Gemelli on Main *Italian*   ▽ 24 | 22 | 20 | $49

Manayunk | 4161 Main St. (Pensdale St.) | 215-487-1230 | www.gemellionmain.com

"Props" ring out for chef Clark Gilbert's "vibrant", French-accented Italian in Manayunk whose "innovative" (if "pricey") menu is anything but the same old, same old, and is backed by "solid wine offerings" and "unique" beer choices; the staff makes you "feel right at home" in "hip", contemporary new digs that locals call a "nice change" for Main Street.

General Warren Inne   25 | 25 | 26 | $51
Restaurant ⊠ *American*

Malvern | General Warren Inne | 9 Old Lancaster Rd. (Lantern Ln.) | 610-296-3637 | www.generalwarren.com

"Well-prepared" Traditional American cuisine is served in a "historic boutique hotel" setting at this Main Line "fine-dining" destination in Malvern where the "great visuals" include a "peaceful" summer terrace and "warm fireplaces in the winter"; with "wonderful" "tableside preparations" of "classics" like Caesar salad and Châteaubriand, most agree that the "gracious", "old-world" service is worthy of a "special night out" that will surely "impress."

Geno's Steaks ●⇻ *Cheesesteaks*   22 | 14 | 18 | $13

East Passyunk | Italian Mkt. | 1219 S. 9th St. (Passyunk Ave.) | 215-389-0659 | www.genosteaks.com

To "diehards" queued "around the building", this 24/7 neon-ringed cheesesteak "landmark" in East Passyunk is a "must experience" despite "rules" for ordering ("speak English") and "lingo" ('wit' means 'with onions') enforced by a "rough-around-the-edges" crew keeping the flame after founder Joey Vento's 2011 passing; there's "no indoor seating", and some say the sandwiches taste even "better late at night" when it's harder to see the "goodness" "drip down your arm."

Georges' Ⓜ *Eclectic*   24 | 24 | 23 | $51

Wayne | Eagle Village Shops | 503 W. Lancaster Ave. (Conestoga Rd.) | 610-964-2588 | www.georgesonthemainline.com

A "delightful, modern take on French bistro fare", backed by a "great wine list", draws Main Line "foodies" to Georges Perrier's "pricey" Wayne Eclectic, where a "helpful" staff ushers guests to "inviting", farmhouse-inspired quarters encompassing three dining areas and a patio; meanwhile, the "beautiful bar" boasts a fireplace and a "lively" (if "noisy") "scene"; P.S. Sunday brings an all-you-can-eat brunch.

	FOOD	DECOR	SERVICE	COST

Georgine's *Italian*

25 | 20 | 24 | $28

Bristol | 1320 Newport Rd. (Steele Ave.) | 215-785-0564 |
www.georgines.com

"Super-sized portions" mean you "always leave" with a "big doggy
bag" from this "classy-but-casual" Bristol Italian, which has been
"around forever" as a "family dinner"–slash-"catering" operation
for those with a "small budget"; "friendly" staffers add to the
"superb" experience, while Friday comedy club nights feature a
dinner-and-show deal.

Gigi Restaurant & Lounge ● *Eclectic*

19 | 17 | 20 | $32

Old City | 319 Market St. (bet. 3rd & 4th Sts.) | 215-574-8880 |
www.gigiphilly.com

This trendy, "upbeat" Old City Eclectic, co-owned by Stephenie
LaGrossa, onetime *Survivor* contestant and wife of Phillies pitcher
Kyle Kendrick, has the tribal council debating "reasonable" prices,
"great" happy-hour specials and "friendly" bartenders vs. "unorga-
nized" servers and chow that some say is "nothing to write home
about"; still, late hours are a plus, and "everyone survives."

Gino's Burgers & Chicken *American*

21 | 18 | 21 | $14

King of Prussia | 611 W. Dekalb Pike (Allendale Rd.) |
610-265-5900
NEW Bensalem | 1606 Street Rd. (bet. Olga & Tyler Aves.) |
215-604-5900
www.ginosgiant.com

It's "nostalgic fun" to feast on burgers and chicken at this "rebirth
of a fast-food legend" in King of Prussia and Bensalem; the signature Giant, a "yummy, if somewhat sloppy flashback", headlines
a "varied" menu that affords what some say is the "best dol-
lar-to-calorie ratio out there", and the "mature staff offers much
better service than the bored teens of yesteryear."

Gino's Pizzeria & Restaurant *Pizza*

24 | 16 | 20 | $19

Norristown | 2401 W. Main St. (Potts Ave.) | 610-539-0155 |
www.myginos.com

This long-running red-sauce "gem" in Norristown has "grown" and
moved next door (perhaps to quell the "fights to get in there") but
"it's not lost the quality and attention to detail"; regulars swear by
"*delizioso*" pizza and parm dishes, "friendly, efficient" service and a
BYO policy that keeps tabs "reasonable."

Girasole *Italian*

23 | 21 | 21 | $50

Avenue of the Arts | Symphony House | 1410 Pine St. (Broad St.) |
215-732-2728

"You can't go wrong" with the "divine" salt-baked branzino or
"excellent" homemade pasta at this "family-run" Italian whose
"refined classics" are served "with a quiet sophistication" in a
Symphony House basement bedecked in Versace; "even the prices
feel like Rome", unless you opt for the $35 prix fixe "value" served
5–6:30 PM Sundays–Fridays.

	FOOD	DECOR	SERVICE	COST

Giuseppe's
Pizza Restaurant *Italian*

| 24 | 19 | 19 | $28 |

Ambler | 46 S. Bethlehem Pike (Woodland Ave.) | 215-628-4616
"Basic" Italian eats "just like grandma made" are what this Ambler
institution does in "spectacular" fashion – and at "reasonable"
prices; even devotees warn "you have to wait" because "reservations mean nothing" (though "favorites" manage to "get seated")
and management is bent on "packing them in", creating a "noisy"
scene some liken to "eating in the middle of a convention center";
P.S. it's open late on Fridays and Saturdays.

Giwa *Korean*

| 21 | 14 | 19 | $18 |

Rittenhouse | 1608 Sansom St. (bet. 16th & 17th Sts.) |
215-557-9830
Usually "packed for good reason", this BYO Korean fast-fooder in
Rittenhouse turns out "crazy good" bibimbop, Korean tacos and
"sizzling stone bowls" for the "eat-in win" – assuming you "find
a seat" in the "tiny", "simple surroundings"; meanwhile, "econo-
my-class" prices are a plus, and the staff "gets to know you if you
are a return customer."

Gnocchi *Italian*

| 24 | 20 | 22 | $30 |

South St. | 613 E. Passyunk Ave. (bet. Bainbridge & South Sts.) |
215-592-8300
"As the name would imply", the "pasta dishes are no-brainers" at
this cash-only Italian off South Street where "BYO keeps prices
low", so "grab a bottle and a date and squeeze on in" to the
"cramped" dining room, where the "personable" staff will "treat
you like one of the family"; P.S. there's a $30 four-course prix fixe
for parties of four or more.

Good Dog Bar *Pub Food*

| 24 | 17 | 19 | $22 |

Rittenhouse | 224 S. 15th St. (bet. Locust & Walnut Sts.) |
215-985-9600 | www.gooddogbar.com
The signature burger with a "molten blue cheese center" and
"excellent" "brew list" set tails wagging at this "chill" and "cheap"
Rittenhouse "hipster" "hangout", which blends the "right mix
of trendy and dive" thanks to "knowledgeable bartenders" and
charming "pics of dogs" on all three floors; despite growling over
the "noisy" scene, a pool table and jukebox help make it an "awesome late-night spot."

Grace Tavern *American*

| 21 | 13 | 20 | $21 |

Southwest Center City | 2229 Grays Ferry Ave. (23rd St.) |
215-893-9580 | www.gracetavern.com
"Eat, chill, drink" is the mantra at this "bargain" "find" in Southwest
Center City boasting a "solid beer selection" and "short but flavorful" Southern-leaning New American menu; while it "can get quite
crowded", regulars relish the "nicely restored" space (including
original 1930s pressed-tin ceilings) and "personal" service.

	FOOD	DECOR	SERVICE	COST

Granite Hill *French* | 19 | 22 | 22 | $40 |

Fairmount | Philadelphia Museum of Art | 2600 Benjamin Franklin Pkwy. (Kelly Dr.) | 215-684-7990 | www.philamuseum.org

Managed by Stephen Starr, the Philadelphia Museum of Art's "elegant" French might be "understated" but it offers a "leisurely" break from "gazing at fine art", with a tasty lunch buffet plus "flavorful" à la carte fare (also served for dinner on Fridays); it's "not cheap", and a few sniff that "the ladies who lunch deserve better."

Great American Pub *American* | ▽ 19 | 16 | 21 | $22 |

Narberth | 101 N. Narberth Ave. (Haverford Ave.) | 610-664-4982 | www.greatamericanpub.net

"You'll feel like a real Narb" as you "grab a burger and watch the game" at this "*Cheers*" of the Main Line, known for "cold beer" and "pub grub with a twist", where you can stay indoors or "eat outside" and "watch the world go by"; it's family-friendly too – if you "bring your kids, no one will notice if they make a mess."

Green Eggs Cafe ⊅ *American* | 25 | 20 | 20 | $19 |

South Philly | 1306 Dickinson St. (Clarion St.) | 215-226-3447
Northern Liberties | 719 N. 2nd St. (Brown St.) | 215-922-3447
Washington Square West | 212 S. 13th St. (Locust St.) | 267-861-0314
www.greeneggscafe.com

The Seussian name alludes to this "arty" American BYO trio's "earth-friendly" approach to serving "inexpensive", "innovative updates" on breakfast and lunch "classics" that leave you "stuffed to the gills"; those who "make it a regular stop" say "if you're brunching, best get here early" – though the "sweetie-pie" staff is "quick" once you're seated; P.S. cash only.

Green Line Cafe ⊅ *Sandwiches* | 21 | 19 | 23 | $9 |

West Philly | 4239 Baltimore Ave. (43rd St.) | 215-222-3431
West Philly | 4426 Locust St. (bet. 44th & 45th Sts.) | 215-222-0799 ⊅
West Philly | 3649 Lancaster Ave. (bet. 36th & 37th Sts.) | 215-382-2143 ⊅
www.greenlinecafe.com

"All the local hipsters" drop into these "cozy", budget-friendly West Philly sandwich joints to "chill on their computers", "hang out with friends" or snag "still-warm-from-the-oven" pastries from "helpful" baristas who pull a "great cup of joe"; with "so many vegan options" and "usually always an open seat", surveyors have "no real complaints."

Green Parrot *American* | 16 | 20 | 18 | $24 |

Newtown | 240 N. Sycamore St. (bet. Durham Rd. & Silo Dr.) | 215-504-7277 | www.greenparrotrestaurant.com

The "crowded", "tavernlike feel" at this American tap in Newtown Borough "certainly is not glamorous" but it's suitable for "a casual meal" while "watching a game" or hanging on the "outdoor patio"; though critics complain that the "pub grub" is "nothing special" and "service can be slow", the "nice amount of microbrews on tap" quells much discontent.

	FOOD	DECOR	SERVICE	COST

Grey Lodge Pub ❶ *Pub Food* | 25 | 22 | 25 | $23 |

Northeast Philly | 6235 Frankford Ave. (bet. Harbison Ave. & Robbins St.) | 215-856-3591 | www.greylodge.com

At this "chill" Northeast Philly tap, a "knowledgeable" staff serves up an "out-of-this-world" selection of "unique" brews plus a "tasty", "reasonably priced" pub grub menu; those who say it's "all about the beer" stick to the downstairs bar rather than the "family"- and "date"-friendly second floor.

🆕 Grill Fish Café Ⓜ *Vietnamese* | - | - | - | M |

West Philly | 814 S. 47th St. (Warrington Ave.) | 215-729-7011 | www.grillfishcafe.com

As a counterpoint to his spacious West Philly fave Vietnam Cafe (and as a third offering beside his Chinatown hit Vietnam Restaurant), Benny Lai has gone next door into a narrow former grocery store for this Viet arrival; seafood specials, many of them grilled, and creative cocktails populate a midpriced menu that's as tight as the modern space is snug.

Grindcore House Ⓢ Ⓜ *Vegetarian*   ▽ | 26 | 25 | 27 | $10 |

Queen Village | 1515 S. 4th St. (Greenwich St.) | 215-839-3333 | www.grindcorehouse.com

Urban "punks" groove on the "organic" coffee and "vegan treats" at this "quaint" South Philly vegetarian where the soundtrack is as "heavy" as a caffeine jolt; while "helpful", the staff will also leave you and "your laptop" to "hang out" in peace.

Gryphon Coffee Co *Coffeehouse*   ▽ | 21 | 21 | 22 | $13 |

Wayne | 105 W. Lancaster Ave. (Wayne Ave.) | 610-688-1988 | www.gryphoncafe.com

Main Line javaheads enjoy "organic, gourmet and gluten-free" goodies backed by "occasional live music" at this "charming", "shabby-refined" coffeehouse in the center of Wayne with "lots of clients and very little room to put them"; insiders warn of "table hogs" who test the patience of "would-be diners" seeking an elusive lunchtime seat.

Guard House Inn Ⓢ *American* | 23 | 22 | 25 | $51 |

Gladwyne | 953 Youngsford Rd. (Righters Mill Rd.) | 610-649-9708 | www.guardhouseinn.com

Owner Albert Breuers "treats you like family" at this "lovely" Traditional American in "the heart of Gladwyne", where Main Line "blue blood mixes perfectly with blue collar" in a "historic", "Civil War"–inspired setting; "reliable", "high-quality" cookery that's "worth every penny" and "timeless" people-watching at a "bar to beat the band" explain why it's a "mainstay."

Gullifty's ❶ *Pub Food* | 17 | 16 | 18 | $23 |

Rosemont | 1149 E. Lancaster Ave. (bet. Franklin & Montrose Aves.) | 610-525-1851 | www.gulliftys.com

A "fusion of college bar and quality family restaurant", this "noisy" "Main Line standby" in Rosemont is "more about the scene" than its "standard pub fare" (though the "extensive" "array of micro-brews" is "enough to make anything taste better"); service can be "slow", but the "wonderful" outdoor patio is "always packed" in the summer, and nearly 40 years in business leads many to conclude "they must be doing something right."

Gypsy Saloon *Eclectic*   21 | 20 | 20 | $31

West Conshohocken | 128 Ford St. (1st Ave.) | 610-828-8494 | www.gypsysaloon.com

There's a "neighbors-only", "drop-in" vibe at this midpriced West Conshy "watering hole" where a "welcoming" staff dishes up "ridiculously tasty" lobster mac 'n' cheese and other Eclectic fare; "delicious cocktails" fuel an "energetic happy hour" while occasional live music "adds to the hipness", and there's also a "quaint patio" fit for a "romantic" night out.

Half Moon   22 | 18 | 22 | $31
Restaurant & Saloon ☒ *American*

Kennett Square | 108 W. State St. (Union St.) | 610-444-7232 | www.halfmoonrestaurant.com

Many surveyors are game to try the "exotic meats" that make this midpriced New American a "unique" but "reliable" choice in Downtown Kennett Square for taking "out-of-town guests" and the "in-laws"; service is "attentive", and the "phenomenal" beer selection on tap fuels a "vibrant bar scene", while the "neat" year-round "rooftop patio" works as an "afternoon retreat."

Han Dynasty *Chinese*   25 | 15 | 19 | $26

Exton | 260 N. Pottstown Pike (Waterloo Blvd.) | 610-524-4002
Royersford | Limerick Square Shopping Ctr. | 70 Buckwalter Rd. (Rte. 422) | 610-792-9600
Old City | 108 Chestnut St. (Front St.) | 215-922-1888
NEW Manayunk | 4356 Main St. (bet. Grape & Levering Sts.) | 215-508-2066
University City | 3711 Market St. (38th St.) | 215-222-3711 | www.handynasty.com

Aficionados advise be sure to "grab your water" and "take extra tissues" to cope with "tongue-numbing", dial-by-number "heat" at Han Chiang's five "affordable" Sichuan destinations, where some fans would "probably trade" their "first-born child" for the "ecstasy-inducing" dan dan noodles; while the contemporary digs leave little impression, opinions of the owner range from "amusing to annoying."

Hank's Place ⊘ *Diner*   23 | 14 | 22 | $17

Chadds Ford | 1625 Creek Rd. (Creek Rd.) | 610-388-7061 | www.hanks-place.net

"Big portions" of "homestyle", "stick-to-your-ribs" diner fare (and the chance you "might rub elbows with" a Wyeth) have 'em "lined up" outside this inexpensive, "cottage-cute eatery" near the Brandywine River Museum in Chadds Ford; loyalists maintain it manages "attentive service in spite of the crowds", but a few demur, dubbing it "touristville."

	FOOD	DECOR	SERVICE	COST

The Happy Rooster ☒ *American* | 18 | 14 | 17 | $34 |

Rittenhouse | 118 S. 16th St. (Sansom St.) | 215-963-9311 |
www.thehappyrooster.net

Opinions are split over this "old-guard, classic watering hole" in
Rittenhouse where decent service and comforting New American
pub grub make it conducive to "medium-priced work lunches";
though critics see "nothing happy" about what they describe as
a "cramped", "noisy" "dive bar", fans find lots of "charm" in the
"quaint" spot.

Hard Rock Cafe *American* | 19 | 24 | 21 | $27 |

Chinatown | 1113-31 Market St. (12th St.) | 215-238-1000 |
www.hardrock.com

"Colorful" surroundings teeming with "crazy" rock 'n' roll memorabilia are the main draw at this "loud", "family-friendly" Chinatown
outpost of the national chain; if the "decent", "basic" American
grub is "nothing to rave about", the "knowledgeable" staff helps
put "tourists and T-shirt shoppers" in a "good mood."

Harvest Seasonal Grill & Wine Bar *American* | 25 | 26 | 24 | $35 |

Glen Mills | Glen Eagle Sq. | 549 Wilmington West Chester Pike
(Marshall Rd.) | 610-358-1005

"Modern"-meets-"rustic" surroundings create an "inviting" aura at
this Glen Mills New American whose shtick is a "seasonally changing", "farm-to-table" menu that keeps almost everything "under 500
calories", including "scrumptious" but "sensible" desserts; given
the "smaller portions", some are "taken back by the prices", but
most consider it a "well-thought-out" experience staffed by "courteous" folks; P.S. a new branch is due on Penn campus in 2012.

HAVANA Restaurant and Catering ● *American/Eclectic* | 21 | 20 | 21 | $36 |

New Hope | 105 S. Main St. (bet. Mechanic & New Sts.) |
215-862-9897 | www.havananewhope.com

"Decent" American and Eclectic fare at moderate prices competes
with the view from the "outdoor patio bar" at this "popular", tropical-
themed hangout on New Hope's Main Street, especially "in good
weather" when "you can easily burn an afternoon" people-watching;
perhaps it "really isn't about the food" confess regulars who come
just for the "fun" of it.

Hawthornes *American* | 24 | 23 | 22 | $22 |

Bella Vista | 738 S. 11th St. (Fitzwater St.) | 215-627-3012 |
www.hawthornescafe.com

With comfortable sofas and "real fire in the fireplace", this "calming" Bella Vista New American could be "your home away from
home – if your fridge held 1,000 bottles of beer" – as befits its
dual purpose as a bottle shop with a "fantastic" variety of suds;
the "tasty, well-priced" cooking "attracts a good-sized crowd" too,
though some warn that the usually "hospitable" service can get
rushed when it's "busy."

	FOOD	DECOR	SERVICE	COST

NEW Heirloom ☒ *American* ▽ 26 | 24 | 25 | $40

Chestnut Hill | 8705 Germantown Ave. (Bethlehem Pike) |
215-242-2700 | www.heirloomdining.com
Chestnut Hill "locals are feeling the love" for chef Al Paris' "fresh",
"farm-to-table" creations at this New American BYO, conveniently
located next to a liquor store; the "beautiful", "rustic" decor creates a "chill" vibe encouraged by servers "who want you to enjoy
yourself", and "reasonable" prices seal the deal; P.S. check out the
three-course Sunday brunch.

Hibachi *Japanese* 24 | 21 | 24 | $29

Springfield | 145 S. State Rd. (Springfield Rd.) | 610-690-4911
Jenkintown | Benjamin Fox Pavillion | 261 Old York Rd.
(Township Line Rd.) | 215-881-6814
Delaware Riverfront | Pier 19 N. | 325 N. Columbus Blvd.
(Callowhill St.) | 215-592-7100
Berwyn | 240 Swedesford Rd. (Valley Forge Rd.) | 610-296-4028
Downingtown | 985 E. Lancaster Ave. (Rte. 30) | 610-518-2910
www.hibachidining.com
"It's like getting dinner and a show" at this midpriced Japanese
teppanyaki chain where the "food is usually the star", cooked
"right in front of your eyes" by "entertaining chefs" who "go out
of their way for your enjoyment"; though a few are tired of the
"tried-and-true shtick", many find it "a lot of fun with a group";
P.S. you "can't beat" the all-you-can-eat sushi, either.

NEW Hickory Lane ▽ 20 | 20 | 21 | $39
American Bistro *American*

Fairmount | 2025 Fairmount Ave. (Corinthian St.) | 215-769-2420 |
www.hickorylanebistro.com
At this Fairmount eatery across from Eastern State Penitentiary,
chef Matt Zagorski (ex Rouge) turns out "satisfying", "spot-on"
New American fare while "professional" service keeps things "on
the right track"; an open kitchen lets diners "see how the food
is prepared", and the only gripe from some is that it's a "little
high-priced for the neighborhood."

High Note Cafe ☒ *Italian* ▽ 23 | 19 | 23 | $34

South Philly | 1549 S. 13th St. (Tasker St.) | 215-755-8903 |
www.highnotecafe.com
"Decent" Southern Italian cuisine shares top billing with occasional
"all-star" singing performances by "hospitable" waiters who "bring
character" to this "homey" South Philly haunt; tabs are "reasonable" and there are live performances by professional musicians
nightly, making it a "unique" "treat" for anyone "with an appreciation of the arts."

High Street Caffe *Cajun/Creole* 26 | 20 | 23 | $33

West Chester | 322 S. High St. (Dean St.) | 610-696-7435 |
www.highstreetcaffe.com
For a "little taste of Bourbon Street all year long", fans tout this
West Chester Cajun-Creole, whose "creative", "mouthwatering"

grub comes with a kick" and there's "wild game" to tempt the "adventurous"; cognoscenti caution it shifts from "cozy" to "cramped and noisy" "during prime hours", but "the wait is never too bad" and "attentive" service helps you "forget you're in a crowded restaurant"; P.S. BYO is offered Sunday–Tuesday.

Hikaru *Japanese*   24 | 21 | 23 | $34

Manayunk | 4348 Main St. (Grape St.) | 215-487-3500
South St. | 607 S. 2nd St. (bet. Bainbridge & South Sts.) |
215-627-7110
www.hikaruphilly.com

"A+ sushi" for "reasonable" prices sums up these "dependable" Japanese twins that have been making people remove their shoes for decades in Manayunk and South Street (there's tatami and regular seating); a few find the "quiet" settings a bit "boring", but many say the "service is awesome."

Hinge *American*   ∇ 27 | 23 | 25 | $23

Port Richmond | 2652 E. Somerset St. (Edgemont St.) |
215-425-6614 | www.hingecafe.com

"Perfect for Sunday brunch" or a "lovely" night out (with a dinner menu that "changes monthly"), this "cozy, classy" Port Richmond BYO serves "fresh" American fare that's not "unnecessarily fussy"; "friendly waitresses" maintain a "welcoming" "neighborhood" vibe, and since it's less than 15 minutes from Center City, it draws "locals" and downtown folks alike.

NEW HipCityVeg *Vegetarian*   - | - | - | I

Rittenhouse | 127 S. 18th St. (Sansom St.) | 215-278-7605 |
www.hipcityveg.com

Healthful, inexpensive vegan fast food (buffalo bella sandwiches, smoked tempeh burger) and fresh smoothies come out quickly at this industrial-looking Rittenhouse Square cafe; there are a handful of tables, but many choose to skip the crowds and bring their eats in nifty recyclable packaging to the park.

Ho Sai Gai Restaurant ☽ *Chinese*   23 | 14 | 22 | $20

Chinatown | 1000 Race St. (10th St.) | 215-922-4930

"Go where the locals go" advise regulars of this Chinatown "mainstay" whose "delightful" treatment of Chinese "classics" and "nice-size portions" make it a "cheap" thrill; the "super-friendly" staff, with chef Cathy Wu as "den mother", adds to the feel-good experience, though tepid scores suggest surveyor indifference to a 2009 top-to-bottom renovation.

Hokka Hokka *Japanese*   ∇ 20 | 20 | 21 | $34

Chestnut Hill | 7830 Germantown Ave. (bet. Moreland &
Springfield Aves.) | 215-242-4489

"You are well taken care of" by an "attentive" staff at this "above-average neighborhood Japanese" in Chestnut Hill, and "with a fire going in the fireplace" it's a "lovely" destination for "fresh" rolls and sashimi plus a tight selection of cocktails, wines and Japanese beers; bento box "deals" at lunch and BYO on Sundays and Mondays also make it a "good value."

NEW Honest Tom's Taco Shop *Mexican*

▽ 23 | 12 | 19 | $9

West Philly | 261 S. 44th St. (Spruce St.) | 215-620-1851
"Less is more" at Tom McCusker's bricks-and-mortar version of his former taco truck in West Philly, where you belly up to the colorful counter for "fresh, savory" burritos and tacos that come out "so quick"; little is said about the "non-decorated storefront" space, but most agree for a "cheap, tasty" bite, it's "awesome."

Honey *American*

27 | 25 | 26 | $50

Doylestown | 42 Shewell Ave. (Main St.) | 215-489-4200 | www.honeyrestaurant.com
At their "romantic" bistro "tucked in a side street" in Doylestown, Joe and Amy McAtee make culinary "magic" with an "ever-changing menu" of "creative" New American small plates that "always offers something new" "without getting weird"; while the "top-shelf prices" may limit it to "special occasions" for some, the "well-informed" staff makes "excellent suggestions" for an experience that "should delight most foodies."

Honey's Sit 'n Eat ⊘ *Jewish/Southern*

25 | 18 | 22 | $20

Northern Liberties | 800 N. 4th St. (Brown St.) | 215-925-1150 | www.honeyssitneat.com
"Down-home" Jewish *essen* meets Southern cooking at this "funky" Northern Liberties "hipster diner" where an "off-the-wall mix" of customers braves the "line out the door" for "fab", "nap-after-your-meal-type" brunches with no judgments ("get a veggie burger with bacon without batting an eye"); "friendly" service "makes you feel at home" – just be sure to bring cash; P.S. a Southwest Center City branch is in the works.

Hop Angel Brauhaus ❷ *American/German*

▽ 21 | 19 | 19 | $22

Northeast Philly | 7980 Oxford Ave. (Pine Rd.) | 215-437-1939 | www.hopangelbrauhaus.blogspot.com
"Yummy" German-American grub, a thirst-quenching "rotation of beers" on the 12-tap system (offered in a variety of pour sizes) and solid service put the oompah into this rustic, Teutonic-tinged American that's "growing into its historic home" – a ye-olde-style building in Northeast Philly; "lunch out in the biergarten" is a treat, while late hours add night-owl appeal.

Hot Diggity! *Sandwiches*

▽ 24 | 18 | 22 | $11

South St. | 630 South St. (bet. 6th & 7th Sts.) | 267-886-9253 | www.thehotdiggity.com
It's "about time for a good hot dog" in the heart of "cheesesteak country" rave cravers of the "customized" wieners and "tasty" Belgian-style fries paired with "out-of-this-world" dipping sauces at this "funky" South Street shop run by "eager-to-serve", "nice

guys" who "love their craft"; mum's the word on decor, but "big ups" go for the "freakin' delicious" vegan dogs and "great soft drink selection."

Hummus *Mediterranean* 19 | 10 | 16 | $13

University City | 3931 Walnut St. (bet. 40th St. & University Ave.) | 215-222-5300 | www.hummusrestaurant.com
Ardmore | 18 Greenfield Ave. (Lancaster Ave.) | 610-645-9500 | www.hummusardmore.com

"They understand value" at this "popular" Mediterranean duo in University City and Ardmore dishing out "generous portions" of "tasty" falafel, Moroccan cigars and of course the "namesake" dish, at "reasonable" prices; "counter service" makes it a "great fast dining option", albeit a "cramped" one (you'll be "snuggled right up to your neighbors while eating").

The Hunan Restaurant Ⓜ *Chinese* 24 | 21 | 24 | $29

Ardmore | 47 E. Lancaster Ave. (Argyle Rd.) | 610-642-3050 | www.hunan-ardmore.com

Maintaining a "serene", "elegant" air, this long-running BYO "family place" in Downtown Ardmore manages to "outclass" the field with "superb", "subtle" Chinese cooking ("not the usual over-breaded and fried food"); it's a "real treat for the price" and "wonderful" service makes it a Main Line "favorite."

Hymie's Merion Delicatessen *Deli* 19 | 12 | 16 | $19

Merion Station | 342 Montgomery Ave. (Levering Mill Rd.) | 610-668-3354

"When your cholesterol level is dangerously low", a trip to this "real-deal" deli "institution" in Merion is in order for "belly buster" sandwiches and "cheap", "huge-portioned platters that your bubbe and zayde would appreciate" in an "unpretentious" room worked by "amusing" waitresses; while naysayers sniff it "will do in a pinch", a trip to the "self-serve pickle bar" reinforces for most how "indispensable" it is.

Il Cantuccio Ⓩ⑨ *Italian* 24 | 17 | 20 | $25

Northern Liberties | 701 N. 3rd St. (Fairmount Ave.) | 215-627-6573
"Superior" basic trattoria fare at "affordable" prices is the draw at this "cozy" Tuscan BYO in Northern Liberties where the "kitchen's in the dining room" (or vice versa) so it's like "eating at your loud Italian aunt's house"; the servers are "friendly", though a few complain that they "rush you" to "turn the tables", while others quip the "decor is from a year before the Flood."

Il Giardino Pizza Cafe *Italian/Pizza* 23 | 15 | 21 | $29

Spring House | 907 Bethlehem Pike (Blue Bell Pike) | 215-646-8034 | www.ilgiardinopizzacafe.com
With its Montco strip-mall location, you might "think you're just in a typical pizza place" but this "neighborhood" "red-sauce" Italian BYO doles out "delicious, innovative" *cucina*; "energetic" staffers "take joy in tempting you with the possibilities", and "huge portions" ensure "plenty of food to take home."

	FOOD	DECOR	SERVICE	COST

NEW Il Pittore *Italian*   26 | 24 | 25 | $63

Rittenhouse | 2025 Sansom St. (bet. 20th & 21st Sts.) |
215-391-4900 | www.ilpittore.com

"Bring your bonus check" to experience Chris Painter's "inventive" takes on modern Italian at his and Stephen Starr's "intimate" storefront "splurge" in Rittenhouse; "portions are small to allow for several courses" (you may find yourself "ordering more than you should"), and meals are enhanced by "smooth wine pairings" and a "lovely" staff that keeps an eye on you "without going overboard."

Il Tartufo ⊅ *Italian*   22 | 20 | 19 | $42

Manayunk | 4341 Main St. (Grape St.) | 215-482-1999
Alfresco aficionados vow the "creative", "home-cooked" Tuscan fare at Il Portico's cash-only sibling in Manayunk tastes even better "outside on the sidewalk underneath an awning" as "people stroll by"; inside, the "tables are packed in" and some say service runs "slow", but most say the eats still make it "worth the visit."

Imperial Inn ● *Chinese*   21 | 15 | 20 | $22

Chinatown | 146 N. 10th St. (bet. Cherry & Race Sts.) | 215-627-5588
The "constant flow" of "craveable" dim sum at this "no-frills" 40-year veteran in Chinatown is "like a continuous cocktail hour at a fabulous wedding" and "cheap prices" mean you get "lots to share"; some critics find it "too Americanized", but while it may "never blow your socks off", for many it's a "consistent standby."

NEW In Riva M *Italian*   - | - | - | M

East Falls | 4116 Ridge Ave. (Kelly Dr.) | 215-438-4848 |
www.in-riva.com
At this industrial-chic Italian by the Schuylkill River in East Falls, chef Arthur Cavaliere digs into his Italian heritage for inspiration after making his mark on other cuisines elsewhere (French at Parc, Spanish at Amada, Mexican at El Vez); wood-fired pizzas, salumi and a few apps make for a simple, moderately priced menu, pairable with a tight wine, cocktail and beer list.

NEW The Industry ● *American*   - | - | - | I

South Philly | 1401 E. Moyamensing Ave. (Reed St.) |
215-271-9500 | www.theindustrybar.com
This casual South Philly New American from the folks behind Good Dog Bar is dedicated to members of the restaurant biz, though all are welcome to try the creative pub food and serious beer selection; the low-key corner space draws a neighborhood crowd, and the kitchen serves from 4 PM to 1 AM to catch both ends of a kitchen shift; P.S. those in the industry get a 20-percent discount.

Inn at Phillips Mill Restaurant ⊅ *French*   25 | 25 | 24 | $49

New Hope | Inn at Phillips Mill | 2590 River Rd. (Phillips Mill Rd.) |
215-862-9919 | www.theinnatphillipsmill.com
"Superior" French cooking "attentively served" in a "charming locale" defines this "elegant" BYO in a historic inn fashioned from an "exquisite old millhouse" in New Hope; there's "always something

a bit unexpected on the menu", which works well for a "special holiday", "especially in winter months with the fire roaring" or for "summer outdoor dining in the candlelit garden" (just don't forget cash or your checkbook).

Irish Pub ● *Pub Food* | 19 | 17 | 21 | $22 |

Rittenhouse | 2222 Walnut St. (20th St.) | 215-568-5603
Washington Square West | 1123 Walnut St. (bet. 11th & 12th Sts.) | 215-925-3311
www.irishpubphilly.com

"Reliable" suds and burgers and "friendly" service make for an "enjoyable" time at these "pleasant" pubs in Rittenhouse and Wash West, where an "older, professional crowd" comes to "unwind" "after work", to be replaced by a "younger" set and a "frat-house" vibe later on; critics rate the fare "one step above fast food" while shrugging at the "generic Irish theme" (and marveling that "they don't serve Guinness").

Iron Abbey ● *American/Belgian* | 22 | 20 | 20 | $27 |

Horsham | 680 Easton Rd. (Jefferson Ave.) | 215-956-9600 | www.ironabbey.com

"'Real' football" (soccer) fans watch matches (games) at the "television-encrusted" bar at this "rare find" in Horsham, where "upscale" Belgian-meets-American pub grub is backed by a "massive beer list" and served by a "knowledgeable staff" in "dark", "cozy" environs; the bargain lunch buffet segues into "amazing" happy-hour specials, and when "noise" levels peak, many retreat into the "adjacent dining room."

Iron Hill Brewery & Restaurant *American* | 22 | 21 | 22 | $28 |

West Chester | 3 W. Gay St. (High St.) | 610-738-9600
Media | 30 E. State St. (bet. Jackson & Monroe Sts.) | 610-627-9000
North Wales | Shoppes at English Vill. | 1460 Bethlehem Pike (Welsh Rd.) | 267-708-2000
Phoenixville | 130 Bridge St. (Starr St.) | 610-983-9333
Chestnut Hill | 8400 Germantown Ave. (bet. Gravers Ln. & Highland Ave.) | 215-948-5600
www.ironhillbrewery.com ●

"There's no better place to be Friday at 5" than these "always busy" local brewpubs whose "bright, open" (maybe a little "corporate") settings permit prime viewing of the brewing process while amping the "noise"; surveyors tout the "inventive" "comfort food" "for the masses" and "down-to-earth" service but add "the beer alone is worth the trip" – so "make sure to get the sampler and a designated driver."

Isaac Newton's ● *American* | 22 | 19 | 21 | $22 |

Newtown | 18 S. State St. (Washington Ave.) | 215-860-5100 | www.isaacnewtons.com

The "constantly changing selection of microbrews and foreign beers" is the big draw at this "classic" "hangout" in Newtown, which "has the feel of a London pub"; families gravitate to "reasonable prices" and "friendly" service and just about "everyone gets what they want" from the "extensive" "all-American" menu.

Isaac's Famous Grilled Sandwiches *American/Sandwiches*
23 | 18 | 21 | $14

Exton | Crossroads Sq. | 630 W. Uwchlan Ave. (Pottstown Pike) | 484-875-5825 | www.isaacsdeli.com
See review in the Lancaster/Berks Counties Directory.

NEW Isabel *Californian/Mexican*
∇ 21 | 18 | 23 | $29

Fairmount | 2601 Pennsylvania Ave. (bet. Aspen & 26th Sts.) | 215-475-8088 | www.isabelbyob.com
The owners of Trio are behind this Cali-Mex BYO in Fairmount's 2601 Parkway condos (across from the Museum of Art); "lots of seafood dishes" and "outta-here" desserts headline the "upscale" menu, on which you'll find "nothing like refried beans and rice", and everything is served in an "attractive" space filled with hand-made wooden tables.

Isabella *Mediterranean*
23 | 20 | 19 | $38

Conshohocken | 382 E. Elm St. (Cherry St.) | 484-532-7470 | www.barisabella.com
The Conshohocken crew is keen on the "tasty" tapas and the "well-stocked bar" at this "small but inviting" "Center City–style" Med where the "seating is tight" and it "gets loud when the crowd builds"; it's a bit "pricey" for some, and others think the service, while "friendly", could use "better pacing."

Ishkabibble's *Cheesesteaks*
25 | 15 | 21 | $11

South St. | 337 South St. (4th St.) | 215-923-4337 | www.philacheesesteak.com
"Crazy name but crazy good" cheesesteaks is what they say about this "old-school" South Street "hole-in-the-wall" (across from the TLA) whose take-out window is a beacon for "those late-night and after-show munchies"; though it's "often overlooked due to flashier places" nearby, it has a "devoted following" for its Spanish fries and 'gremlin' drink (half-lemonade, half-grape), dished out by "friendly" counter folks.

Izumi Ⓜ *Japanese*
26 | 23 | 24 | $36

East Passyunk | 1601 E. Passyunk Ave. (Tasker St.) | 215-271-1222 | www.izumiphilly.com
"Beautiful presentations of mouthwatering sushi" are a "feast for the eyes and palate" at this "edgy" Japanese BYO from the owner of the nearby Paradiso on East Passyunk; adherents also sing the praises of cooked entrees and "comfortable" indoor and outdoor seating, dubbing it a "date-friendly choice."

Jack's Firehouse *Southern*
21 | 22 | 20 | $35

Fairmount | 2130 Fairmount Ave. (bet. 21st & 22nd Sts.) | 215-232-9000 | www.jacksfirehouse.com
Named for its "unique location" in a converted 19th-century firehouse across from Eastern State Penitentiary, this "welcoming"

Fairmount Southern serves up "delicious" BBQ and other "locally sourced", midpriced Southern grub that'll "satisfy the toughest of critics", plus a "whiskey selection that would make any Southerner proud"; it can get "a bit noisy when crowded", but the "quiet" outdoor patio is "sublime."

Jake's and Cooper's
Wine Bar and Restaurant *American*

21 | 20 | 20 | $41

Manayunk | 4365 Main St. (bet. Grape & Levering Sts.) | 215-483-0444 | www.jakesrestaurant.com

Chef-owner Bruce Cooper's side-by-side duo in Manayunk – a rustic wine bar with a "jolly" crowd and a New American "gastropub with class" – appeals to those who "love the option of being able to have a serious dinner or lighter fare"; to some, it's "nothing terribly memorable", but most appreciate the "reasonably priced" chow and "knowledgeable" service.

Jake's
Wayback Burgers *Burgers*

24 | 14 | 21 | $12

Exton | 807 N. Pottstown Pike (Gordon Dr.) | 484-872-8341
Kennett Square | 811 E. Baltimore Pike (bet. Onix Dr. & Schoolhouse Rd.) | 484-732-8171
Northeast Philly | Northeast Village Shopping Ctr. | 9173 E. Roosevelt Blvd. (Welsh Rd.) | 267-388-7692 ◗
Pottstown | 255 Upland Sq. Dr. (bet. Rte. 100 & Sell Rd.) | 484-300-4246
NEW Thorndale | 3483 E. Lincoln Hwy. (Municipal Dr.) | 610-380-9500
NEW Wayne | 369 W. Lancaster Ave. (bet. Eagle Rd. & Strafford Ave.) | 610-688-3332
NEW West Chester | West Goshen Town Ctr. | (bet. 5 Points Rd. & Spring Ln.) | 610-701-7015
Willow Grove | 2720 Easton Rd. (bet. Linden & Willow Aves.) | 215-442-1975
www.waybackburgers.com

"Loyal customers" "always count on" the "hot", "made-to-order" burgers and "real" milkshakes at this affordable, Delaware-based fast-fooder; sure, it "could be updated as far as looks go", but "alert order takers" "give you the warm and fuzzies" with "friendly" service.

Jamaican Jerk Hut *Jamaican*

22 | 16 | 17 | $21

Avenue of the Arts | 1436 South St. (15th St.) | 215-545-8644 | www.jajerkhut.com

"Blink" and you're in Negril at this Jamaican off the Avenue of the Arts where "terrific" oxtail, fried plantains and other "island classics" go perfectly with your BYO "Red Stripe"; a few gripe that the "well-meaning" staff can be "island slow" and it's "tight quarters" with a "minimum of amenity" inside, but if you snag some "open air seating" and soak up the reggae music, "you're good to go."

| | FOOD | DECOR | SERVICE | COST |

NEW Jamonera ● *Spanish* — | — | — | M

Washington Square West | 105 S. 13th St. (Sansom St.) |
215-922-6061 | www.jamonerarestaurant.com

Chef Marcie Turney and owner Valerie Safran (Lolita, Barbuzzo)
have amped up the "party that is 13th Street" in Wash West with
this "warm, intimate" Spaniard serving housemade charcuterie and
a collection of moderately priced tapas and larger plates; it's suitable for a romantic evening or a bite at the copper-top bar where
the "bartenders know their sherry."

Jasmine Asian Bistro *Asian* 22 | 19 | 23 | $20

Glenside | 138 S. Easton Rd. (Glenside Ave.) | 215-885-4333 |
www.jasmineasianbistro-glenside.com

An "awesome vegetarian menu" supplements the "fresh", "consistently good" Chinese fare at this Glenside Asian, a neighborhood
"go-to" where the BYO policy helps keep tabs down; "comfortable seating" and an "accommodating" staff that "makes you feel
welcome" add to the "calming" aura.

J.B. Dawson's *American* 24 | 22 | 23 | $31

Langhorne | Shoppes at Flowers Mill | 92 N. Flowers Mill Rd. (Rte. 213) |
215-702-8119

Dawson's *American*

Plymouth Meeting | 440 Plymouth Rd. (Germantown Pike) |
610-260-0550
www.jbdawsons.com

With "wonderful babyback ribs" and other "tasty" pub favorites,
these "dark", "upscale-casual" Traditional American eateries offer
a "delicious departure from your typical chain"; they're suitable
for "business or pleasure" thanks to "witty" "team service", an
atmosphere of "tranquility" and a "decent" happy hour.

JD McGillicuddy's ● *American* 21 | 19 | 22 | $19

Ardmore | 2626 County Line Rd. (Edgemont Ave.) |
610-658-2626
Manayunk | 111 Cotton St. (Cresson St.) | 215-930-0209
North Philly | 421 N. 7th St. (Willow St.) | 215-925-5310
Roxborough | 473 Leverington Ave. (Ridge Ave.) | 267-335-2672
Upper Darby | 8919 W. Chester Pike (Kirklyn Ave.) | 610-924-0441
www.jdmcgillicuddys.com

"When there's a game on", a "college-age crowd" flocks to this
local chain of "watering holes" where plates of wings and other
"tasty" but "typical" American bar bites join a nightly list of "specials" that help you "relax" "without breaking the bank"; boosters
insist the "loud", "fun" vibe and "fast" service will make you "glad
you went", and late hours are a plus.

JG Domestic *American* 23 | 21 | 22 | $49

University City | Cira Centre | 2929 Arch St. (30th St.) |
215-222-2363 | www.jgdomestic.com

"They have done wonders" in "transforming" the "sterile" lobby
of the Cira Centre (next to University City's Amtrak station) to

FOOD | DECOR | SERVICE | COST

create this "rustic", "farmer's market"–inspired New American, "another winner" from Iron Chef Jose Garces, where an "efficient" staff serves up "interesting" cocktails and "innovative" cuisine that "sparkles"; though a few quip the portions are too small "to feed Kate Moss" and come with "expense-account" tabs, the "superb vibes" prevail for most.

Jim's Steaks ● *Cheesesteaks*   24 | 13 | 18 | $13

South St. | 400 South St. (4th St.) | 215-928-1911
Northeast Philly | Roosevelt Mall | 2311 Cottman Ave. (Bustleton Ave.) | 215-333-5467
West Philly | 431 N. 62nd St. (bet. Callowhill St. & Girard Ave.) | 215-747-6615
Springfield | Stony Creek Shopping Ctr. | 469 Baltimore Pike (Sproul Rd.) | 610-544-8400
www.jimssteaks.com

The "authentic, fabulous" cheesesteaks served by a "charmingly surly" staff at this "no-frills" sandwich chain "embody Philadel-phia" and will "make your cardiologist sing"; expect "lines wrapped around the block" filled with regulars who "can't resist" the "amaz-ing smell" that "you take with you on your clothes" so you "can enjoy the scent all over again."

NEW Joe's Crab Shack ● *Seafood*   23 | 21 | 21 | $34

King of Prussia | King of Prussia Mall | 244 Mall Blvd. (Wills Rd.) | 610-265-2237 | www.joescrabshack.com

When "you're in the mood to get messy", fans recommend "crackin' crabs" at this "family-friendly" seafood chain link next to King of Prussia Mall; a few skeptics liken it to a "flashy remake of your father's Red Lobster", but many report a "good time" in the "noisy", "industrial" setting when the staff starts "line-dancing", creating a "great atmosphere for a party."

Johnny Mañana's *Mexican*   19 | 18 | 17 | $27

East Falls | 4201 Ridge Ave. (Midvale Ave.) | 215-843-0499 | www.johnnymananas.net

Even under new management, this colorful, Day of the Dead-themed East Falls venue draws mixed reactions; while amigos "recommend" it for "large" portions of traditional Mexican fare and "cheap" "mason-jar margaritas" in a setting suited for "relaxing after work" (especially if you snag a seat outside), foes say the "prices are a little steep" for *comida* they deem "average."

John's Roast Pork ⬛ *Sandwiches*   27 | 8 | 19 | $12

South Philly | 14 Snyder Ave. (Weccacoe Ave.) | 215-463-1951 | www.johnsroastpork.com

"Local connoisseurs" queue up early for "first-rate" roast pork sandwiches and cheesesteaks at this family-run "old-school joint" in South Philly that closes at 3 PM (or whenever "they run out"); expect "long lines that move fast" at this "everlasting cornerstone of true Philly food", where "you eat outside on picnic tables or in your car"; P.S. cash only.

	FOOD	DECOR	SERVICE	COST

Jones *American*   23 | 23 | 23 | $30

Washington Square West | 700 Chestnut St. (7th St.) | 215-223-5663
Those "jonesing" for "comfort-food classics" such as "killer mac 'n' cheese" head to Stephen Starr's New American off Washington Square, the "favorite brunch spot" of many; "reasonable" tabs and "accommodating" service suit "families with kids", and if the "comfy", "retro" setting can get "a little too noisy", fans say it makes it seem "just like home" – but "without all the drama."

Jong Ka Jib *Korean*   ▽ 23 | 18 | 19 | $16

East Oak Lane | 6600 N. 5th St. (66th Ave.) | 215-924-0100
The "spicy tofu soup" and other "authentic" Korean dishes are "worth the trip" to this BYO in East Oak Lane; the "traditional" decor and service don't elicit much comment, and "if you go on the weekend", chances are you'll be "seated next to a table of loud kids."

Joseph Ambler Inn *American*   25 | 25 | 25 | $51

North Wales | Joseph Ambler Inn | 1005 Horsham Rd. (bet. Stump & Upper State Rds.) | 215-362-7500
For a "special-occasion night out", the "ambitious", "beautifully presented" New American fare and "superb" service at this "classy", "romantic" inn in North Wales are "worth the price" to fans; housed in a stone bank barn on a 19th-century farmstead, it's "delightful" year-round, although for many summer is the "best time", when you can dine "under the stars" on the patio.

Jose's Tacos ⊠⊄ *Mexican*   ▽ 26 | 16 | 24 | $16

Callowhill | 469 N. 10th St. (Buttonwood St.) | 215-765-2369
This "authentic" taqueria in Callowhill near the Electric Factory and Union Transfer dishes out "large portions" of what many say are some of the "best carnitas in the city", and amigos "can't imagine eating anywhere else"; there's only a handful of tables, but "fast", "friendly" service and modest prices make it a local "gem."

Joy Tsin Lau ❶ *Chinese*   18 | 13 | 16 | $22

Chinatown | 1026 Race St. (bet. 10th & 11th Sts.) | 215-592-7226 | www.joytsinlauchineserestaurant.com
Surveyors report "large groups of Chinese" diners at this "classic" Chinatown dim sum house where the rolling carts are laden with "something for everyone"; though killjoys kvetch about "tired-looking" decor and "so-so" service, many "keep coming back" because the "full experience" is a "great value" – and it's open late too.

Jules Thin Crust *Pizza*   22 | 17 | 20 | $15

Jenkintown | 817 Old York Rd. (The Fairway) | 215-886-5555
Doylestown | 78 S. Main St. (Green St.) | 215-345-8565
Newtown | 300 N. Sycamore St. (bet. Durham & Swamp Rds.) | 215-579-0111
NEW **Wayne** | 114 E. Lancaster Ave. (bet. Louella & Wayne Aves.) | 484-580-8003
www.julesthincrust.com
"Delicious", "organic" "yuppie pies" with "innovative toppings" and "flavorful" thin crusts have a "healthier" spin ("gluten-free op-

tions", etc.) than the "standard thought of American pizza" at this local mini-chain; while some foes fume that the prices are "higher than the product deserves", "quick" counter service compensates.

Kabobeesh *Pakistani*   24 | 9 | 17 | $14

University City | 4201 Chestnut St. (42nd St.) | 215-386-8081
"All those cab drivers cannot be wrong" assert admirers of this Pakistani in University City, where "awesome" kebabs and sha-warma platters are complemented by "amazing accoutrements" such as "flavorful" yogurt-mint chutney; surveyors seem to have overlooked a renovation to the "converted diner car", but "gentle-manly" service gets a shout-out.

Kabuki Japanese Restaurant *Japanese*   26 | 18 | 21 | $28

King of Prussia | 180 E. Dekalb Pike (bet. Henderson Rd. & Saulin Blvd.) | 610-878-9203
"First-rate sushi" draws diners to this "family-oriented" Japanese BYO "on the fringes of the King of Prussia mall"; the "redecorated interior" may address previous complaints about "low light", and while some critics find service "slow", others praise it as "efficient."

Kabul Afghan Cuisine *Afghan*   24 | 18 | 21 | $28

Old City | 106 Chestnut St. (bet. Front & 2nd Sts.) | 215-922-3676 | www.kabulafghancuisine.com
"One of the stars" of Old City eateries, this "comfortable" BYO serves up "satisfying portions" of Afghan fare in a "moody" but "authentic" interior; service that makes you feel like a "guest of the family" is another reason many deem it "a great change of pace."

Kanella ⓜ *Greek*   27 | 18 | 24 | $38

Washington Square West | 1001 Spruce St. (10th St.) | 215-922-1773 | www.kanellarestaurant.com
Konstantinos Pitsillides makes "fabulous things happen" in the kitchen of his "homelike" Greek-Cypriot BYO in Wash West, turn-ing out "soul-warming" seafood that "shakes up your taste buds" and dazzles "adventurous" diners; the "charming" spot is "sublime in its simplicity", bolstered by "attentive, efficient" service and a "great-value" Sunday meze prix fixe.

Karma Restaurant & Bar *Indian*   22 | 18 | 20 | $27

Old City | 114 Chestnut St. (bet. Front & 2nd Sts.) | 215-925-1444 | www.karmaphiladelphia.com
This Old City eatery is "worth a visit" for not only "delicious" Indian staples and a "wonderful" lunch buffet, but also "people-watching" at the bar (where a menu is available late) and the works of local artists hanging on the walls of the "modern and chic" room; "cour-teous" service and "reasonable prices" are additional pluses.

Kaya's Fusion Cuisine ⊠ⓜ *American*   ▽ 25 | 19 | 24 | $34

Havertown | 5 Brookline Blvd. (Darby Rd.) | 610-446-2780 | www.kayascuisine.com
The New American grub "prepared with inspiration and innova-tion" at this "family-run" Havertown BYO "never disappoints",

even when compared to city spots; the "nice" staff harmonizes with the "friendly" ambiance in the "cozy", "funky" storefront, making it an all-around "great find in the suburbs."

NEW KC Prime *Steak* 22 | 21 | 20 | $53
Warrington | 1580 Easton Rd. (Kelly Rd.) | 267-483-8075 | www.kcprimerestaurant.com

At this "comfortable" steakhouse in a former Houlihan's in Warrington, "decent" steaks "come with a salad and sides", so "you're not breaking the bank" to dine here, and the "all-you-can-eat" Sunday brunch also offers value; while a few report that the staff is "still getting its act together", others regard it as a "welcome new addition to the area."

KC's Alley ☻ *Pub Food* 19 | 16 | 20 | $20
Ambler | 10 W. Butler Ave. (Main St.) | 215-628-3300 | www.kc-alley.com

This "comfy", "low-key" Ambler pub "won't hit your wallet hard" and locals laud the "friendly" staff that handles families or big "get-togethers with friends" with equal aplomb; though middling scores suggest the American grub is "nothing special", "consistency" seems to be right up its alley.

Keating's *American* ▽ 22 | 25 | 22 | $36
Delaware Riverfront | Hyatt Regency at Penn's Landing | 201 S. Columbus Blvd. (Dock St.) | 215-521-6509 | www.keatingsrivergrill.com

For many it's all about the "amazing views" of the Delaware at this Traditional American in the Hyatt Regency at Penn's Landing, but "attentive" service, a "tranquil" vibe in the nautical-themed room and a terrace overlooking a marina also make it suitable for "date night"; P.S. it also serves a "nice breakfast buffet."

Kelly's Seafood *Continental/Seafood* 21 | 17 | 23 | $29
Northeast Philly | 9362 Old Bustleton Ave. (Welsh Rd.) | 215-969-5950 | www.kellysseafood.com

After more than a half-century, this "pure blue-collar" seafooder in Northeast Philly still "lives and breathes Philadelphia", with "pleasant" servers toting "reliable" platters (the usual fried oysters, broiled flounder) in somewhat "dark" environs; "bargain" prices and "great early-bird specials" help make it an "excellent value."

Kennett Restaurant Ⓜ☻ *American* 24 | 20 | 23 | $30
Queen Village | 848 S. 2nd St. (Christian St.) | 267-687-1426 | www.kennettrestaurant.com

"Locavore at its best" is how fans describe the "creative", "sustainable" New American fare at this "unassuming" Queen Village tap whose "superb" brick-oven pizza and "vegetarian options" help keep it "packed"; an "accommodating" staff helps you navigate a "fine-tuned beer list", and "good prices" seal the deal.

	FOOD	DECOR	SERVICE	COST

Khajuraho India *Indian*

15 | 14 | 14 | $26

Ardmore | Ardmore Plaza | 12 Greenfield Ave. (Lancaster Ave.) | 610-896-7200 | www.khajurahoindiacuisine.com

Sagging food scores suggest the new owners "have a lot of work to do" in restoring the luster of this Main Line Indian BYO that critics say has "gone downhill", though defenders insist it's doing "fine", with "tasty" fare and "timely" service; others remain "hopeful" and are "willing to give it another shot."

Khyber Pass Pub ◐ *Southern*

23 | 18 | 20 | $23

Old City | 56 S. 2nd St. (Chestnut St.) | 215-238-5888 | www.khyberpasspub.com

This "cozy" "dive bar" in Old City "transports you" to an "outdoor BBQ pit in the South" with "guilty pleasures" ("smoky meats that don't need their homemade sauce", "decadent" mac 'n' cheese) that "taste like home", backed by an "astonishing beer selection"; the staff may "take a minute to warm up", but its "punk (in a good way)" attitude goes over well with the "lively" clientele.

Kildare's ◐ *Pub Food*

20 | 21 | 21 | $22

West Chester | 18 W. Gay St. (High St.) | 610-431-0770
Manayunk | 4417 Main St. (Green Ln.) | 215-482-7242 | www.kildaresirishpub.com

The "cool Irish pub vibe" is the main selling point of these "watering holes" in Manayunk and West Chester with "crowds of recent grads" and "groups of friends" "meeting and mixing" or stepping onto the "killer dance floor"; "solid" pub grub and "friendly" service suffice, while "drinks specials" make this spot "affordable for anyone on a budget."

Kimberton Inn Ⓜ *American*

26 | 26 | 25 | $47

Kimberton | 2105 Kimberton Rd. (Hares Hill Rd.) | 610-933-8148 | www.kimbertoninn.com

"Cozy and elegant", this "quaint country inn" in Chester County conveys "pure luxury in a quiet, unassuming manner", offering a Traditional American menu that may yield "no surprises" but is "consistently outstanding", albeit "costly"; "courteous" service "without hovering" makes "date night" a "treat", while "piano music wafting in from the bar area" amplifies the feeling that you're "stepping back in time."

Kingdom of Vegetarians Restaurant *Chinese/Vegetarian*

▽ 25 | 18 | 25 | $20

Chinatown | 129 N. 11th St. (bet. Arch & Race Sts.) | 215-413-2290 | www.kingdomofvegetarians.com

The mock meat seems "so real you don't realize it's made of vegetable products" marvel fans of this tiny Chinatown "treat" with "so many vegetarian and vegan options" it's "hard to choose" (including dim sum that's "out of this world"); some say the "run-down" digs are not suitable for a "first date", but "low lighting makes blemishes forgivable" and "friendly" service also compensates.

	FOOD	DECOR	SERVICE	COST

Kinnaree ⓜ *French/Thai* ▽ 25 | 16 | 23 | $38

Horsham | 583 Horsham Rd. (Norristown Rd.) | 215-441-5514 |
www.kinnareepa.com

Tony Kanjanakorn's fans from his days at Alisa Cafe have followed
him to his white-tablecloth French-Thai BYO in an "unassuming"
Horsham strip mall, and promise "you will not be disappointed"
with the "lovely" staff and grub that "excites the palate"; the
Sunday–Thursday prix fixe dinners (three courses for $25, four for
$30) are "fantastic" values.

Kisso Sushi Bar *Japanese* 25 | 17 | 24 | $34

Old City | 205 N. 4th St. (Race St.) | 215-922-1770 |
www.kissosushibar.com

The "simple, straightforward" sushi "tastes like heaven" at Alex
Park's "cozy" Japanese BYO in Old City, where it feels like you've
been "invited into the test kitchen of a friendly chef"; there's an
"enjoyable atmosphere" in the "intimate" space, so "grab a bottle
of sake or Riesling and make it a date" – just "make sure to share" a
glass with the "personable" guys at the counter.

Kitchen Bar ❶ *American* 20 | 20 | 20 | $25

Abington | 1482 Old York Rd. (bet. Jericho Rd. & Wheatsheaf Ln.) |
215-576-9766 | www.kitchenbar.net

Is it a "sports bar or a diner"? – this "modern" American in
Abington attempts to cover all the bases with "accommodating"
service and "consistently good" grub (including a late-night menu)
at "moderate prices", plus an "upscale" setting aided by "TVs for
game-watching" and a "nice outdoor area when the weather is
cooperative"; naysayers think it's "trying too hard to be chic" and
runs "so noisy you can't hear yourself think."

Kite & Key ❶ *American* 18 | 17 | 19 | $22

Fairmount | 1836 Callowhill St. (19th St.) | 215-568-1818 |
www.thekiteandkey.com

"Friendly" bartenders "know what they're doing" at this Fairmount
"hot spot" where there's "plenty of beer to choose from" amid a
"top-notch rotating tap selection", which pairs with "fab" American pub grub at "reasonable prices"; the "neighborhood" vibe attracts a "down-to-earth" crowd, and while a few grouse that it gets
"frat-house" loud, many recommend it for a "drink or a light bite."

Knight House Restaurant ⓩ *American* 24 | 22 | 21 | $42

Doylestown | 96 W. State St. (Clinton St.) | 215-489-9900 |
www.theknighthouse.com

Spread out across a multiroom 19th-century building, this old
hatter's house is "worth a trip to Doylestown" to soak in the "nice
atmosphere" and historic appeal while chowing down on "good"
New American fare, including steak and sushi; though called "a bit
expensive" for the area, it's recommended for "meeting friends in
the summer and eating outside."

	FOOD	DECOR	SERVICE	COST

Koo Zee Doo *Portuguese*

25 | 19 | 24 | $40

Northern Liberties | 614 N. 2nd St. (Spring Garden St.) |
215-923-8080 | www.koozeedoo.com

David Gilberg and Carla Gonçalves are a "team to be reckoned
with" at their Northern Liberties Portuguese BYO, where "enormous" portions that "necessitate sharing" are a good "value" – and
it helps to be "adventurous"; expect to be "treated like family" in
an "intimate" space where you'll be "rubbing elbows with your
neighbors" as you're "transported" to "the midst of Lisbon."

Kopper Kettle Takeout ⊅ *Seafood*

23 | 11 | 22 | $23

Langhorne | 1985 Bridgetown Pike (Bristol Rd.) | 215-322-0993 |
www.thekopperkettle.com

You get "a lot for your money" at this circa-1973 seafooder in an
"old house" in Bucks, where you'll find "locals eating huge portions
of well-prepared food" (especially "satisfying" fried goodies like
shrimp and wings); it's run by "friendly" folks, but cognoscenti
caution that the usually "crowded, noisy" dining room won't "impress a date."

NEW Kris *Mediterranean*

- | - | - | |

South Philly | 1100 Federal St. (11th St.) | 215-468-0104 |
www.krisphilly.com

The "sophistication" of the small plates, pastas and entrees at
Kristian Leuzzi's South Philly Mediterranean keeps locals "coming back for more", while $5 apps please happy hour-goers – and
there's a "great choice of wines at reasonable prices" (including
half-price on Mondays); with wood floors and soft lighting, its
"classy" pub setting feels like a "quiet getaway."

La Belle Epoque Wine Bistro Ⓜ *French*

22 | 19 | 21 | $35

Media | 38 W. State St. (Olive St.) | 610-566-6808 |
www.labellebistro.com

"What they do well will please you" say fans of this "intimate
French corner bistro" in Downtown Media that gets a "thumbs-up"
for its "special" crêpe, "fabulous" brunch and "impressive" wine
list, available in two-oz. flights (BYO is also allowed, with a $10
corkage); "accommodating" service is also a "treat", although
some find it "spotty", and while the space is "tight", most consider
it "worth the squeeze."

NEW La Calaca Feliz *Mexican*

▽ 22 | 23 | 21 | $36

Fairmount | 2321 Fairmount Ave. (23rd St.) | 215-787-9930 |
www.lacalacafeliz.com

"Happy" is the apt translation for the mood at this "colorful" Fairmount
Mexican sibling of Cantina Feliz that provides an "upscale" Latin
"lift" to the neighborhood; amigos enjoy sitting beneath Day of the
Dead "murals" to "swoon" over Tim Spinner's "inventive" *comida*
and "long list of specialty cocktails" at the bar ("oh, those margaritas"), and while some find it "a little too pricey", many view it as
a "home run."

	FOOD	DECOR	SERVICE	COST

La Cena ⊠ *Italian* ▽ 26 | 27 | 28 | $33

Bensalem | 2233 Galloway Rd. (Hulmeville Rd.) | 215-639-9969 |
www.lacenarestaurant.com

"For a romantic evening with someone special", fans tout this
Bensalem Italian as a place "well worth going to", its strip-mall
location notwithstanding; "excellent food" and "attentive" service
are why it's "highly recommended" by fans, and "live entertainment" is another "nice touch."

La Collina *Italian* 23 | 20 | 22 | $52

Bala Cynwyd | 37 Ashland Ave. (Jefferson St.) | 610-668-1780 |
www.lacollina.us

Admirers of this "old-school", "upscale" Main Line Italian "hangout" "overlooking Belmont Hills" "love the view" and appreciate "servers in white coats" rolling out "classic" fare in "quaint"
surroundings; contrarians complain about "grumpy" service and
"over-the-top" prices for fare that's "nothing fancy or new", but for
others it remains a "good standby."

La Colombe Torrefaction *Coffeehouse* 24 | 19 | 21 | $9

Rittenhouse | 130 S. 19th St. (bet. Sansom & Walnut Sts.) |
215-563-0860
Avenue of the Arts | 1414 S. Penn Sq. (15th St.) | 215-977-7770 |
www.lacolombe.com

These homebrewed cafes on Rittenhouse Square and across from
City Hall are the "coffeehouse of choice for wannabe intellectuals"
(is that "Jean-Paul Sartre at the next table with an iPad?"); your
"hipster" experience comes with "joke-cracking" baristas (who are
"too cool" for some) pulling "cappuccino as good as in Italy", enjoyed in "inviting surroundings" along with tasty "baked goodies"
that are often "gone by lunch."

Lacroix at
The Rittenhouse *Eclectic* 27 | 27 | 28 | $77

Rittenhouse | Rittenhouse Hotel | 210 W. Rittenhouse Sq. (bet. Locust &
Walnut Sts.) | 215-790-2533 | www.lacroixrestaurant.com

When you want to "propose", "celebrate" or just "pamper yourself", devotees recommend the Rittenhouse Hotel's "top-drawer",
"special-occasion" Eclectic, set in a "cosseted perch" above
Rittenhouse Square; you can "traipse through" chef Jon Cichon's
kitchen where he creates "stunning flavors and textures", including
a "spectacular" Sunday brunch spread, while the "exceptional"
staff treats you like a "visiting dignitary" in a setting that "exudes
class, beauty and romance."

Ladder 15 ☾ *American* 19 | 18 | 18 | $28

Rittenhouse | 1528 Sansom St. (bet. 15th & 16th Sts.) |
215-964-9755 | www.ladder15philly.com

"Great happy-hour specials" are the chief draw of this New
American tavern in a former Rittenhouse firehouse, which also
gets shout-outs for "inventive twists" on "pub grub" since a chef
change in January 2012; to many, it's the "unofficial singles meat

market of Center City" with lines of "pretty young girls and frat boys" as it "goes from bustling to swamped" late at night.

La Famiglia Ristorante ☒ *Italian*   26 | 24 | 25 | $55

Old City | 8 S. Front St. (bet. Chestnut & Market Sts.) | 215-922-2803 | www.lafamiglia.com

For "old-school" dining in Old City, fans head to Giuseppe Sena's "elegant" Italian, where adherents swear you'll feel you've "stumbled into Italy" for grub that's "better then mom's (well, sometimes)", a "dessert cart" on weekends and a "telephone book-sized wine list", all served by a "professional" staff in a "beautiful dining room"; feel free to dress like "you are out to dinner and not going bowling."

La Fontana Della Citta *Italian*   21 | 18 | 21 | $34

Rittenhouse | 1701 Spruce St. (17th St.) | 215-875-9990 | www.lafontanadellacitta.com

"Sizable" portions of "tasty" Italian staples "hit the spot" at this "affordable" BYO option in Rittenhouse, although some shrug that it "won't amaze you, but won't disappoint", either; while the service is "cordial", some report that the servers "rush you out at the end of a meal" during peak times, making it a safe choice for those with tickets to the Kimmel Center.

La Fourno
Ristorante Trattoria ☒ⓜ *Italian*   25 | 18 | 24 | $29

South St. | 636 South St. (bet. 6th & 7th Sts.) | 215-627-9000

A "welcome respite from the carnival" that is South Street, this "unpretentious" Italian may look like "your run-of-the-mill pizza joint" from outside, but inside is a neighborhood "secret" – "homemade" pastas, "wonderful" veal parmigiana and "custom" brick-oven pies served in the "lovely" upstairs dining room where the "owner will often drop by to say hello"; BYO on Tuesday and Fridays nights ramps up the value.

Lai Lai Garden *Asian*   23 | 24 | 24 | $28

Blue Bell | 1144 Dekalb Pike (Skippack Pike) | 610-277-5988 | www.lailaigarden.com

Back on its game (as indicated by a rise in scores), this Blue Bell Pan-Asian delivers "consistently" tasty fare from an "astounding" menu comprising sushi, Thai, Vietnamese, Chinese and Korean; and "polite" service and "beautifully decorated" environs help make it a "family favorite for celebrations."

La Locanda Del Ghiottone ⓜ🕾 *Italian*   25 | 18 | 22 | $32

Old City | 130 N. 3rd St. (Cherry St.) | 215-829-1465

"You can smell the garlic a block away" from this "attitude"-filled Italian BYO in Old City, where "made-to-order" "classics" (mushroom crêpes, mussels) are slung with "panache" by "bossy", "colorful" waiters who are quick to "dish out food as well as quips"; "you really feel like part of the family here", so "don't expect a quick meal" and don't forget the cash.

	FOOD	DECOR	SERVICE	COST

La Na Thai
French Cuisine *French/Thai*

▽ 23 | 18 | 20 | $27

Media | 33 W. State St. (bet. Jackson & Olive Sts.) | 610-892-7787
The kitchen at this "cozy", "affordable" French-Thai BYO in
Downtown Media "balances spicy and savory tastes" so deftly you
may "wish it were acceptable to lick your plate"; some describe
the service as "earnest but not especially polished", and while a
few feel it's "running on automatic pilot" after 12 years, for most it
"rarely disappoints."

The Landing Restaurant and Bar *American*

21 | 22 | 20 | $34

New Hope | 22 N. Main St. (Bridge St.) | 215-862-5711 |
www.landingrestaurant.com
Thanks to its "prime location" on the Delaware, this "cozy",
"scenic" New Hope "tourist magnet" has drawn alfresco diners
since the '70s for a "feast" of "terrific views" from the deck and a
"varied" New American menu providing both "pub meals and fancy
dinners"; still, critics note "there's not a lot of creativity" to the
cooking, and feel you pay a "premium" for the setting.

Landmark Americana
Tap & Grill ● *American*

20 | 21 | 20 | $23

University City | 3333 Market St. (34th St.) | 215-222-4500 |
West Chester | 158 W. Gay St. (Darlington St.) | 610-701-9900
Wayne | 629 W. Lancaster Ave. (Old Eagle School Rd.) | 610-995-1001
www.landmarkamericana.com
"Two words: college kids" describe these "lively" pubs in Glassboro,
West Chester and University City that satisfy cravings for burgers, wings and beer while "watching the game", plus "awesome
daily specials" such as "quizzo nights"; to critics they're "way too
loud" and staffed by servers "with an attitude", though the Wayne
branch opened post-Survey with a Main Line family focus.

L'Angolo Ristorante Ⓜ *Italian*

26 | 16 | 24 | $35

South Philly | 1415 W. Porter St. (Broad St.) | 215-389-4252 |
www.salentorestaurant.com
It's a "tight squeeze", but "no one seems to care" at Davide
Faenza's BYO on a South Philly corner, where the "authentic" Italian
grub is "incredible from start to finish" and "flirtatious Italian
stallion" servers "make you feel like family"; "at least you know the
kitchen is clean", since you walk through it, reinforcing impressions that it's "like dining in Auntie's house" (assuming she's a
"serious" chef).

La Pergola *Eastern Euro./Mideastern*

23 | 14 | 20 | $24

Jenkintown | 726 West Ave. (Johnson St.) | 215-884-7204
"Reliable" Mediterranean fare augmented by "delicious" Eastern
European Jewish "comfort food" comes at "reasonable prices" at
this Jenkintown BYO; "polite", "efficient" service is another plus,
and enthusiasts advise "don't let the outdated '80s decor deter
you", otherwise you'll "miss out on an absolute treat."

NEW La Petite Dauphine ⊘ Dessert/French | – | – | – | I |

Rittenhouse | 2029 Walnut St. (21st St.) | 267-324-5244 |
www.lapetitedauphine.com

Old-fashioned luxury is the mission statement of this spare yet
sumptuous French salon in a Rittenhouse walk-up brownstone,
which starts the day with coffee and pastry and then segues into
light fare (salads, sandwiches); the *pièce de résistance* are the
cheese and dessert carts, making for an affordable BYO feast.

Larry's Steaks ● Cheesesteaks   ∇ 25 | 17 | 20 | $13 |

Wynnefield | 2457 N. 54th St. (Overbrook Ave.) | 215-879-1776
There's "no ambiance to speak of" at this somewhat "overlooked" Wynnefield sandwichery, just "juicy, perfectly cooked
meat" on a roll, including the signature 'belly filler', whose
"name surpasses expectations"; "fast service" and "late-night"
hours also help make it a "local delight" for residents and "St.
Joe's students and staff."

Las Bugambilias Mexican   24 | 20 | 21 | $34 |

South St. | 148 South St. (2nd St.) | 215-922-3190
"Every bite" of Carlos Molina's "refreshingly authentic"
Veracruz-style cuisine is "*delicioso*" declare fans of his "charming" South Street Mexican, and though you should "be prepared
to get cozy with your neighbors", most insist it's "worth the
squeeze"; while some sniff about "pedestrian" service, others
groove to the "Latin music" and "Mexican movie posters and
creative table settings" that set the "lively" mood (with help
from "inventive margaritas").

LaScala's Italian   23 | 22 | 23 | $33 |

Washington Square West | 615 Chestnut St. (7th St.) |
215-928-0900 | www.lascalasphilly.com

NEW LaScala's Pronto Italian

Fairmount | 1501 Spring Garden St. (15th St.) | 215-751-0200 |
www.lascalaspronto.com

"Within a stone's throw of Independence Hall" in Wash West, Rob
LaScala's "classic red-sauce Italian" delights both "hungry tourists
and local office workers", usually "sending them out the door with
a doggy bag"; tabs that are "easy on the pocketbook" and an "inviting" setting give fans that "warm and fuzzy feeling"; P.S. the new
Fairmount sibling opened post-Survey.

Las Cazuelas ⓜ Mexican   24 | 19 | 21 | $29 |

Northern Liberties | 426 W. Girard Ave. (bet. 4th & Lawrence Sts.) |
215-351-9144 | www.lascazuelas.net

"Honest" Mexican "with a gourmet twist" and "low prices" are
the hallmarks of this "pioneer" BYO in Northern Liberties, where
"greetings" from the "happy" staff fill the "cozy", "authentic" setting; if you bring a "bottle of tequila and let them mix you a pitcher
of margs", you'll "feel like you're on a beach somewhere."

	FOOD	DECOR	SERVICE	COST

Las Margaritas *Mexican* — 24 | 22 | 22 | $26

Northeast Philly | 2538 Welsh Rd. (Roosevelt Blvd.) | 215-969-6600
Southampton | 765 2nd St. Pike (Street Rd.) | 215-354-4445
Living up to their name, these Mex twins in Lower Bucks and Northeast Philly are "margarita heaven" thanks to "awesome" drinks that go along with a "huge menu" of "oversized entrees" at "great prices", all worthy of a night out with the "family" or "girl-friends"; though it can get "loud" in the "bright", "festive" settings, "friendly" service helps compensate.

La Stalla *Italian* — 23 | 22 | 22 | $38

Newtown | 18 Swamp Rd. (Eagle Rd.) | 215-579-8301 | www.lastallarestaurant.com
The "Newtown/Yardley crowd" and "suburban *Soprano* wannabes" converge on this "fancy" Italian in a converted barn to share "fam-ily-style" platters of "consistent, fresh" fare served by "attentive", "handsome waiters" (who some say are "slow"); regulars recom-mend the "enclosed porch" and, for a "real show", the outdoor bar where the "Desperate Housewives of Bucks County" and "40-plus singles" gather.

La Stanza Ⓜ *Italian* — ▽ 26 | 22 | 21 | $40

South Philly | 2001 W. Oregon Ave. (20th St.) | 215-271-0801 | www.lastanzapa.com
The *Restaurant: Impossible* treatment "did this place well" say fans of this South Philly trattoria that "always delivers", with "gigantic" portions of "tasty", "upscale" fare served by a staff that "really knows the menu" in a "pretty" setting; don't be surprised if you have "no room for dessert."

La Viola Ⓜ⪚ *Italian* — 24 | 16 | 23 | $32

Rittenhouse | 253 S. 16th St. (bet. Locust & Spruce Sts.) | 215-735-8630
"Reliable" pastas at "amazing prices" and "attentive" service make this cash-only Rittenhouse Italian BYO a "bargain"; along with its sibling across the street, it's "perfect for pre-theater", and while some recommend "earplugs" for the "noise level" in a room so "cramped" some quip all "40-odd patrons have to take turns breathing", most report "leaving with a full belly and a smile."

La Viola Ovest ⪚ *Italian* — 26 | 20 | 24 | $34

Rittenhouse | 252 S. 16th St. (bet. Locust & Spruce Sts.) | 215-735-8630
"Always get the special" and "bring earplugs" are the tips from fans of this "charming", cash-only Italian BYO "offshoot" of La Viola across the street in Rittenhouse, where you're "practically sitting on your neighbor's lap" and may need "a variation of Occupy Wall Street's human microphone" to order; "inventive" grub, "reason-able" prices and "friendly", "welcoming" service make it "a place to go to over and over again."

Le Bec Fin ⌧ *French*

-	-	-	VE

Rittenhouse | 1523 Walnut St. (bet. 15th & 16th Sts.) |
215-567-1000 | www.lebecfin.com

This French landmark has been revived under new ownership
(Nicolas Fanucci, a LBF alum and the former general manager of
the French Laundry) and a new chef (Walter Abrams, ex French
Laundry) who offer go-for-baroque $150 tasting menus (for omni-
vores and vegetarians) in roomier but no less sumptuous quarters;
the downstairs bar has been warmed up and named Chez Georges
in honor of founder Georges Perrier.

Le Castagne *Italian*

24	23	23	$50

Rittenhouse | 1920 Chestnut St. (bet. 19th & 20th Sts.) |
215-751-9913 | www.lecastagne.com

"*Si mangia bene*" sizes up impressions of La Famiglia's "hip, yet
elegant" "little sister" in Rittenhouse whose kitchen adds a "sophisticated" "touch" to Italian cuisine; though some find it "a bit
expensive", most "feel right at home" thanks to a "courteous" staff
and a "romantic", "candlelit" setting with "good table separation."

Lee How Fook Ⓜ *Chinese*

24	12	19	$22

Chinatown | 219 N. 11th St. (Spring St.) | 215-925-7266 |
www.leehowfook.com

This family-owned Chinatown Cantonese does "all the usual
dishes from your corner Chinese joint, but so much better", and at
"rock-bottom prices"; it seems like you place your order and then
"get served 10 seconds later", and many think the place "looks
better" after a renovation, as the next generation took over, though
everything "tastes like grandma is still cooking it."

Lee's Hoagie House *Sandwiches*

24	13	21	$13

Bala Cynwyd | 214 Rock Hill Rd. (bet. Belmont
Ave. & Conshohocken State Rd.) | 610-664-5900 |
www.leeshoagiehouse.com

Abington | 1656 Old York Rd. (bet. Edge Hill & Old Welsh Rds.) |
215-659-3322 | www.leeshoagiesabington.com

Bensalem | 1871 St. Rd. (Hulmeville Rd.) | 215-245-1500 |
www.leesbensalem.com

Horsham | 870 Easton Rd. (Maple Ave.) | 215-674-8000 |
www.leeshoagiehouse.com

East Norriton | 2896 Dekalb Pike (Germantown Pike) |
610-279-0800 | www.leeseastnorriton.com

Northeast Philly | 7328 Castor Ave. (Bleigh Ave.) | 215-742-8111 |
www.leeshoagiehouse.com

University City | 4034 Walnut St. (41st St.) | 215-387-0905 |
www.leeshoagiehouse.com

This "old reliable" hoagie chain is a "tasty value" because they
"never skimp on the meat" (a "half is the size of a regular" in many
other places) and the counter staff "knows how to hustle" if you're
"on your way to a game", but is cool with your "kids racing around"
the shop; fans attest "it's worth going out of your way."

	FOOD	DECOR	SERVICE	COST

Legal Sea Foods *Seafood*   22 | 20 | 21 | $41

King of Prussia | King of Prussia Mall | 680 W. Dekalb Pike (Mall Blvd.) | 610-265-5566 | www.legalseafoods.com

"Top-quality" seafood, including "chowda", "lobster rolls" and "real fried clams with bellies", is "done just right" at this "faithful renditions" of the Boston chain in King of Prussia; some critics find it "overpriced" and demur on the "functional" digs, but a "relaxing bar" and "professional" service compensate.

Lemon Grass Thai Restaurant *Thai*   21 | 17 | 18 | $23

University City | 3630 Lancaster Ave. (36th St.) | 215-222-8042 | www.lemongrassphila.com

Penn students crave this "comfortable", long-running University City Thai for a "peaceful" night out or "meal between classes"; "quick" service, "comfortable" surroundings and the "Evil Jungle Princess" (spicy chicken) all make it "worth the trip."

NEW Lemon Hill *American*   ∇ 23 | 20 | 23 | $33

Fairmount | 747 N. 25th St. (Aspen St.) | 215-232-2299 | www.lemonhillphilly.com

"Delicious" brick-oven American locavore fare and "outstanding cocktails" from Mike Welsh of the Franklin Mortgage & Investment Co. "hit the right notes" at this "beautiful" corner tap in Fairmount; fans call it a "much-needed addition" to the neighborhood, though its "upscale" ambitions come with "Center City prices."

Le Pain Quotidien *Bakery/Belgian*   20 | 18 | 17 | $22

Rittenhouse | 1425 Walnut St. (15th St.) | 215-751-0570
Washington Square West | 801 Walnut St. (8th St.) | 215-253-3114
www.lepainquotidien.us

A "little bit of Brussels" has sprouted in Rittenhouse Square and Washington Square as this Belgian-based boulangerie's "beautifully prepared" sandwiches, salads and bistro plates and "discreet yet efficient" service make for a "good mother/daughter outing or lunch with the ladies"; critics find the menu a bit "precious", the portions "stingy" and the "seats at the communal table" a "pain."

Le Viet *Vietnamese*   24 | 24 | 23 | $30

Bella Vista | 1019 S. 11th St. (bet. Kimball St. & Washington Ave.) | 215-463-1570 | www.levietrestaurant.com

Bruce Cao's "inventive", "dress-up" Vietnamese in Bella Vista showcases a "strikingly modern" "NY ambiance", with "modern glass-tile walls" in lieu of "your usual hanging lanterns", and grub that's "just as sleek"; "helpful" service is another plus, and while it skews "expensive compared with the mom-and-pop places", it's nonetheless a "breath of fresh air" for many.

Le Virtù *Italian*   27 | 22 | 23 | $49

East Passyunk | 1927 E. Passyunk Ave. (bet. McKean & Mifflin Sts.) | 215-271-5626 | www.levirtu.com

"Craveable fresh pasta", "housemade salumi" – "you cannot wrong with anything" on the "rustic" menu at this "casual" yet "elegant"

Abruzzese "destination" in East Passyunk where "the pig head sits in the kitchen in full view" to remind that this is "not your standard red-sauce Italian"; while some think the "servers need more personality", others "feel well cared for", and the "lovely" outdoor garden is an added bonus.

Limoncello Ristorante & Caterers *Italian*   26 | 22 | 23 | $37

West Chester | 9 N. Walnut St. (Gay St.) | 610-436-6230 | www.limoncellowc.com

"Outstanding" Italian "classics" and an "off-the-charts-great" $9.95 weekday lunch buffet bring "crowds" into this "small", "boisterous" West Chester "hot spot" where "nice folks work their tail off to get it right"; devotees find it "too bad that so many people know about it", making "reservations a must."

Little Fish BYOB *Seafood*   28 | 16 | 23 | $44

Bella Vista | 746 S. 6th St. (Fitzwater St.) | 267-455-0172 | www.littlefishbyob.com

Making a big "splash" despite its "tiny" (22 seats) dimensions, Chadd Jenkins' "solid" BYO Bella Vista seafooder hooks fish lovers with its "creative" chalkboard menu and a "superior" Sunday tasting menu full of "fabulous surprises"; fans describe it as a "perfect little hole-in-the-wall" with a "quaint" "Village feel" and "helpful" staff, urging "make reservations early" – "you won't be sorry, if you can get in."

Little Pete's ● *Diner*   19 | 12 | 19 | $17

Rittenhouse | 219 S. 17th St. (Chancellor St.) | 215-545-5508
Fairmount | The Philadelphian | 2418 Fairmount Ave. (bet. 24th & 25th Sts.) | 215-232-5001

Dishing out "big taste at a little price", this "homestyle" diner duo is "as close as you can get to a NY coffee shop without the trip"; the "after-club" crowd with "late-night munchies" packs the cash-only, 24/7 Rittenhouse original while the Fairmount sibling caters to a similarly quirky "cast of characters" – all served by "efficient" though "grumpy" waitresses.

Local 44 ● *American*   20 | 19 | 19 | $20

University City | 4333 Spruce St. (44th St.) | 215-222-2337 | www.local44beerbar.com

The "amazing beer selection" (20 on tap) is a "winner every time" at this "laid-back" University City "haunt", which draws "festive crowds" that "can be a bit crazy on weekends"; the "seasonal" New American fare can be a "home run or swinging miss" (though the vegan seitan Reuben sandwich is the stuff of "dreams") and impressions of the staff run the gamut from "friendly" to "West Philly pretentious."

NEW Loco Pez ●⊄ *Mexican*   ∇ 29 | 23 | 24 | $21

Fishtown | 2401 E. Norris St. (Susquehanna Ave.) | 267-886-8061 | www.locopez.com

"The secret is out" about this "great little Mexibar" tucked into Fishtown, where a "friendly" staff serves up "cheap", "yummy"

Cali-style "mini-tacos" and "spot-on" margaritas to a "sociable" "hipster" clientele; there's "just the right amount of energy" in the "retro" rec-room setting replete with Pez dispensers, a fish tank and pinball machine, making for "good times" all around.

Lolita ⊅ Mexican   26 | 19 | 20 | $39

Washington Square West | 106 S. 13th St. (bet. Chestnut & Sansom Sts.) | 215-546-7100 | www.lolitabyob.com

"Bring your own tequila", order housemade mixers and watch "the fun begin" at this "scene-driven", cash-only Mex BYO in Wash West proffering "well-prepared" carne asada and other delights, served by an "efficient", though some say "unfriendly", staff; it gets "packed" and "loud" in the "tight space", but for fans, that "just makes the party better"; P.S. there's an $18-per-person food minimum and automatic 20% tip on parties of five or more.

London Grill ● American   19 | 17 | 19 | $31

Fairmount | 2301 Fairmount Ave. (23rd St.) | 215-978-4545 | www.londongrill.com

Fairmount's "middle-of-the-road" New American is a "hybrid of a bistro and pub", delivering "craft beers, local color and good fare" in an "intimate" setting, though some report a "harried sense of 'hurry up' during busy times"; outdoor dining is "enjoyable" and the addition of Paris Wine Bar next door allows the menu to pair with Pennsylvania vino.

Lourdas Greek Taverna Ⓜ⊅ Greek   22 | 17 | 22 | $36

Bryn Mawr | 50 N. Bryn Mawr Ave. (Lancaster Ave.) | 610-520-0288 | www.lourdasgreektaverna.com

"As tasty as a trip to the Greek islands and without the default risks" quip admirers of this "small", "unpretentious" Bryn Mawr BYO whose "reliable" Hellenic specialties are "worth seeking out" and served at an "unrushed" pace; a few dissenters sound off that cash-only is "a bit of a drag" and caution "be prepared to share your neighbor's conversation" in the "tiny" space.

Lovash Indian Cuisine Indian   ▽ 21 | 18 | 21 | $24

South St. | 236 South St. (bet. American & 3rd Sts.) | 215-925-3881 | www.lovashrestaurant.com

"Spicy is definitely spicy" at this "cute" South Street Indian BYO serving "freshly prepared" "home cooking", including veggies with a "snap" to them; a "gracious" staff keeps the plates moving in the "casual" setting, making it a "go-to place" for many; P.S. it's open for lunch only on weekends.

Lucky Lab Tavern Pub Food   ▽ 22 | 19 | 22 | $27

Royersford | 312 N. Lewis Rd. (Royersford Rd.) | 610-948-8088 | www.luckylabtavern.com

This cozy, lodgelike Cajun pub in Royersford run by two Louisiana expats maintains its beer-focused past with 26 craft brews on tap while picking up a dog theme (as in decor and weekly "yappy hours" on the patio); parents appreciate the kid-friendly approach, while couples will warm to the two romantic fireplaces.

Luigi's Pizza Fresca *Italian/Pizza* | 23 | 16 | 20 | $12 |

Fairmount | 2401 Fairmount Ave. (24th St.) |
215-769-8888 | www.luigispizzafresca.com
See review in the New Jersey Suburbs Directory.

Macaroni's Restaurant Ⓜ *Italian* | 25 | 23 | 25 | $40 |

Northeast Philly | 9315 Old Bustleton Ave. (bet. Ambassador St. &
Welsh Rd.) | 215-464-3040 | www.macaronis.net
With new decor and an expanded dining area, now you're just eating
"elbows" and not rubbing them at this "top-notch Italian ristorante" in
Northeast Philly that insiders dub an "unexpected little gem" with
"high-quality" grub; it's a "bit pricey for the neighborhood", but the
"spectacular" staff does a "heck of a job" for the "whole family."

Mac's Tavern ◑ *American* | - | - | - | I |

Old City | 226 Market St. (bet. 2nd & 3rd Sts.) | 267-324-5507 |
www.macstavern.com
If everyone seems a bit bright and cheery at this Old City watering
hole, that might be because it's part owned by Rob McElhenney
and Kaitlin Olson, stars of the TV comedy *It's Always Sunny in
Philadelphia*; the look suggests 'Philly dive bar' but the menu runs
more toward gastropub, offering a selection of sandwiches, wings
and five kinds of topped fries, all to pair with 17 beers on tap and
dozens by the bottle.

Mad Mex ◑ *Mexican* | 21 | 21 | 19 | $21 |

University City | 3401 Walnut St. (Sansom St.) | 215-382-2221
NEW **Willow Grove** | 2862 W. Moreland Rd. (Lawnton Rd.) |
267-495-5000
www.madmex.com
"Solid" Mexican grub with "vegan-friendly options" anchors the experience at this "quirky" cantina chain with outposts in University City
and Willow Grove whose "witty attitude" extends from the "strong,
flavorful" "Big Azz margaritas" to the "graffitilike art on the walls";
though "service takes a beating" during prime times, it's "best to
relax and not take anything too seriously."

MaGerks Pub & Grill ◑ *Pub Food* | 20 | 18 | 19 | $22 |

Fort Washington | 582 S. Bethlehem Pike (Rte. 73) |
215-948-3329 | www.magerks.com
The Eastern Montco crowd favors this "decent little pub" in Fort
Washington to "grab a beer and unwind" over a "varied menu" of
"typical grill dishes"; detractors say it's "hit or miss" - despite "lots
of staff, you can never get a drink when you need one."

Maggiano's Little Italy *Italian* | 24 | 23 | 24 | $35 |

Chinatown | 1201 Filbert St. (12th St.) | 215-567-2020
King of Prussia | King of Prussia Mall | 205 Mall Blvd. (Gulph Rd.) |
610-992-3333
www.maggianos.com
"Go hungry" or "bring a second stomach" to this "lively", "family-
style" Italian chain dishing out "tasty", "familiar" dishes in "portions meant for sumo wrestlers" that'll "turn the button on your

pants into a lethal weapon"; "helpful" service helps make up for "long waits" and "elbow-to-elbow" seating, and while some deem the "Americanized" eats "nothing special", others "can't pasta up" the "mountains" of "above-par" fare at "reasonable prices."

Maggio's ● *Italian/Pizza*   22 | 21 | 22 | $27

Southampton | Hampton Sq. | 400 2nd St. Pike (bet. Madison & Rozel Aves.) | 215-322-7272 | www.maggiosrestaurant.com
Whether for "family get-togethers" or "breakfast on the weekend", there's "something for everyone" on the menu at this "crowded" Bucks County bistro boasting "consistent", moderately priced Italian fare (including "tasty" pizzas) and "polite" service; the adjoining sports bar "with every beer you can think of" and a spacious special-event ballroom set it apart from the usual "neighborhood" hangout; P.S. there's takeout and delivery too.

Majolica Ⓜ *American*   28 | 21 | 25 | $49

Phoenixville | 258 Bridge St. (bet. Gay & Main Sts.) | 610-917-0962 | www.majolicarestaurant.com
Cognoscenti urge you to "let your bouche be amused" by chef Andrew Deery's "artistic" treatment of New American cuisine – "amazing flavors not usually found in the suburbs" – at the pricey, "trendsetting" Phoenixville BYO he runs with his wife, Sarah Johnson; between the "lovely, intimate" dining room and "warm" service with "no rush", most say it's an "unpretentious indulgence" that's "worth the trip" for a "special night out."

Makiman Sushi *Japanese/Korean*   21 | 16 | 20 | $25

Northeast Philly | 7324 Oxford Ave. (Rising Sun Ave.) | 215-722-8800
Washington Square West | 1326 Spruce St. (bet. Broad & Juniper Sts.) | 215-546-0180
"Consistently fresh", "filling" sushi, Korean fare and "a ton of vegetarian options" are "great value" "for the price" at these "middle-of-the-road" Japanese-Korean siblings where you'll get "great service with a smile" in homey surrounds; an "all-you-can-eat" deal on Mondays and BYO with no corkage make them a "destination" for budget-conscious fans.

Mal's American Diner *American*   ▽ 20 | 16 | 20 | $16

Skippack | 4006 Skippack Pike (bet. Collegeville & Mensch Rds.) | 610-584-0900
This "basic, basic, basic" '50s-style diner in Skippack does American "staples like meatloaf" well, but it's a "local favorite" for breakfast, whether first thing in the morning or at dinnertime; solid service accommodates BYO, and the patio's a plus during pleasant weather.

Mama Palma's Ⓜ🖘 *Italian*   23 | 16 | 20 | $22

Rittenhouse | 2229 Spruce St. (23rd St.) | 215-735-7357
For an "inexpensive option" near Fitler Square, surveyors "love" the "scrumptious", "brick-oven" pizzas, "solid" beer selection and "comfortable" indoor and sidewalk seating at this "cute", cash-only Italian staffed by an "attentive" crew; while "deciding" on a pie isn't easy, the only real "challenge" is "finding parking."

	FOOD	DECOR	SERVICE	COST

Mamma Maria
Ristorante Italiano *Italian*
▽ 24 | 22 | 25 | $49

East Passyunk | 1637 E. Passyunk Ave. (bet. Morris & Tasker Sts.) | 215-463-6884 | www.mammamaria.info

"Like Sunday dinner at your Italian grandma's house", you'd better "come hungry" to this "legit", "old-world" Italian on East Passyunk where the $55, seven-course prix fixe will "leave you stuffed" (relax, à la carte is an option); "what more could you ask for – oh, a tray of free drinks at the end? you got it!"

Manayunk
Brewery & Restaurant ❷ *Pub Food*
22 | 22 | 21 | $29

Manayunk | 4120 Main St. (Shurs Ln.) | 215-482-8220 | www.manayunkbrewery.com

"Attention, beer lovers" – it's hard to top the seasonal rotation of "new, interesting" brews (some made in-house) served by "attentive" bartenders at this "lively", "cavernous" Manayunk pub whose diverse, "decent" menu encompasses "creative pizza options" and even "sushi" (meanwhile, critics who scorn the "mediocre" mid-priced eats simply advise "start drinking"); while the canal-side deck is "what makes this place" for many, frequent "live music" is certainly a bonus.

Mandarin Garden *Chinese*
24 | 18 | 22 | $25

Willow Grove | 91 York Rd. (Davisville Rd.) | 215-657-3993 | www.mandaringardenrestaurant.com

"Save the trip to Chinatown" confide cognoscenti of this Willow Grove Chinese, because the "delicious" chow here is the "golden standard" for the 'burbs and "inspired" specials keep things fresh; "friendly, efficient" service, "inexpensive" tabs and "pleasant", traditional decor make it a "dependable" favorite.

Maoz Vegetarian *Mideastern/Vegetarian*
23 | 13 | 18 | $11

Washington Square West | 1115 Walnut St. (11th St.) | 215-922-3409
South St. | 248 South St. (3rd St.) | 215-625-3500
www.maozusa.com

Not only do these "cheap, quick" South Street and Wash West branches of a Holland-based Mideast-Vegetarian chain "pack a lot of flavor" into their falafel sandwiches and salads, they let you "load" 'em up with "a variety of toppings" from their "gloriously multicolored salad bar"; "don't expect to be sitting in comfort", but most treat this as an "eat and run" anyway.

Marathon Grill *American*
21 | 18 | 19 | $23

Rittenhouse | 121 S. 16th St. (Sansom St.) | 215-569-3278
Rittenhouse | 1818 Market St. (bet. 18th & 19th Sts.) | 215-561-1818
Marathon on the Square *American*
Rittenhouse | 1839 Spruce St. (19th St.) | 215-731-0800
www.eatmarathon.com

Everyone from "daters to families with children" finds something on the "easy-on-the-budget" New American "comfort-food" menu at this "low-key" local chain whose cred is buttressed by "produce from its own urban farm"; many in Center City consider it "the closest thing to home" with "classy-industrial" looks and "smiles" at the door, though a few complain about "slacking" service.

Marco Polo Ristorante & Bar *Italian* | 22 | 18 | 23 | $40 |

Elkins Park | Elkins Park Sq. | 8080 Old York Rd. (Church Rd.) | 215-782-1950 | www.mymarcopolo.com

An "attentive" staff keeps the cocktails flowing and the patrons happy at this "dependable", "bistro-like" Italian in Elkins Park whose kitchen delivers "quality" while juggling a "sizable number of specials each night" for a "neighborhood" crowd "mostly over 40"; "you can tell it's good when it's busy every night."

Margaret Kuo's *Chinese/Japanese* | 24 | 22 | 21 | $38 |

Wayne | 175 E. Lancaster Ave. (Louella Ave.) | 610-688-7200 | www.margaretkuos.com

A "destination" in Wayne, Margaret Kuo's "beautiful" bi-level Asian teams "tasty" Japanese upstairs with impressively "authentic" Chinese downstairs, and the "care taken to craft the dishes is evident in every bite"; meanwhile, critics urge blocking off a "big chunk of time" in case service is "slow" and warn that "modest portion sizes" can make midrange tabs feel "pretty high."

Margaret Kuo's Mandarin *Chinese/Japanese* | 24 | 22 | 21 | $30 |

Malvern | 190 Lancaster Ave. (Malin Rd.) | 610-647-5488 | www.margaretkuos.com

With "well-prepared" Chinese and Japanese cuisine that's surely "above what you expect to get so far from Chinatown", Margaret Kuo's "popular" Malvern BYO promises an "upscale" experience at moderate tabs (and for folks on a budget, the $8.95 lunch buffet is an "awesome" find); set inside "unpretentious" strip-mall digs, it's a surprisingly "elegant", "well-furnished set of rooms" that suits "groups" and "families", though a few are "turned off" by "slow service and repeated Chinese Muzak."

Margaret Kuo's Media *Chinese/Japanese* | 25 | 23 | 23 | $34 |

Media | 6 W. State St. (Jackson St.) | 610-892-0115 | www.margaretkuos.com

"Impressive," "gourmet"-quality Sino-Japanese fare (including "superb" sushi) anchors Margaret Kuo's "sophisticated", "relaxing" Downtown Media outpost where you could "swear you're in the city" thanks to "professional" service and a revamped setting that combines the "traditional" with "modern, chic" touches; while it merits a "special occasion", the "moderate" prices are still manageable for "midweek" dinner.

Margaret Kuo's Peking *Chinese/Japanese* | 25 | 23 | 24 | $30 |

Media | Granite Run Mall | 1067 W. Baltimore Pike (Middletown Rd.) | 610-566-4110 | www.margaretkuos.com

"Don't let the locale scare you" explain adherents who've been "spoiled for years" at Margaret Kuo's flagship in Media's Granite Run Mall, where a "friendly" staff delivers "high-level" Chinese "delicacies" and "refined" Japanese fare; while the atmosphere is "relaxing", the "quiet" is occasionally broken by a "gong" that sounds for "yet another Peking duck" coming out to the table – indeed, that's hardly "mall food."

Marigold Kitchen ⓂAmerican
26 | 21 | 24 | $47

University City | 501 S. 45th St. (Larchwood Ave.) | 215-222-3699 | www.marigoldkitchenbyob.com

"Bring on the bubbles" declare devotees of this "special-occasion" BYO New American in University City, where chef Rob Halpern's "unreal" experiments in "molecular gastronomy" yield a "surprising succession" of "amuse-bouches" between courses; the "patient" staff "knows every detail of the food", and given the "romantic" setting in a "charming Victorian home", "you won't want to rush."

Marrakesh ⌿ Moroccan
24 | 23 | 22 | $37

South St. | 517 S. Leithgow St. (South St.) | 215-925-5929 | www.marrakesheastcoast.com

Use your "smart phone" to find the "hidden" door of this Moroccan mainstay off South Street where the decor evokes an "exotic vacation" and the staff's "hospitality" makes it a "pleasure" to indulge in a "relaxed", seven-course, $25 "feast"; "you eat with your hands from common dishes", so "go with someone whose company you really enjoy" for a "break from the same old, same old."

Marra's Ⓜ Italian
22 | 15 | 18 | $24

East Passyunk | 1734 E. Passyunk Ave. (Moore St.) | 215-463-9249 | www.marrasone.com

"Comforting", "classic red-gravy" specialties "from A to Z" fill the menu at this "old-school" Italian that's been slinging "brick-oven pizzas" on East Passyunk since 1927; nostalgic "natives" know what to expect: "basic" "bargains" that "make looking for a parking place worth the aggravation" and "casual-cum-rude" service.

Marsha Brown Creole Kitchen Creole/Southern
25 | 26 | 24 | $55

New Hope | 15 S. Main St. (Bridge St.) | 215-862-7044 | www.marshabrownrestaurant.com

For those seeking to "impress guests" or a "date", the "cathedral ceilings" and stained-glass windows of a "former church" create a "religiously grand" "respite from Main Street" at this "pricey" New Hope Creole-Southern whose "delicious" comestibles have devotees "cleaning the plate"; while most appreciate the "informative" service, a few prefer the more "relaxed" vibe when "sitting at the bar" for "oysters on the half shell."

Masamoto Asian Grill & Sushi Bar Asian
▽ 28 | 18 | 23 | $41

Glen Mills | Keystone Plaza Shopping Ctr. | 1810 Wilmington Pike (Baltimore Pike) | 610-358-5538 | www.masamotosushi.com

Even jaded West Coast transplants are impressed with the "superb" sushi bar at this colorful but "unassuming" Pan-Asian BYO in a "run-of-the-mill strip mall" in Glen Mills, which has become the "go-to" among Brandywine Valley sashimi-philes who beg "please God, let them prosper and stay here"; the "portions are great for the price", and what's more, the "owners are always in the house", ensuring "helpful" service with a "minimal wait."

Más Mexicali Cantina ● Mexican
19 | 22 | 21 | $22

West Chester | 102 E. Market St. (Walnut St.) | 610-918-6280 | www.masmexicali.com

Amigos insist "nothing beats" the "delightful" "views of West Chester" from the "rooftop deck" at this "festive", "friendly" Mex; many seem to "come for the drinks but stay for the food", including "cheap, delicious tacos" stuffed with everything from shortribs to tofu; P.S. there's live music or DJs almost nightly.

Matador ●) Mexican/Spanish
21 | 22 | 18 | $38

Wayne | 110 N. Wayne Ave. (Lancaster Ave.) | 610-688-6282 | www.matadorrestaurante.com

It's almost "worth going to work" just "for the happy hour" afterward at this "happening", bi-level Mexi-Spaniard in Downtown Wayne where the "amazing" "tableside" guacamole pairs well with "refreshing" sangria pitchers and "top-shelf margaritas" in an "over-the-top" Spanish setting; naysayers wave the red cape over "inconsistent" service from a staff with "attitude"; P.S. don't miss the monthly flamenco performances.

Matyson ⌧ American
27 | 19 | 24 | $46

Rittenhouse | 37 S. 19th St. (bet. Chestnut & Ludlow Sts.) | 215-564-2925 | www.matyson.com

You can "feel the love" coming from chef Ben Puchowitz's "finely tuned" kitchen in the form of "tantalizing weekly tasting menus" that are "worth the bucks" at this BYO New American "favorite" in Rittenhouse; the "quiet", "intimate" confines can become "too loud" "as the night marches on", and you may "get to know fellow patrons in extremely personal ways", but staffers who "actually enjoy what they are doing" keep the pace.

Max Brenner American/Dessert
22 | 23 | 22 | $30

Rittenhouse | 1500 Walnut St. (15th St.) | 215-344-8150 | www.maxbrenner.com

"If heaven had chocolate instead of clouds", it would be this "kid"- and "date"-friendly "tourist" destination in Rittenhouse whose menu of "sugar rush"–inspiring "deliciousness" is "thicker than most Harry Potter books", and among the savory New American offerings "even the fries are seasoned with cocoa"; while a few complain it's "overpriced", the "decadence" generally makes "scents" for the "sweet-tooth demon that lives in all of us."

Mayfair Diner ● Diner
20 | 17 | 21 | $17

Northeast Philly | 7373 Frankford Ave. (bet. Bleigh Ave. & Tudor St.) | 215-624-8886 | www.mayfairdiner.com

Whether you're "hungover" or satisfying "overnight cravings", the affordable, "above-average" "diner staples" at this 24/7 Northeast

	FOOD	DECOR	SERVICE	COST

Philly "greasy spoon" (established in 1932) will "do ya right"; a bump in scores suggests it's "finally" operating on an "even keel" after an ownership change awhile back, while surveyors attest to "friendly folks" on staff who "provide a decent meal for the cost."

McCormick & Schmick's *Seafood* | 23 | 23 | 23 | $45 |

Avenue of the Arts | 1 S. Broad St. (Penn Sq.) | 215-568-6888 | www.mccormickandschmicks.com

A "perfect mix of fancy and family-oriented", this "upscale" seafood chain offers "something new to try" from a "daily changing menu" and the results are "always cooked perfectly"; while detractors find it "overpriced" and "resting on its reputation", fans laud the "crazy cheap" prices on "bar food" during happy hour and "helpful" service, and tout it as "always a good choice."

McGillin's
Olde Ale House ● *Pub Food* | 18 | 21 | 22 | $22 |

Washington Square West | 1310 Drury St. (bet. Chestnut & Sansom Sts.) | 215-735-5562 | www.mcgillins.com

Leap into a "time warp" at this circa-1860 "landmark" in Wash West, a "great place for a sandwich and a beer" at "amazing prices"; though a "frat-party atmosphere" reigns in a building "where our forefathers dreamed of grandeur", "entertaining characters", "legit karaoke" and "homey" service ensure you "leave with a smile" – and remember, "it's been there forever for a reason."

McKenzie Brew House ● *American* | 21 | 21 | 21 | $26 |

NEW **Berwyn** | Valley Fair | 324 W. Swedesford Rd. (Valley Forge Rd.) | 610-407-4300

Glen Mills | 451 Wilmington West Chester Pike (Ridge Rd.) | 610-361-9800

Malvern | 240 Lancaster Ave. (Conestoga Rd.) | 610-296-2222 www.mckenziebrewhouse.com

"Outstanding" house-brewed beers and "solid" New American grub with "something for everyone" please patrons at this "family-friendly", "sports-bar-feel" brewpub chainlet with three links along the "Route 202 corridor" (Berwyn is the "happening" newcomer with "modern, sleek styling"); it may not be "your foodie delight, but every neighborhood needs one."

Mediterranean Grill *Mediterranean* | 22 | 17 | 20 | $30 |

Bryn Mawr | 870 W. Lancaster Ave. (bet. Merion Ave. & Morris Ln.) | 610-525-2627 **M**

NEW **Wayne** | 232 W. Wayne Ave. (Conestoga Rd.) | 610-225-0002 www.tasteofmainline.com

"Well-prepared" Persian cooking (including "great homemade bread" from a clay oven) and "friendly" service are on offer at these Main Line BYO twins, which fans recommend as "good places for vegetarians"; though a few sniff that it's "not a destination", others tout it as a "good choice for a casual, reasonably quick and reasonably priced dinner."

	FOOD	DECOR	SERVICE	COST

NEW Mekong River *Vietnamese*

- | - | - | I

South Philly | 1120 S. Front St. (Titan St.) | 215-467-6100 |
www.mekongriverphilly.com

This family-run Vietnamese in the Pennsport area of South Philly
boasts a wide-ranging, affordable menu with vermicelli platters
and a dozen different phos; the polished space is slick with wood
and ceramic accents, and will remain BYO until a planned bar is
ready in 2012.

Melograno Ⓜ *Italian*

24 | 20 | 21 | $42

Rittenhouse | 2012 Sansom St. (20th St.) |
215-875-8116 | www.melogranorestaurant.com

"Bring earplugs" and a "great Chianti" to Gianluca Demontis'
"sleek" Italian BYO in Rittenhouse, where "must-have pastas" and
other "rustic" "Roman delights" emerge from his "open kitchen";
though you're "packed in like sardines" and the noise can be
"unbelievable", while occasional "rudeness" is de rigueur, many
conclude it's "in a league of its own."

Melrose Diner ● *Diner*

20 | 15 | 21 | $18

South Philly | 1501 Snyder Ave. (15th St.) | 215-467-6644

"When did the waitresses get so polite?" ask astonished regulars of this "iconic" 24/7 South Philly diner long known for sassy
"attitude" along with "large portions" of "quality" grub; still, for
most it remains a "reliable" "old-school" "treasure" where you're
"entertained by the local populace" and "opinions on Philly sports
teams flow as freely as the great coffee."

The Melting Pot *Fondue*

24 | 23 | 24 | $48

Chinatown | 1219 Filbert St. (bet. 12th & 13th Sts.) |
215-922-7002

King of Prussia | Courtside Sq. | 150 Allendale Rd. (bet. Court Blvd.
& DeKalb Pike) | 610-265-7195
www.meltingpot.com

Offering a "gooey, cheesy and chocolatey" "interactive" experience, these upmarket fondue chain links work for anything from a
"romantic" evening to a "girls' night out"; cynics find the concept
"stuck in the '70s" and even some fans deem it "a little pricey" for
"cook-it-yourself" fare, but service is "eager" and the "ability to
play with your food" makes it an "entertaining" experience.

Memphis Taproom ● *American*

25 | 20 | 23 | $22

Port Richmond | 2331 E. Cumberland St. (Memphis St.) |
215-425-4460 | www.memphistaproom.com

No "Philly bar tour" is complete without a pilgrimage to this
"quaint" "oasis" in Port Richmond from the Resurrection Taproom
and Local 44 team, whose "knowledgeable and unpretentious
bartenders" put 12 craft beers in "rotation"; the New American
menu "caters to vegans and vegetarians" (and "occasionally gets
a little arty with the specials"), while the "hot dog truck" ramps up
the "outdoor beer garden's" "coolness factor."

	FOOD	DECOR	SERVICE	COST

Mendenhall Inn *American*   24 | 25 | 25 | $50

Mendenhall | Clarion Inn at Mendenhall | 323 Kennett Pike
(Hillendale Rd.) | 610-388-1181 | www.mendenhallinn.com
"Innovative theme nights" (including BYO Friday and Sunday) and
"reasonable prices" are drawing attention to this "classy", "quaint"
country inn in the Brandywine Valley whose "relaxing" vibe "feels
like another century"; adherents marvel at "attention to detail"
throughout, as well as the "excellent" prix fixe Sunday brunch
staffed by "pleasant cooks" at various stations.

Mercato ⊄ *Italian*   26 | 19 | 22 | $40

Washington Square West | 1216 Spruce St. (Camac St.) |
215-985-2962 | www.mercatobyob.com
"Imaginative" Italian flavors that may have you "licking the plate"
and frequent "menu changes to keep you coming back" send a
"buzz of electricity" through this cash-only Wash West Italian
BYO; "don't go expecting intimate conversation" in the "claustrophobic" space where the "attentive" staff seals its rep as a "tiny
place with a big heart"; P.S. remember "reservations are honored"
only until 6:30 (when it "fills up quickly").

Meritage Philadelphia 🅂🄼 *American*   24 | 20 | 23 | $47

Southwest Center City | 500 S. 20th St. (Lombard St.) |
215-985-1922 | www.meritagephiladelphia.com
Susanna Foo alum Anne Coll injects "Asian and French" flavors in
her "outstanding" New American cookery at this stylish Southwest
Center City wine bar that doubles as a "foodie's destination" – wit-
ness the "combination of small, medium and large dishes" to encourage sharing, plus a Tuesday vegan tasting menu; "reasonable
prices" and "personable" service seal the deal for most.

Metropolitan American Diner ◐ *American*   ∇ 24 | 22 | 23 | $23

North Wales | 750 Upper State Rd. (Bethlehem Pike) |
215-361-1603 | www.metrodinerbar.com
The name notwithstanding, this "fabulous find" in North Wales
"doesn't feel like a diner", offering an "extensive" New American
menu with whatever "you're in the mood for", including "huge"
all-day breakfasts, and all of it gets "two thumbs up"; the staff is
"eager to please" and doesn't "rush you out", so you can linger
over the "nice beer list" while watching the game at the bar.

Mexican Post *Mexican*   19 | 18 | 19 | $23

Old City | 104 Chestnut St. (Front St.) | 215-923-5233
Logan Square | 1601 Cherry St. (16th St.) | 215-568-2667
Mexican Post Express 🅂 *Mexican*
Logan Square | Comcast Ctr. | 1701 John F Kennedy Blvd. (17th St.) |
267-519-3953
www.mexicanpost.com
"When you need a quick Mexican fix", these "affordable" cantinas
do the trick thanks to a "super bar staff" mixing some of the "best
margaritas around", and "friendly" servers, though the "cafeteria-

| | FOOD | DECOR | SERVICE | COST |

like" environs are "always crowded" and perhaps not suitable for a "romantic date"; some purists, however, sniff that the fare's as "Americanized" as the "Budweiser ads out front."

Mica ⓜ American `24` `21` `23` `$70`

Chestnut Hill | 8609 Germantown Ave. (Evergreen Ave.) | 267-335-3912 | www.micarestaurant.com

Fans find this New American from Blackfish's Chip Roman in Chestnut Hill a "real treat", where the "unexpected combinations" on "awesome" tasting menus resemble "works of art", although a few critics find his dishes "fussy" and full of "too many ingredients"; the service is "friendly" and the "sparse" digs are "comfortable", and while it's "expensive", all agree it's a "big-city experience in a small-town neighborhood."

Mikado Thai Pepper Japanese/Thai `20` `17` `17` `$29`

Ardmore | 64 E. Lancaster Ave. (Argyle Rd.) | 610-642-5951 | www.mikadothaipepper.com

Expect "no surprises and no disappointments" at this "tastefully" decorated Main Line Japanese-Thai where the "good times" roll with "basic" sushi and sashimi and other "reliably decent" Asian selections that "meet expectations"; "accommodating" service is another plus, but "premium prices" give some pause.

Mi Lah Vegetarian Vegan/Vegetarian `23` `14` `21` `$23`

Rittenhouse | 218 S. 16th St. (Walnut St.) | 215-732-8888 | www.milahvegetarian.com

"Uniformly tasty", "one-of-a-kind" vegan and vegetarian dishes at this Asian-inspired Rittenhouse BYO "veggie haven" make omnivores "consider converting" (they certainly "don't miss the meat"); "phenomenal" weekend brunch buffets, "moderate prices" and an "attentive" staff also "impress", and while some report it "can be noisy downstairs", upstairs is quieter.

Mile High Steak & Seafood Seafood/Steak `25` `21` `24` `$45`

Glen Mills | 1102 Baltimore Pike (Painters Crossing) | 610-361-0855 | www.milehighss.com

"Creative" surf 'n' turf selections make this "outstanding" Glen Mills eatery a "special" place in a strip-mall setting; the "maître d' remembers everyone's preferences so well, he'd be an asset in the CIA", while the contemporary space belies the somewhat "lackluster" exterior, all of which add up to an "enjoyable" experience.

MilkBoy Coffee Coffeehouse `18` `17` `18` `$14`

NEW **Washington Square West** | 1100 Chestnut St. (11th St.) | 215-925-6455 | www.milkboyphilly.com ●

Ardmore | 2 E. Lancaster Ave. (Cricket Ave.) | 610-645-5269 | www.milkboycoffee.com

"Green sensibilities" and live music are the hallmarks of these "funky", "friendly" coffeehouse twins; while the Ardmore original rocks the "prototypical cafe" vibe that lets you "chill awhile" over vegetarian-friendly fare on "comfy chairs", the newer Wash West branch is a "bar by night" with "some of the hottest local" acts playing upstairs ("bring your shouting voice") and "cool garage doors" that let the outside in.

Minar Palace Ⓢ Indian ▽ 23 | 18 | 19 | $19

Washington Square West | 1304 Walnut St. (13th St.) | 215-546-9443 | www.minarphilly.com

The "zest you know and love" still surrounds this "consistent" Indian BYO in Wash West, which maintains its "affordable" price points even after switching from plastic to "actual plates and tableware"; followers describe "marvelous" cookery and find the service "less surly" than in the past, although a few naysayers feel it's "not as good as the original" in Rittenhouse that closed in 2006.

Minella's Diner ◑ Diner 20 | 14 | 20 | $19

Wayne | 320 W. Lancaster Ave. (Farm Rd.) | 610-687-1575 | www.minellasdiner.com

In the "high-rent district" of Wayne, this "quintessential" 24/7 diner brings in "crowds" with an "extensive menu" of "reliable" grub at "amazingly low" price tags; "addictive" baked goods and a "super-friendly", "old-school" staff help ensure its standing as a Main Line "mainstay."

Mirna's Cafe Eclectic/Mediterranean 22 | 18 | 21 | $29

Jenkintown | 417 Old York Rd. (West Ave.) | 215-885-2046 Ⓜ
Blue Bell | Village Sq. | 758 Dekalb Pike (Skippack Pike) | 610-279-0500
www.mirnascafe.com

"Large portions" of "well-prepared" Med-focused Eclectic vittles and "great hospitality" from "attentive" waiters are common features of this "pleasant, unassuming" BYO duo; the Jenkintown storefront original is "a little cramped" while Blue Bell boasts "plenty of free parking", and while some kvetch about "noise", for most it's a "safe choice."

🆕 Miss Rachel's Pantry Ⓜ Vegan - | - | - | M

South Philly | 1732 W. Passyunk Ave. (bet. 17th & 18th Sts.) | 215-798-0053 | www.missrachelspantry.com

Vegan caterer Rachel Klein has expanded her business into this quaint, sunny-hued South Philly cafe, serving light breakfast and lunch items during the week (with fair-trade Green Street coffee to wash it down); on Friday and Saturday nights, the space opens up to 12 guests for a prix fixe farm-to-table dinner at a long communal table.

Mission Grill Ⓢ Southwestern 20 | 20 | 21 | $30

Logan Square | 1835 Arch St. (19th St.) | 215-636-9550 | www.themissiongrill.com

"Happy-hour specials" make this midpriced Southwestern with an "upscale feel" off Logan Square a "cozy" "hangout" for "people-watching", a "date" or a "small group of friends" over "better-than-average" comestibles; a few dissenters knock the service as "spotty", but it's popular nonetheless among "corporate types" as a "change of pace" for a "power lunch."

	FOOD	DECOR	SERVICE	COST

Mixto *Pan-Latin*
24 | 23 | 22 | $32

Washington Square West | 1141 Pine St. (bet. Quince & 12th Sts.) | 215-592-0363 | www.mixtorestaurante.com

It's "like being on vacation" at this "laid-back" Pan-Latin with "festive" decor in a "quaint", "old" Wash West building, delivering "mouthwatering" empanadas and other "innovative" *comida* "worth every calorie"; you can "check out all the cute gals and guys" over "cheap bites" during "happy hour" or "snag an outdoor seat and sip a margarita under the trees" where you'll be as "happy as a fly in tequila."

NEW M Kee ⊘ *Chinese*
▽ 23 | 14 | 19 | $11

Chinatown | 1002 Race St. (10th St.) | 215-238-8883

Sinophiles assert the "fantastic roasted meats" and "rice plates" at this "standard" Hong Kong duck house are "worth a trip to Chinatown"; the "friendly", "eager-to-please" staff quickly overcomes language barriers and trumps the narrow, Formica-filled storefront and cash-only policy.

Modo Mio Ⓜ⊘ *Italian*
27 | 17 | 24 | $40

Northern Liberties | 161 W. Girard Ave. (Hancock St.) | 215-203-8707 | www.modomiorestaurant.com

"Every dish pops with flavor" on the $35, four-course Italian 'turista' menus at Peter McAndrews' "modest" BYO trattoria near Northern Liberties, which many deem one of the "best deals in the city"; the service is "knowledgeable", although a few find it "quirky", while others complain that the space's "horrific acoustics" make "lip-reading" necessary; P.S. don't forget cash, and "reservations are a must."

Molly Maguire's
Irish Restaurant & Pub *Pub Food*
19 | 23 | 22 | $27

Phoenixville | 197 Bridge St. (Main St.) | 610-933-9550 ◐
Lansdale | 329 W. Main St. (Wood St.) | 267-263-2109
www.mollymaguirespubs.com

"Irish all the way", these Phoenixville and Lansdale pubs are popular among locals looking for "fun activities after putting the kiddies to bed", with "accommodating bartenders" pulling "pints of Guinness" and "live entertainment several nights" a week in attractive spaces with "spacious" outdoor seating; while the mac 'n' cheese is something "special", critics call out the fare as "uneven" and "kinda pricey"; P.S. a Downingtown location is slated for late 2012.

Monk's Cafe ◐ *Belgian*
24 | 19 | 20 | $28

Rittenhouse | 264 S. 16th St. (bet. Latimer & Spruce Sts.) | 215-545-7005 | www.monkscafe.com

Fans hoist "two mussels-moistened thumbs up" for this "perpetually packed" Belgian bar near Rittenhouse whose "hefty bible of brews" and "charmed" frites satisfy the most demanding "connoisseur"; the "endearing" staff "spills nary a drop while weaving and wiggling" through the "vaguely medieval", "claustrophobic warren of rooms" that feels "like a good, comfortable pair of shoes."

	FOOD	DECOR	SERVICE	COST

Monsu ⓂⒷ *Italian* — 23 | 15 | 21 | $42

Bella Vista | 901 Christian St. (9th St.) | 215-440-0495 |
www.monsurestaurant.com

"One of the hottest tickets in town" is this cash-only,
"easy-on-the-wallet" Italian BYO in Bella Vista from Modo Mio's
Peter McAndrews, where "yummy, filling" Sicilian fare is served by
a "helpful" staff; a few critics carp that "they should ease up on the
salt shaker", and report that "noise can be a problem" in the "tiny"
space, but most who "come hungry always leave satisfied."

Moonstruck *Italian* — 24 | 25 | 24 | $43

Northeast Philly | 7955 Oxford Ave. (Rhawn St.) | 215-725-6000 |
www.moonstruckrestaurant.com

"When you want to impress" in Northeast Philly, fans recommend
this "top-shelf" Italian for its "dependable", "first-rate" fare and
"elegant" airs that work for "business dinners" or an "evening with
friends"; you "never feel rushed out" the door, and while some find
it "expensive", BYO on Wednesday and Sunday and $29 prix fixes
hold the line on pricing.

More Than Just Ice Cream *American/Dessert* — 20 | 13 | 19 | $17

Washington Square West | 1119 Locust St. (bet. Quince & 12th Sts.) |
215-574-0586 | www.morethanjusticecream.com

"The name says it all" at this "hip", "little" "neighborhood joint"
in Washington Square West that serves as a "go-to" lunch and
dinner stop with "well-done" American comfort food, but really
"shines" as a dessertery whose renown is "mile-high apple
pie" ("like your mother tried to make but didn't succeed"); the
"patient" staff stays cool while you choose, so this is a sure bet
to "please kids of all ages."

ⓃⒺⓌ Morgan's Pier ◑ *American* — - | - | - | I

Delaware Riverfront | 221 N. Columbus Blvd. (bet. Race & Vine Sts.) |
215-279-7134 | www.morganspier.com

This urbane beer garden on the pier (formerly known as Rock
Lobster) boasts a new menu courtesy of David Katz (Meme), with
wallet-friendly snacks, sandwiches and tacos designed to pair with
the 40-plus beers on offer; on a clear day, picnic-table diners can
see straight to Camden from the landscaped deck.

Morimoto *Japanese* — 28 | 27 | 26 | $74

Washington Square West | 723 Chestnut St. (bet. 7th & 8th Sts.) |
215-413-9070 | www.morimotorestaurant.com

"Omakase: just do it" urge boosters of this "one-of-a-kind"
Japanese from Stephen Starr and Iron Chef Masaharu Morimoto
in Washington Square West, where legions are tempted to "close
their eyes in rapturous delight" over the "heavenly" fare – but if
they did, they'd miss the "color-changing", "postmodern" setting;
"knowledgeable" service is another plus, and despite "splurge"
pricing, many leave "screaming 'I want Mor-imoto!'"

	FOOD	DECOR	SERVICE	COST

Morning Glory Diner ⊅ *Diner* | 25 | 15 | 20 | $17 |

Bella Vista | 735 S. 10th St. (Fitzwater St.) | 215-413-3999 |
www.themorningglorydiner.com

"Behold the glory" of this "classic", cash-only diner in Bella Vista
whose "mouthwatering" grub ("homemade ketchup") stars in a
"no-frills" corner spot "barely large enough to turn around twice",
where the "funky staff with big smiles" vows to keep it going after
the May 2012 passing of founder "Sam" Mickey; "insane" weekend
lines prompt insiders to quip "go about an hour before you're even
hungry and you might get food before passing out."

Morton's the Steakhouse *Steak* | 26 | 23 | 25 | $70 |

Avenue of the Arts | 1411 Walnut St. (Broad St.) | 215-557-0724
King of Prussia | Pavilion at King of Prussia Mall | 640 W. Dekalb Pike
(bet. Allendale & Long Rds.) | 610-491-1900
www.mortons.com

You "know what to expect" at these links in the Chicago-based
"gold standard" steakhouse chain, where "big slabs" of "mouthwatering" "meat grilled to perfection" and "plentiful portions" of
sides are toted by "unobtrusive staffers who attend to every need";
loyalists offer "three thumbs up" while "swooning" over "hot
chocolate cake", and though this "luxury" may cost "an arm and a
leg", many agree it's "worth the money."

Moshulu *American* | 23 | 25 | 23 | $60 |

Delaware Riverfront | Penn's Landing | 401 S. Columbus Blvd.
(Spruce St.) | 215-923-2500 | www.moshulu.com

"Ahoy!" cry mates of this "beautifully restored" four-masted
barque docked at Penn's Landing whose "over-the-top nautical
theme", "friendly" service and the view of Camden offer "smooth
sailing" for "romance" and "special occasions"; though the New
American chow doesn't "rock everyone's boat", fans insist the
"menu lives up to its unique setting", while the Sunday brunch buffet and "outdoor bar on the deck" are especially see-worthy.

M Restaurant ☒Ⓜ *American* | 23 | 24 | 23 | $52 |

Washington Square West | Morris House Hotel | 231 S. 8th St. (bet.
Locust & Walnut Sts.) | 215-625-6666 | www.mrestaurantphilly.com

All sorts of "gorgeous views" are at work at this "sophisticated",
"low-key" New American in the "historic" Morris House Hotel in
Wash West, including a "romantic" Georgian-style garden that
feels like a "country estate"; add "creative", "beautifully presented" New American fare and "knowledgeable, efficient" service –
it's "definitely adult time."

Mrs. Marty's Deli *Deli* | 18 | 13 | 19 | $16 |

Media | 11 W. State St. (bet. Jackson & Olive Sts.) | 610-566-2888
Broomall | Lawrence Park Shopping Ctr. | 1991 Sproul Rd. |
610-359-1996
www.mrsmartys.com

These functional suburban Jewish twins are renowned for "amazing matzo ball soup" and "corned beef specials that are a reward

for enduring life's knocks"; cynics sniff if it's "NY"-style fressen you're after, you're "nowhere near the target", but "big portions" win the day for most, though some lament they don't "leave much room for one of the tasty-looking desserts."

Ms. Tootsie's
Restaurant Bar Lounge ◐ *Soul Food*

24 | **21** | **19** | **$31**

South St. | 1312 South St. (13th St.) | 215-731-9045
Ms. Tootsie's 2Go ◐ *Soul Food*
South St. | 1314 South St. (13th St.) | 215-731-9045
www.mstootsiesrbl.com

The "outstanding" fried fish, chicken and cornbread will "make any Southerner proud" at KeVen Parker's "modern" South Street soul fooders (restaurant/bar/lounge on one side, take-out cafe on the other); the service is "accommodating", though a few complain that servers "move like snails" through the "cramped" multilevel building, and while some find it "pricey", others insist the feeling of "being way too full" comes at a "reasonable cost."

Mugshots
Coffeehouse & Cafe *Sandwiches*

19 | **16** | **15** | **$12**

Fairmount | 1925 Fairmount Ave. (Uber St.) | 267-514-7145
NEW North Philly | 1520 Cecil B Moore Ave. (Sydenham St.) | 215-232-1116
Brewerytown | 2831 W. Girard Ave. (29th St.) | 215-717-3327 | www.mugshotscoffeehouse.com

These "funky" little coffee shops fuel Brewerytown, Fairmount and North Philly with fair-trade java and locally sourced sandwich options "for all types of eaters, from omnivores to vegans"; critics cry "highway robbery" over the prices and grouse about "slow" service and "people with computers occupying all seats all day."

Murray's Deli *Deli*

19 | **10** | **17** | **$19**

Bala Cynwyd | 285 Montgomery Ave. (Levering Mill Rd.) | 610-664-6995 | www.murraysdeli.com

Though locals still kvetch about a change of owners, this "classic" Main Line Jewish deli seems to be "making a nice recovery", slicing "corned beef so good, NYC is jealous" and layering on "hot pastrami" in portions "enough for two sandwiches"; detractors claim it's "just a sandwich shop" and opinions are split on the service ("friendly" vs. "surly"), but for devotees it's a "dependable" option.

Mustard Greens *Chinese*

24 | **18** | **23** | **$30**

Queen Village | 622 S. 2nd St. (bet. Bainbridge & South Sts.) | 215-627-0833 | www.mustardgreensrestaurant.com

Building its rock-solid rep after more than 20 years by upgrading and installing a bar, chef-owner Bon Siu's "casual" Chinese in a "simple but classy" storefront off South Street is a "neighborhood" fave for "light, heavenly" Cantonese-inspired cuisine with myriad "menu options"; an "attentive" staff and "child-friendly" vibe keep people coming back, even from outside the city.

My Thai *Thai*

19 | 16 | 20 | $25

Southwest Center City | 2200 South St. (22nd St.) | 215-985-1878
For "Thai at its comforting best", "Penn professors" and "neighbor-hood" folk seek out this "relaxed, intimate" BYO that's been on a Southwest Center City corner for more than 20 years; some feel it's "showing its age" and the decor "needs to be updated", but it's "still reliable" for "food to Thai for" and "friendly service."

Na'Brasa Brazilian
Steakhouse *Brazilian/Steak*

25 | 23 | 25 | $48

Horsham | 680 N. Easton Rd. (Jefferson Ave.) | 215-956-0600
www.nabrasa.com
Fans of the Brazilian churrascaria "prepare their stomach" before heading to this "over-the-top" "carnivore heaven" in Horsham where "you could get a great meal on just the salad bar alone" but it's better to await the "devastating array of skewered meats deliv-ered tableside"; the "bland" interior is no match for the "Caipirinha cart" or the "marathon of good eating."

Nam Phuong Restaurant *Vietnamese*

24 | 13 | 19 | $19

Bella Vista | 1100 Washington Ave. (11th St.) | 215-468-0410
"Chandeliers" provide a "touch of class" at this "popular" Bella Vista strip-mall Vietnamese whose "delish cheap eats" come out of the kitchen "almost as quickly as you order them" in an "unas-suming" dining room that reminds some of "the set of an early John Woo movie"; the "servers aren't that attentive, but when you receive the bill you don't mind."

Nan Zhou Hand Drawn
Noodles *Noodle Shop*

26 | 10 | 19 | $11

Chinatown | 1022 Race St. (bet. 10th & 11th Sts.) | 215-923-1550
This cash-only Chinese noodle shop offers one of the best shows in Chinatown: the chef "working his magic" on hunks of dough to pull toothsome strands with "just the right texture", which are then topped with "tender", "nicely braised" meats, "tendons", "fish balls" and the like; the "memorable" delights come at an "unbeliev-ably low price", so regulars don't mind if service seems "indiffer-ent"; P.S. post-Survey, it moved into an upgraded, neon-ringed storefront a block away.

Nectar *Asian*

25 | 26 | 23 | $50

Berwyn | 1091 Lancaster Ave. (Manchester Ct.) | 610-725-9000 |
www.tastenectar.com
With a "breathtaking" Buddha as a focal point and "knowledge-able" staff fetching "world-class" sushi and other Pan-Asian de-lights (including "roasted foie gras" that achieves "divinity"), this "elegant fusion of East meets West" in Berwyn "could be dropped right in the center of Manhattan"; the "high-energy feel" can be "screamingly loud", and a few critics say they "can't justify the price", but believers beckon you to "valet your Porsche", order that "blood orange martini" and "join the crowd."

	FOOD	DECOR	SERVICE	COST

New Delhi Ⓜ *Indian* | 22 | 17 | 20 | $17 |

University City | 4004 Chestnut St. (40th St.) | 215-386-1941 |
www.newdelhiweb.com

"For the price", you "can't beat" the "incredible" all-you-can-eat
buffets that are "constantly being replenished" by "organized"
servers at this "modern" University City Indian (as "the frequent-
ing UPenn crowd can attest"); it's not for those "watching their
weight or trying to eat healthy", so picky types should probably
"order off the menu."

New Harmony Vegetarian | ▽ 25 | 16 | 24 | $17 |
Restaurant *Chinese/Vegetarian*

Chinatown | 135 N. 9th St. (bet. Cherry & Race Sts.) | 215-627-4520
So it's "not the fanciest place" in Chinatown, but this popular
Chinese vegetarian BYO is a rock-"solid" destination for a "large
dumpling section" and a mix of "heavier fried items" and "lighter
options too" – thereby pleasing "omnivores" put off by fake meats;
there's no "dress code or lofty expectations, just the "down to
earth" staff and the prospect of $12 buffets.

New Wave Cafe ◐ *American* | 18 | 15 | 20 | $25 |

Queen Village | 784 S. 3rd St. (Catharine St.) | 215-922-8484 |
www.newwavecafe.com

"Even when they aren't working", the bartenders and servers
at this Queen Village taproom "hang out" there like "family",
solidifying its rep as an "ultimate neighborhood place" with "lots
of big-screen TVs", "decent" New American "pub grub" and a
"better-than-average beer list"; while critics dismiss it as a "waiting room" for the "overflow from Dmitri's across the street", sup-
porters say it can "stand on its own"; P.S. it's open late too.

The Newtown Grill *Italian/Steak* | 18 | 18 | 18 | $36 |

Newtown Sq. | 191 S. Newtown Street Rd. (½ mi. south of West
Chester Pike) | 610-356-9700 | www.thenewtowngrill.com
Surveyors are split over this Newtown Square Italian steakhouse,
with fans insisting it's "well worth seeking out" for "wonderful"
fare, including "bargain" "aged prime steaks", served by a "helpful" staff, while critics counter that it's a "disappointment in every
respect" – "just ok" eats at "downtown" prices and "indifferent"
service; all agree that the "portions are large."

Nick's Old Original | 26 | 15 | 22 | $16 |
Roast Beef Ⓩ◐ *Sandwiches*

South Philly | 2149 S. 20th St. (Jackson St.) | 215-463-4114
Springfield | 10 E. Woodland Ave. (Ballymore Rd.) |
610-690-1112 | www.nicksroastbeef.com
Boosters boast the "best hand-carved roast beef on the planet" is
served at these "classic", "unadvertised gems" in South Philly and
Springfield, Delco, run by the same family for 75 years; "don't be
fooled by the hole-in-the-wall decor", with sides of "gravy fries"
this good, even if your "arteries clog when you walk in", chances
are "you'll die with a smile on your face."

	FOOD	DECOR	SERVICE	COST

Nifty Fifty's *Diner*
23 | 23 | 22 | $16

Folsom | 1900 MacDade Blvd. (Rte. 420) | 610-583-1950
Northeast Philly | 2491 Grant Ave. (Roosevelt Blvd.) | 215-676-1950
Bensalem | 2555 St. Rd. (Knights Rd.) | 215-638-1950
www.niftyfiftys.com

It's "worth blowing your weekend calorie allotment" on "fresh-ground beef burgers", "hand-cut fries" and "milkshakes in every flavor you could imagine" at this "kitschy", neon-trimmed diner chain, a '50s "nostalgic ride" that "really takes you back in every way but the price"; the "noisy", "kid-friendly" confines are "always busy", but "helpful" servers are thankfully "on the ball."

The Night Kitchen
26 | 15 | 21 | $13

Bakery *Bakery/Sandwiches*
Chestnut Hill | 7725 Germantown Ave. (bet. Mermaid Ln. & Moreland Ave.) | 215-248-9235 | www.nightkitchenbakery.com

While "fresh baked goods", including "beautifully decorated, perfectly baked cakes" and "unique desserts" made with "so much love", are the forte of this "memorable" Chestnut Hill bakery, it also offers sandwiches and other "light-lunch" items in a "dedicated" "sit-down" space, served by an "accommodating" staff; it's "especially perfect for a Sunday morning", but the name notwithstanding, it's "barely open past sunset."

943 Ⓜ ⇻ *Argentinean/Italian*
23 | 18 | 22 | $32

Bella Vista | 943 S. 9th St. (bet. Carpenter & Montrose Sts.) | 267-687-2675 | www.cafe943.com

"Personable" chef-owner Pascual Cancelliere's "country-style" Argentinean and Italian "home cooking" comes out of an open kitchen at his "simple but lovely", cash-only BYO located amid the "chaos of the Italian Market"; "accommodating" service and "reasonable" prices also make it "worth the trip."

Nineteen (XIX) *American/Seafood*
23 | 28 | 22 | $50

Avenue of the Arts | Hyatt at the Bellevue | 200 S. Broad St. (Walnut St.) | 215-790-1919 | www.nineteenrestaurant.com

It "feels like a palace" in this "opulent" New American seafood "splurge" on the 19th floor of the Hyatt at the Bellevue, where the "beautiful dining room" with "strings of white pearls" hanging from the "domed" ceiling is surpassed only by "breathtaking views"; a "fantastic" weekend brunch and "wonderful" prix fixe lunch are "musts", and "polite" service seals the deal.

19 Bella *Mediterranean*
25 | 22 | 23 | $38

Cedars | 3401 W. Skippack Pike (Bustard Rd.) | 610-222-8119 | www.19bella.com

Fans call Grant Brown's Cedars Med BYO an "event" wherein you build "wonderful tasting menus" around an "amazing" array of "superb" small plates, served by an "accommodating" staff; though some grouse that the "quaint", "well-attired" space is "cramped" and the tabs "can run up quickly", most feel that they're "onto something special" here.

	FOOD	DECOR	SERVICE	COST

1906 at Longwood Gardens 🖼️Ⓜ️ *American* | 24 | 22 | 23 | $35 |

Kennett Square | 1001 Longwood Rd. (Baltimore Pike) |
610-388-5290 | www.1906atlongwood.com

A "treat" for visitors to Longwood Gardens in Kennett Square, this
eatery offers "outstanding" American lunches and brunches, plus
prix fixe dinners in season, along with "top-notch" service in an
"elegant room" overlooking the conservatory's "glorious" flora;
signature cocktails help fuel "that special feeling", and if a few find
it "overpriced", there's always "the much cheaper cafeteria."

Nodding Head Brewery & Restaurant ⚫ *Pub Food* | 20 | 17 | 19 | $23 |

Rittenhouse | 1516 Sansom St. (bet. 15th & 16th Sts.) |
215-569-9525 | www.noddinghead.com

Yes is the verdict on Monk's "cool" second-story spin-off in
Rittenhouse Square, where "unexpectedly tasty twists on hearty
home-cooked-style bar food", "friendly" service and fair prices
keep 'em "coming back", though "TVs, darts, lots of wood and
bobblehead dolls all over" make 'em stay; oh – and with six or more
"in-house brews" on tap, pal, "just don't be a dummy and order a
Yuengling or a Bud."

🆕 Nomad Pizza Ⓜ️ *Pizza* | - | - | - | I |

South St. | 611 S. 7th St. (Kater St.) | 215-238-0900 |
www.nomadpizzaco.com

A mobile wood-fired pizza operation based in Hopewell, NJ,
has put down Philly roots in a cheerily upbeat, bi-level space off
South Street, where the first floor is dominated by a big-bellied
oven modeled after the original (which sits on a 1949 REO Speed
Wagon) and a projector in the second-floor dining room plays ran-
dom movies; 12 craft drafts and assorted Italian wines wash down
thin-crust, organic pies at wallet-friendly prices.

Nonna's Italian Restaurant *Italian* | 23 | 21 | 21 | $36 |

West Chester | 116 E. Gay St. (bet. Matlack & Walnut Sts.) |
610-430-0203 | www.nonnaswc.com

"Solid classic Italian" – and "not just a menu full of pasta" – is the
bill of fare at this white-tablecloth charmer in West Chester, where
the bartenders serve "a decent sized glass of wine and martini"
and quality makes it right for a "special occasion"; the "tables
crammed together provide for magnificent eavesdropping" – but
watch what you say about the owner, for she's known to "come to
the table to greet guests."

N. 3rd ⚫ *American* | 23 | 20 | 21 | $26 |

Northern Liberties | 801 N. 3rd St. (Brown St.) | 215-413-3666 |
www.norththird.com

Chef Peter Dunmire "transcends pub grub" with "creative" New
American fare (including "possibly the best wings in town") that
brings "beer geeks, foodies and socialites" to this "lively", affordable Northern Liberties tap whose "mismatched, boho decor" is
dimly bathed in lighting that "makes you wonder if they've paid the

electric bill" ("alfresco dining" is "prime"); while "hipster" servers are "friendly", you'll need to "bring your shouting voice" to flag one down; P.S. it's "open late for a nightcap."

Oak Lane Diner *Diner*

19 | 16 | 20 | $21

West Oak Lane | 6528 N. Broad St. (66th Ave.) | 215-424-1026
"Not kitschy, not retro", this "vintage" stainless-steel West Oak Lane diner landmark is the "real deal", serving "hefty" portions of "solid food to solid folks"; it's been "around forever", which "says something about consistency" and "wonderful" service that lets you "make a fast stop" or sit back and "relax" if you like.

Ocean City Restaurant *Chinese*

∇ 22 | 17 | 18 | $20

Chinatown | 234 N. 9th St. (Vine St.) | 215-829-0688
Join the "mostly Chinese patrons" for an "authentic" "feast" of "chicken feet prepared two ways", "hot and sour soup made to order" and other seafood and dim sum specialties at this Chinatown "treat" where modest prices make it a welcome option "for a big group"; however, with so many "carts making their way around, there is no time to analyze the outdated decor" or occasionally "temperamental" service.

Ocean Harbor *Chinese*

23 | 14 | 17 | $21

Chinatown | 1023 Race St. (bet. 10th & 11th Sts.) | 215-574-1398
The "crowds keep coming" as the carts keep rolling at this Chinatown dim sum specialist where "those who love a good deal" "bring ear plugs" and "get there early on weekends" to "pig out" on "cheap", "tasty" morsels; even if you have to "hound" the staff, insiders say "be adventurous" and try "everything at least once."

Oishi *Asian*

27 | 23 | 24 | $30

Newtown | 2817 S. Eagle Rd. (Durham Rd.) | 215-860-5511 | www.eatoishi.com
Bucks Countians "go into cucumber roll withdrawal" if they venture too far from this suburban-"hip", "subway-crowded" Pan-Asian in a "minimalist shopping-center setting" where BYO "helps" keep things "reasonably priced" and staffers "pour their hearts out" to serve up "stellar" sushi and an "eclectic mix of Japanese, Thai and Korean cuisine"; it's "always a packed house on weekends", so "don't even think about showing up without a reservation."

Olce Pizza Grille Ⓜ *Pizza*

∇ 26 | 17 | 22 | $16

Lansdale | 3401 Skippack Pike (Bustard Rd.) | 610-222-3839 | www.olcepizza.com
"Unique varieties" of "incredible", "cracker-thin-crust" pizza make both your taste buds and "your wallet happy" at this "super-cute", rustic BYO owned by a lawyer-turned-pizzaiolo in the Lansdale-area Cedars Country Store shopping complex; it's "not your run-of-the-mill factory", as you can tell from the "handmade" pies that "aren't always round."

	FOOD	DECOR	SERVICE	COST

ld Town Buffet Ⓢ Ⓜ *Asian/Eclectic*   20 | 14 | 18 | $19

bington | 1495 Old York Rd. (bet. Jericho Rd. & Wheatsheaf Ln.) |
5-885-0800

\ buffet is a buffet is a buffet", so middle-of-the-road service and
:cor are "as expected" at these "budget"-friendly, Asian-inspired
od lines in Moorestown and Abington offering "decent", albeit
nass-produced" chow "for the huge eater"; "you will leave full
id satisfied" after sampling "tons of choices", but wearing
xtra-stretchy sweatpants" will give you an advantage.

he Olive Tree   25 | 18 | 23 | $27
Iediterranean Grill Ⓢ *Greek*

owningtown | 379 W. Uwchlan Ave. (Peck Rd.) | 610-873-7911 |
ww.olivetreegrill.com

›u "feel like family as soon as you walk in the door" of this
uaint" Greek BYO in Downingtown, prized for its "consistent",
uthentic" chow, including "char-grilled whole fish that tastes as
it you caught it yourself", topped off with "decadent, homemade
esserts"; an outdoor patio complements the diner-like space,
ut for most, it's the food and service that make it an "experience
cond to none."

›n the Border *Mexican*   22 | 20 | 22 | $23

ensalem | 901 Neshaminy Mall (Rockhill Dr.) | 267-984-4980
(ton | 102 Bartlett Ave. | 484-870-3181
ww.ontheborder.com

.ndless chips" and "awesome margaritas" are among the "guilty
easures" at this "busy", "nothing-fancy" cantina chain that
:rves as a "hangout place for PTO moms" and a "starter Mexican"
:stination "for the kids"; "large portions", "efficient" service and
rices on the low side" are a few reasons the "go-to" is "loved by
any", though wary types warn "keep your expectations low."

›ne Shot Coffee *American*   23 | 23 | 23 | $19

orthern Liberties | 217 W. George St. (American St.) |
5-627-1620 | www.1shotcoffee.com

.wesome" Stumptown joe, "delicious" specialty drinks, "yummy
agels" and more, served by a staff that's "always nice no matter
›w cranky you are" make this "cozy" Northern Liberties cof-
ehouse a "perk-fect" "waker-upper"; a few grouse about the
ieattle-like price tags", but caffeinds tout the "half-hipster, half–
andmother's living room" upstairs lounge where they could sit
ith their laptops "for days if they never closed at night."

›oka Japanese *Japanese*   26 | 23 | 23 | $34

'illow Grove | 1109 Easton Rd. (Fitzwatertown Rd.) | 215-659-7688
oylestown | 110 Veterans Ln. (Main St.) | 215-348-8185
ontgomeryville | 764 Bethlehem Pike (bet. Vilsmeier & Wales
ds.) | 215-361-1119
ww.ookasushi.com

'hey put their own spin" on "eye-popping fresh sushi" at this
osmopolitan" Japanese trio, but there are "lots of options for the

	FOOD	DECOR	SERVICE	COST

non-sushi crowd" too – namely the "awesome" teppanyaki tables with "knife-twirling chefs" providing the "entertainment"; though the staff "could handle rush periods a bit better", it generally offers "good value for the price", and best of all, "no passport is needed". P.S. it's BYO in Willow Grove.

Opa ⌧ Greek 20 | 21 | 19 | $37

Washington Square West | 1311 Sansom St. (13th St.) | 215-545-0170 | www.opaphiladelphia.com

The "sexy", "modern" vibe at this "intimate" Wash West Greek befits its "lively but not too noisy" bar scene that rates it as a "good alternative when everything on 13th Street is packed", even if some cite "below-par" service as "the only negative"; while you may not "throw napkins" over the "nontraditional" menu of "small plates" you'd never find at a "church festival", it's nevertheless "tasty" and "reasonably priced."

The Orchard Restaurant ⌧Ⓜ American ▽27 | 26 | 27 | $68

Kennett Square | 503 Orchard Ave. (Rte. 1) | 610-388-1100 | www.theorchardbyob.com

Gary Trevisani's Kennett Square New American is a "treat for the senses", with "fabulous", "nouveau" cuisine that "will amaze you" in a "sublime, relaxing" space, where "servers make you feel comfortable"; "high" tabs give pause to some, but most agree this "foodies' paradise" is "one of the very best in Chester County."

Oregon Diner ⌧Ⓜ● Diner 19 | 15 | 20 | $17

South Philly | 302 W. Oregon Ave. (3rd St.) | 215-462-5566 | www.oregondinerphilly.com

Phillies fans, families and "sleepy-eyed college students" find "on-point", "call-you-Hon'" service at this no-frills, 24/7 South Philly institution near the sports complex, regarded by "regulars" as their "'old pair of slippers' place to eat" when they "just want to get out but not be out on the town"; the call is "big-portioned, well-priced", "standard diner fare" – just be sure to "save room for the pie."

Osaka Japanese 24 | 22 | 23 | $36

Chestnut Hill | 8605 Germantown Ave. (Evergreen Ave.) | 215-242-5900
Lansdale | 1598 Sumneytown Pike (Reiff Rd.) | 267-222-8308 | www.osakapa.com

From "hands-down" delicious sushi to "entertaining" hibachi, there's quite the "varied" menu at these "relaxed", contemporary Japanese twins in a Chestnut Hill storefront and Lansdale strip mall; though some grumble that "portions are shrinking and the prices are not", "upbeat, professional" service keeps things running smoothly; P.S. Chestnut Hill has live jazz on Tuesdays.

Osteria Italian 27 | 25 | 26 | $55

North Philly | 640 N. Broad St. (Wallace St.) | 215-763-0920 | www.osteriaphilly.com

"Tuscany" is just a "cab ride" away courtesy of this "pricey" North Philly "treasure" where the "bustle and warmth" is "conducive to onversation" and chef Jeff Michaud's "robust", "inventive" Italian ooking makes "every mouthful a delight", from "savory, crispy" izzas and "house-cured" salumi to "creative" handmade pastas natched with a "mouthwatering wine list"; "knowledgeable" ervice orchestrates a "fantastico" experience in which the Vetri amily's "golden touch is apparent."

Ota-Ya

25 | 18 | 23 | $37

apanese Restaurant Ⓜ *Japanese*

lewtown | 10 Cambridge Ln. (Sycamore St.) | 215-860-6814
hough there's "not a lot of fanfare" surrounding these Japanese wins in Bucks and Lambertville, rising ratings reflect "they've eally stepped up their game", exhibiting "more creativity in roll hoices" and lots more to "love" at the hibachi upstairs from campy" staff; a few wish they'd address "tired interior", but in um, the "secret" is out.

Otto's Brauhaus *German*

21 | 17 | 21 | $27

lorsham | 233 Easton Rd. (Pine Ave.) | 215-675-1864 | ww.ottosbrauhauspa.com
Gut, gut, gut" go raves from fans of this time-honored Horsham ierman, who insist it's "the closest thing to Oktoberfest" in Montco, especially for its "outdoor beer garden" and "reasonably riced" Sunday buffet stocked with the best of "wursts"; though s "dining room needs to be updated" and service can be "slower han you like" at "peak times", "lederhosen" and an occasional "ac-ordion" make it a "definite" *ja.*

Oyster House Ⓩ *Seafood*

24 | 22 | 22 | $41

ittenhouse | 1516 Sansom St. (bet. 15th & 16th Sts.) | 15-567-7683 | www.oysterhousephilly.com
Real Philadelphia tradition" lives on at this "modern rustic" ittenhouse fish house under "third-generation" ownership by the Mink family, whose stock in trade is "unpretentious but perfectly resented seafood" and a "bustling" raw bar where you can "get your naster's in oysternomics" at "buck-a-shuck happy hours"; there's good service even when busy", and "except for the Philly accents, ou can pretend you're on the coast of Maine or New Brunswick."

Paesano's Philly Style Ⓩ Ⓜ ⊄ *Italian*

27 | 12 | 20 | $13

lorthern Liberties | 152 W. Girard Ave. (Hancock St.) | 67-886-9556
outh Philly | 1017 S. 9th St. (Kimball St.) | 215-440-0371
ww.paesanosphillystyle.com
here's "no atmosphere" at these Italian sandwich shops in Northern iberties and the Italian Market from Peter McAndrews (Modo Mio, Monsu), but they're where legions find "heaven on a hoagie oll" – "wonderful sloppy things" that let loose an "explosion of fla-or" (get "plenty of napkins"); you may want to "plan on takeout" seating is limited, "decor is a nonissue"), but at least "the only roblem is choosing" among "first-rate" options.

FOOD | DECOR | SERVICE | COST

Palace of Asia *Indian*

21 | 18 | 20 | $25

Fort Washington | Best Western Inn | 285 Commerce Dr.
(Delaware Dr.) | 215-646-2133

The "delicious" "lunch buffet" is a standby for office workers at
this long-running Indian tucked into a Best Western Hotel "in the
midst of a suburban business campus"; despite complaints of a
"dreary", "formal and antiquated" dining room, most agree it's "the
next best thing to a home-cooked" experience.

Palm Restaurant *Steak*

25 | 22 | 23 | $64

Avenue of the Arts | Hyatt at the Bellevue | 200 S. Broad St.
(Walnut St.) | 215-546-7256 | www.thepalm.com

"Classic" to some and "safe and predictable" to others, this Avenue
of the Arts outpost provides a "clubby, red-meat throwback to the
Mad Men era," complete with wall caricatures of notable locals;
a "power lunch" go-to good for big steaks, martinis and "surprisingly great" seafood, the floor's run by a "veteran staff" providing
"old-school service."

Paloma Mexican
Haute Cuisine🈹Ⓜ *French/Mexican*

28 | 21 | 25 | $54

Bella Vista | 763 S. 8th St. (Catharine St.) | 215-928-9500 |
www.palomafinedining.com

Fans predict "you'll keep coming back" to this "cozy", white-tablecloth
Bella Vista BYO for chef-owner Adán Saavedra's "inventive"
"haute" French fare "laced" with the "flavors and spices of Mexico"
and topped off with his "charming" wife Barbara's "homemade
desserts" (the "spicy sorbets alone are worth the visit" to some);
"charming" service, "reasonable" prices and a "quiet" setting with
"ample room" "between tables" seal the deal.

Paradiso Restaurant Ⓜ *Italian*

25 | 23 | 24 | $45

East Passyunk | 1627 E. Passyunk Ave. (bet. Morris & Tasker Sts.)
215-271-2066 | www.paradisophilly.com

Lynn Rinaldi's "vibrant" Italian wine bar on East Passyunk deftly
"mixes fine-dining elegance and casual" ambiance for a "special
dinner or just a night out", featuring "outstanding homemade pastas" and "warm" service, plus niceties such as "Friday night jazz",
"cheese cart" and Sunday BYO option; some note that the "decibel
level" swings between "relaxing" and "impossible."

🆕 Paramour *American*

22 | 27 | 21 | $58

Wayne | Wayne Hotel | 139 E. Lancaster Ave. (Waynewood Ave.)
610-977-0600 | www.paramourwayne.com

For the "glamour of a night out in the city without the drive", Main
Liners head to this "swanky", "upscale" New American that suc-
ceeded Taquet at the Wayne Hotel, where "sophisticated" fare
and "amazing" cocktails are served by an "enthusiastic" staff;
the "beautiful" decor "makes everyone look gorgeous too", which
may be why some deem it the "new spot to find a fortysomething
divorcée", perhaps sipping something at the "sexy bar."

	FOOD	DECOR	SERVICE	COST

Parc *French*

24 | 26 | 23 | $45

Rittenhouse | Parc Rittenhouse | 227 S. 18th St. (Locust St.) |
215-545-2262 | www.parc-restaurant.com

It feels like Stephen Starr "airlifted" this re-creation of a "swanky"
"100-year-old" Paris bistro "straight" from the "sixth arrondisse-
ment" to Rittenhouse Square say fans "swept away" by the "buzzin'
bar", "artsy versions" of classic dishes and "outdoor seats that are
some of the most prized in the city"; the "hustle and bustle make
for a lovely meal" that strikes Francophiles as "perfect – except for
the lack of cigarette smoke."

Parc Bistro *American*

24 | 24 | 23 | $44

Skippack | 4067 Skippack Pike (bet. Church & Store Rds.) |
610-584-1146 | www.parcbistro.com

"Creative" New American fare may be the main draw at this "old
country roadhouse" in Downtown Skippack, but the "lively" but
"comfortable bar" also "packs them in at happy hour" (and "chocolate martinis make you feel amazing"); a "friendly", "knowledgeable" staff keeps proceedings running smoothly whether you're out
on the summer patio or in the homey dining room – in sum, this
bistro "performs."

Paris Wine Bar ⊠Ⓜ *French*

▽ 22 | 19 | 22 | $30

Fairmount | 2303 Fairmount Ave. (bet. 23rd & 24th Sts.) |
215-978-4545 | www.londongrill.com

"Wine connoisseurs" gravitate to this "cozy, sexy and intimate"
Fairmont French bistro that serves only casked Pennsylvania wine,
along with "fresh" grub from the London Grill next door, eliminat-
ing the need to "go into Center City"; devotees credit it with "open-
ing their eyes" to "local products."

Pat's King of Steaks ●⇄ *Cheesesteaks*

23 | 12 | 17 | $13

East Passyunk | 1237 E. Passyunk Ave. (9th St.) | 215-468-1546 |
www.patskingofsteaks.com

"Greasy, cheesy goodness" "wit' a side of South Philly attitude"
draws the hungry to the 24/7 East Passyunk "inventor of the
cheesesteak", where the sandwiches "overflowing with fresh
meat" are known "to cure a hangover at 2 AM" and convert
"vegetarians"; naysayers knock it as "overhyped", but you can still
expect "long lines" and plenty of "tourists expecting abuse" from
the "cranky, Hollywood-casted" window staff.

Pat's Pizza Family Restaurant *Pizza*

23 | 17 | 21 | $17

Boothwyn | 3601 Chichester Ave. (bet. Alan St. & Railroad Ave.) |
610-497-5544 | www.patsfamilyrestaurant.com
See review in the New Jersey Suburbs Directory.

Pattaya *Thai*

▽ 22 | 19 | 21 | $21

University City | 4006 Chestnut St. (40th St.) | 215-387-8533 |
www.pattayacuisine.com

A "diverse menu" and $10.95 early-bird specials (Sunday–Thursday)
make this airy, contemporary University City Thai a "popular

dinner spot for U. Penn students"; "very nice" service and "fast delivery" also put it on the dean's list for many.

Peace A Pizza *Pizza*   21 | 14 | 19 | $13

Ardmore | 4 Station Rd. (bet. Lancaster Dr. & Montgomery Ave.) | 610-896-4488
King of Prussia | 143 S. Gulph Rd. (bet. Dekalb Pike & King of Prussia Rd.) | 610-962-9900
Rosemont | 1125 E. Lancaster Ave. (bet. Franklin St. & Roberts Rd.) | 610-581-7010
Springfield | 1178 Baltimore Pike (bet. Sproul Rd. & Woodland Ave.) | 610-328-7437
www.peaceapizza.com

"Awesome salads" and "specialty" "yuppie" pizzas are the draws at this "family-oriented" mini-chain offering "something for everyone", with "lots of choices for toppings"; though some gripe that the "teenage staff is not always fully engaged" and "atmosphere is a bit lacking" in the "standard" digs, for most the "creative" "spin on traditional pizza" makes for a "happy meal."

Penang ◐ *Malaysian/Thai*   25 | 18 | 21 | $24

Chinatown | 117 N. 10th St. (bet. Arch & Cherry Sts.) | 215-413-2531
Perhaps the "happiest and happening-est place in Chinatown", this "spacious", "modern" Malaysian whips up "orgasmic offerings" in "giant woks" in an open kitchen, while guests "relax" in "spacious", industrial-chic surroundings; "incredibly fast" service is another plus, and "you won't spend a ton of money."

Penne Restaurant & Wine Bar *Italian*   18 | 18 | 19 | $36

University City | Inn at Penn | 3611 Walnut St. (36th St.) | 215-823-6222 | www.pennerestaurant.com
This "upscale" Italian at University City's Inn at Penn is "geared to Wharton profs" (and visiting "moms and dads"), with "great homemade pastas" and "interesting wines" served by a "cordial" staff in a "pretty" setting; critics wish it had a "more interesting menu" and carp about "inexperienced" service, but the consensus seems to be that while "you can do better", you can also "do a whole lot worse."

Pepperoncini Restaurant & Bar *Italian*   21 | 16 | 21 | $33

Conshohocken | 72 Poplar St. (bet. Elm & Hectors Sts.) | 610-941-7783

Pepperoncini Sotto *Italian*

Phoenixville | 184 Bridge St. (bet. Main & Star Sts.) | 484-924-8429
"Delicious" fare "like you would find in Rome" and "reasonable" prices draw an "interesting mix of white and blue collars" to these "friendly neighborhood" Italians in Conshy and Phoenixville; the newer spot in Phoenixville has an "underground location" that's "easy to walk by."

Perch Pub ● *American* ▽ 22 | 20 | 22 | $26

Avenue of the Arts | 1345 Locust St. (Broad St.) | 215-546-4090 |
www.perchpub.com

An "ever-changing", "fantastic beer selection on tap" complements "surprisingly sophisticated" American grub at Joe Varalli's
second-story pub overlooking the Avenue of the Arts; "friendly"
service, "nice views from the huge windows" and a "cute"
bird-themed decor all give it a "homey", "relaxing" feel.

Percy Street Barbecue *BBQ* 22 | 19 | 22 | $29

South St. | 900 South St. (9th St.) | 215-625-8510
Logan Square | Comcast Ctr. | 1701 John F Kennedy Blvd. (17th St.) |
215-964-9014
www.percystreet.com ⑤

For "authentic Texas BBQ in the heart of Philly", 'cuennoisseurs
head to this "family-friendly" South Street smokehouse where Erin
O'Shea's "otherworldly" brisket and ribs and "incredible pecan
pie" are served, along with an "extensive" "all-can" beer list, in a
"saloon" setting "complete with sticky floors"; the branch at the
Shops at the Comcast Center is a food court outlet.

Persian Grill *Persian* 19 | 16 | 20 | $30

Lafayette Hill | 637 Germantown Pike (Crescent Ave.) |
610-825-2705 | www.persiangrille.net

"Terrific" kebabs and other "light, tasty" entrees are "the real
thing" at this "family-owned" Persian in Lafayette Hill; service
is "personal" yet "professional", and the ambiance is "quiet and
homey", which help quell grumbles about "pricey" tabs.

NEW Pescatore Ⓜ *Italian* ▽ 27 | 21 | 25 | $40

Bala Cynwyd | 134 Bala Ave. (Montgomery Ave.) | 610-660-9400 |
www.pescatorebyob.com

Afishionados assert the "eastern Main Line could use about a doz-
en more places like this" Bala Italian BYO from Thomas Anastasi (a
scion of the Anastasi Seafood clan), whose "ambitious" "changing
chalkboard menu" features "amazing seafood" and "traditional
South Philadelphia fare"; "personal" service and "elegant" environs
add to the "enjoyable experience."

P.F. Chang's China Bistro *Chinese* 24 | 23 | 22 | $32

Glen Mills | Shoppes at Brinton Lake | 983 Baltimore Pike (Brinton
Lake Rd.) | 610-545-3030
Warrington | Valley Sq. | 721 Easton Rd. (Street Rd.) | 215-918-3340
Plymouth Meeting | 510 W. Germantown Pike (Hickory Rd.) |
610-567-0226
Collegeville | Providence Town Ctr. | 10 Town Center Dr.
(Collegeville Rd.) | 610-489-0110 ⑤
www.pfchangs.com

"Even the pickiest eater" can appreciate the "tasty", "modern"
spins on Chinese food at this "dependable", "allergy-aware"
upmarket chain whose "dan dan noodles could cure the world's
problems"; while it runs like a "well-oiled machine", it "doesn't feel

like an assembly line", though some quip "everything is meant to be shared – including conversation" – in the "crowded" environs.

Philadelphia Bar and Restaurant *Cheesesteaks/Seafood*
∇ 22 | 20 | 23 | $25

Old City | 120 Market St. (Letitia St.) | 215-925-7691 | www.philadelphiabarandrestaurant.com

This "open, airy" Old City American is making a "good name for itself" with "friendly bartenders", a deft mix of "classic" pub grub and comfort food and an "extensive beer selection"; there's a "great crowd" early in the evening to "grab a drink" after work.

Phillips Seafood *Seafood*
24 | 23 | 22 | $44

Logan Square | Sheraton City Center Hotel | 200 N. 17th St. (Race St.) | 215-448-2700 | www.phillipsseafood.com

"Awesome" crab cakes and raw bar offerings "prepared wonderfully" are the calling cards of this expense-account Baltimore-based seafooder in the Sheraton City Center near Logan Square; though a few gripe it's "overpriced", it's still "nice for a chain restaurant" and a good value at "happy hour."

Phil's Tavern ☻ *American*
22 | 14 | 21 | $26

Blue Bell | 931 Butler Pike (Skippack Pike) | 215-643-5664 | www.thephilstavern.com

You get "enough food in one serving to feed three people" at this "bustling", "neighborly" Blue Bell "watering hole" serving a "huge menu" of American "not-exactly-health food"; though decor is "warped in the '80s", a crowd of "mixed ages" gets "comfortable" in the "casual", "friendly" ambiance.

Pho Cali *Vietnamese*
∇ 22 | 13 | 19 | $13

Chinatown | 1000 Arch St. (10th St.) | 215-629-1888

"Generous" bowls of "tasty", affordable pho are the way to go at this "cheerful" Viet "hole-in-the-wall" in Chinatown; a few wish a "smile" could come with the "fast, efficient" service, but the "soul-warming" soup makes it "the place to go" for many.

Phoebe's Bar-B-Q *BBQ*
∇ 20 | 8 | 18 | $20

Southwest Center City | 2214 South St. (bet. Grays Ferry Ave. & 22nd St.) | 215-546-4811 | www.phoebesbbq.com

"Holy smokes", this "friendly" Southwest Center City BBQ is a "homey fallback" for "solid" 'cue with "legit" sauce and sides that'll "get your attention as well"; it's a "hole-in-the-wall, literally", which is why many use it for "takeout only."

Pho Ha *Vietnamese*
∇ 26 | 12 | 18 | $10

Bella Vista | 610 Washington Ave. (bet. 6th & 7th Sts.) | 215-599-0264

Surveyors report a "mostly Vietnamese clientele" at this cash-only Bella Vista pho specialist, a good sign "it's pretty darned authentic"; the plain decor "does not detract one iota from the wonderfully flavorful, freshly prepared" fare, served at speeds that "make Mickey D's look like it's napping."

Pho 75 ⊄ *Vietnamese*

24 | 10 | 19 | $12

Northeast Philly | 823 Adams Ave. (Roosevelt Blvd.) |
215-743-8845
South Philly | 1122 Washington Ave.F (bet. 11th & 12th Sts.) |
215-271-5866

"It's pho me" squeal phonatics of these "bare-bones" Vietnamese
noodle shops in Northeast Philly and South Philly dishing out "delicious" varieties that "arrive at your table before your butt hits the
seat"; bring cash, and prepare for a "full belly for days."

Pho Xe Lua *Vietnamese*

▽ 25 | 11 | 20 | $14

Chinatown | 907 Race St. (9th St.) | 215-627-8883

Phonatics "look for the neon train in the window" of this Chinatown
Vietnamese, where "there isn't much to look at" otherwise; still,
"you can't go wrong" with the "amazing soups and noodles", and
while some say the "excellence of the food is inversely proportional
to the service", many consider it the "best value for your dollar and
taste buds"; P.S. closed Wednesdays.

Piccolo Trattoria *Italian*

23 | 18 | 21 | $27

Newtown | 32 West Rd. (Eagle Rd.) | 215-860-4247
Langhorne | Shoppes at Flowers Mill | 144 N. Flowers Rd. (Maple Ave.) |
215-750-3639
www.piccolotrattoria.com

"Large portions" of "yummy" Italian fare are a "tremendous value"
at these "casual" BYO twins in Bucks that seem to work best for
"lunch with the lady friends" or a "date without kids"; while some
report "spotty" service and a setting straight off an "assembly line
from Restaurants 'R' Us", for most the "food is what counts."

NEW Pickled Heron ⊠⊄ *French*

- | - | - | M

Fishtown | 2218 Frankford Ave. (Dauphin St.) | 215-634-5666 |
www.thepickledheron.com

Todd Braley and Daniela D'Ambrosio''s "farm-to-table" French
cookery is a "nice addition to Fishtown", and their cash-only BYO
in a lovingly restored row house hums with "serious eaters" feasting on charcuterie and other all-from-scratch dishes; you'll get a
"thank you" at the table from the chef-owners, who grow some of
their own produce in their backyard garden.

Pietro's Coal Oven Pizzeria *Pizza*

23 | 18 | 20 | $25

Rittenhouse | 1714 Walnut St. (bet. 17th & 18th Sts.) |
215-735-8090
South St. | 121 South St. (bet. Front & Hancock Sts.) | 215-733-0675
www.pietrospizza.com

"Deliciously thin", "artisan" coal-fire-oven pizzas, pasta "sent from
the heavens" and "yummy" salads, all at a price "that won't cost
you your whole paycheck", are part of the appeal of this "charmingly tacky", family-friendly Italian mini-chain; you can linger over
wine, or "get in and out fast" – either way, the "neighborhood vibe"
"leaves national chains in the dust."

	FOOD	DECOR	SERVICE	COST

Pietro's Prime *Steak*

24 | 24 | 24 | $45

West Chester | 125 W. Market St. (Darlington St.) |
484-760-6100 | www.pietrosprime.com

There's a "cosmopolitan" yet "casual" feel at work at this upmarket West Chester meatery where boosters rave about "incredible" steaks "done to perfection", an "extensive wine list" and "top-notch" service; while a few feel it's "overpriced" and "not worth the hype", most regard it as a "very good steakhouse for the suburbs" and worthy of a "special occasion."

Pistachio Grille Ⓜ *American/Mediterranean*

21 | 17 | 19 | $40

Maple Glen | 521 Limekiln Pike (Norristown Rd.) | 215-643-7400 |
www.thepistachiogrille.com

An "unexpected delight" in a strip mall, this "upbeat" Maple Glen BYO is a "nice find" for "well-made" New American grub with a Med influence and a "long list of specials" "worth trying"; while some grouse about "slow" service and find it "disappointing for the price", others declare it a "winner."

Pizzeria Stella *Pizza*

24 | 20 | 22 | $27

Society Hill | 420 S. 2nd St. (2nd St.) | 215-320-8000 |
www.pizzeriastella.net

"Craveable", "melt-in-your-mouth" pizzas with "thin, fluffy" crusts are the calling card of Stephen Starr's "cool"-meets-"rustic" wood-fired pizzeria in Society Hill, where an "informative" staff guides you to something "yummy" (the black truffle–and–egg–topped Tartufo might be the "best thing to happen to Philly since the signing of the Declaration"); the "quaint little bar" is "a hit with the misses."

Pizzicato *Italian*

22 | 18 | 20 | $29

Old City | 248 Market St. (3rd St.) |
215-629-5527 | www.pizzicatoristorante.com

You can "taste the authenticity" at these "decent" trattoria twins whose "fresh" fare can be mixed and matched (order an "entree", an "unusual pizza combination" or "three appetizers for dinner"); the vibe feels "more upscale than a neighborhood Italian place", though some report "sporadic" service; P.S. Marlton is BYO, while Old City has a full bar and sidewalk dining.

P.J. Whelihan's ◑ *Pub Food*

21 | 19 | 20 | $23

Blue Bell | 799 Dekalb Pike (Skippack Pike) | 610-272-8919 |
www.pjspub.com

See review in the New Jersey Suburbs Directory.

Plate Restaurant & Bar *American*

16 | 18 | 16 | $37

Ardmore | Suburban Sq. | 105 Coulter Ave. (Anderson Ave.) |
610-642-5900 | www.platerestaurant.com

The "real housewives of the Main Line" drop into this "reservedly elegant" New American in Suburban Square for lunch or a "late-afternoon bite" on the side patio, perhaps accompanied by a "specialty martini"; critics clamor over "big prices" for "ho-hum" grub, but most agree it's the "classiest option" in the complex.

	FOOD	DECOR	SERVICE	COST

The Plough & the Stars *Pub Food* | 21 | 22 | 21 | $31 |

Old City | 123 Chestnut St. (2nd St.) | 215-733-0300 |
www.ploughstars.com

"Super for families, a date or just a wee pint or two", this "welcoming" pub in a high-ceilinged former bank is the "perfect getaway" from the rest of Old City, what with its "inviting fireplace" and "lovely staffers"; "delicious lunch and dinner offerings" "prove that not all Irish food is bland and boring."

Pod *Asian* | 24 | 25 | 24 | $42 |

University City | 3636 Sansom St. (bet. 36th & 37th Sts.) |
215-387-1803 | www.podrestaurant.com

"Sushi meets Star Trek" at Stephen Starr's "higher-end" Pan-Asian "space-age canteen" in University City, whose "futuristic" motif pleases "visiting Penn parents and up-and-coming students with deep pockets"; the "awesome" sushi conveyor belt and dining pods may seem "gimmicky" to some, but "ridiculously tasty" eats and "polite" service put this one in the "win" column for most.

Popi's Italian Restaurant *Italian* | 27 | 23 | 24 | $38 |

South Philly | 3120 S. 20th St. (Penrose Ave.) | 215-755-7180 |
www.popisrestaurant.com

For a "nicer than usual" Italian meal near the stadiums in South Philly, *amici* tout this "romantic" trattoria where "quality" fare is "exquisitely presented" and the staff "treats you like an old friend"; sure, you may take a "hit to the wallet", but when you add "Sinatra tunes" from a "singer in the bar" and lots of "neighborhood warmth", you have the "perfect" makings for a "first date."

Porcini 🗷 *Italian* | 25 | 15 | 24 | $38 |

Rittenhouse | 2048 Sansom St. (bet. 20th & 21st Sts.) |
215-751-1175 | www.porcinirestaurant.com

This "unpretentious", "shoebox-size" Italian salon in Rittenhouse "hits all the right notes" – "lovingly prepared" fare, "dedicated owners who pamper you", BYO policy and "they take reservations and credit cards"; it's "close quarters, so keep the gossip to a minimum", but for fans, the "result is intimacy rather than annoyance."

Positano Coast *Italian* | 23 | 24 | 23 | $38 |

Society Hill | 212 Walnut St. (2nd St.) | 215-238-0499 |
www.positanocoast.net

Warm weather can't come often enough for fans of this "sexy" Italian "oasis" in Society Hill, where "open-air dining is taken to a new level" in a setting that evokes an "impressive portrait" of the "Amalfi coast"; the "creative" small plates work just as well in the lounge, and the "friendly," staff makes sure it's a "terrific place to hang out."

Primavera Pizza Kitchen *Pizza* | 19 | 21 | 20 | $30 |

Ardmore | 7 E. Lancaster Ave. (Cricket Ave.) | 610-642-8000 |
www.primaverapizzakitchenardmore.com

Piezani assert you can "bank on solid" "pizzas and pastas" and "efficient" service at this Italian utilizing the grand bones of a century-old bank branch in Ardmore; while it may not "blow your mind", and some feel it "needs updating", it's "reasonably priced" and a quick "walk from the train station."

The Prime Rib *Steak*   27 | 27 | 27 | $66

Rittenhouse | Radisson Plaza-Warwick Hotel | 1701 Locust St. (17th St.) | 215-772-1701 | www.theprimerib.com

"Classy but not stuffy", this "dressy" meatery in the Warwick plays its "elegant supper club" airs to the hilt, complete with a "baby grand and stand-up bass" (is that "the Rat Pack spotted in a corner booth"?); legions love the "luscious steaks" and "divine" seafood proffered by "genteel waiters" padding in on the "leopard-print carpet" – in sum, it "doesn't disappoint."

PrimoHoagies *Sandwiches*   25 | 13 | 20 | $13

Ardmore | 157 W. Lancaster Ave. (Church Rd.) | 610-645-5500
Conshohocken | 113 W. Ridge Pike (bet. Butler Pike & North Ln.) | 610-828-3075
Dresher | 1650 Limekiln Pike (Dreshertown Rd.) | 215-542-7746
Media | 132 E. Baltimore Pike (Valleybrook Rd.) | 610-565-7000
Northeast Philly | 2417 Welsh Rd. (Roosevelt Blvd.) | 215-677-3888
Rittenhouse | 2043 Chestnut St. (21st St.) | 215-496-0540 🗷
South Philly | 1528 W. Ritner St. (Mole St.) | 215-463-8488
Richboro | 130 Almshouse Rd. (2nd St. Pike) | 215-355-0160 | www.primohoagies.com

"Amazing" "sesame-seeded rolls" are the key to the signature sandwiches at this "no-frills" sandwichery, while the "perfect amount of meat, condiments and toppings" yield an "awesome hoagie", albeit a bit on the "expensive" side; still, whether you call them "subs or heros", you "always leave happy."

Pub & Kitchen ❶ *American/European*   24 | 21 | 21 | $32

Southwest Center City | 1946 Lombard St. (20th St.) | 215-545-0350 | www.thepubandkitchen.com

"Awesome" burgers headline the menu of "novel, fresh" Euro-American pub fare at this Southwest Center City hot spot; a "lively late-20s early-30s scene" takes up the "farmhouse"-like space most nights, and while some complain the servers can be "a little snarky", most consider them "top-talent" who "remember your name and your drink."

Pub of Penn Valley ❶ *Eclectic*   20 | 15 | 21 | $25

Narberth | 863 Montgomery Ave. (Gordon Ave.) | 610-664-1901 | www.pubofpennvalley.com

Ordering the "above-average bar fare" is the way to go advise regulars at this "convivial" "neighborhood" Eclectic in Narberth where you often brave "long wait times" for grub that "won't break the bank"; service is "friendly", but insiders warn that those who "overstay their welcome get the evil eye."

	FOOD	DECOR	SERVICE	COST

Pub On Passyunk East ⬤ *Pub Food* | 18 | 17 | 20 | $19 |

East Passyunk | 1501 E. Passyunk Ave. (Dickinson St.) |
215-755-5125 | www.pubonpassyunkeast.com

"P.O P.E." is the acronym for this "hipster mother hive" in East
Passyunk, a "great little dive" with an "amazing beer list" that's
"rotated pretty frequently" and poured by "witty bartenders";
"veggie selections" abound on the "nontypical bar" menu, which
lends itself to an "easy meal."

Public House at Logan Square ⬤ *American* | 17 | 18 | 18 | $29 |

Logan Square | 2 Logan Sq. (18th St., bet. Arch & Cherry Sts.) |
215-587-9040 | www.publichousephilly.com

Updated American pub grub "done with flair" and an address
"near the Franklin Institute" make this pub/restaurant a "great
post-museum" option, but by evening it morphs into a "vibrant bar
scene" that starts "jamming during happy hour"; descriptions of
the service vary from "witty" to "grumpy", and critics find the fare
"overpriced for the quality" and warn of a "fratty" scene with lots
of "Jersey Shore types", especially on weekends.

Pumpkin Ⓜ⇋ *American* | 27 | 19 | 24 | $43 |

Southwest Center City | 1713 South St. (17th St.) | 215-545-4448 |
www.pumpkinphilly.com

"It's all about the food" at this BYO "charmer" on South Street,
where Ian Moroney's "local, fresh" and "beautifully plated"
New American cuisine "never disappoints", featuring "creative
combinations that shock in a good way"; the "gracious" staff is
"attentive, not oppressive", the "recently redesigned", though still
"minuscule", space "works well" and many tout the Sunday night
five-course prix fixe as the "best deal in town."

NEW Pure Fare *Sandwiches* | ▽ 22 | 17 | 21 | $12 |

Rittenhouse | 119 S. 21st St. (bet. Sansom & Walnut Sts.) |
267-318-7441 | www.purefare.com

Offering "healthy lunch options" in Center City, this sandwich
specialist turns out "fresh", "creative" fare that's "delicious and
guilt-free", and while some find it "surprising" that it's pre-pre-
pared, it's "served with a smile" in "clean, cute" environs with
limited seating; a few find the prices "high" for what you get, but
others give it an "A+ for value."

PYT ⬤ *Burgers* | 24 | 20 | 19 | $21 |

Northern Liberties | Piazza at Schmidt's | 1001 N. 2nd St.
(Germantown Ave.) | 215-964-9009 | www.pytphilly.com

A "Chuck E. Cheese's for hipsters" tucked into Northern Liberties'
Piazza, this affordable burgertory-cum-bar offers up an "original" menu of "crazy concoctions", from "kickass, wacky burgers"
to "amazing" "boozy milkshakes"; while opinions are split on
the service ("super-nice" vs. "fail" with "attitude"), most agree
"awesome" outdoor seating and weekend DJs will help keep "your
inner child satisfied."

	FOOD	DECOR	SERVICE	COST

Q BBQ & Tequila ● *BBQ*   20 | 17 | 19 | $23

Old City | 207 Chestnut St. (bet. 2nd & Strawberry Sts.) |
215-625-8605 | www.qoldcity.com

"BBQ + tequila = awesome" sums up this "affordable" Old City
smokehouse for 'cuennoisseurs who laud the "interesting" lineup
of "quality" 'cue, "amazing" burritos and a "great variety of tequilas"; service is "fast" and "friendly" in the "comfortable" setting,
and while a few find the fare merely "serviceable", others prize it
as a "good-value", "low-cost option in an overpriced area."

Qdoba Mexican Grill *Mexican*   20 | 15 | 19 | $12

Rittenhouse | 1528 Walnut St. (16th St.) | 215-546-8007
University City | 230 S. 40th St. (Locust St.) | 215-222-2887
Bala Cynwyd | Bala Cynwyd Shopping Ctr. | 33 E. City Ave.
(Conshohocken State Rd.) | 610-664-2906
North Philly | 1600 N. Broad St. (Oxford St.) | 215-763-4090
Springfield | 1054 Baltimore Pike (Riverview Rd.) | 610-543-4104
Rittenhouse | 1900 Chestnut St. (19th St.) | 215-568-1009
Washington Square West | 1105 Walnut St. (11th St.) | 215-629-2900
www.qdoba.com

A "quick and cheap" way to "fix a craving" for Mexican, this chain
lets you "customize your own taco or burrito" with a "huge variety"
of options that are "healthier and more flavorful than other"
fast-food offerings; critics find the fare "average" and demur at the
"strip-mall atmosphere", but for others "on the run", it'll do.

Race Street Cafe ● *American*   23 | 20 | 21 | $25

Old City | 208 Race St. (Bread St.) | 215-627-6181 |
www.racestreetcafe.net

Feeding bar-goers long "before Old City was cool", this "hidden
gem" offers "everything you look for in neighborhood dining" –
"exceptional" American fare with an "unexpected gourmet" bent,
"one of the better beer lists in the area" and "friendly" service in a
"cozy, comfortable" setting; "regulars abound" at stools and tables
in the rustic space as well as on the sidewalk, where the "outdoor
seating is fantastic."

Radicchio Cafe *Italian*   26 | 20 | 24 | $37

Old City | 402 Wood St. (4th St.) | 215-627-6850 |
www.radicchio-cafe.com

"No pretensions and no reservations" at this "long-standing" Old
City Italian, just "reliable", "wonderful" fare "prepared simply and
traditionally"; regulars warn "you'll always wait on a weekend
night" due to the "small, intimate" (some say "cramped") space,
but "sincere service" and a "lively, congenial vibe" help make it
"worth the hassle", and BYO makes it "very affordable."

Radice *Italian*   23 | 21 | 21 | $47

Blue Bell | Village Sq. | 722 W. Dekalb Pike (Rte. 73) |
610-272-5700 | www.radicerestaurant.com

A "suburban jewel" in Blue Bell, this "upscale" Italian offers a
"varied menu" of "beautifully plated, well-prepared" small plates,

pizzas and entrees; the "ultramodern, all-white" decor belies the unassuming strip-mall location, while the "attentive staff" recognizes loyalty – "a few trips and you're family."

Ralph's Italian Restaurant ⊘ *Italian* 23 | 18 | 22 | $37

Bella Vista | Italian Mkt. | 760 S. 9th St. (bet. Catharine & Fitzwater Sts.) | 215-627-6011 | www.ralphsrestaurant.com
Sure, it's "not cutting-edge", but "America's oldest family-owned Italian restaurant" is a "fixture" for "soothing old-fashioned favorites" and a "classic South Philly" vibe; service is "friendly" and "quick", and while you'll be "sitting elbow to elbow" with "tourists" in a room some find "cramped" and "dreary", fans "love every minute of it"; P.S. "remember, cash only."

Randi's Restaurant
and Bar ◐*American/Italian* 23 | 20 | 22 | $31

Northeast Philly | 1619 Grant Ave. (Welsh Rd.) | 215-677-7723 | www.randisrestaurantandbar.com
Fans insist "you'll never get a bad plate of food" at this Northeast Philly Italian serving "generous portions" of "reasonably priced" fare, served by an "attentive" staff; the ambiance is "wonderful" in the spacious digs where you're almost "always able to get a table", and bar patrons have a good time "singing along with the piano man" on weekend nights.

Rangoon Burmese Restaurant *Burmese* 24 | 15 | 22 | $24

Chinatown | 112 N. 9th St. (bet. Arch & Cherry Sts.) | 215-829-8939 | www.rangoonrestaurant.com
"One of Chinatown's not-so-hidden gems", this "low-key" Burmese offers a "good alternative to typical Chinese" with its "incredible selection" of "unique" dishes "a Burmese mother would cook", including "outstanding" thousand-layer bread; "economical" pricing and "swift, cordial" service help make it a "rare treat."

Raw Sushi & Sake Lounge *Japanese* 23 | 21 | 19 | $40

Washington Square West | 1225 Sansom St. (bet. 12th & 13th Sts.) | 215-238-1903 | www.rawlounge.net
For "sushi done right", fans head to this Wash West Japanese for an "interesting" lineup of "tasty", "fresh" fin fare, served in "sultry", "upscale" surroundings; angst over "awfully high" prices is assuaged somewhat by "courteous" service.

Ray's Cafe &
Tea House ⊠ *Taiwanese/Tearoom* ▽ 25 | 12 | 24 | $19

Chinatown | 141 N. 9th St. (bet. Cherry & Race Sts.) | 215-922-5122 | www.rayscafe.com
The "sublime" siphon coffee at this "family-owned" Taiwanese tearoom in Chinatown is "fresh, strong and delicious", while the teas are "excellent", and they're complemented by treats such as the "delectable dumpling sampler" and "heaven-sent" cookies; "Grace, the owner, lives up to her name", so admirers advise "don't be fooled" by the "hole-in-the-wall" digs.

FOOD | DECOR | SERVICE | COST

Ray's Restaurant & Malt Shop *Diner* 18 | 16 | 18 | $16

Norristown | 14 E. Germantown Pike (Dekalb Pike) |
610-279-3555 | www.raysdiner.com

"Big portions" of diner fare will have you "bringing home a doggy
bag" from this affordable Norristown eatery where fans advise you
"save room" for its "yummy" desserts and malt-shop treats; critics say there's "not much to be excited about" on the "extensive"
menu and pan the "'50s-inspired" digs as a "cliché."

Reading Terminal Market *Eclectic* 26 | 17 | 20 | $16

Chinatown | Reading Terminal Mkt. | 51 N. 12th St. (bet. Arch &
Filbert Sts.) | 215-922-2317 | www.readingterminalmarket.org

Open since 1892, this historic market – a "one-stop shopping center" and Eclectic "foodie heaven" in Chinatown – is an "indispensable" culinary hub offering a "melting pot of different cuisines"
that represents "all the best of Philadelphia"; there's "wonderful
people-watching" too, and though some vendors are knocked as
"pricey and touristy", the overall experience is an "absolute must."

Redstone American Grill ● *American* 23 | 24 | 22 | $37

Plymouth Meeting | Plymouth Meeting Mall | 512 W. Germantown Pike
(Hickory Rd.) | 610-941-4400 | www.redstonegrill.com

A "warm" vibe, especially when it comes to the "casual, comfy"
outdoor seating area, separates these "great-looking" Marlton and
Plymouth Meeting outposts of an "upscale" American chain from
surrounding "sleepy suburban spots", and while the "expansive",
midpriced menu seems geared to "meat lovers", there are also
"slightly more unique" options at play, including a "fabulous
brunch"; expect "long waits for service on weekends", though most
say the "eats are worth it."

Relish Ⓜ *Southern* 26 | 25 | 25 | $32

West Oak Lane | 7152 Ogontz Ave. (Homer St.) | 215-276-0170 |
www.relishphiladelphia.com

Guests should "come hungry" to this "cool", "cozy" West Oak
Lane venue where a "friendly" staff dishes up moderately priced
Southern "comfort food done with style" to an "urban, mature
crowd" that expects to "eat, hear jazz and be merry"; "excellent
live entertainment" is certainly a highlight, though there's plenty to
"love" about the Sunday brunch too.

Rembrandt's ● *American* 22 | 18 | 20 | $28

Fairmount | 741 N. 23rd St. (Aspen St.) | 215-763-2228 |
www.rembrandts.com

Thanks to new owners who "take their food seriously", this
"ancient neighborhood taproom" has been "transformed" – and
"what an improvement" rave Fairmount locals enamored with the
"outstanding" draft list and an affordable American menu that's
"growing more adventurous" while retaining "hearty" classics; service "keeps the crowds happy" in a "comfortable" "hangout" that's
finally "found its mojo."

	FOOD	DECOR	SERVICE	COST

Restaurant Alba ☒ *American / Italian*   27 | 24 | 25 | $54

Malvern | 7 W. King St. (Warren Ave.) | 610-644-4009 |
www.restaurantalba.com

Among the higher-end Italian-American options on the Main Line,
this "locavore's delight" serves up a "distinctive" menu with "wonderful attention to detail", matched by "gourmet-level" service that
delivers a "terrific dining experience"; the "cozy, warm" setting is
augmented by the dynamic open kitchen, where guests can get a
"great view" of dishes coming off the wood-fired grill.

Resurrection Ale House ● *American*   23 | 19 | 21 | $27

Southwest Center City | 2425 Grays Ferry Ave. (Catharine St.) |
215-735-2202 | www.resurrectionalehouse.com

The "continuously changing" beer selection is "second to none" at
this "hard-to-find" Southwest Center City "gastropub" where staffers who "really care" serve up "some of the best fried chicken in
town" plus other "inventive" American dishes that go well beyond
"normal pub fare"; though a few deem it "too fancy" for a "neighborhood tavern", a "blend of hipsters and professionals" "comes
back for more, and more, and more."

Revolution House ☒ *American*   ▽ 22 | 23 | 23 | $27

Old City | 200 Market St. (2nd St.) | 215-625-4566 |
www.revolutionhouse.com

For a "pre-Phillies-game" bite, "family dinner" or "romantic drink",
aficionados find "prompt" service and "sophistication without
stuffiness" at this "updated rustic" Old City bi-level boasting Ital-
ian-tinged New American fare and manageable tabs; it's "worth" a
visit just for the "laid-back" "outdoor deck on nice nights."

NEW Rex 1516 *American*   - | - | - | M

Rittenhouse | 1516 South St. (15th St.) | 267-319-1366 |
www.rex1516.com

Jet Wine Bar's midpriced in Rittenhouse offers "delicious plates" of
vegetarian-friendly, Southern-accented American fare, along with
a "great beverage selection"; the bluesy, "sexy" space features a
bar reclaimed from the Frank Furness–designed Rittenhouse Club.

Ristorante Castello *Italian*   ▽ 26 | 20 | 23 | $42

Blue Bell | Montgomery Commons | 721 Skippack Pike (Wales Rd.) |
215-283-9500 | www.ristorantecastello.com

The Italian cooking is "still the thing" at this BYO "sleeper" in
sleepy Blue Bell after a post-Survey move from North Wales (not
reflected in the Decor score); "marvelous" pastas and "excellent fresh fish" shine on the "sophisticated" menu, while "warm,
friendly servers" keep the "focus on the food and the guests."

Ristorante La Buca ☒ *Italian*   23 | 19 | 20 | $47

Washington Square West | 711 Locust St. (bet. 7th & 8th Sts.) |
215-928-0556 | www.ristlabuca.com

Seems like this Washington Square stalwart has "been there forever", dishing out "consistent", "homey" Italian fare in an "old-world"

	FOOD	DECOR	SERVICE	COST

atmosphere; critics find it "tired" and in "need of updating", while opinions are divided on the service ("genuinely helpful" vs. "rude"), but for many it remains a "neighborhood favorite."

Ristorante Panorama *Italian*   24 | 23 | 23 | $47

Old City | Penn's View Hotel | 14 N. Front St. (Market St.) | 215-922-7800 | www.panoramaristorante.com

Amici assert this "high-end" eatery in the Penn's View Hotel "is the place" in Old City for "wonderful", "reliable" Northern Italian cooking, a "huge by-the-glass wine selection" and "knowledgeable" service; the feel "can be frantic", and some find the digs "dated", but most understand why it's so "hard to get in without a reservation."

Ristorante Pesto 🅼 *Italian*   26 | 22 | 25 | $40

South Philly | 1915 S. Broad St. (bet. McKean & Mifflin Sts.) | 215-336-8380 | www.ristorantepesto.com

"Classic Italian" cuisine with some "creative twists" comes in "generous" portions at this "crown jewel" of South Philly, where the "friendly" staff treats you "like family"; the chandelier-illuminated dining room is "welcoming", though some find it "cramped" and "loud", but most profess that the "wonderful" eats "always bring them back"; P.S. though it serves liquor, you can BYO (wine only) corkage-free.

Ristorante Primavera of Wayne *Italian* 22 | 21 | 22 | $38

Wayne | 384 W. Lancaster Ave. (Conestoga Rd.) | 610-254-0200 | www.ristoranteprimaveraofwayne.com

Located just outside Downtown Wayne, this "Main Line standard" dishes out "dependable", "well-prepared" Italian fare in a "pretty", "relaxing" white-tablecloth setting; "attentive, friendly" servers foster a "*Cheers*"-like atmosphere, and despite some cracks about the average "age of the patrons", most agree you "cannot go wrong" here; P.S. there's valet parking at dinner.

Ristorante San Marco 🆉 *Italian*   26 | 24 | 22 | $51

Ambler | 504 N. Bethlehem Pike (Dager Rd.) | 215-654-5000 | www.sanmarcopa.com

"Exceptionally high standards" in the kitchen make this "sophisticated" Ambler Italian a "spectacular find" for either dinner or a "lovely lunch", with "delectable homemade pastas" and "perfectly prepared fresh fish" headlining the "cut-above" menu; "formal, attentive" servers work the contemporary Colonial room, and there's nightly "live piano music" in the bar.

🆕 Rittenhouse Tavern 🅼 *American*   - | - | - | E

Rittenhouse | Philadelphia Art Alliance | 251 S. 18th St. (Manning St.) | 215-732-2412 | www.rittenhousetavern.com

'Approachable elegance' is the theme at this upscale American brasserie in the historic Art Alliance mansion/exhibition hall on Rittenhouse Square, where chefs Nicholas Elmi (Le Bec Fin) and Ed Brown are plating refined, locally sourced modern fare; in addition to the baroquely styled, business-appropriate dining room, there's a transporting outdoor garden for warm-weather dining.

	FOOD	DECOR	SERVICE	COST

Riverstone Cafe *American* — 21 | 22 | 21 | $32

Exton | Whiteland Towne Ctr. | 150 N. Pottstown Pike (Rte. 100) | 610-594-2233 | www.riverstonecafe.com

"Something different" for Exton, this New American exudes a "high-class" feel despite its location "right off the highway", thanks to an "amazing" martini list, "terrific fresh oysters" (available buck-a-shuck style on Wednesdays) and a tapas menu full of "imaginative flavor combos"; it's run by "nice people", and despite complaints about "noisy" acoustics, most are "never disappointed"; P.S. some call the brunch buffet the "best in Chester County."

Roadhouse Grille *American* — ▽ 20 | 19 | 22 | $38

Skippack | 4022 Skippack Pike (Collegeville Rd.) | 610-584-4231 | www.roadhousegrille.net

Many are "pleasantly surprised" by the steaks and seafood at this seemingly "typical steakhouse" in Skippack Village, where the staff "always has a smile", the outdoor patio is "wonderful in warm weather" and "you can't beat" the bargain bar menu; while a few sniff that it's "nothing special", others "have not been disappointed" here.

Rock Bottom
Restaurant & Brewery ❶ *Pub Food* — 21 | 20 | 21 | $25

King of Prussia | Plaza at King of Prussia Mall | 1001 King of Prussia Plaza (bet. Dekalb Pike & Mall Blvd.) | 610-337-7737 | www.rockbottom.com

Whether you want to "escape from the hordes" of "worn-down shoppers" or "just want a beer and a burger", fans tout this "chill" brewpub-cum-sports bar in the Plaza at King of Prussia for its "great house-brewed beers" and pub grub "prepared with care" at "reasonable" prices; some shrug at the "average" eats and "typical bar scene", but many consider it a "must if you're at the mall."

Roller's at Flying Fish Ⓜ⇪ *Eclectic* — 22 | 17 | 19 | $37

Chestnut Hill | 8142 Germantown Ave. (Hartwell Ln.) | 215-247-0707 | www.rollersrestaurants.com

Open since 1982, Paul Roller's Chestnut Hill "mainstay" is as "consistent as ever" even though he "adds new things constantly" to the locally sourced Eclectic menu, which also includes old standards such as the "wonderful" broiled tilapia; a few feel the digs could use "a coat of paint", and while the service is "friendly", to some the place sometimes appears "understaffed."

Roman Delight *Italian* — 21 | 17 | 22 | $21

Warminster | 255 E. Street Rd. (Louis Dr.) | 215-957-6465 | www.romandelightwarminster.com

"So much food", with "plenty to take home", comes out of the kitchen at this "family" Italian in Warminster that maintains "consistent quality", even if it may not "knock your socks off"; "moderate" prices, "friendly, efficient" service and an outdoor patio help many overlook the "typical pizzeria" setting.

	FOOD	DECOR	SERVICE	COST

Rose Tattoo Cafe *American*   24 | 23 | 23 | $42

Fairmount | 1847 Callowhill St. (19th St.) | 215-569-8939 |
www.rosetattoocafe.com

"Comforting in its refusal to change with the times", this Fairmount
New American "takes advantage of local markets" in crafting a
"delightful" menu with "something for every taste", which is served
by a "caring, thoughtful" staff; "seemingly modest" ("dreary" to
some) on the outside, the "Victorian-style row house" has lots of
"mystique" and "charm" inside, plus an abundance of "live plants"
providing a lush "rainforest view."

Rose Tree Inn ⬧ *American*   ▽ 25 | 21 | 24 | $45

Media | 1243 N. Providence Rd. (Rte. 1) | 610-891-1205 |
www.rosetreeinn.net

A "cozy" golden-era Media staple that recently came under new
ownership, this American gets high marks for its "great seafood"
and staff that makes you "feel comfortable and valued"; the revamped interior provides a fresh backdrop for lovers of "dance and
jazz" in the often "crowded" but "never-noisy" bar area.

Rosey's BBQ Ⓜ *BBQ*   19 | 13 | 18 | $20

Jenkintown | Jenkintown Square Shopping Ctr. | 505 Old York Rd.
(Rydal Rd.) | 215-885-8600
Ambler | 9 N. Main St. (Butler Ave.) | 215-646-7427 |
www.roseysbbq.com

"Take a friend and share a platter" of Memphis-style BBQ at this
BYO smokehouse duo that gets shout-outs for "tasty ribs", "killer
mac 'n' cheese" and "live blues on weekends"; some feel the minimalist digs make them "better for takeout than eat-in", while some
find the fare merely "ordinary."

Rouge *American*   23 | 22 | 20 | $42

Rittenhouse | Rittenhouse Sq. | 205 S. 18th St. (bet. Locust &
Walnut Sts.) | 215-732-6622 | www.rouge98.com
The "original Rittenhouse bistro", this "sophisticated" New American is popular for its "mouthwatering" burgers, plus "entertaining
people-watching" from "see-and-be-seen" sidewalk tables with
"lovely" views of the park; the "dark", "atmospheric" room is
"elegant", but a bit "cramped", while the service is "top-notch",
though a few see red over "snobby" attitudes.

NEW Route 6 *Seafood*   23 | 25 | 22 | $49

Fairmount | 600 N. Broad St. (Mt. Vernon St.) | 215-391-4600 |
www.route6restaurant.com

A "way-upscale seafood shanty" executed with "traditional New
England" style, Stephen Starr's Fairmount fish house seems
plucked "straight out of Cape Cod", boasting a "big space" "beautifully done in shades of gray", where "fresh, well-prepared" fin fare,
including raw bar specialties and "phenomenal whole lobster",
is served; surveyors report "intense noise levels", and some carp
that the "servers need some serious training", but most declare it
a "winner" overall.

Royal Tavern ◗ *American*

26 | 18 | 21 | $22

Bella Vista | 937 E. Passyunk Ave. (bet. Carpenter & Montrose Sts.) | 215-389-6694 | www.royaltavern.com

Fans say this "go-to gastropub" in Bella Vista is "super-crowded for a reason", namely, an "abundant" menu of "inventive" American bar food that "caters to both carnivores and vegans", plus daily specials, backed by a "diverse drink list" and "many beers on tap"; a "hip environment" and "service with a smile" help ameliorate "considerable" waits.

R2L ◗ *American*

23 | 28 | 23 | $62

Rittenhouse | Residences at Two Liberty Pl. | 50 S. 16th St. (Chestnut St.) | 215-564-5337 | www.r2lrestaurant.com

When you want to feel "elite", fans recommend Daniel Stern's flagship on the 37th floor of Two Liberty Place, where "amazing views" and an "iconic" art deco room set the stage for "interesting" New American fare, a "great wine list" and "attentive" service; there's a "sexy" scene in the "vibrant bar" area, and while a few find it "overpriced", many deem it an "excellent" choice for a "special night."

Ruby's Diner *Diner*

19 | 20 | 19 | $18

Ardmore | Suburban Sq. | 5 Coulter Ave. (Anderson Ave.) | 610-896-7829

King of Prussia | Plaza at King of Prussia Mall | 160 N. Gulph Rd. (bet. Dekalb Pike & Mall Blvd.) | 610-337-7829

Glen Mills | Brinton Lakes Shopping Ctr. | 919 Baltimore Pike (Brinton Lake Rd.) | 610-358-1983

www.rubys.com

While these "retro" diners take you "back to the '50s and '60s" with their "burger-and-shake" approach that's decidedly "cholesterol-laden", they also offer a selection of "healthier lifestyle choices" (e.g. "gluten-free rolls and veggie burgers"); service is "prompt", though a few find it "hit-or-miss", and others warn the "kid-friendly" setting can translate to a "loud" dining experience.

NEW Russet Ⓜ *American*

- | - | - | M

Rittenhouse | 1521 Spruce St. (bet. 15th & 16th Sts.) | 215-546-1521 | www.russetphilly.com

A "wonderful addition" to Philly's ever-expanding BYO scene, this "quiet", "creative" New American in Rittenhouse is run by a "husband-and-wife team that knows how to cook and host", serving a "farm-to-table" menu with French and Italian accents, including housemade charcuterie; housed in an old brownstone, the homey digs feature reclaimed furniture and tables made with recycled barn wood.

Rustica *Pizza/Sandwiches*

26 | 17 | 24 | $12

Northern Liberties | 903 N. 2nd St. (Poplar St.) | 215-627-1393 | www.rusticaphilly.com

"Grabbing a slice is always nice" at Northern Liberties' go-to "gourmet-pizza" joint where piezani "pay a little more" for "taste-explosion" pies with "killer" flavor combinations and a "crazy mix of toppings"; "courteous, attentive" service is another plus, and while the hole-in-the-wall probably "won't win awards for romanticism", "you're going for the pizza", after all.

Ruth's Chris Steak House *Steak*

25 | 23 | 24 | $69

Avenue of the Arts | 260 S. Broad St. (Spruce St.) | 215-790-1515
King of Prussia | 220 N. Gulph Rd. (Mall Blvd.) | 610-992-1818
www.ruthschris.com

"Consistency and excellence" are the hallmarks of this "expensive" meatery chain that provides "bang for your steakhouse buck" with "sizzling", "out-of-this-world" steaks that stand up to those of "most NYC testosterone-powered houses"; the staff is "interested in your comfort and satisfaction", while the setting is "fancy enough to make a date special."

Rybread *Sandwiches*

24 | 18 | 23 | $11

Fairmount | 2319 Fairmount Ave. (bet. 23rd & 24th Sts.) | 215-769-0603 | www.rybreadcafe.com

The "made-to-order sandwiches and panini" at this cafe in Fairmount are a "nice alternative to hoagies" and are served by "genuinely nice" folks; you "order at the counter" from the chalkboard menu in the "bright", "Lilliputian-size" space adorned with road-trip photos, and there's also a "cute, tiny" outdoor patio.

Sabrina's Cafe *Eclectic*

25 | 18 | 22 | $21

Bella Vista | 910 Christian St. (bet. 9th & 10th Sts.) | 215-574-1599
University City | Drexel University, Ross Commons | 229 N. 34th St. (Powelton Ave.) | 215-222-1022

Sabrina's Cafe & Spencer's Too *Eclectic*

Fairmount | 1804 Callowhill St. (18th St.) | 215-636-9061 | www.sabrinascafe.com

"Bring friends to share" "huge portions" of "consistently" "terrific" breakfasts and brunches at this "homey" Eclectic–New American trio with a "bohemian" "funky diner" vibe; "decadent" stuffed French toast and other "clutch" morning fare that could "quell any hangover" is brought by a "caring" staff, and while there's often a "long wait", the "vibrant crowd" insists it's "more than worth it."

Saffron Indian Kitchen *Indian*

24 | 17 | 22 | $27

Bala Cynwyd | 145 Montgomery Ave. (bet. Bangor & Tregaron Rds.) | 484-278-4112
Ambler | 60 E. Butler Ave. (Ridge Ave.) | 215-540-0237 | www.saffronofphilly.com

"Traditional" Indian fare comes "as mild or spicy as you like" and served by an "enthusiastic" staff at this "popular" local BYO duo that's "a cut above" generic curry houses; it "won't hurt your wallet, but may hurt your ears" when packed with boisterous diners, though the "soft-colored" decor is a "nice departure" from the typical Indian dining room.

	FOOD	DECOR	SERVICE	COST

Salento ⓜ *Italian* ▽ 23 | 18 | 24 | $35

Rittenhouse | 2216 Walnut St. (23rd St.) | 215-568-1314 |
www.salentorestaurant.com

The Rittenhouse sibling of South Philly's L'Angolo offers the "refreshing warmth of southern Italian pastas and hospitality" with its
"flavorful, authentic" regional Puglian fare served by an "attentive, personable" staff; the ambiance is "warm and inviting" in the
"modest", rustic space, and "BYO is a bonus."

Saloon Restaurant 🚫 *Italian/Steak* 26 | 24 | 25 | $60

Bella Vista | 750 S. 7th St. (bet. Catharine & Fitzwater Sts.) |
215-627-1811 | www.saloonrestaurant.net

You'll "feel important" at this "upscale" Bella Vista steakhouse, a
"perennial favorite" since 1967, where steaks and "old-style" Italian dishes are "cooked and served to perfection" in a "loud, brassy"
setting by "beautiful" waitresses; while some think it's been
"somewhat overtaken" by the competition, many insist it "lives up
to its fine reputation" as "one of the best Philly has to offer."

Salt & Pepper 🚫ⓜ◐ *American* ▽ 25 | 20 | 24 | $43

East Passyunk | 1623 E. Passyunk Ave. (Tasker St.) |
215-238-1920 | www.saltandpepperphilly.com

Fans of this "charming" New American feel the "move to East
Passyunk did it well", and now it fits the "definition of 'neighborhood gem'", thanks to "simple" but "flawlessly executed" fare,
"friendly" service and a "warm, inviting" setting with a "local vibe";
it's "not cheap", but you get "plenty on the plate" and the wine list
provides "good value" (it's no longer BYO).

ⓃⒺⓌ Sammy Chon's ▽ 25 | 16 | 23 | $22
K-Town BBQ *Korean*

Chinatown | 911 Race St. (bet. 9th & 10th Sts.) | 215-574-1778 |
www.ktownbbq.com

See review in the New Jersey Suburbs Directory.

Sampan *Asian* 25 | 23 | 22 | $45

Washington Square West | 124 S. 13th St. (bet. Sansom & Walnut Sts.) |
215-732-3501 | www.sampanphilly.com

Michael Schulson's "offbeat takes" on "modern" Pan-Asian fare, in
the form of "interesting small plates", "succeed remarkably" at his
"cool, trendy" Washington Square West establishment, which also
offers what some say is the "best happy hour in town"; a "great
soundtrack" plays in the "sexy" setting with an open kitchen,
where "friendly" service helps foster a "relaxed atmosphere."

Sang Kee Asian Bistro 🚫 *Chinese* 24 | 19 | 22 | $28

Wynnewood | 339 E. Lancaster Ave. (Wynnewood Rd.) |
610-658-0618 | www.sangkeeasianbistro.com

The "mob scene tells the story" of Michael Chow's midpriced
Wynnewood outpost, which is "always crowded, for good reason" – namely, "attractively presented", "above-average" spins
on Chinese classics, served by an "accommodating" staff in an

"upscale but unfussy" contemporary setting; while you need to "be prepared to wait" and brace for "over-the-top" noise levels, most agree the "food's worth it."

Sang Kee Noodle House ⊭ Chinese   23 | 17 | 19 | $22

University City | Sheraton University City | 3549 Chestnut St. (36th St.) | 215-387-8808 | www.sangkeenoodlehouse.com

"Tasty", "handsomely presented" Chinese eats come "cheap and fast" at this duo from Michael Chow in University City and Cherry Hill, where there's "something on the menu for everyone"; most report a "pleasant experience", but they "can get busy at lunch" and there are often "lines out the door on weekends", which is why some "recommend takeout."

Sang Kee   25 | 11 | 19 | $20
Peking Duck House ⊭ Chinese

Chinatown | 238 N. 9th St. (Vine St.) | 215-925-7532 | www.sangkeechinatown.com
Chinatown | Reading Terminal Mkt. | 51 N. 12th St. (bet. Arch & Filbert Sts.) | 215-922-3930 | www.readingterminalmarket.org

"For decades", Michael Chow's Chinatown "classic" (and his take-out "gem" in Reading Terminal) has been dishing out "consistently outstanding", "inexpensive" Chinese eats, including "succulent" duck, "out-of-control good" soups and "phenomenal" wontons; just remember – "they only take cash", and "no one goes here for ambiance."

Sannie Japanese Chinese   Chinese/Japanese   ▽ 24 | 23 | 21 | $24

Northeast Philly | Bustleton Cottman Shopping Ctr. | 2117 Cottman Ave. (Large St.) | 215-722-6278

A "nice break" from the pizzerias and fast-food chains, this Northeast Philly combo spot is a "good neighborhood option" for Chinese or Japanese, including "fresh" sushi, "before or after a movie next door" or for takeout; it's "nicely decorated" and the staff is "pleasant", although some find the service "slow."

Santucci Square Pizza   Pizza   25 | 20 | 22 | $19

Bella Vista | 901 S. 10th St. (Christian St.) | 215-825-5304
Northeast Philly | 4010 Cottman Ave. (Frankford Rd.) | 215-281-2900
Northeast Philly | 901 Tyson Ave. (Whitaker Ave.) | 215-934-5868
Port Richmond | 2313 E. Venango St. (Aramingo Ave.) | 215-288-2900
www.santuccis.com

Joe Santucci's   Pizza/Sandwiches

Northeast Philly | 4050 Woodhaven Rd. (bet. Knights & Millbrook Rds.) | 215-281-2900 | www.joesantuccisquarepizza.com

For a "different kind of pizza", piezani head to this affordable, "family-friendly" pizzeria chain for the Santucci clan's square, sauce-on-top pies; the service is "pleasant", and it "doesn't have to look pretty, because the pizza is the only reason to go."

	FOOD	DECOR	SERVICE	COST

Savona *Italian*

FOOD 26 | DECOR 26 | SERVICE 24 | COST $67

Gulph Mills | 100 Old Gulph Rd. (Rte. 320) | 610-520-1200 | www.savonarestaurant.com

"One of the most sophisticated" dining experiences on the Main Line is how fans describe this "destination" Italian in Gulph Mills, where Andrew Masciangelo's "outstanding", "creative" cuisine is complemented by a seemingly "limitless selection" of wines; the service is "professional" ("stiff" to some), while the setting is "elegant and intimate", and if "sky-high prices" make you dizzy, the "more casual" Bar Savona is a "moderate" option.

Sawatdee *Thai*

∇ 15 | 13 | 17 | $27

Rittenhouse | 1501 South St. (15th St.) | 215-790-1299

While its name may mean 'hello' in Thai, this Rittenhouse BYO offers good buys in the form of "unbeatable" lunch specials; surveyors are mum on the lime-green digs, while some critics express "disappointment" in the fare and suggest "more heat" is needed.

Sazon Restaurant & Cafe Ⓜ ⑳ *Venezuelan*

∇ 24 | 20 | 23 | $25

Northern Liberties | 941 Spring Garden St. (10th St.) | 215-763-2500 | www.sazonrestaurant.com

It "feels like you're in another country" at this Northern Liberties Venezuelan BYO on a "hip block" of Spring Garden, turning out "meals to remember" consisting of "authentic" dishes that "warm the soul" (including several gluten-free options), topped off by "incredible desserts and hot chocolate"; it's run by "likable" folks who provide "attentive" service in the "inviting, warm" setting.

ᴺᴱᵂ Sbraga *American*

27 | 24 | 24 | $64

Avenue of the Arts | 440 S. Broad St. (Pine St.) | 215-735-1913 | www.sbraga.com

A "*Top Chef* creates a top restaurant" is the story line of Kevin Sbraga's New American located "steps from the Kimmel Center", where the TV "winner" provides "affordable fine dining" with a "bargain" prix fixe of "mind-bending" small plates; an open kitchen anchors the "trendy" rustic space (which can get "noisy"), while the "friendly", "knowledgeable" staff works hard to ensure a "memorable evening."

Scannicchio's *Italian*

25 | 18 | 24 | $42

South Philly | 2500 S. Broad St. (Porter St.) | 215-468-3900 | www.scannicchio.com

"Reservations are a must" at this South Philly Italian BYO, a popular "pre-concert or -game" stop where the "focus is on the food"; a "friendly", "accommodating" staff makes you feel "welcome" in the "comfy", if somewhat "limited", space and helps you navigate the "wide-ranging menu" that's "sure to please everyone."

Schlesinger's *Deli*

20 | 15 | 19 | $17

Rittenhouse | 1521 Locust St. (16th St.) | 215-735-7305 |
www.schlesingersdeli.com

An "old-fashioned Jewish deli with all the trimmings", this
Rittenhouse spot is a "traditional" operation in the "home-
made-food-from-your-bubbe" vein, where "gigantic" sandwiches
and more are "served efficiently" by "friendly" folk; a few sniff that
the emphasis is "more on quantity than quality", but most deem it
a "very nice" nosh.

Scoogi's Classic Italian *Italian*

21 | 18 | 20 | $29

Flourtown | 738 Bethlehem Pike (Arlingham Rd.) | 215-233-1063 |
www.scoogis.com

A "popular local institution", Flourtown's "nice neighborhood
Italian" remains a "reliable" choice for "casual" dining, with
"lots of good choices" of "traditional" eats; while it may "not be
distinguished", "affordable" prices and a "relaxing" vibe make it
especially "good for groups."

Seasons Pizza *Pizza*

21 | 18 | 21 | $18

Aston | 2755 Weir Rd. (bet. Pennell & Richard Rds.) |
610-485-1000 | www.seasonspizza.com

A "reliable" option for "decent" pizzas, this chain also serves other
entrees such as cheesesteaks "seasoned just right" and "great
fried chicken"; critics sniff that the 'za is "not like what you'd get
from NYC", but "fast" service and delivery and affordable prices
make it a "family-friendly" choice for many.

Seasons 52 *American*

24 | 25 | 24 | $38

King of Prussia | Plaza at King of Prussia Mall | 160 N. Gulph Rd.
(bet. Dekalb Pike & Mall Blvd.) | 610-992-1152 | www.seasons52.com
"Flavorful, local" American dishes, all "under 500 calories", and
"guilt-free" "dessert shooters" attract a "health-conscious" crowd
to these Cherry Hill and King of Prussia links of a national chain;
some grumble it's a bit "overrated", but most say the "beautiful decor", "top-notch" service and "piano bar" with "live music"
contribute to a "romantic", "relaxing" experience.

Serafina *Italian*

16 | 18 | 16 | $39

Rittenhouse | 10 Rittenhouse | 130 S. 18th St. (Sansom St.) |
215-977-7755 | www.serafinarestaurant.com

Positioned on one of the "hottest corners" in Rittenhouse, this
"NYC offshoot" may be "more of a see-and-be-seen" destination
than pizzeria; while critics carp about "expensive" prices, "tight
tables" and "clipped" (albeit "prompt") service, most find the
Northern Italian fare "steadily good", if not "groundbreaking."

Seven Stars Inn 🅼 *Steak*

26 | 22 | 25 | $55

Phoenixville | 300 Ridge Rd. (Hoffecker Rd.) | 610-495-5205 |
www.sevenstarsinn.com

Phoenixville's pre-Revolutionary inn, a "small-town restaurant"
known for "Fred Flintstone–sized" servings of steak and seafood,

may be "rough on the checkbook" but it's "well worth it" to fans, especially for special occasions; "elegant food" and "excellent service" win over both locals and tourists, who aren't "embarrassed to take a doggy bag home" for "a week of leftovers."

1750 Bistro *American*   25 | 22 | 23 | $33

Lansdale | Holiday Inn Lansdale | 1750 Sumneytown Pike (Towamencin Ave.) | 215-368-3800 | www.1750bistro.com
"Excellent" American fare, including "amazing sandwiches", and "friendly", "helpful" service in a "cool", modern setting with "art deco" touches make this bistro in the Lansdale Holiday Inn a solid bet for a "business" lunch or "relaxing" dinner; Friday nights attract a local crowd "out to have fun."

NEW Shake Shack *Burgers*   - | - | - | I

Rittenhouse | 2000 Sansom St. (20th St.) | 215-809-1742 | www.shakeshack.com
Crowds are already flocking to the new outpost of Danny Meyer's NYC-based burger and hot dog empire just off Rittenhouse Square for affordable, quick-serve patties and dogs, as well as custard concoctions laced with local ingredients; the cheery, eco-friendly space boasts reclaimed brick floors, recycled wood furnishings and a living green wall on the front of the building.

Shangrila *Asian*   ▽ 23 | 20 | 23 | $30

Devon | 120 Swedesford Rd. (Valley Forge Rd.) | 610-687-8838 | www.shangrila120.com
Serving some of the "best sushi on the Main Line", this Asian fusion specialist in Devon delivers beyond the raw fish department with an "extensive menu" that includes tempura platters, stir-fries and Thai specialties; service is "friendly and fast" in the quiet venue that also offers "quality takeout."

Shere-E-Punjab *Indian*   26 | 21 | 23 | $22

Drexel Hill | Drexeline Shopping Ctr. | 5059 State Rd. (City Ave.) | 484-452-8140
Media | 208 W. State St. (bet. Orange St. & Veterans Sq.) | 610-891-0400
www.shereepunjab.com
Fans "have dreams" about "wonderfully seasoned and perfectly portioned" Indian fare at this Delaware County duo where the "fragrant aromas of jasmine and coriander" greet visitors to the "surprisingly good" lunch buffet and "close-quarters" dinner service; mild-to-wild-spiced dishes are "tailored to your tastes" and come at "acceptable prices."

Shiao Lan Kung ● *Chinese*   ▽ 23 | 6 | 18 | $23

Chinatown | 930 Race St. (bet. 9th & 10th Sts.) | 215-928-0282
The "immaculate kitchen" at this Chinatown BYO "delivers satisfaction" in the form of dumplings in "sauce so good it's drinkable", "fat, fresh oysters" and the house specialty "salt-baked" seafood; so what if the ambiance is "near zero"– aficionados assert the "food brings you back"; P.S. late hours are a plus.

	FOOD	DECOR	SERVICE	COST

Ship Inn *Seafood/Steak*

| 21 | 23 | 21 | $39 |

Exton | 693 E. Lincoln Hwy. (Ship Rd.) | 610-363-7200 |
www.shipinn.net

A "charming" Exton destination founded as a travelers' public
house in the late 18th century, this "off-the-beaten-path"
steak-and-seafooder is a "good drive" for many, but most feel
the unique "historic" decor and "beautiful atmosphere" are
"well worth" the haul, and "above-average" food and service
seal the deal.

Shiroi Hana *Japanese*

| 25 | 21 | 23 | $38 |

Rittenhouse | 222 S. 15th St. (bet. Locust & Walnut Sts.) |
215-735-4444 | www.shiroihana.com

Still "excellent after all these years", this midpriced Rittenhouse
Japanese has been dishing out "solid, no-frills sushi" and a
"wonderful selection of entrees" since 1984; "timely", "attentive"
service and "no loud music" in the "bright, clean" setting put diners in a "mellow" mood.

Siam Cuisine *Thai*

| 23 | 15 | 21 | $32 |

Doylestown | Buckingham Green Shopping Ctr. | 4950 York Rd.
(Hwy. 202) | 215-794-7209 | www.siamcuisinepa.com

Fans are "never disappointed" by the "consistent", midpriced eats
at this strip-mall Thai in Doylestown, where the owner "can be
found greeting each guest warmly" in the "small, quaint" setting; a
few feel it "needs some updating", while spice lovers find the fare
"on the bland side" and advise "speaking up if you want them to
bring the heat."

The Sidecar
Bar & Grille ● *Eclectic*

| 24 | 19 | 21 | $23 |

Southwest Center City | 2201 Christian St. (22nd St.) |
215-732-3429 | www.thesidecarbar.com

A "focused", "well-executed menu" of "creative" Eclectic eats pairs
well with a "rotating" lineup of draft beers and "extensive bottle
list" at this "low-key" gastropub in Southwest Center City, which
attracts a "diverse crowd" (but "watch out for the hipsters"); "super-friendly" service is a plus, and the upstairs bar is a "fantastic
addition", although it means it's "only getting busier", especially
on weekends, which can be "madness."

Silk City ● *American*

| 24 | 20 | 22 | $23 |

Northern Liberties | 435 Spring Garden St. (bet. 4th & 5th Sts.) |
215-592-8838 | www.silkcityphilly.com

Fans "go for the fried chicken" and other "interesting, unique"
American comfort-food offerings at this diner-cum-"hipster bar"
in Northern Liberties offering an "awesome" outdoor beer garden,
"live music and a happening dance scene", as well as "meatloaf
and mashed potatoes like mom used to make"; "friendly" service
and "reasonable" prices are additional reasons that it's become
a "Philly staple."

	FOOD	DECOR	SERVICE	COST

The Silverspoon *American*   ▽ 23 | 18 | 23 | $37

Wayne | Eagle Village Shops | 503 W. Lancaster Ave.
(bet. Eagle & Old Eagle School Rds.) | 610-688-7646 |
www.silverspoonwayne.com

Preparing "elegant" American fare in Wayne, this "unpretentious" BYO offers Main Liners an "innovative" menu of seasonal fare made with market-driven ingredients, which is served with guidance from a "knowledgeable staff"; though small, the "light and airy" quarters include a "fantastic" outdoor option in season, and though some find it "a tad overpriced", to most the "charming" package shows "lots of promise."

Singapore Kosher   ▽ 27 | 19 | 26 | $16
Vegetarian Restaurant *Chinese/Vegetarian*

Chinatown | 1006 Race St. (bet. 10th & 11th Sts.) | 215-922-3288 |
www.singaporevegetarian.com

Both vegetarians and "meat eaters" report "amazing" experiences at Peter Fong's kosher Chinese vegetarian in Chinatown, where an "insanely huge" menu of "awesome" meatless fare is "masterfully prepared with flair" and served by an "exceptionally friendly" staff; a "cozy" setting with a "down-to-earth" vibe completes the picture.

Sitar India *Indian*   23 | 16 | 19 | $17

University City | 60 S. 38th St. (bet. Chestnut & Market Sts.) |
215-662-0818 | www.sitarindiacuisine.net

A "go-to for students", this University City Indian offers "unbelievable buffets" (with "lots of vegetarian options") at lunch and dinner "for unbelievable prices", and while the fare may be "toned down for the American palate", it's "still complex and interesting"; "friendly" service and "tasteful" surroundings add to the value.

63 Bistro ☒ *American*   25 | 22 | 24 | $34

North Wales | Montgomery Commons | 1200 Welsh Rd. (Wales Rd.) |
267-263-4088 | www.63bistro.com

Chef Ted Scholl's "creativity and interesting ingredients" shine on the BBQ-centric American menu at this "quaint" BYO bistro in an "unassuming" North Wales strip mall, where you'll "need extra time" choosing from among the "mouthwatering" offerings; "affordable" tariffs, a "welcoming" staff and a "relaxing" vibe make it a good bet when you want to "catch up with friends."

Sketch *Burgers*   28 | 20 | 24 | $15

Fishtown | 413 E. Girard Ave. (Columbia Ave.) | 215-634-3466 |
www.sketch-burger.com

'Super-messy burgers" and other "comfort-food" classics are "worth the hike" to this Fishtown "joint" where diners doodle while they wait and seating options include "vintage church pews"; Kobe beef and even vegan patties plus sauces that add "the right amount of sloppy, fatty goodness" are a testament to the kitchen's "creativity", and while it all "might cost a few bucks more", "personal, passionate" service seals the deal.

	FOOD	DECOR	SERVICE	COST

Slack's Hoagie Shack *Sandwiches*   23 | 13 | 21 | $13

Springfield | 158 Baltimore Pike (Homestead Ave.) | 610-338-0112
Willow Grove | 1019 Easton Rd. (Fitzwatertown Rd.) |
215-659-8917 | www.slackshoagies.com

A "go-to place for the work-a-day crowd," this hoagie chain layers "fresh and chewy rolls" with enough meat to "bust your belly", while "great steaks", "amazing" chicken wraps and "perfectly fried" french fries also get a shout-out; "nice employees" provide "quick service", and most "always leave satisfied."

Slate ⓂⓄ *American*   ▽ 21 | 22 | 21 | $35

Rittenhouse | 102 S. 21st St. (bet. Chestnut & Sansom Sts.) |
215-568-6886 | www.slatephiladelphia.com

A "late-night find tucked away" off Rittenhouse Square, this "under- the-radar" gastropub is a popular post-shift stop for "restaurant industry folks" for its "simple" New American fare "brought up to a new level"; the "inviting, tasteful" space is usually populated with "enough people to keep it interesting", but "not too crowded", although some gripe that the staff can appear "dis-tracted" at times.

Slate Bleu *French*   ▽ 26 | 21 | 24 | $48

Doylestown | 100 S. Main St. (Green St.) | 215-348-0222 |
www.slatebleu.com

For "French bistro done right", Francophiles head to this "quiet gem" in Doylestown, where "rustic flavors, execution and love abound" on a "scrumptious" menu of both "traditional offerings" and more "imaginative" small- and medium-sized plates; service is "attentive but not overbearing" in the upscale-casual space.

SLiCE *Pizza*   23 | 13 | 20 | $15

South Philly | 1180 S. 10th St. (Federal St.) | 215-463-0868
Rittenhouse | 1740 Sansom St. (18th St.) | 215-557-9299
www.slicepa.com

This pizzeria duo may be a "bit more expensive than your average pizza place, but it's worth it" for "pizza as it should be" – a "thin, toothsome crust" and toppings with "strong flavors"; "fast", "super-friendly" service makes up for lack of ambiance, and while slices are the forte, the sides and salads "are no slouch" either.

Sly Fox
Brewhouse & Eatery *Pub Food*   19 | 16 | 20 | $25

Phoenixville | 520 Kimberton Rd. (bet. Pothouse & Seven Stars Rds.) |
610-935-4540 | www.slyfoxbeer.com

"Pleasant" staffers really know their "flavorful" beers (at least a dozen, including some brewed on-premises) at this "bright" Phoenixville brewpub whose "happy-hour specials" often come with a musical backdrop and menu includes "different spins on sandwiches"; a few naysayers, noting the 2010 move across the road, quip that the new digs "make me feel like I should be paying a late fee on my DVD rental."

	FOOD	DECOR	SERVICE	COST

Smith & Wollensky ● *Steak*
25 | 22 | 24 | $66

Rittenhouse | Rittenhouse Hotel | 210 W. Rittenhouse Sq. (bet. Locust & Walnut Sts.) | 215-545-1700 | www.smithandwollensky.com

"No unpleasant surprises" are in store at the Rittenhouse Hotel outpost of the "classic" steakhouse chain, where "glorious steaks" are served by a "friendly" staff; the primo-location room with a "great view of Rittenhouse Square" is a "lovely place from which to people-watch"; of course, the "upscale" experience "will cost you."

Smokin' Betty's *American/BBQ*
22 | 20 | 20 | $26

Washington Square West | 116 S. 11th St. (Sansom St.) | 215-922-6500 | www.smokinbettys.com

Fans "have never been disappointed" by the "respectable" BBQ and "creative New American" cooking at this Wash West eatery that "brings the South to Sansom Street"; the "decor is simple" in the "spacious" industrial setting that can get "really noisy", and while the staff is "friendly", some report that service can be "on and off."

Snockey's Oyster & Crab House *Seafood*
21 | 13 | 18 | $29

South Philly | 1020 S. 2nd St. (Washington Ave.) | 215-339-9578 | www.snockeys.com

As "old-fashioned" as it gets, this century-old South Philly "icon" opened three weeks after the Titanic sank in 1912, and has been serving "delectable oysters" and "fresh seafood" ever since; don't "expect anything fancy" from the tiled-wall space, just "friendly" service and a "good selection" of "market"-fresh fin fare.

Sola ⊠Ⓜ *American*
27 | 22 | 25 | $52

Bryn Mawr | 614 W. Lancaster Ave. (Penn St.) | 610-526-0123 | www.solabyob.com

"Consistently classy", this "haute" New American BYO in Bryn Mawr offers "imaginative", "beautifully presented" cuisine and "congenial" service in a "cozy", if somewhat "cramped" space, where you'll espy the local "social register" indulging in a "laid-back evening" with a "pinch of elegance"; a post-Survey ownership change may not be reflected in the scores, however.

Solefood ● *Seafood*
▽ 25 | 24 | 26 | $44

Washington Square West | Loews Philadelphia Hotel | 1200 Market St. (12th St.) | 215-231-7300 | www.loewshotels.com

"Fancier than the name lets on", this seafooder in the Loews near City Hall is a "surprise" to many, with "excellent", "perfectly cooked" fin fare and a staff that pays "lovely attention" to diners; though it may "look like a hotel restaurant", the "huge" dining room gets high marks for the "relaxed", "chic" ambiance.

The Sorella Rose Bar and Grille *American*
▽ 18 | 16 | 16 | $31

Flourtown | 1800 Bethlehem Pike (Mill Rd.) | 215-233-0616 | www.sorellarose.com

Surveyors report a "pleasant experience" at this veteran American in Flourtown, where "good food" comes with "reasonable pricing"; set

	FOOD	DECOR	SERVICE	COST

in a former hotel dating back to 1811, it "has a bed-and-breakfast feel to it", and some think it "needs a makeover", although the outdoor patio is "relaxing and enjoyable" when you're "sharing a bottle of wine with the one you love."

Sorrento's Italian Restaurant *Italian*   25 | 18 | 24 | $26

Lafayette Hill | 449 Ridge Pike (Chestnut St.) | 610-828-8093
If you want "good old-fashioned Italian comfort food", "but don't want to break the bank", *amici* tout this casual BYO in Lafayette Hill, where the cooking is "better than mom's" and comes in "portions that would make grandma proud"; "warm, friendly" service and a "charming atmosphere" make up for the plain stand-alone digs, and many consider it a "dependable" option for "any occasion."

South Ocean *Chinese/Japanese*   ∇ 26 | 19 | 26 | $21

Flourtown | 1664 Bethlehem Pike (Mill Rd.) | 215-836-8188 | www.southoceanpa.com
A "nice neighborhood place" in Flourtown, this Chinese-Japanese BYO is a "gem" quietly producing what fans say is some of the "best Asian food in the area", and while it may cost "a few dollars more" than others, most agree it's "well worth the price"; "impeccable" service is another reason it "gets crowded on weekends."

South Philadelphia Tap Room ❶ *American*   25 | 20 | 20 | $24

South Philly | 1509 Mifflin St. (bet. 15th & 16th Sts.) | 215-271-7787 | www.southphiladelphiataproom.com
The "kitchen is always on point" at this South Philly "rock star" serving "banging" American pub grub ("delightful wild boar tacos") and "way too many beers to name" in a "classy" setting with a "chill atmosphere"; the servers strike some as "edgy," but are generally "helpful" and "friendly", all of which make it a solid place for a "date" or "dinner and drinks before games."

South St. Souvlaki Ⓜ *Greek*   23 | 15 | 22 | $21

South St. | 509 South St. (bet. 5th & 6th Sts.) | 215-925-3026 | www.southstreetdinerphilly.com
It's "not fancy or trendy", but this "well-known" South Street Greek has been an "ace in the hole" for many since 1977, offering "flavorful" Hellenic fare at "reasonable" prices in a "genuine" setting; "friendly", "accommodating" service also helps make it a "solid dining selection."

Southwark Restaurant Ⓜ *American*   23 | 22 | 22 | $45

Queen Village | 701 S. 4th St. (Bainbridge St.) | 215-238-1888 | www.southwarkrestaurant.com
"Creative", "well-executed" New American fare featuring "local ingredients" and "old-timey mixed drinks" in a "lovely" old-school setting make this Queen Village watering hole a "best bet" for many; aficionados advise "trust the servers", for they're "extremely knowledgeable", and "don't order anything with vodka if you're not prepared for a fight."

	FOOD	DECOR	SERVICE	COST

Sovana Bistro Ⓜ *French/Mediterranean* — 28 | 23 | 26 | $53

Kennett Square | 696 Unionville Rd. (Rte. 926) | 610-444-5600 |
www.sovanabistro.com

Enthusiasts encourage city folk to "get in your Zipcars", pronto,
because this "contemporary" Kennett Square destination is "worth
the ride into the country" for "surprising, original" French-Med fare
that reflects "great use of locally grown or raised" ingredients –
predictably, the "tiny tables" are "packed at all hours"; account-
ing for the "quality" eats, "first-class" service and optional BYO,
"prices are not bad", but "bring extra cash" anyway.

🆕 SoWe Bar Kitchen ● *American* — - | - | - | M

Southwest Center City | 918 S. 22nd St. (Carpenter St.) |
215-545-5790 | www.sowephilly.com

The name refers to 'Southwest Center City' (though locals know
it as Graduate Hospital) at this stylish neighborhood bistro, with
an affordable American menu that covers everything from burgers
to chile-rubbed duck breast; the weathered oak bar and woodsy
accents lend a rustic vibe to the intimate space.

Spampinato's Italian Restaurant *Italian* — ∇ 21 | 18 | 19 | $30

Conshohocken | 16 E. 1st Ave. (Harry St.) | 610-825-3151 |
www.spampinatosrestaurant.com

Simple, "good food" in the Italian-American image (antipasti,
chopped salads, pasta, etc.) is the play at this Conshohocken gravy
parlor; it's an altogether "friendly neighborhood environment",
and while decor is a bit plain, the outdoor courtyard, known as The
Grotto, is a "pleasant" option.

Spamps Restaurant *Steak* — 19 | 17 | 17 | $30

Conshohocken | 16 E. 1st Ave. (Harry St.) | 610-825-4155 |
www.spampsrestaurant.com

"Young professionals crowd" this Eclectic steakhouse in Conshohocken, where "always-fresh" sushi shares space on the menu
with steak and seafood specialties; the raw fish can be "excellent"
and "BOGO" (buy one, get one) nights help keep tabs down on big
orders; while the overall look and decor can seem "a bit schizo-
phrenic" (perhaps due to the attached traditional Italian Spampi-
nato's), service, at its best, is "accommodating."

Spasso Italian Grill *Italian* — 25 | 21 | 25 | $35

Old City | 34 S. Front St. (bet. Chestnut & Market Sts.) |
215-592-7661 | www.spassoitaliangrill.com

"Blink and you could miss" this "unassuming" Italian hidden on
Front Street in Old City where the cooking, while not cutting-edge,
would "make grandma proud"; the "rustic and pleasant" interior is
a fitting backdrop to "homemade pasta" and specialty whole fish,
and the "spacious" room ensures you "don't feel cramped"; service
is "upscale, yet friendly", which some interpret as "over the top",
but in a good way.

	FOOD	DECOR	SERVICE	COST

Spicy Thai *Thai*
▽ 27 | 21 | 25 | $22

Doylestown | 54 E. State St. (bet. Donaldson & Pine Sts.) | 215-345-5351 | www.spicethaicuisine1.com

This Doylestown neighborhood Thai is a "gem" for a bite before a movie at the nearby County Theater; heat levels of house specialties such as "Chu chee duck" and "ginger fish" are easily adjustable, and service at the BYO is "super-polite" and "prompt"; be sure to "reserve ahead", though, for tables on busy weekend evenings.

NEW Spiga Restaurant ⊠ *Italian*
- | - | - | M

Washington Square West | 1305 Locust St. (13th St.) | 267-273-1690 | www.spigaphiladelphia.com

This casual offering from the owners of Le Castagne serves a broad menu of modern Italian small plates, brick-oven pizzas and wood-fired grilled meats at pleasantly modest prices; the earthy atmosphere (exposed brick, reclaimed wood) reels in families and couples from across Washington Square West.

Sprig & Vine Ⓜ *Vegan*
▽ 27 | 22 | 25 | $29

New Hope | Union Sq. | 450 Union Sq. Dr. (York Rd.) | 215-693-1427 | www.sprigandvine.com

New Hope's innovative vegan restaurant crafts plant-based plates that "would satisfy the hungriest carnivore", including a "mouth-watering" Reuben; service is "accommodating", and the feel is "upscale but relaxed" with a handsome, eco-friendly interior.

Spring Mill Cafe Ⓜ *French*
25 | 23 | 24 | $44

Conshohocken | 164 Barren Hill Rd. (bet. Ridge Pike & River Rd.) | 610-828-2550 | www.springmill.com

"Tucked safely away from the traffic and noise", this "elegant" Conshy BYO flies you to "the French countryside, without the hassle of airport security"; classic bistro fare "with a Moroccan touch" is served "without attitude" in a "quirky" and "quaint" converted farmhouse brimming with "continental ambiance"; while a few may whisper it's past its prime, its "romantic" appeal lives on.

NEW Square Peg ● *American*
- | - | - | I

Washington Square West | 929 Walnut St. (10th St.) | 215-413-3600 | www.squarepegrestaurant.com

The crew from Cuba Libre is behind this spiffy, industrial-chic diner next to Jefferson Hospital on a busy corner in Washington Square West, where chef Matt Levin (ex Adsum, Lacroix) is turning out edgy American grub, e.g. fried chicken tacos and other options for abandoning your diet; the cocktail and beer lists are designed to keep 'em coming into the late hours.

Square 1682 ● *American*
22 | 24 | 20 | $49

Rittenhouse | The Palomar | 121 S. 17th St. (Sansom St.) | 215-563-5008 | www.square1682.com

Set in a "knockout" bi-level space in the Hotel Palomar near Rittenhouse Square, this "hip, stylish" entry deals in "innovative"

New American cuisine with frequent menu changes that "keep things appealing" for regulars, even if some snipe about "small portions" and "expensive" tabs; with "a little more effort" to improve "disjointed" service, it could emerge as "a destination."

St. Stephens Green ● Irish 22 | 18 | 22 | $26

Fairmount | 1701 Green St. (17th St.) | 215-769-5000 |
www.saintstephensgreen.com

Staffed by a "friendly, knowledgeable" crew, this Emerald Isle–inspired Fairmount tappie puts a "quirky" spin on "traditional pub food" that "complements" its "superb" beer selection, and prices are "reasonable"; designed by an Irish architect, the "warm, inviting" interior features a "cozy" fireplace, while the "picturesque" outdoor seating is "a great bet for a summer night."

Standard Tap ● American 23 | 18 | 19 | $27

Northern Liberties | 901 N. 2nd St. (Poplar St.) | 215-238-0630 |
www.standardtap.com

Still a local "benchmark", this Northern Liberties gastropub attracts an "amazing cast of characters" with its "always-changing" chalkboard menu of "delicious" American eats and 20-plus beers on tap (with a "focus on local") at "reasonable" prices; "service can be hit-or-miss" but "tattooed servers add a little something" to the experience, whether you're listening to the "awesome jukebox" downstairs, hanging "near the fireplace" on the "cozy" second floor or enjoying the "lovely" rooftop patio.

NEW Stateside American ∇ 27 | 23 | 23 | $40

East Passyunk | 1536 E. Passyunk Ave. (Cross St.) |
215-551-2500 | www.statesidephilly.com

The best thing to hit East Passyunk in some time, this tiny, "noisy" American "small-plates joint" facing the Singing Fountain is "popping" thanks to "lively cuisine" that's "well priced for the quality", plus a drink list that "rocks" (check out the "great bourbon selection"); fans are likewise impressed by the "neato" industrial interior and service that remains "impeccable" even on a "crowded night."

Stella Blu ☒ American 24 | 20 | 21 | $39

West Conshohocken | 101 Ford St. (Front St.) | 610-825-7060 |
www.stellablurestaurant.com

You "won't leave feeling blue" if you order the signature lobster mac 'n' cheese (devotees say it's "to die for") at this "busy" West Conshohocken "find" serving an array of midpriced New American eats and an international wine list; service is "fast", though stylish decor and weekly live music and DJs give reason to linger.

Stella Sera Italian ∇ 26 | 22 | 23 | $35

Chestnut Hill | 8630 Germantown Ave. (Bethlehem Pike) |
215-248-1980 | www.stellasera.com

The "homemade pasta is just this side of heaven" at this Chestnut Hill BYO dishing up "scrumptious", moderately priced Italian fare to a crowd of "interesting locals"; top-notch service and "cozy" decor add up to a "memorable experience" when you just want to "go with friends and relax."

Steve's Prince of Steaks ⊘ *Cheesesteaks* | 25 | 13 | 20 | $13

Northeast Philly | 7200 Bustleton Ave. (St. Vincent St.) | 215-338-0985
Northeast Philly | 2711B Comly Rd. (Roosevelt Blvd.) | 215-677-8020
Langhorne | 1617 E. Lincoln Hwy. (Highland Pkwy.) | 215-943-4640
www.stevesprinceofsteaks.com

A slightly-less-famous local cheesesteak "favorite", this "nothing-fancy", cash-only trio packs plenty of "quality meat" into "fresh, tasty rolls" for "no-frills" sandwiches with "lots of flavor"; the "hard-nosed" staff is "quick", so it helps to "know what you want before you get to the window."

The Stone Rose Restaurant ● *American* | ▽ 25 | 23 | 23 | $36

Conshohocken | 822 Fayette St. (bet. 8th & 9th Aves.) |
484-532-7300 | www.thestoneroserestaurant.com

This midrange Conshohocken American might "look like a pub" to some, but it distinguishes itself with "consistent" "upscale comfort food" showcasing "local ingredients" and a "fabulous" wine selection delivered by servers who are "great at making recommendations"; though most keep the "upbeat" neighborhood hub "in the rotation", "atrocious acoustics" give pause to potential regulars.

Su Xing House *Chinese* | ▽ 27 | 21 | 25 | $17

Rittenhouse | 1508 Sansom St. (bet. 15th & 16th Sts.) |
215-564-1419 | www.suxinghouse.com

You "hardly realize" it's "meatless" muse mavens of the "healthy", "flavorful cuisine" at this Rittenhouse vegetarian Chinese where the "decor is lovely for a place that doesn't look so exciting" from the sidewalk; accommodating service, "budget prices" and BYO further cement its reputation as a "go-to."

Sullivan's Steakhouse *Steak* | 26 | 24 | 24 | $57

King of Prussia | King of Prussia Mall | 700 W. Dekalb Pike (Mall Blvd.) |
610-878-9025 | www.sullivanssteakhouse.com

The "mouthwatering" meat and other "classic" steakhouse fare at these "swanky" chain links in King of Prussia and Wilmington can "take you back to an elegant time" where "you might expect to bump into Fred Astaire"; "professional" service, an "excellent" wine list, "knockout martinis" from the "hopping" bar and live nightly jazz help justify "expense-account" tabs.

Supper Ⓜ *American* | 25 | 23 | 23 | $50

South St. | 926 South St. (10th St.) | 215-592-8180 |
www.supperphilly.com

"Comfort food meets fine dining" at Mitch and Jennifer Prensky's "modern rustic" South Street New American, where they "take fresh, local ingredients seriously" on a "soulful", Southern-influenced menu ("yay for duck fat fries!") served by a "knowledgeable" crew in "spacious", "nicely appointed" bi-level digs; the all-around "delightful" dining experience is "a bit on the pricier side", though, so some "only go if someone else is paying the bill."

	FOOD	DECOR	SERVICE	COST

Susanna Foo's Gourmet Kitchen *Asian*   24 | 23 | 22 | $47

Radnor | Radnor Financial Ctr. | 555 E. Lancaster Ave. (Iven Ave.) |
610-688-8808 | www.susannafoo.com

Culinary "living legend" Susanna Foo's eponymous Radnor
Pan-Asian is still considered the "gold standard" for "gourmet yet
homey" fare that's "not your typical" Chinese ("delicious dumplings" remain a "highlight"); those who "miss the old Downtown
location" quibble with "consistency" and service that can be "lacking enthusiasm", but the "sleeker", "newer suburban digs" are still
"worth the drive" to devotees.

Swann Cafe ◐ *American/French*   25 | 25 | 25 | $57

Logan Square | Four Seasons Hotel | 1 Logan Sq. (Benjamin Franklin
Pkwy.) | 215-963-1500 | www.fourseasons.com

"The ambiance is the draw" at this casual alternative to the Four
Seasons' opulent Fountain, a "charming room with a fireplace"
encouraging guests to "sit for hours" and relish "elegant" New
American and French cuisine presented by an "attentive but not
overly pushy" staff; fans likewise "enjoy the ritual of high tea"
and a "decadent" Sunday brunch, even if a few critics complain a
"swann dive" in quality makes it all feel "overpriced for what little
you now get."

Sweet Lucy's Smokehouse *BBQ*   25 | 15 | 19 | $19

Northeast Philly | 7500 State Rd. (bet. Bleigh Ave. & Rhawn St.) |
215-333-9663 | www.sweetlucys.com

"Wonderfully tender, smoky" pork, ribs and chicken teamed with
"moist" cornbread and other "traditional sides" lure "ardent BBQ
fans" to this Northeast BYO rendition of a "Southern smokehouse"
where a "fast, courteous" counter staff dishes up "large portions"
at a "reasonable price"; "big eaters" overlook the "plain" ware-
house setting to earmark Monday nights for an all-you-can-eat
"pig-out" that's an "amazing deal" worthy of "stretchy pants."

Sycamore Ⓜ *American*   28 | 22 | 25 | $45

Lansdowne | 14 S. Lansdowne Ave. (Baltimore Ave.) |
484-461-2867 | www.sycamorebyo.com

"Local ingredients" shine on chef Sam Jacobson's "wonderfully
inventive" New American tasting and prix fixe menus at this BYO
"gem" in a "low-key" Lansdowne storefront where the "owner's
belief in service is inspiring"; a "first-class" cheese course, "wonderful" sticky toffee pudding dessert and "incredible" "cocktail
mixers" are pluses, leaving "high prices" as the only complaint.

Table 31 🗷 *Italian*   22 | 22 | 21 | $53

Logan Square | Comcast Ctr. | 1701 John F. Kennedy Blvd. (17th St.) |
215-567-7111 | www.table-31.com

Set in "upscale" confines in the Comcast Center, Chris Scar-
duzio's "stylish" Italian equally appeals to the "power-lunch",
"happy-hour" and special-occasion crowd with "tasty" and
"well-presented" fare via a "knowledgeable" staff; the "warm but
sophisticated ambiance" can be enjoyed in the "elegant" dining

room, "happening bar" or "wonderful" outdoor plaza, and most are
willing to pay "high prices" for the "quality."

Tacconelli's Pizzeria Ⓜ ⇗ *Pizza*   26 | 14 | 20 | $19
Port Richmond | 2604 E. Somerset St. (bet. Almond & Thompson Sts.) |
215-425-4983
Devotees "genuflect" when they walk into this cash-only BYO in
its original "nondescript" Port Richmond location or South Jersey
offshoot; a "national favorite" earning accolades for decades, the
"must go-to" is famous for its call-ahead policy to "reserve your
dough" – a practice some find a little "strange" – but it's the "standard setting" thin-crust pies that get the most attention.

Tai Lake Restaurant ⦿ *Chinese*   23 | 12 | 18 | $25
Chinatown | 134 N. 10th St. (bet. Cherry & Race Sts.) |
215-922-0698 | www.tailakeseafoodrest.com
"Fresh fish" is still "swimming in the tank" when you enter this
"authentic-as-it-gets" Chinatown "late-night" haunt where the
kitchen turns out "perfectly prepared" Cantonese seafood "until
3 AM"; most "don't care" about the unremarkable decor and occasionally "lax" service, considering the "bargain" tabs and the
option to BYO without corkage.

Talula's Garden *American*   27 | 27 | 25 | $63
Washington Square West | 210 W. Washington Sq. (Walnut St.) |
215-592-7787 | www.talulasgarden.com
"Oohs and ahs" fill the "farmhouse-chic" confines of this "spectacular" collaboration between Aimee Olexy (Talula's Table) and
Stephen Starr, where the "wonderfully inventive" American cuisine
showcases the "best ingredients the season has to offer", including
a "can't-miss cheese plate"; "impeccable" servers "lead you to
exactly what you want", and in summer the "gorgeous garden" is
"perfect" for a "magical meal" that's "well worth" the "high price."

Talula's Table *European*   28 | 24 | 28 | $92
Kennett Square | 102 W. State St. (Union St.) | 610-444-8255
"The tough part is getting in" to Aimee Olexy's "outstanding"
European BYO in a Kennett Square market, where groups of eight
to 12 sit at the sole table for the "superb" eight-course prix fixe
that delivers an "educating experience for the taste buds"; you'll
need "deep pockets" and reservations "a year in advance", but the
"staff couldn't be friendlier" and most agree this "one-of-a-kind"
package "deserves all the accolades it receives."

Tamarind *Thai*   25 | 16 | 23 | $23
South St. | 117 South St. (Hancock St.) | 215-925-2764
An "incredible find" on the party end of South Street, this "consistently excellent" BYO offers "fabulous" Thai fare ("and plenty of
it") at wallet-friendly prices; "attentive" but "quick" service means
there's "not too much lingering" in the "quaint" confines, but
insiders still "recommend calling ahead to reserve a table" to avoid
joining the crowds "champing at the bit" for a seat on weekends.

Tamarindos Mexican Restaurant Ⓜ *Mexican*

25 | 18 | 23 | $32

Broad Axe | Homemaker's Shopping Plaza | 36 W. Skippack Pike (Butler Pike) | 215-619-2390 | www.tamarindosrestaurant.com
"Free margaritas" are the first words from fans of "dedicated owner" Fernando Sauri's Broad Axe BYO, but "wonderfully creative" Mexican cooking that transcends "run-of-the-mill" tacos is the real hook; the "well-versed" staff "knows every detail of every dish", and though the "sparse" strip-mall setting can be "loud", this "great find" comes "without a hefty price."

Tampopo *Japanese/Korean*

22 | 14 | 19 | $18

Rittenhouse | 104 S. 21st St. (bet. Chestnut & Walnut Sts.) | 215-557-959 🖪
University City | 269 S. 44th St. (bet. Locust & Spruce Sts.) | 215-386-3866
www.tampoporestaurant.com Ⓜ
It's "less about the atmosphere" and more about the "tasty, flavorful" fare at these Asian "fast-food" twins dispensing "delicious" Japanese-Korean dishes in "simple" Rittenhouse and University City settings; the "utilitarian" approach (you "bus your own trays") and "cheap" tabs are "perfect for college students", and they even offer a "discount if you bring your own" bowl.

Tango *American*

22 | 22 | 22 | $39

Bryn Mawr | 39 Morris Ave. (Lancaster Ave.) | 610-526-9500 | www.tastetango.com
You can "watch the trains go by outside your window" from dining-car-inspired booths at this "charming" Bryn Mawr "standby" across from the SEPTA station, where "consistent" New American fare is peppered with Mexican specialties; "always pleasant" servers and "typical prices for the area" make it a moderate option "for a romantic evening."

NEW Tapestry ❶ *American*

▽ 25 | 21 | 25 | $30

Queen Village | 700 S. 5th St. (Bainbridge St.) | 215-923-1620
"Beer, booze and bites" is the mantra at this Queen Village brewpub armed with a varied American menu to complement the "exceptional selection" of "unique pints" poured by its "knowledgeable staff"; with "reasonable" tabs and an "outstanding" atmosphere to keep it "hopping", acolytes advise you to "get there early" to claim real estate in the "cozy interior."

Taqueria La Michoacana *Mexican*

▽ 24 | 17 | 22 | $24

Norristown | 301 E. Main St. (Arch St.) | 610-292-1971
"Remarkable guacamole" is one of "many delights" on the "extensive" Mexican menu at this "family-friendly" "gem" in a somewhat "depressed" part of Norristown where the "amazing and fresh" fare satisfies even "native" diners; "authentic decorations" spruce up the "comfortable" setting, while the "engaging" staff and "reasonable" prices add appeal.

	FOOD	DECOR	SERVICE	COST

Taqueria La Veracruzana ● *Mexican* ▽ 24 | 10 | 19 | $14

Bella Vista | 908 Washington Ave. (9th St.) | 215-465-1440
"Delicious and filling" Mexican "snack food" (tacos and quesadillas) is the primary export of this Bella Vista BYO; the inside is "nothing fancy", but the food, served in "huge portions", "more than makes up for simple decor"; service can be "a bit slow", but most find the fare "worth the hassle."

NEW Tashan *Indian* 25 | 25 | 23 | $51

Avenue of the Arts | 777 S. Broad St. (Catharine St.) |
267-687-2170 | www.mytashan.com
"Bollywood buzz with upscale Indian" fare sums up this Tiffin offshoot on Avenue of the Arts that "could make an Indian foodie out of anyone" with its "creative spin" and nontraditional approach; far from "lamb vindaloo territory", this is fusion gone "to nirvana" in a "snazzy" setting where servers who are "excited to share their knowledge" help make the "pricey" experience "worth every penny."

Tavern 17 ● *American* 18 | 19 | 18 | $31

Rittenhouse | Radisson Plaza-Warwick Hotel | 220 S. 17th St. (Chancellor St.) | 215-790-1799 | www.tavern17restaurant.com
"A cheap night of fun" can be arranged at this "noisy" tavern attached to Center City's Radisson Plaza-Warwick, where the "tasty" New American eats offer "good value", and happy-hour deals can make for a "bargain meal"; some warn of "erratic" service while shrugging at fare that's "neither terrible nor great", and recommend this one for "just some drinks and snacks" in the bar.

Tavolo ▣ *Italian* 24 | 22 | 25 | $46

Huntingdon Valley | 2519 Huntingdon Pike (Welsh Rd.) |
215-938-8401 | www.augustocuisine.com
"Top-notch service" may be the big sell of Augusto Jalon's "consistent" Italian BYO in Huntingdon Valley, but fans declare the "well-prepared", "beautifully presented" cooking "well above average" too; the "upscale", "classy" space in an old Victorian house rounds out the "impeccable" experience.

Teca *Italian* 25 | 24 | 24 | $39

West Chester | 38 E. Gay St. (Walnut St.) | 610-738-8244 |
www.tecawc.com
Sippers say this "modern" Italian small-plater offering "delicious" food and an "awesome" wine list "in the heart of West Chester" "has only gotten better over the years", leading the area's "gastronomic growth"; with a "high-style scene inside and out" (and somewhat "high cost" too), it's the "rare adult place" in a college town, complete with solid service.

Ted's Montana Grill *American* 21 | 20 | 20 | $29

Warrington | Valley Sq. | 1512 Main St. (bet. Hwy. 611 & Street Rd.) |
215-491-1170 | www.tedsmontanagrill.com
This Warrington outpost of Ted Turner's "alternative" to the big steakhouse chains is "the place to go for an introduction to bison",

	FOOD	DECOR	SERVICE	COST

serving a "stampede" of American dishes ("terrific burgers") based around the lean meat, and trumpeting "healthier eating" with a "salute to the environment"; the "earthy" Craftsman-style setting is "enjoyable" with often "quick" service, and it's "not too expensive" either.

Teikoku *Japanese/Thai* 24 | 23 | 22 | $43

Newtown Sq. | 5492 W. Chester Pike (bet. Delchester & Garrett Mill Rds.) | 610-644-8270 | www.teikokurestaurant.com

In Newtown Square, "hardly a hotbed of fine international cuisine", this "clean, modern" Asian combo turns out "fabulous sushi and sashimi" and other "beautifully prepared", "delicious" Japanese and Thai dishes in a "lovely" space (with adjoining tatami room) reminiscent of a "Japanese teahouse"; service gets mixed marks and some feel it's "high-priced", though the "lunchtime bento box is a bargain."

10 Arts *American* 24 | 25 | 23 | $54

Avenue of the Arts | Ritz-Carlton Hotel | 10 S. Broad St. (Penn Sq.) | 215-523-8273 | www.10arts.com

Beneath a "soaring ceiling" in an "opulent former bank", this "fancy-schmancy" Eric Ripert–run American "splurge" delivers "romantic" dinners and "power lunches" while "bringin' on the Ritz" – the Ritz-Carlton on the Avenue of the Arts, that is; though some grouse about the "acoustics" and prices (note: "happy hour costs you less"), many laud the "friendly" service and insist the "sophisticated" food hasn't slipped despite the departure of *Top Chef* alumna Jennifer Carroll.

Ten Stone ❶ *American* 18 | 15 | 19 | $22

Southwest Center City | 2063 South St. (21st St.) | 215-735-9939 | www.tenstone.com

"Better-than-average" American pub grub gets a boost from a "revolving, seasonal beer list" and bartenders who "take a genuine interest" in brews to match your taste at this Southwest Center City "neighborhood bar" that's "always packed with college kids" playing darts and pool; though critics call the food and service "variable", most find it a "cheap", "comfy" place to "watch a game, have a burger" or go for a "worthwhile" Sunday brunch.

Tequilas *Mexican* 26 | 25 | 25 | $41

Rittenhouse | 1602 Locust St. (16th St.) | 215-546-0181 | www.tequilasphilly.com

A Rittenhouse "institution", this "upscale" Mexican from David Suro (who also owns the Siembra Azul distillery) turns out "fresh, clever" cuisine and "out-of-this-world" margaritas prepared by some of the "most knowledgeable tequila bartenders north of the border"; "beautiful", "hacienda"-style surroundings and "entertaining" servers amp up the "lively atmosphere" ("go with a crowd"), but it's an equally worthy choice for a "serious meal."

	FOOD	DECOR	SERVICE	COST

Teresa's Cafe *Italian*

23 | 17 | 22 | $31

Wayne | 124 N. Wayne Ave. (Lancaster Ave.) | 610-293-9909
The "BYO of choice" in Downtown Wayne, this long-running Italian is a "nice place for a date or celebration", or just "reliably good" "neighborhood eating" for "reasonable" tabs; a "responsive" staff keeps "regulars" "happy" – so don't be surprised by a "loud" din during peak hours.

Teresa's Next Door ● *Belgian*

23 | 19 | 21 | $30

Wayne | 124 N. Wayne Ave. (Lancaster Ave.) | 610-293-9909 | www.teresas-cafe.com
The pub grub "strays from the normal humdrum" at this larger, liquor-licensed counterpart to Teresa's Cafe in Downtown Wayne, plating up cheeses, game burgers, frites and mussels "right out of Brussels" to go with a "tremendous", "mostly Belgian" beer selection; bartenders who "really know their business" add to the "cool" vibe, though the noise level can "make conversation difficult."

Tex Mex Connection ● *Tex-Mex*

24 | 23 | 24 | $24

North Wales | 201 E. Walnut St. (2nd St.) | 215-699-9552 | www.texmexconnection.com
The kitchen "puts its own twist on the classics" at this inexpensive North Wales Tex-Mex that's "been around a long time" and continues to "do it right"; margaritas "to die for" and "awesome" decorations make it extra "festive", and while the bar gets "smoky", the upstairs dining room is smoke-free; P.S. loyalists "love" that it's certified "green."

Thai Kuu *Asian/Thai*

∇ 22 | 20 | 21 | $29

Chestnut Hill | 35 Bethlehem Pike (Germantown Ave.) | 267-297-5715 | www.thaikuu.com
"Unique", "memorable" interpretations of Thai dishes come out of the kitchen of this Chestnut Hill BYO; the dining room is "small" and "intimate" ("cramped" to some), with modern furnishings and other "nice" touches, while "fast service" and "good value" complete the picture.

Thai L' Elephant *Thai*

25 | 22 | 23 | $29

Phoenixville | 301 Bridge St. (Gay St.) | 610-935-8613 | www.thailelephant.com
A "small-town big restaurant" is how "Thai enthusiasts" characterize this Phoenixville BYO serving a "great selection" of "authentic" dishes that are "beautifully presented" and come in "huge portions"; the space is "wonderfully welcoming", though a few find it a "little too trendy", while others gripe about "slow" service.

Thai Orchid *Thai*

25 | 19 | 24 | $25

Berwyn | 556 Lancaster Ave. (Waterloo Ave.) | 610-651-7840 | www.thaiorchidberwyn.com
"Not your traditional mall Thai", this Berwyn BYO "woos" aficionados with "authentic, savory" specials as well as "excellent" renditions of "standards" such as pad Thai; fans "love cozying up"

in the "small, intimate" space "with a bottle of wine from home" to pair with the "fresh, delicious" fare.

Thai Orchid Blue Bell *Thai* 25 | 21 | 23 | $29

Blue Bell | Blue Bell Shopping Ctr. | 1748 Dekalb Pike (Township Line Rd.) | 610-277-9376 | www.thaiorchidofbluebell.com

"Attention to detail" is evident in the "spicy and exotic", yet "comforting" Thai cuisine at this Blue Bell BYO that makes some "want to sail over to Thailand"; the "attractive", "wood-paneled" interior exudes a "very calm feeling", while the staff is "courteous and helpful", all of which make it "enticing" "despite the strip-mall location"; P.S. it's a sibling of Conshy's Chiangmai.

13th Street Gourmet Pizza ◑ *Pizza* 24 | 18 | 22 | $24

Washington Square West | 209 S. 13th St. (Walnut St.) | 215-546-4453 | www.13streetpizza.com

"Melt-in-your-mouth" pizzas with a side of "unforgettable" "people-watching" make this "cool" Washington Square West storefront parlor a "reliable" destination, especially "after the bars close" (it's open until 4 AM); a "friendly" staff that "aims to please", "low" prices and an "upbeat" vibe also make it worth trying "at least once."

Three Monkeys Cafe ◑ *American* 24 | 23 | 23 | $25

Northeast Philly | 9645 James St. (Grant Ave.) | 215-637-6665 | www.3monkeyscafe.com

"Simians are everywhere" at this "unique, out-of-the-way" "neighborhood bar" in Northeast Philly, which attracts a "younger crowd" with its "fun" vibe and "awesome" American eats, including the "sinful" Mighty Joe Young burger; set in a renovated antique store, the space boasts an "amazing" outdoor patio that "transports you to Key West", while "friendly" service ensures a "good time."

333 Belrose Bar & Grill ☒ *American* 23 | 20 | 22 | $41

Radnor | 333 Belrose Ln. (King of Prussia Rd.) | 610-293-1000 | www.333belrose.com

"Fantastic java pork tenderloin" and other "sophisticated" New American dishes "amaze the taste buds" of "bigwigs" and "ladies who lunch" at this "clubby" Radnor "hangout", where you can impress a "date" or "out-of-towners" on the "lovely" "outdoor patio", or join a "mature crowd" for "happy hour"; some find it "a bit pricey", and grouse about the "noise", while others advise "arrive early" or you'll "duke it out for parking"; P.S. the Decor score may not reflect a post-Survey renovation.

NEW 320 Market Cafe ☒ *American* 24 | 21 | 23 | $22

Media | 21 W. State St. (bet. Jackson & Olive Sts.) | 610-565-8320 | www.the320marketcafe.com

"Consider yourself warned" – the pico de gallo is "addictive" and the affordable American grub is "off-the-hook" at this "trendy" Delco "mini-mart", where you order at a "deli counter" and snag a table in the "chic" cafe (or "grab a delicious bite and go"); "helpful" staffers dole out "hints of humor" along with "samples" to ward off the "wait", which can be "long sometimes."

Tierra Colombiana *Colombian/Cuban* 26 | 22 | 24 | $27

North Philly | 4535 N. 5th St. (3 blocks south of Roosevelt Blvd.) | 215-324-6086

The "phenomenal" Colombian and Cuban fare comes in "outrageously large portions" at this "South American delight" in North Philly, where the "authentic" cooking "never deviates from its intended flavors"; "friendly", "attentive" service and weekend salsa dancing ramp up its "bang for the buck", and while it's "not in the best of neighborhoods", for many it's "worth the trek."

Tiffin *Indian* 22 | 14 | 18 | $24

Northern Liberties | 710 W. Girard Ave. (Franklin St.) | 215-922-1297
Mount Airy | 7105 Emlen St. (Mt. Pleasant Ave.) | 215-242-3656
Elkins Park | Elkins Park Sq. | 8080 Old York Rd. (Church Rd.) | 215-635-9205
Wynnewood | Wynnewood Shopping Ctr. | 50 E. Wynnewood Rd. (Williams Rd.) | 610-642-3344
Bryn Mawr | 847 W. Lancaster Ave. (Merion Ave.) | 610-525-0800
www.tiffin.com

For "reliable" Indian fare at "reasonable" prices, this BYO chain is a "go-to" option for many, where your food comes out "fast", though some report "spotty" service; "sparse" decor and "loud" acoustics make delivery or takeout the default for many, and while some find it "just ok", others insist you "can't beat the value."

Ting Wong Restaurant ⊄ *Chinese* ▽ 24 | 7 | 15 | $14

Chinatown | 138 N. 10th St. (Race St.) | 215-928-1883

"You don't go for the service or decor" at this tiny Chinatown sit-down, but rather the "large portions" of "wonderful pork", "superb" chicken and other "real Chinese" dishes according to those in the know; so what if the digs are "unimpressive" and the staff is "unfriendly" – you get your food "fast and cheap."

Tinto *Spanish* 27 | 24 | 24 | $56

Rittenhouse | 114 S. 20th St. (Sansom St.) | 215-665-9150 | www.tintorestaurant.com

This "impeccable" Rittenhouse Basque is Iron Chef "Jose Garces at his best", showcasing "innovative" pintxos (small plates) that are "huge in flavor" and "remain true to Spanish spirit", enhanced by selections from an "amazing wine list" and served in an "intimate", "comfortable" cellarlike space; "informed" staffers help create a "convivial", "more personal" vibe than at some of his other operations, and though it's "not cheap", most consider it a "winner."

Tír na nÓg ● *Pub Food* 19 | 20 | 19 | $25

Logan Square | The Phoenix | 1600 Arch St. (16th St.) | 267-514-1700 | www.tirnanogphilly.com

Surveyors raise a glass of "perfectly pulled Guinness" and say "*sláinte!*" to this "charming" Logan Square bar doling out "decent pints" to go with "good Irish food alongside American favorites";

despite reports of hit-or-miss service, the room has a real "pub feel" and it's an "awesome place for socializing" with folks of "all stripes" – just "don't expect to hear the people you're dining with when a soccer game is on."

ⓃⒺⓌ The Tomato Bistro *Italian*   ∇ 22 | 25 | 21 | $26

Manayunk | 102 Rector St. (Main St.) | 215-483-2233 | www.thetomatobistro.com

Located in a "beautifully renovated" space above the more casual Couch Tomato Cafe in Manayunk, this candlelit Italian specializes in shareable bites and gourmet pizzas served by a "friendly" staff; while some are "not impressed" and grouse that "the portions are way too small for the price", others are won over by the "helpful" service and "great atmosphere."

Tony Luke's *Cheesesteaks*   26 | 13 | 20 | $14

South Philly | 39 E. Oregon Ave. (Front St.) | 215-551-5725 ☾
Springfield | Springfield Mall | 1250 Baltimore Pike (Sproul Rd.) | 610-543-1693
South Philly | 26 E. Oregon Ave. (Delaware Expy.) | 215-465-1901
www.tonylukes.com ☾

"A don't-miss tradition" by the stadiums, this purveyor of "superior" cheesesteaks, "knock-your-socks-off" roast pork and other "sublime" South Philly sandwiches "exploding with meat" (and "provolone so sharp it'll make ya bleed") has spread to multiple locations, including a full-service bar across from the original (on 39 Oregon); despite "long lines", the "yell-your-name" service is "fast" – just "don't go here for the ambiance."

Tony's Place *Italian/Pizza*   26 | 19 | 25 | $16

Northeast Philly | 6300 Frankford Ave. (Tyson Ave.) | 215-535-9851 | www.tonystomatopies.com

With its "long history in the community" (since 1951), this "iconic" Northeast Philly Italian "pizza tavern" is a prime "neighborhood gathering place" for savoring "awesome" thin-crust "tomato pies" "fresh out of the oven"; so "don't be fooled by the dive-bar facade" – even if the "rest of the menu is average to good", the saucy "original" specialty makes up for any shortcomings.

Tortugas Mexican Eatery ⊅ *Mexican*   ∇ 23 | 17 | 20 | $22

Collegeville | 305 2nd Ave. (Park Ave.) | 610-489-0600 | www.tortugasmv.com

Those seeking tasty Mex "outside the city" "love the nachos", "spicy" salsa and "huge" plates at this "little cafe tucked away in a Collegeville strip mall"; though a few "miss the BYO" policy, others don't mind sipping margaritas with the affordable grub, served by a solid staff.

Toscana 52 *Italian*   24 | 24 | 22 | $37

Feasterville | 4603 Street Rd. (Lincoln Hwy.) | 215-942-7770 | www.toscana52.com

Touted for its "terrific", "moderately priced" Tuscan menu and "weekly specials" highlighting regional Italian, this "*delizioso*" destination with a "fabulous" setting and "informed" service "stands out against against a backdrop of bland chain restaurants" in Feasterville; since the "biggest problem is the crowds", guests agree "it's good – when you can get in the door."

Totaro's Restaurant *Eclectic*   24 | 17 | 23 | $41

Conshohocken | 729 E. Hector St. (bet. Righter & Walnut Sts.) | 610-828-9341 | www.totaros.com

It may look like a "dive", but this "comfortable" taproom and adjoining restaurant "tucked away" in Conshohocken is a "find" for the "creative choices" on its Eclectic menu featuring "fantastic" pastas and game; a "responsive" staff adds to the "friendly" vibe, and while some note that "high" prices can add up, you'll still find "value for the quality."

Trappe Tavern ◑ *American/Pub Food*   21 | 16 | 22 | $19

Trappe | 416 W. Main St. (5th Ave.) | 610-489-8686 | www.trappetavern.com

Drawing a "younger crowd", this "noisy" Trappe "sports bar" still manages to be a "family- friendly" destination for a "casual meal" from its "interesting" American menu that's "not just standard pub grub"; the "friendly" staff, appealing outdoor deck and live entertainment prove it has more to offer than just "great drink prices."

Trattoria Giuseppe *Italian*   25 | 21 | 20 | $32

Newtown Sq. | 4799 W. Chester Pike (Rockridge Rd.) | 610-353-4871 | www.mussotra.com

"Expect to wait" "even with a reservation" at this perpetually "jammed" Newtown Square BYO designed to evoke a Sicilian piazza, where patient patrons "keep coming back" for "luscious" Italian offerings like "homemade pasta" and "amazingly fresh fish"; "attentive service" appeases the "crowd", and moderate tabs are "worth every penny."

Trattoria San Nicola *Italian*   24 | 20 | 23 | $38

Paoli | 4 Manor Rd. (Lancaster Ave.) | 610-695-8990 | www.tsannicola.com

You'll find "little change in the menu" and that's the way Paoli regulars like it at this "dependable" "neighborhood Italian" where "perfectly prepared" dishes are "reasonable for the quality"; if some find the old-world atmosphere a little "gaudy", a "welcoming" staff and "charming bartender" help ensure it's "worth returning"; P.S. BYO on Sundays.

Trattoria Totaro ⓩ *Italian*   ▽ 25 | 20 | 24 | $33

Conshohocken | 639 Spring Mill Ave. (7th Ave.) | 610-828-7050 | www.conshohockenrestaurant.com

Set in a "quiet" stretch of Conshohocken, this modest chef-owned "corner BYO" boasts "phenomenal" Italian fare including "homemade pastas" and other "quality meals" like osso buco; "friendly service" makes it a "memorable" choice for a "reasonably priced" celebration while complimentary sangria Mondays–Fridays lends a festive touch.

Trax Restaurant & Cafe 🈲Ⓜ *American* | 24 | 18 | 22 | $37

Ambler | 27 W. Butler Pike (Maple St.) | 215-591-9777
With its "neat location in an old train station", it's not surprising that this "intimate" Ambler BYO maintains a "flair for the unusual" with a "top-notch" American "menu that changes constantly" and highlights local produce (including ingredients grown in on-site); "superb" service keeps things on track, and while some complain of "bad acoustics" that detract from the overall "value", others note you "gradually get accustomed" to it.

Tre Scalini Ⓜ *Italian* | 27 | 19 | 23 | $40

East Passyunk | 1915 E. Passyunk Ave. (bet. McKean & Mifflin Sts.) | 215-551-3870
Ask a regular and they'll tell you this East Passyunk BYO is "as close as it gets to Italy in Philly", serving "old-fashioned, authentic" cuisine delectable enough to make guests leave their "plates so clean they don't need washing"; the "understated" atmosphere is embellished by "interesting drama" from the colorful clientele, while "accommodating" servers "never fail you."

🆕 The Trestle Inn ❶ *American* | ▽ 21 | 24 | 21 | $27

Callowhill | 339 N. 11th St. (Callowhill St.) | 267-239-0290 | www.thetrestleinn.com
"Meat, beer, go-go girls – what else does one need for a good night out?" posit fans of this "sinfully wicked" "hipster" bar in Callowhill, where the "excellent drink selection" and "awesome" atmosphere "make the place", though it does serve up "delicious" mac 'n' cheese and other "small" bites; go-go dancers are a nod to its previous iteration as a strip club, and it also offers weekend DJs and live music.

TreVi Pizza Pasta BYOB Ⓜ *Italian* | ▽ 27 | 20 | 26 | $28

Glenside | 21 E. Glenside Ave. (Easton Rd.) | 215-884-9100 | www.trevibyob.com
The "excellent" thin-crust pizzas and pastas smothered in "home-made" sauces "reflect a proud tradition" at this contemporary Italian BYO in Glenside where regulars "recommend reservations"; "reasonable prices" and welcoming service add further appeal for "everyone in the family."

Tria ❶ *Eclectic* | 24 | 22 | 23 | $30

Rittenhouse | 123 S. 18th St. (Sansom St.) | 215-972-8742
Washington Square West | 1137 Spruce St. (12th St.) | 215-629-9200
Tria Wine Room *European*
University City | Left Bank | 3131 Walnut St. (31st St.) | 215-222-2422
www.triacafe.com
"Diverse wine choices" from "off the beaten vine" plus equally ambi-tious beers are served alongside "cool cheeses" and other Eclectic and European small plates (but "no big dinners") at this "neat little" trio; "classy" and "chill", the venues can seem "cramped" due to limited seating, but staffers' "can't-go-wrong" recommen-dations make amends, as does the "excellent value."

	FOOD	DECOR	SERVICE	COST

Trieste Italian Restaurant *Italian* ▽ 27 | 20 | 26 | $24

Prospect Park | 641 Chester Pike (bet. Amosland Rd. & Lincoln Ave.) |
610-534-8191 | www.triesterestaurant.com

If this Prospect Park "landmark" seems "a little dated", that's
because the "comfortable, sweet and delicious" joint ("just like
mom's kitchen") has been around since 1960, and they've used
the time to perfect their "down-home flavors"; "good, consistent
gravy" is the lifeblood, but the "old-fashioned" favorite does plenty
of other things well too, including "outstanding" service.

Trio *Asian* 25 | 19 | 23 | $30

Fairmount | 2624 Brown St. (Taney St.) | 215-232-8746 |
www.triobyob.com

A "bit off the beaten path" in Fairmount sits this "well-kept secret"
(perhaps a testament to the near-"impossible" parking conditions), an "understated" Asian fusion eatery with a 'heavy Thai'
influence; "great staples and specials" boast "new twists" and
"accommodate vegans" as well as meat and seafood lovers; the
triple-floored white-tablecloth BYOB features a popular "outside
deck for dining" on nicer evenings.

Triumph Brewing Co. ● *American/Eclectic* 20 | 21 | 20 | $29

New Hope | 400 Union Sq. Dr. (Main St.) | 215-862-8300
Old City | 117 Chestnut St. (2nd St.) | 215-625-0855
www.triumphbrewing.com

"High-end pub cuisine" and brewed-on-premises beer to wash
it down are the deal at this Eclectic pair, where rustic, industrial
decor (exposed beams of salvaged wood and steel juxtapose
upholstered barstools) reads "trendy without overdoing it"; large
chalkboards post daily specials but the "old bar standbys" (burgers, fish 'n' chips and the like) are "not neglected", and "knowledgeable" staffers are on hand to help you select suds to pair with
your meal; P.S. there's frequent live music in both spots.

Trolley Car Diner & Deli *Diner* 20 | 16 | 20 | $18

Mount Airy | 7619 Germantown Ave. (Cresheim Valley Dr.) |
215-753-1500 | www.trolleycardiner.com

Trolley Car Café *Diner*

East Falls | 3269 S. Ferry Rd. (bet. Kelly Dr. & Ridge Ave.) |
267-385-6703 | www.trolleycarcafe.com

"Solid diner fare" is served in this Mount Airy "standby" housed
in an actual trolley car (the newer East Falls outpost is bricks and
mortar); there's "a little bit of everything" at these family-friendly
spots ("careful, they have ice cream", but also a "deep" beer list),
and while the decor's "old-school", it "caters to kids" and parents
seeking "cheap" eats; P.S. East Falls offers on-site bike rental.

12th Street Cantina ⊠Ⓜ *Mexican* 24 | 19 | 21 | $22

Chinatown | Reading Terminal Mkt. | 1136 Arch St. (bet. 11th &
12th Sts.) | 215-625-0321

"Line up early" or "don't expect to find a seat during the lunch
rush" at this "no-frills" Mexican in the "middle of busy Reading

Terminal Market", a "second home" for many, thanks to "reliably" "fresh" *comida,* including "delicious" burritos that'll "keep you full all day"; the staff "gets you the food", but "nothing more", and some find it a "tight squeeze" inside, but most agree you "can't beat" it for an "affordable" "quick" bite.

Twenty Manning Grill *American*   23 | 21 | 21 | $42

Rittenhouse | 261 S. 20th St. (bet. Locust & Spruce Sts.) | 215-731-0900 | www.twentymanning.com

The menu of "gorgeous, easy" fare is "always interesting" at Audrey Claire Taichman's Rittenhouse New American, which attracts a "lively" "blend of neighborhood regulars and new faces" with its "solid" cooking and "stellar" service; it's set in a double brown-stone with a "stylish" look, and while the mood is usually "relaxed", some gripe that it can get so loud "you can't hear yourself think."

The Twisted Tail ● *Southern*   ∇ 23 | 22 | 23 | $31

Society Hill | 509 S. 2nd St. (Lombard St.) | 215-558-2471 | www.thetwistedtail.com

"Everything works together" at this bi-level Southern in Society Hill, where "everything works together" – i.e. "wonderful cock-tails", "tasty" BBQ and live blues (five nights a week) – to keep guests "comfortable and happy"; a "friendly" staff smoothly man-ages the transition from a "mellow" dinner to an energetic night out, and moderate tabs add allure.

211 York ⊠Ⓜ *American*   24 | 21 | 24 | $37

Jenkintown | 211 Old York Rd. (bet. Greenwood & Summit Aves.) | 215-517-5117 | www.211york.com

Fans of Timothy E. Papa's rustic bistro on Jenkintown's strip attest his "original", "moderately priced" New American cuisine has "got-ten better" over time and is "worth every cent and more", and the "attentive, friendly" staff seems "genuinely glad you're there"; the interior is "elegant" and "comfortable", though some fret that the exterior looks too much "like a bar", and not enough people "know there's good food inside."

NEW Ulivo *Italian*   ∇ 25 | 19 | 21 | $36

Queen Village | 521 Catharine St. (Passyunk Ave.) | 215-351-1550 | www.ulivophila.com

The "pillowy" ricotta gnocchi will "make you feel like every Italian dish you've tasted before was just practice" at this midpriced Queen Village newcomer whose chef-owner, Joe Scarpone, made his mark at the now-defunct Sovalo; besides "superb" pastas, the menu also highlights "in-season" dishes, while "friendly" service maintains the "cozy" atmosphere (even if the "sound level" can make it "tough to talk").

Umai Umai ⊠ *Asian*   27 | 22 | 24 | $34

Fairmount | 533 N. 22nd St. (Brandywine St.) | 215-988-0707 | www.umaiumai.com

Armed with the rare ability to "convert non-sushi eaters", this Fairmount Asian "treat" works its "magic" with "beautiful, creative arrangements" that "make the crowd go crazy" – and BYO lets you "save on drinks and still indulge"; with "attentive" service and "modern" decor, it's "intimate" enough to be a "date spot" (just be sure to "make reservations, even during the week").

Union Trust *Steak*

24 | 26 | 24 | $64

Washington Square West | 717 Chestnut St. (bet. 7th & 8th Sts.) | 215-925-6000

Expect to be "blown away" by the "beautiful", "regal" setting – a "glamorous old bank" with "soaring" ceilings – at this "expense-account" steakhouse in Wash West where the food is "equally impressive", particularly "top-notch steaks" and "fantastic" selections from the raw bar; service is "on point" too, and while a few complain that it "doesn't quite deliver" for such a "high-end" experience, most consider it an "indulgence" that's "worth it."

Urban Saloon ◐ *Pub Food*

16 | 16 | 16 | $22

Fairmount | 2120 Fairmount Ave. (21st St.) | 215-232-5359

"Plenty of seating, tons of TVs" and "great beers on tap" make this Fairmount gastropub across from the Eastern State Penitentiary a "perfect destination for sports spectators", with a "large selection" of "solid bar food"; while some critics find the "sport-bar" scene full of "frat-boy types" "lame", others recommend it for a "night to just have fun or a day when you need an afternoon Bloody Mary."

Valanni *Mediterranean*

23 | 21 | 20 | $42

Washington Square West | 1229 Spruce St. (bet. 12th & 13th Sts.) | 215-790-9494 | www.valanni.com

"Pre-theater" diners and "small-plate" samplers flock to this "gay-friendly" Wash West "mainstay" for "beautifully presented" and "creative" Mediterranean dishes shuffled by a "scrumptious staff"; raters reveal that while it's "relaxing" for dinner, the "trendy" quarters turn clubby at night when too many "divine cocktails" can amount to "pricey" tabs.

Varalli *Italian*

23 | 21 | 23 | $45

Avenue of the Arts | 231 S. Broad St. (Locust St.) | 215-546-6800 | www.varalliusa.com

The "last of the classics" along the evolving Avenue of the Arts, this "vivacious" Northern Italian "maintains its quality" through "delicious" and "elegant" fare "with a seafood slant"; "efficient" servers "accommodate every need" to keep customers "comfortable", and the $35 early-bird prix fixe "deal" helps make it "perfect" "for pre-theater dining."

NEW Vedge ⊠ *Vegetarian*

28 | 28 | 28 | $47

Washington Square West | 1221 Locust St. (Camac St.) | 215-320-7500 | www.vedgerestaurant.com

Rich Landau and Kate Jacoby make you "forget images of hippies and heavy-handed meat substitutes" with "inventive, delectable" vegan and vegetarian small plates featuring "astoundingly fresh" veggies at their "elegant" successor to Horizons, set in a "charming "old mansion" in Washington Square West; "gorgeous" decor and "excellent" service add to its allure, and while a few gripe about "pricey" "small portions", the "extraordinary" fare makes even "hard-core carnivores" "consider giving up meat."

Verdad Restaurant & Tequila Bar *Spanish*   21 | 20 | 19 | $43

Bryn Mawr | 818 W. Lancaster Ave. (Bryn Mawr Ave.) | 610-520-9100 | www.verdadrestaurant.com

"Crowds" gather at this "lively" Bryn Mawr Nuevo Latino–Spanish for "innovative and tasty" tapas and "even better tequila" via a "knowledgeable" staff; while dissenters warn of "ultrasmall and ultrapriced" plates, fans of the "fun atmosphere" dub it "Center City dining in the 'burbs."

NEW Vernick Food & Drink Ⓜ *American*   – | – | – | E

Rittenhouse | 2031 Walnut St. (21st St.) | 267-639-6644 | www.vernickphilly.com

Returning to his hometown after years with Jean-Georges Vongerichten, chef Gregory Vernick has set up a bi-level American in a Rittenhouse brownstone, serving a pricey menu of simple, polished classics (roasted Amish chicken, braised beef check); the chic, Euro-inspired setting includes a six-seat counter at the open kitchen and sunny window seating on the second floor.

Vetri Ⓩ *Italian*   29 | 25 | 28 | $202

Washington Square West | 1312 Spruce St. (bet. Juniper & 13th Sts.) | 215-732-3478 | www.vetriristorante.com

Acolytes attest "heaven on earth" can be found in an "unassuming" townhouse in Washington Square West, home of Marc Vetri's flagship Italian, a "gastronomic tour de force" that's "high-end" "without being ostentatious", offering "sublime" cuisine and "professional" service; while you may have to "raid your 401(k)" given a prix fixe–only menu that starts at $155, it's on just about "everyone's bucket list."

Via Napoli *Italian*   23 | 22 | 22 | $29
(fka Italian Bistro)

Northeast Philly | 2500 Welsh Rd. (Roosevelt Blvd.) | 215-934-7700 | www.vianapoli.com

After a reboot under a new name with "cool", "freshened" decor, the former Italian Bistro in Northeast Philly is like eating at "grandma's house", complete with "big pasta dishes that will fill your fridge with leftovers", and surveyors see real "improvement" as the waiters have left the "Tony Soprano" shtick behind; "reasonable" prices make this a "keeper."

Victor Cafe *Italian*   22 | 23 | 26 | $41

South Philly | 1303 Dickinson St. (bet. Clarion & 13th Sts.) | 215-468-3040 | www.victorcafe.com

"A must-visit for lovers of la dolce vita, tasty Italian, and opera" this South Philly "institution" has been serving "delectable pasta" with a side of "arias sung by the servers" since 1918; while the "food is secondary" to the "built-in entertainment", the "old-fash-ioned atmosphere" provides a "one of a kind" experience "worth the price of entrees" and even "skeptics" are "won over."

Victory Brewing Co ❶ *Pub Food* 22 | 20 | 21 | $25
Downingtown | 420 Acorn Ln. (Chestnut St.) | 610-873-0881 | www.victorybeer.com

No surprise, the "spectacular" beer is "the star" at this Downingtown pub from the Victory microbrewery, but some find the pub grub "equally impressive", including "serious BBQ" and "excellent" pizzas; even when the industrial setting gets "crowded and loud", service remains "consistently solid", one more reason it's a "local favorite."

Vietnam Café *Vietnamese* 25 | 23 | 24 | $26
West Philly | 816 S. 47th St. (Baltimore Ave.) | 215-729-0260 | www.eatatvietnam.com

Whether for a "date night or a family dinner", Vietnam's West Philly outpost dishes similarly "reliable", "well-prepared" Viet fare and "strong" drinks in "polished" quarters; "sweet" servers know the "menu:" and ensure "fast turnover", and the "easy-to-find free parking" is a "definite bonus", making it a "real asset" to the Baltimore Avenue corridor.

Vietnam Palace *Vietnamese* 23 | 18 | 21 | $25
Chinatown | 222 N. 11th St. (bet. Race & Vine Sts.) | 215-592-9596 | www.vietnampalace.net

"Vibrant flavors run wild" at Nhon T. Nguyen's "chic" Vietnamese retreat in Chinatown where "delicate" vermicelli bowls, "fresh and crispy spring rolls" and "wonderful" charbroiled meats help "transport you to another world"; "attentive service" is "always quick", and despite an "upscale" feel, you can "dine like a prince for next to nothing."

Vietnam Restaurant *Vietnamese* 26 | 19 | 21 | $25
Chinatown | 221 N. 11th St. (bet. Race & Vine Sts.) | 215-592-1163 | www.eatatvietnam.com

Proselytizers urge you to "bring people who say they don't like Vietnamese food" and "watch them change their opinion" at this "Chinatown mainstay" where "huge portions" of "top-notch soups" and other "crazy-good" eats are served by a "happy group" of "friendly, if not fully fluent" servers; the digs are small but "clean and inviting", making it an "all-around win" in most people's books.

Villa Barolo *Italian* 25 | 23 | 23 | $39
Warrington | 1373 Easton Rd. (Bristol Rd.) | 215-491-9370

Hong Kong native Chef Lo "does it all" at his Warrington Italian offering "fantastic" standards as well as "unusual" game offerings ("ostrich, kangaroo and elk") that give you the "chance to try new things"; "wonderful decor" and "pleasant" service from an "experi-enced" staff are further evidence of a "well-run" operation, and the only knock is that the room can get "noisy" at times.

Villa di Roma ⊗ Italian
25 | 14 | 21 | $29

Bella Vista | Italian Mkt. | 936 S. 9th St. (bet. Christian St. & Washington Ave.) | 215-592-1295

You get "just what you expect" from this family-owned "institution" "in the heart of the Italian Market" – "homemade", "genuine Eye-talian" eats, including the "best meatballs", served "with minimum fuss" by "colorful South Philly waitresses" who've "been there forever"; the space has "no frills, but who needs them?"; P.S. cash only.

Village Whiskey ◑ American
26 | 21 | 22 | $34

Rittenhouse | 118 S. 20th St. (Sansom St.) | 215-665-1088 | www.villagewhiskey.com

A "perfect burger" and "duck-fat fries" – "who could ask for anything more?" ponder patrons of Jose Garces' Rittenhouse "upscale" American-cum-whiskey bar, where "well-trained mixologists" prep "throwback" cocktails and the patties are "perfectly seasoned and cooked to order"; the rest of the "bar-food" menu is similarly "excellent", served by a "knowledgeable, helpful" staff, but be warned that it's "tough to get a table" in the "narrow" space where seating is "elbow-to-elbow."

Vintage Bar & Grill American
23 | 21 | 22 | $30

Abington | 1116 Old York Rd. (Susquehanna Rd.) | 215-887-8500

The kitchen at this Abington watering hole demonstrates a "unique talent for creating unusual" American pub grub, which is backed by an "excellent beer selection"; the "friendly staff and owners treat you like family" in the conventional "dark", "neighborhood-bar" setting, which can get "very noisy when it's busy."

Vito's Pizza Pizza
24 | 15 | 21 | $17

King of Prussia | 580 Shoemaker Rd. (Gulph Rd.) | 610-265-1277

Piezani promise the "slice of your life" at this pizzeria duo in King of Prussia and Cherry Hill, where sandwiches and cheesesteaks are "big hits" as well; sure, there's "no decor to speak of", but it doesn't seem to deter the crowds, as the cashier "can't put money into the cash register fast enough."

NEW Walnut Street Supper Club Italian
▽ 22 | 26 | 26 | $34

Washington Square West | 1227 Walnut St. (13th St.) | 215-923-8208 | www.1227walnut.com

Showtune fans "love the concept" of this Washington Square West supper club (an overhaul of the former Portofino) where "all the staff sings" when they're not serving "big" plates of "enjoyable", "reasonable" Italian cuisine; the glitzy, '40s-style room brings back an "era when being a lady and gentleman were required", so even if some think the ambiance outshines the food, it fits the bill as a "beautiful" "date place."

	FOOD	DECOR	SERVICE	COST

Warmdaddy's ● *Soul Food* 24 | 23 | 23 | $35

South Philly | RiverView Plaza | 1400 S. Christopher Columbus Blvd.
(Reed St.) | 215-462-2000 | www.warmdaddys.com
Whether it's "date night, ladies' night or happy hour", music
fans swear by this South Philly lounge, known for its "live blues
and R&B", "Sunday jazz brunch" and soul food that's "as close
to grandma's homemade as can be"; some knock the "cramped"
seating and "cover charge", but most enjoy the "friendly" service,
"reasonable" prices and "chilled-out vibe."

Washington Crossing Inn *American* 22 | 23 | 23 | $39

Washington Crossing | 1295 General Washington Memorial Blvd.
(General Knox Rd.) | 215-493-3634 | www.washingtoncrossinginn.com
At the site of George Washington's daring American Revolution-
ary maneuver, this "impressively historic" Bucks County inn has
"retained its charm", with Colonial surroundings and working
fireplaces upping its "romantic" appeal; opinions are mixed on
the somewhat "expensive" Traditional American fare ("beautifully
prepared" vs. "dated"), though a "helpful" staff and garden dining
lend a "lovely" touch.

Washington House *American* 27 | 26 | 27 | $37

Sellersville | 136 N. Main St. (Temple Ave.) | 215-257-3000 |
www.washingtonhouse.net
Attached to the Sellersville Theater, this "popular" "gem" in a
"homey" circa-1742 landmark building offers a "terrific" "seasonal" menu of "elegant" Traditional and New American dishes
complemented by a "plentiful bar selection"; "antique but casual"
surroundings set the tone, service is "tops" and prices "reasonable", so most "thoroughly enjoy" it.

Water Works Ⓜ *Mediterranean* 21 | 27 | 22 | $54

Fairmount | 640 Water Works Dr. (Kelly Dr.) | 215-236-9000 |
www.thewaterworksrestaurant.com
The "breathtaking view" at this "special-occasion" staple in
Fairmount's historic water works "overlooking the Schuylkill River"
provides an "incomparable" backdrop for enjoying "tasty" Mediterranean fare "by candlelight" in the "elegant" interior or on the
terrace that "feels like Europe"; though "swift" service and clever
touches like an international bottled water list add appeal, the
"stunning setting" is the "star" of this "pricey" "treat."

White Dog Cafe *Eclectic* 23 | 23 | 22 | $39

University City | 3420 Sansom St. (bet. 34th & 36th Sts.) |
215-386-9224 ●
Wayne | 200 W. Lancaster Ave. (Bellevue Ave.) | 610-225-3700
www.whitedog.com
"Still top dog" after 30 years, this University City "mainstay" and
its newer Wayne offshoot "delight" patrons with "gorgeously
prepared", "seasonal" Eclectic dishes made with "all-local ingredients", plus a "great wine and beer selection"; while some feel it's
"deceptively expensive", "overcrowded" and "noisy", others find

the "whimsical" "doggy decor", "lively" atmosphere and "attentive" service "charming"; P.S. "make a reservation!"

White Elephant Restaurant Thai   23 | 22 | 24 | $33

Huntingdon Valley | 759 Huntingdon Pike (bet. Rockledge Ave. & Shady Ln.) | 215-663-1495 | www.whiteelephantrestaurant.com
"Wonderfully surprising flavors" emerge at this "affordable" Thai BYO "hidden" in a Huntingdon Valley strip mall where "lovely and delicious" dishes complement the "pleasant" and, yes, pachyderm-themed setting; "exemplary service" from "informative" staff turns first-timers into regulars "coming back for more."

William Penn Inn   25 | 25 | 25 | $47
Restaurant American/Continental

Gwynedd | William Penn Inn | 1017 Dekalb Pike (Sumneytown Pike) | 215-699-9272 | www.williampenninn.com
For "classy, upscale dining", fans assert "you can't go wrong" with this circa-1714 "special-occasion" inn in Gwynedd, where the "sounds of a harp" add a "special touch" in the "beautiful" dining room; "experienced", "friendly" servers deliver "fantastic" American-Continental fare (including a "fabulous" early-bird prix fixe), and while some find it "pricey" and "stuffy", most agree it "deserves its top-notch reputation"; P.S. the Thursday buffet in the tavern is an affordable "treat."

Winberie's American   21 | 19 | 21 | $27

Wayne | 1164 Valley Forge Rd. (bet. Anthony Wayne Dr. & Swedesford Rd.) | 610-293-9333 | www.selectrestaurants.com
As "reliable as soft comfy shoes", this chain-link "standby" in Wayne offers "casual" American eats at "reasonable prices", with "no unpleasant surprises", served in an airy cafe setting; while many recommend it for a "quick bite", critics find the fare "dull" and the service "hit-or-miss."

Wine Thief Neighborhood Bistro American 21 | 20 | 21 | $30

Mount Airy | 7152 Germantown Ave. (Mt. Airy Ave.) | 215-242-6700 | www.winethiefbistro.com
At this Mount Airy bistro, the "small" but "surprisingly clever" New American menu appeals to "vegetarians and carnivores" alike, and it's backed by a "nice wine-by-the-glass selection"; service is "friendly", though some say it's "not the fastest", and the mood is "relaxed" in the "cute, inviting" space.

Winnie's Le Bus Manayunk American   21 | 19 | 21 | $26

Manayunk | 4266 Main St. (bet. Green & Shurs Lns.) | 215-487-2663 | www.lebusmanayunk.com
A "vegetarian-friendly" menu of "hearty yet healthy", "basic" New American fare and a "friendly" staff that "accommodates quirky requests" make this Manayunk spot a "solid choice" for dining "with family or friends"; "be prepared to be squished" during the popular weekend brunch, when there's "often a wait", and "never pass up the bread basket."

	FOOD	DECOR	SERVICE	COST

Wok Chinese Seafood
Restaurant *Chinese/Seafood*

22 | 20 | 21 | $24

Rittenhouse | 1613 Walnut St. (16th St.) | 215-751-9990 |
www.wok2wok.com

"Delightful Chinese" cooking that "isn't overpriced" is the draw at
this Rittenhouse eatery, which comes recommended for a "nice
dinner with your family"; there's "lots of space" in the "adorable"
digs, which some find "a bit dated", while service is "organized."

World Cafe Live *Eclectic*

19 | 21 | 20 | $24

University City | 3025 Walnut St. (bet. 30th & 31st Sts.) |
215-222-1400 | www.philly.worldcafelive.com

Whether at the "awesome" University City or "fabulous" Wilmington
venue, it's the "music experience we all want but rarely get", a
"sit-down dinner during a live performance" in "trendy, electric"
settings with "phenomenal" acoustics; "friendly" servers bring out
Eclectic fare that "really holds up to the other amenities" according
to some, while others sniff "you don't go for the food."

Xilantro *Mexican*

18 | 21 | 19 | $42

Wayne | 103 N. Wayne Ave. (Lancaster Ave.) | 484-580-8415 |
www.xilantro.com

Specializing in "high-quality tequila" and "upscale" Mexican cuisine, this "sophisticated" (if "noisy") haunt in Downtown Wayne
earns "high marks for creating a place you want to go" with "cool
decor" accented by "glowing neon" and margaritas that are "as
good (and dangerous) as they come"; meanwhile, the food is
"inconsistent", and though the style of cuisine is "sorely needed"
in the area, the prices aren't exactly welcoming to some; P.S. check
out the "sidewalk scene" from the patio.

Xochitl ◐ *Mexican*

23 | 21 | 22 | $37

Society Hill | 408 S. 2nd St. (bet. Lombard & Pine Sts.) | 215-238-7280
www.xochitlphilly.com

Promising "something to fill your mouth, other than its name" (say
it *so-cheet*), this "homey", "intimate" Society Hill Mexican boasts
an "innovative" menu with plenty of "lighter, healthier options",
plus "mad tasty margaritas" ("call the cab or prepare to hang for a
while" so you don't miss out); an "attentive", "friendly" crew caters
to a "young crowd" that doesn't seem to mind if it's "a bit loud."

Yangming *Chinese/Continental*

25 | 22 | 23 | $38

Bryn Mawr | 1051 Conestoga Rd. (Haverford Rd.) | 610-527-3200 |
www.yangmingrestaurant.com

"Keeping up the quality year after year", this "classic old-guard
haunt" in Bryn Mawr "deserves every honor" bestowed upon it say
loyalists who "never tire" of the "impeccably presented" Manda-
rin-Continental dishes (especially "Peking duck carved tableside")
at surprisingly "decent" prices; "top-notch", "professional" service
and an "elegant" atmosphere further make it a "treat", even if
popularity has made it perpetually "crowded."

	FOOD	DECOR	SERVICE	COST

Yardley Inn *American*

24 | 23 | 23 | $41

Yardley | 82 E. Afton Ave. (Delaware Ave.) | 215-493-3800 |
www.yardleyinn.com

Set in a "Revolutionary-era inn" with a "charming" perch "overlooking the Delaware River", this "venerable Yardley fixture" promises a "casual-chic" dining experience with "creative" New American cooking and a "busy" bar fit for "people-watching"; "be prepared to pay for it", of course – just know that the "personable" staff "works hard to please" and may even "remember you" the next time.

Zacharias
Creek Side Cafe ⓜ *American*

▽ 23 | 22 | 22 | $38

Worcester | Center Point Shopping Ctr. | 2960 Skippack Pike
(Valley Forge Rd.) | 610-584-5650 | www.zachariascreeksidecafe.com
Named for the creek that flows behind it, this upscale-casual Worcester BYO fosters a "wonderful experience" for dining "inside or out", on a "superior" New American menu distinguished by Mediterranean touches; with "attentive service" and moderate prices adding to the "terrific surprise", the only thing causing complaint is the "noise level."

Zahav *Israeli*

27 | 24 | 26 | $51

Society Hill | 237 Saint James Pl. (2nd St.) | 215-625-8800 |
www.zahavrestaurant.com
A "breath of fresh international air", Michael Solomonov's "one-of-a-kind" Society Hill Israeli "blends traditional food" (think "heavenly hummus") with "modern techniques" for "delectable combinations" to "keep your tongue guessing"; a "responsive" staff elevates the "casual" setting and guides diners through the journey – a "splurge", but an "adventure" that acolytes assert "everyone must try."

Zakes Cafe *American*

25 | 16 | 20 | $27

Fort Washington | 444 S. Bethlehem Pike (Lafayette Ave.) |
215-654-7600 | www.zakescafe.com
"Save room" for the "deliciously evil desserts" after lunch at this "quaint" Fort Washington BYO set in a "charming old house", where the "thoughtfully crafted" New American fare is distinguished by an "Asian influence"; insiders insist the "taste compensates" for the "small", "cramped" quarters, as do the "helpful" staff and "unbeatable" prices; P.S. dinner is served Wednesday–Saturday, with a "fab" prix fixe Wednesday–Thursday.

Zama *Japanese*

26 | 22 | 22 | $48

Rittenhouse | 128 S. 19th St. (bet. Sansom & Walnut Sts.) |
215-568-1027 | www.zamaphilly.com
Maki mavens contend Hiroyuki 'Zama' Tanaka (ex Pod) "raises the bar for sushi" at his "sleek" Japanese off Rittenhouse Square, and some declare his "creative", "elegant" fin fare some of "the best" in the city, "chopsticks down"; a "friendly" staff adds to the "relaxing atmosphere", and while the "high-end" package comes with a "high cost", the initiated insist it's "worth the bucks."

	FOOD	DECOR	SERVICE	COST

Zavino Wine Bar Pizzeria *Pizza*   25 | 20 | 23 | $28

Washington Square West | 112 S. 13th St. (Sansom St.) |
215-732-2400 | www.zavino.com

"Outstanding", "innovative" pizzas and an "excellent wine selection"
give this "teeny, tiny" Wash West "gem" its cheeky name, while
"tasty" small plates also shine; "reasonable" prices and "attentive"
service are pluses, but a "no-reservations" policy and a "cramped"
space add up to "obnoxious" waits and an "always packed" room.

Zento *Japanese*   26 | 17 | 24 | $37

Old City | 132 Chestnut St. (2nd St.) | 215-925-9998 |
www.zentocontemporary.com

After a move to "more spacious quarters", the sushi "continues to
be excellent" at this "stellar" Old City Japanese, and a Decor score
spike indicates that the new space is a "step up" from the previous
"shoebox"; the prices are "steep", but most feel you "get what you
pay for"; P.S. it now serves liquor, but you can still BYO.

Zesty's *Mediterranean*   23 | 18 | 21 | $30

Manayunk | 4382 Main St. (Levering St.) | 215-483-6226 |
www.zestys.com

"Wonderful" Med fare reels in regulars at this midpriced Manayunk
"hole-in-the-wall" where the "polite"staff keeps the wine flowing;
the contemporary space includes a "nice bar area" as well as a patio where you can "enjoy the beautiful weather" in warmer months.

Zinc Ⓜ *French*   26 | 23 | 25 | $45

Washington Square West | 246 S. 11th St. (bet. Locust & Spruce Sts.) |
215-351-9901 | www.zincbarphilly.com

"Close your eyes" and you just might "hear the boats on the Seine"
at this "tiny", "expensive" Wash West bistro, "the kind of place you
want to keep a neighborhood secret"; it's a "cozy, lovely setting"
for "unabashedly French" cuisine, and while service is "informal",
it's nevertheless "charming" enough to make you "feel special."

Zocalo Ⓩ ◑ *Mexican*   21 | 20 | 20 | $32

University City | 3600 Lancaster Ave. (36th St.) | 215-895-0139 |
www.zocalophilly.com

"In the heart of University City", this "moderate" Mex dishes up
"delicious" grub in a "cozy" space "kicked up a few notches" by an
appearance on Gordon Ramsay's *Kitchen Nightmares*; servers seem
"genuinely happy to see you", and in nice weather, there's no better
place for "amazing margaritas" than the "quaint, relaxing" patio.

Zorba's Tavern Ⓜ *Greek*   24 | 16 | 23 | $27

Fairmount | 2230 Fairmount Ave. (bet. 22nd & 23rd Sts.) |
215-978-5990 | www.zorbastavern.com

It's like dining at "your Greek relatives' house" at this Fairmount
Hellenic BYO where "flavorful" "comfort food" is served by a "friendly" staff in a "welcoming" setting; the "plain" digs notwithstanding,
the fare is "good enough to take out-of-towners", while the prices
are "reasonable enough to come here often."

Lancaster/Berks Counties

TOP FOOD

27 | Green Hills Inn | *Amer./French*
26 | Lily's On Main | *Amer.*
Gibraltar | *Med./Seafood*
Belvedere Inn | *American*
Gracie's 21st | *Eclectic*

TOP SERVICE

28 | Green Hills Inn
25 | Gibraltar
Bird-in-Hand
The Log Cabin
Good 'n Plenty Restaurant

TOP DECOR

27 | El Serrano
25 | Gracie's 21st Century Cafe
24 | Lily's On Main
The Log Cabin
Green Hills Inn

BEST BUYS

1. Jake's Wayback Burgers
2. Qdoba
3. Isaac's
4. Exeter Family Rest.
5. Bird-in-Hand

Annie Bailey's Irish Pub & Restaurant ● *Irish*

23 | 23 | 21 | $25

Lancaster | 28-30 E. King St. (bet. Duke & Queen Sts.) | 717-393-4000 | www.anniebaileysirishpub.com

"Reliable", "authentic" Irish chow (fish 'n' chips, bangers and mash) and an "excellent suds selection" keep this pub in Downtown Lancaster "busy" with a mostly "younger crowd" that's unfazed by the "high" "noise level"; "efficient", "friendly" service, a "Dublin"-like atmosphere and a "great" outdoor deck are pluses.

Belvedere Inn *American*

26 | 23 | 23 | $42

Lancaster | 402 N. Queen St. (Lemon St.) | 717-394-2422 | www.belvedereinn.biz

A "well-executed" menu that "changes often", "personable" service and "fabulous" ambiance in a Victorian setting make this upscale Lancaster New American a "happy place"; "weekend jazz" at Crazy Shirley's, the upstairs lounge, is a "hoot" and "sets the stage for a fun evening."

Bird-in-Hand Family Restaurant ⊠ *PA Dutch*

25 | 19 | 25 | $21

Bird-in-Hand | 2760 Old Philadelphia Pike (Ronks Rd.) | 717-768-1500 | www.bird-in-hand.com

For a "true Lancaster County experience", "stuff yourself silly" with "wholesome" Pennsylvania Dutch "home cookin'" at this "reasonably priced" "tourist" mecca, where you can opt for the smorgasbord or order off the menu; the "bang for the buck" keeps it "busy", especially on weekends, when "long waits" are common, but the staff maintains a "friendly" atmosphere.

Blue Pacific Sushi & Grill *Asian*

24 | 20 | 23 | $32

Lancaster | 1500 Oregon Pike (Lititz Pike) | 717-393-9727 | www.bluepacificrestaurant.com

Still on a roll after more than a decade, this midpriced Japanese in Lancaster County appeals to mall shoppers and others with "perfect portions" of "consistent" sushi and other "fresh" Asian selections; "friendly" service is another plus, and if some find the space "nothing to rave about", it's "clean" and "easy to get to."

El Serrano *Nuevo Latino*

23	27	23	$29

Lancaster | 2151 Columbia Ave. (Rte. 741 S.) | 717-397-6191 | www.elserrano.com

Fans feel like they're "miles from Amish country" at this Nuevo Latino on the outskirts of Lancaster, where the "chairs, tables, doors and even the brass decorations are handmade in Peru"; with "authentic" south-of-the-border dishes that are a "labor of love" plus "good margaritas" and "summer music in the courtyard", it feels like a "party at every meal."

Exeter Family Restaurant ● *Diner*

21	16	23	$15

Reading | 4800 Perkiomen Ave. (Grace St.) | 610-370-5131 | www.exeterfamilyrestaurant.com

With "fast and friendly service" and 350 seats, there's seldom a "long wait" at this "pleasant", "comfortable" 24/7 diner outside Reading; "genuine family atmosphere" makes it a favorite of those "meeting friends" – especially for "affordable" breakfasts that are "served all day."

Gibraltar *Mediterranean/Seafood*

26	23	25	$47

Lancaster | 931 Harrisburg Ave. (Race Ave.) | 717-397-2790 | www.gibraltargrille.com

"Exquisite", "Philadelphia-quality" Med seafood, housebaked artisanal breads and a 300-label wine list delight transplanted city folks at this Lancaster eatery overseen by an "attentive, knowl-edgeable" staff; "high ceilings carry conversations up and away" in a "relaxing" space suited to a "special occasion", and while it's on the spendy side, most agree "you get what you pay for."

Good 'n Plenty Restaurant 🅇 *PA Dutch*

24	19	25	$25

Smoketown | 150 Eastbrook Rd. (Rte. 30) | 717-394-7111 | www.goodnplenty.com

"If you want to splurge" on fried chicken, buttered noodles and other "excellent down-home cooking served family-style", head to this traditional Pennsylvania Dutch set in a 19th-century Lancaster County farmhouse where you'll "share the victuals while making new friends"; with manageable tabs, seating for 500, a bakery and a gift shop, it's a bus-trip standby.

Gracie's 21st Century Cafe 🅇 🅜 *Eclectic*

26	25	23	$63

Pine Forge | 1534 Manatawny Rd. (King St.) | 610-323-4004 | www.gracies21stcentury.com

Fans crank up the GPS and seek out chef-owner Gracie Skiadas' "hard-to-find" Eclectic "gem" outside Pottstown, which is still putting out "inventive" grub after a quarter-century; it's one of the more "romantic, stellar experiences" out there, though the "pricey" tabs are more palatable "if someone else is picking up the bill."

	FOOD	DECOR	SERVICE	COST

Green Hills Inn ⓩ *American/French*   27 | 24 | 28 | $54

Reading | 2444 Morgantown Rd. (off Morgantown
Expwy.) | 610-777-9611 | www.greenhillsinn.com

Still regarded as the "class" act of the Reading dining scene, this
"elegant" country inn (first established as a tavern in 1805) maintains its "traditional" approach with a "pricey", "well-prepared"
Franco-American menu and "professional" service that ensures a
"wonderful dining experience"; while some lament that it's "doing
nothing to attract younger diners", others value its "consistency."

Haydn Zug's ⓩ *American*   ▽ 25 | 23 | 23 | $38

East Petersburg | 1987 State St. (Rte. 72) | 717-569-5746 |
www.haydnzugs.com

Jumbo lump crab cakes, steaks and other midpriced Traditional
American dishes are complemented by a "wine list with exceptional values" at this "dependable dining" option in "charming" East
Petersburg; around for more than four decades, it has a "Colonial
atmosphere" that feels timeless; P.S. lunch only on Saturdays.

Iron Hill Brewery & Restaurant *American*   22 | 21 | 22 | $28

Lancaster | 781 Harrisburg Ave. (bet. College & Race Aves.) |
717-291-9800 | www.ironhillbrewery.com
See review in the Philadelphia Directory.

Isaac's Famous   23 | 18 | 21 | $14
Grilled Sandwiches *American/Sandwiches*

Lancaster | The Shoppes at Greenfield | 565 Greenfield Rd. (Rte. 30) |
717-393-6067
Ephrata | Cloister Shopping Ctr. | 120 N. Reading Rd. (Martin Ave.) |
717-733-7777
Lancaster | Sycamore Ct. | 245 Centerville Rd. (Rte. 30) | 717-393-1199
Lancaster | Granite Run Sq. | 1559 Manheim Pike (Rte. 283) |
717-560-7774
Strasburg | Shops at Traintown | 226 Gap Rd. (Rte. 896) | 717-687-7699
Lititz | 4 Trolley Run (Rte. 501) | 717-625-1181
Wyomissing | Village Sq. | 94 Commerce Dr. (bet. Papermill &
State Hill Rds.) | 610-376-1717

Isaac's Downtown &
The Pickle Bar *American/Sandwiches*

Lancaster | 25 N. Queen St. (King St.) | 717-394-5544 |
www.isaacsdeli.com

This "kid-friendly" American chain with a "bird theme" is in fine
feather thanks to "inventive" sandwiches on just about every kind
of bread (including pretzel rolls), "fresh" soups and "satisfying"
sides; some find the decor a "little dated", so it's "fine for quick
takeout" when you have to fly.

▮▮▮▮ Jake's Wayback Burgers *Burgers*   24 | 14 | 21 | $12

Lancaster | 2481 Lincoln Hwy. E. (bet. Eastbrook Rd. & Willowdale Dr.) |
717-435-9408 | www.waybackburgers.com
See review in the Philadelphia Directory.

| | FOOD | DECOR | SERVICE | COST |

J.B. Dawson's *American*

24 | 22 | 23 | $31

Lancaster | Park City Ctr. | 491 Park City Ctr. (Rte. 30) | 717-399-3996

Austin's *American*

Reading | 1101 Snyder Rd. (Van Reed Rd.) | 610-678-5500
www.jbdawsons.com

See review in the Philadelphia Directory.

Jimmie Kramer's Peanut Bar ⌧● *American*

24 | 20 | 23 | $29

Reading | 332 Penn St. (bet. 3rd & 4th Sts.) | 610-376-8500 |
www.peanutbar.com

"Nostalgia rules" at this "homey", "well-attended" "gem" that's
been in Downtown Reading seemingly "forever" (or at least "since
your grandparents were kids"), dishing up American eats at
"reasonable" prices; given that "you can throw peanut shells on the
floor", it's probably "not the place for a romantic dinner", but "attentive, chatty" bartenders help foster a "relaxed" atmosphere.

Lily's On Main *American*

26 | 24 | 24 | $35

Ephrata | Brossman Business Complex | 124 E. Main St. (Lake St.) |
717-738-2711 | www.lilysonmain.com

"Interesting combinations" and "game platters" add a spark to
this New American located above an old-time movie theater in
Ephrata; "excellent" service and a "beautiful" "NYC deco" space
generate an aura of "cool" that makes it "unique for the area";
P.S. on Tuesday nights, a movie comes free with dinner.

The Log Cabin Ⓜ *American*

23 | 24 | 25 | $37

Leola | 11 Lehoy Forest Dr. (Log Cabin Rd.) | 717-625-2142 |
www.logcabinrestaurant.com

The "cozy" feel has returned to this "quaint", stone-and-beam,
white-tablecloth destination in Lancaster County that was re-
opened by former employees; while some say it's "pricey", "fast
service" and "excellent" eats in the "rustic, elegant" setting make it
a "great place for a date."

Miller's Smorgasbord & Bakery *PA Dutch*

24 | 19 | 22 | $32

Ronks | 2811 Lincoln Hwy. E. (Ronks Rd.) | 717-687-6621 |
www.millerssmorgasbord.com

It's "all you can eat – and there is a lot" at this "cute" Pennsylvania
Dutch in Lancaster County that sates buffet lovers with "delicious"
offerings "with all the trimmings", and "lighter eaters" with à la
carte options; the friendly staff makes you feel like you're "eating
at grandma's on a Sunday", and when it gets "crowded", many hit
the gift shop for "local crafts and souvenirs."

Plain & Fancy Farm *PA Dutch*

22 | 16 | 22 | $24

Bird-in-Hand | 3121 Old Philadelphia Pike (bet. Harvest &
Old Leacock Rds.) | 717-768-4400 | www.plainandfancyfarm.com

"You must enjoy eating close with people you don't know" at
this kitsch-filled, pass-the-platter Pennsylvania Dutch in a
Lancaster County farmhouse; the $19.95 all-you-can-eat special of
"home-country cooking" is not only "family-style" but "family-ori-

ented", and in a non-Amish twist, coupons are available online; P.S. à la carte dining is also available.

The Pressroom Restaurant *American* — | — | — | M

Lancaster | 26 W. King St. (Prince St.) | 717-399-5400 | www.pressroomrestaurant.com

The local newspaper magnate Steinman family has taken a page from their history in theming this old-time New American near Penn Square; amid the richly appointed mahogany decor are high ceilings, art deco booths, frosted-glass partitions, marble and the occasional mellow live act, and the outdoor dining includes views of a 20-ft. waterfall.

Qdoba Mexican Grill *Mexican* 20 | 15 | 19 | $12

Lancaster | Park City Ctr. | 387 Park City Ctr. (Ring Rd.) | 717-299-4766 | www.qdoba.com

See review in the Philadelphia Directory.

Shady Maple Smorgasbord ⊠ *PA Dutch* 24 | 20 | 23 | $21

East Earl | 129 Toddy Dr. (28th Division Hwy.) | 717-354-8222 | www.shady-maple.com

The "hot and plentiful selection" of Pennsylvania Dutch fare at this "Amish-Mennonite gut-buster" buffet is "worth the drive" to Lancaster County – especially if you're "coming off a hunger strike"; sure, the "oversized cafeteria" is "teeming with tourists", but "unbeatable comfort food" and "do-it-yourself" service leave many locals in a "food trance."

Stoudts Black Angus Restaurant and Pub *American* 25 | 20 | 21 | $37

Adamstown | 2800 N. Reading Rd. (Pennsylvania Tpke.) | 717-484-4386 | www.stoudtsbeer.com

Adjacent to the popular Adamstown microbrewery, this "little gem" dishing up "delicious" American fare encompasses a Victorian-style dining room and traditional pub decorated with "plenty of old breweriana"; top-notch service keeps the "super-fresh" drinks flowing, making it a "truly great beer destination"; P.S. be sure to "take a tour of the brewery" before or after you eat.

New Jersey Suburbs

TOP FOOD

28	Zeppoli	*Italian*
27	Sagami Japanese	*Japanese*
	Sapori Trattoria	*Italian*
	Arugula	*Italian*
	Filomena Lakeview	*Italian*

TOP SERVICE

26	Filomena Lakeview
	The Capital Grille
	Jasmine Oriental Cuisine
	Fuji Japanese Restaurant
	Kitchen Consigliere Cafe

TOP DECOR

26	Filomena Lakeview
25	The Chophouse
	The Capital Grille
	Fleming's Prime Steakhouse
	Terra Nova

BEST BUYS

1. Animo Juice
2. Luigi's Pizza Fresca
3. Alfred's Tomato Pie
4. Five Guys
5. PrimoHoagies

Akira *Japanese*

`25` `23` `25` `$29`

Voorhees | Eagle Plaza Shopping Ctr. | 700 Haddonfield Berlin Rd. (White Horse Rd.) | 856-566-0888

Akira 2 *Japanese*

Moorestown | 45 E. Main St. (Mill St.) | 856-802-3888
www.akiranj.com

"Fresh", "inventive" sushi at these neon-ringed Japanese twins in Moorestown and Voorhees satisfies even "picky" patrons at "business lunches and weekend dinners", while families find the "entertainment value" of the "hibachi chefs" "priceless"; "lovely" staff, BYO and "respectable" "prices" complete the picture.

A Little Cafe 🅢🅜 *Eclectic*

`25` `19` `19` `$37`

Voorhees | Plaza Shoppes | 118 White Horse Rd. (Burnt Mill Rd.) | 856-784-3344 | www.alittlecafenj.com

While Marianne Powell's "charming" Voorhees Eclectic BYO may be as "tiny" as advertised, devotees happily endure the "close quarters" for her "flavorful", "amazing" fare; the moderate prices are "appropriate", and while critics complain of "attitude" and "feeling rushed" when it "gets busy", others counter that "attentive" service is part of the "marvelous culinary experience."

Al Dente Italiana *Italian*

`22` `21` `22` `$31`

Moorestown | 1690 Nixon Dr. (Rte. 38) | 856-437-6593 | www.aldenteitaliana.com

An open kitchen dishes out "generous" portions of "freshly made" Italian fare at this midpriced BYO in Moorestown, but be sure to "allow room" for gelato "to die for" counsel fans; "pleasant" service and an "airy", "attractive" space in a "redone furniture store" do the trick "whether you're with the kids", a "date" or spouse.

Alstarz Sports Pub ● *Eclectic*

`22` `21` `20` `$26`

Bordentown | 140 Rte. 130 S. (Rte. 206) | 609-291-0200 | www.alstarzbarandgrill.com

"Friendz" head to this Bordentown sports bar from the Mastoris diner family to "meet and greet" or "watch the games" over a "wide variety" of "enjoyable", "affordable" Eclectic pub grub; "attentive" service is another plus, and while it can feel like an "echoing airplane hangar" whenever the "music's rocking", you can always dine outside and "relax."

Amelia's Tea & Holly Ⓜ *Tearoom* ∇ 25 | 28 | 25 | $22

Mullica Hill | 26 S. Main St. (Church St.) | 856-223-0404 | www.ameliasteasandholly.com

At this "charming" Mullica Hill tearoom, "three-tiered plates" brimming with "fabulous tea sandwiches, fresh scones and scrumptious desserts" are washed down with tea served in "beautiful china pots", making for a "relaxing lunch" or "leisurely" afternoon repast; "courteous" staffers who "go out of their way to accommodate special requests" complete the picture; P.S. you can also shop for "tchotchkes" in the gift shop.

Andreotti's Viennese Cafe *Italian* 22 | 19 | 21 | $34

Cherry Hill | Pine Tree Plaza | 1442 E. Rte. 70 (Covered Bridge Rd.) | 856-795-0172 | www.andreottis.com

A "favorite with romantics", "ladies" who "lunch" and "foodies alike", this "cosmopolitan" Italian "mainstay" in a Cherry Hill strip mall frames "tasty", "consistent" meals with comp "appetizers" and trays of "home-baked" pastries from the "spectacular" bakery; the "wine shop on the premises is a plus", as is the "timely" service, and don't be surprised by "spot sing-alongs" from the "happy bar crowd"; P.S. there's live music and dancing on Saturdays.

Angelo's Pizzeria & Ristorante *Pizza* 25 | 20 | 24 | $18

Mount Laurel | 878 Union Mill Rd. (Morning Glory Dr.) | 856-778-7222
Mount Laurel | 200 Larchmont Blvd. (Hainesport Rd.) | 856-231-8777
www.angelospizza.biz

"Crusty" "New York"–style pizza that "never disappoints", "reasonable" prices and a staff that's "on the ball" make these Mount Laurel strip-mall parlors "go-to" choices for many; while critics find them as "nondescript as an office reception area", the "bang for the buck" is "more than enough" to compensate.

Angelo's Pizza *Pizza* 25 | 20 | 24 | $20

Woodbury | 627 N. Broad St. (Walnut St.) | 856-845-3450

"Excellent" pizzas and "fabulous sandwiches" are "served fresh and hot" at this joint" down the street from Underwood Memorial Hospital in Woodbury; sure, the decor's a "bit lacking", but it's run by "friendly" folks who foster a "warm atmosphere" and make it a "great place for a family meal."

Animo Juice *Mexican* 23 | 18 | 21 | $12

Haddonfield | 113 Kings Hwy. E. (bet. Mechanic & Tanner Sts.) | 856-427-9070 | www.animojuice.com

"Eat without the guilt" advise fans of this Haddonfield smoothie shop-cum-burrito bar that offers "excellent", "revitalizing" "fresh juice combinations", "light", "healthy" Mex options and "friendly" service; although the digs are unremarkable, most agree that for an "inexpensive" lunch, "this place is a must."

Anthony's Creative Italian Cuisine 🖬 *Italian*   24 | 22 | 24 | $32

Haddon Heights | 512 Station Ave. (bet. Atlantic Ave. & White Horse Pike) | 856-310-7766 | www.anthonyscuisine.com
"Homemade" Italian comfort food "so good, it should be patented" makes this "cute" BYO in Haddon Heights a "solid option", particularly for the $25 prix fixes Tuesdays–Thursdays; the "lovely staff" provides "wonderful" service in the "contemporary" space, and those in the know advise the "second floor" is better for a "relaxed" "night out."

Antonietta's 🗷🖬 *Italian*   23 | 22 | 23 | $26

Runnemede | 212 N. Black Horse Pike (3rd Ave.) | 856-312-9000 | www.antoniettas.com
"Fresh" "homemade Italian specialties" and "prompt" service keep 'em coming "back again" to Antonietta Romano's contemporary bistro-slash–watering hole in Runnemede; some critics, though, find it "too pricey" given the "small", "corner-bar" setting that can get "loud" at times.

Anton's at the Swan 🖬 *American*   24 | 23 | 24 | $45

Lambertville | Swan Hotel | 43 S. Main St. (Swan St.) | 609-397-1960 | www.antons-at-the-swan.com
"Treat yourself and someone you love" to an "intimate dinner" "rich in flavors" at this "old-world" American in a Lambertville inn "tucked away off the main tourist routes"; whether you're seated beside the "cozy fireplaces" or outside on the "darling" patio, the staff "tries to make you feel like a regular"; P.S. many regard the bar as one of the "best in Hunterdon County."

Ariana *Afghan*   23 | 20 | 22 | $27

Voorhees | Eagle Plaza Shopping Ctr. | 700 Haddonfield Berlin Rd. (White Horse Rd.) | 856-784-1100 | www.restaurantariana.com
See review in the Philadelphia Directory.

Arugula *Italian*   27 | 25 | 25 | $37

Sewell | 373 Egg Harbor Rd. (bet. Bentley Dr. & Greentree Rd.) | 856-589-0475 | www.arugularestaurant.net
Though it flies "under the radar", this white-tablecloth Sewell BYO serves "inspired", "modern" Italian cuisine full of "amazing flavor combinations" in a contemporary space with the "atmosphere of a city restaurant"; the staff is "always cheerful", and while you should "be prepared to spend some moolah" (unless you go for the "early-bird" prix fixe), most agree it's "worth a return visit."

Aunt Berta's Kitchen 🖬 *Soul Food/Southern*   ∇ 26 | 17 | 25 | $17

Oaklyn | 639 White Horse Pike (Greenwood Ave.) | 856-858-7009 | www.auntbertaskitchen.com
For fans, this Oaklyn Southerner is like "going to grandma's house on Sundays", assuming your grandmother whips up "fresh, flavor-

ul" soul food with a healthful bent, plus "wonderful" desserts that
are "well worth the cellulite"; the "friendly, helpful" staff "makes
you feel right at home", and while some report "parking problems",
most find it an "enjoyable" experience.

Bahama Breeze Caribbean 22 | 23 | 21 | $28

Cherry Hill | Cherry Hill Mall | 2000 Rte. 38 (Haddonfield Rd.) |
856-317-8317 | www.bahamabreeze.com
See review in the Philadelphia Directory.

Baja Fresh Mexican Grill Mexican 21 | 15 | 19 | $13

Mount Laurel | Centerton Sq. | 10-A Centerton Rd. (Union Mill Rd.) |
856-802-0892
Voorhees | Echelon Vill. Plaza | 1120 White Horse Rd. (bet. Executive Dr. &
Haddonfield Berlin Rd.)
Cherry Hill | Garden State Park | 2000 Marlton Pike West
(bet. Garden State Blvd. & Haddonfield Rd.)
www.bajafresh.com
When in the mood for "copious amounts of food for pretty cheap",
amigos tout this *"bueno"* chain for its "fresh", "customized" bur-
itos and tacos that are a "step above regular Mexican fast food";
sure, it's "not for dates", and some find the fare "sterile" and decor
"lacking", but for "families with children" and those on a budget, it
"never disappoints."

Barnsboro Inn American 23 | 20 | 22 | $34

Sewell | 699 Main St. (Center St.) | 856-468-3557 |
www.barnsboroinn.com
The "rustic" decor, "slanted floors" and "historical atmosphere"
at this circa-1776 inn in Sewell make you feel "like you're stepping back in time"; while a few think it needs to be "brought into
the 21st century", for most, the "reasonably priced" "homestyle"
cooking and "personable" service make it a "nice place to go out
with friends for a relaxing night."

Barone's Tuscan Grille Italian 24 | 21 | 23 | $28

Moorestown | 280 Young Ave. (Main St.) | 856-234-7900 |
www.baronestuscangrille.com

Villa Barone Italian

Collingswood | 753 Haddon Ave. (bet. Frazer & Washington Aves.) |
856-858-2999 | www.villabaronesite.com
Maple Shade | 112 W. Main St. (bet. Lippincott & Terrace Aves.) |
856-779-0100 | www.baronerestaurants.com
"Silly big" portions of "classic Italian dishes" and "friendly,
down-to-earth" service are the hallmarks of these "understated"
South Jersey BYOs; "reasonable" prices and a "relaxing" ambiance
also make them a "solid" choice for many.

Barrington Coffee House Coffeehouse ▽ 26 | 19 | 24 | $27

Barrington | 131 Clements Bridge Rd. (Haines Ave.) |
856-573-7800 | www.barringtoncoffeehouse.com
"Exceptional" breakfast sandwiches, "great cappuccino" and
"sweet-as-pie" service make for lots of "happy campers" at this

Barrington coffee shop, a "frequent stop" on many people's "morning routes"; by night it morphs into a music venue, hosting live acts, songwriting sessions and a Thursday open-mike night.

Bella Pizza Cafe *Italian/Pizza*   ▽ 24 | 13 | 20 | $16

Delran | 100 Brown St. (bet. Chestnut & Front Sts.) |
856-461-1480 | www.bellapizzacafe.com
Fans insist this "family-operated and -oriented" Italian in Delran is "well worth the trip to the 'burbs" for affordable "amazing pizzas" and other "down-home" eats; there are only "a few tables" and some report "no atmosphere to speak of", but most consider takeout to be the "staple of its business" anyway.

Bell's Tavern ⊟ *American/Italian*   23 | 16 | 22 | $27

Lambertville | 183 N. Union St. (bet. Buttonwood & Elm Sts.) |
609-397-2226 | www.bellstavern.com
"Good, simple" "red-gravy" Italian and "consistent" American pub fare "with prices to match" appeals to "locals and tourists" alike at this "comfortable" Lambertville tap; though it can get "somewhat noisy" and "crowded", the "friendly" atmosphere makes it a "cut above what you'd expect."

Benihana *Japanese*   23 | 21 | 22 | $37

Pennsauken | 5255 Marlton Pike (McClellan Ave.) |
856-665-6320 | www.benihana.com
See review in the Philadelphia Directory.

Big John's *Cheesesteaks*   22 | 12 | 19 | $15

Cherry Hill | 1800 Rte. 70 E. (bet. Fulton St. & Marlton Pike W.) |
856-424-1186 | www.bigjohns.com
The cheesesteak "moved across the river" to this "classic" South Jersey sandwich shop duo serving "tasty", "humongous" versions of Philly's signature sandwich, and the free pickle bar is a "real winner"; some fault it for "inconsistency", and decry the "dark, dreary" digs – but "you're not going for the atmosphere", after all.

Bistro at
Cherry Hill *American*   25 | 18 | 23 | $24

Cherry Hill | Cherry Hill Mall | 2000 Rte. 38 (Haddonfield Rd.) |
856-662-8621
Cherry Hill Mall shoppers "skip the food court" and instead belly up to this "cute" American bistro situated in the "old Woolworth's lunch counter", where "amazing" fare is "plated as you would expect in a classy restaurant" and served "fast"; no surprise, the "people-watching" is "fantastic", though some fret that it "needs more seating", and others demur at dining while "annoying teenagers scream behind you."

Bistro di Marino Ⓜ *Italian*   26 | 21 | 24 | $30

Collingswood | 492 Haddon Ave. (Crestmont Terrace) |
856-858-1700 | www.bistrodimarino.com
"A+ Italian cuisine" that's "worth every calorie" comes out of Jimmy Marino's kitchen at his "low-lit" BYO in Collingswood; it's

like a "holiday" in the "charming" "backyard garden", which works for a "date" or a "little party", especially on Thursday nights when there's live jazz.

Black Horse Diner ● *Diner*

23 | 18 | 23 | $18

Mount Ephraim | 152 N. Black Horse Pike (George St.) | 856-742-8989 | www.blackhorsediner.com

"After a night of dancing" and "you're really hungry", this "dependable" 24/7 diner in Mount Ephraim will still be turning out "heaping platters" of "down-home cooking" while "friendly" servers are "happy to bring more coffee as long as you want"; more sedate types counter that "breakfast is the best bet" here.

Blackbird Dining

22 | 17 | 20 | $41

Establishment Ⓜ *French/Italian*

Collingswood | 714 Haddon Ave. (bet. Collings & Irvin Aves.) | 856-854-3444 | www.blackbirdnj.com

Showcasing his "creative" "home cooking", Alex Capasso's "simple yet chic" French Italian BYO in Downtown Collingswood is a "great date place" with a "cool" vibe; "bargain" specials and "fast" service are further pluses, but some feel it "lost its spark" after the move to its current digs, where critics report enduring "unbelievable noise levels" and "knocking elbows with neighbors."

Blue Claw Crab

26 | 18 | 22 | $34

Eatery *Seafood*

Burlington | 4494 Burlington Pike (bet. Campus Dr. & Van Skiver Pkwy.) | 609-387-3700 | www.crabeatery.com

"Don't forget your bib", for you might get "messy" as you "throw back" "excellent crabs" of "all types" at this "cute", "shack-y" Burlington seafooder that also serves "fresh, delicious" fin fare; the digs may be "kitschy" to some, but "friendly" service, "reasonable" prices and BYO add to an overall "awesome experience."

Blue 2O *Seafood*

22 | 24 | 23 | $40

Cherry Hill | 1906 Marlton Pike W. (Mercer St.) | 856-662-0297 | www.blue2Oseafoodgrill.com

"Beautiful" decor with a "blue-ocean" theme and "attentive" service that's "not overbearing" create an "upscale atmosphere" with a whiff of "romance" at this Cherry Hill seafooder with a "lively bar scene"; afishionados "have no complaints" about the "quality" fin fare, but some find it "a tad pricey."

Blueplate *American*

23 | 15 | 22 | $26

Mullica Hill | 47 S. Main St. (High St.) | 856-478-2112 | www.blueplatenj.com

"Small-town diner by day", James Malaby's "relaxed" BYO in Mullica Hill morphs into a "trendy", "adventurous" American at night, turning out "interesting" dishes featuring "locally grown ingredients", which are served by a "friendly" staff; though many are cool to the "so-so", "no-frills" digs, most agree it's "worth a visit any time of day."

	FOOD	DECOR	SERVICE	COST

Bobby Chez ⓜ Seafood
25 | 17 | 22 | $25

Cherry Hill | Tuscany Mktpl. | 1990 Marlton Pike E. (Old Orchard Rd.) | 856-751-7575
Collingswood | 33 W. Collings Ave. (Haddon Ave.) | 856-869-8000
Mount Laurel | Centerton Sq. | 32 Centerton Rd. (Marter Ave.) | 856-234-4146
Sewell | 100 Hurffville Crosskeys Rd. (Glassboro Cross Keys Rd.) | 856-262-1001
www.bobbychezcrabcakes.com

"Amazing crab cakes" are the stock-in-trade of these "modern" South Jersey seafood shops, which "live up to their great expectations" with "huge", "fresh" offerings that contain "very little filler"; "dingy" digs reflect its primary "take-out" function, and the service is usually "fast", although some say it can be "slow", because they get so "crowded."

Bobby Ray's American
▽ 24 | 20 | 21 | $24

Pennsauken | 6324 Westfield Ave. (Cove Rd.) | 856-356-2072 | www.braysplace.com

Fans want to meet the owner and "shake his hand" for this spacious Pennsauken sports bar serving "quality" (if a "tad expensive") American pub grub and "great drink specials" served by "cute bartenders"; quizzo nights, DJs and occasional live music add to the "fun."

NEW Bobby's Burger Palace Burgers
24 | 20 | 20 | $16

Cherry Hill | Cherry Hill Mall | 2000 Rte. 38 (Haddonfield Rd.) | 856-382-7462 | www.bobbysburgerpalace.com
See review in the Philadelphia Directory.

Bomb Bomb BBQ
Grill & Sandwich Factory ⓜ BBQ/Sandwiches
24 | 18 | 24 | $26

Glassboro | 22 High St. E. (Main St.) | 856-243-5119 | www.bombbombgrill.com
See review in the Philadelphia Directory.

Bonefish Grill Seafood
24 | 22 | 23 | $36

Deptford | 1709 Deptford Ctr. Rd. (Almonessen Rd.) | 856-848-6261
Marlton | 500 Rte. 73 N. (bet. Baker Blvd. & Lincoln Dr.) | 856-396-3122
www.bonefishgrill.com
See review in the Philadelphia Directory.

Botto's Italian Line Italian
25 | 20 | 23 | $34

Swedesboro | 1411 Kings Hwy. (bet. Auburn & Moravian Church Rds.) | 856-467-1570 | www.bottos.com

"Superb" Italian chow is served in a "homey" setting with a "South Philly" feel at this "family-owned" white-tablecloth restaurant in Swedesboro, where the staff makes "you feel like a king"; it's an "invigorating place to be on the weekends" with "live bands", while "bar specials" make it a popular "nightspot for drinks."

	FOOD	DECOR	SERVICE	COST

Braddock's Tavern ⓜ *American*   22 | 23 | 22 | $43

Medford | 39 S. Main St. (Union St.) | 609-654-1604 |
www.braddocks.com

Housed in a circa-1844 "Colonial house you always wanted but
couldn't afford", this "classy" American in the "lovely town" of
Medford serves "solid" chow in a dining room full of "old-time
charm", while the more laid-back downstairs tavern offers a menu
with some more "modern twists"; some find the prices "a little
high", but "friendly" service and an "elegant" ambiance make it
suitable for a "romantic evening."

Brio Tuscan Grille *Italian*   23 | 24 | 24 | $34

Cherry Hill | Towne Place at Garden State Park | 901 Haddonfield Rd.
(Graham Ave.) | 856-910-8166
NEW Marlton | Promenade at Sagemore | 500 Rte. 73 S. (bet. Brick Rd. &
Marlton Pkwy.) | 856-983-0277
www.brioitalian.com

"A chain for people who hate chains", this semi-"upscale"
"shopping-center" Italian fills the bill whether for "family dining"
or "dates", with "something for everyone" on the menu, "courteous" service and a "comfortable" setting that feels like a "private
home"; while it's "dependable to a fault", some find it a "smidge
pricey", though it does offer "unbelievable" "happy-hour" deals.

The British Chip Shop *British*   24 | 23 | 24 | $18

Haddonfield | 146 Kings Hwy. E. (Kings Ct.) | 856-354-0204 |
www.thebritishchipshop.com

"Dieters beware" the "generous portions" of "fresh" fish 'n' chips
and other "fantastic" eats at this British BYO in Haddonfield, which
"puts to rest the idea that the Brits eat a bland, boring diet"; while
the "authentic" setting is a bit "snug", the servers are "friendly and
well versed on the menu"; P.S. it also offers a "proper tea without
all of the frilliness of many tea shops."

Brother's Pizza *Pizza*   26 | 16 | 22 | $16

Cinnaminson | Acme Plaza Shopping Ctr. | 1105 Rte. 130 S.
(Riverton Rd.) | 856-829-6474 | www.brotherspizzaonline.com
Piezani "drive out of their way" for the "excellent" pizzas (including
"gluten-free") at this modest BYO parlor in a Cinnaminson strip
mall, which also serves "great cheesesteaks" and "typical" Italian
offerings; "nice service" and "reasonable prices" are additional
reasons it's "highly recommended" by many.

Bruno's Restaurant & Pizza *Italian*   25 | 19 | 24 | $24

Haddonfield | 509 Hopkins Rd. (Lafayette Rd.) | 856-428-9505
Haddonfielders laud the "amazing" pizzas and "homemade" Italian
eats at this "family-oriented" eatery where the "generous portions"
usually wind up as "another meal for the next day"; while the digs
may look like your "basic pizzeria", "attentive" service helps make
the experience "enjoyable", and the "liquor store next door" makes
for "easy BYO."

	FOOD	DECOR	SERVICE	COST

Cafe Fontana *Italian/Pizza*   ∇ 22 | 19 | 20 | $30

Maple Shade | 30 E. Main St. (Forklanding Rd.) | 856-321-1301 |
www.cafefontana.com

You get "a lot of food for your money" (including "delicious gnocchi") at this midpriced BYO Italian in Maple Shade, and it's served
by a "friendly" staff; a few find the space "a bit outdated", but it
does have outdoor seating and a ballroom that seats up to 250.

Café Gallery *Continental*   23 | 24 | 23 | $44

Burlington | 219 High St. (Pearl St.) | 609-386-6150

"Get a seat by the window" at this "charming" Continental on the
Delaware River in Burlington and "watch the riverboats" or gaze at
the "original artwork" on the walls; "wonderful" Sunday brunches,
"attentive" service and a "romantic" ambiance complete the picture.

Caffe Aldo Lamberti *Italian/Seafood*   25 | 24 | 24 | $46

Cherry Hill | 2011 Marlton Pike W. (Haddonfield Rd.) |
856-663-1747 | www.caffelamberti.com

The "swanky" Lamberti flagship in Cherry Hill is "always dependable" for an "outstanding meal" of "refined" Italian seafood in
"unbutton-your-jeans"-size portions, served by an "attentive"
staff; the "eye-catching" space with "low lighting" is "great for a
date night" or "business lunch to impress a client", and while the
"middle-age" crowd flashing "Rolexes" and "fancy cars" generate
some eye-rolls, most regard it as a "classic."

Caffe Galleria *Eclectic*   ∇ 23 | 21 | 22 | $28

Lambertville | Lambertville House Hotel | 32 Bridge St. (Union St.) |
609-397-2400 | www.caffegalleria.com

There's "something for everyone" at this Eclectic in the Lambertville House Hotel, serving "reasonably priced" breakfast, lunch
and dinner fare, plus "awesome" desserts, all made with "fresh
ingredients"; though a few gripe about the "claustrophobic" space,
"friendly", "old-school" service puts most at ease.

California Pizza Kitchen *Pizza*   22 | 18 | 20 | $23

Cherry Hill | Cherry Hill Mall | 2000 Rte. 38 (Cherry Hill Mall Dr.) |
856-910-8121 | www.cpk.com

See review in the Philadelphia Directory.

The Capital Grille *Steak*   26 | 25 | 26 | $65

Cherry Hill | Cherry Hill Mall | 2000 Rte. 38 (Haddonfield Rd.) |
856-665-5252 | www.thecapitalgrille.com

See review in the Philadelphia Directory.

Cap'n Cat Clam Bar *Seafood*   24 | 12 | 21 | $28

Voorhees | Eagle Plaza Shopping Ctr. | 700 Haddonfield Berlin Rd.
(Whitehouse Rd.) | 856-435-2287

It might not "look like much", but this Voorhees strip-mall BYO
dishes out the "freshest" seafood without "a lot of frills", which
is "as good as you'd get at a fancy-schmancy restaurant"; "fair"
prices and "friendly" service also make up for the "plain" digs, and
it "must be doing something right", since it's "always packed."

	FOOD	DECOR	SERVICE	COST

Cap'n Cats
Clam Bar & Tavern ◐ *Seafood*

27 | 16 | 23 | $33

Deptford | 1416 Crown Point Rd. (Hessian Ave.) | 856-853-1844

For an "awesome night of seafood" or just a "few drinks" in a "comfortable", "low-key" atmosphere, fans tout this Deptford bar-cum-"old-time clam house" serving "excellent" fin fare (plus a house cocktail sauce that'll "clear your sinuses"); it's "not fancy, but that's reflected in the price."

Carriage House *American*

▽ 21 | 20 | 22 | $28

Voorhees | 1219 Gibbsboro Rd. (White Horse Rd.) | 856-783-1100 | www.carriagehousevoorhees.com

Owner Sue Fulton "makes you feel at home" at her "quaint" lakeside American in Voorhees where there are enough "antiques and homemade items" to "make you feel you're eating at your grandmother's"; "friendly" service, "homemade" fare and "good value for your money" make it a "family favorite."

Casona Ⓜ *Cuban*

24 | 22 | 21 | $31

Collingswood | 563 Haddon Ave. (Knight Ave.) | 856-854-5555 | www.mycasona.com

Amigos attest "you can't go wrong with anything on the menu" of "authentic" Cuban eats at this "unpretentious" Collingswood Cuban BYO; it's a "treat" to dine and "people-watch" from the wraparound porch of the circa-1905 house, and while some report "hit-or-miss" service and "extreme noise levels", others insist the "top-notch" fare is "totally worth leaving the city for."

Charlie Brown's Steakhouse *Steak*

23 | 21 | 22 | $29

Woodbury | 111 N. Broad St. (bet. Hunter St. & Red Bank Ave.) | 856-853-8505

Maple Shade | 114 E. Main St. (Spruce Ave.) | 856-779-8003

Mount Holly | 1920 Burlington Mount Holly Rd. (Burrs Rd.) | 609-265-1100

www.charliebrowns.com

For fans, happiness is the "terrific" salad bar that "dominates" an altogether "yummy" bill of fare at this "old-fashioned" steakhouse chain; a "welcoming" bar atmosphere is conducive to "hanging and watching the game", and while some say good grief to "dim" lighting and somewhat "old-fashioned" decor, fans insist you'll have "little chance of being disappointed."

The Cheesecake Factory *American*

24 | 22 | 23 | $30

Cherry Hill | Marketplace at Garden State Park | 931 Haddonfield Rd. (off Rte. 70) | 856-665-7550 | www.thecheesecakefactory.com

See review in the Philadelphia Directory.

Chez Elena Wu *Chinese/Japanese*

22 | 21 | 22 | $31

Voorhees | Ritz Shopping Ctr. | 910 Haddonfield Berlin Rd. (bet. Laurel Oak Blvd. & White Horse Rd.) | 856-566-3222 | www.chezelenawu.com

Fans of this Voorhees BYO applaud the "variety" of "delicately flavored" dishes on its "contemporary" Sino-Japanese menu and "friendly" service; the "white-tablecloth" setting is "more upscale than one might expect" from its "unassuming" strip-mall locale, and while some lament that it's "not what it used to be" when Elena Wu herself owned it, others insist it's still "better than the usual take-out place."

Chickie's & Pete's ● *Pub Food*   23 | 22 | 22 | $26
Bordentown | 183 Rte. 130 (Ward Ave.) | 609-298-9182 |
www.chickiesandpetes.com
See review in the Philadelphia Directory.

Chick's Tavern ⊠ *Pub Food*   ▽ 24 | 18 | 25 | $23
Bridgeport | 231 E. 4th St. (Ford St.) | 610-279-9606 |
www.chickstavern.net
"If you're not here for the mussels you're in the wrong place" advise fans of this Bridgeport watering hole, whose "large portions" of "simple", "homemade" pub grub and happy-hour specials constitute some of the "best deals in town"; while the basic bar setting elicits no comment, fans praise the "pleasant owners" who make you feel "like one of the family."

China House *Chinese*   ▽ 28 | 22 | 27 | $21
Woodbury | 565 N. Evergreen Ave. (Red Bank Ave.) |
856-384-1188 | www.chinahousewoodbury.com
"Don't be fooled by the diner look from the outside" urge enthusiasts of this Woodbury Chinese, offering a "different variety" of "exceptional" dishes, including "awesome" sushi, and "courteous" service in a space with "above-average" decor; it's "not the kind of place you'd expect to find in a strip mall."

The Chophouse *Seafood/Steak*   26 | 25 | 25 | $59
Gibbsboro | 4 Lakeview Dr. S. (Clementon Rd.) | 856-566-7300 |
www.thechophouse.us
Situated in a "pretty, multilevel stand-alone" building with lakeside views, this "classy" surf 'n' turf "gem" in Gibbsboro promises "more than just great steaks", offering options "for the seafood crowd" along with a "well-chosen wine list"; servers "go out of their way to please", but at a price, as many find the experience too "expensive" for anything other than "special occasions."

Clancy's Pub ● *Pub Food*   20 | 18 | 22 | $21
Brooklawn | 304 Crescent Blvd. (Creek Rd.) | 856-456-4100
Sewell | 485 Woodbury Glassboro Rd. (Lambs Rd.) |
856-589-8989
www.clancyspubs.com
A "relaxed environment" makes locals "feel welcome" at these "low-key" South Jersey pubs boasting "awesome" outdoor seating, dozens of TVs and "reasonably priced" pub grub, including affordable lunch and dinner specials, with occasional live music adding to the "fun"; still, some find them "just ok" and "nothing special."

Club Diner ❶ *Diner* ▽ 24 | 19 | 24 | $20

Bellmawr | 20 N. Black Horse Pike (Chestnut Ave.) |
856-931-2880 | www.theclubdiner.com

Neon buzzes 24 hours a day at this "classic old diner" (circa 1946)
in Bellmawr, a clear shot to the Ben Franklin and Walt Whitman
Bridges; "friendly", "chatty" servers deliver "plentiful" portions of
"surprisingly delicious", "reasonably priced" comfort food that'll
"help sober you up" after a late night.

Coastline Restaurant ❶ *American* 19 | 16 | 21 | $27

Cherry Hill | 1240 Brace Rd. (bet. Kresson Rd. & Marlton Pike) |
856-795-1773 | www.coastlinenj.com

A "helpful, friendly" crew dishes up "huge portions" of midpriced
American eats (including an "awesome Sunday brunch") at this
long-running Cherry Hill "favorite" where "dated" decor doesn't
deter a "mostly older crowd" that shows up for "drinks and dancing"; skeptics sniff that the dining experience is "entirely secondary" to the "booze and loud music."

Coconut Bay Fusion Cuisine *Asian* ▽ 21 | 21 | 20 | $24

Voorhees | Echelon Village Plaza | 1120 White Horse Rd.
(bet. Executive Dr. & Haddonfield Berlin Rd.) | 856-783-8878 |
www.coconutbayfusion.com

The "strip-mall locale doesn't do justice" to the "interesting"
Pan-Asian fusion at this Voorhees BYO according to fans, who
deem it a "step above most others in South Jersey"; "reasonable
pricing", "knowledgeable" service and a "pleasant, quiet" atmosphere complete the picture.

Coffee Works *Coffeehouse* ▽ 21 | 19 | 20 | $11

Voorhees | 8109 Town Center Blvd. (Echelon Rd.) | 856-784-5282 |
www.coffee-works.com

Fans believe this coffeehouse in Voorhees Town Center "deserves
all the best" for its "great selection" of "tasty" joe, "sandwiches,
salads and quesadillas", and "pleasant", "super-fast" service;
"quiet" environs ("except for live music nights") make it a "good
place to meet friends."

Colonial Diner *Diner* 20 | 13 | 20 | $17

Woodbury | 924 N. Broad St. (Edith Ave.) | 856-848-6732

"What more could you ask for from a Jersey diner?" ponder fans of
this "familylike" Woodbury eatery dishing out "great breakfasts"
and other "down-home meals", served "with a smile"; though
some quip the "decor looks as old" as its name, most acknowledge
that it's been a "staple in the community" since the 1970s.

Connie Mac's ❶ *Irish/Pub Food* ▽ 19 | 14 | 18 | $20

Pennsauken | 8000 S. Crescent Blvd. (bet. Central Hwy. & Park Dr.) |
856-910-1255 | www.conniemacs.com

The "local-yokel crowd" gravitates toward this pub in Pennsauken
where it's "all about the Irish nachos" and other "affordable" "happy-hour" snacks, plus a "decent" number of beers to choose from;

it really comes together during a "ballgame" when multiple TVs are on, though fans also enjoy "sitting outside on the back deck."

Cool Dog Cafe   *American*   22 | 17 | 20 | $15

Cherry Hill | 2091 Marlon Pike E. (bet. Old Orchard Rd. & Split Rock Dr.) | 856-424-0400 | www.thecooldogcafe.com

Hot dogs "done right" and "sliders with the best and most unusual toppings you will find" "earn the 'cool' in the name" of this Cherry Hill sandwich shop whose enormous menu is a "refreshing change" for a "fast lunch"; whether you take out or "hang out", most concur "you don't go here" for the strip-mall decor.

Coriander: An Indian Bistro   *Indian*   26 | 22 | 23 | $27

Voorhees | Ritz Shopping Ctr. | 910 Haddonfield Berlin Rd. (bet. Voorhees Dr. & White Horse Rd.) | 856-566-4546 | www.coriandernj.com

At this BYO in Voorhees, the chef brings "plenty of heat" to "classic" dishes from "various parts of India", but the "spicing is well adjusted to non-Indian tastes"; a "large selection of both vegetarian and meat" offerings is served by a "professional" staff in a "bright, colorful" setting, adding up to an "outstanding" experience that merits a "drive from Philly."

Cross Culture   *Indian*   ▽ 25 | 21 | 24 | $29

Haddonfield | 208 Kings Hwy. E. (bet. Haddon Ave. & Mechanic St.) | 856-428-4343
Lambertville | 13 Klines Court (Bridge St.) | 609-397-3600

"Authentic", "gourmet Indian" fare in an attractive setting makes this BYO trio a "delightful" find "outside a large city", and locals in Doylestown, Haddonfield and Lambertville are glad to have them "in their backyards"; fans rate the service "excellent", if a bit "serious", and the only gripe is that the "prices seem a little on the steep side."

Cucina Carini   *Italian*   ▽ 22 | 21 | 22 | $31

Mount Laurel | 1373 Hainesport Mount Laurel Rd. (Moorestown Mt. Laurel Rd.) | 856-439-1941

The "parking lot always seems full" at this "small" Italian BYO in Mount Laurel, a popular "standby" for "fresh" dishes and take-out pizza; the mood is "friendly" in the "comfortable", "homey" (literally, it's a "renovated home") digs, adding to its "great value."

Curran's Irish Inn ● *American*   24 | 21 | 22 | $22

Palmyra | 5 W. Broad St. (Cinnaminson Ave.) | 856-314-8241 | www.curransirishinn.com

"Fantastic wings", "excellent local entertainment" and "efficient" service – "for the win!" enthuse fans of this Palmyra American pub; there's "always a friendly atmosphere with familiar faces" among a mostly "middle-aged" crowd, while daily specials and happy-hour deals make it a "must-visit place" for many.

	FOOD	DECOR	SERVICE	COST

Dream Cuisine Cafe 🖼️Ⓜ️ *French*   ▽ 25 | 16 | 20 | $46

Cherry Hill | Tuscany Mktpl. | 1990 Marlton Pike E. (Old Orchard Rd.) | 856-751-2800 | www.dreamcuisinecafe.net

Surveyors report "they take their time" in the open kitchen at this "unpretentious" Cherry Hill French BYO, so don't go "if you are in a hurry", but almost all agree the "outstanding", "reasonably priced" cuisine justifies the "leisurely" pace; it's a "diamond in the rough", which some say "deserves a better home" than its "sleepy strip-center" location.

Dúbh Linn Square ● *Irish*   20 | 23 | 22 | $25

Bordentown | 167 U.S. Hwy. 130 (Ward Ave.) | 609-298-7100

Cherry Hill | 482 E. Evesham Rd. (Short Hills Dr.) | 856-520-8312 www.dubhlinnsquare.com

A "beautifully crafted" bar is the centerpiece of the "eye-catching" decor (bartenders in kilts are another "sight") at this Irish pub duo serving "amazing black-and-tans" and "solid" pub grub; though some critics pan the fare as "inconsistent" and the scene as "faux" Gaelic, most agree it "transitions well into the nightlife scene", adding "best nights to go are when live bands are playing."

El Azteca *Mexican*   22 | 14 | 21 | $20

Mount Laurel | Ramblewood Shopping Ctr. | 1155 Rte. 73 (Church Rd.) | 856-914-9302 | www.elaztecaonline.com

See review in the Philadelphia Directory.

El Sitio Grill & Cafe *Pan-Latin/Steak*   ▽ 24 | 20 | 23 | $32

Collingswood | 729 Haddon Ave. (Fern Ave.) | 856-240-1217 | www.elsitiocollingswood.com

A "wonderful addition to the Collingswood community", this family-owned and -operated Pan-Latin steakhouse offers "interesting", Ecuadorian-influenced steaks and such, plus service with "warm smiles", at "fair" prices; the "roomy", inviting setting is "the perfect place for a date" even if a few think that the "acoustics need to be tempered."

Elements Cafe Ⓜ️ *American*   25 | 21 | 24 | $35

Haddon Heights | 517 Station Ave. (White Horse Pike) | 856-546-8840 | www.elementscafe.com

"Whimsical" "small plates" pack "big taste" at this "romantic" New American BYO in Haddon Heights, which locals regard as both the "embodiment of a neighborhood gem" and an "escape" from chains; a "knowledgeable" staff helps you build a meal from the frequently changing menu, and the $15 Sunset dinners (4:30–6:30 PM Tuesdays–Thursdays) are an "amazing" deal.

Elevation Burger *Burgers*   21 | 13 | 19 | $12

Moorestown | Moorestown Mall | 400 Rte. 38 (bet. Lenola Rd. & Nixon Dr.) | 888-291-4620 | www.elevationburger.com

See review in the Philadelphia Directory.

| | FOOD | DECOR | SERVICE | COST |

Famous & Original King of Pizza *Pizza* | 26 | 15 | 21 | $15 |

Cherry Hill | 2300 Rte. 70 (Cornell Ave.) | 856-665-4824 |
www.thefamouskingofpizza.com

"Long live the king" exclaim loyalists who practically "live in the parking lot" of this Cherry Hill pizzeria, which has been dishing out "awesome NY-style pies" since 1976; lukewarm reactions to decor and service notwithstanding, most agree it's "worth the traffic on Route 70 to get a fix" of its "saucy, cheesy glory."

Farnsworth House ● *Continental* ∇ | 23 | 17 | 22 | $33 |

Bordentown | 135 Farnsworth Ave. (Railroad Ave.) |
609-291-9232 | www.thefarnsworthhouse.com

This bi-level Continental mainstay in the "attractive little town" of Bordentown turns out "tasty", "well-presented" dishes, including "typical" "red-sauce Italian offerings", and backs it with a "good beer selection"; smooth service makes for a "relaxing" meal, and while some say "there are more exciting places" in town, most find the experience "enjoyable."

The Fat Tomato Grill ☒ *Italian* ∇ | 26 | 21 | 25 | $26 |

Berlin | 175 Rte. 73 (bet. Oak & Tauton Aves.) | 856-768-8811 |
www.thefattomatogrill.com

Berliners boast about their "local hangout", this Italian BYO that's ideal for nights when "kids want pizza and adults want a great piece of fish or beef"; "excellent specials" and "awesome desserts" shine on the menu, and the "visible, involved" owner ensures "amazing service" in the "charming" setting that belies its strip-mall location.

Femmina Italian Grill *Italian* ∇ | 26 | 22 | 24 | $27 |

Medford | 408 Stokes Rd. (Schoolhouse Dr.) | 609-714-8800 |
www.femminaitaliangrill.com

The "well-prepared" Italian grub at this Medford BYO is "amazing" in terms of "quality and quantity", because you always "get two more delicious lunches out of dinner"; "accommodating" service comes with Bocelli playing in the background of the "tidy" space; P.S. it offers $12.99 early-birds for diners 55 and older.

Fieni's Ristorante *Italian* ∇ | 27 | 20 | 27 | $34 |

Voorhees | 800 S. Burnt Mill Rd. (Britton Pl.) | 856-428-2700 |
www.fieni.com

The "home-cooked" eats coming "straight from an authentic Italian kitchen" and "attentive" service at this "cozy" Voorhees BYO are worthy of a "special dinner" according to fans; the "converted ranch-house" digs are "comfortable", if "dated", and most recommend calling ahead because this "gem" "fills up quickly."

Filomena Cucina Italiana *Italian* | 27 | 24 | 25 | $38 |

Clementon | 1380 Blackwood Clementon Rd. (bet. Laurel &
Little Gloucester Rds.) | 856-784-6166 | www.filomenascucina.com

South Jerseyans groove on the "old-fashioned" gnocchi and other "homemade-tasting" pasta specialties at this "wallet-friendly" Ital-

FOOD | DECOR | SERVICE | COST

ian in Clementon whose "fine-dining atmosphere" features "help-ful" service that's "immediate without hovering", a rustic setting and live entertainment Tuesdays–Saturdays; the desserts "look gorgeous", though it's a challenge to "leave room to try them."

Filomena Lakeview *Italian*   27 | 26 | 26 | $36

Deptford | 1738 Cooper St. (Almonesson Rd.) | 856-228-4235 | www.filomenalakeview.com

"Classic dishes" "your nona would enjoy" are served by "waitress-es full of energy" at this rustic, "comfortably elegant" Italian in an old Deptford inn; "cozy and warm", it's like the "restaurant in the Billy Joel song", "perfect for a date", a "special occasion" or just a "nice night out", without "spending a lot of money."

Five Guys Burgers & Fries *Burgers*   24 | 14 | 20 | $13

Mount Ephraim | Audubon Shopping Ctr. | 130 S. Black Horse Pike (Mt. Ephraim Ave.) | 856-672-0442
Voorhees | Eagle Plaza Shopping Ctr. | 700 Haddonfield Berlin Rd. (White Horse Rd.) | 856-783-5588
Deptford | 2000 Clements Bridge Rd. (Rte. 42) | 856-845-5489
Sicklerville | 493 Berlin Cross Keys Rd. (Williamstown Erial Rd.) | 856-875-5558
Moorestown | East Gate Sq. Shopping Ctr. | 1650 Nixon Dr. (Rte. 38) | 856-866-0200
www.fiveguys.com

If you're determined to "dive head-first off your diet", fans tout this hamburger chain's "sloppy-licious" patties and "addictive" "greasy fries", with "free peanuts" and "friendly" counter service thrown in for good measure; even if "no extra cash was wasted on the basic decor", many deem it "one of the best things to happen to Philly since the Declaration of Independence."

Fleming's Prime Steakhouse & Wine Bar *Steak*   26 | 25 | 25 | $62

Marlton | 500 Rte. 73 N. (bet. Baker Blvd. & Lincoln Dr.) | 856-988-1351 | www.flemingssteakhouse.com

Fans ponder "what's not to love" about these suburban links of the "clubby", "testosterone-filled" steakhouse chain where "premium" beef is schlepped by "seasoned waiters" who take "customer service to old-time levels" amid "elegant" surroundings; whether it's a full-on, "expense-account" dinner "splurge" or just "awesome happy-hour drinks and noshes", most "go home happy."

Forno Pizzeria & Grille *Pizza*   ▽ 23 | 16 | 22 | $21

Maple Shade | 28 S. Church Rd. (Kings Hwy.) | 856-608-7711 | www.fornopizzeria.com

"Creative specials" and no-frills counter service make this "invit-ing" Maple Shade trattoria an "easy choice" for pizza or other "casual" Italian grub "on short notice"; an "interesting" antipasto bar offers you "a little of this, a little of that", while outdoor seating and a "friendly" atmosphere help make this a solid option that's "not fast food."

	FOOD	DECOR	SERVICE	COST

45th Street Pub ● *Pub Food* | 22 | 19 | 22 | $29 |

Edgewater Park | 4303 S. Rte. 130 (Cooper St.) | 609-877-5610
Pennsauken | 2545 45th St. (Federal St.) | 856-488-4578
www.45thstreetpub.com

"Kid-friendly before 8 PM", these "laid-back" "hometown" sports bars in Edgewater Park and Pennsauken are often packed with "groups of friends" in their "20s and 30s" who come for "tasty" burgers and wings, nightly "beer specials" and DJs Thursdays–Saturdays; while many praise the "pleasant" staff, others find the service "less than stellar", and sure, the digs are "nothing fancy", but they're "not holes-in-the-wall, either" (Edgewater Park boasts outside seating).

Francesco's Cucina Italiana ● *Italian* | ▽ 26 | 18 | 24 | $41 |

Berlin | 15 Rte. 73 (Pump Branch Rd.) | 609-561-1296 |
www.francescos73.com

This "family-owned" white-tablecloth Italian has the power to "surprise first-time diners" given that it's tucked away in "obscure" Berlin; "authentic" grub is backed by a "superb" wine list, and you needn't "be afraid to order something not on the menu" because owner Francesco Diodati and staff provide "excellent service."

Frank's Time Out *Pizza/Sandwiches* | ▽ 23 | 14 | 21 | $14 |

Berlin | 2 Rte. 73 S. (Berlin Cross Keys Rd.) | 856-768-7222 |
www.frankstimeout.com

Berlin locals deem this South Philly–style BYO pizzeria a "good choice" for "delicious" pies, sandwiches and other "quick bites" "cooked fresh when you order" at the counter; for some it's a "two-night-a-weeker" while others make time on nights they crave a Chicago-style deep-dish pizza or just "don't feel like cooking."

Franzone's Pizzeria & Restaurant *Italian/Pizza* | 25 | 13 | 21 | $17 |

Bridgeport | 501 Dekalb St. (5th St.) | 610-275-0114 |
www.kingofprussia.com

Local piezani "go out of their way" for the "thin-crust" pizza at this Bridgeport "institution" where pizzaioli "put the cheese on first", then "swirl" on a "sweet sauce" and "bake it to yummy perfection"; while the digs are unremarkable, "you are never rushed and the service is like family."

Fuji Japanese Restaurant Ⓜ *Japanese* | 27 | 23 | 26 | $46 |

Haddonfield | Shops at 116 | 116 Kings Hwy. E. (Tanner St.) |
856-354-8200 | www.fujirestaurant.com

Well-traveled chef Matt Ito brings an "upscale" "slice of Japan" to Haddonfield at his "cozy", "modern" BYO in an indoor mall; fans urge you to "get the omakase" because he "won't steer you wrong" – it's a "superb journey when you have a few hours to spend" in a "relaxed, no-rush atmosphere", and "every chopstickful is a divine experience."

	FOOD	DECOR	SERVICE	COST

Full Moon *Eclectic* — 22 | 17 | 22 | $25

Lambertville | 23 Bridge St. (Union St.) | 609-397-1096

An "extremely popular" stop for "quick, low-key" breakfasts and lunches, this Lambertville Eclectic serves a daytime menu full of "slightly exotic offerings", plus the "unique" once-a-month 'Full Moon' dinners (served on nights when the moon is full); a rotating collection of artwork from local artists grace the otherwise basic space; P.S. closed Tuesdays.

Gaetano's *Cheesesteaks* — 24 | 14 | 21 | $16

Berlin | 437 Rte. 73 N. (Commerce Ln.) | 856-753-1919 | www.gaetanosberlin.com

"Huge sandwiches for huge appetites" are the hallmarks of this humble Berlin eatery whose "amazing" cheesesteaks at "reasonable" prices ("without any language rules") make it a "great lunch stop", although seating is limited; "consistent quality" makes it a "solid value."

Gaetano's of Penny Packer *Cheesesteaks/Pizza* — ∇ 23 | 12 | 22 | $16

Willingboro | 224 Pennypacker Dr. (Sunset Ln.) | 609-871-6861 | www.gaetanospennypacker.com

"Philadelphia has nothing" on this Willingboro spot popular for its "real cheesesteaks", pizzas and other sandwiches "to die for"; "affordable" prices and "courteous, professional" service are further reasons many "make a point of stopping in."

GG's Restaurant Ⓩ *American* — ∇ 25 | 23 | 25 | $58

Mount Laurel | DoubleTree Guest Suites Mount Laurel | 515 Fellowship Rd. (Rte. 73) | 856-222-0335 | www.ggsrestaurant.com

"For a grown-up night out", this polished, "white-tablecloth gem" in a Mount Laurel DoubleTree offers "first-class" New American fare and "efficient" service, plus an added "bonus", a pianist supplying "great dinner music" most nights of the week; if the "bar scene can get noisy", part of that may be the shock of some locals who "find it hard to believe" they're in a hotel.

Giumarello's Ⓜ *Italian* — 26 | 24 | 25 | $46

Westmont | 329 Haddon Ave. (Maple Ave.) | 856-858-9400 | www.giumarellos.com

Aficionados assure us "you can't make a bad choice" from the "scrumptious" Northern Italian menu at this "relaxing" Westmont haunt where "high rollers" "flock" for "a romantic dinner or business lunch" – or the "fantastic bar scene" at happy hour; an "enthusiastic" staff, a solid wine list and "live music on some nights" make it a "perfect special-occasion" destination.

Golden Dawn Diner ⬤ *Diner* — 20 | 16 | 21 | $18

Burlington | 4387 U.S. Hwy. 130 (McNeil St.) | 609-877-2236 | www.goldendawn130.com

The "friendly" staff keeps the "hot coffee coming" at this "typical" diner that's been plying travelers in Burlington for nearly 60 years with "hearty portions" of decent fare; there's "a bit of everything" on the inexpensive menu, and it's open late every night.

Hamilton's Grill Room *Mediterranean*   26 | 23 | 24 | $50

Lambertville | 8 Coryell St. (bet. Lambert Ln. & Union St.) | 609-397-4343 | www.hamiltonsgrillroom.com

Jim Hamilton's "romantic", "hard-to-find" Med in Lambertville seldom "disappoints" with "great flavors" and "attentive but not overbearing" service, and while the menu's "pricey", "BYO keeps tabs down"; whether you opt for "pleasant outdoor dining" with views of the Delaware River Canal or enjoy the "lovely decor" inside, insiders suggest a "pre-dinner drink" at the bar across the courtyard.

Happy Buffet *Chinese*   ∇ 24 | 22 | 23 | $27

Audubon | Black Horse Pike Shopping Ctr. | 130 Black Horse Pike (Nicholson Rd.) | 856-310-1888

Fans feel "happy" indeed when they head home with a "full stomach" from this Chinese buffet next to Wal-Mart on Black Horse Pike in Camden County; the "crazy selection" of "hot, tasty" treats comes at "reasonable" prices too, while "attentive" service contributes to a "no-hassle" dining experience.

Harrison House Diner *American*   18 | 15 | 19 | $18

Mullica Hill | 98 N. Main St. (Richwood Rd.) | 856-478-6077 | www.harrisonhousediner.com

This "homey" Mullica Hill diner is like "going back in time", dishing up "ample portions" of all-American fare from a "varied" menu; sure, it's "nothing fancy", but "fair" prices and "quick", "friendly" service make it an easy option for locals who "don't want to cook."

The Harvest ● *American*   ∇ 22 | 22 | 20 | $24

Cinnaminson | 2602 Rte. 130 (New Albany Rd.) | 856-829-4499

Those "on a budget" flock to this 24/7 Cinnaminson "hometown" diner for New American eats and "blue-plate specials" that yield "a meal for the next day"; it's not big on looks, but with a "huge choice in menu options", "breakfast all day" and "sweethearts" for waitresses, it's "everything a Jersey diner should be."

Healthy Garden & Gourmet Pizza *Pizza*   ∇ 22 | 12 | 19 | $19

Voorhees | 200 Haddonfield Berlin Rd. (bet. Essex & Mercer Aves.) | 856-616-9300 | www.healthygardencafe.com

Aficionados insist the "modest setting gives no indication of just how good the food is" at this "casual" Voorhees pizzeria serving up "delicious" pies, "huge" salads, wraps and other "nutritious" grub, including "lots of great vegetarian dishes"; though service can be "a little slow", wallet-friendly prices make up for it.

High Street Grill *American*   ∇ 21 | 17 | 20 | $30

Mount Holly | 64 High St. (bet. Brainerd & Garden Sts.) | 609-265-9199 | www.highstreetgrill.net

It's "easy to become a regular" at this "pleasant", brick-walled bi-level in Mount Holly where a "friendly" staff delivers midpriced

New American fare that "doesn't stop at pub food"; there's "always something going on", often fueled by the "amazing craft beer selection" or "live music" in the "dim" downstairs tavern, more reasons many "cannot wait to go back."

Hollywood Cafe ◐ *American* 21 | 21 | 21 | $22

Woodbury Heights | 904 Mantua Pike (Cherry Ave.) | 856-251-0011 | www.thehollywoodcafeandsportsbar.com

From "breakfast to surf 'n' turf", this "upbeat" "retro" "hangout" in Woodbury Heights has you covered - it's an "affordable", "family-friendly" diner featuring "quick" service and a vintage Corvette on display, backed by a sports bar perfect for "celebrating the end of the week", all giving off a "faux-Hollywood" sheen; "management makes the effort to remember regulars" too.

Holy Tomato M ⊭ *Pizza* 24 | 19 | 23 | $14

Blackwood | 9 S. Black Horse Pike (Church St.) | 856-228-1234 | www.holytomatogourmetpizza.com

"Outstanding" pies made with "thin crust and fresh ingredients" make this "adorable", "affordable" cash-only tomato-pie outlet in a home in Blackwood a "refreshing change from the chains"; the digs are "cute", if a "little tight", and the "great girls behind the wheel" work to ensure you "never leave disappointed" (tip: "eat in and then take out more").

Il Fiore *Italian* 27 | 20 | 25 | $31

Collingswood | 693-695 Haddon Ave. (Collings Ave.) | 856-833-0808

"That line down Haddon Avenue" leads to this "charming" Collingswood BYO whose "fabulous", "reasonably priced" Italian fare is "well worth the wait - and there will be one"; "don't plan on a private conversation" because the "tables are close" so just pretend you're at a "dinner party with strangers", albeit one with "attentive" servers and "doggy bags."

Illiano Cucina *Italian* ▽ 24 | 22 | 23 | $23

Medford | 200 Tuckerton Rd. (Taunton Rd.) | 856-985-2721 | www.illianocucina.com

The "garlicky good" bruschetta that comes in the bread basket is "worth the trip alone" to this "dependable" red-sauce Italian BYO in Medford; the "apps and entrees are large, delicious and reasonable", while the "friendly" staff is "like family."

IndeBlue *Indian* 27 | 22 | 24 | $29

Collingswood | 619 Collings Ave. (White Horse Pike) | 856-854-4633 | www.indebluerestaurant.com

"Not your everyday Indian", this "moderately priced" Collingswood BYO showcases chef-owner Rakesh Ramola's "sophisticated", "exceptional" dishes, which are prepared "as spicy as you want it"; "knowledgeable" service in a "relaxed", "modern" setting adds to its allure, and while many Philadelphians consider it "worth the $5 toll" on the Ben Franklin Bridge, a Wash West branch slated to open in 2012 will save them the expense.

	FOOD	DECOR	SERVICE	COST

Inn of the
Hawke Restaurant *American*

▽ | 20 | 20 | 22 | $33

Lambertville | 74 S. Union St. (Mt. Hope St.) | 609-397-9555
"You'll find the locals" at this "inviting" Lambertville tavern where the American pub grub and beer selection are "worthy of your attention"; outfitted like an English pub (with a working fireplace), it's purportedly haunted, but the living are all "friendly", and there's "great" outdoor dining in the summer.

Iron Hill Brewery
& Restaurant ❷*American/Pub Food*

22 | 21 | 22 | $28

Maple Shade | 124 E. Kings Hwy. (Lenola Rd.) | 856-273-0300 |
www.ironhillbrewery.com
See review in the Philadelphia Directory.

Jasmine Oriental Cuisine *Asian*

27 | 19 | 26 | $21

Medford | Sharp's Run Plaza | 175 Rte. 70 (Jennings Rd.) |
609-654-8818 | www.jasmineorientalcuisine.com
"Don't tell anyone" about this Medford BYO plead loyalists, for it's "already too hard to get in on the weekend", thanks to "top-notch", "inexpensive" Asian grub that's "difficult to find in South Jersey"; "if you're looking for elegant decor, this is the wrong place", but "service with a smile" compensates.

Joe Pesce *Italian/Seafood*

22 | 18 | 21 | $38

Collingswood | 833 Haddon Ave. (bet. Collings Ave. & Cuthbert Blvd.) |
856-833-9888 | www.joepescerestaurant.com
Aficionados advise the "fresh grilled whole fish" is the "best bet" at this midpriced BYO Italian seafooder in Collingswood where "everything is cooked to order" and served by a "personable", "enthusiastic" staff; romantics also recommend the "intimate", nautical-themed space as "great for a first date."

Joe's Peking
Duck House Ⓜ⇱ *Chinese*

24 | 12 | 20 | $24

Marlton | Marlton Crossing Shopping Ctr. | 145 Rte. 73 S. (Rte. 70) |
856-985-1551 | www.joespekingduckhouse.com
"Top-notch" Chinese "basics" such as dumplings and wonton soup – along with "amazing" duck, plus lunchtime and weekend dim sum – are a "pleasant constant" at this cash-only Sino spot in a Marlton strip mall; the "quality of the food" and "friendly, professional" service outshine the "simple, spare" decor, while BYO helps keep it "inexpensive."

Johnny's Pizza *Pizza*

▽ | 22 | 16 | 18 | $21

Cherry Hill | 717 Kings Hwy. N. (Chapel Ave. E.) | 856-667-3232 |
www.johnnyspizzacherryhill.com
"Pizza is spelled j-o-h-n-n-y-s" for fans of this BYO parlor that's "been there forever" in Cherry Hill; "fast", "friendly" service and "good prices" in basic surroundings make it a popular option for those nights "when the whole family gets together."

	FOOD	DECOR	SERVICE	COST

The Kibitz Room *Deli* | 25 | 12 | 19 | $21 |

Cherry Hill | Shoppes at Holly Ravine | 100 Springdale Rd. (Evesham Rd.) | 856-428-7878 | www.kibitzroom.com

"Bring a big appetite or at least one friend" to this "family-friendly" deli in Cherry Hill, home of "tasty", "traditional heart-clogging" "Jewish soul food" in "Goliath portions", which "you order at the counter"; "New York prices" may rattle a few, but then again, "if you leave here hungry there is something wrong with you."

King of Pizza *Pizza* | 22 | 14 | 20 | $16 |

Berlin | 3 S. White Horse Pike (Berlin Cross Keys Rd.) | 856-753-8797 | www.thefamouskingofpizza.com

For tasty "thin-crust" pizzas and "even better wings", piezani rely on these "consistently good", no-frills Camden County parlors; some find them just "ok" and consider the royal moniker "just a name", but most agree they're fine for a "quick meal" on a budget.

Kitchen Consigliere Cafe *Italian* | 27 | 19 | 26 | $26 |

Collingswood | 8 Powell Ln. (Haddon Ave.) | 856-854-2156 | www.kitconcafe.com

"Delish" Southern Italian fare – by way of South Philly – is the name of the game at this "cute", modestly priced Collingswood BYO where owner Angelo Lutz "comes out and talks to every table", adding an "entertaining" side to the "people-watching"; the "waitresses aren't syrupy sweet" but they are "helpful with food suggestions", one more reason it's a "date-night" favorite.

Kunkel's Seafood & ▽ | 24 | 24 | 26 | $42 |
Steakhouse Ⓜ *Seafood/Steak*

Haddon Heights | 920 Kings Hwy. (bet. Black Horse & White Horse Pikes) | 856-547-1225 | www.kunkelsrestaurant.com

With wine lockers, twin fireplaces and prix-fixe options, this "dressy" surf 'n' turf BYO in Haddon Heights is a "wonderful" choice; "you can count on" "awesome" eats and "attentive" service, so be sure to "make a reservation" and "save room for dessert."

Kuzina *Greek* | 23 | 15 | 21 | $28 |

Cherry Hill | Sawmill Vill. | 404 Marlton Pike E. (Kings Hwy.) | 856-429-1061 | www.kuzinabysofia.com

"Greek done right" is how fans describe this "quaint yet elegant" Cherry Hill strip-mall charmer where they "enjoy every bite" of chef-owner Sofia Karakasidou-Khoury's "top-notch" chow, served in "plentiful portions" by an "attentive" staff; BYO keeps prices "reasonable", and if you forget your bottle, the nearby WineWorks shop will deliver to your table.

La Esperanza *Mexican* | 25 | 20 | 24 | $24 |

Lindenwold | 40 E. Gibbsboro Rd. (White Horse Pike) | 856-782-7114 | www.mexicanhope.com

"There's always a crowd" at this "bright-pink", family-owned cantina in Lindenwold, thanks to "amazing", "authentic" Mexican cuisine and "tasty" margaritas you want to "drown in"; service comes "with a smile", though a few feel "rushed", and "reasonable" prices are one more reason not to "drive all the way to Philly."

La Locanda *Italian*   ▽ 26 | 20 | 24 | $40

Voorhees | Echelon Village Plaza | 1120 White Horse Rd. (bet. Executive Dr. & Haddonfield Berlin Rd.) | 856-627-3700 | www.lalocandaonline.com

The "impeccably prepared" whole fish is "always a pleasure" and the rest of the menu is "solid" at this Italian BYO in Voorhees, where the service is "courteous" and the white-tablecloth setting belies its strip-mall location; a few gripe that there's "always a wait, even with reservations", but many declare it a "winner" overall.

Lambertville Station *American*   21 | 23 | 22 | $39

Lambertville | 11 Bridge St. (Delaware River) | 609-397-8300 | www.lambertvillestation.com

Multiple choices are available at this Lambertville American housed in a Victorian-era train station – a "chic wine bar" in the cellar, a "townies'" pub, an outdoor "pickup" spot "overlooking the canal" and "elegant" dining rooms "for tourists"; "solid" grub (including an "unusual" game menu in winter) and "friendly" service make it a "dependable" "standby" for many.

Landmark Americana Tap & Grill ❶ *American/Pub Food*   20 | 21 | 20 | $23

Glassboro | 1 Mullica Hill Rd. (Main St.) | 856-863-6600 | www.landmarkamericana.com

See review in the Philadelphia Directory.

La Vita's Pizza *Pizza*   ▽ 25 | 19 | 22 | $17

Moorestown | 121 W. Main St. (Church St.) | 856-235-0052 | www.lavitaspizza.com

"New York taste without that New York attitude" is the line on this Moorestown pizzeria that earns props for "unique pizza choices" (25 on display at one time) and "outstanding" delivery; South Jerseyans may give it the Bronx cheer, though, for billing its large sandwiches as 'heroes', since it's south of I-195.

Library IV *Steak*   26 | 21 | 24 | $41

Williamstown | 1030 N. Black Horse Pike (Lake Ave.) | 856-728-8064 | www.libraryiv.com

This long-running South Jersey chophouse will "never go out of style" as fans find it "fun" to "pick their cut of beef" at the "window" from the chefs and then hit the "superior salad bar"; a "homey" vibe, "terrific prices" and "keep-it-simple" approach are a "recipe for success" that works for either a "casual dinner" or "special occasion."

Lilly's On the Canal Ⓜ *Eclectic*   23 | 21 | 22 | $38

Lambertville | 2 Canal St. (Bridge St.) | 609-397-6242 | www.lillysgourmet.com

"Entirely dependable", this "casual" Eclectic BYO overlooking the Delaware Canal in Lambertville is worth a "walk across the bridge from New Hope" for "quality" sandwiches, signature eggplant fries and "stupendous desserts" toted by an "experienced" staff from the "open kitchen"; the "lovely" patio and two-story waterfall wall are "delightful in nice weather."

🆕 Little Louie's BBQ *BBQ*   – | – | – | I

Collingswood | 505 Haddon Ave. (Crestmont Terrace) | 856-854-0600 | www.littlelouiesbbq.com

Said Louie is a cartoon dachshund, and his sniffer points to all manner of barbecue from assorted regions at this Collingswood BYO, done up kitschy with old movie posters and a 70-in. flat-screen; chef Gerald Dougherty's longtime white-tablecloth past shows clearly in his out-there specialties, which include smoked duck and 'BBQ spaghetti.'

The Little Tuna *Seafood*   24 | 21 | 24 | $33

Haddonfield | 141 Kings Hwy. E. (Haddon Ave.) | 856-795-0888 | www.thelittletuna.com

Marcus Severs' "adorable" BYO seafooder works its "small-town" charms in "arty" Haddonfield, with an "efficient" staff putting out "loving prepared" fare in a "casual-elegant black-and-white" space on the main drag; the three-course early-birds (3–6:30 PM daily) are a "steal" for $19.99, so cognoscenti plead "let's just keep this our little secret, ok?"

Lobster Trap *Seafood*   ∇ 22 | 21 | 21 | $35

Pennsauken | 5300 N. Park Dr. (McClellan Ave.) | 856-663-3537

Although the signature dish doesn't come from the nearby Cooper River, adherents shell out praise for this "affordable" seafooder in Pennsauken's park offering a "wonderful view of the rowers" and "comfortable" seating; most praise the "simple fare done well", though a few wish it could be "stepped up a notch."

Luigi's Pizza Fresca *Italian/Pizza*   23 | 16 | 20 | $12

Marlton | 529 Old Marlton Pike W. (Cropwell Rd.) | 856-810-8888
Burlington | 1700 Columbus Rd. (Neck Rd.) | 609-239-8888 | www.luigispizzafresca.com

"Real" "thin-crust" "New York pizzas" and "hearty" panini get thumbs up at these "affordable" Italian bistros in South Jersey and Fairmount run by "friendly people" who "know their regulars"; even for those who detect "no ambiance" in the "casual" settings, it's a "reliable delivery go-to."

Luna Rossa Biagio Lamberti Ⓜ *Italian*   ∇ 28 | 25 | 25 | $30

Turnersville | 3210 Rte. 42 (Woodlawn Ave.) | 856-728-4505 | www.lambertis.com

For "consistently good" Italian fare like your "grandparents used to make", admirers recommend Biagio Lamberti's BYO in Turnersville, and while it's part of the Lamberti stable, it's "not cookie-cutter" and "kind" management assures a "nice night out"; the modern art deco setting includes an outdoor patio.

	FOOD	DECOR	SERVICE	COST

Maggiano's Little Italy *Italian* | 24 | 23 | 24 | $35 |

Cherry Hill | Cherry Hill Mall | 2000 Rte. 38 (Haddonfield Rd.) |
856-792-4470 | www.maggianos.com
See review in the Philadelphia Directory.

Makiman Sushi *Japanese/Korean* | 21 | 16 | 20 | $25 |

Medford | 185 Rte. 70 (Marlton Pike) | 609-654-7772 |
www.makimanonline.com
See review in the Philadelphia Directory.

Mandarin Buffet *Chinese* ∇ | 21 | 17 | 19 | $17 |

Cherry Hill | 1631 N. Kings Hwy. (Marlton Pike) | 856-857-1151
The all-you-can-eat buffet "never disappoints" at this spacious
Cherry Hill Chinese with seemingly "something for everyone", including "fresh seafood" and "sushi"; "quick", "kind" service keeps
things moving along, while BYO boosts the overall "value."

Mandarin Inn *Chinese* ∇ | 25 | 19 | 25 | $21 |

Sewell | 390 Hurffville Crosskeys Rd. (Egg Harbor Rd.) |
856-582-9055
Even after 25 years, there's "always something new to try" at this
"family-owned" Chinese in Sewell, where "you're not hungry 30
minutes later – you get a lot of good food at a reasonable price";
adherents will steer you to the Japanese side of the menu for "the
all-you-can-eat sushi days."

Manon Ⓜ ⇪ *French* ∇ | 26 | 20 | 22 | $47 |

Lambertville | 19 N. Union St. (Bridge St.) | 609-397-2596
Jean-Michel and Susan Dumas "won't settle for anything but excellence" at their "funky" BYO French in Lambertville, so it's "hard to
beat" the "rustic" Provençal classics, "even if you have to share
them with neighbors" (it's so "convivial" that "tables are touching",
though a reproduction of Van Gogh's "Starry Night" on the ceiling
keeps chins up); loyalists overlook the "big prices" and cash-only
policy to declare it a "serious winner."

Mastoris ● *Diner* | 22 | 16 | 21 | $26 |

Bordentown | 144 Rte. 130 (Rte. 206) | 609-298-4650 |
www.mastoris.com
If you "get hungry near Exit 7" of the New Jersey Turnpike, this
"crowded" Bordentown "diner with a capital D" dishes up "plentiful
servings" of midpriced American "comfort food" that distracts
from the "dated" decor; "good-natured" servers cater to "people in
suits and sweats" who pop in to devour "free cheese and cinnamon
breads" from the "awesome on-site bakery" and expect to "leave
with a doggy bag."

McCormick & Schmick's *Seafood* | 23 | 23 | 23 | $45 |

Cherry Hill | Garden State Park | 941 Haddonfield Rd. (Rte. 70) |
856-317-1711 | www.mccormickandschmicks.com
See review in the Philadelphia Directory.

	FOOD	DECOR	SERVICE	COST

Medport Diner ● *Diner* `21` `14` `21` `$18`

Medford | 122 Rte. 70 (bet. Hartford Rd. & Old Marlton Pike) |
609-654-4001

The "typical diner staples" plus at this 24/7 Medford coffee shop
"can't be beat late at night"; the retro digs are "comfortable" and
you're "treated like family" "any time of the day."

Megu Sushi *Japanese* `25` `21` `21` `$29`

Cherry Hill | Tuscany Mktpl. | 1990 Marlton Pike E. (Old Orchard Rd.) |
856-489-6228

Moorestown | 300 Young Ave. (bet. Centerton Rd. & County Rd. 537) |
856-780-6327

www.megusushi.com

Cherry Hillers and Moorestownians "fill their sushi void" at these
"charming"-meets-modern Japanese BYOs whose "creative" combos
are complemented by "lovely" service that "hums when it's busy";
it's "not super-pricey", and Sunday and Monday sushi deals bring
down the tabs considerably; P.S. Cherry Hill also serves hibachi.

Mélange @ Haddonfield Ⓜ *Cajun/Italian* `26` `23` `25` `$40`

Haddonfield | 18 Tanner St. (Kings Hwy.) | 856-354-1333 |
www.melangerestaurants.com

"Fabulous" Cajun and Italian dishes share the spotlight at Joe Brown's
"white-tablecloth", "Big Easy"–themed Haddonfield BYO; the chef
table-hops to be sure you have everything "before you need it",
along with his "attentive" staff, while an "upscale" vibe is in play on
the patio – all of which make it worthy of a "special occasion."

Metro Diner ● *American/Diner* ▽ `21` `21` `22` `$21`

Brooklawn |100 Rte. 130 (Browning Rd.) | 856-456-3690 |
www.metrodinernj.com

It's hard to knock the "pleasant" folks serving the "high-quality"
American diner grub at this "roomy", "modern" eatery in Brooklawn;
"large portions" of breakfast and dinner specials and "excellent
variety" on the menu help make it a "family favorite."

Mexican Food Factory *Mexican* `22` `19` `21` `$27`

Marlton | 601 W. Rte. 70 (Cropwell Rd.) | 856-983-9222

Amigos of this "colorful" cantina in Marlton praise its "authentic"
Mexican comida as "more than tacos", and it's backed by "tasty
drinks" that go down even easier on the "gorgeous" back patio; the
interior is "nothing fancy", save the Frida Kahlo prints on the walls,
and while a few gripe that the "seats could be padded", the "attentive" staff works to keep you comfy otherwise.

Mikado *Japanese* `24` `20` `22` `$32`

Cherry Hill | 2320 Marlton Pike W. (Union Ave.) | 856-665-4411
Maple Shade | 468 S. Lenola Rd. (Kings Hwy.) | 856-638-1801
Marlton | Elmwood Shopping Ctr. | 793 Rte. 70 E. (Troth Rd.) |
856-797-8581
www.mikado-us.com

At this South Jersey teppanyaki trio, the chefs show off a "sense
of humor" while indulging in "creative flair", while the sushi guys

pack rolls "tight with fresh, delicious fish"; while reactions are mixed to the "austere" setting, service is "efficient", the prices are "affordable" and the grill show is "always popular with the kids."

Mozzarella Grill *Italian/Pizza* 22 | 21 | 22 | $22

Sewell | 415 Egg Harbor Rd. (Green Tree Rd.) | 856-589-1000 | www.mozzarellagrill.net

Washington Township locals who crave a "quick snack" or a "relaxing" repast seek out this "homey" Italian BYO in the Acme Shopping Center whose specialty is a "sunset menu" that "fills your belly" for $12.95; the digs are "cozy without being cramped", and the service is "friendly but not in your face."

New Berlin Diner *Diner* ▽ 21 | 17 | 22 | $17

Berlin | 117 S. White Horse Pike (bet. Berlin Cross Keys & Jackson Rds.) | 856-767-7066 | www.newberlindiner.com

"Friendly" service makes it easy to stop at this Berlin diner for a "large selection" of "omelets", "sandwiches" and other staples dished up in "good portions"; it may have that "typical" retro look, but its "excellent value" gives it all-around "family" appeal.

Nick's Pizzeria   25 | 20 | 24 | $17
& Steakhouse *Italian/Pizza*

Clayton | 4 N. Delsea Dr. (Greentree Rd.) | 856-881-3222
Glassboro | 644 N. Delsea Dr. (Heston Rd.) | 856-307-1100
Sicklerville | 579 Cross Keys Rd. (Sicklerville Rd.) | 856-740-0707
Williamstown | 47 S. Main St. (Garwood Ave.) | 856-728-3322
www.nickspizzaonline.com

These "simple", "reasonably priced" Italian "staples" in South Jersey have been turning out "awesome pizza and wings" for decades, earning a "devoted bunch of customers" who count on them for "quick working lunches" and "delivery that's always on time"; thanks to "sociable employees" who keep up with the "status of orders", they're generally a "safe bet" (and BYO as well).

Nifty Fifty's *Diner* 23 | 23 | 22 | $16

Clementon | 1310 Blackwood Clementon Rd. (Millbridge Rd.) | 856-346-1950
Turnersville | 4670 Black Horse Pike (Fries Mill Rd.) | 856-875-1950
www.niftyfiftys.com

See review in the Philadelphia Directory.

Norma's Eastern   24 | 17 | 23 | $21
Mediterranean Cuisine *Mideastern*

Cherry Hill | Barclay Farms Shopping Ctr. | 995 Rte. 70 E. (Kings Hwy.) | 856-795-1373 | www.normasrestaurant.com

Chef-owner Norma Bitar's "dynamite" Middle Eastern fare bridges borders ("Israeli salad side by side with Lebanese salad") at her "inviting", "affordable" Cherry Hill BYO where "pleasant" service makes "foodies" feel like they're eating "in her home" (though the "weekend belly dancer" can get "overwhelming"); "after you're inspired by your tasty meal", check out the "authentic" items at the "attached mini-grocery."

	FOOD	DECOR	SERVICE	COST

Nunzio Ristorante Rustico *Italian* | 26 | 23 | 25 | $38 |

Collingswood | 706 Haddon Ave. (Collings Ave.) | 856-858-9840 | www.nunzios.net

Amid gorgeous frescoes and a courtyard evoking the old country, Nunzio Patruno's eponymous Collingswood trattoria provides "up-graded" "homemade" Italian flavors for "discerning palates" and "charming' service, positioning it as a "jewel" among the town's Restaurant Row; adherents call it a "treat" though there's too much of a good thing – "popularity", which "occasionally" "detracts from the total experience."

Old Town Buffet *Asian/Eclectic* | 20 | 14 | 18 | $19 |

Moorestown | 401 W. Rte. 38 (Lenola Rd.) | 856-608-6880
See review in the Philadelphia Directory.

Ollie Gators Pub ❶ *Cajun*   ∇ | 23 | 19 | 23 | $24 |

Berlin | 2 Rte. 73 S. (Berlin Cross Keys Rd.) | 856-768-9400 | www.olliegators.com

It feels like Mardi Gras year-round at this Cajun-themed Berlin sports bar that rocks the Bourbon Street and gator theme hard, keeping the drinks flowing with nightly specials and dishing up a "wide variety" of tasty grub at "reasonable" prices; "fast service" is another plus, and while it's "a little out of the way" for some, fans insist it's "always a fun time" for "lunch, dinner and late-night."

On the Border *Mexican* | 22 | 20 | 22 | $23 |

Mount Laurel | 4160 Church Rd. (bet. Rte. 73 & Springdale Rd.) | 856-437-5360 | www.ontheborder.com
See review in the Philadelphia Directory.

Oriental Pearl *Chinese*   ∇ | 27 | 19 | 24 | $20 |

Haddonfield | 215 Kings Hwy. East (Friends Ave.) | 856-427-6985
This pleasant "staple" in a Haddonfield storefront "pulls off a variety of Asian cuisines", including "fantastic sushi" and some of the "best suburban Chinese for miles" according to fans; add BYO and "friendly and courteous staff", and it's a bona fide "find."

Ota-Ya Japanese Restaurant Ⓜ *Japanese* | 25 | 18 | 23 | $37 |

Lambertville | 21 Ferry St. (Union St.) | 609-397-9228 | www.ota-ya.com
See review in the Philadelphia Directory.

Ott's Tavern ❶ *American/Pub Food* | 21 | 18 | 21 | $20 |

Delran | 3112 Bridgeboro Rd. (bet. Castelton & Hartford Rds.) | 856-764-8100

Ott's on the Green
Bar & Grill ❶ *American/Pub Food*

Sewell | 340 Greentree Rd. (bet. Egg Harbor Rd. & McClure Dr.) | 856-589-1776

Ott's Restaurant ❶ *American/Pub Food*

Medford | 656 Stokes Rd. (Nelson Dr.) | 609-654-2700
www.ottsrestaurants.com

It's the tasty "bar food and good beer" at "relatively cheap prices" at these "super-friendly" South Jersey "hometown" pubs that draw locals happy to put up with a "wobbly table" or two to "run into someone they know", join "trivia night" or check out the "flat-screens" when they "crave" a Phillies game; some grouse about "suburbanites trying to be urbane" and crowding the outdoor bar, but otherwise it "feels like home."

Palace Diner ● *Diner* ▽   20 | 17 | 22 | $21

Berlin | 100 N. Rte. 73 (Walker Ave.) | 856-767-5061 | www.thepalacediner.net

"Your good old Joisy diner" delivers a "delicious" "breakfast" and "quality" coffee, "served hot and cheerfully" to Berliners – even "at 4 AM" (there's 24-hour service); "prices are very reasonable", service is "fast" and "they give you so much food you need a doggy bag" – in short, "what you'd expect" from a "no-frills" diner.

Palace of Asia *Indian*   22 | 19 | 20 | $22

Cherry Hill | 2389 Rte. 70 W. (bet. Hampton Rd. & Lexington Ave.) | 856-773-1200 | www.palace-of-asia.com

"Not pretentious, not hip", this Indian duo in Cherry Hill and Wilmington is simply satisfying with a solid buffet and "a range of specialties from both north and south of the subcontinent"; service goes "above-board to satisfy", but as menu options are myriad, cognoscenti counsel "take someone who knows what they are ordering for the best experience."

Passariello's Pizzeria & Italian Eatery *Italian/Pizza*   ▽ 22 | 15 | 18 | $15

Moorestown | 13 W. Main St. (bet. Chester Ave. & Church St.) | 856-840-0998

Voorhees | 111 Laurel Oak Rd. | 856-784-7272 | www.passariellos.com

"Gigantic portions" of above-average Italian cuisine from a "steam table" at these "cafeterialike" trattorias in Moorestown and Voorhees can form the basis of an "informal dinner"; some find the "freaky ordering system" to be "such a pain", but devotees rave about the "large selection" on the menu.

Pasta Pomodoro Sewell *Italian*   ▽ 27 | 13 | 23 | $22

Sewell | 404 Egg Harbor Rd. (bet. Greentree Rd. & Greenwood Dr.) | 856-256-7799 | www.pastapomodoro-bygiovanni.com 🖂

The "inexpensive", "home-cooked" Italian grub is "out of this world" and served by a "friendly, efficient" staff at this Italian BYO in Washington Township; surveyors report being "packed in like sardines" in the warmly decorated room (which is slated for expansion in 2012), but fortunately it makes for "amazing" takeout.

Pasta Pomodoro Voorhees *Italian*   ▽ 21 | 16 | 21 | $27

Voorhees | Eagle Plaza Shopping Ctr. | 700 Haddonfield Berlin Rd. (White Horse Rd.) | 856-782-7430 | www.pastapomodoronj.com

The celiac-aware have nothing but praise for this contemporary "neighborhood" Italian BYO in a Voorhees shopping center, offering a gluten-free menu "just as delicious as the regular menu", including "divine" apps and "fresh" salads; "reasonable prices" and an owner who "makes you feel welcome" seal the deal.

Pat's Pizza Family Restaurant *Pizza*   23 | 17 | 21 | $17

Cherry Hill | 2298 Chapel Ave. (bet. Cooper Landing Rd. & Garden State Dr.) | 856-779-1111
Cinnaminson | 2700 Rte. 130 N. (bet. Riverton & New Albany Rds.) | 856-303-2323
Mullica Hill | 104 N. Main St. (Earlington Ave.) | 856-223-9977 |
National Park | 702 Hessian Ave. (Grove Ave.) | 856-853-6060
Runnemede | 325 N. Black Horse Pike (bet. 3rd & 4th Aves.) | 856-939-2600
Swedesboro | 1423 Kings Hwy. (bet. Allen St. & Grant Ave.) | 856-467-1188
www.patsfamilyrestaurant.com

"It seems no matter where you go" in the area, you can find one of these "wholesome" pizzerias that are a "huge step above the run-of-the-mill lunch spots", serving pies and sandwiches "loaded with meat and toppings" in "art deco–meets–the '60s digs; "reasonable prices" and workers with a "smile and great jokes" "go a long way."

Peking Buffet *Chinese*   ∇ 21 | 17 | 18 | $17

Glassboro | 753 Delsea Dr. N. (Burr Ave.) | 856-881-4055 | www.pekingbuffetnj.com

"Come hungry" to this Glassboro Chinese buffet that's popular among "college kids", offering a "ton of options" "suitable for even the pickiest eaters" (notably "soft-serve ice cream") and price ranges from $6.99 at lunch to $12.49 at weekend dinner; tip: "wear a stretch waistband", or order off the à la carte menu.

Penn Queen Diner ◑   20 | 15 | 20 | $20

Pennsauken | 7349 N. Crescent Blvd. (bet. Cove Rd. & Union Ave.) | 856-662-1928 | www.pennqueendiner.com

"It's nice to see the same people dining and working there after all these years" claim regulars of this "classic New Jersey diner", approaching its 50th anniversary in the shadow of the Betsy Ross Bridge; though some find it merely "so-so", many cheer the menu with "something for everyone", "no long waits" and waitresses who "seem to remember you."

P.F. Chang's China Bistro *Chinese*   24 | 23 | 22 | $32

Marlton | Promenade at Sagemore | 500 Rte. 73 S. (bet. Brick Rd. & Marlton Pkwy.) | 856-396-0818 | www.pfchangs.com
See review in the Philadelphia Directory.

Phily Diner ◑ *Diner*   22 | 20 | 20 | $20

Runnemede | 31 S. Black Horse Pike (Clements Bridge Rd.) | 856-939-4322 | www.philydiner.com

Though it "looks more like a nightclub" (with a "sports-bar" adjunct), this shiny, "vintage" testament to neon in Runnemede "brings diner food to a new level" according to fans, who talk up the "out-of-this-world dessert case"; "prompt", "friendly" service helps make it a "good value."

| | FOOD | DECOR | SERVICE | COST |

Pho Eden ⌷ *Vietnamese* ▽ 24 | 10 | 18 | $14

Cherry Hill | 1900 Greentree Rd. (Springdale Rd.) | 856-424-0075
"Amazing, authentic" Vietnamese fare keeps them "coming back" to this "very affordable" Cherry Hill BYO where the "filling" pho are "meals in themselves" – often "with leftovers"; despite "minimal service and lack of decor", adherents bill it as a "neighborhood restaurant worth driving to."

Pietro's Coal Oven Pizzeria *Pizza* 23 | 18 | 20 | $25

Marlton | 140 Rte. 70 W. (Rte. 73) | 856-596-5500 |
www.pietrospizza.com
See review in the Philadelphia Directory.

Pizzicato *Italian* 22 | 18 | 20 | $29

Marlton | Promenade at Sagemore | 500 Rte. 73 S. (bet. Brick Rd. & Marlton Pkwy.) | 856-396-0880 | www.pizzicatoristorante.com
See review in the Philadelphia Directory.

P.J. Whelihan's *Pub Food* 21 | 19 | 20 | $23

Cherry Hill | 1854 Marlton Pike E. (Greentree Rd.) | 856-424-8844 ●
Haddonfield | 700 N. Haddon Ave. (Ardmore Ave.) |
856-427-7888 ●
Maple Shade | 396 S. Lenola Rd. (Kings Hwy.) |
856-234-2345 ●
Medford Lakes | 61 Stokes Rd. (Tabernacle Rd.) | 609-714-7900
Sewell | 425 Hurffville Cross Keys Rd. (Regulus Dr.) |
856-582-7774 ●
www.pjspub.com
"Guilty pleasures" abound at these "always crowded", "upscale sports bars", including "outrageous wings", lots of TVs, "skimpily clad waitresses and an extensive beer selection"; foodies may dismiss it as a "glorified Friday's or Chili's", but fans retort "it is what it is: noisy with reasonably decent food – it ain't Le Bec Fin, guys."

Ponzio's *Diner* 21 | 16 | 20 | $22

Cherry Hill | 7 Rte. 70 W. (Kings Hwy.) | 856-428-4808 |
www.ponzios.com
Philadelphians don't mind "paying the $5 bridge toll" to hit this "mega-popular" Cherry Hill "model of a diner" where "large portions" of American eats and "overindulgent bakery items" are slung by an "attentive" staff; in business since 1964, it's "still the place to see and be seen" and a popular "meeting spot for pols and boldface names."

The Pop Shop *American* 23 | 21 | 21 | $18

Collingswood | 729 Haddon Ave. (Collings Ave.) | 856-869-0111 |
www.thepopshopusa.com
"Not the place to go for a quiet evening", this "kitschy", "retro" soda fountain–slash–"playground" in Downtown Collingswood that's a "blast" "right out of the '50s"; a "helpful" staff shleps "yummy" American "comfort food" and "extra-creamy shakes" in a "loud, crowded" setting.

	FOOD	DECOR	SERVICE	COST

PrimoHoagies *Sandwiches* 25 | 13 | 20 | $13

Berlin | 421 Rte. 73 (bet. Cushman & McClellan Aves.) |
856-719-2121
Cherry Hill | 826 Haddonfield Rd. (bet. Graham & Hollis Aves.) |
856-662-1010
www.primohoagies.com
See review in the Philadelphia Directory.

The Pub *Steak* 24 | 19 | 22 | $36

Pennsauken | 7600 Kaighns Ave. (Crescent Blvd.) | 856-665-6440 |
www.thepubnj.com
"It doesn't get more Jersey" than this "old-world steakhouse"
in Pennsauken that's "so retro it's almost ironic", where "huge
portions" of "awesome" charcoal-grilled red meat are served in a
"large" room that looks like a cross between a "medieval castle"
and a "bingo parlor"; though the "no-nonsense" servers "get the
job done like clockwork", some caution "beware of long waits."

Redstone American Grill ● *American* 23 | 24 | 22 | $37

Marlton | Promenade at Sagemore | 500 Rte. 73 S. (bet. Brick Rd. &
Marlton Pkwy.) | 856-396-0332 | www.redstonegrill.com
See review in the Philadelphia Directory.

Rick's Ⓜ *Italian* ∇ 23 | 15 | 21 | $35

Lambertville | 19 S. Main St. (Ferry St.) | 609-397-0051 |
www.ricksitalian.com
It's a "neighborhood favorite for good reasons" say Lambertville
locals who love this "homey" Italian's "tasty" red-sauce dishes and
"pleasant", "cozy" setting, complete with red-and-white check-
erboard tablecloths; reservations are only accepted for parties of
four or more, which means "the wait can be long", but at least a
BYO policy "keeps the cost down."

Ritz Seafood Ⓜ *Asian/Seafood* 24 | 17 | 22 | $38

Voorhees | Ritz Shopping Ctr. | 910 Haddonfield Berlin Rd.
(bet. Laurel Oak Blvd. & White Horse Rd.) | 856-566-6650 |
www.ritzseafood.com
For "fresh fish prepared well" (including some "unusual types"),
with a Pan-Asian touch, finatics head to this "Voorhees favorite";
"friendly" service is another plus, but its location next to the Rave
Cinema means the "cozy" room can get "hectic" and "crowded
before movie time."

Robin's Nest *American* 25 | 22 | 23 | $32

Mount Holly | 2 Washington St. (White St.) | 609-261-6149 |
www.robinsnestmountholly.com
"Top dining in an unexpected place" is how fans describe this
"charming" American housed in a "quaint Victorian" overlooking
Rancocas Creek in Mount Holly; "lovely presentations" of "excel-
ent" dishes at "reasonable prices" impress, but many feel the
desserts are the "main stars", and "you can tell they really care"
from the "friendly service."

Rode's Fireside
Restaurant & Tavern *American/BBQ*

▽ 21 | 18 | 21 | $24

Swedesboro | 533 Kings Hwy. (Paulsboro Rd.) | 856-467-2700 | www.rodesfireside.com

"Where the locals go" in Swedesboro, this "nice little" American offers a "little bit of everything", "from sandwiches to seafood and BBQ", at budget-friendly prices; "friendly" service and a "comfortable", "rustic-cabin" setting, complete with eponymous fireplace, complete the picture.

Sagami
Japanese Restaurant Ⓜ *Japanese*

27 | 17 | 23 | $35

Collingswood | 37 W. Crescent Blvd. (bet. Haddon Ave. & White Horse Pike) | 856-854-9773

There are "no fancy takes" at this Collingswood institution where the sushi chefs are "devoted to amazing fish" and a "wonderful staff" provides "helpful, polite" service; decor is "like a typical Tokyo restaurant", and while a few quibble that the "cavelike environs" could use "upgrading", most shrug "who cares when the sushi is this good?"

Sage Diner
Restaurant ❶ *Diner*

18 | 14 | 18 | $19

Mount Laurel | 1170 Rte. 73 (Church Rd.) | 856-727-0770 | www.sagedinernj.com

"All that you love about Jersey diners" can be found at this Mount Laurel veteran, according to fans – a "huge menu", "large, comfortable booths" and servers who'll have you "looking at your food in minutes" after you order; critics say it's "seen better days", citing "inconsistent" eats and "dated" decor.

Sakura Spring *Chinese/Japanese*

26 | 23 | 24 | $27

Cherry Hill | 1871 Marlton Pike E. (Greentree Rd.) | 856-489-8018 | www.sakuraspring.com

For a "nice change" of pace, fans head to this Cherry Hill Chinese-Japanese for midpriced, "top-quality" eats, including "over-the-top" sushi and other "fantastic" Asian and Thai dishes; "friendly" service and "quiet", "roomy" environs complete the picture, and while it's a bit "hard to find", most agree it's "worth the trouble."

Sal & Joe's Spaghetti &
Pizza House *American/Italian*

▽ 24 | 16 | 25 | $19

Maple Shade | 300 S. Lenola Rd. (Old Kings Hwy.) | 856-234-3130 | www.salandjoes.com

"Generous portions" of "typical pizza place stuff" as well as "wonderful-tasting entrees" and "outstanding" sandwiches make this Italian BYO in Maple Shade a popular go-to spot for "dinner with the family"; the mall space is a "bit of a hole-in-the-wall", but "reasonable prices" and a "casual" vibe compensate.

	FOOD	DECOR	SERVICE	COST

Sammy Chon's K-Town BBQ 🖾 *Korean*
▽ 25 | 16 | 23 | $22

Cherry Hill | 404 Marlton Pike E. (Kings Hwy.) | 856-216-0090

Sammy Chon's K-Town Express ◑ *Korean*

Cinnaminson | The Shoppes at Cinnaminson | 127 Rte. 130 S.
Cinnaminson Ave.) | 856-829-8280
www.ktownbbq.com

"You don't need to know anything about Korean food" at this
affordable chainlet where the "nicest owners" and "gracious" servers are "happy to explain" the "well-prepared" choices from the
extensive, graphic menu"; a few demur at the "dinerlike setting",
but for most it's "all about the kalbi."

Sang Kee Noodle Cafe *Chinese*
23 | 17 | 19 | $22

Cherry Hill | 1601 Kings Hwy. N. (Marlton Pike) | 856-310-2388 |
www.sangkeenoodlehouse.com
See review in the Philadelphia Directory.

Sapori Trattoria Italiana *Italian*
27 | 22 | 26 | $38

Collingswood | 601 Haddon Ave. (Harvard Ave.) | 856-858-2288 |
www.sapori.info

Chef-owner Franco Lombardo is a "master at combining flavors",
and his "creative" cuisine is showcased at his midpriced Italian
BYO in Collingswood, where "adventuresome" diners "skip the
menu and ask him to cook" a tasting prix fixe; "lack of parking is
the only drawback", as "professional service" and a "well-decorat-
ed" rustic space round out the "delightful experience."

Seasons Pizza *Pizza*
21 | 18 | 21 | $18

Stratford | 1014 N. White Horse Pike (bet. Cooper & Darmouth Aves.) |
856-783-9333 | www.seasonspizza.com
See review in the Philadelphia Directory.

Seasons 52 *American*
24 | 25 | 24 | $38

Cherry Hill | Cherry Hill Mall | 2000 Rte. 38 (Haddonfield Rd.) |
856-665-1052
See review in the Philadelphia Directory.

Siam Thai Restaurant 🖾⇥ *Thai*
▽ 23 | 15 | 22 | $26

Lambertville | 61 N. Main St. (bet. Coryell & York Sts.) | 609-397-8128
"Servers treat you like old friends" at this "surprising gem in Lambertville", but it's the Thai fare that "shines"; though a few grouse
that the "simple" room "gets very loud with crowds", for most,
dinner is a "relaxing experience" and "lunch is an excellent deal."

Silver Diner ◑ *Diner*
20 | 18 | 20 | $18

Cherry Hill | 2131 Rte. 38 (bet. Haddonfield Rd. & Mall Dr.) |
856-910-1240 | www.silverdiner.com

While the "traditional chrome decor" might scream "classic South
Jersey diner", this Cherry Hill BYO is "not your typical diner", offering a "health-conscious", "updated" menu with an emphasis on
"locally supplied foods" and "fresh produce"; "friendly" service and
"comfortable" digs add to its allure.

	FOOD	DECOR	SERVICE	COST

Siri's Thai French Cuisine *French/Thai* | 24 | 20 | 21 | $37 |

Cherry Hill | 2117 Rte. 70 W. (bet. Beideman & Washington Aves.) | 856-663-6781 | www.siris-nj.com

An "unexpected treasure" in a "highway strip mall", this "serene" Thai-French BYO in Cherry Hill offers a "cosmopolitan" menu of "innovative fusion" cooking; "courteous" service is another plus, and while some feel the digs "could use an update", others find th space "comfortable."

Skeeters Pub ❶ *Pub Food* | ▽ 23 | 20 | 23 | $21 |

Blackwood | 7 Coles Rd. (Black Horse Pike) | 856-227-2314 | www.skeeterspub.com

Blackwood's sports bar scores a home run with some for its "high-quality bar food" and "cheap domestic drafts"; "fast and consistent" servers sprint, serving "big fat wings" and "greasy-spoon burgers" to a "pumped" crowd, "packed with jerseys"; and for those who need a breath of fresh air while they watch the game, there's a TV-outfitted patio.

Station House Restaurant *American* | ▽ 25 | 23 | 24 | $19 |

Haddon Heights | 602 Station Ave. (bet. Atlantic & 7th Aves.) | 856-547-5517

A "favorite breakfast place" in Haddon Heights, this is an "old restaurant with food that never gets old", transporting AM eaters "back in time" even though it's only been open since '02; "very nice" but low-key interior touches are augmented by "friendly service."

Steak 38 Ⓜ *Steak* | 23 | 17 | 22 | $46 |

Cherry Hill | 515 Rte. 38 (Cuthbert Blvd.) | 856-662-3838 | www.steak38cafe.com

Original owner Joe DiAmore has teamed up with 'Barnacle Ben' Blumberg to make this "crowded" Cherry Hill "favorite" feel "just like the supper clubs of the past" with "friendly" servers ferrying "superb steaks", seafood, "tableside Caesar salad" and other "classic foods"; though some say it's "a little pricey", it's nevertheless a "charming" throwback that leaves guests "delighted."

Tacconelli's Pizzeria Ⓜ⇕ *Pizza* | 26 | 14 | 20 | $19 |

Maple Shade | 450 S. Lenola Rd. (Rte. 38) | 856-638-0338 | www.tacconellispizzerianj.com

Devotees "genuflect" when they walk into this cash-only BYO in its original "nondescript" Port Richmond location or South Jersey offshoot; a "national favorite" earning accolades for decades, the "must go-to" is famous for its call-ahead policy to "reserve your dough" – a practice some find a little "strange" – but it's the "standard setting" thin-crust pies that get the most attention.

The Taproom & Grill *American/Pub Food* | ▽ 22 | 20 | 22 | $27 |

Haddonfield | 427 W. Crystal Lake Ave. (MacArthur Blvd.) | 856-854-4255 | www.taproomgrill.com

Haddonfielders "highly recommend" this "lively" watering hole where a "family-friendly" American "pub menu" teams up with great craft beers on tap" for a "filling meal" at a "good price"; solid servers work the "huge space", which gets a boost from live music on weekends and an outdoor deck.

Taylors ● *American* ▽ 18 | 16 | 17 | $32

Williamstown | 2021 N. Black Horse Pike (Berlin Cross Keys Rd.) | 856-875-9700 | www.taylorsbarandgrill.com
"Typical bar-and-grill" food is served at this Williamstown pub that's more of a sports bar with a "nightclub atmosphere" than an "outright dinner spot"; reasonable prices and "decent" service placate the clientele, who expect no more than a "fun night out."

Terra Nova *American* 27 | 25 | 25 | $34

Sewell | 590 Delsea Dr. (bet. Bethel Mill Rd. & Parke Pl. Blvd.) | 856-589-8883 | www.terranovawineanddine.com
It's rare to find "high-quality Italian and sushi in the same place", but this moderately priced New American in Sewell offers just that, along with a raw bar and abundant wines (including 50 by the glass) in a spacious "Napa-esque atmosphere"; "pleasant" and "friendly", it's solid for a "business meeting", "fancy dinner" or just "hanging out" over "drinks and apps" (and "sushi happy-hour specials") on the more casual bar side.

Thai Basil *Thai* ▽ 22 | 22 | 23 | $31

Collingswood | 653 Haddon Ave. (bet. Lincoln & Woodlawn Aves.) | 856-833-0098 | www.thaibasilcollingswood.com
"Yummy" traditional eats are the hallmark of this quaint Collingswood Thai, where "super-good" classics emerge from the kitchen and are delivered by "nice, attentive" servers (who don't mind a bit if you "explain your spice level"); the warmly decorated space features rich red walls and cozy booths that can be reserved ahead.

That's Amore ● *Italian* ▽ 23 | 20 | 21 | $31

Collingswood | 690 Haddon Ave. (Collings Ave.) | 856-869-5683 | www.ilovethatsamore.com
Fans are "full of *amore*" for the Italian fare at this low-key Collingswood BYO that's a local destination for "Sunday gravy" and "fresh pasta"; the service is "friendly", and if some find the surroundings a bit "tacky", low-budget prices increase the "love"; P.S. the Chef's Table offers a "way to sample several dishes."

Tokyo Hibachi & Sushi Buffet *Japanese* ▽ 26 | 21 | 25 | $29

Deptford | 1692 Clements Bridge Rd. (Westville Almonessen Rd.) | 856-848-8289 | www.tokyodeptford.com
Offering an "extensive" buffet of "well-made sushi" plus "great" hibachi items, this "family-friendly" Japanese in Deptford makes it easy for groups of all tastes to "get what they want to eat" for a moderate price; the atmosphere's fairly "average", but "pleasant, attentive" service is a perk.

	FOOD	DECOR	SERVICE	COST

Tokyo Mandarin *Chinese/Japanese*   27 | 21 | 24 | $22

Deptford | 1907 Deptford Center Rd. (Beckett Rd.) | 856-374-053.
Glassboro | 370 Delsea Dr. N. (High Hill Rd.) | 856-881-7599
Logan Township | 525 Beckett Rd. (High Hill Rd.) | 856-467-1308

Mandarin Oriental Inc *Chinese/Japanese*

Mullica Hill | 141 Bridgeton Pike (Rte. 581) | 856-223-9886
www.themandaringroup.com

South Jersey's multilocation buffet is "superior" in the food department, excelling at "the combination of Chinese and Japanese" dishes that characterizes the approach of many area competitors; the selection chases "quality over quantity", and "they are accommodating" to special requests, as well; service "needs some help" in the "small but cozy" spaces.

Tomo Sushi   ▽ 28 | 19 | 27 | $20
Japanese Restaurant *Japanese*

Glassboro | 806 Delsea Dr. N. (Charles III Dr.) | 856-582-6699
Glassboro's "all-you-can-eat" destination provides "quality" sushi and other Japanese bites for a "value" you "can't beat" (and BYO keeps it "cheap" too); service is "super-friendly" and "streamlined", though it does get "busy" so "be prepared to wait" if you show up during peak lunch and dinner hours.

NEW Tony Luke's *Cheesesteaks*   26 | 13 | 20 | $14

Sicklerville | Crossings at Twin Oaks | 683 Berlin-Cross Keys Rd.
(bet. Johnson Rd. & Redbud Dr.) | 856-875-8700 | www.tonylukes.com
See review in the Philadelphia Directory.

The Tortilla Press *Mexican*   25 | 21 | 24 | $25

Collingswood | 703 Haddon Ave. (Collings Ave.) |
856-869-3345

Tortilla Press Cantina

Merchantville | 7716 Maple Ave. (Haddonfield Rd.) |
856-356-2050 | www.thetortillapress.com

"Amazing", "modern" riffs on traditional south-of-the-border cooking featuring "fresh, local ingredients" attract amigos to these "hip", "reasonably priced" South Jersey Mexicans; an "outgoing staff" handles crowds with ease and while the Collingswood original is BYO, the Merchantville outpost offers "excellent margaritas" from the "full-service bar" which make the "wait on weekends" more tolerable.

Toscana *Italian*   23 | 23 | 21 | $28

Mullica Hill | 127 Bridgeton Pike (bet. Walnut Ln. & Wheatley Blvd.) |
856-478-2288 | www.toscanamullicahill.com

At this "rare food find in Mullica Hill", "delicious" brick-oven pizzas and entrees cooked "over the wood-fired grill" exemplify the "country Italian" approach; with a "family" following, it can get "a little loud" at times, but the "nice setting" and "warm" service kee it comfortable, while BYO makes it extra budget-friendly.

FOOD · DECOR · SERVICE · COST

Toscano's Ristorante *Italian*
▽ 26 | 23 | 23 | $41

Bordentown | 136 Farnsworth Ave. (Park St.) | 609-291-0291 |
www.toscano-ristorante.com

"The garlic bread is reason enough to come" to this Bordentown
date-destination, but the "delicious" menu of "traditional Italian
entrees" mixed with "unusual options" is an even better one;
though the "small" space is "normally packed", the staff makes
"you feel like you're the only people" there, precisely why it's an
ideal (if expensive) "choice for a special night."

Tre Famiglia Ⓜ *Italian*
26 | 19 | 24 | $40

Haddonfield | 403 N. Haddon Ave. (bet. Hawthorne & Rhoads Aves.) |
856-429-1447 | www.trefamiglia.com

So "light" they're like "pillows of air", the "great homemade
gnocchi" are just an taste of the "presents to your palate" at this
"inviting" Italian BYO in Haddonfield that's "filled with family" (just
expect it to be "loud when busy"); from midrange tabs to "courteous", "helpful" service, "everything about it shouts yes."

Tree House *Sandwiches*
▽ 23 | 26 | 24 | $20

Audubon | 120 W. Merchant St. (Atlantic Ave.) | 856-547-3270 |
www.treehousecoffee.net

Besides simply being a good place "to get work done", Audubon's
cutesy, warm "hometown coffee shop" serves affordable grub
"with a healthy twist", including casual breakfast options and
creative sandwiches solidifying it as "an area favorite"; the
"kid-friendly" environment also plays host to open-mike nights and
traditional Irish music performances.

Treno *Italian*
22 | 23 | 21 | $29

Westmont | 233 Haddon Ave. (Crystal Lake Rd.) | 856-833-9233 |
www.trenopizzabar.com

With its "homey", "comfortable" interior, "fantastic" enclosed
patio and service that supports an all-around "family-friendly"
vibe, this "upscale neighborhood hangout" in Westmont is "on the
culinary map" for "delicious, rustic Italian fare", including an "awesome" selection of wood-fired pizzas; "you can get a decent beer
or glass of wine" too, and tabs are quite affordable.

Umi Japanese Cuisine & Bar *Japanese*
▽ 28 | 26 | 27 | $39

Somerdale | 11 N. White Horse Pike (Somerdale Rd.) |
856-783-8868 | www.umisushi.com

"From start to finish, this is the place to eat" in Somerdale, an "enjoyable" Japanese option that keeps sushi lovers "satisfied" with
"fresh", "memorable" creations and plenty of "tasty sake"; "you
would expect to pay much more" for it all, especially since the staff
is "always so pleasant", and secluded tatami rooms supplement
the main seating area.

	FOOD	DECOR	SERVICE	COST

Villari's Lake Side *Italian*

22 | 22 | 22 | $30

Sicklerville | 2375 Sicklerville Rd. (Garwood Rd.) | 856-228-5244 |
www.villarislakeside.com

The "lakeside view" is the star at this Sicklerville Italian boasting
an "awesome" patio "overlooking the water" that works for happy
hour or a "night with your significant other"; the interior, by con-
trast, strikes some as "a bit dated", and surveyors are split on the
food – fans find it "wonderful", while critics pan it as "subpar."

Vitarelli's Pizza & Restaurant *Italian*

23 | 18 | 23 | $22

Cherry Hill | 1250 Kings Hwy. N. (Daytona Ave.) | 856-429-9088 |
www.vitarellisnj.com

Though it's "hard to find", fans insist this Cherry Hill Italian is
"worth looking for", citing "huge portions" of "simple", "hearty"
fare, including "homemade soups" that merit a "half-hour drive";
"fast, friendly" service adds to the "good value", though the
"old-style" setting makes it "better for takeout" for some.

Vito's Pizza *Pizza*

24 | 15 | 21 | $17

Cherry Hill | 1500 Berlin Rd. (Browning Ln.) | 856-429-9244 |
www.vitospizzapie.com

See review in the Philadelphia Directory.

West Side Gravy Ⓜ *American*

▽ 20 | 16 | 18 | $26

Collingswood | 714 Haddon Ave. (bet. Collings & Irvin Aves.) |
856-854-3444 | www.westsidegravynj.com

Adjoining his more formal Blackbird Dining Establishment inside a
former Woolworth's, this "ode to comfort food" from chef/owner
Alex Capasso lures curious Collingswooders with "inventive" riffs
on American standards via "fast service"; some are won over by
the "cool choices" but critics call it "overpriced" for the "homey"
offerings and sparse "high school cafeteria" setting.

Westmont Family
Restaurant & Diner *Diner*

23 | 17 | 23 | $14

Westmont | 317 Haddon Ave. (Maple Ave.) | 856-854-7220 |
www.westmontdiner.com

Westmont well-wishers "double-dog-dare you to walk away hungry" from this "swell" family-run diner where "generous portions"
of "homemade" "comfort food" provide a "delicious" meal at a "fair
price"; with a "dedicated staff" that's "friendly but not intrusive"
the only downside is that the "small" setting "gets crowded fast."

Whistlers Inn ● *American/BBQ*

▽ 23 | 19 | 21 | $21

Cinnaminson | 901 Rte. 130 S. (Riverton Rd.) | 856-786-8776 |
www.whistlersinnnj.com

"If you want to stay away from the chains" raters "recommend"
this "lovable neighborhood bar" and barbecue turning out "fabulous wings" and "to die for" ribs from its on-site smokehouse; a
"friendly" staff satisfies hungry crowds in the "English pub"-like
interior or "popular outdoor deck" and "reasonable prices" complete the picture.

	FOOD	DECOR	SERVICE	COST

Whitman Diner *American*
23 | 21 | 22 | $19

Turnersville | 4990 Rte. 42 (Johnson Rd.) | 856-228-4449 |
www.thewhitmandiner.com

A "solid" spot for "fantastic" all-day breakfasts and other
"home-cooked" American eats, this Turnersville stalwart has
"stepped it up over the years," adding "upscale" touches and a
lounge to its "retro" diner digs; service is "quick and friendly" and
if some find prices "a little much" it helps that most meals "come
with enough food for two."

Wild Wings *Chicken*
▽ 21 | 18 | 20 | $21

Pennsauken | 4909 Westfield Ave. (Browning Rd.) | 856-661-9422

"Wings any way you want" is the straightforward specialty of
Pennsauken's "affordable" chicken shack where the signature
dish (spiced mild to "amazingly hot") pairs well with "good fried
pickles" and a "sports atmosphere"; the "crowd is loud even when
games aren't on" but fans of the "friendly" vibe "recommend" it–
especially for lunch.

Yellow Submarine *Cheesesteaks*
▽ 21 | 13 | 21 | $14

Maple Shade | 710 N. Forklanding Rd. (Orchard Ave.) |
856-667-2110

While it's hard not to "love a sub shop named after a Beatles
song", admirers of this specialist in Maple Shade are mostly in it
for the "delicious cheesesteaks", "hoagies" and "freshly cut fries",
served by "pleasant" folks; some think the "cute little spot" "could
be better on the inside", but most see it as a "pick-up-and-go"
option anyway.

Yokohama Japanese Restaurant *Japanese*
▽ 27 | 25 | 27 | $33

Maple Shade | 300 S. Lenola Rd. (Old Kings Hwy.) |
856-608-8812 | www.yokohamacuisine.com

"Artistic sushi and sashimi" is the star at this Maple Shade Japanese, which also offers "interactive" "dinner and a show" at its
teppanyaki tables; the mood is "cozy" in the "upscale, modern"
setting, which is equally suitable for "a quiet date night" or "a
casual family dinner", and "outstanding" service brings it all home.

NEW Zeppoli *Italian*
28 | 19 | 25 | $43

Collingswood | 618 Collings Ave. (Richey Ave.) | 856-854-2670 |
www.zeppolirestaurant.com

"NJ folk hit the lottery with this Italian heavyweight" BYO in
Collingswood from Vetri alum Joey Baldino, whose "Sicilian soul
food" is "sophisticated, refined and flavorful" (the eponymous
pastries are as "light as a feather"); many grouse about "cramped,
noisy" conditions in the storefront space, which is graced with
black-and-white photos of the old country, but most concur the
"food and service make up for it."

Wilmington/Nearby Delaware

TOP FOOD

28 | Green Room | *French*
27 | Mikimotos | *Asian/Japanese*
     Culinaria | *American*
     Soffritto Italian Grill | *Italian*
26 | Capriotti's | *Sandwiches*

TOP DECOR

29 | Green Room
26 | Firebirds Wood Fired Grill
25 | Krazy Kat's Restaurant
     Pizza by Elizabeths
     Harry's Seafood Grill

TOP SERVICE

28 | Green Room
26 | Soffritto Italian Grill
     Moro
25 | Culinaria
     Eclipse Bistro

BEST BUYS

1. Brew HaHa!
2. Lucky's Coffee Shop
3. Jake's Wayback Burgers
4. Capriotti's
5. Five Guys

Anthony's Coal Fired Pizza ⌧Ⓜ *Pizza*   24 | 20 | 22 | $21

Wilmington | 5611 Concord Pike (Zeigler Ln.) | 302-477-1488 |
www.anthonyscoalfiredpizza.com
See review in the Philadelphia Directory.

Back Burner   24 | 21 | 23 | $33
Restaurant & Bar ⌧ *American*

Hockessin | 425 Hockessin Corner (Old Lancaster Pike) |
302-239-2314 | www.backburner.com
The "pumpkin mushroom soup is a full meal" at this Hockessin
New American offering "artfully done" eats and "pleasant" service
in a "charming", "country" setting; while a few find it "overpriced"
and feel it "needs an update" after 32 years, many others tout it as
their "go-to place" for a "great business lunch or romantic dinner."

Big Fish Grill *Seafood*   24 | 22 | 23 | $32

Wilmington | 720 Justison St. (Beech St.) | 302-652-3474 |
www.bigfishriverfront.com
"Tasty", "fresh seafood" "done right" at "not such a big price"
makes for happy diners at these "upbeat", "super kid-friendly"
fish houses in Glen Mills and along the Riverfront in Wilmington
(siblings of the original in Rehoboth Beach, Delaware); it's often
"noisy" and "bustling", but the staff "can handle a big crowd" and
also "accommodates special requests", making it a "great catch."

Blue Parrot   23 | 21 | 21 | $24
Bar & Grille ➊ *Cajun*

Wilmington | 1934 W. 6th St. (Union St.) | 302-655-8990 |
www.blueparrotgrille.com
There's "plenty to please a pepperhead" at this New Orleans
themer in Downtown Wilmington serving "spot-on" Cajun chow at
"value prices" in a "Mardi Gras" setting with a "lively", "welcoming" vibe; "awesome" live music is a "highlight" for many, but some
complain that "service slows considerably" and "conversation"
becomes futile when bands play.

	FOOD	DECOR	SERVICE	COST

Brew HaHa! *Coffeehouse* | 22 | 19 | 23 | $12 |

Wilmington | Branmar Plaza | 1812 Marsh Rd. (Silverside Rd.) | 302-529-1125

Wilmington | Shops of Limestone Hills | 5329 Limestone Rd. (bet. Ocheltree Ln. & Stoney Batter Rd.) | 302-234-9600

Wilmington | 835 N. Market St. (bet. 8th & 9th Sts.) | 302-777-4499 ⑤

Wilmington | Concord Gallery | 3636 Concord Pike (Lebanon Rd.) | 302-478-7227

Greenville | Powder Mill Sq. | 3842 Kennett PikeB (Buck Rd.) | 302-658-6336

Wilmington | Rockford Shops | 1420 N. Dupont St. (Delaware Ave.) | 302-778-2656

Newark | Main St. Galleria | 45 E. Main St. (bet. Academy St. & College Ave.) | 302-369-2600

Newark | Christiana Hospital | 4755 Ogletown Stanton Rd. (Churchmans Rd.) | 302-733-2739

www.brewhaha.com

'In a world of too many bad coffeehouses", this "laid-back" cafe chain is the "go-to" spot for fans, thanks to "friendly", "well-trained baristas" who are "appreciative" of your business as they pour "outstanding" drinks; "inventive" sandwiches, "yummy" treats and a "comfortable" atmosphere complete the picture.

Capers & Lemons ❷ *Italian* | 24 | 24 | 24 | $34 |

Wilmington | The Commons at Little Falls | 301 Little Falls Dr. (Lancaster Pike) | 302-256-0524 | www.capersandlemons.com

"Well worth the trip to the middle of nowhere", this "stylish" Wilmington bistro offers "creative", "first-rate" Italian cuisine and "top-notch" service in "spacious", "inviting" surroundings that are suitable for a "business luncheon or a romantic dinner"; outdoor seating is another plus, and it's a "pleasure to browse" in the adjacent gourmet food market.

Capriotti's
Sandwich Shop *Sandwiches* | 26 | 14 | 23 | $13 |

Newark | Newark Shopping Ctr. | 614 Newark Shopping Ctr. (Chapel St.) | 302-454-0200 | www.capriottis.com

See review in the Philadelphia Directory.

Charcoal Pit *Burgers* | 22 | 16 | 21 | $15 |

Wilmington | 2600 Concord Pike (Woodrow Ave.) | 302-478-2165 ❷

Wilmington | 714 Greenbank Rd. (Kirkwood Hwy.) | 302-998-8853

www.charcoalpit.net

This "Wilmington institution" "gets it right" with "mouthwatering" hamburgers and "awesome" milkshakes at "fair prices", though opinions are split on the service ("speedy" vs. "spotty"); the Concord Pike original is "frozen in the 1950s", making it the "cheapest time travel going", while the Prices Corner branch doubles as a sports bar with big-screen TVs.

FOOD | DECOR | SERVICE | COST

Chelsea Tavern ● *American* — 23 | 22 | 20 | $24

Wilmington | 821 N. Market St. (bet. 8th & 9th Sts.) |
302-482-3333 | www.chelseatavern.com

Though its location across from Wilmington's Grand Opera House
is "ideal for theatergoers", "most appreciate happy hour" at this
bustling gastropub thanks to its "long list" of beers (30-plus on
tap, 90 bottled) and "stiff drinks"; still, fans praise the "outstanding" American grub, "attractive" decor and "dynamic" service, not
to mention tabs that won't "break the budget."

China Royal ⓜ *Chinese* — 21 | 16 | 21 | $25

Wilmington | 1845 Marsh Rd. (Silverside Rd.) | 302-475-3686

A bounce-back in Food score suggests this long-running North
Wilmington Chinese has regained its footing; though there's a
"large" menu of "traditional" offerings, regulars recommend asking
"the chef to prepare a dinner for you as if it were for his family" –
either way, "well-prepared" grub comes out in "plentiful" portions,
served by an "attentive" staff.

Claymont Steak Shop *Cheesesteaks* — 24 | 14 | 21 | $13

Claymont | 3526 Philadelphia Pike (bet. Manor Ave. & Wiltshire
Rd.) | 302-798-0013
Newark | 57 Elkton Rd. (Amstel Ave.) | 302-453-9500
www.claymontsteakshop.com

Delawareans insist Philly has "meat-envy" over the "superior",
"meaty" cheesesteaks at this sandwich duo; "flat-screen TVs"
enhance the dine-in experience, abetted by a "friendly" staff that
slings 'em "fast" and sells meat so you can "make your own at
home" – all told, most agree it's "worth the drive."

Columbus Inn *American* — 22 | 23 | 21 | $40

Wilmington | 2216 Pennsylvania Ave. (Woodlawn Ave.) |
302-571-1492 | www.columbusinn.com

This Wilmington landmark draws a mixed reaction – to fans, it's
an "inn" spot bathed in "understated elegance", with a "trendy"
New American menu that includes "satisfying" renditions of the
"classics", backed by a "solid" wine list; critics clamor that the
"food quality is not up to the prices" and "service needs to be more
attentive", and posit that it "can't figure out" what it "wants to be"
since its extensive 2010 renovation.

Corner Bistro *Eclectic* — 24 | 22 | 24 | $30

Wilmington | Talleyville Towne Shoppes | 3604 Silverside Rd.
(Concord Pike) | 302-477-1778 | www.mybistro.com

This Northern Wilmington strip-mall bistro looks "just a little bit
more grown-up" since a fall 2011 renovation, and adherents say it
hasn't missed a step with Eclectic chow that "never fails to please"
backed by a solid "selection of wines by the glass"; the "attentive",
but not "intrusive", staff keeps things moving, whether you're "celebrating an event", entertaining "out-of-town visitors" or making a
"quick stop" before or after shopping.

Culinaria ⊠Ⓜ *American* | 27 | 23 | 25 | $33

Wilmington | Branmar Plaza | 1812 Marsh Rd. (Silverside Rd.) | 302-475-4860 | www.culinariarestaurant.com

"Looks are deceiving" observe fans of this "hip" American "hidden in a shopping center" in North Wilmington, which has "kept its edge" over the years while turning out "consistently delish" grub from an "innovative" menu; a few find the no-res policy for parties of four and fewer "infuriating", but "attentive" service and an "attractive" setting help make it a "wonderful find" for most.

Dead Presidents Pub & Restaurant ◐ *American* | 21 | 20 | 22 | $19

Wilmington | 618 N. Union St. (7th St.) | 302-652-7737 | www.deadpresidentspub.com

There's a "true pub feel" at this Oval Office–themed "white-collar hangout" near Trolley Square in Wilmington where the "interesting" American menu with "lots of choices", including "terrific" lamb sliders, and daily happy-hour specials win a solid majority of votes; the service is "friendly", and some pundits describe the decor as "tacky in a good way."

Deep Blue Bar & Grill ⊠ *Seafood* | 25 | 22 | 24 | $39

Wilmington | 111 W. 11th St. (bet. Orange & Tatnall Sts.) | 302-777-2040 | www.deepbluebarandgrill.com

You "get your money's worth" at this "upbeat" seafooder in the middle of Downtown Wilmington in the form of "creative" fare and "top-notch wine selections" whether you're grabbing "a drink and snack at the bar" or a "full meal in the dining room"; the "experienced" staff will get you "out in time for the theater", while "imaginative signature cocktails" help fuel a "lively" happy hour.

Domaine Hudson *American* | 26 | 24 | 25 | $49

Wilmington | 1314 N. Washington St. (bet. 13th & 14th Sts.) | 302-655-9463 | www.domainehudson.com

Even after an ownership change in 2011, this "classy" Wilmington New American "continues to excel", with a "knowledgeable" staff recommending "dead-on pairings" of wines from a "staggering" list and "fresh, inventive" fare ("save room for that cheese plate"); the mood is "chill" in the "comfortable", "intimate" space, and while some gripe about "small portions for the money", many consider it an "all-around top-notch" experience.

Eclipse Bistro *American* | 25 | 23 | 25 | $40

Wilmington | 1020 N. Union St. (bet. 10th & 11th Sts.) | 302-658-1588 | www.eclipsebistro.com

"Inventive and inspired" Traditional American fare that "would hold its own in NYC or LA" (notably the short rib tacos) keep this "low-key" Downtown Wilmington bistro "always crowded, but deservedly so"; "attentive" waiters are "on top of their game" in the "pleasant" contemporary setting, making it a "wonderful place for a date or an anniversary."

FOOD | DECOR | SERVICE | COST

El Tapatio Mexican Restaurant *Mexican*   25 | 18 | 21 | $21

Wilmington | 1700 Philadelphia Pike (Delaware Ave.) |
302-791-9566 | www.eltapatiode.com

"*Yo quiero*" coo fans of this North Wilmington "order-by-number"
cantina, where a "reasonably priced" "Mexican food fix" and "fabulous" frozen margaritas are ferried by "friendly" waiters who offer
"speedy service"; though it's housed in "a former convenience
store" many find the "colorful" interiors appealing.

NEW Ernest & Scott   - | - | - | M
Taproom 🅾🌙 *Eclectic*

Wilmington | 902 N. Market St. (bet. 9th & 10th Sts.) |
302-384-8113 | www.ernestandscott.com

American beer and complementary eats are celebrated at this
Downtown Wilmington New American, an ode to Hemingway and
Fitzgerald, whose friendship had some roots in the area; 28-ft.
ceilings and arched architectural trusses (holdovers from the
building's former occupant, the Delaware Trust Bank) create an
impressive setting a short walk from the Grand, Du Pont and World
Cafe Live; an outdoor seating area is in the works.

Feby's Fishery *Seafood*   24 | 19 | 23 | $31

Wilmington | 3701 Lancaster Pike (bet. Centre & Dupont Rds.) |
302-998-9501 | www.febysfishery.com

"Good values" and "healthy portions" abound at this "unpretentious" "go-to" seafooder in Wilmington where "friends gather"
Tuesdays and Thursdays for $34.99 all-you-can-eat Dungeness
crabs, "oysters at the bar" and fin finds "prepared any way you like
it", all "fresh from the market next door"; the digs are "homey", if
"uninspiring" to some, and many laud the "friendly" service.

Firebirds Wood Fired Grill *American*   25 | 26 | 24 | $32

Newark | 1225 Churchmans Rd. (Continental Dr.) | 302-3667577- |
www.firebirdsrestaurants.com

See review in the Philadelphia Directory.

FireStone   22 | 22 | 22 | $27
Roasting House *American*

Wilmington | 1105 S. West St. (Water St.) | 302-658-6626 |
www.firestoneriverfront.com

A "low-key place to get to know someone" over dinner, this Wilmington New American "right on the riverfront" also boasts an outdoor bar with a fire pit that turns into one big "meet market" with a
"summer-party atmosphere"; "awesome salads" and "stupendous
desserts" shine on a menu that's "completely on par", and live
music Wednesdays–Saturdays completes the picture.

Five Guys Burgers & Fries *Burgers*   24 | 14 | 20 | $13

Wilmington | 3234 Kirkwood Hwy.
(Newport Gap Pike) | 302-998-2955 | www.fiveguys.com

See review in the New Jersey Suburbs Directory.

	FOOD	DECOR	SERVICE	COST

Green Room *French*

| 28 | 29 | 28 | $56 |

Wilmington | Hotel du Pont | 42 W. 11th St. (Market St.) | 302-594-3154 | www.hoteldupont.com

"Dining perfection" sums up the Hotel du Pont's "elegant" French on Wilmington's Rodney Square, where you'll "feel like royalty" (or perhaps "a du Pont") feasting on seasonally "updated", "world-class" cuisine, including a "heavenly" Sunday brunch, amid a "Gilded Age" atmosphere; "impeccable" service and an "extensive wine list" complete the "outstanding" experience, which is "worth the drive" for a "special occasion"; P.S. jacket required on Friday and Saturday evenings.

Harry's Savoy Grill *American*

| 25 | 23 | 24 | $46 |

Wilmington | 2020 Naamans Rd. (Foulk Rd.) | 302-475-3000 | www.harrys-savoy.com

"Top-notch" prime rib is one reason fans call Xavier Teixido's "classy" Wilmington New American "institution" an "outstanding choice for beef lovers"; there's a "wonderful wine list" too, and while it can all be "a bit pricey", the "congenial" staff and "see-and-be-seen" vibe in "dark-wood gentleman's-club" confines make it "worth it" for "special occasions."

Harry's Seafood Grill *Seafood*

| 26 | 25 | 25 | $49 |

Wilmington | 101 S. Market St. (Shipley St.) | 302-777-1500 | www.harrysseafoodgrill.com

"Tantalizing" seafood reels in regulars at this "urban-chic" fish house (sibling of Harry's Savoy Grill) "right on the riverfront" in Wilmington, where the "pricey" tabs are alleviated by "happy-hour specials"; "welcoming" service enhances the vibe for a "business dinner, if you don't mind the background noise", and there's a "great crowd in the summertime, especially outside."

Hibachi *Japanese*

| 24 | 21 | 24 | $29 |

Wilmington | 5609 Concord Pike (Naamans Rd.) | 302-477-0194
Bear | 1160 Pulaski Hwy. (bet. Bear Corbitt & Walther Rds.) | 302-838-0414
Newark | Astro Shopping Ctr. | 216 Kirkwood Hwy. (Meadowood Dr.) | 302-456-3308
www.hibachidining.com

See review in the Philadelphia Directory.

The House of William and Merry Ⓜ *American*

| ∇ 25 | 20 | 25 | $46 |

Hockessin | 1336 Old Lancaster Pike (Valley Rd.) | 302-234-2255 | www.williamandmerry.com

"Creative", "well-prepared" New American fare that "changes with the seasons" (including four-course chef's tastings and Sunday prix fixe options) has made a destination of this mod mom-and-pop "newcomer" in a century-old Hockessin farmhouse; though some carp about the "small" room that gets "noisy" quickly, "wonderful" service ensures most leave "full of merry."

Iron Hill Brewery & Restaurant ● *American*

22 | 21 | 22 | $28

Newark | Traders Alley | 147 E. Main St. (bet. Chapel & Haines Sts.) | 302-266-9000
Wilmington | 710 S. Justison St. (Beech St.) | 302-472-2739
www.ironhillbrewery.com
See review in the Philadelphia Directory.

Jake's Wayback Burgers *Burgers*

24 | 14 | 21 | $12

Wilmington | Roselle Ctr. | 2401 Kirkwood Hwy. (Rte. 141) |
302-994-6800 | www.jakeshamburgers.com
See review in the Philadelphia Directory.

Jasmine Asian Cuisine *Asian*

23 | 19 | 20 | $27

Wilmington | Concord Gallery | 3618 Concord Pike (Mt. Lebanon Rd.) | 302-479-5618 | www.jasminede.com
Feast on "creative" sushi rolls and a "well-balanced fusion" of "interesting" Pan-Asian flavors "without breaking the bank" at this spacious Wilmington strip-maller; "polite" service, a slew of specialty cocktails and weekly live vocal performances brighten the "relatively hip" vibe.

Kid Shelleen's Charcoal House & Saloon ● *American*

20 | 17 | 20 | $26

Wilmington | 1801 W. 14th St. (bet. Lincoln & Scott Sts.) |
302-658-4600 | www.kidshelleens.com
Wilmingtonians talk up the "big beer selection" at this "vibrant" New American "hangout" with a "warm, welcoming" atmosphere and an "Irish twist" on the menu; even with a "decibel level way above 11", most find it a "decent place to drink" but some rate the fare just a "step up from bar and grill", and suggest "sticking to the pub basics."

Krazy Kat's Restaurant *French*

25 | 25 | 24 | $50

Montchanin | Inn at Montchanin Vill. | 528 Montchanin Rd. (Kirk Rd.) | 302-888-4200 | www.krazykatsrestaurant.com
"Don't wait for a special occasion" to check out this "unique" "hideout" in the "peaceful" "château countryside" of suburban Wilmington, where "inventive" French plates, a "fine" Sunday brunch and an "extensive wine list" are served by a "caring", "charming" staff; the "whimsical", cat-centric decor is not for everyone, though – it's either "exquisite" or like eating "in a closet of one of the New Jersey Housewives."

Lamberti's Italian Grill & Bar *Italian*

23 | 22 | 21 | $36

Wilmington | 514 Philadelphia Pike (Marsh Rd.) | 302-762-9094 |
www.lambertis.com

Tutto Fresco *Italian*

Wilmington | Prices Corner Shopping Ctr. | 1300 Centerville Rd. (Kirkwood Hwy.) | 302-995-6955 | www.tuttofrescode.com
It "smells just wonderful when you walk into" these Wilmington Italians serving "big hearty plates well done", whether you're keeping it simple or venturing into more "adventurous" territory; "ef-

ficient" service maintains a "pleasant atmosphere" that's "great for families", and the "amount of food for the money" is a "bargain."

La Tolteca *Mexican* 23 | 19 | 22 | $19

Wilmington | Fairfax Shopping Ctr. | 2209 Concord Pike (Rte. 141) | 302-778-4646

La Tolteca Express *Mexican*

Wilmington | Talleyville Towne Shoppes | 4015 Concord Pike (bet. Brandywine Blvd. & Silverside Rd.) | 302-478-9477
www.lastoltecas.com

There's "hardly a wait" at these "comfortable" Mexican twins in Wilmington dishing out a "huge variety" of "burritos" and other "guilty pleasures" (the "house hot sauce is divine") at "reasonable" prices; the "friendly" staff "accommodates children well", but grown-ups need to "keep an eye out for margarita specials that'll have you wondering what happened the next day."

Lucky's Coffee Shop *American* 23 | 20 | 23 | $13

Wilmington | Talleyville Towne Shoppes | 4003 Concord Pike (Silverside Rd.) | 302-477-0240 | www.luckyscoffeeshop.com
A "real taste of Americana" awaits at this "kid-friendly", "'60s"-themed diner in Wilmington's Talleyville Towne Shoppes, where "huge portions" of "mom's kitchen" classics come from an "open kitchen" and "make you want to go home and take a nap afterward"; while the staff is "generally on the ball", cognoscenti caution "be prepared to wait."

The Melting Pot *Fondue* 24 | 23 | 24 | $48

Wilmington | Independence Mall | 1601 Concord Pike (bet. Murphy & Weldin Rds.) | 910-256-1187 | www.meltingpot.com
See review in the Philadelphia Directory.

Mexican Post *Mexican* 19 | 18 | 19 | $23

Wilmington | 3100 Naamans Rd. (Shipley Rd.) | 302-478-3939 | www.mexicanpost.com
See review in the Philadelphia Directory.

Mikimotos *Asian/Japanese* 27 | 24 | 24 | $41

Wilmington | 1212 N. Washington St. (12th St.) | 302-656-8638 | www.mikimotos.com
Ballyhooed as one of the "best sushi" spots in Wilmington with "tons of special rolls to choose from", this "swanky" Japanese–Pan-Asian pumps up the jam with a half-price weekday "happy hour", but even at full freight, acolytes simply "close their eyes and point to the menu, knowing it will be delicious"; a "lively" bar" and "amazing" service add to its "classy" allure.

Moro 🗷Ⓜ *Italian* 26 | 22 | 26 | $43

Wilmington | 1307 N. Scott St. (bet. 13th & 14th Sts.) | 302-777-1800 | www.mororestaurant.net
Michael DiBianca's "superb pastas" and "fresh versions of comfort food" at his high-style Italian in Downtown Wilmington headline a menu that "changes weekly" (including tasting and à la carte op-

tions); a "wonderful wine selection" and "top-notch" service also help make it a place "where you want to take someone special."

Mrs. Robino's *Italian* 22 | 15 | 22 | $22

Wilmington | 520 N. Union St. (bet. 5th & 6th Sts.) | 302-652-9223 | www.mrsrobinos.com

"As red gravy as it gets", this "old family favorite" has been "filling" Wilmingtonians with "fantastic" Italian chow "made with love" for nearly 75 years; it's "like eating at mom's kitchen table" in the "cramped" "row home" stocked with "old-school wine glasses and place mats from the '70s", where "waitresses call you hon'" and send you off "with a doggy bag."

Orillas Tapa Bar & Restaurant ⑤Ⓜ *Spanish* ▽ 26 | 23 | 25 | $32

Wilmington | 902 N. Market St. (bet. 9th & 10th Sts.) | 302-575-9244 | www.orillastapasbar.com

Some of the "best noshing" in Downtown Wilmington comes courtesy of Julio Lazzarini, whose "tiny" Spaniard whips up "creative", "chock-full-of-flavor" tapas that are a "fun break from the traditional"; "just watch what you order because a filling meal will start tugging on your wallet", making "wine specials" that much more important.

Palace of Asia *Indian* 22 | 19 | 20 | $22

Wilmington | 3421 Kirkwood Hwy. (bet. Greenbank Rd. & Newport Gap Pike) | 302-994-9200 | www.palace-of-asia.com

See review in the New Jersey Suburbs Directory.

Piccolina Toscana *Italian* 26 | 21 | 24 | $36

Wilmington | 1412 N. Dupont St. (Delaware Ave.) | 302-654-8001 | www.piccolinatoscana.com

The majority concurs that chef-owner Dan Butler made the right call "reinventing" Wilmington's Toscana Kitchen into an Italian small-plate "hot spot", citing its "incredible menu you want to try everything on" and "well-priced wine list"; despite solid service scores, a few think the staff could use "some training", but almost all agree the overall "quality is back."

Pizza by Elizabeths *Pizza* 25 | 25 | 23 | $28

Greenville | Greenville Ctr. | 3801 Kennett Pike (Buck Rd.) | 302-654-4478 | www.pizzabyelizabeths.com

"Outstanding" "custom pizzas" and other "top-quality" fare with a healthful bent are on offer at Betsy LeRoy and Betty Schneider's "casual-chic" Greenville pizzeria "destination"; "accommodating", "spot-on" service makes it a "great girls'-night-out spot", and for those who find the space "a little too pink and lace", the "exquisitely decorated" Cork bar is a "respite."

Rasa Sayang *Malaysian* ▽ 25 | 19 | 23 | $28

Wilmington | Independence Mall | 1601 Concord Pike (Foulk Rd.) | 302-543-5286 | www.rasasayangusa.com

"Originality prevails" on the menu of "fragrant, wonderfully spiced" Malaysian fare at this eatery in North Wilmington's Independence Mall, where the "friendly" staff is "incredibly quick" with your order; sure, some think the setting "isn't all that special" and the seating may be "cramped", but for most it's a "great bargain" that "rarely disappoints."

Seasons Pizza *Pizza* | 21 | 18 | 21 | $18 |

Edgemoor | 1524 Philadelphia Pike (bet. Holly Oak Rd. & Willow Ln.) | 302-793-0505 | www.seasonspizza.com
See review in the Philadelphia Directory.

Soffritto Italian Grill Restaurant *Italian* | 27 | 24 | 26 | $34 |

Newark | 1130 Kirkwood Hwy. (Red Mill Rd.) | 302-455-1101 | www.soffrittogrill.com

"Not your usual Italian", this Newark eatery "frequented by locals" maintains a "high level" of cooking with its "handcrafted" takes on "comfort food" that are "seasoned to please"; "knowledgeable" servers are "eager to take your order" in the "quiet", "pleasant" surroundings that are suitable for "business meetings", while "reasonable" prices seal the deal.

Stoney's British Pub ● *British* | 21 | 20 | 20 | $21 |

Wilmington | 3007 Concord Pike (Cleveland Ave.) | 302-477-9740 | www.stoneyspub.com

Doing a "bloody good" job of re-creating an "authentic British" vibe in the heart of Wilmington, this "quaint", inexpensive watering hole offers up "real English beers and ciders", a "fantastic assortment of single-malt whiskeys" and "hearty" "pub standards" "done correctly" (regulars "recommend" the "great fish 'n' chips"); "friendly" service and "European football" on the big-screen TV add to the "comfortable" experience.

Sullivan's Steakhouse *Steak* | 26 | 24 | 24 | $57 |

Wilmington | Brandywine Town Ctr. | 5525 Concord Pike (Naamans Rd.) | 302-479-7970 | www.sullivansteakhouse.com
See review in the Philadelphia Directory.

2 Fat Guys *American* | 24 | 19 | 23 | $22 |

Hockessin | 701 Ace Memorial Dr. (Rte. 41) | 302-235-0333
Greenville | Greenville Ctr. | 3801 Kennett Pike (Buck Rd.) | 302-543-4053
www.2fatguys.net

In keeping with their name, these "bustling", "no-frills" Northern Wilmington strip-mall twins turn out "huge portions" of "inventive", "reasonably priced" American grub, including "fresh" burgers and "tasty" wings, suitable for "your buds" or "family"; "friendly" servers keep "peanuts on the tables", but some quip that they also "need to hand out energy drinks to counteract the need to sleep afterwards."

Union City Grille *Steak* | 23 | 19 | 24 | $36 |

Wilmington | 805 N. Union St. (8th St.) | 302-654-9780 | www.unioncitygrille.com

"The service can't be beat" at this relaxing, contemporary Wilmington steakhouse where there's "a good deal of variety" on the

FOOD | DECOR | SERVICE | COST

American menu but the focus is "mouthwatering" meat complemented by "hearty, delicious" sides (visit on Sundays to take
advantage of the $2-an-ounce "name your cut" filet special); the
boozy end of the experience is strong, as well, spearheaded by a
"tremendous bar."

Walter's Steakhouse *Steak*

23 | 21 | 24 | $49

Wilmington | 802 N. Union St. (8th St.) | 302-652-6780 |
www.walters-steakhouse.com

This independent "classic American steakhouse" in Wilmington
holds its own against the big chains with "steaks done right" (the
"best" prime rib, a "pretty ballin'" porterhouse), "awesome" sides
and an "old-fashioned" "family" atmosphere; the savvy staff will
recommend "the perfect wine to go with dinner", completing what
most call a "satisfying" experience for a suitably upscale price.

Washington Street Ale House ● *Pub Food*

22 | 21 | 21 | $25

Wilmington | 1206 Washington St. (12th St.) | 302-658-2537 |
www.wsalehouse.com

A "wide choice of craft beers" accompanies the "upscale pub food"
at this airy Wilmington watering hole, a "safe bet" for a "casual
meal" served in "generous", "efficient" style; it's "lively" for sure –
just prepare yourself for the "cacophonous din of suburban mating
rituals" coming from the "always-buzzing" bar area; P.S. "tables by
the fireplace are great in the winter."

World Cafe Live at The Queen ⊠ *American*

19 | 21 | 20 | $24

Wilmington | Queen Theater | 500 N. Market St. (5th St.) |
302-994-1400

See review in the Philadelphia Directory